W9-BKW-981

History
of
North Carolina

Volume I
From 1584 to 1783

The Reprint Company
Spartanburg, South Carolina

This Volume Was Reproduced
From A 1925 Edition
In The
North Carolina Collection
University of North Carolina
Chapel Hill

The Reprint Company
Post Office Box 5401
Spartanburg, South Carolina 29301

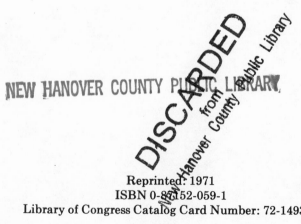

Reprinted: 1971
ISBN 0-87152-059-1
Library of Congress Catalog Card Number: 72-149340

Manufactured in the United States of America on long-life paper

Very Truly Yours

S. A. Ashe

History
of
North Carolina

BY

SAMUEL A'COURT ASHE

In two Volumes

VOLUME I
FROM 1584 TO 1783

GREENSBORO, N. C.:
CHARLES L. VAN NOPPEN, Publisher
1925

DEDICATION

To Thomas Jordan Jarvis:

In taking a retrospect of past events I recall that you and the lamented William Laurence Saunders and myself were fellow soldiers in the long war; that we shared in the anxieties of the Reconstruction period; that we were together in the important work of 1870-72, when you, as Speaker of the House, held the most commanding position among our friends; that from that time onward we were co-laborers in every effort that promised to promote the welfare of the people; that we suffered together in disappointments and enjoyed together many glorious victories; that during the six years of your useful and brilliant administration we were in constant co-operation, and in complete sympathy in all matters of public concern; and that since then, our cordial friendship has continued without interruption, save that Saunders has rested from his labors. Recalling those long years of association, when we were animated by common hopes and subject to the same anxieties—in remembrance of that eventful period—

I dedicate this volume to you and to the memory of our departed friend, it being an early fruitage of his important state publications, the preparation of which was made possible by your own cordial concurrence; and I inscribe your names on this page in recognition of your great services to the people of North Carolina and in token of my friendship.

S. A. Ashe.

PREFACE

At different times in the past the public were led to hope
that Judge Murphey, Governor Graham or Governor Swain
would prepare a History of North Carolina, but these distinguished investigators into historical subjects had not the
leisure, or they were deterred by the labor that such a work
would entail. Fortunate would it have been had the literature of the State been enriched by such a contribution from
any one of those illustrious citizens.

And yet it is to be observed that it is only in more recent
years that the great mass of original documents bearing on
our history has been collected and made accessible to
students. The publication by the State of twenty-six volumes of a thousand pages each of this material has thrown
such light on matters formerly obscure that the story of our
people can now be much more accurately written than ever
before.

It was the fortune of the writer to have been familiar
with these documents before they were made public by the
State, and to have carefully considered those of any particular import. An investigator into original sources of
North Carolina history for many years, he was naturally the
co-laborer of Colonel Saunders in his great work, and he
was also somewhat concerned in preparing the Prefatory
Notes of the State Records. It is then with some confidence that he offers the result of his protracted labors to the
public.

As this work is based almost exclusively on the State
publications, nearly every statement relating to North Carolina has for its support a contemporaneous document.

Every one owes something to the community of which he
is a member, and the author in performing the self-imposed
task of preparing this History of North Carolina feels that
he is only paying a small part of the natural obligations
resting on him as a citizen of the State. In the execution
of his design he has sought to present the past with unswerving fidelity. Animated by an ambition to do his work so

thoroughly that posterity will value it, he has closely investigated all subjects, and, as far as practicable, has brought together the circumstances bearing on transactions concerning which there have been differences of opinion.

The history of North Carolina abounds with incidents that illustrate the high patriotism of our people, their manhood, their constancy and their endurance. It has been with pride that the author has sought to perpetuate the record of those events and to enforce on posterity the lessons they inculcate, while preserving the memory of those useful citizens who have contributed to the public welfare.

The author makes acknowledgment to Dr. Stephen B. Weeks for valuable suggestions, for his assistance in reading proof and for his indefatigable labor in verifying references. It is largely due to his critical acumen, to his scholarly taste and to his unsparing labor that this volume will be found so free from defects.

Acknowledgment should also be made to Mr. Charles L. Van Noppen, the publisher, for his zealous interest. He has not considered the cost but has been animated by a patriotic purpose to be instrumental in the production of a work which he hopes will gratify the people of the State.

THE AUTHOR.

RALEIGH, N. C., *June* 1, 1908.

CONTENTS

THE FIRST EPOCH—1584-91

RALEIGH'S EXPLORATIONS AND COLONIES

CHAPTER I

CONTEMPORANEOUS DOCUMENTS

CHAPTER II

EXPLORATIONS, 1584

CHAPTER III

LANE'S COLONY, 1585-86

CHAPTER IV

WHITE'S COLONY, 1587-91

SECOND EPOCH—1629–63

PERMANENT SETTLEMENT

CHAPTER V

CHARTERS AND COLONIAL OFFICERS

CHAPTER VI

BEGINNINGS OF PERMANENT SETTLEMENT IN ALBEMARLE

CHAPTER VII

SETTLEMENT ON THE CAPE FEAR

THIRD EPOCH—1663–1729

PROPRIETARY GOVERNMENT

CHAPTER VIII

ADMINISTRATIONS OF DRUMMOND AND STEPHENS, 1664-69

CHAPTER IX

CARTERET'S ADMINISTRATION, 1670-73

CHAPTER X

ADMINISTRATIONS OF JENKINS AND MILLER, 1673-78

CHAPTER XI

ADMINISTRATIONS OF HARVEY, JENKINS, WILKINSON AND SOTHEL, 1679-89

CHAPTER XII

ADMINISTRATIONS OF LUDWELL, JARVIS, ARCHDALE, HARVEY
AND WALKER, 1689-1704

CHAPTER XIII

THE EXCLUSION OF THE QUAKERS

CHAPTER XIV

THE CARY REBELLION

CHAPTER XV

The Tuscarora War

CHAPTER XVI

Eden's Administration, 1714-22

CHAPTER XVII

Administrations of Burrington and Everard, 1724-31

FOURTH EPOCH—1729-65

NORTH CAROLINA AS A ROYAL PROVINCE

CHAPTER XVIII

BURRINGTON'S SECOND ADMINISTRATION, 1731-34

CHAPTER XIX

JOHNSTON'S ADMINISTRATION, 1734-52

CHAPTER XX

DOBBS'S ADMINISTRATION, 1754-65

FIFTH EPOCH—1765-75

CONTROVERSIES WITH THE MOTHER COUNTRY

CHAPTER XXI

TRYON'S ADMINISTRATION, 1765-71: THE STAMP ACT

CHAPTER XXII

Tryon's Administration, 1765-71 : The Regulation

CHAPTER XXIII

Social Life at the Opening of the Revolution

CHAPTER XXIV

MARTIN'S ADMINISTRATION, 1771-75

CHAPTER XXV

MARTIN'S ADMINISTRATION, 1771-75—*Continued*

CHAPTER XXVI

THE MECKLENBURG RESOLVES, MAY 31, 1775

CHAPTER XXVII

THE PROVINCIAL COUNCIL, 1775-76

CHAPTER XXVIII

THE PROVINCIAL COUNCIL, 1775-76—Continued

SIXTH EPOCH—1775-83

THE WAR FOR INDEPENDENCE

CHAPTER XXIX

THE PROVINCIAL COUNCIL, 1775-76—Continued

MAPS AND ILLUSTRATIONS, VOL. I

SIR WALTER RALEIGH

HISTORY OF NORTH CAROLINA

THE FIRST EPOCH—1584-91

RALEIGH'S EXPLORATIONS AND COLONIES

CHAPTER I

CONTEMPORANEOUS DOCUMENTS

Extracts from contemporaneous writings relative to the discovery of Virginia.—Explorations.—Localities.—Attempted settlements at Roanoke, and the fate of the Lost Colony.—The Croatans.

[Richard Hakluyt, a lecturer on geography at Oxford, began about the year 1580 to devote himself particularly to a study of the geography of America, collecting all manuscript accounts of voyages to that unknown country, translating and publishing them. In 1598 he gave to the world his greatest work, "The Principal Navigations, Voyages, Traffiques and Discoveries of the English Nation" (London, 1598-1600, three volumes). In the third volume of this valuable collection are found the reports and narratives of those concerned in Sir Walter Raleigh's explorations and colonies in Virginia. The author has made such extracts from them as are of particular interest in connection with this work.]

THE FIRST VOYAGE

Made to the Coasts of America, with Two Barks, Wherein Were

Captains

M. PHILIP AMADAS

and

M. ARTHUR BARLOW,

Who Discovered Part of the Country now Called
VIRGINIA,
Anno 1584.

Written by One of the Said Captains and Sent to Sir Walter Ralegh, Knight, at Whose Charge and Direction the Said Voyage Was Set Forth.

1584

[This account was written by Barlow, and as it is addressed to Sir Walter Raleigh, its preparation was completed after Raleigh was knighted, which was subsequent to the return of the expedition.]

Extracts

Barlow's
Narrative,
Hakluyt,
III, 301

The 27th day of April in the Year of our Redemption 1584, we departed from the west coast of England with two barks well furnished with men and victuals.

The second of July we found shoal water . . . and keeping good watch and bearing but slack sail, the fourth of the same month we arrived upon the coast, which we supposed to be a continent See also
Goldsmid's
edition of
Hakluyt,
Early
English
Voyages,
II, 169
et seq. and firm land, and we sailed along the same a hundred and twenty English miles before we could find any entrance or river issuing into the Sea.

The first that appeared to us we entered, though not without some difficulty, and cast anchor about three harquebus-shot within the haven's mouth, on the left hand of the same; and after thanks given to God for our safe arrival thither, we manned our boats and went to view the land next adjoining and to take possession of the same, in the right of the Queen's most excellent Majesty, as rightful Queen and Princess of the same, and after delivered the same over to your use according to her Majesty's grant and letters patent under Her Highness' great seal. Which being performed according to the ceremonies used in such enterprises, we first landed, very sandy and low towards the water side, but full of grapes, etc. We passed from the seaside towards the tops of those hills next adjoining, but being of mean height, and from thence we beheld the sea on both sides to the North and to the South, finding no end any of both ways. This land lay stretching itself to the West, which after we found to be but an island twenty miles long and not above six miles broad.

We remained by the side of this island two whole days before we saw any people of the country: the third day we espied one small boat rowing towards us, having in it three persons. This boat came to the island side, four harquebus-shot from our ships: and there two of the people remaining, the third came along the shore side towards us, and we being then all within board, he walked up and down the point of the land next to us. . . . They are of colour yellowish, and their hair black for the most part: and yet we saw children that had very fine auburn and chestnut coloured hair.

The next day there came unto us divers boats, and in one of them the King's brother accompanied by forty or fifty men. . . .

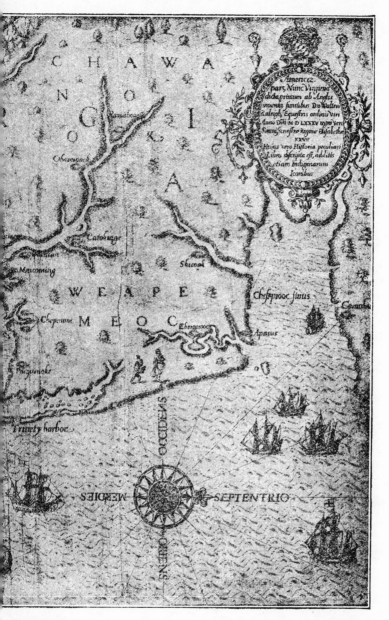

His name was Granganimeo, and the King is called Wingina, the country Wingandacoa.

After they had been divers times aboard the ships, myself and seven more went twenty miles into the river that runs towards the city Skicoak, which river they call Occam; and the following evening we came to an island which they call Roanoak, distant from the harbor by which we entered seven leagues:* and at the north end thereof, there was a village of nine houses built of cedar and fortified round about with sharp trees to keep out their enemies, and the entrance into it made like a turnpike; when we came towards it, standing near into the water's side, the wife of Granganimeo, the King's brother, came running to meet us very cheerfully and friendly. . . .

Beyond this island is the mainland; and over against this island, falls into this spacious water, the great river called Occam by the inhabitants, on which stands a town called Pomeiock, and six days' journey from the same is situated their greatest city called Skicoak.

Into this river falls another great river, called Cipo. . . . Likewise there descendeth into this Occam, another river called Nomopana; on the same side thereof stands a great town called Choanook, and the lord of that town and country is called Pooneno. This Pooneno is not subject to the King of Wingandacoa.

Beyond this country is there another king whom they call Menatonon. Towards the Southwest, four days' journey, is situated a town called Sequotan, which is the Southernmost town of Wingandacoa, near unto which six and twenty years past there was a ship cast away, whereof some of the people were saved, and those were white people, whom the country people preserved. And after ten days remaining in an out island, uninhabited, called Wocokon, with the help of some of the dwellers of Sequotan, fastened two boats of the country together and made masts unto them and sails of their shirts and departed. . . . Adjoining to this country aforesaid, called Secotan, begins a country called Pomouik, belonging to another king whom they called Piamacum; and this king is in league with the next king adjoining towards the setting of the sun, and the country Newsiok, situate upon a river called Neus; and these kings have mortal war with Wingina, King of Wingandacoa.

When we first had sight of this country, some thought the first land we saw to be the continent, but after we entered into the haven we saw before us another mighty long sea; for there lieth along the coast a tract of islands, two hundred miles in length, adjoining to the sea, and between the islands, two or three entrances. When you entered between them (these islands being very narrow for

*Twenty-one miles.

1584

the most part, as in most places six miles broad, in some places, less; in few, more,) then there appeared another great sea, containing in breadth in some places forty, and in some fifty, in some twenty over, before you come unto the continent; and in this enclosed sea are above a hundred islands of different bignesses, whereof one is sixteen miles long. . . .

[After remaining in this new country about six weeks making discoveries, and establishing friendship with the natives, these explorers, highly delighted, set sail for England accompanied by two Indians, Wanchese and Manteo, and arrived at home about the middle of September.]

THE VOYAGE

made by

SIR RICHARD GREENVILLE

for

SIR WALTER RALEGH

to

VIRGINIA

in the year 1585

Extracts

1585,
Grenville's
Narrative,
Hakluyt,
III, 307

The ninth day of April 1585, we departed from Plymouth, our fleet consisting of the number of seven sails; the Tiger, the Roebuck, etc.

The 23d of June we were in great danger of a wreck on a breach called the Cape of Fear. The 24th we came to anchor in a harbor; the 26th we came to anchor at Wocokon. The 29th we weighed anchor to bring the Tiger into harbor, where through the unskillfullness of the master whose name was Fernando, the Admiral struck on ground and sunk. The 3d day of July we sent word of our arrival at Wocokon to Wingina at Roanoak.

The 6th, Master John Arundall was sent to the main and Manteo with him; and Captain Autry and Captain Boniton the same day were sent to Croatoan, where they found two of our men left there

32 men at
Croatoan
20 days

with thirty others by Captain Raymond twenty days before. The 8th Captain Autry and Captain Boniton returned with two of our men, found by them, to us at Wocokon.

The 11th day, the General accompanied by divers gentlemen in

1585

his tilt boat; Master Lane with twenty others in the new pinnace; Captain Amadas with ten others in a ship-boat, and Francis Brook and John White in another ship boat, passed over the water from Wocokon to the mainland, victualled for eight days; in which voyage we first discovered the towns Pomeiok, Aquascogok and Secotan; and also the great lake called by the savages Paquique.

On the 12th, we came to Pomeiok: the 13th we passed by water to Aquascogok: the 15th we came to Secotan: the 16th we returned thence, and one of our boats with the Admiral was sent to Aquascogok to demand a silver cup, which one of the savages had stolen from us, and not receiving it according to his promise, we burned and spoiled their corn, all the people being fled.

The 18th, we returned from the discovery of Secotan, and the same day came aboard our fleet riding at Wocokon.

The 21st, our fleet anchoring at Wocokon, we weighed anchor for Hatorask.

The 27th, our fleet anchored at Hatorask and there we rested.

The 29th, Granganimeo, brother to Wingina, came aboard the Admiral and Manteo with him.

The 2d of August the Admiral was sent to Weapomeiok.

The 5th Master Arundell was sent for England.

The 25th our General weighed anchor and set sail for England, leaving one hundred and seven men under the government of Master Ralph Lane.

AN ACCOUNT

Of The Particulars Of The Employments Of

THE ENGLISHMEN

Left in Virginia by

RICHARD GRANVILLE,

Under the Charge of

MASTER RALPH LANE,

General of the Same;

From the 17th of August, 1585, until the 18th of June, 1586,

At Which Time They Departed the Country.

Sent and Directed to

SIR WALTER RALEGH.

1585

1585,
Lane's
Account,
Hakluyt,
III, 311

First, therefore, touching the peculiarities of the country, you shall understand that our discovery of the same has been extended from Roanoak (the same having been the place of our settlement or inhabitation) into the South, into the North, into the Northwest and into the West.

The uttermost place to the southward of any, Secotan, being from estimation four score miles distant from Roanoak. The passage from thence was through a broad sound within the main, the same being without kenning land and yet full of flats and shoals.

To the Northward our fartherest discovery was to the Chesipeans, distant from the Roanoak about one hundred and thirty miles; the passage to it was very shallow and most dangerous. . . .

There be sundry Kings whom they call Weroances, and countries of great fertility, as the Mandoages, Tripanicks and Opossians, which all came to visit the Colony of the English, which I had for a time appointed to be residents there.

To the Northwest, the fartherest place of our discovery, was to Chawanook, distant from Roanoak of about one hundred and thirty miles. Our passage thither lay through a broad sound, but all fresh water; and the channel of great depth. The towns about the water's side, situated by the way, are the following: Passaquenoke, "the woman's town," Chepanoc, Weapomeiok, Muscamunge, and Metackwem, all those being under the jurisdiction of the King of Weapomeiok, called Okisco. From Muscamunge, we entered into the river and the jurisdiction of Chowanook; there the river begins to straighten until it comes to Chowanook and then groweth to be as narrow as the Thames between Westminster and Lambeth.

Between Muscamunge and Chowanook, upon the left hand as we pass thither, is a goodly highland, and there is a town which we call the blind town, but the Savages call it Ohanoak. It has a very goodly cornfield belonging to it. It is subject to Chowanook. Chowanook itself is the greatest province and seignory lying upon that river, and the very town itself is able to put seven hundred fighting men into the field, besides the forces of the province itself.

1586

The King of the said province is called Menatonon. In March 1586, amongst other things he told me that going a three days' journey in a canoe, and then descending to the land, you are within four days' journey to pass over land Northeast to a certain King's country whose province lays upon the Sea. . . . Very near (Chowanook) directly from the West runs a most notable river, and in all these parts most famous, called the river Moratoc. This river opens into the broad sound of Weapomeiok: and whereas the river Chowanook, and all the other sounds and bays, salt and fresh, show no current in the world in calm weather, but are moved alto-

1586

gether with the wind, this river of Moratoc has so violent a current from the West and Southwest, that it made one almost of opinion that with oars it would scarcely be navigable.

On the 8th day of June came advertisement to me from Captain Stafford, lying at my Lord Admiral's Island, that he had discovered a great fleet of three and twenty sails, but whether they were friends or foes, he could not yet discern. He advised me to stand upon as good guard as I could. The 9th of the same month he himself came unto me, having that night before and that same day travelled by land twenty miles. He brought me a letter from the General, Sir Francis Drake. The tenth day he arrived in the road of our bad harbor; and coming there to anchor on the eleventh day, I came to him.

[The above account was written by Lane. On the 19th of June, 1586, the whole colony embarked in the fleet of Sir Francis Drake and arrived in Portsmouth on the 27th of July. Among the colonists was Thomas Hariot, who wrote and published an extended account of the natural productions of Virginia, and of the nature and manners of the people inhabiting there. Philip Amadas was deputy governor and admiral of the country. Thomas Cavendish was also one of the colonists. Extracts from Drake's narrative follow.]

Drake's narrative, 1586

1586, Drake's Narrative, Hawks' Hist. of North Carolina, I, 139

The 9th of June, upon sight of one special great fire (which are very ordinary all along this Coast even from the Cape of Florida hither) the General sent his skiff to the shore where they found some of our English countrymen. (that had been sent thither the year before by Sir Walter Raleigh) and brought one aboard, by whose direction we proceeded along to the place which they make their port. But some of our shipps being of great draught, unable to enter, we anchored all without the harbor in a wild road at Sea, about two miles from the shore. From whence the General wrote letters to Master Ralph Lane, being Governor of those English in Virginia and then at his fort, about six leagues from the road, in an island which they call Roanoak: wherein especially he showed how ready he was to supply his necessities and wants which he understood of, by those he had first talked withall.

The morrow after, Master Lane himself and some of his Company coming unto him, with the consent of his Captains, he gave them the choice of two offers, that is to say: either he would leave a ship, pinnace and certain boats, with sufficient masters and mariners, together furnished with a month's victual, to stay and make further discovery of the country and coasts, and so much victual likewise that might be sufficient for the bringing of them all (being one hundred and three persons) into England, if they thought good after such time, with any other thing they would desire, or that he might be able to spare; or else, if they had made sufficient discovery already, and did desire to return unto England, he would give them passage. But they, as it seemed, being desirous to stay, accepted very thankfully and with great gladness, that which was offered first. Whereupon the ship being appointed and received into charge by some of their own company sent into her by Master Lane, before they had received from the rest of the fleet the provision appointed them, there arose a great storm (which they said was extraordinary and very strange) that lasted three days together, and put all our fleet in great danger to be driven from their anchoring upon the coast. For we broke many cables and lost many anchors: and some of our fleet which had lost all (of which number was the ship appointed for Master Lane and his Company) was driven to put to Sea in great danger, in avoiding the coast and could never see us again until we met in England. Many also of our small pinnaces and boats were lost in this storm. Notwithstanding all this, the Generall offered them (with consent of his Captains) another ship, with some provisions, although not such a one for their turns as might have been spared before, this being unable to be brought into their harbor.

Or else, if they would, to give them passage into England, although he knew he should perform it with greater difficulty than he might have done before.

[A few days after their departure Sir Richard Grenville with his relief ships arrived, but finding the colony gone, left fifteen men in the fort to hold possession.]

THE FOURTH VOYAGE

Made to

VIRGINIA,

With Three Ships, In The Year

1587.

Wherein was Transported the Second Colony.

Extracts from White's narrative 1587

[This is an account of the arrival in Virginia of the Lost Colony.]

In the year of Our Lord 1587, Sir Walter Raleigh, intending to 1587, White's Narrative, Hakluyt, III, 340 persevere in the planting of his country of Virginia, prepared a new Colony of one hundred and fifty men to be sent thither, under the charge of John White, whom he appointed Governor, and also appointed under him twelve Assistants, unto whom he gave a charter, and incorporated them by the name of Governor and Assistants of the "Citie of Raleigh in Virginia."

Our fleet being in number three sails, namely, the Admiral (the Lion), a ship of one hundred and twenty tons, a fly-boat, and a pinnace, departed the six and twentieth of April from Portsmouth. The eighth of May, we weighed anchor at Plymouth and departed for Virginia. The sixteenth, Simon Ferdinando, Master of our Admiral, lewdly forsook our fly-boat, leaving her distressed in the bay of Portugal. . . . About the sixteenth of July we fell in with the main of Virginia, which Simon Ferdinando took to be the Island of Croatoan, where we came to anchor, and rode there two or three days; but finding himself to be deceived, he weighed and bare along the coast, where in the night, had not Captain Stafford* been more careful in looking out than our Simon Ferdinando, we had been all cast away upon the breach, called the Cape of Fear; for we were come within two cables length upon it; such was the carelessness and ignorance of our Master. The two and twentieth of July we arrived safe at Hatorask, where our ship and pinnace anchored; the Governor went aboard the pinnace, accompanied with forty of his best men, intending to pass up to Roanoke forthwith, hoping there to find those fifteen Englishmen, whom Richard Greenville had left there the year before, with whom he meant to have some conference concerning the state of the country and savages, meaning after he had done so to return again to the fleet, and pass along the coast to the bay of Chesepiok, where we intended to make our seat and fort, according to the charge given us, among other directions in writing, under the hand of Sir Walter Raleigh; but as soon as we were put with our pinnace from the ship, a gentleman by the means of Ferdinando, who was appointed to return for England, called to the sailors in the pinnace, charging them not to bring any of the planters back again, but to leave them in the island, except the Governor and two or three others as he approved; saying that the Summer was far spent, wherefore he would land all the planters in no other place. Unto this were all the sailors

*In the pinnace.

both in the pinnace and ship persuaded by the Master, wherefore it booted not the Governor to contend with them, but passed to Roanoke, and the same night at sunset went aland on the island, in the place where our fifteen men were left, but we found none of them nor any sign that they had been there, saving only we found the bones of one of those fifteen, which the savages had slain long before. . . . The same day order was given that every man should be employed for the repairing of those houses which we found standing, and also to make other new cottages for such as should need.

The 25th, our fly-boat and the rest of our planters arrived all safe at Hatorask, to the great joy and comfort of the whole company. . . . The eighth and twentieth George Howe, one of our twelve Assistants, was slain by divers savages, which were come over to Roanoak, either of purpose to espy our company, and what number we were, or else to hunt deer, whereof were many in the island. . . . On the thirtieth of July, Master Stafford and twenty of our men passed by water to the Island of Croatoan with Manteo, who had his mother and many of his kindred dwelling in that island, of whom we hoped to understand some news of our fifteen men, but especially to learn the disposition of the people of the country towards us, and to renew our old friendship with them. . . . We also understood of the men of Croatoan that our man, Master Howe, was slain by the remnant of Wingina's men, dwelling then at Dasamonquepeuc, with whom Wanchese kept company; and also we understood by them of Croatoan, how that the fifteen Englishmen left at Roanoak the year before, by Sir Richard Greenville, were suddenly set upon by thirty of the men of Secota, Aquoscogoc, and Dasamonquepeuc. . . .

Manteo christened Aug. 13, 1587

The 13th of August, our savage Manteo, by the commandment of Sir Walter Raleigh, was christened in Roanoak, and called Lord thereof and of Dasamonquepeuc, in reward of his faithful service.

Virginia Dare, born August 18, 1587

The 18th [of August] Eleanor, daughter to the Governor, and wife to Ananias Dare, one of the Assistants, was delivered of a daughter in Roanoak, and the same was christened there the Sunday following, and because this child was the first Christian born in Virginia, she was named Virginia. By this time our ships had unladened the goods and victuals of the planters, and began to take in wood and fresh water, and to new caulk and trim them for England; the planters also prepared their letters and tokens to send back into England. . . . At this time some controversies arose between the Governor and Assistants about choosing two out of the twelve Assistants, which should go back as factors of the company into England; the next day, the 22d of August, the whole company, both of the Assistants and planters, came to the Governor, and with

one voice requested him to return himself into England for the 1587
better and sooner of obtaining supplies and other necessaries for
them; but he refused it, and alledged many sufficient causes why
he would not. . . . Also he alledged, that seeing they intended to To remove
remove fifty miles further up into the main presently, he being then fifty miles
absent, his stuff and goods might be both spoiled, and most of them in the interior
pilfered away in the carriage. . . .

[Eventually White was persuaded to return to England. On 27 Aug., 1587
the seventh and twentieth of August the admiral and the fly-boat
weighed anchor and set sail for England, where they arrived in
November. The pinnace remained in the sound.]

The names of all the men, women and children which safely
arrived in Virginia and remained to inhabit there 1587.

White's Narrative

John White	John Bright	Hugh Pattenson
Roger Bailey	William Dutton	Martin Sutton
Ananias Dare	Maurice Allen	John Farre
Chrystopher Cooper	William Waters	John Bridger
Thomas Stevens	Richard Arthur	Griffin Jones
John Sampson	John Chapman	Richard Shabedge
Clement Taylor	William Clement	James Lasie
William Sole	Robert Little	John Cheven
John Cotsmur	Hugh Tayler	Thomas Hewet
Humphrey Newton	Hugh Wildye	William Berde
Thomas Colman	Lewes Wotton	Henry Brown
Thomas Gramme	Michael Bishop	Richard Tompkins
Thomas Butler	Henry Rufoote	Charles Florrie
Edward Powell	Henry Dorrell	Henry Payne
John Burdon	Henry Mylton	William Nichols
James Hinde	Thomas Harris	John Borden
Thomas Ellis	Thomas Phevens	Michael Myllet
William Browne	Mark Bennett	Thomas Smith
Dionys. Harvie	John Gibbes	Richard Kemme
Roger Pratt	John Stillman	Thomas Harris
George Howe	Robert Wilkinson	Richard Taverner
Simon Fernando	John Tydway	John Earnest
Nicholas Johnson	Ambrose Viccars	Henry Johnson
Thomas Warner	Edmund English	John Starte
Anthony Cage	Thomas Topan	Richard Darige
John Jones	Henry Berry	William Lucas
William Willes	Richard Berry	Arnold Archand
John Brooke	John Spendlove	John Wright
Cuthbert White	John Hemington	Thomas Scott

Names of colonists

John Wyles	Alice Chapman	Thomas Smart
George Martyn	Emma Merimoth	George Howe
Peter Little	—— Colman	John Pratt
Bryan Wyles	Margaret Lawrence	William Wythers
	Joan Warren	
Women	Jane Mannering	Children born in **Vir-**
Eleanor Dare	Rose Payne	**ginia**
Margery Harvie	Elizabeth Viccars	Virginia Dare
Agnes Wood		—— Harvie
Winifred Powell	**Boys and Children**	
Joyce Archard	John Sampson	Savages that were in
Jane Jones	Robert Ellis	England, and re-
Elizabeth Glane	Ambrose Viccars	turned home to
Jane Pierce	Robert Archard	Virginia with them
Audry Tappan	Thomas Humphrey	Manteo Towaye

[Although this list purports to embrace the names of those who remained in Virginia, yet John White and Simon Ferdinando returned to England, and George Howe was murdered before White's departure. Neither physician nor minister is mentioned as such, yet doubtless this colony was accompanied by a minister, as Manteo and Virginia Dare were "christened."]

THE FIFTH VOYAGE

of

M. JOHN WHITE

into the

WEST INDIES

and parts of America called

VIRGINIA

in the Year 1591

[This narrative was communicated to Hakluyt in February, 1593, and printed by him in 1598.]

On the 20th of March, the three ships, Hopewell, the John Evangelist and the Little John put to Sea from Plymouth with two small shallops. . . .

The third of August, we stood again in for the shore, and at midday we took the height of the same. The height of that place

we found to be 34 degrees of latitude. Towards night we were
within three leagues of the low sandy islands of Wokokon.
On Monday, the 9th of August, the storm ceased and we had
very great likelihood of fair weather. Therefore we stood in again
for the shore, and came to anchor at eleven fathoms in 35 degrees
of latitude, within a mile of the shore, when we went on land on
the narrow sandy island, being one of the islands west of Wokokon.
Between the main, as we supposed, and that island, it was but a
mile over, and three or four feet deep in most places. On the
12th in the morning we departed from thence, and towards night
we came to anchor at the Northeast end of the island of Croatoan,
by reason of a breach which we perceived to be out two or three
leagues into the Sea: here we rode all that night. This breach
is in 35½* degrees and it lays at the very Northeast point of Croatoan where goes a part out of the main Sea into the inner waters,
which part the island from the main land.

Aug., 1591.
White's
Narrative,
Hakluyt,
III, 350

The 15th of August, towards evening we came to an anchor at
Hattorask in 36⅓ degrees, in five fathoms of water, three leagues†
from the shore. At our first coming to anchor on this shore we
saw a great smoke rise in the Isle Roanoak, near the place where
I left our Colony in the year 1587, which smoke put me in good hopes
that some of the Colony were there expecting my return out of
England.

The 16th and next morning, our two boats went ashore and
Captain Cooke and Captain Spicer and their Company with me, with
intent to pass to the place at Roanoak, where our countrymen
were left. . . . But before we were half way between our ship
and the shore, we saw another great smoke to the Southwest of
Kindrick's Mounts: we therefore thought good to go to that second
smoke first. But that which grieved me more, was that when we
came to that smoke, we found no man, nor sign that any had been
there lately, nor yet any fresh water in all this way to drink.

Being thus wearied with this journey, we returned to the harbor
where we left our boats, who in our absence had brought their
casks ashore for fresh water. So we deferred our journey to Roanoak till next morning, and caused some of those Sailors to dig in
the sand hills for fresh water, whereof we found very sufficient.
That night we returned aboard with our boats and our whole
Company in safety. The next morning it was 10 o'clock aforenoon
before we put from our ships, which were then come to an anchor
within two miles of the shore. The Admiral's boat first passed
the breach but not without some danger of sinking. For at this

*Really about 35°.   †Nine miles.

time the wind blew at Northeast and direct into the harbor so great a gale that the Sea broke extremely on the bar and the tide went very forcibly at the entrance. Captain Spicer came to the entrance of the breach with his mast standing up and was half passed over, but by the rash and indiscreet steerage of Ralph Skinner, his master's mate, a very dangerous sea broke into their boat and overset them quite. There were eleven in all; seven of the chiefest were drowned; among them, Captain Spicer and Ralph Skinner. . . . Our boats and all things filled again, we put off from Hattorask, being the number of nineteen persons in both boats. But before we could get to the place where our planters were left, it was so exceedingly dark that we overshot the place a quarter of a mile, where we espied towards the North end of the island, the light of a great fire through the woods, to the which we presently rowed. When we came right over against it, we let fall our grapnel near the shore, and sounded with a trumpet a call, and afterwards many familiar English tunes of songs, and called to them friendly; but we had no answer. We therefore landed at daybreak, and coming to the fire, we found the grass and sundry rotten trees burning about the place. From thence, we went through the woods to that part of the island directly over against Dasamonquepeuc; and from thence we returned by the water side, round about the North point of the island until we came to the place where I left our Colony in the year 1586. In all this way, we saw in the sand the print of the Savages' feet of two or three sorts trodden in the night; and as we entered upon the sandy banks, upon a tree, in the very brow thereof, were

Fair Roman letters, "C. R. O."
curiously carved these fair Roman letters, "C. R. O." which letters presently we knew to signify the place where I should find the planters seated, according to a secret token agreed upon between them and me at my last departure from them; which was that in any way they should not fail to write or carve on a tree or posts of the doors the name of the place where they should be seated; for at my coming away, they were prepared to remove from Roanoak fifty miles into the main.

Therefore at my departure from them in Anno 1587, I willed them that if they should happen to be distressed in any of those places, that then they should carve over the letters or name a + in this form. But we found no such sign of distress. And having well considered of this, we passed toward the place where they were left in sundry houses; but we found the houses taken down and the place very strongly enclosed, with a high palisade of great trees, with curtains and flankers very fort-like; and one of the chief trees or posts at the right side of the entrance had the bark taken off and five feet

"Croatoan"
from the ground in fair capital letters was graven "Croatoan,"

without any cross or sign of distress. This done, we entered into the palisade, where we found many bars of iron, two pigs of iron; four iron fowlers; iron locker shot, and such like heavy things, thrown here and there, almost overgrown with grass and weeds. From thence, we went along the water side, towards the point of the Creek, to see if we could find any of their boats or pinnaces, but we could perceive no sign of them nor any of the last falcons or small ordnance which were left with them at my departure from them.

At our return from the Creek, some of our sailors meeting us, told us that they had found where divers chests had been hidden, and long sithence digged up again and broken up, and much of the goods spoiled and scattered about, but nothing left of such things as the Savages knew any use of undefaced. Presently Captain Cooke and I went to the place, which was in the end of our old trench made two years past by Captain Amadas—where we found five chests that had been carefully hidden of the planters, and of the same chests three were my own: and about the place many of my things spoiled and broken, and my books torn from the covers, the frames of some of my pictures and maps rotten and spoiled with rain, and my armour almost eaten through with rust. This could be no other than the deed of the Savages, our enemies at Desamonquepeuc, who had watched the departure of our men to Croatoan, and as soon as they were departed, digged by every place where they suspected anything to be buried, but although it much grieved me to see such sport of my goods, yet on the other side, I greatly joyed that I had surely found a certain token of their safe being at Croatoan, which is the place where Manteo was born and the Savages of the island our friends.

When we had seen so much of this place as we could, we returned to our boats, and departed from the shore towards our ships with as much speed as we could, for the weather began to be overcast and very likely that a foul and stormy night would ensue. Therefore, the same evening, with much danger and labor, we got ourselves aboard. . . .

The next morning it was agreed by the Captain and myself with the master and others, to weigh anchor and go for the place at Croatoan where our planters were, for that then the wind was good for that plan, and also to leave that cask with fresh water on shore on the island until our return. So then they brought the cable to the capstan, but when the anchor was almost apeak the cable broke, by means whereof we lost another anchor, wherewith we drove so fast unto the shore that we were forced to let fall a third anchor, which came so fast home that the ship was almost aground by Kenrick's Mounts; so that we were forced to let slip the cable end for end. And if it had not chanced that we had fallen into a channel of deeper water close by the shore than we accounted of, we could never have gone clear of the point that lies to the Southward of Kenrick's Mounts.

Colonists abandoned

It was therefore determined that all should go for St. John or some other island to the Southward for fresh water. And it was further proposed that if we could any ways supply our wants of victuals and other necessaries either at Hispaniola, St. John or Trinidad, that then we should continue in the Indies all winter following, with hope to make two rich voyages of one, and at our return, to visit our Countrymen at Virginia.

The Captain and the whole Company in the Admiral (with my earnest petitions) thereunto agreed, so it rested only to know what the master of the Moonlight, our consort, would do therein. But when we demanded them if they would accompany us in that new determination, they alledged that their weak and leaky ship was not able to continue it, wherefore the same night we parted, leaving the Moonlight to go directly to England, and the Admiral set his course for Trinidad, which course we kept for two days.

[Later they changed their course and went after the Spaniards, and after many adventures finally reached Plymouth October 24th.]

References to the colony, 1591-1709

Letter of Sir Walter Raleigh to Sir Robert Cecil

Whereas as I wrote unto yow in my last that I was goun to Weymouth to speak with a pinnes of mine arrived from Virginia, I found this bearer, Captayne Gilbert, ther also, who went on the same voyage. But myne fell 40 leaugs to the west of it, and this bearer as much to the east; so as neither of them spake with the peopell. But I do sende both the barks away agayne, having saved the charg in sarsephraze woode; but this bearer bringing sume 2200 waight to Hampton, his adventurers have taken away their

Aug. 21, 1602 Edwards' Life of Raleigh, II, 251

parts and brought it to London. I do therefore humblie pray yow to deal withe my Lord Admirale for a letter to make seasure of all that which is come to London, either by his Lordship's octoretye or by the Judge: because I have a patent that all shipps and goods are confiscate that shall trade their without my leve. And whereas Sassaphraze was worth 10s., 12s. and 20s. per pound before Gilbert returned, his cloying of the market, will overthrow all myne and his own also. He is contented to have all stayde: not only for this present; but being to go agayne, others will also go and destroy the trade, which otherwise would yield 8 or 10 for one, in certainty and a return in XX weeks. . . .

I beseich yow, favor our right: and yow shall see what a prety, honorabell and sauf trade wee will make.

Yours ever to serve yow,
W. RALEGH.

[William Strachey was secretary of the colony of Virginia, and his "Historie of Travaile into Virginia Britannia" was apparently written after the colony had been seated at Jamestown six years—in 1613.]

The men, women and children of the first plantation at Roanoke were by practize and commandment of Powhatan (he himself persuaded thereunto by his priests) miserably slaughtered, without any offense given him, either by the first planted (who twenty and od years had peaceably lyved intermyxed with those Savages and were out of his territory) or by those who nowe are come to inhabit some parte of his desarte lands.

Southward they [Newport's exploring party] went to some parts of Chowanook and the Mangoangs, to search there those left by Sir Walter Raleigh, which parts—to the towne of Chesepeak—hath formerly been discovered by Mr. Harriott and Sir Ralph Lane.

The high land is in all likelihoodes, a pleasant tract, and the mould fruitful, especially what may lye to the Southward, where at Peccarecamek and Ochanahoen by the relation of Machumps,* the people have houses built with stone walls, and one story above another, so taught them by the English who escaped the slaughter at Roanoke, at which time this our Colony, under the conduct of Captain Newport, landed within the Chesepeake Bay, where the people breed up tame turkeys about their houses, and take apes in the mountains, and where at Ritanoe the Weroance Eyanoco perserved seven of the English alive, four men, and two boys and one younge mayde (who escaped and fled up the river of Choanook) to beat his copper, etc.

[Powhatan] seems to command south and north from the Mangoangs and Chowanoaks, bordering upon Roanoke and the old Virginia, a town pallisadode standing at the north end of the bay.

He doth often send unto us to temporize with us, awaiting perhaps a fit opportunity (inflamed by his furious and bloody priests) to offer us a taste of the same cup which he made our poor countrymen drink of at Roanoke.

[In "The True and Sincere Declaration" made by the governor and councillors of the Jamestown settlement in December, 1609—they speak of having] intelligence of some of our nation planted by Sir Walter Raleigh, yet alive, within fifty miles of our fort, who

*An Indian of Powhatan's tribe who had been to England.

1613

1613. William Strachey's Travaile into Virginia, 85

Strachey, 26

Strachey, 48

1609. The True and Sincere Declaration

1608

Brown's
Genesis,
I, 349

can open the womb and bowels of this country; as is testified by two of our Colony sent out to seek them, who (though denied by the savages speech with them) found Crosses and Letters, the Characters and assured Testimonies of Christians, newly cut in the barks of trees.

[The discovery of these characters recently cut in the barks of trees at that time locates some of Raleigh's colony within fifty miles of Jamestown in 1608. The narrative continues:]

What he knew of the Dominions, he spared not to acquaint me with, as of certain men cloathed at a place called Ochanahonan, cloathed like me.

[And again:] We had agreed with the King of Paspehegh to conduct two of our men to a place called Panawicke, beyond Roanoke where he reported many men to be apparelled. We landed him at Warraskoyack, where playing the villain and deluding us for rewarde, returned within three or four days after, without going further.

Smith's
True
Relation.

Brown's
Genesis,
I, 184
February,
1608

[Smith sent from Warraskoyack, Master Scitlemore and two guides to seek for the Lost Colony of Sir Walter Raleigh.

Alexander Brown has found and embodied in his work a rude drawing sent by Francis Nelson from Virginia in 1608 to illustrate Smith's "True Relation," and the same year sent to Spain from London.

On this map, on the Chowan, or on the Nottoway, falling into the Chowan River, Ochanahonan is placed: and on the Tar, or upper Pamlico River, "Pakrakanick" is located: and near it is a legend: "Here remayneth 4 men clothed that came from Roanoak to Ochanahonan." Between the Chowan and the Moratoc (Roanoke River) on this map is a legend: "Here the King of Paspehegh reported our men to be, and wants to go." And that region is marked "Pananiock."

On the map, the point Warraskoyack, from which Master Scitlemore and two guides started, and where Smith landed "the King of Paspehegh to conduct two of our men to a place called Panawicke, beyond Roanoke," is on a stream that probably is intended to represent Nansemond River.

December,
1608

This map was drawn on the relation of some Indian. The Indians of the James River had no connection with those farther south. Powhatan's jurisdiction did not extend over the Chowanists or the Mongoaks. The Indian who gave the information on which the drawing was based probably had but little familiarity with the localities, knowing about the rivers but nothing of the coast. He knew that the first river was the Chowan and its tributaries; that the next was the Moratoc, and that farther on there was a third— the Tar. He probably knew nothing of the sounds. He placed the chief town of the Chowan Indians on the northeast side of the Chowan River, and Ochanahonan on the other side. It seems to the author of this work that Ochanahonan is probably the town called by Lane Ohanoak. On DeBry's map this town is placed above the town of Chowanoak, but in Lane's narrative it is located below that town.

1608

The Indian account places Pananiock, where White's colony settled, between the Moratoc and the Chowan rivers, but as the Indian was probably not acquainted with the waters of the sound, and only knew that the Moratoc discharged itself some distance below the Chowan, he inaccurately indicates that both emptied into the ocean. In that he was mistaken; but he probably was correct in locating the settlement north of the Moratoc River. It was between the mouth of the Moratoc and the Chowan that Lane observed the "goodly highlands," and that location being substantially "fifty miles in the interior" from Roanoke Island, it is there we would expect to find the place of permanent settlement. And it is there that the Indian relation places it.

After the massacre, "four men and two boys and one young mayde" escaped and fled up the river of Chowanoak, and were preserved by the Weroance at Ritanoe. This flight could have been readily made from a point north of the Moratoc River. It is also stated that four men came to Ochanahonan. If there were still other fugitives than those preserved at Ritanoe, their journey through the woods would also indicate that Pananiock was on the north of the Moratoc.]

Lawson's suggestions

Lawson's History of North Carolina, 108

1709

The first discovery and settlement of this country was by the procurement of Sir Walter Raleigh, in conjunction with some public spirited gentlemen of that age, under the protection of Queen Elizabeth; for which reason it was then named Virginia, which begun on that part called Roanoke Island, where the ruins of a fort are to be seen at this day as well as some old English coins which have been lately found, and a brass gun, a powder horn and one small quarter-deck gun made of iron staves, which method of making guns might very probably be made use of in those days for the convenience of infant colonies.

A further confirmation of this we have from the Hatteras Indians who either then lived on Roanoke Island or much frequented it. These tell us that several of their ancestors were white people and could talk in a book as we do: the truth of which is confirmed by gray eyes being found frequently amongst these Indians and no others.

They value themselves extremely for their affinity to the English and are ready to do them all friendly offices. It is probable that this settlement miscarried for want of timely supplies from England, or through the treachery of the natives: for we may reasonably suppose that the English were forced to cohabit with them for relief and conversation: and that in process of time, they conformed themselves to the manners of their Indian relations; and thus we see how apt human nature is to degenerate.

The Hatteras Indians

1585

[The Hatteras Indians in 1585 were not under the same government as the savages on the mainland. They were a different tribe; and they were so few in numbers and so poor that when Lane was making a counterplot against Pemisapan and pretended that he was going to make a journey to Croatoan, he asked to be furnished with men to hunt for him while there, and with four days' provisions to last during his stay. No subsistence could be gotten from the Croatoans. A century later, in Lawson's time, that tribe had but sixteen fighting men, and even if all of these had a strain of English blood in them, their white ancestors might have been but a very small fraction of the English colonists. The tribe was still further reduced during the Indian War of 1711-15, when it adhered to the English. It lingered about its old home, suffering the fate of other small tribes, gradually becoming extinct. In 1763 some of the Hatteras and Mattamuskeet Indians were still living on the coast of Hyde, where a reservation had been set apart for them. Because names borne by some of the colonists have been found among a mixed race in Robeson County, now called Croatans, an inference has been drawn that there was some connection between them. It is highly improbable that English names would have been preserved among a tribe of savages beyond the second generation, there being no communication except with other savages. If English names had existed among the Hatteras Indians in Lawson's time, he probably would have mentioned it as additional evidence corroborating his suggestion deduced from some of them having gray eyes, and from their valuing themselves on their affinity to the English. It is also to be observed that nowhere among the Indians were found houses or tilled lands or other evidences of improvement on the customs and manners of the aborigines. When this mixed race was first observed by the early settlers of the upper Cape Fear, about 1735, it is said that they spoke English, cultivated land, lived in substantial houses, and otherwise practised the arts of civilized life, being in these respects different from any Indian tribe. In 1754 they were described as being on "Drowning Creek, on the head of Little Peedee, fifty families, a mixed crew, a lawless people, possessed the lands without patent or paying quit rents; shot a surveyor for coming to view vacant lands, being enclosed in great swamps." From that time to the present these people have remained in their settlement on Drowning Creek. It is worthy of remark that in 1754 they were not considered Indians, for the military officers of Bladen County particularly reported that there were no Indians in that county. Whatever may have been their origin and the origin of their English names, neither their names

1709

C. R., VI, 995

The Croatans

1754

C. R., V, 161

nor their English manners and customs could have been perpetuated from the time of the Lost Colony without exciting some remark on the part of explorers, or historians. Apparently that community came into being at a later date. Yet it is to be observed that many persons believe them to be the descendants of the Lost Colony; and the Legislature has officially designated them as "Croatans," and has treated them as Indians.*]

*The subject of the connection of these Croatans with the colonists has been ably discussed by Mr. Hamilton McMillan and by Dr. Stephen B. Weeks, who maintain that view with much plausibility.

CHAPTER II

Explorations, 1584

England claims rights in America.—Sir Humphrey Gilbert.—
Walter Raleigh's charter.—The landing of Amadas and Barlow.—
The spot uncertain.—The savages kindly.—Explorations.—Fortu-
nate return.—The new land named Virginia.—Conditions in America.

England claims rights in America

1486

Six years before the discovery of America the Portu-
guese, the most adventurous sailors of that age, had already
explored the coast of Africa and had turned the Cape of
Good Hope in their search for a route to the Indies. The
fortunate issue of the expedition undertaken by Columbus
under the patronage of Ferdinand and Isabella gave to Spain
a claim to the New World and opened a door for a serious
clashing of interest between those two faithful supporters of
the Catholic religion; and to settle their differences and to
establish their respective rights of dominion, Pope Alexander VI in 1493 issued a papal bull dividing the undiscovered regions of the earth between them. Drawing an
arbitrary line on the map of the world running a hundred
leagues west of the Azore Islands, he apportioned to Portugal
all to the east of it and, depriving Spain of any interest in
Africa, allotted to that country the whole of the New World
"west and south of Spain." And by a treaty, the next year,
this line was fixed three hundred and seventy leagues west
of the Cape Verde Islands.

Alexander's Bull

England, however, did not recognize that arbitration as
binding upon her and claimed the Atlantic coast of America,
by virtue of the discoveries of the Cabots, who, in 1497, had
coasted along it from Labrador to Florida. From that time
onward there were occasional movements made by English
navigators for exploration, trade, and even colonization, that,
however, had no practical result. Although among the
great fleet of vessels that were employed in the Newfound-

Cabot

land fisheries there were generally to be found fifty or more bearing the English flag, it was not until Elizabeth's time that an attempt was made at English colonization. During her reign England made a marvellous advance in wealth, in manufactures and in population; and a spirit of enterprise was manifested by her merchants no less than among those bold soldiers and seamen who sought fame and fortune in battling against the Catholic Spaniards on land, and despoiling their richly laden vessels on the sea.

One of the most notable of the enterprising heroes who made her reign illustrious was Sir Humphrey Gilbert, whose great capacity and services had been rewarded by his appointment as lord lieutenant of Ireland.

Gilbert

But he had other claims to royal favor. Her lustful father having beheaded her mother, and having cast her off in infancy as illegitimate, Elizabeth, the queen, while having slight regard for her father's kin, stood loyally to her mother's. In her girlhood days she had fallen to the care of Mrs. Catherine Ashley, a connection on her mother's side, to whom she declared that she owed more for kindness and preservation than she could have done to her own mother. And this woman, for whom the queen cherished such warm gratitude, was the aunt of Sir Humphrey Gilbert. So beyond his undoubted ability and merit there was an influence favorable to him at court. In June, 1578, Sir Humphrey sought and obtained from the queen a patent to explore and settle any part of the New World not already occupied by a Christian prince, and to possess it for himself and his heirs, with power and dominion over the same—a right royal grant to any subject of the realm. He associated with himself in this enterprise his younger half brother, Walter Raleigh, and in June, 1583, sailed from England with five vessels and landed in Newfoundland. Raleigh, however, did not accompany him, but wrote to him just previous to his departure expressing the queen's great interest in the enterprise. "I have sent you," he wrote, "a token from her Majesty, an ancor guided by a lady, as you see; and farther, her Highness willed me to sende you worde that she wished you as great good-hap and safety to your ship, as if herself were ther in parson, desiring you to have care of your sealf,

1578

1583

as that which she tendereth; and therefore for her sake, you must provide for it accordingly. Farther, she commandeth that you leve your picture with me."

Surely Gilbert stood well with the woman his aunt had reared, she "desiring him to have care of himself, as of that which she tendereth." But Elizabeth's fears were prophecies. That barren, frozen, inhospitable shore was not favorable for colonization, and the vessel that bore the intrepid navigator, overwhelmed in a fearful tempest, went down at sea, and the brave Sir Humphrey perished.

Raleigh

But even that great misfortune did not dismay the enterprising spirit of Raleigh. As a young man, a volunteer soldier of fortune, he had fought in the ranks of Protestantism against the French and Spanish legions of intolerant Catholicism. For some years he had served in the Irish War, where he had displayed heroism and bravery, and had also led his band and had put to the sword six hundred Spanish and Italian troops, after surrender, in Smerwick Bay; a bloody butchery. Appearing at court as bearer of despatches, his pronounced views as to the thoroughness with which a war of extermination should be waged accorded so well with Elizabeth's own policy that she called him her "Oracle." A month later the command of a band of footmen in Ireland became vacant, and the queen, in

Edwards' Life of Raleigh

April, 1582, issued her command to the general-in-chief: "But chiefly that Our Pleasure is to have Our servant, Walter Rawley, trained sometime longer in that Our realm for his better experience in martial affairs, and for the especial care that We have to do him good, in respect of his kindred, that has served Us, some of them (as you know) near about Our person, these are to require you that the leading of the said band may be committed to the said Rawley; and for that he is for some considerations by Us excused to stay here, Our pleasure is that the said band be, in the meantime, until he repair into that Our realm, delivered to some such as he shall depute to be his Lieutenant there." That was the year before Sir Humphrey lost his life, Raleigh being kept at court under the eye of the queen, "for the especial care she had to do him good." But interested in this matter of colonization, he did not let it slumber.

1584

The disastrous ending of his brother's attempt did not deter him. Although the queen made no such princely grant to any other than Kate Ashley's kin, Raleigh speedily obtained a new patent for himself; and at great expense he fitted out at London two barks to transport, as his guests, a goodly number of merchants, nobles and notable sailors, to discover an eligible location for a colony in the warmer latitudes bordering on Florida.* Having sailed from the Thames, his vessels took their final departure from the west coast of England on April 27, 1584, and sought the shores of America by the southern route. Reaching the Canaries by May 10th, a month later they arrived at the West Indies, where they lingered a few days, and then entered the Gulf Stream on their northward course. On July 2d they found shoal water off Cape Fear; and then shortening sail, the captains, Amadas and Barlow, proceeded cautiously until, July 4th,† they arrived upon the coast.‡ Watching for a harbor and an entrance, they coasted along one hundred and twenty miles before they discovered one, but finally north of Cape Hatteras they discerned a breach and came to anchor at its mouth. With grateful hearts, the company assembled and piously returned solemn thanks for their safe arrival; and then they eagerly manned their boats and made their landing on the south side of the inlet. This first landing place of the English on the coast of Virginia was apparently at the mouth of Trinity Harbor, as depicted on the maps of the explorers, about twenty miles north of Roanoke Island, and well within what has since been known as Currituck Sound. It was forty miles north of Hattorask Inlet, which afterward became the roadstead of the colonists.

The Landing, July 4, 1584, O.S.

*Jean Ribault had published in London his account of "Terra Florida" in May, 1563, and on the dispersal of his colony later, the survivors having put to sea in a small boat were picked up by an English vessel and brought to England. (Brown's "Genesis.")

†By the reckoning then in use the longest day in the year fell on July 3d. This arrival on the coast was one day after the longest day of the year.

‡John Verazzani, a Florentine, sixty years before having sailed from Madeira, on January 17, 1524, "through the assistance of Heaven and the goodness of his ship, discovered a new land never before seen by any man, either ancient or modern." The point he reached was this immediate locality where Raleigh's captains first saw the land.

On reaching the solid ground, amid great rejoicing and with ceremonial pomp, according to the custom of the times, they took possession of the land in right of their sovereign, the Queen of England, and formally delivered it over to the use of Walter Raleigh.

The ceremony of taking possession Amadas and Barlow deemed of such high importance that they made a record of the particular gentlemen and men of account who were present as witnesses of it, so that no question might be made of their queen's rightful title to the country. Being now in possession, and having the English flag waving over the soil of this new dominion, they proceeded to look about them and view the land. With wonder they noted the abundance of grapes that grew even on the sands of the beach, where the surge of the sea overflowed them; and in all places else; on the hills and in the plains, on every little shrub and climbing even up the branches of the high cedars. Then with hurried footsteps they passed from the seaside to the tops of the adjacent hills, and with amazement beheld the broad sea stretching away on both sides as far as the eye could reach. They found later that where they were was an island some six miles wide and about twenty long, a part of the sand banks that separated the sound from the sea. "After we had entered into the haven," wrote Barlow in his narrative of the exploration, "we saw before us another mighty long sea; for there lies along the coast a tract of island two hundred miles in length; and between these islands two or three entrances; these islands being very narrow, for the most part only six miles broad; then entering, there appeared another great sea, in breadth in some places forty and fifty miles and in some twenty miles before you come to the continent; and in this enclosed sea near a hundred islands, whereof one is sixteen miles long."

As yet all was solitude. The face of nature was unbroken by the hand of man. For two days they saw no evidences of human life; but on the third day after their arrival they discovered a boat in the sound containing three savages, who cautiously approached and held communication with them. These being favorably received, and delighted with the little presents given them, the next day forty or fifty

AN INDIAN VILLAGE
(From the John White Drawings)

others visited the ships and exchanged commodities. It may be observed in passing that the aborigines of America were not generally called Indians by English writers until about the year 1600; at that time they were spoken of only as savages. But although so called, the natives were found to be gentle in their disposition and not unfriendly, and themselves copper-colored, their admiration was unbounded at the white skins of the strangers, their apparel and their great ships, while the thunder and lightning from their muskets filled them with awe.

A few days later Barlow proceeded in his boat to Roanoke Island, the distance being seven leagues, or about twenty miles, and visited Granganimeo, brother to the King Wingina, who lived with his wife in great state on that island. The country was called by the natives Wingandacoa; and on the mainland were Secotan, Newsiok, and other territories. For six weeks the explorers remained, making excursions in all directions. July and August are delightful months in those landlocked sounds, and all were charmed by the natural advantages of that region as a place for settlement. The beautiful flowers, the magnificent forests, the noble watercourses, the abundance of game, the new and valuable plants, possessing medicinal properties, all combined to make this summer land appear to be a glorious home for the proposed colony. And it must be remembered that the company on board the ships had been especially selected as men of experience for the purpose of ascertaining a desirable location for the English settlement.

At length, taking specimens of the natural products, the prized sassafras and the fragrant tobacco, and accompanied by two young Indian men, Manteo and Wanchese, Amadas and Barlow spread their sail and turned their prows homeward, reaching England safely about the middle of September. The happy return of the explorers caused much enthusiasm in England. Manteo and Wanchese excited widespread interest among all classes, while the accounts given by Amadas and Barlow and their companions of the new land they had found led many to look with longing eyes toward such an alluring country. Elizabeth, pleased at being mistress of so fair a realm, and gratified at Raleigh's success,

conferred knighthood on him as a mark of her favor, and
at his solicitation named his possessions in America Virginia,
as a memorial of herself, who had remained through life a
virgin queen, and Parliament manifested its applause and
its hope of important commercial benefits by confirming and
ratifying the queen's patent with all of its high powers and
exclusive privileges.

Conditions in America

Many years before, the Spaniards had explored and
claimed Florida; and when, in 1564, a French settlement
had been made on the river May by some Huguenots under
Ribault, at Fort Carolina, the Catholic Spaniards asserted
dominion and put them to the sword. In Canada, at the far
north, the French had made explorations and claimed the
possession, but between Florida and Canada the wilderness
was unbroken; and when Amadas and Barlow landed on
the sandy shore near Cape Hatteras and raised there the
meteor flag of England and took possession of the country
for the English-speaking race, it was the first step in a series
of events of the utmost consequence to mankind. The limits
of Virginia were the undefined bounds of Canada at the
north, and of Florida at the south; the Atlantic on the one
hand and the South Sea on the other; and that vast expanse,
so long a solitude, was in the course of time to become the
home of the greatest of all the nations of the earth.

Fortunate, indeed, was it for America and for humanity
that this first lodgment on our stormy coast was by a race
devoted to the Protestant faith, ardently attached to freedom
and personal liberty, and trained to the usages and customs
of the realm of England. Different certainly the world's
history would have been had Raleigh not blazed the way
in English colonization, and had the dominion of the Spaniards under the papal bull of Alexander been permanently
established throughout the Atlantic slope of America.

Ribault's
Colony, 1564

CHAPTER III

Lane's Colony, 1585-86

Lane's colony.—Arrival at Wokokon.—Secotan visited.—Aquascogoc burned by Grenville.—Disembarkation at Hattorask.—Settlement at Roanoke.—Fort Raleigh.—Explorations.—Manteo friendly.—
Wanchese hostile.—The peril of famine.—Lane penetrates the
Chowanoak; seizes Skyco; ascends the Moratoc.—Food exhausted.—
The Indian conspiracy.—The hostiles gather at Dasamonquepeuc.—
Lane strikes a blow and secures safety.—The arrival of Drake.—The
departure of the colonists.—Arrival of Grenville's fleet.—Fifteen
men left to hold possession.

The first colony

Hastening to lay the foundations of a regal domain and   1585
with an eager anticipation of rich returns from his commercial dealings, Sir Walter now prepared a second expedition, which was to transport a hundred colonists for settlement in Virginia. Provisions were collected for a year's
subsistence, by which time a new supply was to be furnished.
The colonists were to be under the authority of Ralph Lane,
as governor, who was chosen for this important post because
he had already given the world assurance of his bravery,
capacity, and resourcefulness. Among the enterprising men
of that day he ranked high for energy, courage and versatile
powers. Barlow, who, years before, had served with
Raleigh in Flanders, was again to be with the party, and was
to remain in Virginia as admiral; while Cavendish, afterward famous as a bold and skilful navigator, Thomas
Hariot, highly distinguished as a mathematician and scien-
tist, and John White, whose maps and admirable sketches,
made in Virginia, are still extant, and who was deeply interested in the work of colonization, were likewise members of
the company. At length, the preparations being completed,
a fleet of seven vessels, all small, however, and capable of
entering the inlets of the Virginia sounds, under the command of Sir Richard Grenville, a kinsman of Sir Walter
Raleigh, and famous for his skill and bravery, set sail from
Plymouth on April 9, 1585. After various adventures that

caused delay, the fleet passed the Cape Fear on June 23d, and two days later came to anchor at Wokokon, now known as Ocracoke, southwest of Cape Hatteras. One of the vessels, under Captain Raymond, had, however, preceded the others, and having reached the vicinity twenty days earlier, had disembarked thirty-two men at Croatoan, a part of the sandbanks nearer the cape, that island also being called the "Admiral's Island," and Cape Hatteras itself was known as Cape Amadas.

Exploration on the mainland

Some ten days were spent in examining the vicinity, and then, on July 11th, a considerable party embarked in four large boats, and taking provisions for eight days, passed over to the mainland, bordering on Pamlico Sound. They visited the Indian town of Pomeiok, and the great lake, Paquipe, and the town of Aquascogoc, and then Secotan, and explored the rivers of that region. During the expedition an Indian at Aquascogoc stole a silver cup from Sir Richard Grenville, and not restoring it, according to promise, Sir Richard went back from Secotan to that town for the purpose of regaining it; but the Indians had fled. So Sir Richard, to punish the theft, burned and spoiled their corn, which set those savages at enmity with the English.

Having gained some familiarity with those southern parts, the admiral weighed anchor, and turning the cape, reached Hattorask Inlet, having previously advised King Wingina at Roanoke Island of their coming. The colonists were accompanied by Manteo and Wanchese. The former had been strengthened in his friendship for the English, but the latter, whether because of apprehensions of their great power, which he had beheld in England, or because he belonged to that tribe on the Pamlico whose corn Sir Richard had destroyed, displayed an unfriendly disposition toward them.

Arriving at Hattorask, the settlers disembarked on August 17th, and landed on Roanoke Island. Who now can enter fully into the feelings of those first adventurers, who in that summer time made their lodgment in the New World! The unknown country, the placid waters of the great sound, the delightful atmosphere and brilliant sunshine,

and their difficult intercourse with the untutored savages
who gathered around them—with their strange color, manners, and customs—and themselves so far removed from
their distant homes—must have been constant subjects of
reflection, mingling pleasure and apprehension, gratifying
their spirit of adventure, and fostering hopes of personal
reward, but ever startling them with the extreme novelty
of their situation. A week after the landing Grenville took
his departure, leaving the colonists established on Roanoke
Island.

Fort Raleigh on Roanoke Island

Lane at once began the erection of dwelling houses at a
convenient point on the northern end of the island, and constructed a fort there, which he called Fort Raleigh; and
from there excursions were made in every direction to get a
better acquaintance with the country and its products. To
the southward they went eighty miles to Secotan, that lay
near the mouth of the Neuse; to the north they reached the
Chesipeans, some fifteen miles inland from the head of
Currituck Sound, and temporarily a small number of the
English established themselves in that region. From those
Indians, as well as from information derived from those
on the Chowan, Lane learned that there was a larger and
better harbor not far distant to the northward. On the
west they penetrated to Chowanoak, a large Indian town
on the Chowan River, and in that region they found an
Indian sovereign, or Weroance, who ruled about eight hundred warriors, having subject to him eighteen towns. These
towns, however, never consisted of more than thirty houses,
and generally of only ten or twelve. The houses were made
with small poles fastened at the top, the sides being covered
with bark, and usually about twenty feet long, although some
were forty and fifty feet, and were divided into separate
rooms.

In these explorations the colonists ascended the various
rivers emptying into the sound, and became familiar with the
adjacent country. Hariot devoted himself to the study of
the natural history of the region and wrote a valuable account of the animals, the vegetables, the plants, and the trees

Lane
explores

1536

found there, and White made many sketches that are still preserved in the British Museum.

Famine threatens the colonists

Among the savages, Ensinore, the old father of Wingina and Granganimeo, and Manteo were friendly with the white strangers; but the other chieftains were not favorable to them, although their bearing was not openly hostile. Granganimeo unfortunately died shortly after the arrival of the colonists, and upon that event Wingina, the king, according to some usage, took the name of Pemisapan, and as time passed he began to intrigue against the English, in which he was joined by Wanchese, Terraquine, Osacan, and other head men of the Indians. Relying on an additional supply of provisions by

The spring of 1586

Easter, the colonists had been improvident, and by spring had exhausted their stock, and the planting time of vegetables and corn had hardly come when they found themselves without food. Their reliance now, temporarily at least, was on the corn of the Indians, and that was difficult to obtain. Their situation had become one of peril, especially as the Indians were reluctant to supply them. Pemisapan, understanding their difficulties, and at heart their enemy, now warily devised a plan for their destruction. He instilled into the Chowanists and into the Mangoaks, a strong and warlike tribe inhabiting the region on the Moratoc, or Roanoke River, that the English were their enemies; and then he informed Lane that the Mangoaks had much corn and that there were rich mines of gold and copper and other minerals in their country, and that they possessed stores of pearls and precious stones. This appealed strongly to Lane's cupidity, and he eventually determined to visit them, and applied to Pemisapan for guides, and three Indians

Lane's expedition up the Moratoc

besides Manteo were assigned to accompany him. So in March Lane set out on his expedition, taking the pinnace and two smaller boats, with some fifty or sixty men. He visited all the towns on the water's edge, and was especially pleased with some high land seen before reaching Chowanoak, subject to that king, where there was a goodly cornfield and a town called Ohanoak. Arriving at Chowanoak, he found a considerable assemblage there, the King Menatonon and his people being under apprehension that the English were enemies to them. Although Lane as a precautionary measure seized the person of the king and his young son, Skyco, he, nevertheless, was able to disarm their fears, and during a sojourn of two days with them obtained considerable information concerning the Mongoaks and their country, and also learned that by ascending the Chowan two days in a boat he would be within a four days' journey, by land, of a king's country that lay upon the sea. Obtaining some corn from Menatonon, and keeping Skyco as a hostage for further kindness, he sent the young Indian prince in the pinnace to the fort, and with the remaining boats and forty men pushed on up the Moratoc. His progress was slow, and he observed the difference between the strong current of that river and the sluggish waters of the great estuaries of the broad sound of Weapomeiok, as the country north of Albemarle Sound was then called.

The Mongoaks proved hostile, and when he had ascended the river two days, having progressed about thirty miles, they made an attack that was, however, easily repulsed. Then penetrating into the country, Lane found that the savages withdrew before him, removing all their corn and leaving nothing on which his men could subsist. His provisions being nearly out, he left it to the men to determine whether they should return or proceed; but they had two large mastiffs with them, and the men, declaring that the dogs prepared with sassafras would be good for two days' food, would not then abandon the expedition; and so they pushed on farther, but without any favorable result. At length, in danger of starvation, and their strength failing, they turned down stream, and in one day reached an island at the mouth of the river.

Their provisions now were entirely exhausted; but here, because of a heavy wind raising great billows in the sound, they were constrained to remain the whole of the next day. It was Easter eve; and Lane says they truly kept the fast. But Easter morn brought them new hope, and the storm ceasing, they entered the sound, and by four o'clock reached the Indian town of Chepanum (apparently on Durant's Neck, between Little and Perquimans rivers), which they

1586

found deserted; but fortunately there were fish in the weirs that furnished timely food; "for some of our company of the light-horsemen were far spent," those sailors who managed the canoes or light boats since called gigs being facetiously designated as "light-horsemen."

The next morning, refreshed and strengthened, they resumed their journey and returned to Roanoke in safety.

The Indians become hostile

In their absence, Pemisapan had stirred up the neighboring Indians to enmity against the remaining colonists, and hoping that his devices for the destruction of Lane's party had succeeded, he sought to strengthen the resolution of his followers by declaring that Lane and his party had either died of starvation or had been cut off by the Mongoaks. Ensinore, who had urged more friendly counsels, had unfortunately died toward the end of March, and there was now no influence to counteract Pemisapan's hostility; and urged by him, the Indians would no longer render any assistance in the way of obtaining either fish or other food, and the situation of the colony was becoming extremely critical. The protracted absence of Lane's party added to their despondency, while it gave color to the report of their destruction. Such was the deplorable condition on the island when Lane's reappearance, contrary to the prophecies of his enemies, together with the accounts given by the Indians who had accompanied him of the ease with which he had overcome those Mongoaks who had fought him, caused a reaction in favor of the whites, and the Indians once more began to set weirs for them and aided them in planting corn, the planting season having now arrived. Still, until relief should come from England, or the crops just planted should mature, the colonists had to rely on such supplies as they could gather for themselves. In this extremity resort was had to the oyster beds found in the sound; and the better to subsist, the men were divided into small companies, and located at different points. Captain Stafford and twenty others were sent to Croatoan, where, while getting oysters, they could watch for the approach of the expected vessels

Pemisapan plots

INDIANS COOKING FISH
(From the John White Drawings)

bearing relief; at Hattorask a dozen more were stationed for the same purpose, while every week companies of fifteen or twenty were sent to the mainland to hunt for food. Thus they managed to exist through the month of May, waiting and watching in vain for the promised supplies from home.

In the meantime, Pemisapan, while preserving a friendly guise, began to plot anew against them, and instigated the hostile Indians to take the whites at a disadvantage, falling upon them while scattered and cutting them off in detail. To carry out this scheme he proposed to hold a great assembly of Indians, to last a month, by way of solemnizing the death of his father, Ensinore. This meeting was to be held on the mainland, at Desamonquepeuc, opposite Roanoke Island; and besides seven hundred neighboring warriors, it was to be attended by an equal number of the Mangoaks and Chesipeans, who were to come and lie secretly in the woods until the signal fires should give them the order to rise. As a part of the same plan, it was arranged that Terraquine, one of Pemisapan's chieftains, with twenty men, should set fire to the thatched roof of Lane's house, and when he should come out, they were to murder him. Another leader and squad were to deal with Hariot the same way; and, similarly, all of the principal men of the colony were to be surprised and overcome. Toward the end of May the neighboring Indians began to assemble on Roanoke Island, the night of June 10th being the time appointed for the others to meet and carry into effect the murderous plot.

Skyco, being the son of a king, on reaching the island had been taken by Pemisapan to reside with his own family, and as the young prince was held a prisoner and was deemed hostile to the English, the plot became known to him; but Lane had treated him with kindness and consideration, and the young boy in gratitude revealed to him all the details of the conspiracy. Confronted with such an emergency, Lane's strength of character and resolution promptly displayed itself. Had he been a weaker man, not so resourceful, the colonists would probably have fallen victims to Indian strategy.

Skyco reveals the plot

Lane's strategy

Pemisapan had gone over to the mainland, ostensibly to see about his growing corn crops, but really to attend to collecting the hostile Indians. Lane, realizing that safety could only be secured by the death of this wily foe and of his coadjutors, resolved on an immediate stroke. He sent him word to return to the island, for having heard of the arrival of his fleet at Croatoan, he himself proposed to go there; and he wished Pemisapan to detail some of his men to fish and hunt for him at Croatoan, and he also wanted to purchase four days' supply of corn to take with him. Pemisapan, however, did not fall into the trap; but while promising to come, postponed doing so from day to day, waiting for the assembling of the hostile Indians. At length, on the last of May, all of Pemisapan's own people having begun to congregate on the island, Lane determined to wait

no longer. So that night he ordered "the master of the light-horsemen," as he termed his chief boatman, with a few others to gather up at sunset all the canoes in the island, so as to prevent any information being conveyed to the mainland. As the "light-horsemen" were performing this duty, they saw a canoe departing from the island, and in seizing it two of the savages were killed. This aroused the Indians who were present, and they at once took themselves to their bows and the Englishmen to their muskets. Some few of the savages were killed in the encounter and the others fled down the island. At dawn the next morning, with the "light-horsemen" and a canoe carrying twenty-five others, with the "colonel of the Chesipeans," and "the sergeant major," Lane hastened to the mainland, and sent word to Pemisapan that he was coming to visit him, as he was about to depart for Croatoan, and wished to complain of the conduct of Osacan, who the night before had tried to convey away the prisoner Skyco, whom he had there handcuffed. The Indian king, ignorant of what had happened on the island, and not suspecting any hostile purpose, received Lane and his attendants, who, coming up, found him surrounded by seven or eight of his principal Weroances, together with many other warriors.

1586

As soon as they met, Lane gave the agreed signal, "Christ, our Victory," and immediately the colonel of the Chesipeans, the sergeant major, and their company opened fire, and Pemisapan and his chief men were slain and the others dispersed. A blow so sudden and terrible paralyzed the Indians; the plot was abandoned and the danger averted.

Drake arrives and the colonists return to England

A week later, on June 8th, the colony was thrown into an ecstasy of excitement by the hasty arrival of a messenger from Stafford, who reported seeing off Croatoan a fleet consisting of more than twenty vessels; but war had the year before broken out between Spain and England, and it was not at first known whether the ships belonged to friends or foes. The next day, however, Stafford himself came, having walked twenty miles by land, bringing a letter, proffering food and assistance, from Sir Francis Drake, then at Hattorask, who had just returned from sacking Santo Domingo, Cartagena and St. Augustine. With a joyful heart, Lane hastened to the fleet "riding at his bad harbor"; and Drake proposed to leave him a sufficient supply of provisions and a small vessel that could pass the inlet and lie within the sound. But before the necessary arrangements were completed a terrific storm came up that lasted three days, and the vessel which was to have been left was blown to sea and did not return; and much damage was done to the other ships of the fleet, and many pinnaces and smaller boats were entirely lost. After the storm had abated, Drake offered to leave another vessel, but he then had none that could enter the harbor; so the ship, if left, would have had to remain on the perilous coast. As an alternative proposition Drake offered to take the colonists aboard and transport them to England. After consideration, it was deemed best to accept this last offer, and the different companies into which the colony had been broken being again collected, they embarked on June 19th and safely reached Portsmouth on July 27th. Thus, after a nine months' residence, ended the first attempt to plant a colony on Roanoke Island.

End of the first colony

In the meantime, a bark bearing advice that a new fleet was coming had been despatched from England, and somewhat later Sir Richard Grenville sailed with three vessels freighted with supplies and bringing other colonists. The first bark arrived immediately after the departure of Lane, and finding the settlement abandoned, returned to England; but when Sir Richard came, a fortnight later, he remained three weeks searching for the settlers and making explorations; and then putting fifteen men in the fort, with an ample supply of provisions, he sailed away on a cruise against the Spaniards.

CHAPTER IV

White's Colony, 1587-91

Raleigh's Embarrassments

The unexpected return of Lane's colonists greatly disappointed Raleigh. His efforts at exploration and colonization had involved great expenditures. He had already disbursed forty thousand pounds in the enterprise, a sum approximating in this age half a million dollars, and that at a period when there was no great accumulation of wealth in England. He had now been at court some years and was a member of Parliament; and his fine powers and accomplishments, his versatility of genius and varied learning, commended him to the high favor of the queen, who gave substantial evidence of her inclination to push his fortunes. In 1584 she had bestowed on him a grant of twelve thousand acres of forfeited land in Munster, Ireland, which he attempted to colonize with English tenants and where he employed a large force in cutting timber for market, which, however, did not turn out a profitable enterprise. Also, beginning in the same year, he received annually for five years profitable grants allowing him to export quantities of broadcloth from England—a sort of monopoly; and he likewise obtained a lucrative monopoly in the grant of the "farm of wines," vesting in him the power of selling licenses for the vending of wine and, in some measure, of regulating the price of that commodity throughout the kingdom. Some months after Lane's return, on the attainder of Anthony Babbington,

1585

Edwards'
Life of
Raleigh

the queen was also pleased to bestow on Raleigh all of the estates that had come to the Crown by the attainder, which gave him rich manors and broad acres in five counties of England. In July, 1585, when the war broke out with Spain, he was created Lord Warden of the Stannaries (Cornwall and Devon) and Vice-Admiral of Cornwall and Devon; and two years later he was appointed captain of the Queen's Guard, the office of a courtier, to succeed Hatton, who was to become Lord Chancellor. But neither his outlays in Ireland nor his expenditures for Virginia had yielded him any return, while his living at court, where he indulged in magnificent display, involved large expenses.

The Citie of Raleigh in Virginia

1586

Such were his circumstances when Lane's colony returned to England in the fall of 1586. But unwilling to abandon the enterprise and still hoping for profit from establishing a trade in Virginia, he now determined to associate merchants with him who would share the profits and the expenses. At that time some of the wealthy merchants of London were looking with eager eyes for new avenues of trade and commerce. Chief among these was Thomas Smith, whose subsequent enterprises led to his receiving knighthood at the hands of his appreciative sovereign; and of their number was Richard Hakluyt, to whom posterity is indebted for the collection and publication of many narratives of exploration and discovery in that interesting period. To Smith and eighteen other merchants who risked their money in the enterprise Raleigh granted free trade forever with his colony in Virginia, and to thirteen others he assigned the right of governing the colony. Of these John White, who had been in all the previous expeditions to Virginia, was constituted the governor, and the other twelve, who also were to accompany the colony, were nominated his assistants; among them Ananias Dare and Dionysius Harvie, who carried their wives with them, and the former of whom was White's son-in-law. / These thirteen Raleigh, by patent, under the powers contained in his own charter, on January 7, 1587, erected into a corporation under the name of "The Governor and Assistants of the Citie of

The
corporation

Raleigh in Virginia"; and the nineteen merchants were made members, "free of the corporation."

A permanent settlement attempted

These preliminaries being arranged, a new colony was collected, consisting of one hundred and twenty-one persons, of whom seventeen were women, twelve apparently being wives accompanying their husbands, and nine being children. On April 26, 1587, three vessels bearing the colonists left Portsmouth for Plymouth; and on May 8th finally took their departure from that port for Hattorask, where, after many adventures, two of them arrived on July 22d, and a few days later the other. Raleigh had given written directions that after taking in the fifteen men left by Grenville the vessels were to proceed to Chesapeake Bay, where a new settlement was to be made, and such was the purpose of Governor White. But when White with a part of his men had left the ship to visit Roanoke Island for the purpose of taking off the fifteen men, Ferdinando, the admiral, influenced the sailors to say that they could not be received back into the ship, thus constraining all the colonists to disembark. At sunset White's boat reached the island, but the only trace he could find of the men left by Grenville was the bones of one that lay unburied where he had been slain. The fort had been razed down, but the cottages were still standing, some of the outer planks, however, being torn off. . Forced to remain there, White set the men at once to work to repair the buildings and to construct others. The colonists had hardly gotten established in their new homes, when George Howe, one of the assistants, having strayed off two miles from the fort catching crabs on the shore opposite the mainland, was set upon by some savages, receiving sixteen wounds from arrows, and was slain. This was an evidence of hostility that White at once sought to allay. He sent Stafford with twenty men, accompanied by Manteo, who along with another Indian, Towaye, had gone to England and had now returned, to Croatoan, where Manteo's mother and kindred were; and from these friendly Indians it was learned that some savages from the mainland had taken the men left by Grenville unawares, had killed some of them.

set fire to the house where they had taken refuge, and driven them from the island; they taking their boat and going to an island near Hattorask, after which they had never been seen. They also said that it was a remnant of Wingina's men dwelling at Dasamonquepeuc who had slain Howe. To establish more amicable relations with these hostile Indians, the Croatoans were requested to go over to their towns and proffer them the friendship of the English, who promised to forgive and forget all past offences; and it was agreed that this embassy was to return with the answer within seven days. At the end of the time, no answers being received, White deemed it best to strike a blow to show that the colonists were to be dreaded. At night, accompanied by Stafford and twenty-four men and Manteo, he crossed over to Dasamonquepeuc and secreted his force near the Indian town; and early in the morning he opened fire on some Indians discovered there. Unfortunately, these were not the hostiles, who, fearing punishment for the murder of Howe, had fled, leaving their corn standing in the fields; but they were some of the Croatoans who had gone there to gather the corn. White, disappointed in his revenge, despoiled the fields and returned home. The colony being now settled, on August 13th a ceremony was performed at Roanoke that gave expression to the gratitude of Raleigh and the colony for the faithful and friendly services of Manteo.

The baptism of Manteo and Virginia Dare

By command of Sir Walter, the rite of baptism was administered to Manteo, and there was conferred on him the order of Knighthood; and he was created Lord of Roanoke and Dasamonquepeuc. And five days later another interesting event occurred, the birth of the first English child born in America. On August 18, 1587, Eleanor Dare, wife of Ananias Dare and a daughter of the governor, gave birth to a daughter, who the next Sunday was christened Virginia, because she was the first Christian born in the new country. A few days later, also, was born to Dionysius Harvie and his wife, Margery, a child, whose name, however, has not been preserved.

The colonists to remove into the interior

It was now discovered that certain other particular sup-

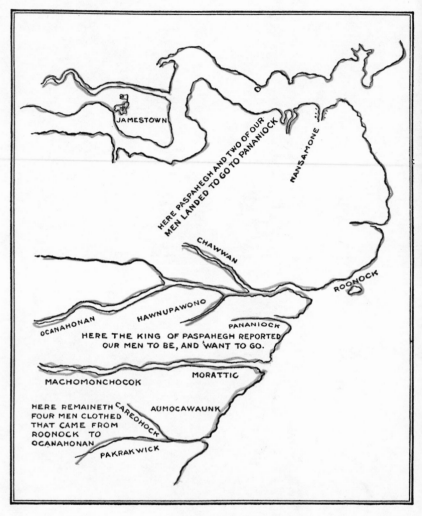

THE LOST COLONY

1587

plies were needed, as this was intended to be a permanent settlement; and there was consultation as to who should return with the fleet to obtain them. It was finally determined that White himself would answer the purpose best, and he agreed to go with the vessels back to England. But before his departure it was resolved that the colony should remove to some point about fifty miles in the interior; and it was agreed that they would, on departing from the island, leave some sign indicating their location; and if in distress, a cross would be the sign. It is probable that this point, fifty miles in the interior, where the colony was to locate, was the highland near Ohanoak, where there were goodly cornfields and pleasant surroundings.

At length, the fleet being ready to sail, on August 27th, after a month's sojourn with the colony, White embarked and departed for England. On the return voyage he met with many perilous adventures, but finally, about the middle of October, made land at Smerwick, on the west coast of Ireland, and in November reached Hampton. With him came to England still another Indian, who, accepting Christianity, was baptized at Bideford Church; but a year later died, and was interred there. When the colonists receded from White's view, as he left the shores of Virginia, they passed from the domain of history, and all we know is that misfortune and distress overtook them; and that they miserably perished, their sad fate being one of those deplorable sacrifices that have always attended the accomplishment of great human purposes.

Doyle, English in America, I, 72

Conditions in England on White's arrival

On White's arrival, in November, 1587, seeking aid for the colony, doubtless the merchants and others who had ventured their means with Raleigh in this last attempt at colonization and trade in Virginia, were willing to respond; but there were rumors of the preparation in Spain of a great Armada to invade England, and an order had been issued forbidding the departure of any vessel from any English port. In that period of excitement and alarm, the necessities of the distant colonists were of less moment than the pressing matters at home. Still Raleigh, exerting his per-

1588

sonal influence, obtained a license for two small vessels to sail, and on April 25, 1588, White departed with them from Bideford for Virginia. The captains, however, were more intent on a gainful voyage than on the relief of the colonists, and betook themselves to the hazardous business of making prizes. At length one of them, meeting with two ships of war, was after a bloody fight overcome and rifled, despoiled and disabled, and she returned to England within a month; and three weeks later, the other, equally badly served, came home without having completed the voyage. Soon after-

The Invincible Armada, July 21-29, 1588

ward, the great Armada appeared, and Raleigh was among those who made havoc of the Spanish galleons in the "morris dance of death," that, beginning in the straits, lasted around the north of Scotland and on the coast of Ireland. Immediately on his return he was challenged to mortal combat by the queen's favorite, the handsome boy, Essex, and for a time retired to Ireland in seclusion. But soon all his powers and resources were employed in distressing Spanish commerce and in taking rich prizes, while England was again and again threatened with Spanish invasion. In the following March, 1589, because, perhaps, both of his public employments and of the greater facilities of the merchants to care for the colonists, he transferred his rights in Virginia

Doyle, English in America, I, 72 ; Edwards' Life of Raleigh, I, 91

by an assignment or lease to Thomas Smith, White and others, and relinquished his interest in the colony. What particular efforts these merchants made to relieve the planters are not recorded; but White afterward mentioned "having at sundry times been chargeable and troublesome to Sir Walter for the supplies and relief of the planters in Virginia." Because of the inhibition of the sailing of merchant ships from England, no opportunity presented for White to return to Virginia until early in 1591. He then ascertained that John Watts of London, merchant, was about to send three vessels to the West Indies; but when they were ready to depart, a general stay was again commanded of all ships throughout England. Taking advantage of this circumstance, White applied to Sir Walter to obtain a special license for these vessels to sail, on condition that they would transport a convenient number of passengers with their furniture and necessaries to Virginia. The license was obtained by Raleigh, but the condition was not observed; and the only passenger they would take was White himself, and no provisions for the relief of the colonists.

White sails for Roanoke

Leaving Plymouth on March 20, 1591, they sailed for the West Indies and sought to make prizes, and had some desperate encounters. Eventually, on August 3d, they reached Wokokon, but were driven off by a storm. On Monday, the 9th, however, the weather being fair, they returned and anchored and went on shore, obtaining a supply of fresh water and catching great stores of fish. On the morning of the 12th they departed, and toward night dropped anchor at the north end of Croatoan. The next morning they sounded the inlet there, and then, on August 15th, came to anchor at Hattorask, seeing a great smoke on Roanoke Island. The next morning, after directing signal guns to be fired, to warn the colonists of their presence, they entered the inlet; but observing a great smoke toward the southwest, they landed and proceeded to it, only to meet with disappointment. Returning to their vessels, the morning following they set off again; but on passing the bar one of the boats was upset, and seven of the crew, including the captain, the mate and the surgeon, were drowned, and the remaining men protested against proceeding further. Distressing, indeed, was the situation of White and unpropitious the outlook of a journey begun with such a calamity. But at length the men reluctantly yielded and the boats proceeded to the island, arriving after night, anchoring off the shore and sounding a trumpet call and familiar tunes to evoke a response. But all in vain. No answer came, although in the distance a firelight was seen. At break of day they landed and hastened to the fire, finding no sign of the English. Then pressing across the island, they skirted along its western shore until they came to the north point near where the settlement had been. There on the shore they found a tree on which had been cut the Roman letters C. R. O. With despondent C. R. O. hearts they proceeded to the place of settlement, and saw that the houses had been taken down and the place strongly enclosed with a high palisade of great trees, very like a

1591

fort; and on a tree was cut the word "Croatoan," but without the cross or sign of distress. The boats were gone; the pieces of light ordnance had been taken away, only some of the heavier pieces remaining, and the fort was all grown up with grass and weeds, as if long since deserted. A trench in which White had buried his boxes had been opened and his maps and property scattered, and his armor lay on the ground, almost eaten through with rust. It was a scene of

Croatoan

desolation. There was still a hope, yet it must have been but faint, that the colonists could be found at Croatoan. White had just sailed along that island and had anchored at its northern end and had beheld no sign of the presence of any English there. Returning to the inlet, it was, however, determined to go again to that island. But after they had weighed anchor, the design was relinquished; and one vessel returned to England and the other steered for the West Indies. From that time onward the English who settled in Virginia were known as Raleigh's Lost Colony. They were not forgotten, but were never discovered.

Raleigh's efforts to relieve the colony

Edwards' Life of Raleigh

Greater enterprises now absorbed Raleigh, who had become one of the most heroic of that splendid company of heroes who brought lustre to the Elizabethan Age; but still, between 1587 and 1602, it is said that he sent out no less than five expeditions to seek his unfortunate company in Virginia. In 1602 he bought a ship, hired a crew, placed

Mace

it under the command of Samuel Mace, who had twice before sailed for Virginia, and in March sent it forth to search for the colonists. Mace struck Virginia forty leagues southwest of Hatteras, and spent a month trading with the Indians as he scoured along the coast; but without going to Croatoan or Hattorask, he returned to Weymouth in August. Raleigh hastened there to meet him, and found in the same harbor another vessel likewise just arrived from Virginia, but which had missed Roanoke also, by forty leagues to the northward. He, however, proposed to send them both away again, having saved the cost in the sassafras they brought, which he claimed because of his ownership of the land under his patent, no one having the right,

he asserted, to trade in Virginia except by his license. The
next year Richard Hakluyt, one of the grantees in the charter
of the City of Raleigh, formally applied to Sir Walter for
permission to sail to northern Virginia; but in the spring
of that year, 1603, Elizabeth died, and before the summer
had passed Raleigh was arrested for treason.

1603

Jamestown settled—The Roanoke colony disappears

In the meantime the spirit of enterprise which had been
stimulated by Raleigh's efforts at colonization had grown,
and Thomas Smith and a few other London merchants, in
1599, had laid the foundations of the East India Company,
whose great success led, in 1606, to the formation of another
corporation, called the Virginia Company, with two divisions, at the head of one division being Thomas Smith, now
knighted, and other London merchants and gentlemen who
had been associated with Raleigh in his enterprise; and
on December 19, 1606, Christopher Newport set sail with
one hundred and forty-three immigrants and, on May 13th,
settled Jamestown. The next year Newport was directed
to make an expedition to find Raleigh's Lost Colony.

Virginia
Company,
1606

1607

The fate of White's colonists

The colonists, warned by previous mishaps, certainly
brought with them sufficient supplies to last until a crop
would mature in the fall of 1588, and they did not neglect
to begin their planting operations.

On his return White found no sign of any planting on
Roanoke Island; nor was there evidence of any conflict
with the savages—no graves, no butchery. The dwellings
had been taken down and removed, and the light ordnance
had been carried away. The growth of weeds indicated that
two seasons had passed since the removal, and apparently the
spot had not been revisited by the colonists in many months.

On his departure for England, the avowed intention was
for the colonists to settle fifty miles in the interior; and when
he coasted along Croatoan leisurely he observed no sign of
their presence on the shore. Instead of establishing themselves on that barren sandbank, exposed to the attacks of the
Spaniards, with no inviting streams, nor fertile fields, nor
shady forests, they looked westward for a secure and agreea-

ble location for their permanent settlement. Fifty miles would have brought them to the "goodly highlands, on the left hand between Muscamunge and Chowanoak," where the Indians already had fertile cornfields; and there, according to Indian statements of different sources, they appear to have seated themselves on what are now the pleasant bluffs of Bertie County.

Several vessels were at different times despatched to search for them; but none of these entered the great sounds. At length, after Jamestown was settled, Newport in 1608 was specially directed to make an exploration to discover them. An expedition by water did not proceed far and was without result. A searching party by land penetrated to the territory of the Chowanists and Mangoaks, but did not find the colonists.

Smith in his "True Relation" (1608) repeats information derived from the king of the Paspehegh Indians, who resided above Jamestown, to the effect that there were men apparelled like himself at Ochanahonan, which seems to have been on the Nottoway; and that there were many at Panawicke, a region apparently between the Chowan and Roanoke rivers. Five years later, William Strachey, the secretary of the Jamestown colony, gave some account of the missing colonists derived from Machumps, a friendly Indian of considerable intelligence, who had been to England and who came freely and often to Jamestown. At Peccarecamek and Ochanahonan, the Indians had houses built with stone walls, one story above another, having been taught by the English who escaped the slaughter at the time of the landing at Jamestown. And at Ritanoe there were preserved seven of the colonists, four men, two boys and a young maid, who having escaped, fled up the Chowan.

For more than twenty years the colonists were reported to have lived peaceably with the Indians and to have intermixed with them in their locality, beyond the territory of Powhatan; and then on the arrival of the colonists at Jamestown, Powhatan, persuaded by his bloody priests, procured their slaughter, he being present on the occasion. Some escaped; but none ever had communication with the Jamestown settlers.

Peccarecamek was apparently on the upper Pamlico, or Tar River; and perhaps a trace of English blood might be found in the aggressiveness and fierceness of the Indians of that region a century later.

Traces of the colonists

If others were preserved on the sandbanks, as they might well have been, escaping in their pinnace through the waters of the sound, a trace of them possibly came down to posterity through their intermixture with the Hatteras Indians. That small tribe had always been friendly with the whites: and as late as 1709, grey eyes were found among them and they cherished a friendship with the English because of their affinity, according to their own traditions. /Yet there were other opportunities for an admixture of the races. Thirty-two men of Captain Raymond's company were among them twenty days before the arrival of Lane's colony, and the following summer Captain Stafford and twenty men were with them until Drake came in June, and doubtless others were stationed there the next year to keep watch for the expected return of White, until all hope had expired. Other than these possible traces no memorial has ever been discovered of the existence of the Lost Colony, whose mournful fate, involved in mystery, has ever been a fruitful theme of song and story.

THE SECOND EPOCH—1629-63

PERMANENT SETTLEMENT

CHAPTER V

CHARTERS AND COLONIAL OFFICERS

The charters.—The concessions.—The Lords Proprietors and their successors.—The Palatines.—The governors, speakers of the Assembly, and chief justices.

Carolana

1629

C. R., I, 5

Sir Robert Heath's Patent—30th of October, 1629.

By this grant Charles I conveyed to his Attorney-General, Sir Robert Heath, Knight, his heirs and assigns forever so much of the Continent of America as lay between 31 and 36 degrees of North latitude,—"to have, exercise, use and enjoy in like manner as any Bishop of Durham within the Bishopric or County Palatine of Durham in our Kingdom of England ever heretofore had, held, used, or enjoyed, or of right, ought or could have, hold, use, or enjoy. And by these presents we make, create and constitute the same Sir Robert Heath, his heirs and assigns, true and absolute Lords and Proprietors of the region and territory aforesaid."

"Know that we . . . do erect and incorporate them into a Province, and name the same Carolana, or the Province of Carolana." "Furthermore know ye that we do give power to the said Sir Robert . . . to form, make and enact and publish what laws may concern the public state of said Province or the private profit of all according to the wholesome directions of, and with the counsel, assent and approbation of the Freeholders of the same Province."

"Furthermore lest the way to honours and dignityes may seem to be shutt, etc. do for ourselves, our heirs and successors give full and free power to the aforesaid Sir Robert Heath, Knight, his heirs and assigns to confer favours, graces and honours upon those well-deserving citizens that inhabit the aforesaid Province, and the same with whatever titles and dignityes (provided they be not the same as are now used in England) to adorne at his pleasure."

GREAT SEAL OF THE LORDS PROPRIETORS OF CAROLINA

The charter to the Lords Proprietors

1663

First and
second
charters of
Charles II,
1663, 1665

By the first charter, King Charles II on the 20th day of March, 1663, granted to the grantees, the same territory conveyed to Sir Robert Heath in 1629, and in large measure granted the same powers; such, for instance, as that the grantees, with the consent of the freemen, should make laws, etc., and that they might bestow titles of nobility, not being the same as those in use in England; and also authorizing freedom in religion. The second grant made the 30th of June, 1665, extended the territory conveyed so as to embrace "as far as the north end of Currituck River, or Inlet, upon a straight, westerly line to Weyanoke Creek, which lies within or about the degrees of 36 and 30 minutes northern latitude; and so west, in a direct line, as far as the south seas; and south and westward as far as the degrees 29, inclusive." In other respects the charters were the same; except the provision establishing religious freedom is somewhat fuller in the second.

The original Lords Proprietors

Edward Hyde.	Anthony Lord Ashley.
George Monk.	Sir George Carteret.
William Lord Craven.	Sir William Berkeley.
John Lord Berkeley.	Sir John Colleton.

After Clarendon's death, his share was bought in 1679 by Seth Sothel, on whose death in 1694, it was assigned to Thomas Amy, a London merchant, who had been very active in promoting colonization. Eventually this share passed to Honorable James Bertie, after whom the county of Bertie was named.

The devolution of
the shares

The share of the Duke of Albemarle was acquired by John Granville, Earl of Bath, who dying in 1701, was succeeded by his son, John Lord Granville. In 1709 the Duke of Beaufort acquired this share and devised it to James Bertie in trust for his sons, Henry and Charles Somerset. His name appears in a county and in the seaport town called in his honor, when he was Palatine.

The Earl of Craven's share, he having no descendants, passed to his grand-nephew, William Lord Craven, whose son William, Lord Craven, succeeded him. That name is also perpetuated in a county.

The share of John Lord Berkeley came to his son, John, an admiral of great merit; but it had been forfeited, and in April, 1698, was sold to Joseph Blake, on whose death it descended to his son of the same name.

On the death of Shaftesbury, his share passed to his son, Lord Ashley.

1663 – 1776

George Carteret dying in 1679, was succeeded by his infant son, who was represented by the Earl of Bath. This second George Carteret dying about 1695, was succeeded by his son, George Carteret, who at the time of the purchase by the Crown in 1729, was lieutenant-governor of Ireland, and in 1742 overthrew Walpole's administration and became prime-minister. About that time, on the death of his mother, the Countess of Granville, he became Lord Granville. He would not sell his share to the Crown, and in 1744 it was set apart to him in the northern half of North Carolina. After the Revolution it was held by the State, although his heirs brought suit to recover it, but failed in the courts.

On the death of Sir William Berkeley, 1677, his share was sold by his widow to John Archdale for his son Thomas. Afterward in 1684 she and her husband, Philip Ludwell, sold it again to Sir Peter Colleton for 300 pounds. Sir Peter purchased it for himself and three other Proprietors and the title was conveyed to Thomas Amy in trust for them.

In 1705 this share was acquired by John Archdale, who in 1709 conveyed it to John Dawson, his son-in-law. Later it was sold by decree of the Court of Chancery and purchased by Hugh Watson as trustee for Henry and James Bertie.

Sir John Colleton's share on his death in 1666 descended to his son, Sir Peter, who held it until 1694, and who was succeeded by his son, Sir John Colleton. All of the shares were bought by the Crown in 1729, except that of Sir George Carteret.

Palatines

McCrady's South Carolina, I, 716

1. Duke of Albemarle, October 16, 1669.
2. John Lord Berkeley, January 20, 1670.
3. Sir George Carteret, February 5, 1679.
4. William Earl of Craven, November 20, 1680.
5. John Earl of Bath, April, 1697.
6. John Lord Granville, January 10, 1702.
7. William Lord Craven, 1708.
8. Henry Duke of Beaufort, November 8, 1711.
9. John Lord Carteret, August 10, 1714, and he so continued until the sale to the Crown in 1729.

John Lord Berkeley did not attend the meetings of the Proprietors after 1671, Shaftesbury being then the particular manager.

Governors of Albemarle under the Proprietary Government

William Drummond, appointed October, 1664—October, 1667.
Samuel Stephens, appointed October, 1667. Died December, 1669.
Peter Carteret, appointed October, 1670. Left colony May, 1673.

John Jenkins, president of council, appointed May, 1673.
Thomas Eastchurch, appointed November, 1676. Never qualified.
Thomas Miller, appointed 1677. Deposed by Culpepper.
John Culpepper, in power, 1677-78.
Seth Sothel, appointed 1678. Captured by Algerines.
John Harvey, appointed February 5, 1679. Died August, 1679.
John Jenkins, president of council, appointed November, 1679.
Henry Wilkinson, appointed February 16, 1681.
Seth Sothel, arrived 1682. Deposed fall of 1689.

Governors of North Carolina under the Proprietors

Philip Ludwell, appointed December 5, 1689.
Thomas Jarvis, deputy, 1691-94.
Thomas Harvey, deputy, July, 1694—July, 1699.
John Archdale, governor, 1695.
Henderson Walker, president of council, 1699-1704.
Robert Daniel, deputy governor, 1704-05.
Thomas Cary, deputy governor, 1705-06.
William Glover, president of council, 1706-08.
Thomas Cary, president of council, 1708—January, 1711.
Edward Hyde, governor, January, 1711—September, 1712.
Thomas Pollock, president of council, September, 1712-14.
Charles Eden, governor, 1714-22.
Thomas Pollock, president of council, 1722.
William Reed, president of council, 1722-23.
George Burrington, governor, 1724-25.
Sir Richard Everard, governor, 1725-31.

Governors of North Carolina under the Crown

George Burrington, February 25, 1731—November, 1734.
Gabriel Johnston, November, 1734—July, 1752.
Nathaniel Rice, president, July, 1752—January, 1753.
Matthew Rowan, president, January, 1753—November, 1754.
Arthur Dobbs, November, 1754—March 28, 1765.
William Tryon, March, 1765—June 30, 1771.
James Hasell, president of council, July 1, 1771—August, 1771.
Josiah Martin, August, 1771. Expelled 1775.

Speakers of the Assembly

George Catchmaid, 1666.
Thomas Eastchurch, 1675.
Thomas Cullen, 1676.
John Porter, 1697.
Edward Moseley, 1708.
William Swann, 1711.
Edward Moseley, 1715.
Edward Moseley, 1722.
Maurice Moore, 1726.
John Baptista Ashe, 1727.

Thomas Swann, 1729.
Edward Moseley, 1731.
William Downing, 1734.
John Hodgson, 1739.
Sam Swann, 1743.
John Campbell, 1755.

Sam Swann, 1756.
John Ashe, 1762.
John Harvey, 1766.
Richard Caswell, 1770.
John Harvey, 1772-75.

Chief justices of North Carolina

Christopher Gale, 1712.
Tobias Knight, 1717.
Frederick Jones, 1718.
Christopher Gale, 1722.
Thomas Pollock, 1724.
Christopher Gale, 1724.
William Smith, 1731.
John Palin, 1732.
William Little, 1732.
Daniel Hanmer, 1733.

William Smith, 1734.
John Montgomery, 1743.
Edward Moseley, 1744.
Eleazar Allen, 1749.
Enoch Hall, 1749.
James Hasell, 1750.
Peter Henley, December 5, 1755.
Charles Berry, 1758.
James Hasell, 1765.
Martin Howard, 1766-76.

CHAPTER VI

Beginnings of Permanent Settlement in Albemarle

Conditions in America.—Virginia under the treaty with Parliament.—Roger Green's explorations.—The king of Roanoke Island. —Permanent settlement on the Carolina Sound.—The Restoration. —The Cape Fear explored.—Berkeley receives instructions as to Carolina.—The name Albemarle.—The Quakers.—The grant of the Lords Proprietors.—William Drummond, governor of Albemarle.— The second grant.

Conditions in America

The disturbed condition of England prior to her civil war led to an immense emigration to the New England plantations, and at the close of that period of unrest, marked by the execution of the king in 1649, settlements had extended into Rhode Island, Connecticut and New Hampshire. Maryland also had prospered, and Virginia's population, which in the first years after settlement increased but slowly, numbered twenty thousand souls, and extended far into the interior and well along the sluggish waters of the Nansemond.

The region south of the thirty-sixth parallel, which under the name of Carolana had, in 1629, been granted by King Charles I to his attorney-general, Sir Robert Heath, had not been settled; and the wilds of Carolana remained unoccupied save by the copper-colored aborigines.

While the civil war was raging at home, the Puritans of New England adhered to Parliament, but Virginia remained faithful to the Crown, winning by her loyalty the name of the Old Dominion; and upon the death of his father, Charles II, then in exile, transmitted to Sir William Berkeley, who had been the royal governor for a decade, a new commission confirming his authority.

Virginia under the treaty

Parliament, however, was not indifferent to the attitude of those colonies that continued to sustain the monarchy, and its power being fully established at home, in convenient

1652

season took measures to assert its supremacy in Virginia. On one hand, it threatened war; in the other it held out the olive branch of peace, offering terms that could hardly be refused. The Old Dominion preferred peace, and a formal treaty was agreed to in 1652 that secured to Virginia almost complete independence. The Assembly obtained the right of choosing all the officers of the colony, including the governor, who had formerly been appointed by the Crown, and of defining their duties and privileges. It also secured the high power of regulating commerce, and, without regard to the British navigation acts, it declared that trade should be absolutely free with all nations at peace with England. The right of suffrage was extended to all freemen, and "Dissenters" had full religious liberty; but under one clause of the treaty the prayer-book was not to be used in the churches. Of churches, there were none except in the very heart of the colony, and ministers were so few that a bounty was offered for their importation.*

Bancroft,
I, 231

Thus between the treaty of peace, in 1652, and the Restoration, in 1660, the Old Dominion enjoyed a republican government, and local independence. Indeed, Virginia has the distinction of having been the first community in the world whose government was organized on the principle of manhood suffrage, where all freemen, without exception, had an equal voice in the government, and their representatives chose the administrative officers and controlled public affairs. It was near the close of a decade of growth under the favorable influences of virtual independence, that the increasing population led to an overflow of the inhabitants into the territory north of the Albemarle Sound, and perhaps the movement was quickened by some apprehensions that the downfall of the Commonwealth, then imminent, would usher in a new era of religious intolerance.

Roger Green's exploration

The Nansemond penetrates near to the head waters of the Chowan, and before 1653 Roger Green† had explored

*In 1658, while the Dissenters still held sway, Quakers were banished.

†Roger Green is mentioned as "Clarke," by which he is understood to have been a clergyman, and it may be, if he was a member of the

that fertile region, and some of the inhabitants of Nansemond were considering a removal to that attractive country.
Green obtained from the General Assembly of Virginia a
grant of ten thousand acres for the one hundred persons who
should first seat on the Roanoke and on the lands on the
south side of the Chowan; and "as a reward for his own
first discovery and for his encouraging the settlement,"
he was granted a thousand acres for himself. But while his
enterprise may have led to the subsequent settlement, no
memorial of his being concerned in it has come down to posterity. The waters of the great sound had been explored
and were well known to Virginians, and about the year **Bennett and Drew in Carolina, 1646**
1646 two expeditions had been made from Virginia against
the Indians on the sound: one by land, under General Bennett, and the other by water, under Colonel Drew. Drew's
vessels entered Currituck Sound and proceeded as far as
the Chowan River. At the mouth of Weyanoke Creek he
had an encounter with the Indians, with whom, however, he
soon established a peace; and shortly afterward Henry
Plumpton, who had been on that expedition, together with
Thomas Tuke and several others, purchased from the **C. R., I, 676**
Indians all the land from the mouth of Roanoke River to
Weyanoke Creek. But they did not take possession, and
no settlement was made at that time.

In 1654, Francis Yardley, then governor of Virginia, **Explorations, 1654**
mentioned in a letter that small sloops were employed in
visiting the sounds of Carolina, and in hunting and trading
for beavers. In that year such a vessel, having left a couple
of her crew near Lynnhaven, where Yardley resided, he sent
his son and some other men to hunt for the sloop. These
visited the ruins of "Sir Walter Raleigh's fort" on Roanoke
Island, then in a good state of preservation, and had
friendly intercourse with the king of the Roanoke Indians,
whom they induced to visit the governor at his home. **The king of Roanoke Island**
When the king of Roanoke came to Lynnhaven, he brought
with him his wife and one son, and during their sojourn

Church of England, he was seeking to lead his flock to new homes,
where they could use the prayer book without restraint.

there they all accepted Christianity and were baptized. Yardley sent six carpenters to Roanoke Island to build an English house for the king, whose son remained at Lynnhaven to be taught to "read out of a book." With the cooperation of this king, an extensive exploration was then made throughout the eastern portion of Carolina, where a Spaniard was found living among the Tuscarora Indians, and a purchase was made from the Indians of the territory drained by three rivers, covering a large scope of country, which probably lay north of Albemarle Sound. There were further explorations, and in 1656 the General Assembly of Virginia commissioned Colonel Thomas Drew and Captain Thomas Francis to make discoveries between Cape Hatteras and Cape Fear.

Permanent settlement on the Carolina Sound

But whatever settlement was then in contemplation, it was probably arrested by an outbreak of the Indians, who now began active hostilities on the northern confines of Virginia. In 1656, several fierce tribes, known as the Rechahecrians, several hundred strong in warriors, established themselves near the falls of the James, and in a great battle defeated the forces sent against them. But while this disaster and the Indian depredations to the northward for a time checked any movement to establish distant plantations in the wilderness, yet when peace was restored and the desire to seek new locations again began to be felt, the favorable situation of the region bordering on the Carolina Sound speedily attracted the attention of the adventurous pioneer. On the south it was protected by the wide sound; on the north and east the Indians were but few and had much intercourse with the whites; on the west were the Tuscaroras, who although a strong and brave nation, were not unfriendly in their disposition. Their hunting grounds that lay southward toward the Neuse had not been encroached upon, while many traders, trafficking in their furs, supplied them freely with those commodities they desired. Distant from the vicinity of the fierce and troublesome tribes of the upper James, the mild climate and fertile soil of the region bordering on the landlocked sounds near Nansemond offered many inducements to settlers, and so it came about that in 1659, or thereabouts, the permanent settlement of Carolina began. It was a movement so natural that the particulars are not recorded in the local annals of the time. A few active spirits, perhaps more adventurous than their neighbors, resolved to make new homes in a more attractive locality. It was no great company, perhaps a dozen or twenty men, who may have come from Nansemond through the wilderness, or may have brought their supplies and implements for house building by water from some convenient point in Virginia. The roll of these companions in the enterprise of establishing "new plantations" to the southward has not been preserved, and only incidentally have the names of some of them been recorded. All we know is that they came not as conquerors, writing their names in blood on the scroll of Fame, nor yet were they exiles from the habitations of mankind for conscience' sake. It was a time of peace in Virginia, when the freemen still governed themselves, chose their own officers and made their own laws. It was not oppression that drove these first settlers into the wilderness. They were not discontented with the democratic-republican institutions under which they were living. They were not fleeing from the ills of life, nor plunging into the primeval forest to escape the tyranny of their fellow-men. But they were bold, enterprising, hardy Virginians, nurtured in freedom's ways, who were wooed to this summer land by the advantages of its situation. The movement involved no great change. It was merely a removal of a few miles beyond the outlying districts of Nansemond, with water communication to the marts of trade on the Chesapeake. Nor did they come without the sanction of the Indians, who were to be their neighbors in these "new plantations." They bought their land from the king of the Yeopims with the consent of his people, and their doorsills were not stained with blood, nor were their spirits tortured with apprehensions of butchery. They came in peace and were received as friends by the native inhabitants who surrounded them. Among the earliest who were seated were

1661
Durant,
1662

John Battle, Dr. Thomas Relfe, Roger Williams and Thomas Jarvis; and with the first who came was George Durant, who, however, did not select a plantation at once, but spent two years in exploring, and bestowed much labor and cost in finding out the country, with its rivers, channels, passages, and conveniences, and then he bought from Kilcocanen, king of Yeopim, with the consent of his people, a tract on Roanoke Sound, upon a point then known as Wikacome, but ever since called Durant's Neck. This conveyance bears date March 1, 1661, but as the English year then began on March 25th, that date may answer to March, 1662. In this deed, Kilcocanen mentions that similar purchases had previously been made by other settlers; and a few months later Durant purchased a second tract from the friendly king of the Yeopims.*

Durant at once began his clearing, and as the location of any previous settlement has not been ascertained, Durant's Neck is the oldest known clearing in Albemarle.

Quickly after the arrival of these first pioneers others were attracted to the "new plantations." Lawson, writing about fifty years later, mentions that "the first settlement was by several substantial planters from Virginia and other plantations; and the fame of this newly discovered country spread through the neighboring colonies and in a few years drew a considerable number of families to join them." Among those who followed, buying Indian titles, were George Catchmaid, of Treslick, Gentleman; John Harvey and Captain John Jenkins.

1665

Thomas Woodward, the surveyor-general and a member of the council when the government was first established in Albemarle, writing to the Proprietors on June 2, 1665, refers to the quitrent exacted by them, and says that the people will not "remove from Virginia upon harder conditions than they can live there . . . it being land only that they come for." Woodward also mentions that he had been many years endeavoring and encouraging the people to seat Albe-

*Recorded in Book A, Perquimans County Records.

marle, and that "those that live upon a place are best able 1665
C. R., I, 100
to judge of the place, therefore the petition of the General
Assembly that was here convened will deserve your Honor's
serious consideration."

It appears that the people were drawn to Albemarle because
of the land, but protested against paying a higher quitrent
than was exacted of them in Virginia, and they gave expression to their wishes in a petition of the Assembly at the
first session held in Albemarle.

These early purchases were made on the supposition that
the lands were beyond the limits of Virginia, and the first
settlers probably thought they would be free from the payment of quitrents and other public charges. They believed
themselves outside the bounds of the Old Dominion and
within the wilds of Carolina. Of Carolina the Commonwealth had taken no notice, but now the Commonwealth itself
had passed away, and the change in the mother country
inaugurated changed conditions in the forests of the
Roanoke.

The Res-
toration

The House of Commons, that half a century before had
emphasized, by the Petition of Right, its unswerving and
resolute purpose to maintain constitutional liberty, was the
wealthiest body that had ever assembled in England. It
fully represented in the purses of its members the property
of the kingdom. After varying developments, active hostilities subsequently began between the Long Parliament
and the king, and in the course of the struggle the army
under the control of the Independents came to be the ruling
element, Oliver Cromwell, as its general, attaining supreme
power. By excluding a large number of the House of
Commons; by abolishing the House of Lords; by parcelling
out England into satrapies governed absolutely by his major-
generals, who systematically levied forced contributions from
the inhabitants, and by controlling parliaments at will,
Cromwell laid the foundation for a widespread sentiment in
favor of a return to the old constitution. In deference to

this public demand, he contrived a simulation of the three estates, and he himself became Protector, representing the sovereign; and in semblance he established a House of Lords, appointing to it nobles of his own creation. But the military influence controlled by the Independents dominated, and the discontent continued to grow in volume and intensity. Property that had opened the struggle with Charles I now cast about for some hope of security, and the Presbyterians equally with the Churchmen were ready to try the Stuarts once more as an escape from the domination of the Independents. Such were the conditions on Cromwell's death, when his son Richard succeeded to his office, but could not wield his power. The army, recognizing Richard's feebleness, fell away from him, and Cromwell's system, losing its military support, tottered to its fall. The end of the protectorate had come. At a call from the army the "bloody rump," which Cromwell had disbanded and suppressed, again met, while cries for a free Parliament rang throughout the kingdom. General Monk, in command of the forces in Scotland, maintaining an impenetrable silence, twice purged his army of Independent zealots, and marched rapidly to London, where he arrived in February. Under the lead of Ashley Cooper, a man of great wealth and of superior talents, who had espoused the cause of constitutional liberty but had separated himself from Cromwell's government, the majority of the Long Parliament who had been ejected by Pride's Purge, after many years of exclusion, in March, 1660, forced their way back to their seats, and after calling for the election of a new Parliament, adjourned *sine die* that body which had survived through so many years of turmoil and revolution. The new Parliament, known as the "Convention Parliament," met on the 25th of April. Ashley Cooper hastened with a delegation to Holland to invite Charles to occupy his throne. Monk, still sphinxlike, controlled his fifty thousand red coats—the uniform of Cromwell's Ironsides—who, appalled, in gloomy silence submitted to the complete and final overthrow, by their own general, of the

power they had so long wielded in governing the Commonwealth. Within a month Charles had landed, largely owing
his restoration to Ashley Cooper's management and to
Monk's resolute control of the hostile army; to Clarendon's
counsel, and to the fidelity of loyal friends, who never forsook his cause.

The Cape Fear explored

While these events were stirring England to its very foundation, and, by the overthrow of the Independents, the suppression of the Republicans and the restoration of the
monarchy, had prepared the way for a new exodus from the
mother country, perhaps because of the favorable reports
spread abroad concerning the summer land of the "new
plantations," attention was drawn to Carolina as a desirable
location for a new colony. From the north and the south
alike now came explorers. Massachusetts had at different
times projected colonies to the southward, and her vessels
traded along the coast and up the Chesapeake, and after
an exploration of the Cape Fear River, perhaps as early
as 1661, an association was formed in Massachusetts to
establish a plantation there, and the assistance of some London merchants was invoked with the expectation that they
would supply the needed capital. But if New England was
looking to a more temperate climate with a view to colonization, there were adventurers at Barbadoes who were likewise
casting longing eyes to the shores of Florida, as they then
usually called Carolina. Barbadoes had been settled by the
English in 1625, and during the civil war many Royalists
found refuge there, and a considerable number of prisoners
taken in battle were transported thither, so that the population had become numerous, and some of the more active
spirits were intent on bettering their fortunes in a new settlement. Captain William Hilton, with his vessel, the *Adventure,* was despatched by John Vassall and others from
Barbadoes to explore the Carolina coast, and he had ascended

1663

Letter of
P. Colleton,
August 12,
1663,
C. R., I, 39

New
Englanders
on Cape
Fear

the Cape Fear and had made a favorable report of it. Shortly afterward the first of the proposed settlers from New England came to the Cape Fear, but perhaps because Hilton had made his exploration and their title would be disputed, without locating permanently they turned loose their cattle on the cape, and having deposited in a box a paper writing in which they sought to disparage that region, they returned home and spread evil reports of both the soil and the harbor. Some other vessels had followed them from New England, but these also returned without making a settlement.

Berkeley receives instructions about Carolina

C. R., I,
36 et seq.

While these movements looking to a settlement in Carolina were in progress, Sir William Berkeley was again governor of Virginia. That devoted loyalist had been removed from office when the Old Dominion yielded to the authority of Parliament in 1652, but after the abdication of Richard Cromwell and before the Restoration, he had been elected governor by the General Assembly, and was holding his office at the will of the Virginians when Charles regained his throne. The following year he visited England to pay his court to the restored monarch, returning to Virginia in November, 1662.

While in England he represented the situation of the settlers on Carolina, or Roanoke Sound, as it was sometimes called, who had purchased their lands and received deeds from Kilcocanen, and regarded themselves as beyond the borders of Virginia, and he received particular directions to ignore the Indian titles and to require the inhabitants who had settled there to take out patents from him under the Virginia laws. Pursuant to this authority, immediately on his return, in the autumn of 1662, Sir William announced that the inhabitants on Roanoke Sound should no longer hold under Indian titles, and he required all who had seated land in the "new plantations" to take out patents from him and pay the usual quitrent. Patents were at once taken out by Thomas Relfe for lands on the south side of Pasquotank River adjoining Thomas Keele's land; and by Robert Peele for land on Pasquotank River; by John Harvey for land on Chowan River, and another patent for two hundred and fifty acres by John Harvey on the River Carolina adjoining Roger Williams's land, Harvey having brought seventeen persons into the colony; by Captain John Jenkins, who had brought in fourteen persons, for seven hundred acres, being a neck bounded on the south by the River Carolina and on the north by Perquimans River and on the west by the great swamp that divides it from Thomas Jarvis's land; and by George Catchmaid for fifteen hundred acres adjoining Captain Jenkins, who brought in thirty persons. Dr. Relfe had brought with him fifteen persons, and the others a greater or a less number.

Another patent was issued to George Catchmaid for Durant's Neck, including George Durant's land. Durant had induced Catchmaid to come and seat adjoining his premises, and when Berkeley's instructions were made known, Catchmaid undertook to obtain a patent for Durant as well as for himself, but instead of doing so, he took out one patent covering both premises. He thereafter executed an agreement to make a conveyance to Durant, which led to a lawsuit, the record of which is full of historical interest.

Doubtless there were many other such patents issued to those who had purchased Indian titles; but these serve to preserve the names of some of the earlier settlers, and they show that they did not come empty-handed, but, as Lawson says, they were men of substance, each attended by a considerable retinue of servants. George Durant came to be one of the most influential inhabitants of Albemarle.

George Catchmaid, Gent., of Treslick, became the first speaker of the Assembly and his widow married Timothy Biggs, who afterward became one of the early Quakers and

1662

Early
Settlers

C. R., I, 59
et seq.

MSS. Office
Sec. of State

1663
was the first surveyor of customs. John Jenkins became governor, as did John Harvey; Dr. Thomas Relfe attained the age of ninety, and has descendants still living in Albemarle, and Thomas Jarvis was deputy governor, 1691-94, and there are Peeles also in that section, and many Battles in the State. A little later Roger Williams's executrix married Edward Haswell. There are two grants on record for land embraced in two of the above patents, one to Thomas Relfe, the other to John Harvey, adjoining the lands of Roger Williams, for which a grant was issued sixteen years later to John Varnham, being near Skinner's Point, formerly known as Moseley's Point.

Local names

It will be observed that in these patents issued before the end of September, 1663, by Governor Berkeley, the sound itself, once called Roanoke Sound, was designated as the Carolina River, its mouth being at the inlet. In London the Proprietors named it the Albemarle, saying that it had been the Chowan River, and Colleton Island was near its mouth; while the Roanoke, the Chowan, Pasquotank and Perquimans rivers were already known by those names.

*Grant of
Colleton
Island to
Sir John
Colleton,
C. R., I,
54, 55, and
the grants to
Harvey and
others,
59 et seq.*

The only inlet mentioned at that time was Roanoke, in the vicinity of Colleton Island; but Ocracoke Inlet was then known to exist, and it was thought to be a bolder one than Roanoke. By that time the old Hatteras and Croatan inlets had closed; and a new breach had broken through the banks opposite the upper portion of Roanoke Island.

The Quakers

So far as the records show, the actual settlement began about 1659, about the time when New England and Virginia were frowning at the new sect, the Friends, then attracting attention because of their stubborn opposition to some of the established usages of society and government. But that was a coincidence rather than cause and effect. At that time the number of Quakers in Virginia must have been very small. The Society of Friends was introduced into that colony by Elizabeth Harris, who arrived in 1656, and, remaining but a few months, returned to England the next year. In March, 1660, the General Assembly prohibited any Quaker from coming into the province, and that adverse legislation extended to the Albemarle region equally with the other portions of Virginia. Nor, indeed, did any Quakers come to Albemarle seeking refuge and a haven. Ten years after the settlement, Edmundson came from Virginia to Carolina and reached the place he intended, Henry Phillips's house, by the Albemarle. "He and his wife," wrote Edmundson in his journal, "had been convinced of the truth in New England, and came here to live, and, not having seen a Friend for seven years before, wept for joy to see us." Up to 1672 Phillips and his wife were the only Quakers in Albemarle. On the other hand, it affirmatively appears that the settlement was brought about by the ordinary inducements of a favorable location, as Lawson expressly states; and it may be that the Albemarle country offered some inducements in the way of security against the hostility of the Indians, whose depredations had checked the expansion of the colony on the James. The savages beyond Nansemond were not so numerous and were more gentle, and the great sounds afforded protection from the southward; while Fort Christiana, on the upper Meherrin, gave security from that quarter. There was, however, a breadth of some thirty miles intervening between the inhabited parts of Virginia and the Albemarle settlement where the Indians roamed at will.

Edmundson's Journal, 1671-72

The grant to the Lords Proprietors

Seeing that the time was ripe for colonizing Carolina, Governor Berkeley doubtless conceived the idea of securing some advantage from it for himself and others who had suffered because of their loyalty to their sovereign. Application was made to the king for a grant of Carolina to Sir William, his brother, John Lord Berkeley, Sir John Colleton, then at the Barbadoes, who had spent £140,000 in the king's cause, and a number of other gentlemen whose valuable services the king might well have rewarded by such a princely gift; and on March 24, 1663, the grant was secured. The grantees were persons of the highest consequence. Edward Hyde, Earl of Clarendon, the most illustrious of the king's friends, whose daughter had married the king's brother; General Monk, who, having restored the monarchy and placed Charles on the throne, had been created Duke of Albemarle; William Earl of Craven, a military officer of great merit, who had advanced large sums to Charles; Ashley Cooper, afterward created Earl of Shaftesbury, who had led the Parliament, as Monk had controlled the army; and Sir George Carteret, esteemed the best seaman of his day, who, like Colleton and the two Berkeleys, had ever been devoted to the fortunes of the Stuarts.*

These grantees were constituted absolute Lords Proprietors of Carolina, with full powers of government such as appertained to the Palatine County of Durham, and to create dignities, the grant being similar to that of Sir Robert Heath, the only limitation being that the laws should not be repugnant to the laws of England. Six weeks after the grant was issued the Lords Proprietors held their first meeting and formed a joint-stock company, and provided by general contribution for transporting colonists and for the payment of their expenses. But as soon as publicity was given to the issuing of this grant, its validity was questioned because the same territory had formerly been bestowed on Sir Robert Heath; and Samuel Vassall claimed that he had an assignment from Sir Robert for the southern half of Carolina for a term of years not then expired, and Sir Robert Greenfield's heirs claimed the other half; while the heirs of the Duke of Norfolk declared that Sir Robert took his grant originally in trust for their ancestor; and Maltravers, Earl of Arundell and Surrey, likewise set up an interest. There is some reason to believe that in 1639 a permanent settlement

---

*Lord John Berkeley and Sir George Carteret also became the owners of New Jersey in 1664.

was attempted. William Hawley appeared in Virginia as governor of Carolina, and leave was granted by the Virginia legislature that he might colonize it by carrying a hundred persons from Virginia, freemen, being single and disengaged from debt, and it was said that Arundell was at considerable expense in planting several parts of the country, but was prevented from accomplishing his design by the civil war breaking out in England. The assertion of a title older than the grant to the Lords Proprietors interfered with their contemplated arrangements, and at their instance the grant to Sir Robert Heath was annulled by the Privy Council; but notwithstanding this proceeding, the title to Carolina years afterward was claimed by Dr. Coxe, who in a memorial to King William III traced his right through different conveyances, and who declared that he had explored and surveyed a large portion of the country, and his son, Daniel Coxe, published an account and map of the territory, which he still called *Carolana*.

Bancroft, I, 130

William Drummond governor of Albemarle

As soon, however, as the title of the Proprietors was assured, in September following, they vested in Sir William Berkeley the power to appoint a governor for all that part of their province which lay on the northeast side of the River Chowan, now named by them the Albemarle River, the Proprietors being aware that settlements had been made in that territory. This, then, is the date of the first use of the name Albemarle in connection with Carolina. The Proprietors, in September, 1663, changed the name of "Chowan River," by which they meant "the waters of the sound as far as Roanoke Inlet," to Albemarle River, while the same expansive waters had also been called the Carolina River; and earlier, the Roanoke River. The date when Governor Berkeley discontinued issuing patents for land in Albemarle in the name of the king under his instructions as governor of Virginia was apparently December 25, 1663; after that the patents for land there were issued under the direction

Albemarle named, Sept., 1663

1664

of the Lords Proprietors as being in Carolina. The first patents, being under the Virginia law, reserved a rent of one farthing per acre, according to the Virginia custom; those issued after December 25, 1663, under the instructions of the Lords Proprietors, were at the greater rate of half penny per acre. But although Governor Berkeley had been

C. R., I, 238

issuing patents for the land on the Albemarle as subject to his authority as governor of Virginia, and as not being within the limits of Carolina, yet after the grant to himself and associates he seems to have refrained from asserting the claim of Virginia to the plantations on the Chowan and Pasquotank and to have allowed the Lords Proprietors to proceed as if that territory were within their domain. He visited the new settlement the following summer, and conformably to their direction, appointed necessary officers and organized the government, and he either appointed William Drummond, a Scotchman, then a resident of Virginia, to be the governor, or recommended him for that post. The Lords Proprietors having speedily considered plans for the government of their province, determined to form counties forty miles square, each of which was to have its own governor; and they proposed to lay off such a county on the Chowan

Drummond
governor,
Oct., 1664

and to call it Albemarle. It is probable that in October, 1664, they gave effect to this purpose, and at that time made out and transmitted to Drummond his commission as governor of the county of Albemarle, for on January 7, 1665, they mentioned in a letter to him that they had previously sent him by Peter Carteret his commission as governor of Albemarle County, but had by mistake stated that it was to contain forty square miles instead of being forty miles square; and their plans seem to have contemplated that the term of office for the governor should be three years; and in

C. R., I, 93

October, 1667, a successor was appointed to Drummond. Later, one Nathaniel Batts was mentioned as having been governor of Roanoke, and he may have been appointed to that office by Governor Berkeley under the instructions of the Lords Proprietors, Roanoke Island not being within

Albemarle County as originally laid off, and authority having been given to Berkeley to establish two separate governments, one for each division of territory.

The second grant

Probably it was in connection with the organization of the new government that attention was sharply drawn to the fact that the Albemarle settlement was not in Carolina, but was really within the boundaries of Virginia. The Lords Proprietors, becoming aware that the limits of Carolina just touched the northern shore of the sound and did not embrace the plantations that had been settled, hastened to apply to the king for an extension of their grant some thirty miles further northward, and on June 30, 1665, the king was pleased to make this addition to their possessions, and issued a second grant or charter, extending Carolina to 36 degrees 30 minutes north latitude, which has ever since been the dividing line between the two territories; and also extending it two degrees further to the southward.

CHAPTER VII

SETTLEMENT ON THE CAPE FEAR

The settlement on the Cape Fear.—Hilton's explorations.—The New England Association.—The first settlement.—Sir John Yeamans, governor.—Conditions at Charlestown.—Yeamans sails from Barbadoes.—An Assembly at Cape Fear.—An Indian war.—Dissatisfaction. —The Cape Fear River abandoned.—A new Charlestown on Ashley River.—Slavery in the colonies.—The Indian inhabitants

The settlement of the Cape Fear

1662

The evil reports set afoot in 1662 by the New Englanders in regard to the Cape Fear soon reached Barbadoes, and the persons there who had in contemplation a settlement on that river thought it expedient, before proceeding further, to cause a more particular investigation to be made of that locality. Colonel Modyford and John Vassall, the chief promoters, again engaged the services of Hilton, who with Anthony Long and Peter Fabian, as representatives of the association, in August, 1663, set sail on the *Adventure* upon a new mission of discovery and particular exploration. They skirted the coast from September 29th to October 2d without finding an entrance, and when they were in the vicinity of Cape Fear a violent storm came up, and they were carried by the strong current of the Gulf Stream nearly up to Hatteras. Returning, they reached the outer roads of Cape Fear on October 12th, and then visited the cape, expecting to find the cattle left there by the New Englanders. But the cattle could not be found. Doubtless the Indians had feasted upon them. A fortnight later they entered the harbor, and finally came to anchor at the junction of what they called the Main River and Green River, where the town of Wilmington now is. They ascended in their boats the northeast branch, naming certain localities Turkey Quarter, Rocky Point, and Stag Park; and likewise the northwest branch, and Clarendon River, which they called

Hilton
makes a
second
expedition

October,
1663

C. R., I, 71

1663

Hilton; and while they found much poor land and many pine barrens, and along the streams extensive marshes, on the whole they were pleased with the locality as being suitable for a settlement. Indeed, no region is more attractive than the Cape Fear in autumn. The soft, moderate climate, the fine vegetation, the numerous flowers, the towering pines, were all calculated to impress the explorers most favorably. After a delightful experience of six weeks spent in exploration, they turned their backs and dropped down to Crane Island, about four leagues from the entrance of the harbor, where they purchased the river and the adjacent land from Wat Coosa, the king of the neighboring Indians, and his chief men, and established friendly relations with them. On December 4th they weighed anchor and turned their prow southward for Barbadoes, where they arrived after a perilous voyage of sixty days. In their report they strongly denounced the disparaging statement made by the New Englanders concerning the Cape Fear lands, and they gave a renewed impetus to the projected enterprise.

But while these steps were being taken at Barbadoes, the New England Association had not remained inactive. Still purposing to establish a colony on the Cape Fear, they sought the aid of London merchants to furnish means and supplies, and to secure settlers from England, and were taking measures to make the enterprise a success. Such was the situation when it became known that Carolina had been granted to the Lords Proprietors, and that terms of settlement and title must be obtained from them.

When this information was received, the London adventurers who were associated with the New Englanders hastened to apply to the Lords Proprietors for the terms on which a settlement could be made, and obtained assurances of liberal treatment. The Proprietors, however, claimed the privilege of appointing the governor, and this was not satisfactory to the New Englanders, who had always enjoyed the right of choosing their own governors, and objected to any other mode of appointment. But this difference it

C. R., I, 36

was hoped might be reconciled. Indeed, the Proprietors were eager to promote the settlement of their possessions, and were active and energetic in doing so, considering the pressing demands upon them of their high public employment.

Hardly had they entered upon their negotiations with the New Englanders, however, when on August 12th they received a communication from Barbadoes, signed by Colonel Thomas Modyford and Peter Colleton, who were cousins of the Duke of Albemarle, detailing the designs of the Barbadoes adventurers and applying for terms of settlement. With these two applications pending, the Proprietors, buoyant with the prospects, hastened to respond, and on August 25th they published their first declarations and proposals to all that will plant in Carolina. They authorized that the first settlement should be on Charles River, as Cape Fear River was then named; and announced that the colonists were to make their own laws by their assemblymen, by and with the advice and consent of the governor and council. Freedom and liberty of conscience in all religious and spiritual things were absolutely granted. They sought particularly to satisfy the New Englanders, who, being Independents, demanded the right of electing their governor and all other officers, by agreeing that the settlers, before embarking, should present to them the names of thirteen of the actual settlers, of whom one would be selected for governor, and six more for the council; and at the end of every three years the inhabitants should in like manner present thirteen persons from whom the governor and council should be selected.

But even this was not satisfactory to the London agents of the New Englanders, who insisted that the governor must be elected by the people. The Proprietors, however, disregarded this demand, and, hopeful of final acquiescence, sought to consolidate the different interests, and to have the adventurers or promoters at Barbadoes associate with them those in New England and such persons in London, the

C. R., I, 39

The declarations and proposals

C. R., I, 43

Bermudas and other islands in the Caribbean Sea as could be induced to engage in the enterprise.

These efforts were in some measure successful. The conflicting claims of New England and Barbadoes were reconciled, and an association, of which Henry Vassall was the London agent, was formed to make the settlement. Vassall with much persistency continued negotiations for better terms, and finally secured concessions which he thought would be acceded to, and transmitted them to Barbadoes. The promoters at Barbadoes now applied themselves with such diligence to the work of preparation that on May 29, 1664, the first instalment of colonists disembarked on the banks of the Cape Fear and established themselves at the mouth of the creek since known as Old Town Creek, and thither soon came accessions from New England, and the settlement was apparently on a permanent and solid basis. The river as early as August, 1663, was called the Charles River, in honor of King Charles, and the new town was named Charlestown. Five months after this settlement, in October, 1664, at the time when the county of Albemarle was laid off, the county of Clarendon was established on the Cape Fear, and John Vassall was appointed surveyor and Robert Sanford register of that county.

But among the Barbadoes adventurers were some who were not favorable to the location on the Cape Fear, and preferred a settlement further to the southward. The Proprietors themselves entertained similar views, and dwelt upon the necessity of establishing a colony at Port Royal. While willing to foster all projects, they regarded with particular favor this new movement. Chief among the promoters of it were Colonel John Yeamans, his son, Major William Yeamans, Colonel Edward Reade and Captain William Merrick, and these and their associates were supposed to have the greatest influence at Barbadoes. Sir John Colleton, one of the Proprietors who had resided in that island, was a staunch friend of Colonel Yeamans, and recommended that he should be selected to manage the details of

May 29, 1664
Settlers
from New
England
and
Barbadoes

C. R., I, 156

County of
Clarendon

C. R., I, 75

1664

organizing the colony. Resolved on this course, the Proprietors ignored the negotiations they had had with Henry Vassall as the agent of the association for the settlement of Cape Fear and determined to treat with Major William Yeamans, who, in the name of his father and eighty other adventurers, made proposals for the exploration of the coast and for establishing a colony further to the southward.

C. R., I, 94
Yeamans
governor
of
Clarendon
County

The negotiations being concluded, the Proprietors, in order to strengthen the probabilities of success, sought and obtained knighthood for Colonel Yeamans, who at their instance was created baronet, and on January 11, 1665, they appointed him governor of Clarendon County and of all of Carolina to the southward and commissioned him lieutenant-general, and invested him with full powers of control. Contemporaneously with this appointment, the Yeamans association, including some who had been interested in the colony already settled on Cape Fear and other associates in England, New England, the Leeward Islands and the Bermudas, agreed on their part that before the last day of September, 1665, they would provide two ships with ordnance and munitions and provisions to make a settlement south of Cape Romania, there to settle and erect a fort. These measures being taken looking to colonization, the Lords Proprietors now promulgated their "concessions" and agreement with all who should settle at Albemarle, at Clarendon, and at a county to be established further south, which was to be called Craven.

C. R., I, 78

C. R., I, 79

"The Concessions"

Conditions at Charlestown on Cape Fear

C. R., I,
154-156

The Vassall colony at Cape Fear had now been seated a year and a half, and the additions had been so considerable that a publication intended to promote it claimed that the population was already eight hundred. It is said they brought with them from the Barbadoes cotton seed, which, with corn and pulse, they planted; and that in their clearings they felled much timber, which was profitably shipped to Barbadoes; and they erected their houses and built forts, and

made much progress toward establishing permanent plantations. But despite the influx of population, they were still
dependent on others for provisions, clothing, and necessaries.
Besides, they had early incurred the enmity of the Indians
by sending away some of the Indian children under pretence of instructing them in learning and in the principles
of the Christian religion; and although the Indians had
no guns, only bows and arrows, they annoyed the settlers
and killed their cattle. The fall of 1665 thus found them
in a bad case, in want of provisions, clothing and munitions,
but they were hopeful of speedy relief and were anxiously
expecting the arrival of the governor with needed succors.

Yeamans sails from Barbadoes

For some time great preparations had been making at
Barbadoes to carry into effect the agreement with the Lords
Proprietors. Sir John Yeamans had secured a frigate of
his own, the associated adventurers purchased a sloop, and
the Lords Proprietors bought a fly-boat, the *Sir John,* of
one hundred and fifty tons, which were to be used in the
expedition. On the fly-boat were stored the munitions and
the provisions and the armament for the fort, a part being
twelve cannon, a present from the king. By October, all
being in readiness, the governor and his little fleet set sail
for Cape Fear. On the way the vessels were separated
by a great storm, in which the frigate lost her mast and
came near foundering. But eventually, early in November,
they all came to anchor before the mouth of Charles River.
Suddenly, however, a fresh gale swept them from their
insecure anchorage and drove them to sea; and upon their
return the *Sir John* stranded upon the outer shoals of the
bar, where she was soon broken to pieces by the violence of
the waves. Those on board fortunately were saved; but
the provisions and clothing, the magazines of arms, the
powder and the king's cannon were all lost.

Undismayed by his misfortunes, Yeamans began at once
to repair his frigate, which with the sloop had gotten safely

1664

Lawson, 127
C. R., I, 137

The king's
gift

November,
1665
C. R., I, 119

1665

into the river, and proposed to send her back to Barbadoes for recruits, while he awaited the result of an exploration to the southward by Robert Sanford in the sloop. But the necessities of the colonists, heightened by the loss of the provisions on the fly-boat, led to a great clamoring that the sloop might be sent to Virginia for their immediate relief To this Sir John assented, and having arranged for the exploration to be made later by Sanford, he himself returned to Barbadoes in his disabled frigate. The sloop reached Virginia and obtained a supply of provisions, but on the return voyage it was driven on shore at Cape Lookout by a violent storm and was cast away. All of the crew except two, however, escaped in their boat, and after many perils contrived to reach the plantations on the Chowan.

An Assembly at Cape Fear

While Sir John was still at Charlestown, probably in December, 1665, an Assembly was held for Clarendon County, he and his council participating; and an address was prepared to be sent to the Lords Proprietors detailing the grievances of the colony and asking for redress. Although Sir John at first agreed to join in this petition, at the last he withheld his signature. In it the Assembly, of which John Vassall seems to have been speaker, and the council complained of the terms set out in "the concessions"; that the rent was too high; that the method of laying off the land was not satisfactory; and that the penalty of forfeiture if a man were not kept on every hundred acres was unreasonable. They rehearsed that they had come to Cape Fear notwithstanding the obloquy resting upon it, and were promised large holdings of land by those acting for the Lords Proprietors; that after they had embarked upon the enterprise the negotiations with their agent for terms had been interrupted by the agreement made with Major William Yeamans, and now that misfortune had overtaken those acting under that agreement they had lost all interest in sustaining the colony. They therefore prayed that the negotiations

C. R., I, 146
1665 or 1666

which had been interrupted might be again taken up "with us and with the adventurers of Old and New England"; and they promised, "when supported by freedom, to trample on all difficulties." And they warned the Proprietors that, being deserted by all, only ruin awaited them, and that they were utterly unable either to proceed or retire without aid, and this they could hope to receive only upon obtaining the terms originally asked.

From this address and other circumstances it appears that the settlement had been chiefly made from New England, and that when the Proprietors declined to allow them to elect their own governor the New England association refused to proceed; while the adventurers at Barbadoes chiefly looked to the proposed settlement further to the southward. Such was the situation of the colonists in the winter of 1665, eighteen months after the first landing, when Sir John Yeamans was for a short time at Charlestown; the Indians hostile, their cattle being destroyed, constantly menaced by danger, provisions scarce, clothing needed, and influences preventing supplies being furnished them, while they themselves were dissatisfied with the terms of settlement offered by the Lords Proprietors. Still, there was some trade, the colonists having lumber to send out, and an occasional vessel visited Charlestown; and one evening in June, Robert Sanford together with some seventeen other inhabitants sailed southward, exploring the coast as far as Port Royal, finding many places that were favorable for settlement, uniting good lands and an excellent harbor with security against attack by the Indians. And, indeed, he reported that he observed an emulation among the Indians to secure the friendship of the English, and this notwithstanding they knew that the colonists at Clarendon were in actual war with the Cape Fear Indians and had sent away many of them. On their return, after a month spent in exploration, their accounts seemed to have increased the dissatisfaction among the inhabitants at Charlestown, who in sending their address to England insisted that "because

1666

C. R., I, 121

1666   they had settled in the worst locality, the heaviest terms
should not be exacted from them."

C. R., I, 144   John Vassall seems to have been in charge of the colony,
and in August, 1666, his cousin, Henry Vassall, their agent
in London, again sought a hearing by the Lords Proprietors.
He remonstrated with them that after agreeing with him on
terms of settlement, they ignored those negotiations and
entered into a different agreement with Major Yeamans,
Vassall   and that the colonists were dissatisfied. He renewed his
solicitations for the terms originally agreed on, and declared
that many in England, in New England, the Barbadoes and
those actually at Cape Fear now awaited the issue of his
last appeal in their behalf. If his demands should be
assented to, he said, a good ship was ready to sail with men
and provisions, with the likelihood of other ships following
in the spring. But otherwise the whole design would be
abandoned and those on the place, he asserted, would give
up the settlement.

The Cape Fear River abandoned

Vassall's warning seems to have been unheeded. Sir John
Colleton, one of the most active of the Proprietors, lay dead.
Albemarle was off the coast of Holland fighting the greatest
sea battle of that era. The other Proprietors were too
closely engaged to give much attention to Carolina. As
time passed the situation at Clarendon grew steadily worse.
C. R., I, 160   In November, John Vassall sent an agent, Whitaker, to give
an account of the condition of the colonists, but he was taken
prisoner either by the French or the Dutch, and his mission
failed. Vassall wrote that he "had not heard a word from
any of the Proprietors since he received his commission by
Mr. Sanford," in November, 1664. But the settlers still
had friends in Massachusetts. The General Court of Massa-
C. R., I, 161   chusetts, touched by their distress, imposed a general tax
for their benefit throughout that colony, and for a season the
necessities of Charlestown were relieved. Such measures,

however, were only palliatives and not remedies. The causes 1667 of discontent continued without abatement.

Vassall, who had spent much of his means in the enterprise, was greatly interested that it should not fail.

He sought to keep the colonists together, and for a time succeeded. But at length they found a way by land to Albemarle, and neither his arguments nor his authority could longer prevail to quiet them. He therefore detained the first vessel that came in until he could collect others to take them all away together. Some went to Virginia, but the larger part returned to Boston; so, in September, 1667, three years after the landing of the colony, Charlestown was deserted and Clarendon County again became a solitude. Vassall himself stopped in Nansemond, Virginia, and from there, on October 6, 1667, he wrote to Sir John Colleton, of October, 1667 C. R., I, 159 whose death he had not heard, a touching letter: "I presume you have heard of the unhappy loss of our plantation on Charles River, the reason of which I could have never so well understood had I not come hither to hear—how that all who came from us made it their business to exclaim against the country as they had rendered it unfit for a Christian habitation; which hindered the coming of the people and supplies to us, so as the rude rabble of our inhabitants were daily ready to mutiny against me for keeping them there so long. . . . And, indeed, we were as a poor company of deserted people, little regarded by any others and no way able to supply ourselves with clothing and necessaries, nor any considerable number to defend ourselves from the Indians; all of which was occasioned by the hard terms of your concessions, which made our friends that set us out from Barbadoes to forsake us; so as they would neither supply us with necessaries nor find shipping to fetch us away. Yet had we had but £200 sent us in clothing, we had made a comfortable shift for another year. And I offered to stay there, if but twenty men would stay with me, till we had heard from your Lordships; for we had corn enough for two years for a far greater number, and though the Indians had killed our cattle, yet we might have defended ourselves. But I could not find six men that would be true to me to stay, so was constrained to leave it, to my great loss and ruin."

Thus the fair beginning of a settlement was defeated by some unreasonable quibbling over a few acres of land in a vast wilderness, and over the mode of appointing a governor for a distant colony hedged in by the perils of Indian warfare; while the troubles of the colonists themselves were intensified by their selling into slavery Indian children and also such Indian captives as fell into their hands during the war that followed that act of heartless tyranny and treachery.

A new Charlestown on the Ashley

However, the Lords Proprietors were not entirely inactive. Indeed, their prospects were now improved, for Spain by a treaty executed in 1667 abandoned her claim to Carolina and conceded to England her colonial possessions and the right to trade in those waters. So contemporaneously with the abandonment of Cape Fear the Proprietors fitted out a vessel under the command of Captain William Sayle, and sent him to make another exploration of the coast. After his return with a favorable report of Port Royal, the Proprietors, having formed themselves into a stock company, made a great effort and raised twelve thousand pounds, with which they prepared two vessels amply stored with provisions and arms, and bearing a considerable number of emigrants. They appointed Sayle governor, and the expedition, departing from England, arrived at Port Royal in 1670.

But after a year spent in that locality, the settlers were led to remove to the west bank of the Ashley River, some miles from its mouth, where they began a new Charlestown. Within a year, however, Sayle succumbed to disease. West, who was the mercantile agent of the Proprietors, hoped to succeed him, but Yeamans, being a landgrave, was entitled to be governor, and taking up his residence in Carolina, as-

sumed the reins of government, and continued to be governor
for five years, when, because of dissatisfaction with him, he
was retired and West was made a landgrave and appointed
governor. In 1679 the present city of Charleston* was laid
off at the junction of the Ashley and Cooper rivers, and the
colony removed thither; the government offices were established there, and it soon became a thriving and prosperous
community.

Slavery in the colonies

When in 1494 Pope Alexander VI, at the request of Portugal and Spain, apportioned the New World between them,
Spain was forbidden any possessions east of the one hun-
dredth meridian, and could have no foothold in Africa. So
after the trade in negroes was begun, Spain looked to English
enterprise to supply her colonies with negro laborers, and a
considerable traffic in negroes sprung up. Later, when England established colonies of her own, white labor was
obtained either by contract, the men engaging for a limited
period of bondage, or by the purchase of those who had been
condemned to servitude for some infraction of the law.
Every rising against the government, either in England,
Ireland, or Scotland, was followed by the transportation of
large numbers of the unfortunate malcontents to the colonies,
where they were either sold or bestowed as a gift upon some
favored planter. In Virginia, the whites held in bondage
were chiefly indented servants, under contract for a term
of years, although from time to time those condemned to
penal servitude, in some instances at their own request, were
sent there. The demand for labor in the "new plantations"
being great, a thriving trade was done in indented servants,
kidnapped children and condemned persons; and since in
the course of this horrid business many outrages occurred, the
subject received the attention of the Board of Trade, of
Parliament, and of the courts. In 1620, an English vessel,
having captured some negroes on board of a Spanish ship

*For nearly a century it was called Charlestown.

1659

fell in with a Dutch man-of-war, which took possession of the negroes, twenty in number, and stopping at Jamestown the Dutch commander traded them for needed provisions.

Slaves in
New
England

In 1638 the first importation of negroes was made into New England at Boston, and contemporaneously with this, at the end of the Pequod War, Massachusetts and the other New England colonies enslaved their Indian prisoners, selling the men to the islands in the Caribbean Sea, but keeping the women and maids among themselves. From that period both Indians and negroes were used as slaves among the English colonists. In 1631 the African Company was chartered to transport negro slaves from Africa to the Spanish colonies, and soon after the Restoration, 1662, the second African Company was chartered, with exclusive rights to carry on the slave trade, the Duke of York and

Royal
African
Company

other nobles being at the head of it. Twelve years later this company was supplanted by the Royal African Company, composed of the king, his brother the Duke of York, and other notables, among them four of the Proprietors of Carolina.

C. R., III,
115

When Queen Anne came to the throne she specially directed that the Royal African Company should take care that a sufficient supply of merchantable negroes should be furnished at moderate rates, and the slave trade grew to enor-

The
Asiento, 1713

mous proportions. In 1713 England entered into a contract with Spain, known as the "Asiento," for the exclusive right of supplying the Spanish colonies with negroes for thirty years; and the stock in the company holding this franchise was taken, one-fourth by the King of Spain, one-fourth by Queen Anne, and the other half by her favored friends. To maintain this exclusive right of carrying on the slave trade England engaged in sundry wars, and at the Peace of Utrecht she required that it should be solemnly engrafted into the treaty.

As early as the settlement of Albemarle the institution of slavery had been well established, and there were whites, Indians, and negroes held to bondage. The Indian tribes themselves sold their prisoners taken in their neighborhood

1659

wars to the colonists. And as in Africa wars were con-   1659
tinually carried on to secure slaves for the slave marts, so
in America wars were fomented to obtain Indian prisoners
to be sold into slavery. Beginning in Massachusetts, this
practice of capturing and enslaving Indians led to the destruction of the first settlement on the Cape Fear and to
many of the wars in South Carolina, and it stimulated the
South Carolina Indians to come to the aid of North Carolina in 1712, the captives taken at that time being sold in the
West Indies and in New England. Indeed, so many were
sent to Connecticut that the governor and council forbade
the importation of any more Tuscaroras for fear that in   Conn. Col.
Rec., V, 516
connection with the neighboring tribes they would be a
source of danger to that colony. At the time of the settlement of Albemarle there were two thousand negro slaves
in Virginia, while the white indented servants were four
times that many. In 1683 the white servants were sixteen
thousand, while the negroes were but three thousand.

The Indian inhabitants

The aborigines of North Carolina at the time of the settlement consisted of many different tribes of Indians, each
having its own language. Near the great lakes of the
North were the Algonquins and the Iroquois. Some of
these moved southward and became inhabitants of North
Carolina. The Indians of the South are supposed to have
come from across the Mississippi River, and they extended
into North Carolina. Not only did these differ from the
northern Indians in language, but they were not so barbarous and they had made more progress from the savage
state. One of the tests now applied to determine whether a   Indian
civilization
tribe was of southern or northern origin is its pottery and
its ornamentation. It is said that the northern Indians
had made such a slight advance that none of their pottery
was decorated by a curved line. Pottery bearing curved
ornamentation has been found in western North Carolina
and also in eastern Carolina, and in a general way it has

1659

Rep. Bu.
Eth., XX,
147, 159

been said that a line drawn from Hatteras marked the boundaries of the southern and northern Indians. There is reason to believe that the southern Indians occupied North Carolina and were measurably expelled by fierce tribes from the north, except along the coast.

The Indians on the Cape Fear were Congarees. The Hatteras and Coranines were southern Indians, and perhaps also the Chowanoaks, who afterward became known as Meherrins. The Mongoaks, later the Tuscaroras, the Woccoons, and perhaps the Pamlicos, were northern Indians. The Catawbas were southern. In 1656 the Rechahecrians came from the north, fought with the Virginians, and passed southward into the mountains. It is supposed they became the Cherokees, who have been ascertained to be of northern origin.* Tradition assigns several points in the Haw and Deep River country as scenes of great battles between the northern and southern Indians.

Indian
origins

Brickell in 1729 went on a mission to the Indians in that part of the province, and in December, 1752, when Bishop Spangenberg explored the lands on the upper Catawba, he found the remains of an Indian fort, as also "tame grass, which is still growing about the old residences on the northeast branch of Middle Little River."

C. R., V, 9

There was always antagonism between the northern and southern Indians, and the Catawbas were at constant war with the Tuscaroras. Not only were the tribes destroyed by their continual wars, but they were exterminated by disease. The Pamlicos, that had been very numerous, about 1694 were swept away by an epidemic, and later the Catawbas were destroyed by the smallpox. Other tribes met with a similar fate.

The Indians have left many memorials of their former existence in North Carolina, which, however, have not been carefully preserved. One intelligent investigator, Dr. Dillard, says: "One of the largest and most remarkable Indian mounds in eastern North Carolina is located at Bandon, on

*Now classed as Iroquois.

the Chowan, evidently the site of the ancient town of the
Chowanokes, which Grenville's party visited in 1585, and
was called Mavaton. The map of James Wimble, made in
1738, also locates it at about this point. The mound extends
along the river bank five hundred or six hundred yards, is
sixty yards wide and five feet deep, covered with about one
foot of sand and soil. It is composed almost exclusively of
mussel shells taken from the river, pieces of pottery, ashes,
arrow-heads and human bones. . . . Certain decorations
on their pottery occur sufficiently often among the Indian
tribes of the different sections to be almost characteristic of
them. A sort of corncob impression is found on a great deal
of Chowan pottery and also in Bertie. There are also pieces
with parallel striations, oblique patterns, small diamond patterns formed by transverse lines, evidently made by a sharp
stick. Some are decorated with horizontal lines, while a
few are perfectly plain. In the deposits on the Chowan
River, at the site of the ancient Chowanoke town of Mavaton, the decorations on the pottery are both varied and
artistic. . . . I have never seen so many distinct patterns occurring in the same mound as at Avoca, left there by
the Tuscaroras. The ancient Tuscarora town of Metackwem
was located in Bertie County just above Black Walnut Point,
and most probably at Avoca, from the extensive deposits
there."

THE THIRD EPOCH—1663–1729

PROPRIETARY GOVERNMENT

CHAPTER VIII

ADMINISTRATIONS OF DRUMMOND AND STEPHENS

The settlement of Albemarle.—Governor Drummond.—The first Assembly.—Conditions at Albemarle.—The concessions.—Cessation of tobacco planting.—An Indian war.—Changes in the Proprietors.—Stephens governor.—The great deed.—Act of Assembly.—The marriage act.

The settlement of Albemarle

1662

The excellence of the location, the salubrity of the climate, and the fertility of the soil soon drew to Albemarle considerable accessions of population. Lawson says that the first who came found the winters mild and the soil fertile beyond expectation, producing everything that was planted to a prodigious increase; that the cattle, horses, sheep, and swine, breeding very fast, passed the winter without any assistance from the planter; so that everything seemed to come by nature, the husbandman living almost void of care and free from those fatigues which are absolutely necessary in winter countries for providing necessaries; and the fame of this new-discovered country spread through the neighboring colonies and speedily drew other families to it.

Indeed, it was a location abounding in attractions for the hardy pioneer. The great Albemarle River, as they called the sound, its mouth being Roanoke Inlet, while furnishing in its wide expanse a protection from the southern Indians, offered an unfailing supply of fish and game. The broad Chowan was likewise a protection from the Tuscaroras, whose hunting grounds lay on the west and down to the waters of the Neuse. On the east and north were only two small tribes, one of which gave some trouble in 1666, but was

SEAL OF THE COUNTY OF ALBEMARLE, 1669–1689, AND
CONTINUED IN USE AS THE SEAL OF THE PROVINCE
OF NORTH CAROLINA UNTIL THE PURCHASE
BY THE CROWN IN 1729. THIS REPRO-
DUCTION IS SLIGHTLY LARGER
THAN THE ORIGINAL;
REVERSE IS BLANK

1663

so speedily conquered that the war left no mark on the infant settlement. The pioneers on their separated plantations felt no alarm, and were quite free from Indian depredations. In natural advantages Albemarle was incomparable.

"Most of the plantations," says Lawson, "enjoy a noble prospect of large and spacious rivers, pleasant savannahs, and fine meadows, with their green liveries interwoven with beautiful flowers of most glorious colors, hedged in with pleasant groves of the famous tulip-tree, stately laurels and bays, myrtle, jessamine, woodbine and honeysuckle, and other fragrant vines and evergreens, whose aspiring branches shadow and interweave themselves with the loftiest timbers, yielding a pleasant prospect, shade and smell; proper habitations for the sweet singing birds that melodiously entertain such as travel through the woods of Carolina." Lawson, History of North Carolina, 110

Drummond governor

Sir William Berkeley in the fall of 1663 received from the other Proprietors instructions to organize a government at Albemarle, and was authorized to appoint a governor for the settlers on the northern and another for the southern shore of the sound* if he should deem it expedient. The following summer he visited the settlement, then confined chiefly to the waters of the Chowan, and appointed William Drummond governor, and later the Lords Proprietors sent a commission and instructions to Drummond, whose term would seem to have begun in October, 1664. Berkeley was also instructed to appoint six councillors to act with the governor, and all other necessary officers; and the governor and councillors together with the freemen or their deputies were to make all laws, which were to be transmitted to the Lords Proprietors within a year for their approval or disapproval. These laws as enacted were to be in force until they should be disapproved by the Proprietors. C. R., I, 50 Chalmers in Carroll's Coll., II, 283

Oct., 1664

*George Fox, in his Journal, 1672, speaks of Nathaniel Batts, who had been "governor of Roanoak." He had probably been appointed governor under this authority for the southern division. He was buried at Batts's Island, near Durant's Neck.

The governor was to issue all grants for lands, and the secretary was to record them, and these grants, like those in Virginia, were to be void if the land should not be seated in three years. A rent of half a penny an acre was to be paid each year, but rent was not to be exacted for a period of five years. The governor for his compensation was to have the sole trade of furs until some other means of payment should be arranged. Governor Drummond was a Scotchman who had been long settled in Virginia, and was well acquainted with the vicissitudes of pioneer life. He was a man of education, of integrity, and well fitted for his office. Although sparsely settled, Albemarle was now not an unbroken wilderness.

Population had flowed in, some of the planters being men of large means, bringing with them from ten to thirty persons; and shortly after the government was organized, not later than the spring of 1665, the first Assembly was held, and the little settlement became a self-governing community, a pure democracy, the entire body of the inhabitants acting for themselves, and not through the instrumentality of representatives.

Spring of 1665

Such was the beginning of the organized government of Albemarle. At that first session a petition was drawn up to be forwarded to the Lords Proprietors, the subject-matter being that the settlers should continue to hold their lands as they had done under the Virginia law, paying only a farthing an acre rent, and that not in cash, but in commodities, as was the practice in Virginia. The quantity of land one could take up was dependent on the number of persons he brought into the settlement, and the patents issued show that some of the early settlers were accompanied by a numerous retinue.

C. R., I, 101

C. R., I, 252

As an illustration of the early influx of population, a remonstrance drawn up fourteen years after the settlement was signed by twenty-one persons, who stated that most of them had been inhabitants since 1663 and 1664. These had become Quakers, while there was only one family of that

1664

faith in the settlement in 1672. In 1666 quite a number of settlers came from the Bermuda Islands, and, establishing themselves on Pasquotank River, found employment in shipbuilding. Trading vessels also began to frequent the waters of Albemarle, the first large ship of which we have a record coming in during the winter of 1664. It was Captain Whittly's vessel, which appears to have been employed by the Proprietors in connection with their colonization. She entered the sound through Roanoke Inlet, and when she came in found fifteen feet of water, but on going out had but eleven feet, and notwithstanding the channel had been marked out, she grounded several times. "So uncertain are all these inlets," remarks Thomas Woodward, who was then the surveyor of the colony.

Ship-
building
1666

The concessions

The system of government at Albemarle was soon afterward still further perfected by the provisions specified in the concessions, bearing date January, 1665, which formulated a general plan, covering all the counties established in the province. All acts of the Proprietors were to be authenticated by the great seal of the province, kept at London, while each county was to have its own proper seal, and that designed and adopted for Albemarle continued in use as the seal of North Carolina until after the purchase by the king, in 1729. All grants and deeds for land were to be acknowledged or proved by the oath of two witnesses and recorded, and the conveyance first recorded was to be effectual, notwithstanding any prior unrecorded conveyance. This provision, now so common, was then unknown to the English law. It had its origin in Holland, and had been adopted by the settlers in Massachusetts. It was a marked improvement on the English system of ascertaining and perpetuating titles. In those first days of settlement, the population being inconsiderable, the freemen were either themselves to meet in General Assembly or were to come together and elect twelve deputies to represent them.

C. R., I, 79

All officers were to swear to bear true allegiance to the king, and to perform their duties faithfully, or were to subscribe a declaration to that effect in a book. There was full liberty of conscience, but the General Assembly was to have power to appoint as many ministers or preachers as they should see fit, giving, however, to all persons the right to have and to support any other ministers or preachers they might please.

Each person coming in during the first year should be entitled to have eighty acres of land for himself, and the same quantity for his wife and every dependent capable of bearing arms, and forty acres for each servant. And servants, after their term of servitude, should have an equal right for themselves. But after the first year only sixty acres were to be allowed instead of eighty. These grants of land, while in fee, were subject to a yearly quitrent payable to the Proprietors. The rent, half a penny an acre, was to be paid in money. As an inducement to settlers, however, the first payment of rent was postponed until the year 1671.

Thus, with full liberty of conscience guaranteed, with an agreement that those who did not feel disposed to take an oath of allegiance might merely subscribe a declaration of their fealty, with a stipulation that no tax should be levied or collected except by act of their General Assembly, and that the Assembly, in the absence of the governor or his deputy, might choose a president in his stead, and with an Assembly elected by themselves vested with full power to ordain laws and establish courts and appoint officers to enforce them, the freemen of Albemarle enjoyed every liberty they desired, and being blessed with bountiful harvests, led easy, quiet lives in their sylvan homes.

The development of the "new plantations" progressed rapidly. In addition to their corn and wheat, supplies and provisions necessary for their subsistence and comfort in the wilderness, the planters also raised tobacco; and so considerable was the production of this commodity that when Maryland, in June, 1666, proposed a cessation from planting tobacco for one year, the agreement was made dependent not merely on the acceptance of Virginia, but by "the new plantations" at Albemarle as well.

An Indian war

Agreeably to that invitation, Governor Drummond and Thomas Woodward, who had been appointed a commissioner to represent the General Assembly, met the other commissioners at James City on July 12th and agreed on a plan, which in order to be effective was to be ratified by their respective legislatures, and the ratifications were to be exchanged by the last of September. The General Assembly of Albemarle met, George Catchmaid, Gent., being the speaker, and passed the desired act; but about that time there was an Indian outbreak and the colony was in peril, and because of the Indian invasion the act ratifying the agreement could not be transmitted within the period limited. However, the delay was only for a few days, and the failure to send the act forward by the day fixed was held immaterial. So by act of Assembly no tobacco was planted during the year 1667.

In October of that year Drummond's term of three years came to its close, and after an admirable administration that capable governor, whose name is perpetuated in that of the beautiful lake in the great Dismal Swamp, gave place to his successor. Drummond retired to Virginia, where ten years later, having engaged in Bacon's rebellion, in January, 1677, he fell into the hands of Governor Berkeley and was summarily executed by that insensate and exasperated tyrant.

Drummond hanged by Berkeley, 1677

Changes in the Proprietors

In the meantime notable changes had occurred among the Lords Proprietors. Clarendon, who, being Lord Chancellor, was held responsible by the people of England for all the improper measures of the court since the restoration, had become very unpopular; while his severe virtue, no less than his opposition to all schemes looking to the toleration of the

Catholics, had rendered him disagreeable to Charles. In 1667 he became an object of the king's bitter hatred because he ventured to thwart the passionate purpose of that lascivious monarch. On August 30th of that year his seals of office were demanded by Charles, and a month later, out of common hatred, articles of impeachment were presented by the popular leaders against him, and he was charged by the Commons at the bar of the House of Lords with high treason generally, without any allegations being specified.

On such a general charge the Lords refused to proceed; but Clarendon saw that his friends had fallen away, and that both the opposing factions were bent on his destruction, and so, seeking safety in flight, he retired to the continent. A bill of perpetual banishment was passed against him, and he sojourned in Europe until his death, in 1674, his last years being employed in literary work. Such was the closing of the honorable career of this devoted adherent of the Stuarts, but a true Protestant and an honest Englishman.

Sir John Colleton had died in 1666, and Sir Peter Colleton succeeded to his place among the Proprietors. Albemarle, the skilful general and brave admiral, who, when London was deserted by all during the great plague of 1665, had given the world an additional illustration of his intrepidity by remaining at his post in charge of the stricken city, had, in 1666 and 1667, won famous victories at sea, and then, falling ill with dropsy, lingered until December, 1669, when

his son, Christopher, Duke of Albemarle, succeeded him. Sir George Carteret was vice-chamberlain to his Majesty's household, and Sir John Berkeley was at his post as lord lieutenant of Ireland, while his brother, Sir William, remained governor of Virginia.

Stephens governor

In October, 1667, the Lords Proprietors appointed Captain Samuel Stephens governor, and sent him for instructions a copy of the concessions published in 1664. So far as the government of Albemarle had conformed to the concessions there were no changes in the administration. Up to 1667 Albemarle had not been laid off into precincts, but the freemen of the settlement chose twelve deputies, called in the legislation of 1666 "committee," to represent them; and the General Assembly, composed of the governor, his council, appointed by himself, and the representatives of the people, sat together as one body and enacted laws and had the power to establish courts and define their jurisdiction.

Of Stephens we know but little. His relations with the Proprietors and people seem to have been pleasant. He became the owner of Roanoke Island, and otherwise identified his interests with the growth of the colony. The governor and council held a court for the county, which exercised chancery powers, and had jurisdiction over estates. They sat without pay, but it is probable that considerable gain was made by way of compensation for public service by a monopoly of trade with the Indians.

That Stephens was a gentleman of culture and standing may well be surmised from what is known of his wife; and in like manner it appears that Harvey and some of the other settlers in Albemarle were the equals in social condition of the best of the Virginia planters of that time. Such was the real character of the original settlement, made, as Lawson asserts, by men of substance.

The Great Deed

It was during Stephens's administration that the Lords Proprietors were pleased to answer favorably the petition of the Grand Assembly of 1665, so termed, perhaps, because when the petition was prepared the people had not elected delegates, but themselves assembled under the instructions to Governor Berkeley; and for many years the legislative body of Albemarle continued to call itself "the Grand Assembly."

On May 1, 1668, under the seal of the province, the Lords Proprietors, in response to this request, granted that the inhabitants of Albemarle should hold their lands upon the same terms and conditions as the people of Virginia, by which the rent became only a farthing an acre and was payable in commodities at a fixed price and not in money. This concession was regarded so highly that the instrument containing it was called "The Great Deed," and in after years it played an important part in North Carolina matters, and for many years the General Assembly required that it should be securely kept in the personal possession of the speaker of the house.

The Great
Deed

At the session of the Assembly held in 1669 there were passed seven acts that have come down to us. One of these recites that no provision had been made for defraying the expenses of the governor and council in time of the courts, and "as the General Assembly thinks it unreasonable that they should spend their time in the service of the county and not have their charges borne, therefore every one who brings a suit in court and is cast shall pay thirty pounds of tobacco" as a sort of tax fee to pay the expenses of the governor and council. Prior to that the governor and council composed the only court held, for as no precincts had been laid off, there were no precinct courts.

Legislation
of 1669

In order that Albemarle should not be behind Virginia in offering inducements to settlers, an act was copied from the Virginia statutes prohibiting the institution of any suit for any debt against a person who should come into Albemarle until after five years had elapsed from his arrival.

In 1642 Virginia had passed a similar law, which was formally re-enacted by the Virginia Assembly in 1663, and the settlers in Albemarle coming from Virginia brought with them the remembrance of this legislation as a Virginia institution; and, indeed, similar laws were adopted in other colonies. There were no ministers in the colony, and but few in Virginia; so an act was then passed that legalized marriage as a civil institution, and provided that a marriage solemnized by the governor or any of his council in the presence of three or four of the neighbors, the certificate thereof being registered by the secretary, should be a valid

The
Virginia
debtor law

marriage, and any person violating such a marriage should be punishable as if it had been performed by a minister. This marriage law was born of the necessity of the case; and as it was founded in reason, the civil marriage thus instituted at Albemarle has since been adopted by all of the enlightened states of the American Republic. These acts were transmitted to England for the approval of the Lords Proprietors, and meeting with their approbation, received their sanction and became the law in the colony.

CHAPTER IX

Carteret's Administration, 1670-73

The Fundamental Constitutions.—Changes introduced by them.—
The first meeting under the Grand Model.—Carteret governor.—
The Grand Model in practice; The precincts.—The nobility.—The
Palatine's Court.—The Quakers.—First dissatisfaction.—Carteret
sails for England.—John Jenkins deputy-governor.—Visits from
Edmundson and Fox.

The Fundamental Constitutions

1669

The banishment of Clarendon and the long illness of
Albemarle made an opening at court for the higher rise
of Lord Ashley, a man of superior mental powers and
capabilities. He had inherited great wealth, had been studious in the law and in the sciences, and, possessing a strong
influence with the people, soon attained the highest position
and power among the statesmen of England. A Presbyterian and somewhat of a free thinker, among his intimates
was John Locke, the scholar and philosopher, with whom he
contracted a friendship based on their common sympathy
with civil and philosophical freedom. In 1667 Locke became
his secretary, and took up his abode in Ashley's residence.

The rise of Shaftesbury

The Lords Proprietors had requested Ashley to prepare a
permanent constitution for Carolina, and in the summer of
1669 a rough draught was submitted to them of that famous
instrument which has come down to posterity as Locke's
Fundamental Constitutions or the Grand Model of Government. This instrument was adopted and signed by the
Lords Proprietors on July 21, 1669.

The purposes avowed in it were to provide for the better
settlement of the government, to establish the interests of
the Proprietors with equality and without confusion, to
conform the government agreeably to the English monarchy,
and to avoid erecting a numerous democracy in their
province.

England had just passed through the experiment of the Commonwealth, the course of which was marked by many deplorable excesses. The Proprietors had seen stalwart republicans, seeking an escape from evils of their own creation, unite in offering a crown to Cromwell, and had witnessed the establishment of a monarchy clothed with arbitrary power under the specious title of Protector; and most of them had suffered severely in their fortunes and in their persons during those convulsions; and now that the ancient constitution of the kingdom had been restored, largely through their own instrumentality, they wished to avoid erecting an unsteady and unrestrained democracy in their possessions. They were themselves of the nobility, and possessed in Carolina under the grant of the king even the regal powers that were enjoyed by the owners of the Palatine County of Durham. Not unnaturally, they sought to guard their individual rights and privileges. As there were eight Proprietors, to establish equality among them was a chief care. Eight great offices were created: one, the Palatine, was assigned to the oldest Proprietor, and upon his death the next in seniority succeeded him. The Palatine was the executive, and the other Proprietors were to be the admiral, chamberlain, chancellor, constable, chief justice, high steward, and treasurer of the province. Carolina was to be divided into counties, and there was to be an hereditary nobility established in each county consisting of one landgrave and two caciques. The other inhabitants were freemen and leetmen, as the landholders were called in the county of Durham; and the institution of negro slavery was recognized. An alien by subscribing the Fundamental Constitutions thereby became naturalized, but no person over seventeen years of age could have any benefit or protection of the law who was not enrolled as a member of some religious profession acknowledging the Deity.

The eight great offices

Each county was to be laid off into eight seignories, eight baronies, and four precincts, and every precinct was to be subdivided into six colonies. One of the seignories was to be the property of each Proprietor. It was to contain 12,000 acres, and was to descend to his heirs male, with some provision in case of failure of heirs. Four of the baronies, 12,000 acres each, were for the landgraves, and each cacique was to have two baronies. Each precinct was

Divisions of the land

to embrace 72,000 acres, and each of its six colonies was to contain 12,000 acres. The land in the precincts could be bought and sold at pleasure by the owners, but whoever purchased it had to pay a yearly quitrent of a penny an acre to the Lords Proprietors. Within the precincts, by special grant, a holding of 3000 acres might be erected into a manor, with certain powers and privileges vesting in the lord of the manor, and in that case, being once erected into a manor, it could be sold in fee only in its entirety, and no parcel of it could be conveyed for a longer period than twenty-one years. Provision was made for leetmen within the manors, baronies,

Leetmen

and seignories. A person became a leetman by voluntarily entering himself as such in the proper court. On the marriage of a leetman the lord was required to give him ten acres of land for his life, subject to a rent of not more than the eighth part of the yearly produce of the ten acres. The children of leetmen were to remain forever as their parents were ; and they were not to live off of the land of their

Freemen

particular lord without license obtained from him. Being subjects of their lord, all their controversies were to be tried in the leet courts of their lord, who had a feudal jurisdiction over them. Thus, besides negro slaves the inhabitants were to be leetmen attached to the land, freemen, and nobles.

Nobles

That the nobles should be properly maintained, they were to have no power to alienate their property and dignity, which must forever descend undivided to their heirs male, but this provision was not to go into effect until the year 1700.

The system of government was cumbersome and complex. The Palatine and the other seven Proprietors, being the great officers, formed what was designated the Palatine's Court. This body was, however, executive rather than judicial. It had power to call parliaments, to pardon all offences, to elect all officers, to negative the acts of Parliament, and generally was vested with all the powers granted to the Proprietors, except as was otherwise limited in the Fundamental Constitutions. In this court, any Proprietor being absent, he could be represented by his deputy.

Each of the other great officers also had a court composed of himself, six councillors, and twelve assistants chosen from among the landgraves, caciques, and such commoners or freemen as were designated; and to each of these courts a particular jurisdiction was allotted.

Superior to these courts, however, was the Grand Council, composed of the Palatine, the seven other great officers, and the forty-two councillors. To this council was assigned the power to determine controversies between the courts, and to make peace and war, leagues and treaties with the Indians, and to raise forces for war. It also had authority to prepare matters to be adopted in Parliament, and no act could be proposed in Parliament unless it had first passed the Grand Council.

The Parliament was to consist of the Proprietors or their deputies, the landgraves and the caciques, and one freeholder from each precinct chosen by the freeholders. These were to sit in one room, each member having one vote. Parliament was to meet on the first Monday of November every second year in the town it last sat in, without any summons. And in order to elect members the freeholders of each precinct were to meet on the first Monday of September every two years and choose their representatives.

Under the concessions the people had a right to elect assemblymen on the first day of each January, and this new provision investing them with the constitutional right to elect a parliament every other September, to convene in November without any call from the governor, was founded in the severe experiences of the English people during the troubles of the recent past, and was a change from English methods largely favorable to the liberties of the people. In after years it became the foundation of a famous enactment known as the Biennial Act of 1715, which, however, merely continued in force the former practice.

The general court

In every county there was to be a general court, held by the sheriff and one justice from each precinct. Appeals lay from this court in important civil cases and in criminal cases to the Proprietors' court; and in every precinct there was to be a court consisting of a steward and four justices, who should judge all criminal cases except treason, murder, and other offences where the punishment was death, and except criminal cases against the nobility; and also all civil causes whatsoever, but with appeal to the county court in important cases. To try treason, murder, and other offences punishable with death, a commission for itinerant judges was to issue twice a year, who were to hold assizes in each county with the sheriff and four justices with appeal to the Proprietors' court. There were grand juries for the criminal courts, and in all courts causes were determined by a jury of twelve men, but a majority verdict was sufficient, unanimity not being required.

While the nobles had great places provided for them, there were thus open to the freemen avenues to distinction in a judicial career, as members of Parliament, as assistants in the great courts, and as councillors. But lawyers were

Lawyers discountenanced

discountenanced, and it was declared a vile thing to plead a cause for money. The purpose of this provision was, possibly, to build up a clientage for the great lords and add to their importance. While appeals were allowed, a new trial in the same court was forbidden, and all manner of comments and of expositions on any part of the law was absolutely prohibited. But at the end of a hundred years every law was to be void. There were one hundred and twenty sections of the Grand Model, or Constitutions as Locke called them, and every part of them was to remain sacred and unalterable forever, and every inhabitant was to take an oath to support them.

Among the provisions of the Fundamental Constitutions

1669

were some innovations on English customs that were not
without merit. There was to be in each precinct an officer
called the register, in whose records should be enrolled all
deeds, judgments, and conveyances which concerned any
land in the precinct, and until registered such conveyances
had no force. And in every seignory, barony, and colony
there was to be a registry for recording all births, marriages,
and deaths; and no marriage was to be lawful, no matter
what contract or ceremony was used, until both parties
mutually owned it before the register, and he had recorded
it, together with the names of the parents.

Registration of land and of social statistics

In regard to religion, while freedom of conscience was
allowed, yet it was enacted that no man should become a
freeman of Carolina or have any estate or habitation within
it "that doth not acknowledge a god, and that god is to be
publicly and solemnly worshipped"; and while no person of
the age of seventeen years could have any protection of
the law unless a member of a church, yet any seven persons
agreeing in any religion could constitute a church or profession on which they should bestow some name to distinguish it from others.

Religion

The changes introduced by the Constitutions

Some of the administrative provisions of the Grand Model
were not unlike those that had been in use in Albemarle from
the first. Others were easy to introduce. But the establishment of new orders of nobility with the powers and privileges
accorded them and the subdivision of the counties as proposed were utterly impracticable.

The details of what the philosopher Locke and his coadjutor, a sagacious man of business and practical statesman,
deemed a perfect plan of government were worked out with
great care and particularity. But political institutions to fit
the needs of a community must be the reasonable outgrowth
of actual conditions, developed through the natural operation of influences that affect the thoughts, habits, aspirations, and life of the people. Although the Grand Model

won high applause upon its publication in Europe, it did not excite enthusiasm in Carolina. As a theoretical adjustment of forces in government, establishing on a secure basis a conservative aristocracy and perpetuating a monarchical system along with guarantees of popular freedom, it was doubtless superior to any European government of that era. But it was not suited for freemen inhabiting a wilderness. For the chief aim in view, the establishment of a practical government in Carolina, it was a strange admixture of unmitigated folly and theoretical wisdom. The provision ordaining a nobility was probably not offensive to the inhabitants of Albemarle. The people of every nationality were at that period accustomed to class distinctions, which entered largely into the social life of their country, and an order of nobility could not have been disagreeable to Englishmen in any colony. But the plan was too elaborate to be put into successful operation, and, except in some unimportant particulars, it was not attempted in Albemarle. A century later, when a constitution was to be framed by practical statesmen for a continent, the outline of a system, a few general grants of power, a few denials of authority by way of limitation, sufficed to establish a government that has evoked the admiration of mankind.

The margin note reads: The limitations of the Constitutions

The first meeting under the Grand Model

C. R., I, 179

The principal features of the Grand Model having been agreed on, a rough draft of it was, in July, 1669, transmitted to Albemarle. The first meeting of the Proprietors after its adoption was held in October, 1669, at the Cockpit, a government office near Whitehall, where Lord Ashley's public business was commonly transacted, where the Board of Trade held its sessions, and where later Princess Anne resided until called to the throne. There were present all of the Proprietors except Clarendon and Sir William Berkeley. Albemarle, being the oldest of the Proprietors, became the first Palatine. At a second meeting two months later, January, 1670, it was resolved that instructions should be sent to Carolina to put the new model into operation. Before that, however, Albemarle had, in December, passed away, and Lord John Berkeley succeeded to the office of Palatine. At this meeting the acts of the General Assembly of 1669, that had been transmitted to the Lords Proprietors for their confirmation, were approved, and they were redrafted to conform to the requirements of the Grand Model, and were then returned to Albemarle, where they were passed for the second time on October 15, 1670.

C. R., I, 183

Carteret governor

At this meeting, too, John Locke and Sir John Yeamans were appointed landgraves; and Lord Berkeley, exercising his prerogative as Palatine, deputized Samuel Stephens, the former governor, to be his deputy and to continue in as governor. But about December of the year 1669 Stephens died, and the council in Albemarle having, in such an emergency, the power and right to fill the vacancy, chose as governor Peter Carteret, a kinsman of Sir George Carteret, who had settled in Albemarle in 1664; and Carteret entered actively on the duties, and as governor held with the council a called session of the county court, being the general court for the county, in July, 1670, at which time administration was granted on the estate of Stephens to John Culpepper, as attorney for Sir William Berkeley, whose marriage with the widow may already have been solemnized. That council, previously appointed by Governor Stephens under his commission and instructions, was composed of Colonel John Jenkins, John Harvey, Major Richard Foster, and Captain Thomas Cullen, some of the other councillors not being in attendance.*

Stephens dies, Dec., 1669

*At a called court held July 15, 1670, at the house of Samuel Davis, for the county of Albemarle, there were present the Hon. Peter Carteret, governor and commander-in-chief; Colonel John Jenkins, John Harvey, Major Richard Foster, Captain Thomas Cullen, councillors; and the following was adopted: Whereas, Mr. John Culpepper, Gent., attorney for Sir William Berkeley, governor, and captain-general of Virginia, petitioned to this court for letters of administration on the estate of Captain Samuel Stephens, deceased, he putting in security to save the court harmless,

1670

The news of the death of Stephens apparently reached England before the instructions prepared for him at the January meeting of the Proprietors had been sent, and so later in the year Carteret was appointed governor and his instructions were sent him, together with a copy of the Grand Model, which had been completed and fully perfected on March 1, 1670.

On September 27th of that year a general court was held for the county of Albemarle, there being present the same councillors, together with Francis Godfrey and John Willoughby.

The Grand Model in practice: The precincts

C. R., I, 181

In the instructions directed to Carteret as governor the Proprietors said they were not able to put the Grand Model fully into practice, "but intending to come as nigh to it as· we can," Carteret was directed to observe it as far as practicable. These instructions, therefore, varied from the Grand Model and also varied from the existing system at Albemarle in several particulars. Among the directions given to Carteret was one that a writ should be issued to the four precincts of Albemarle for the election in each of five representatives for a general assembly, the division into four precincts having been made conformably to the rough draft of the Grand Model sent over in July, 1669.* Under the concessions, and under Stephens's instructions in 1667, the inhabitants were to choose twelve deputies, until "districtions of the county should be made," and then each "distriction" should choose two representatives. That would

Grand Model vs. the existing system

MSS. Records at Edenton

it is ordered that the said Culpepper have orders of administration granted him. Whereas, Andrew Woodward was summoned to this court of chancery, and being required to give his oath upon inquiry of what he knew to be the estate of Samuel Stephens, deceased, he wilfully denied and refused to give his oath, wherefore the court ordered that he remain a close prisoner. On September 27, 1670, a general court was held at the same place, which seems to have been at that time the convenient point of meeting.

*The names of three of these precincts were Carteret, Berkeley and Shaftesbury; the name of the fourth is now not positively known.

indicate that at least six subdivisions were then in contemplation; now the county was divided into four precincts,
as required by the Grand Model, each electing five representatives. Such was the origin of the right of the Albemarle precincts to have five representatives, which they
continued to enjoy, despite all antagonism, until the adoption
of the state constitution in 1776.*

The nobility

Five persons appointed by the Lords Proprietors, who
theoretically were to represent the nobility, were to sit with
the twenty representatives chosen by the people to form
an Assembly. After the Assembly had chosen a speaker, it
was to elect five persons, who were to join the five deputies
appointed by the Lords Proprietors to form the governor's
council, the governor himself being the deputy of the Palatine. And this council of ten was to have the power of the
Grand Council in the Grand Model. The governor and the
five deputies were to form the Palatine's Court, and were
vested with the jurisdiction and powers conferred on that
court. Particular authority was conferred on the governor
and council to establish courts for the administration of
justice; and all the inhabitants were to take an oath of
allegiance and of submission to the form of government.

Such were the instructions to Governor Carteret, in 1670,
to put the Grand Model into operation "as nigh as may be,"
and in several particulars to alter the existing government
in order to do so, and to require the submission of the
people to it under the sanction of an oath. Carteret, who
early settled in Albemarle, and was so esteemed that he
had been speaker of the Assembly, and whose qualifications
were such that he had served as secretary of the general
court, sought to give effect to his instructions and put into
operation the changes indicated. The county had already

*In 1665, the freemen themselves met in Grand Assembly; in 1666,
they assembled and appointed members to represent them; and this
was continued until the precincts were established, when the election
was by precincts.

been laid off into four precincts, which were now permanently established. The governor and deputies held their Palatine's Court, the council was increased by five commoners chosen by the Assembly, and in other respects attempts were made to follow the instructions of the Proprietors.

The Grand Model in its complex entirety was not at all adapted to a few scattered planters in a new settlement; nor were its provisions that erected a class of landed aristocracy in harmony with the spirit of liberty and of equality which **Value of the Grand Model** would naturally be fostered in a remote wilderness. But it contained some important principles of liberty which thus became engrafted in the fundamental constitution of the colony, and whose maintenance was in after years of great interest to the people. Although it did not go into operation in all its parts, yet in some respects the frame and system of government conformed to it. The governor was the representative of the Palatine, the deputies were appointed from among the people, and the Assembly elected five persons to sit with them; the precinct courts, the general courts and courts of chancery were now held conformably to the fundamentals; and every second year, in September, the people elected their deputies to sit in the legislature without any writ; and the Assembly met in November.

The Quakers: Edmundson and Fox

It was during Carteret's administration, in 1672, that William Edmundson, a preacher of the new sect, the Friends, visited Albemarle, and the first religious meeting was held in the forests of Carolina. Accompanied by two woodsmen to guide him through the wilderness, Edmundson passed on horseback beyond the confines of the Nansemond settlements, and on the third day reached the house of Henry Phillips, the only Quaker then in Albemarle. Phillips and his wife had been convinced in New England, and coming to Carolina about 1665 had not seen a Friend for seven years. When Edmundson made himself known, they wept for joy. Word was speedily sent to the neighbors to come at noon to hear

1672

the preacher, and many came. For a dozen years those who had first seated in that remote locality had been without church privileges, had not assembled in prayer, nor heard a preacher of the Word. Edmundson, accustomed to the observance of the proprieties, was shocked that they brought their pipes and sat smoking during the religious service. But while their forest breeding impressed him that they were not religious, yet he found the way to their hearts, and several at once received the "Truth with gladness." Truly, those were glad hearts that were converted and brought into communion with this apostle of repentance preaching that the inner light was a revelation of the Holy Spirit. On the third day Edmundson, well pleased with Carolina, returned to Virginia. But a few months later he was followed by the very head and founder of the faith, George Fox. Fox reached Bennett's Creek toward the last of November, and taking a canoe, proceeded to the Chowan and then to Edenton Bay; and there, obtaining a larger boat, went on to Governor Carteret's. The governor and his wife "received them lovingly," and Carteret courteously accompanied him two miles through the wilderness. Thirty miles more brought Fox to the residence of Joseph Scot, one of the assemblymen, where they had a precious meeting; and a few miles further they reached the home of the secretary of the colony, who had previously accepted the Quaker faith. For three weeks Fox lingered among these people of the forest, whom he described as tender and loving and receptive of the truth, holding meetings to which they flocked. The seed fell on good ground. The faith of the zealous and earnest evangelist, who appealed so effectively to the consciences of his hearers, took firm root in Albemarle. No other religious meetings were held calling the people into communion and at once ministering to their human needs and satisfying their spiritual longings. It was in sympathy with the solitude of their surroundings and the quietude of their daily life. There had been naught to disturb the restfulness of the people or to inflame their passions. Content-

Edmundson preaches

C. R., I, 217

Fox visits Carolina

1672

ment prevailed. The administration of their government had
been of the people and for the people. Their assemblies met
regularly, and the laws were of their own making.

The first dissatisfaction

C. R., I, 219

The
Assembly
of 1672

At the session of 1672 at least fifty-four acts were passed,
which may, however, have embraced all former laws then
re-enacted. The fifty-fourth prohibited the sale of rum at a
greater price than twenty-five pounds of tobacco per gallon;
for the unit of value was the pound of tobacco, and taxes,
rents, and debts were all payable in that commodity. This
attempt to regulate prices, interfering with the freedom of
trade, was soon found to be inexpedient, because if the
traders could not make a greater profit on the rum, they
would not bring in other commodities that were more necessary to the inhabitants. The next year, therefore, the act
was repealed.

Notwithstanding those features of the Grand Model that
were inimical to freedom, there was probably no opposition
to the introduction of the administrative changes which
Carteret, under his instructions, put into operation. The
people, few in number, somewhat scattered, occupied with
their industries, probably did not at first greatly concern themselves with those provisions of the new constitution that
were not to be carried into effect at once among them; but
when they were required to take an oath to support it and
to abide by it, and when one of its unalterable provisions
was that their rent per acre, instead of one farthing per
acre, payable in commodities, should be as much silver as is
contained in a penny, they exhibited signs of dissatisfaction.

The Great
Deed
appealed to

They had just secured by the Great Deed the concession for
which they had petitioned years before, that their rent should
be like that in Virginia, and the proposed change must have
aroused indignation. In the records of Perquimans is an
entry showing that Francis Toms, Christopher Nicholson,
and William Wyatt, being Quakers, did subscribe the
Fundamental Constitutions, but they added a protest, how-

ever, that by accepting the Grand Model they should not be disannulled of the gracious grant given by the Lords Proprietors in their Great Deed to hold their lands according to the tenure of Virginia. Doubtless this protest but expressed the common sentiment of all the inhabitants.

Besides, just at this time there were other causes of discontent arising from the navigation laws and customs duties, which if enforced would seriously interfere with the trade of the colony. But whatever was the occasion, dissatisfaction pervaded the settlement—a dissatisfaction so pronounced that Carteret could not stem it. The new element introduced into the council by the admission of five inhabitants appointed by the Assembly now changed the attitude of that body toward public measures and virtually brought it under the rule of the people themselves. The council was no longer in harmony with the governor.

Carteret's efforts to compose differences were fruitless; he wearied of the attempt, and finally laid down his office and abandoned the colony. Before May, 1673, he sailed for England, leaving the administration, it is said, in ill order and worse hands.

Carteret resigns

On May 25th, at a council held at the house of Thomas Godfrey, Carteret was absent and Colonel John Jenkins presided as deputy governor.

CHAPTER X

Administrations of Jenkins and Miller, 1673-78

The navigation acts.—The Board of Trade.—The people murmur.—Other causes of dissatisfaction.—An Indian war.—The tobacco duty resisted.—The administration compromises.—Miller arrested.—Eastchurch goes to England.—Governor Jenkins deposed.—Eastchurch appointed governor.—Bacon's rebellion in Virginia.—A government by the people.—Eastchurch deputizes Miller.—Opposition to the navigation acts.—Durant resolves to revolt.—Miller acts resolutely.—Durant returns to Albemarle.—The crisis arrives.—The revolt proceeds.

The navigation acts

1660

Since the opening of the century there had been rapid progress in the art of manufacturing and in the development of the commercial interests of England. Fierce wars had been waged for the expansion of trade and for the establishment of commercial supremacy. The early navigation acts, strengthened by Cromwell's legislation, were initial movements in a system intended to secure the mercantile prosperity of England. And as the enterprising Dutch were now proving successful competitors in the colonial trade, there was in 1660 a further enactment, aimed at Holland, that all importations into the plantations should be in English ships. Because of that prohibition, Dutch vessels were no longer seen in American harbors, and the carrying trade was secured. But still there was direct intercourse between the colonies and European ports, and the London merchants did not reap all the advantage of the colonial trade. So three years later English statesmanship took a further step. The importation of European commodities into the colonies was prohibited unless shipped from England. In the interest of the London merchants, it was

1663

virtually enacted that the colonies could obtain foreign goods only from them. Still there was unrestrained trade between the colonies themselves. The Englishmen in New England could freely barter with their fellow-subjects of Albemarle, and that, indeed, was the chief source of supply for that colony. And it may be that the New England merchants evaded the navigation acts, and that a part of the European commodities brought to Albemarle had not come by way of London. At any rate, the growing mercantile importance of New England attracted attention, and in 1672 a blow was aimed to cripple it. An act was passed abridging the freedom of inter-colonial traffic.

A duty was imposed on tobacco and certain other enumerated articles when exported from one colony to another. And tobacco was the staple in which payments were made. It was the basis of bills of credit. The duty imposed was a penny a pound, and to that extent the tax lessened the value of tobacco as a debt-paying commodity in the inter-colonial trade. Indeed, tobacco from the first had been the subject of particular regulation. Its culture in England was forbidden, and Charles I had taken to himself the entire production of the English colonies, at a price fixed by himself, and it paid a duty on being brought into England. If any obtained at Albemarle by the New England merchants was shipped to the continent, the king lost his taxes and New England obtained funds from abroad to pay for European commodities to be clandestinely brought into the colonies. To stifle this trade and to secure more funds for the deplenished purse of a needy sovereign this export tax was imposed, and it was to be collected by officers of the Crown. Indeed, the entire regulation of colonial affairs, being claimed as a royal prerogative, had on the Restoration been committed to the king's Privy Council. When Ashley became chancellor of the exchequer, in 1668, ever active in promoting national advancement, he procured the appointment of a Council of Commerce, to whom was assigned special charge of the colonies. In 1672 Ashley became lord high

Tobacco shipped to New England taxed

1672
chancellor and was created Earl of Shaftesbury, and in the same year this export tax was laid on tobacco.

The Board of Trade

But the Council of Commerce was inefficient, and later it was dissolved and its functions were transferred to a new board appointed to take charge of all matters relative to trade and the foreign plantations; and the immediate care of these affairs was committed to a few selected members, Origin among them being Shaftesbury, Craven, Berkeley, and Colleton, four of the Proprietors of Carolina, while Landgrave Locke was their secretary. Such was the origin of this board that continued until the Revolution to manage the affairs of the American colonies. At the time of its creation the colonies were free to export their products, except tobacco and some other enumerated articles, in English ships, to the West Indies and elsewhere, and to import rum and salt and produce in return; and European commodities imported by one colony from England could be reshipped to another; tobacco could be exported from one colony to another on the payment of the export tax, and upon its importation into England an import duty was to be paid. But while these were the regulations, they had not been enforced. No customs officers had been appointed for Albemarle, and there had been no interference with the trade that enterprising New Englanders had established with Albemarle. Now there was to be a change; but Shaftesbury was no longer on the board.

1673
His zealous efforts to arrest the advance of Catholic influences had, in 1673, separated him from the other great officers of state, and in September of that year, having been dismissed from the office of lord chancellor, he became the popular leader and the central figure in the contest against Shaftesbury the measures of the court. Having carried through Parliament a bill forbidding Catholics to come within ten miles of London, the king, who was largely under Catholic influ-

ences, dismissed him from the Privy Council and ordered him to leave London.

1675

The people murmur

It was fifteen years after the axe of the first settlers had rung in the clearings of Albemarle before any order "by the king's command" was heard in Carolina. Then came commissions for one Copeley and one Birch to be the king's collector of customs and his surveyor of customs; and in case these appointees should not be in the colony, the governor was directed to fill the offices by his own appointment. Copeley and Birch did not appear and claim their commissions, so the duty of appointment devolved on John Jenkins, then president of the council and acting governor. Opposition was at once manifested to this first step toward putting in force the navigation acts and trade regulations that had not been previously observed in Albemarle. But Jenkins and the other deputies managed to reconcile the people to it, and the appointments were made. Timothy Biggs, the deputy of Earl Craven, who had married the widow of Speaker Catchmaid, was appointed surveyor of customs, and Valentine Byrd, the collector. Byrd was a man of consequence and of wealth, and lived in style, as the inventory of his estate filed on his death a few years later indicates.* He entered on his duties, but probably was not exacting or thorough in their performance. It was said that many hogsheads of tobacco went out tax free marked as "bait for the New England fishermen," and European com-

C. R., I, 291

C. R., I, 292

---

*In 1680 we have the inventory of Captain Valentine Byrd, who was one of the grandees of the time, and here we come upon "fine Holland sheets," and "diaper napkins," and "table cloaths," and "silver tankards and spoons," "dressing boxes," "mirrors," "books," "a coach," and "lignum-vitæ punch bowl," with a rich account of household articles in the shape of "warming pans," "beds and bedding," "chairs and tables," clearly demonstrating that Captain Valentine Byrd was a man well-to-do in this world; and if not very comfortable, had no one to blame but himself, for he had men servants and maid servants, negroes, Indians, and white convicts, and lands well stocked and good tenements thereon, all of which he left to his wife, who afterward gave both it and herself to the first leader of rebellion, and became Madame Culpepper.

Hawks, II, 578

modities were allowed to be landed that did not come under a London manifest. Still ostensibly the law was observed in Albemarle, but it was a constant cause of irritation.

In the meantime other circumstances led to discontent and apprehension among the inhabitants. There were rumors that the rents were to be raised, and also that the province was to be divided among the Proprietors, and that Albemarle was to be allotted to Sir William Berkeley. It would have been repugnant to the freemen of Albemarle to be cast under the dominion of any single Proprietor; but when their ruler was to be Berkeley, whose tyranny in Virginia was drawing the inhabitants into revolt, the suggestion was abhorrent to them, and the Assembly in November, 1675, adopted a remonstrance to the Lords Proprietors on the subject.

In addition to these troubles an Indian war now set in. Some of the savages who had been waging a murderous warfare on the northern borders of Virginia fled to the Meherrins and stirred them up to hostilities, and they began to roam in the wilderness between Albemarle and Nansemond, and committed several murders that aroused the people. Fortunately, just when needed, Captain Zack Gilliam came into port from London with his armed ship, the *Carolina,* bringing a cargo among which was a supply of arms and ammunition, and a force was organized to suppress the Indians. In the prosecution of this war, which lasted for more than a year, as the council said later, "by God's assistance, though not without the loss of many men," the Meherrins were wholly subdued, and were removed from their territory on the south side of the Meherrin River, which they had occupied under a treaty made by commissioners appointed by King Charles II, to a reservation at the mouth of the Meherrin River, and on the north side, although after that some of them planted corn and built cabins on old fields of the Chowanoak Indians on the south side of the river.

On the return of the force from this campaign against the Meherrins the people, with arms in their hands, demanded

The Remonstrance

An Indian war
C. R., I, 658

Meherrins subdued, 1676-77

The tobacco duty resisted

that the export tax on tobacco shipped to another colony should not be collected. Here was incipient rebellion. The grievance to be redressed was not because of the Proprietary government, but it arose under the laws of England. The purpose of the English statesmen was to build up England's greatness by constraining the colonies to trade at London and by preventing inter-colonial trade in tobacco. The New England traders, it was alleged, were adept in evading these regulations. Vessels leaving England would stop at Ireland and obtain a quantity of linen; others would call by the Canary Islands and take in wine. There was nothing immoral in the act itself. It had always been proper and lawful, but now it was sinful because prohibited in the interest of the London merchant. And so with tobacco. It was entirely proper to export it from Albemarle direct to London without any export duty, but if used to pay a debt in New England it was burdened with an export tax. Its value as a debt-paying medium, if used in the New England trade, was lessened a penny a pound in the interest of the London merchant. The coast trade was natural, but it was not helpful to London, therefore it must be stifled. Such was the argument of the English statesmen. The men of Albemarle were not of that mind. They preferred to consult the advantage of Albemarle. The law they objected to was not of their making. It was not for their benefit. It was disadvantageous to their community. It was imposed on them without their consent by men across the Atlantic to promote their own selfish interests. It was not submitted to with complacency. Oppressive and unjust legislation bears the same fruit in every age. There are evasions by artifice and then revolt. Hogsheads of tobacco were clandestinely exported, and then the people with arms in their hands took an open stand against the enforcement of the law. Chief among those who led the opposition was George Durant, who had become one of the most influential men in Albemarle, and who had a considerable quantity of tobacco for shipment to New England; and in alliance with him were

Tobacco export laws

Armed rebellion

1676   Richard Foster, one of the council; Patrick White, William Crawford, and Valentine Byrd himself.

The administration compromises

C. R., I, 292   The few councillors and officials who felt constrained to support the law were unable to cope with a determined community. They therefore effected a compromise. Without authority, they offered to reduce the export tax to a farthing the pound. That was assented to, and Byrd was allowed thereafter to peacefully discharge his duties, but even then The law evaded probably he used no great vigilance as the king's officer. And, indeed, it was afterward alleged against him that he allowed much tobacco to be exported without the payment of any duty, and even winked at the importation of European manufactures that had not come by way of England.

And now came some episodes that in the uncertain and unsteady light thrown upon them and the shifting relations of the actors cannot be certainly accounted for, and the causes can only be surmised.

Thomas Miller, an apothecary, but a person of some consideration, was often in drink. There seems to have been bad blood between him and Jenkins, the president of the council. It is said a conspiracy was formed by Jenkins and Miller arrested John Culpepper, who had once been the surveyor-general of Carolina, to charge him with uttering treasonable words against the king's person and the monarchy, as well as blasphemy. Early in 1676 he was arrested by Jenkins and the C. R., I, 269, council and held under a guard of soldiers, put in irons 314 and thrown into prison. Then, doubtless on their application to Berkeley, that rank Royalist issued a mandate for Miller's removal to Virginia to be tried before him and his council. The Albemarle Assembly, however, was no party to this proceeding, and it heard evidence in opposition to the charges. Miller, on being carried to Virginia, was acquitted by Berkeley and his council, and he caused his attorney, Henry Hudson, to institute an action for damages against Culpepper, and then in May Miller took shipping for London, bearing with him a remonstrance to the Proprietors adopted by the Assembly in the preceding November, and also a subsequent address adopted in March, relative to the deposition of Jenkins, and assuring the Proprietors of their fidelity to them.

About the same time Thomas Eastchurch, speaker of the Assembly, also sailed for London. He had had a case in one of the courts, of which Captain John Willoughby was a member, in which the court decided adversely to him, and on his proposing to appeal to the Lords Proprietors Willoughby denied the appeal, declaring that his "court was the court of courts and the jury of juries." Willoughby is alleged to have been a great tyrant. For his tyrannical conduct and oppression he was cited before the Palatine's Court, but he beat the officer of that court and refused to attend; thereupon he was declared in contempt and outlawed, and the succeeding General Assembly put a price on his head, and he fled to Virginia and remained there until the government of Albemarle subsequently became unsettled.

It would seem that Jenkins's course toward Miller, and perhaps his willingness to have the custom duty on tobacco collected, led to charges of misdemeanor against him, and the General Assembly deposed him from his office as president of the council and imprisoned him and sent by Miller to the Proprietors for instructions. There was a conflict between the Assembly and Governor Jenkins, who was nevertheless sustained by a majority of the council. Nor were the Proprietors satisfied with the conduct of their own deputies, who in several particulars had disregarded their wishes and in some instances had thwarted them. The Proprietors had directed that towns should be laid off and built at Roanoke Island and elsewhere, so that trade could be centred at certain points instead of being carried on in a desultory way at the landing places of the planters. They had also directed that a way by land should be opened to the settlement on the Ashley; and they had particularly enjoined that plantations should be settled on the south side of the

1676

Eastchurch goes to England

Governor Jenkins deposed, May, 1676

1676

sound. None of these instructions had been obeyed, and the councillors had prevented any settlement on the south side of the sound, because that would have interfered with their individual trade with the Indians in that direction, which they had engrossed. Indeed, Thomas Cullen, one of the deputies, was accused of furnishing the Indians with pistols and with arms and ammunition, and because of that charge he fled from the colony.

Eastchurch appointed governor

C. R., I,
228-233

In the fall of 1676 Eastchurch and Miller arrived in London, and the Proprietors at once took their matters into consideration. Eastchurch was not merely a gentleman of good fame, but was related to Lord Treasurer Clifford, one of the Board of Trade, who had solicited his appointment as governor. The Proprietors finding that he was a very discreet and worthy man, was speaker of the Assembly and much interested in the prosperity of the colony, November 21, 1676, appointed him governor. They also, in a letter to the Assembly, approved its action in regard to Jenkins, and expressed their appreciation of the respect shown for themselves by the Assembly.

The spirit
of self-gov-
ernment

Difficult indeed was the situation of those Proprietors who were members of the Board of Trade and in duty bound to see his Majesty's customs collected, and were yet interested in preserving quiet in their province, where the people were evading the payment of that tax in defiance of the royal authority, and, emboldened by the progress of Bacon's revolution in Virginia, were likewise manifesting a purpose to govern themselves.*

*In May, 1676, because of Berkeley's supineness in not checking Indian hostilities, many of the Virginians embodied under the leadership of Nathaniel Bacon and marched against the Indians; this proceeding being in defiance of Governor Berkeley's wishes, on the 29th of the month he proclaimed them rebels. The next month an Assembly met, and Berkeley having promised to issue a commission to Bacon as commander of the forces against the Indians, all differences were quieted. But later the governor refused to abide by the agreement, and withheld the promised commission. Bacon hurriedly marched his troops to Jamestown, surrounded Berkeley and de-

If any one could reconcile the conflicting elements in Albemarle, Shaftesbury wisely surmised that he must be found among those who were in favor with the Assembly. So having appointed Speaker Eastchurch governor, he procured Miller's appointment as collector of customs, for Miller's cause had been espoused by the Assembly, and he had borne their letters to the Proprietors, and on his account they had imprisoned and deposed John Jenkins, the president of the council.

A year had elapsed since the Assembly had by the deposition of Jenkins taken the administration into its own hands, and still the Proprietors did not hasten to interfere. Shaftesbury, now grown to be the greatest of all subjects, had persistently declined the overtures of the king, and had resolutely agitated to secure safeguards for Protestantism and liberty. In 1677 a mismove led to his arrest and imprisonment in the Tower, and all his applications for a *habeas corpus* being denied, he was only released by the king's order the following year.

Government by the people

Eastchurch deputizes Miller

The new governor dallied in England, and it was not until toward June, 1677, that Eastchurch and Miller departed for Albemarle. And even then, instead of sailing direct for Virginia, they embarked in a vessel bound for the island of Nevis, in the Caribbean Sea. There Eastchurch fell in with a lady of attractive person and with a considerable

Eastchurch stops at Nevis

manded the fulfilment of the promise. The governor complied; but shortly afterward revoked the commission as being obtained under compulsion, and raised an army to take Bacon, who was again proclaimed a rebel. In September the contending forces met at Jamestown, and Berkeley was routed and fled. Bacon thereupon called a new Assembly. But on the first day of October he fell a victim to fever contracted in the trenches of Jamestown. After his death Berkeley soon re-established his authority and terrorized the Virginians by his unsparing cruelties and excessive executions. On January 29th, however, Herbert Jeffreys arrived from England, bringing a commission as lieutenant-governor, and accompanied by a regiment of soldiers. Berkeley sailed for England in April, and smarting under the king's disapprobation, soon after his arrival died of a broken heart.

1677

fortune, and, remaining to pay his addresses, commissioned Miller, who had been appointed deputy, to be president of the council, and despatched him in advance to settle affairs by the time of his own arrival.

C. R., I,
278, 292
Miller
arrives
July, 1677

In July Miller reached Albemarle, and having exhibited his commissions, was quietly admitted into his various offices and assumed the reins of government. All the inhabitants again took the oath, or, being Quakers, subscribed it, of allegiance to the king, fidelity to the Proprietors and submission to the established government. The Indians being still hostile, Miller during the summer carried on a campaign against them, and eventually they were overcome.

As collector of customs Miller appointed deputies in every precinct, among them Timothy Biggs, who were very active in collecting the export tax on tobacco and in seizing any European commodities that had not come from England; and, indeed, the ship *Patience* was seized for unlawfully bringing in such goods.

Opposition
to the
navigation
laws

This zealous enforcement of these odious laws again occasioned discontent among the inhabitants, who had acquiesced in Valentine Byrd's easier administration. And then it began to be rumored that Byrd was to be held accountable for great sums and much tobacco that he ought to have had in possession, as well because of what he had collected as because of what he had failed to collect. Such demands interested not merely Byrd, but all exporters of tobacco who had profited by the reduction of the tax to a farthing the pound.

Durant resolves to revolt

C. R., I,
258, 286

Perhaps it was because of this probable demand that the idea of revolt had suggested itself to Durant, whose interest lay in not disturbing the existing situation. He being in London subsequent to the appointment of Eastchurch and Miller, had plainly told the Proprietors that Eastchurch should never be governor, and rather than that he would revolt. Bold, self-reliant, and masterful must have been that untitled woodsman when standing face to face with the great earl and the other powerful noblemen who owned Carolina he had warned them that Eastchurch should never be governor, but that he would keep him out by force and arms. Whatever principle had been settled in England by the Restoration, in Albemarle Durant still held that government should be by consent of the governed. And his purpose to revolt against Eastchurch's administration was openly declared in Albemarle.

Of this Miller doubtless had timely information, and his arbitrary measures while acting as governor may have been taken because of it. He made limitations on the choice of assemblymen, and succeeded in having himself invested with the power of imposing fines at his own pleasure. Armed with this authority, he issued warrants to have some of the most considerable men in the colony brought before him dead or alive, setting a price upon their heads, and for his own protection he surrounded himself with a guard of soldiers. Such desperate measures indicate apprehension of trouble; and, indeed, as they were reasonably calculated to excite a conflict, Miller must have considered that revolt was imminent and that the better way to meet it was by resolution and a show of force rather than by temporizing. Forewarned, he doubtless thought to overawe those who had not already attached themselves to the leaders of the opposite faction by a show of determined conduct.

Miller acts resolutely
C. R., I, 249, 287

On December 1, 1677, the *Carolina* came into port from London with George Durant on board, who found Gilliam a willing ally in his plans. Gilliam himself had a grievance against some of the Proprietors, who had turned him out of a considerable employment in Hudson's Bay, and wished them evil. His son also seems to have had a vessel plying from Albemarle to New England, and while the *Carolina* and her consorts took in cargoes for London, there may have been illicit traffic to which all the shipmasters were parties. A person described as the New England ambassador had been in Albemarle, and rumors were set afloat to inflame the

Durant returns to Albemarle
C. R., I, 292

Dec., 1677

1677

Purpose
of the
rebellion

people. It does not appear that there was harbored a design to throw off allegiance to the king or to deny the authority of the Lords Proprietors, but rather to impede the enforcement of the navigation acts and the collection of the tax on tobacco shipped to New England. The laws relating to trade bore hard upon them, and the Revolutionists proposed to prevent their operation. If necessary to that end, they would subvert the administration and set up a government of their own, and thus at least for a time escape from the rule of those who would enforce the regulations that bore so heavily upon their trade. Such appears to have been the purpose of the confederates, who drew into their measures nearly all the leading inhabitants, except alone the deputies and those holding employment under Miller. The occasion for the outbreak followed swift upon the arrival of the *Carolina.* That ship was well armed, "a pretty vessel," carrying several cannon, and could defy any force Miller could bring against her. She now brought in a cargo composed in part, as the year before, of arms and ammunition, swords and pistols for sale to the farmers of Albemarle.

The crisis arrives

C. R., I, 297   Coming to anchor off Captain Crawford's landing, no sooner had Gilliam gone ashore than Miller charged him with having carried off his last cargo of tobacco without paying the tax, and demanded the payment now of a thousand pounds. Gilliam refused to make this payment, alleging that the tobacco had been carried to London and the tax was paid there. He was at once arrested and his papers seized; and Miller having thus begun his proceedings, hastened that night aboard the *Carolina,* and with cocked pistols sought to arrest George Durant, charging him with treason. This step precipitated the crisis. It led at once to a resolute purpose to overthrow the administration. The men of Albemarle, trained in their sequestered homes to prompt action, now boldly took an open stand. The leadership was conferred on John Culpepper, a man of energy and enterprise, and the movement has been known to history as the "Culpepper Rebellion." A report was quickly spread abroad that Gilliam was about to depart and carry all his cargo away, and the inhabitants would lose the chance of trading with him. Such a misfortune, it was declared, concerned all the people, and to prevent it a revolution was necessary.

C. R., I, 293

Valentine Byrd, with Culpepper and other coadjutors, immediately embodied a force and seized the person of Timothy Biggs, deputy collector of customs, and arrested him on the charge of murder. The next day a force of forty armed men seized Miller and two other deputies and put them in irons, charging them with treason. Culpepper, who is said to have had considerable experience in insurrection in several of the colonies, now despatched instructions to Richard Foster, who, although one of the council and a deputy, was in alliance with the confederates to arrest Hudson, the deputy collector in Currituck, and to seize his papers and bring him to George Durant's house. And a proclamation, called the Remonstrance of the Inhabitants of Pasquotank, was on the same day, December 3d, prepared and sent to the other precincts, setting forth their justification for the revolt. In it the confederates averred that the occasion of securing the records and imprisoning the president was that thereby the country might have a free Parliament, by whom their grievances might be sent home to the Lords Proprietors. Miller they charged with having denied a free election and with cheating the country out of one hundred and thirty thousand pounds of tobacco, besides the expense of "near twenty thousand pounds of tobacco he had brought upon us by his piping guard," and they recited his conduct toward Captain Gilliam and Durant, "and many other injuries, mischiefs and grievances he hath brought upon us, that thereby an inevitable ruin is coming upon us (unless prevented), which we are now about to do; and hope and expect that you will join with us therein and subscribe this."

Biggs and Miller arrested

The Remonstrance of Pasquotank

Dec., 1677
C. R., I, 248

C. R., I, 249

CHAPTER XI

ADMINISTRATIONS OF HARVEY, JENKINS, WILKINSON AND SOTHEL, 1679-89

The revolt successful.—A government by the people.—Victory brings moderation.—Quiet succeeds the storm.—The revolt against arbitrary power and the navigation acts.—The Proprietors dilatory.—The increase of Albemarle.—The Proprietors acquiesce. —Seth Sothel sent to govern.—John Harvey governor.—Miller flees.—Durant dominant.—Biggs retires to Virginia.—The Quakers appeal to the Proprietors for protection.—Harvey dies; succeeded by Jenkins.—Culpepper tried, but acquitted.—Shaftesbury in exile.—Albemarle to observe the law.—Wilkinson governor.— Sothel arrives.—John Archdale visits Albemarle.—A view of the situation.—Sothel becomes a tyrant.—He is expelled.

The revolt successful

1677
C. R., I, 242, 303

The Revolutionists, having appealed to the country for support, lost no time in dallying. A supply of arms was obtained from the *Carolina,* and Culpepper conducted a force to Chowan, where he seized the marshal and all the records in his possession.

C. R., I, 299

After keeping Miller and the other prisoners about a fortnight at Crawford's house, the Revolutionists proceeded by water to George Durant's, being accompanied by several boats filled with armed men. As they passed the *Carolina* she, with all her flags and pennons flying, saluted them by firing three of her great guns. At Durant's some seventy men had assembled, and Foster, with an additional party, soon arrived with their prisoner from Currituck. A search was now made for the seal of the colony, which was found, together with Miller's commission and other public documents, concealed in a hogshead of tobacco. Being in possession of the great seal and of the public records, and the old officers deposed and in prison, Durant, Culpepper and their associates proceeded to establish a government and to order matters their own way.

Dec., 1677

A government by the people

An Assembly of eighteen members was elected, which deputed five of its members (John Jenkins and Valentine Byrd being among the number) to sit with Foster, one of the Proprietors' deputies, and form a court for the trial of the prisoners, who were charged with treason. A grand jury was formed and a petit jury was being summoned when the proceedings were interrupted by the receipt of a proclamation issued by Governor Eastchurch, warning them to desist and return to their homes. Eastchurch had reached Virginia eight days before, and on learning of the revolt, hastened to demand that the Revolutionists should disperse and be obedient to lawful authority. The trials were adjourned and a force was despatched to prevent Eastchurch from coming into Albemarle; and, as Durant had threatened, they kept him out by force of arms. Disappointed and baffled, Eastchurch invoked the aid of the governor of Virginia, there being in that province the troops sent from England to suppress Bacon's Rebellion, and permission was given him to enlist volunteers. To meet this new danger that threatened them the Revolutionists organized a larger force, and to obtain the necessary funds seized the customs money which Miller had collected, and deposed him as collector and elected Culpepper in his stead, following a precedent that had just been set in Virginia, where the Assembly elected a collector to fill a vacancy. But while collecting recruits and organizing his forces Eastchurch fell ill with fever, and within a month died in Virginia. With his death all apprehension of immediate interference with their plans passed away. Durant and his coadjutors were masters of Albemarle. All of the deputies but Foster being arrested, and all opposition overcome, the Revolutionists now proceeded more slowly and with greater caution.

Their success had been obtained by boldness and resolution, and it was complete; but looking to the future, they realized that their situation called for the exercise of wisdom

C. R., I, 297, 299

C. R., I, 298

C. R., I, 298

Victory brings moderation

and discretion.   The interrupted trials were not resumed.
Miller was conveyed to William Jennings's plantation at the
upper end of Pasquotank River, where a log house ten feet
C. R., I, 300   square was built for his prison, and there he was confined,
not being allowed either writing material or intercourse with
any friend.   Similar prisons were constructed for each of
the other prisoners, and precautions were taken to prevent
any of them communicating with England.   But Biggs contrived to escape, and, succeeding in his efforts to reach Virginia, hastened to England.   To counteract his representations to the Proprietors, the Assembly was convened and
two commissioners were despatched to explain their pro-
Commis-   ceedings and to conciliate the Proprietors by promising all
sioners sent
to England   manner of obedience to their authority, but they were to
enlarge on the tyranny of Miller and to insist strongly for
right against him.   Chalmers says that these agents were
Culpepper and Holden, but apparently he is in error.   Somewhat later Holden, who had been in England, returning to
Virginia stopped in Boston, and while there wrote to the commissioners of customs about what had taken place in Albemarle, and mentioned that he had never seen and did not
know Culpepper.   It is said that one of these commissioners
was quickly despatched, Gilliam providing the funds, and
that the other, George Durant, was to sail in the *Carolina*
after measures to insure safety were perfected. Shortly afterward they were both together in London.

C. R., I, 288   In the meanwhile there was established in Albemarle what
A free
government   Culpepper called "the government of the country by their
own authority and according to their own model."   The
people had at last a free Parliament.   Thomas Cullen was
speaker, and among the members were John Jenkins, Alexander Lillington, Thomas Jarvis, Henry Bonner, William
Jennings, Anthony Slocumb, John Varnham, William Crawford, Richard Sanders, Patrick White, and Valentine Byrd,
and other substantial men.   Byrd's career was, however,
fast drawing to a close, and within a year the troubles of
Albemarle had ceased for him.

Foster, one of the deputies, and the assistants chosen by the Assembly to act with the deputies in forming the grand council, were co-operating with the Revolutionists, and these, under the direction of Durant and Culpepper, managed the public business. While Harvey and many others may have been inactive, yet it does not appear that there was any substantial opposition to the revolt.

The revolt one against arbitrary power and the navigation laws

As neither the king's authority nor that of the Proprietors was denied, the Revolutionists did not regard themselves as being in rebellion. Indeed, at one time, when some of the people set up a cry that they would have no lords nor landgraves nor caciques, the leaders quickly hushed them and told them that that would not do. They justified their action on the claim of right to protect themselves from the arbitrary exercise of power by Miller; and as to that, the Proprietors found that they had cause for their action. But before Miller came as deputy-governor Durant had declared his purpose to keep Eastchurch out, and he took measures in preparation for the revolt. From the attending circumstances it reasonably appears that the original purpose was to escape from a too rigid enforcement of the navigation laws and custom duties, and to this end Culpepper was chosen collector. The annual tax on tobacco was £3,000, and that was the stake at issue. Indeed, just at that time strenuous efforts had been made to obtain from the king a repeal of this export duty. And while Charles, to show his favor to Carolina, did at his own charge send two vessels to convey some foreign Protestants to the province, and remitted some of the duties and restraints of trade, and might have granted this particular request, he was persuaded not to do so by his commissioners of customs, who strongly recommended against it because they foretold the exemption asked for would occasion abuses more easy to prevent than to abolish.

Purpose of the revolt

Thus the outbreak in Albemarle in 1677 was of the same color and similar in origin to the outbreak on the continent

Forerunner of the Revolution

a century later, which in the course of its progress developed into a struggle for separation and independence.

Therefore, while the Revolutionists established courts and held parliaments and maintained order and otherwise carried on the functions of government, his Majesty's customs were not collected with vigilance and exactness.

Biggs

Timothy Biggs, although a Quaker, was by no means submissive to his opponents. Indeed, the Quaker faith in its early days did not have the exact cast that it subsequently assumed. On reaching London, he sought to persuade the Proprietors to put down the Revolution by force. In particular he urged that a ten-gun vessel could not be resisted, and that sufficient volunteers could be obtained in Virginia to rout the rebels. But the Proprietors were not of his mind. They did not choose to engage in such a conflict. Indeed, at that time it would have been difficult for them to have subjugated the people of Albemarle united in determined resistance.

The increase of Albemarle

The colony had grown. The tithables, being the working hands between sixteen and sixty years of age, numbered fourteen hundred, of whom, however, one-third were women and negro and Indian slaves. Although the Proprietors had bestowed but little attention on Albemarle, but had devoted their efforts to promote the growth of their new town on the Ashley, the neglected settlement was more populous and more prosperous than the southern colony. The planters

Extent in 1677

were spread out from the Chowan to Currituck Sound; and besides a superfluity of provisions, of grain and cattle, their annual crop of tobacco was 800,000 pounds, which sufficed to secure the needed European commodities. And the discontent was general. Perhaps it was heightened because at this time, tobacco being very low, Virginia by act of Assembly undertook to prevent the Albemarle crop from being marketed through her ports, and prohibited any of it from being brought into that province. A measure so unfriendly was exasperating. Efforts had been made to establish local markets at different points on the Albemarle

shores, where the tobacco could be taken on board the vessels
for shipment, and the Proprietors had given directions to
lay off towns at Roanoke Island and elsewhere, but all such
endeavors to establish centres of trade had proved futile.
The tobacco was loaded at the farms of the producers. There
were no villages in the settlement. The public business was
transacted at private houses, and while George Durant's
house was a place of meeting, yet other points were equally
convenient. There was no locality where an attack by an
armed force could have availed to subdue the inhabitants.
The prudence of Durant now bore its fruits. The Proprietors rejected the proposal of the warlike Biggs, and
listening to the commissioners of the people, took the other
alternative. They sought to co-operate with the inhabitants;
and accepting the assurance of the envoys that they had
no purpose to antagonize legitimate authority, made efforts
to establish order and government at Albemarle on a firmer
footing.

While remonstrating and threatening that they would
maintain their government with force, if need be, and would
punish to the extent of the law any new outbreak, they
declined to antagonize the revolutionary leaders, and pursued the wiser and better way of preserving friendly relations
with their colony. Clarendon was now dead, and his share
in Carolina had been purchased by Seth Sothel, who at that
time stood well in the esteem of the other Proprietors. It
was thought that the presence of a Proprietor would invest
the administration with greater dignity and tend to allay the
factional strife and dissensions that had been involved in the
course of the Revolution. The commissioners representing
Durant and his associates, perhaps glad to embrace such an
easy solution of their difficulties, promised on the part of
the people the utmost submission to Sothel if he should
come as governor.

And so it was arranged that he should be the new governor; and, the more certainly to remove former difficulties,
the Proprietors had Miller's commission as collector of cus-

Sothel
captured

toms revoked, and Sothel was appointed to succeed him. He early sailed for his new government, but misfortune befell him during the voyage. The Algerines, whose piratical crafts were then scouring the seas near the Mediterranean, overhauled his vessel and took him prisoner. Efforts were at once made to secure his release by ransom, but for a time they were in vain.

John Harvey governor

1679

The Proprietors, to establish a temporary government, in February, 1679, appointed John Harvey governor until Sothel should be released, and obtained for Robert Holden the appointment of collector, at the same time appointing him a deputy and conferring on him a commission to make an extensive exploration of Carolina to the mountains. Holden had been a follower of Bacon in the Virginia rebellion, but was pardoned and was then in England. In June he reached Boston, bearing the commissions for Harvey and for the other deputies. There he remained ten days examining into the methods of the New England traders, and he reported that a half dozen traders controlled all the tobacco raised at Albemarle, brought it to Boston, whence it was shipped as bait and illegally conveyed to Europe, and the king's customs were defrauded. A few weeks later he arrived at Albemarle, followed fast by Timothy Biggs, who resumed his functions as surveyor of the customs.

Miller flees

In August Harvey was acting as governor, and at a Palatine's Court held by him, on affidavits covering the charges against Miller by Jenkins in 1675, the deposed collector was again arrested, but broke jail and made good his escape to England. The old deputies had been reappointed, and the council and courts were substantially composed of the same members as under Miller's administration. Associated with the council to form the general court, Crawford, Blount, and Varnham were assistants chosen by the Assembly, being the same assistants elected before the outbreak in 1676. And these were members of the Revolutionary Assembly chosen

1679

at Durant's house when Miller was deposed. Harvey, the governor, had not been an active participant on either side; but that he was not unfriendly with the Revolutionists is indicated by his appointment of George Durant and Alexander Lillington as justices for the precinct of Berkeley, with authority to hold the precinct court, which, besides a civil, had a criminal jurisdiction attached to it.

George Durant was now the attorney-general, and continued to be the most influential person in the colony; and as the Proprietors had condoned the excesses of the Revolutionists, he felt his power, and his enemies dreaded it. Biggs, as Miller's deputy collector and zealous supporter, had been an object of especial malevolence; and, moreover, there was probably some personal ill-will between him and Durant, growing out of Catchmaid's taking a patent in 1662 for Durant's premises; for although Catchmaid had entered into an agreement to convey to Durant, he had never done so, but the legal title had under his will vested in the widow, and on her marriage to Biggs, although he and Durant had come to an accounting, the matter was not closed.

Durant dominant C. R., I, 313

Biggs was tenacious of his rights, a man of stubborn obstinacy, who realized his own importance as a king's officer, and he was fully satisfied with the honesty of his own purposes and of the dishonest purposes of the leaders of the Revolution. Smarting under a sense of the injuries and wrong he had suffered, for which the Proprietors had provided no redress, he declined to be complacent toward the new administration. Harvey having shown favor to Durant and his coadjutors, whose influence was still dominant in Albemarle, Biggs persuaded some of the other deputies to join him in withdrawing from the council, sought to interfere with the orderly collection of the customs by Holden and prevailed on a number of his Quaker adherents to leave the colony and seek refuge in Virginia.

Biggs retires to Virginia

In the early days of the Revolution the Quakers had sided with Biggs and James Hill, who were deputies and the most considerable men of their faith. Being called on to join the

The Quakers appeal to the Proprietors for protection

1679
C. R., I, 252
people in revolt, they had refused. Thereupon they were required to surrender their guns; and when they held their religious meetings it was alleged that they were plotting against the revolutionary government. Their numbers had increased considerably, not merely by conversion in Albemarle, but probably by accessions from abroad. In 1676 Edmundson, who had again visited the colony in that year, wrote in his journal concerning them: "The people were tender and loving; and there was no room for the priests, for Friends were finely settled, and I left things well among them." When Harvey's administration began, and the government, instead of being under the influence of Biggs, as they had hoped, was seen to be controlled by the popular faction, their disappointment was great, and entertaining apprehensions for their personal safety, they were led to

The Quaker remonstrance, 1679
abandon their homes. In September, 1679, a number of them joined in a remonstrance to the Lords Proprietors, setting forth their innocence of any turmoil and trouble and vindicating themselves from aspersion. They declared that "these persons by whom we have suffered are still breathing forth their threats against us; they having received an act of grace and indemnity, as they call it. And now that the heads of that sedition are elected to sit in Parliament, and some of them are of the court, and so consequently to become our judges, we shall be the objects for them to execute their vengeance upon;" and they appealed to the Proprietors for protection.

John Jenkins succeeds Harvey as governor

The Proprietors sought to compose these differences among the inhabitants of their province, and while allowing to the dominant faction the powers of government, required that the minority should be protected from ill-usage. In the appointment of Harvey they seem to have chosen wisely, and after the first ebullition of dissatisfaction by the adherents of Biggs and Miller had subsided the administration seems to have been guided into calmer waters; but Harvey was not

1679

destined to see the full fruition of his efforts to adjust differences. After a term of six months he died in office, and the
council elected John Jenkins to be governor in his stead, Harvey dies
Jenkins being in office in February. But the change in
administration produced no alteration in policy, and quiet
continued to prevail while Jenkins was governor.

Miller having made good his escape, on reaching England Culpepper
acquitted
laid his case before the commissioners of customs, and proceedings were had that resulted in the arrest, in February,
1680, of Culpepper, who at that time was in England, on
the charge of rebellion and of embezzling the customs. Culpepper admitted the facts alleged against him, but prayed
for a pardon; and if not pardoned, he desired to be tried in
Carolina. His requests were not granted, and he was
arraigned and was on trial for treason when Shaftesbury
appeared as a witness and declared that at the time of the
Revolution there was no legal government in Albemarle;
that neither the governor nor the government was legal
according to the Constitutions of Carolina; and that taking
arms against them could not be treason; and that the Parliament elected by the people was legal, the people having
a right to choose a Parliament every two years of their own
motion and without any writ; and that the disorder in Albemarle was not treason, but a mere riot. And so on Shaftes- C. R., I, 33,
bury's testimony that Miller had obtained possession of the
government without legal authority, and that it was not
rebellion in the people to dispossess him, Culpepper was
acquitted by the jury. 1680

Shaftesbury in exile

This was about the last appearance of Shaftesbury in connection with the affairs of Carolina. In 1679 he had attained
the zenith of his great career. His unswerving purpose had
been to obtain security for Protestantism and constitutional
liberty, and he became the head of a strong party devoted
to those objects. In order to check the growth of Catholic
influences, he had made strenuous endeavors to have the

queen removed from court, and to have James, Duke of York, the king's brother, dismissed from the council and excluded from the succession, and the Duke of Monmouth, a Protestant, declared legitimate so that he would succeed to the throne. In these efforts he failed; but he succeeded in forcing through Parliament the Habeas Corpus Act, which required immediate action on the part of any judge to whom an application for the writ might be made—since become the very palladium of Anglo-Saxon freedom. An election for Parliament occurring in 1681, he prepared instructions to be handed by the constituencies to their representatives, insisting on the exclusion of James, the limitation of prerogative, and security against popery and arbitrary power; and he again appealed to the king to legitimatize Monmouth. But the king instead seized him and committed him to the Tower. In October he offered to retire to Carolina if released. Charles, however, was relentless, and had him indicted for high treason; but the grand jury ignored the bill. Charles, still bent on his destruction, managed to secure the appointment of men of his own selection as sheriffs of London, and these picked the jurymen. Shaftesbury at length realized that he could not escape the vengeance of his enemies and fled in disguise to Holland, where he died in January, 1683.

Henry Wilkinson governor

Albemarle
to observe
the laws

Although Albemarle was now in repose, the Crown continued to complain of the seizure of the customs funds and the non-observance of the navigation acts. So the Proprietors agreed that steps should be taken to ascertain how much Miller's estate had been damaged and also promised that there should be an efficient government maintained in Albemarle; and particularly that the customs laws should not be evaded.

In February, 1681, the Proprietors appointed Captain Henry Wilkinson, then in London, governor of Albemarle, and gave him instructions to choose, with the consent of the council, four able, judicious men who had not been concerned in the late disorders, who with him should be a court to try all disputes growing out of these troubles; and he was also directed to ascertain the damages suffered by the king's officers; and in his instructions there was power conferred on the council to elect a governor should he die in office. Sir William Berkeley having died, the Proprietors directed Governor Wilkinson not to admit any deputies for that share, they claiming that as Berkeley had not conveyed it in his lifetime, it devolved to his associates, and they asserted that Sir William had never paid a penny toward the settlement of Carolina. Later, however, four of them— Albemarle, Craven, Carteret, and Colleton—purchased the right of Sir William's widow, then the wife of Colonel Philip Ludwell, paying him £300 for it, and had it conveyed to Thomas Amy in trust for them. In 1686 it appears that Thomas Archdale, a minor son of John Archdale, had the title to Lord John Berkeley's share; Amy to Sir William's, and Sothel to Clarendon's; and Sir Peter Colleton was the Palatine. Wilkinson had been selected as governor because of his reputation for prudence, which led to a hope that he would be able to reconcile conflicting interests in Albemarle.*

The devolution of the shares

The Proprietors, who were men of affairs, realized that the inhabitants of Albemarle had the purpose to manage their own concerns, and although they recognized the duty of protecting their officers and deputies who had striven to maintain their authority and to enforce the king's mandates, yet they considered it was best to pursue a conciliatory course rather than one of exasperation. Efforts were made to heal existing dissensions. An act of oblivion was passed, but with a saving clause in regard to the payment of the money that ought to have been collected for the king and to make satisfaction for the injuries sustained by Miller, whose property had been seized and destroyed; and the Assembly levied a tax to repay the customs money they had seized and used to carry on the Revolution. On the governor and council

The moderate policy of the Proprietors

C. R., I, 328, 329

*Wilkinson on his appointment was created a cacique.

1683

the Proprietors urged moderation. "We hope," they said, "your own interest, as well as our injunction, will induce you to use your utmost endeavors to settle order among yourselves, without which you can never expect an increase of

C. R., I, 283

trade or strength. And these considerations ought so far to prevail that we shall not be constrained to use force to reduce the seditious to reason, since it is the good of the inhabitants we most desire and not the taking away of any man's life and estate."

Sothel arrives

But little, however, had been done toward redressing the injuries of those who suffered in their estates during the Revolution when Wilkinson's administration suddenly closed.

C. R., I, 346

Seth Sothel, after a long detention by the Turks, had been ransomed, and after a sojourn in England, in 1683 he sailed for Albemarle and assumed the government. Blank deputations had been signed to be filled out by him with the names of persons unconcerned in former differences; and he was instructed, with the consent of the council, to appoint three discreet persons not concerned in the disorders to form a court to try all actions growing out of those disturbances. But instead, he appointed, according to the complaint of Timothy Biggs, the very persons who had injured that unpopular official, and Biggs alleged that he could obtain no redress.

Archdale visits Albemarle

John Archdale, one of the Proprietors, perhaps in right of his son, a man of education and of fine character, who, like Penn and other men of capacity, wealth, and social standing, had accepted the faith of George Fox, was then in Albemarle, and Sothel was instructed to confer with him

C. R., I, 350, 351

about making these appointments. He was also directed to establish a county court for Albemarle, and to appoint a sheriff who should hold the court as under the Fundamental Constitutions, a court of criminal jurisdiction. At that time, also, a receiver was appointed to collect the rents for the Proprietors, the governor himself having before that been charged with the duty of collecting them. And among other changes that occurred about this time, 1684, the names of the precincts were changed to Currituck, Pasquotank, Perquimans, and Chowan.* Even at that early date some complaint was made against Sothel that he engrossed to himself the perquisites of the secretary and other inferior officers; and Colonel Ludwell, who owned a plantation in Albemarle, complained that it was withheld from him by Sothel on the pretence that it was forfeited.

In 1686 Sothel was out of Albemarle, and John Archdale seems to have been conducting the administration. One of Archdale's letters gives a slight view of the colony at that time. "For the present," he writes, "we have not immediate opportunities to send to England, by reason there is no settled trade thither. . . . The country produces plentifully all things necessary for the life of man. . . . We at present have peace with all nations of the Indians." The Tuscarora king was very desirous to cut off a nation of Indians called the Matchapungoes, which Archdale prevented, and he hoped that he would have the country at peace with all the Indians and with one another; but the people were very fearful of falling into some troubles again should he leave them before the return of Sothel, and therefore he was remaining beyond his intention.

It was about this time also that the Coranines, a bloody and barbarous tribe, were cut off by a neighboring nation, and that the Pamlico Indians fell victims to some dreadful plague, which opened the way for a settlement south of Albemarle Sound.

On the death of Charles II, in 1685, his successor, King James, at first made promises of protecting the charters of the colonists, but soon steps were taken to bring them more immediately under the control of the Crown. Proceedings were begun to annul most of the Proprietary grants. The Proprietors of Carolina wisely avoided any controversy, and

*The precincts bore their old names in 1680.

1684

MSS.
Records
Off. Sec.
State

C. R., I,
351, 352

A view
of the
situation

Hawks, II,
378

The
charters
threatened

1688

their charter was not disturbed. Sothel seems to have governed acceptably to the people, although not observing his instructions, until after Archdale left for England. Then he entered on a career that has been described as infamous.

Sothel becomes a tyrant

Being a Proprietor, he assumed to be above the law. He seized upon the estates of some of the inhabitants without any process from the courts, and arbitrarily imprisoned some of the people. He used his authority to fill his purse, imprisoning men illegally and releasing them on the payment of money.

C. R., I, 369

Thomas Pollock and George Durant became victims. Durant was charged with speaking words reflecting on him, was seized and thrown into prison, and as the price of his release Sothel exacted a bond for the payment of a sum of money, which not being paid, he seized on Durant's estate

Durant opposes him

without process of law. That was more than Durant would stand. The point of endurance was passed. The revolution of 1688, by which the people of England had driven King James from the throne, doubtless had its influence in determining the action in Albemarle. Durant and Pollock rose to right their wrongs. They seized the governor and confined him in a log prison ten feet square, intending to send him to England for trial. But Sothel sought to avoid that. He entreated them instead to submit his case to the General Assembly. This assented to, an Assembly was convened in 1689, and he was tried and convicted of many mean and despicable crimes, and of oppression, tyranny, extortion, and taking bribes. The solemn judgment passed on him was that he should abjure the country for twelve months

Sothel impeached and expelled 1689 C. R., I, 362

and his government forever. On receiving information of these proceedings, the Proprietors, in December, 1689, suspended him from the office of governor and appointed

Ludwell governor of North Carolina, 1689

Colonel Philip Ludwell to succeed him. On leaving Albemarle Sothel went to Charleston and assumed the reins of government as a Proprietor, but fell into such courses there that he was deposed by the Proprietors and instructed to return to London.

CHAPTER XII

Administrations of Ludwell, Jarvis, Archdale, Harvey and Walker, 1689-1704

Philip Ludwell, governor of North Carolina.—Gibbs's claim.—Thomas Jarvis appointed deputy.—Ludwell governor of all Carolina.—His instructions.—Changes in the system.—Conditions in Albemarle.—Proprietors prepare rent roll.—Ludwell gives effect to the Great Deed.—Thomas Harvey deputy-governor.—John Archdale governor of Carolina.—The arrival of the Huguenots.—Erection of Bath County.—The line between Carolina and Virginia in dispute.—Pirates harbor in all the colonies.—Parliament directs that governors should be approved by the king.—Henderson Walker governor.—Changes in Albemarle.

North Carolina: Ludwell governor

The inhabitants of Albemarle were now extending the settlement to the west and south. The limits of the county had been defined by the sound and five miles beyond, and the time had come for an extension. The two settlements at Charleston* and at Albemarle were spoken of as South Carolina and North Carolina. Albemarle was called North Carolina by the Virginia council in 1688, and in commissioning Governor Ludwell, December 5, 1689, the Proprietors appointed him "governor of that part of the province lying north and east of the Cape Fear." No longer was there to be a governor of Albemarle; but the province was divided into two governments, the one north and east of the Cape Fear and the other south and west of that river. Ludwell was the first governor of North Carolina. In his instructions he was authorized to appoint a deputy-governor, and he appointed Thomas Jarvis, who had been one of the first seaters, about 1659, to act as his deputy.

But the administration was disturbed by the claim of Captain John Gibbs, of Currituck, who on June 2, 1690, issued a proclamation declaring Ludwell to be an impostor, and

*Charlestown on the Ashley was incorporated as Charleston in 1783.

1689

C. R., I, 357

C. R., I, 360

Albemarle gives place to North Carolina

C. R., I, 361

C. R., I, 467

Gibbs claims the government

1690

C. R., I, 363

challenging any one who would maintain Ludwell's title to meet him in single combat, and promising to "fight him in this cause as long as my eyelids shall wag." He also with a body of armed men invaded Albemarle, and broke up the courts and seized two of the magistrates and carried them off. His claim to be governor perhaps grew out of an election by the council after the removal of Sothel by the Assembly, for he invited the new deputies appointed by the Proprietors to meet with him along with the other councilmen chosen by the Assembly. His position was so strong that Governor Ludwell, who was in Virginia, represented to Governor Nicholson of that province the desirability of his intervention, and a month later Nicholson reported to the Crown officers at home that he had quieted the stirs in Carolina for the present, but that the people were mutinous, and how long they would remain quiet was uncertain. In the meantime, both Ludwell and Gibbs repaired to London to have the Proprietors determine their claims, and Gibbs lost his cause.

Thomas Jarvis deputy governor

MSS.
Records
Office
Sec. State

C. R., I,
373-380, 381

In the interim, between November, 1690, and November, 1691, Thomas Jarvis was acting as governor by appointment of Ludwell. In November, 1691, Craven, as Palatine, appointed Colonel Ludwell governor of all Carolina, with power to appoint a deputy-governor for North Carolina, and instructions were sent him not based on the Fundamental Constitutions, but "suitable to our charter from the Crown." The Fundamental Constitutions were largely abandoned. It was contemplated to have but a single parliament for the entire province, the representatives from Albemarle County meeting with those of the southern counties, such being the wording of the charter; but that being impracticable, the system of government in Albemarle was not thus altered.

Changes in
the system

Theretofore a governor had been appointed by the Proprietors for the northern colony; now, however, the governor of Carolina was authorized to appoint a deputy-governor for the northern as well as for the southern colony.

1691

Another change made under his instructions was that the
Assembly no longer elected five commoners to sit in the council, but the council was to be composed merely of the governor and deputies. The governor and council were to establish
courts and appoint the judges to hold them, the council itself
being a court of appeals and of chancery, and also a Palatine's Court. The former title had been the grand council,
held by "the governor and lords deputies and the rest of the
members of the council of state." A new court system was   New court
under these instructions established, and two of the council   system
and some particular assistants were appointed to hold a general court; while the precinct courts continued to be held by
the justices and the sheriff of the precincts. Somewhat later
a change was made in the general court, and justices were
appointed and commissioned to hold that court, being sworn
in by the governor.

In their public instructions the Proprietors preserved the   C. R., I, 381
appearance of adhering to the Grand Model, but by private   Influence of
directions they allowed Governor Ludwell to ignore it in   the Grand
                                                             Model in
many particulars. In Albemarle the changes introduced in   North
attempting to conform to it had been neither disagreeable   Carolina
to the people nor oppressive in their consequences. While
in some measure the framework of the administration was
based on the system, its more peculiar features were entirely
ignored. It mattered little that the governor and council
should be called the Palatine's Court; that the grants should
be issued in the name of the Palatine and the other Lords
Proprietors, an innocent innovation that continued until the
purchase by the Crown in 1729, and generally the people
of Albemarle were content. In South Carolina the situation
was different. There the Proprietors had spent a large
amount of money in fostering the settlement, had, pursuant
to their chartered powers, created landgraves and caciques,
and efforts had been made to enforce some of the particular   Influence of
provisions of the Fundamental Constitutions that were seri-   the Grand
                                                              Model in
ously objected to by the inhabitants, whose dissensions and   South
violent proceedings caused the Proprietors more trouble and   Carolina

1693

anxiety by far than the alleged turbulence of Albemarle; and to smooth over matters, Ludwell was directed to consult the wishes of the inhabitants in conducting the government at Charleston.

Harvey,
deputy-
governor

Having authority to appoint a deputy for Albemarle, Ludwell at first continued Thomas Jarvis, and then appointed Thomas Harvey. He was, however, much in Albemarle himself, and while there acted as governor.*

Conditions in North Carolina

Little clash-
ing with
Proprietors

With Ludwell's administration a new era began in the North Carolina settlement. For more than a dozen years it now enjoyed undisturbed repose. Indeed, there had never been much clashing between the people and the Proprietors. In great measure the inhabitants governed themselves, the Proprietors being represented by some of the planters, whose interests were identified with those of the colony, while the governors were frequently selected from among the people. If there were any turbulent spirits, with the exception of Captain Gibbs, who asserted a claim to be governor and who

Character of
the people

lived very near the Virginia line, they manifested turbulence only on provocation. If occasionally a governor was deposed and imprisoned, it was because of offences and in vindication of freedom; and truly in tracing their story one finds remarkable illustrations of the sufficiency of their manhood to solve the problems of government. Even in the most trying times government was never dissolved; and while the will of the people was enforced, anarchy did not supplant

MSS.
Records
Off.
Sec. State

*Dr. Hawks, II, 495, mentions Alexander Lillington as acting as governor or president of the council. The author has not found that record. Jarvis was governor in November, 1690, and in November, 1691. Ludwell was present and acting as governor in November, 1693, and in April, 1694; Thomas Harvey in July, 1694; Ludwell in August; Harvey in September; John Archdale in July, 1695; and Thomas Harvey in April, 1696. In 1693 Alexander Lillington was "High Sheriff" of Albemarle County, and as such Governor Ludwell ordered him in November, 1693, to make proclamation, that all persons in Albemarle could have their land under the Great Deed of 1668, which led to Ludwell's removal from office.

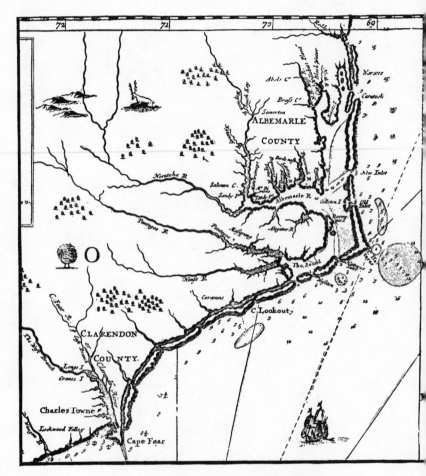

LEA'S NEW MAP OF CAROLINA, 1695

law. If in 1677 the Revolutionists ran into excesses and, not content with seizing their enemies, destroyed their property, it was in a moment of exasperation. Order was quickly restored. Courts were organized and the machinery of government at once established on a new basis. For the most part the inhabitants had no quarrels with the Proprietors; but they did seek in every way to escape from the oppression incident to the enforcement of the trade regulations and custom laws.

The collection of the quit rents had from time to time been postponed, and the rent charged under the Great Deed was not onerous. But now perhaps the Proprietors were more intent on reimbursing themselves for their outlay, and the payment of quit rents became of interest. A rent roll of Albemarle prepared apparently about 1694 showed 146 planters, some of them with several plantations, the average holding being about 275 acres; altogether, about 40,000 acres in farms, and probably a population of 4000.

MSS. Records at Edenton

Ludwell recognizes Great Deed

In November, 1693, Ludwell issued a proclamation to the effect that under the Great Deed lands in Albemarle were to be granted at the same rate as in Virginia, subject to quit rents of only a farthing an acre; and he directed Alexander Lillington, the high sheriff of Albemarle County, to give notice thereof to the people of Perquimans. Fault was found with him for reserving that low rent, and for assenting to a new form of deed, that was considered to be in derogation of the rights of the Proprietors. He justified his action by declaring that it was in conformity with the Great Deed; but the Proprietors questioned the authenticity of that document, no copy of it having been retained in England, and they quickly revoked his commission. Still Ludwell continued to exercise the functions of governor in North Carolina during the years 1693 and 1694; and when he was not present Thomas Harvey was the deputy governor. To succeed Ludwell as governor of Carolina, Thomas

MSS. Off. Sec. State

1693
Smith,* a planter in South Carolina, was, in 1693, created a landgrave and appointed governor. He seems to have continued Harvey in office, for the latter conducted the administration when no governor was present until his death, on July 3, 1699.

But Smith was hardly established in his government before he represented to the Proprietors that the dissensions in South Carolina were so great that no one could heal them except one of the Proprietors; and in August, 1694, John Archdale was prevailed on to come over as governor.

John Archdale governor

In the following June Archdale reached Albemarle, where a daughter, the wife of Emanuel Lowe, resided. While there he exercised the functions of governor. But after a short sojourn he passed on to Charleston, leaving Harvey in the administration. Because of the concessions made to Albemarle in the Great Deed, Archdale was directed to limit that county strictly to the territory north of the sound and east of the Chowan, and a higher rent was to be exacted for land beyond those boundaries.

C. R., I, 391

Already settlements had been made elsewhere, and the western shores of the Chowan were well occupied. In 1691 some of the Huguenots who had originally settled on the James River, being attracted by the warmer climate, came to Carolina and located on the Pamlico, where they prospered so satisfactorily that constant accessions were made to their numbers. Indeed, population was now extending itself rapidly to the southward.

Huguenots, 1691

C. R., I, 472
Archdale
County
After Archdale became governor, the Pamlico region was called by the council Archdale County in his honor; but at a Palatine's Court held on December 9, 1696, he being then in North Carolina, and presiding, an order was passed that inasmuch as several persons had seated themselves on Pam-

---

*It was about this time that a grant of 40,000 acres of land was issued to Smith, and located on the Cape Fear River, and perhaps it was then in contemplation to make a settlement on that river; but if any were made, no evidence of it has been preserved.

ico River, a writ of election was to issue to them as Pamlico Precinct, in Bath County, to choose two assemblymen. The change of name was made in compliment to John Lord Granville, Earl of Bath, a Proprietor, who possessed the share originally belonging to the Duke of Albemarle, and who on the death of Craven, in 1699, became the Palatine. The precinct of Pamlico was thus organized in 1696. Later Wickham Precinct was established on the south of Albemarle Sound, and before 1708 a third precinct was established south of Pamlico Sound, called Archdale.

1696
Bath
County.
Lawson's
map
C. R., I, 472

From North Carolina Archdale returned to England, leaving Harvey his deputy in North Carolina, and appointing Joseph Blake his deputy for South Carolina. Blake was a nephew of the great admiral, and had once before been deputy-governor at Charleston. His father, being a dissenter and fearful of persecution in England, had years before removed to South Carolina. A few years earlier the South Carolina Assembly had made a strong remonstrance against some of the provisions of the Fundamental Constitutions, and in 1691 and 1693 they had been annulled; but in 1698 the Proprietors, after consultation with Major Daniel, reformed the Constitutions, reducing them to forty-one articles, eliminating the provisions about leet men and leet courts, and making other changes, particularly with regard to courts, and they sent a copy of the amended Constitutions to Governor Blake by Colonel Daniel.

Harvey
deputy
governor

C. R., II,
852

The Consti-
tutions
revised

These Constitutions had been operative in North Carolina only in some particulars, and the changes now made in them were not of much interest to the inhabitants; but this amended copy seems to have been considered in the colony as taking the place of that originally sent over. The administration in North Carolina was, however, in conformity with the instructions to the governors rather than in close adherence to the Fundamental Constitutions; and the court system was modified under Archdale's government, and apparently other changes were made about the time this new copy of the Constitutions came over. Earlier, the general court had been

C. R., III,
453

held by the governor and the council, with some assistants.
Now a commission was issued to two of the council, one
of whom was to be present at the court, and to some assistants.   The first commission of this sort was to Samuel
Swann and William Glover, and one of them was to hold
the court, there being in attendance one or more of the other
judges or justices.   The title of chief justice was not specifically bestowed on either at that time, and its earliest use
appears to have been in 1713.

The line between Carolina and Virginia disputed

About the year 1680 the uncertain location of the dividing
line between Albemarle and Virginia began to attract attention.   Some of the inhabitants of lower Norfolk and Currituck had taken out their grants from the Virginia authorities
and had paid their annual dues to Virginia; but now Albemarle claimed payment from them, and on their application
that the line should be established, the Virginia officials
pleaded ignorance of the second grant to the Proprietors,
which extended their territory thirty miles to the northward.
But proof being furnished, in 1692 the surveyor of Virginia
ascertained substantially where the line 36° 30' would run,
and as the Old Dominion would lose considerable population
and property, her authorities stubbornly resisted every
attempt to have the question settled, and urged that the king
should buy Albemarle and attach it to Virginia, saying that
£2,000 would be a fair price.

Pirates infest the coast

Indeed, there was always some ground for apprehension
that the grant to the Proprietors would be annulled and their
province be taken from them.   Complaints were made that
pirates found ready access to Carolina, and that the governors for bribes issued illegal commissions to sea rovers; and
the evasion of the navigation acts was a continual source of
trouble.   These allegations, however, applied to South Carolina rather than to Albemarle, while there was yet greater
cause for scandal at Philadelphia and in all the northern

governments. Still, there was one particular charge made against North Carolina. "Thomas Harvey," said Randolph, 'put masters to great charges because of their vessels not being registered, though the time limited for registering them was not expired." This, however, would seem to indicate that Harvey was too exacting in demanding a compliance with the law. Another complaint Randolph makes against Albemarle is: "The tobacco made in that province is generally carried to Boston or to the islands near to Connecticut colony, where it is carried to Scotland, etc., which fraud ought speedily to be prevented." In this it would seem that the Albemarle authorities were entirely within the law, as it was clearly their right to ship their tobacco to Boston and Connecticut, and if the traders of those northern marts afterward smuggled the tobacco into Scotland, Holland, and Ireland against the law, the offence ought not to be laid at the doors of North Carolinians. Mr. Randolph continues: "During Governor Harvey's government his Majesty's ship, the *Hady,* was driven ashore upon the sands between the inlets of Roanoke and Currituck. The inhabitants robbed her and got some of her guns ashore and shot into her sides and disabled her from getting off. The actors were tried, and one of the chief was banished. Henderson Walker, the present governor, in no sort fit for the office." The conclusion does not appear to be well drawn from the premise. The affair happened in Harvey's time, and the government was active. That the bankers were thrifty is undeniable, as the name "Nag's Head"* would indicate. Still so notorious were the evasions of the revenue laws in all the Proprietary governments that in 1689 it was proposed in Parliament to take cognizance of the colonies in America and bring them more directly under the control of the king.

1698

C. R., I, 541, 546

Complaints against Albemarle

C. R., I, 547

---

*The name "Nag's Head" is said to have been derived from a practice of the bankers fastening a lantern to the head of a horse, which as the horse walked at night would have the appearance of a light on a ship gently moved by the waves, thus alluring vessels to the shore. There was also a "Nag's Head" on the southern coast of England, so named from the same practice.

1699

For the proper enforcement of the trade regulations it was deemed necessary that the governor and other chief officers should be appointed with the king's concurrence; but this direction at the time was not observed by the Proprietors. At length, in 1697, Parliament enacted that not only should the governors of the colony be approved by the king, but they should take certain oaths of office before qualifying. So when, in March, 1699, Governor Harvey appointed Daniel Akehurst and Henderson Walker commissioners to arrange with the Virginia authorities for establishing the dividing line, Governor Nicholson refused to recognize Harvey's authority because he had not taken the required oaths of office.

C. R., I, 506

Henderson Walker governor

It was during this correspondence that the governor of Virginia alleged that runaways escaping from Virginia were harbored in North Carolina, which brought out an indignant denial by Henderson Walker, who in July succeeded Harvey as governor. In his reply Governor Walker said: "I assure you that neither our laws nor our practice deserves such an imputation of evil neighborhood. Neither are there any runaways harbored here that we can discover by diligent inquiry; nor shall any such thing be suffered so far as it is in our power to prevent it." Governor Walker, whose skill as a letter writer suffers nothing by comparison with that of the governor of Virginia, then recited the laws in force in Albemarle, and specified some particular runaways who had come into the settlement, but had perished in the uninhabited parts of the country; and he expressed the belief that the same fate had befallen others seeking to escape into South Carolina. He did not rest easy under this suggestion of his Virginia neighbors.

1699

C. R., I, 514

Changes in Albemarle

In the course of time Colonel Jenkins, Valentine Byrd, the Harveys and many of the old leaders in Albemarle had passed

1700

away and other men had risen to prominence. Durant died in 1691, at the age of sixty-nine, while Sothel, after an unsettled life still marked by devious ways, made his exit in 1693, leaving a widow in Albemarle. Thomas Jarvis, one of the first seaters, and deputy-governor in 1691 and subsequently, passed away in the spring of 1694. Alexander Lillington, who had figured largely in the Culpepper Rebellion, and whose family connection came to be the most influential in the settlement, after marrying a third wife in 1695, succumbed to disease two years later, at the age of fifty-three, Governor Thomas Harvey soon following him. 1699 But Thomas Relfe, also one of the first seaters, was still living, and survived until 1707, being then ninety-three years of age. He was one of those who made the first clearings before the name Albemarle was ever heard of on the shores of the river Carolina.

Major Sam Swann was now a resident of Perquimans, a member of the council, judge of the general court, and collector of customs, and Colonel Thomas Pollock, Henderson Walker, William Glover, and John Porter (speaker of the Assembly) were at the close of the century among the most influential inhabitants.

Life in the colony

A letter written about the close of the century by William Gale from Perquimans gives some insight into the affairs in Albemarle at that time. Mr. Gale was just setting out on a four months' voyage to the Cape Fear, whither he had sent a shallop's load of goods to trade with the Indians. Apparently he intended to pass up that river and go as far westward as the mountains to establish an Indian trade there. A well-qualified Indian trader, he says, "secures for himself a comfortable living in this world." "All sorts of English goods are here very valuable, especially nails, carpenter's tools, hoes, axes, all sorts of linings, powder and shot, hats, stockings, and what else is requisite to make a sortable store." The most direct route of communication from England was

S. R.,XXII, 732

by London ships bound for York River. Of the Indians he said, "they live in small towns and bark cabins, palisadoed in with two or three rows of stakes. Every town or nation has its particular king and different language. They have some notion of the flood, but very obscure. They offer the first fruits of everything they eat to the devil, by whom they cure diseases, and act several strange things, as laying the wind." He mentioned some thirteen different tribes, with whom he was well acquainted and had very free commerce. "If Henry Ramsbottom was here and would work, he might live a companion for the best. His trade would bring him in £300 per annum. Others might do very well. Our greatest

grievance is want of books and pleasing conversation. The Quakers are here very numerous, but as for Independents, Anabaptists, Presbyterians, and other sectaries, they have little or no place here. Most who profess themselves doctors and attorneys are scandals to their profession. The decay of Christian piety is in such large characters that he who runs may read. The second of January last it pleased God to make me happy in a son, who bears the name of his grandfather, but he has still the unhappiness to be unchristened, to my great grief, the only minister we have had of the Church of England having left us before my son was born, but it was no loss to religion, for he was ye monster of ye age."

The inventories of deceased persons filed in court afford some information of the style of life and the value of house-

hold goods. Pewter dishes were in common use. A dozen pewter plates were valued at about £1. Holland sheets at fifty shillings a pair for fine ones, and thirty shillings for coarser ones, while Osnaburg sheets were five shillings a pair. A feather bed and bolster at £6. Fifteen yards of kersey at something less than £2. Plain shoes at three shillings per pair. A fowling piece at £1 10s. Iron pots were valued at four shillings a pound. A hand mill for grinding meal was £6; a broad axe four shillings and a handsaw two shillings. Sheep were valued at ten shillings; cows at thirty shillings, and shoats at five shillings. Negro men were valued at £35 sterling; negro women at £30, and children at £10. Mary, an Indian, was thought to be worth £20; and a white woman servant, probably indentured, at £2 per year for the time she had to serve. At that time cotton appears to have been cultivated. Lawson says: "The women Lawson, 142 make a good deal of cloth of their own cotton, wool and flax: some of them keeping their families, though large, very decently apparelled, both with linens and woollens, so that they have no occasion to lay their money out for clothing." But trading vessels came in often, bringing merchandise, which was paid for in produce, rather than money. There were hatters, and others skilled in different trades in the colony. Tar, pitch, corn, tobacco, etc., had a debt-paying value fixed by law. While most of the houses were of wood, there were some of brick; the lime being made from oyster shells. The women, says Lawson, are well featured and "have very brisk, charming eyes. They marry very young, some at thirteen or fourteen; and are very fruitful, most houses being full of little ones. The girls are not bred up to the wheel and sewing only, but the dairy and the affairs of the house they are very well acquainted withal."

CHAPTER XIII

The Exclusion of the Quakers

Albemarle at the opening of the new century.—Religious affiliations.—The Quakers.—Nathaniel Johnson governor of Carolina.—
The Church party in South Carolina.—Major Daniel succeeds Henderson Walker.—The Quakers excluded from office.—The Constitution ignored.—A new church law.—Daniel removed.—Succeeded by
Cary.—The colony grows.—Virginia disputes the boundary.—John
Porter's voyage to England.—He obtains redress.—New elements
in the controversy.—Porter breaks with Glover.—Two governments contending.—Both call the Assembly.—Glover departs to Virginia.—Cary in possession.—The government orderly. . . .

Albemarle at the opening of the new century

1701

In a decade of entire repose, undisturbed by any dissensions, the administration being by the people and for the
people, and quiet and orderly government prevailing, the
settlement had grown in population and in importance. The
more influential families were attracted to Chowan, while in
Pasquotank and Perquimans the Quakers had considerably
increased. Their numbers may have been swollen by some
few additions from abroad, but Governor Walker in 1703
attributed their growth entirely to the preachers who yearly
came to Albemarle to encourage and exhort to Quaker prin-

C. R., I,
572

ciples. And there were none to dispute with or to oppose
them, for there were no churches in Albemarle and no preach-

May 24, 1689

ers. In England, before the Toleration Act was passed, in
William and Mary's reign, there was some persecution of
non-conformists and dissenters, to whom the freedom of
conscience guaranteed by the charter and laws was an in-
ducement to remove to Carolina, but they located near
Charleston. There was no great influx of population to
Albemarle from beyond the seas. Accessions had come from
Virginia and the neighboring colonies; and even if they

were originally adherents of the Church of England, in the absence of religious ministrations their affiliations became weakened; and, indeed, those born in Albemarle, who had never attended any religious services, could have had but slight attachment to any church. There were no missionary societies then in the world, and other than the travelling Quaker preachers, there were no missionaries. But about the close of the century the Bishop of London, to whose jurisdiction the colonies had been assigned, sent Dr. Bray to Maryland to settle some differences, and he becoming interested in the religious condition of the colonists, established the Society for the Propagation of the Gospel in Foreign Parts, and sought to have ministers sent to America. By correspondence he inspired zeal among some of the churchmen in Albemarle, which doubtless was heightened by the general religious revival incident to the Pope's having proclaimed the year 1700 as a year of jubilee.

In that year the first minister of the Church of England C. R., I, 572 was sent to Albemarle, Mr. Daniel Brett, who on his arrival conducted himself satisfactorily, but soon began such a course as brought trouble and grief to the churchmen and strengthened the antagonism of those opposed to that communion. With the opening of the new century Governor Walker and other churchmen, in order to procure some religious services in the colony, made strenuous efforts to elect an Assembly that would establish parishes and provide for the erection of church buildings and the maintenance of ministers. And the Assembly of 1701 passed such an act. By it vestrymen were appointed in every precinct, who were, besides other duties, to erect church buildings and collect the assessments for church purposes. In Chowan, where the adherents of the Church of England predominated, the vestry met that fall and made provision for a "reader" and for erecting a chapel, which was completed the next year. Later other chapels were erected.

In April, 1703, Mr. Blair was ordained to go to Albemarle, C. R., I, 600 and the next January reached the settlement. By that time

1703
a "reader" had been established in three of the precincts; but there were a great many children to be baptized, "whose parents would not condescend to have them baptized with

Blair, 1704
godfathers and godmothers." Besides the Quakers, Mr. Blair found many who would be Quakers, but were deterred by the moral life the Quakers enjoined; others were in faith like Presbyterians, and had preachers who baptized among them, without, however, having any manner of orders; and lastly the Church of England people, who were the fewest

C. R., I, 600, 603
in number. The four old precincts were divided by rivers along whose banks for a distance of some twenty miles lay the plantations; and between Pamlico and Albemarle there were fifty miles of desert without any inhabitants. The Indians were numerous, and on visiting their towns he found many who could speak English and seemed to be fond of their white neighbors. Mr. Blair would have remained in the settlement, but no adequate provision being made for his maintenance, he soon returned to England, suffering the mishap of being taken prisoner by the French on his way.

C. R., I, 708
A few years later Mr. Gordon gave a more extended account of the inhabitants. Chowan, as it was the largest

Gordon, 1708
of the old precincts, was the thinnest peopled. It contained no Quakers or other dissenters; but the people were very ignorant, there being few who could read and write.

The Quakers

The Quakers in Perquimans were numerous, extremely ignorant, proud and ambitious, and consequently ungovernable. Many persons had accepted that faith, being willing to embrace any religion rather than have none at all. Pasquotank also was largely peopled by Quakers. The roads, bad enough everywhere, were worst there, but it was closer seated than the other precincts and relatively more populous. In their way of living, the people of Pasquotank had much the advantage of the other inhabitants, being more industrious, careful, and cleanly; but above all, says Mr. Gordon, "I was surprised to see with what order, decency, and seri-

ousness they performed the public worship, considering how 1703
ignorant the people are in the other parishes." One of the
distinctive principles of the Quaker faith was that preaching
should be but the outpouring of the spirit; that one should
preach only as the spirit moves him; and on principle they
were opposed to a paid ministry, and also to paying tithes
to support ministers. The Quakers in Albemarle were therefore violently opposed to the new church law, that imposed 1701
on them the duty of contributing to the support of paid
pastors, and as the next election for assemblymen after the
adoption of that law drew nigh, they made the repeal of that C. R., I, 572
Mr. Blair
act an issue. But about that time the act was returned by
the Lords Proprietors, annulled and disapproved by them,
because the provision made for the maintenance of the
ministers was inadequate; and so it ceased to have effect C. R., I, 601
without the necessity of repeal by the Assembly.

Nathaniel Johnson governor of Carolina

In South Carolina Governor Moore had led an expedition
against Florida, but on his return a faction arose violently
opposed to his administration, so in June, 1702, Lord Granville, the Palatine, appointed Sir Nathaniel Johnson, who
was then residing in South Carolina, to be governor.

Under a recent act of Parliament, because of the trade 1695
regulations, a bond was required of the new governor, and
he offered as his bondsman Thomas Cary, a merchant of
that province, who later was to figure largely in North Carolina affairs.

In their instructions to Governor Johnson the Proprietors
required him to observe the Fundamental Constitutions as
modified in 1698. There was, however, no change made in
administrative methods in Albemarle.

But while the direction to enforce the Constitutions brought The Church
party in
South
Carolina
no trouble in Albemarle, a period of great unrest and dis-
order now began, based on religious opinions. The same
differences among Churchmen that marked that period in
England had found their way to the forests of Carolina.

Church
uniformity
in South
Carolina

There were those who cried out for conformity, while others advocated toleration. Johnson's appointment was the signal for a great show of zeal by the High Church party in South Carolina, whose leaders were closely associated with Moore and sustained his administration while the opposing faction demanded a rigorous examination into the matters connected with the Florida expedition. By great activity, Moore's friends secured a majority in the Assembly, and by one vote carried through a bill rigidly excluding all dissenters from the Assembly; and when this act came before the Proprietors for ratification, although violently opposed by some, it was approved by Colleton and by Granville, whose intolerance and arbitrary spirit were in full sympathy with its provisions, and notwithstanding Archdale strenuously objected, Granville also signed for Carteret and Craven, and it went into operation.

Major Daniel succeeds Walker

Robert
Daniel
deputy -
governor

In April, 1704, Governor Walker died, and Governor Johnson sent Major Daniel, who was a landgrave, from South Carolina to be deputy-governor. Major Daniel had established for himself an enviable reputation for bravery and experience in business. He had won laurels during the war with the Indians and Spaniards at the south, and was highly esteemed. Some of the neighboring tribes now giving trouble, he called a council of their chiefs and agreed with them for a firm peace, one of the articles being that the English were not to furnish rum to the Indians.

The
Quakers
excluded
from office

Up to that time the Quakers had not been required to take oaths in Carolina, being excused by the original concessions and by the Fundamental Constitutions; but soon after Daniel's arrival in the colony the act of Parliament imposing the oaths of allegiance to Queen Anne, who had just come to the throne, was transmitted to him, and he tendered them to the members of the council and other officers of the government. They were such oaths as most dissenters could take; but the Quakers would take no oath whatsoever, and

C. R., I,
709

1704

insisted on their constitutional right to sign a declaration of like tenor in a book. This privilege was now denied them, and they were excluded from their places under government. And when the Assembly met the same proceedings were had, and the house was thus purged of Quakers. A large part of the population was denied the right to hold office. It was in effect a revolution, changing without legal sanction the constitution of Albemarle.

It was inconsistent with the Grand Model, subversive of the fundamental constitution of the colony and utterly repugnant to those practices and customs which had their origin in the earliest lodgment in the wilderness and had grown with the growth of the settlements as the woof and warp of the rights of the people. The whole foundation on which Wm. Gordon's statement, C. R., I, 708-715 the political structure of the colony rested was wiped away by this requirement of an oath of office to be taken after the prevailing English fashion; for it is to be observed that it was not until the eighth year of George I, twenty years later, that the affirmation of Quakers was received in England in lieu of the customary oath. But on this new requirement Governor Daniel insisted, and, carrying his design into execution, he drove the Quakers from the house and thus secured a pliant majority, who followed his leadership.

A new law for establishing the Church was enacted, and, A new church law 1704 to secure it against the possibility of repeal, he determined to exclude Quakers from future assemblies, and to this end he caused an act to be passed prescribing an oath of office to be taken by way of qualification for membership. And so the church act was passed beyond the power of repeal.

But the violence of this course resulted in commotion. C. R., I, 709 The Quakers were not disposed to be deprived by this parliamentary proceeding of the political rights they had hitherto enjoyed in the colony. They were numerous in The Quakers resist Pasquotank and Perquimans, and by uniting with the Presbyterians and other dissenters in Bath, they were superior in power to the Church party, who were in the majority only in Chowan and Currituck. Such an alliance seems to have

1705

been formed, and an effort was made to secure the removal of Governor Daniel, and they soon had the satisfaction of obtaining an order for his suspension.

Thomas Cary governor

Cary succeeds Daniel, 1705

Again was Governor Johnson called on to appoint a deputy-governor, and this time he selected Thomas Cary, a merchant doing business in South Carolina, who came to his new charge in 1705.

When the legislature assembled to meet Cary, the law passed the year before requiring an oath of office to be taken by the members was still on the statute-book, but it seems to have been expected that Cary would either ignore that law altogether, or, not enforcing it strictly so far as the Quakers were concerned, would admit them to seats on their making affirmation after the custom of that sect. Cary, however, followed the same course that had led to Daniel's downfall.

He disappointed all the favorable expectations that had been raised by the change of governors, and augmented the inquietude of the colony by proceeding still further in the line of the new departure.

C. R., I, 709

The Assembly met him in November, but the members refusing to take the oaths, he dissolved it and called a new election. When the new Assembly met, applying the law which required an oath of office with rigorous exactness, he excluded the Quaker members and obtained a majority that would sustain his measures. He then caused an act to be passed imposing a fine on any person who should enter into an office before taking an oath of qualification and another declaring void the election of any person who should promote his own candidacy.

With these provisions in force, not only were the Quakers debarred from entering into an office, but the election of any Presbyterian or other dissenter who was objectionable might be declared void on the slight pretext that he had promoted his own election.

Step after step had been successfully taken to bind the

Assembly hand and foot. Inflamed by Cary's proceedings, the opponents of these measures hastened to send John Porter to England to seek a redress of grievances.

The colony grows

In the meantime the growth of the colony, especially to the southward, had continued. The town of Bath was laid off in 1704. The precinct of Pamlico, established ten years earlier, was in 1705 limited from Moline's Creek five miles west of the mouth of Pungo to the westward up the Pamlico; and from Moline's Creek north and east was Wickham Precinct; while all south of Pamlico River, including the settlers on the Neuse, was Archdale Precinct. It was in Archdale Precinct on the Trent that the Huguenots had located. Lawson says: "Most of the French who lived at that town on James River (Mannakin Town) are removed to Trent River, where the rest were daily expected, in August, 1708." There they made very good linen cloth and thread and raised considerable quantities of hemp and flax, being well established. They were accompanied by their pastor, Richebourg.

C. R., I, 629

C. R., iii, 453

Lawson's Hist. of N. C., 141

These precincts were each allowed two representatives in the Assembly. The influx of population was chiefly from Virginia, and so great was the movement that the commissioners of trade and plantations at London directed an inquiry into its causes and how it might be prevented. Among the new accessions was John Lawson, an Englishman, who landed at Charleston in 1700 and journeyed through the interior near the sites of Salisbury and Hillsboro, then eastward to Pamlico, and he remained in the colony studying its natural history. He returned to England in 1707 and published "A New Voyage to Carolina" in 1709 (later reprinted as the "History of North Carolina"), with a map of the province at that time. He returned to Albermarle as surveyor-general in 1711.

John Lawson

C. R., I, 703

Another important accession was Edward Moseley, Gent., probably an Englishman, perhaps from the Barbadoes, who

Edward Moseley

1706
came into the province about 1704 and soon began to play a prominent part in public affairs, being surveyor-general, and in 1705 a member of the council.*

Hawks, II, 139
Governor Daniel, who was a landgrave, located near Bath Town, a region which was now attracting many of the new settlers; but others pushed up the Chowan, where they came in contact with the Meherrin Indians, who were forcibly dispossessed of their lands and moved farther to the northward, a proceeding which again involved a dispute with Virginia about the dividing line.

The Chowan Indians had formerly, by grant from the Yeopims, occupied the land on the south of Meherrin River, and after the Indian war of 1675, in which they were sub-dued, they were required to locate farther eastward. The Meherrin Indians settled on the north side of that river and then roamed on the south side, where they eventually had plantations. In 1706 they were ordered to abandon these plantations and move to the north side. Not obeying these directions, Colonel Pollock, who had possessions on the west side of the Chowan, with a force of forty-six men seized many of them and brought them to terms. The government of Virginia complained of this proceeding, de-claring that the land along the Meherrin was in its terri-tory, and that the Carolinians had no right to locate the Indians upon it; but being doubtful of its claim, the Vir-ginia surveyor was directed to secretly run a line 36° 30' to see where it really was. He probably discovered enough to remain quiet, for when the dividing line was established later the Virginia claim was shown to be erroneous.

C. R., I, 658

The Indians reduced

John Porter's voyage to England

Oct., 1706
The prime objects Porter had in view appear to have been the restoration of the rights of the Quakers to hold office, the setting aside of the laws requiring the assemblymen to

*On May 7, 1703, the treasurer of South Carolina paid Edward Moseley £5 15s. for transcribing the catalogue of the library books at Charlestown. On August 4, 1705, Edward Moseley married the widow of Governor Walker.

1706

ake an oath of office, and the restoration of the privilege of he colony to choose its own governor from among the ouncil. He had hardly reached England before Cary left Albemarle and returned to South Carolina, where he remained for more than a year, not coming back to his government until after Porter himself had returned, and during his bsence William Glover, a member of the council, administered the affairs of the colony.

MSS.
Records
Off. Sec.
State

C. R., I, 698

Porter's visit to England was well timed. He found public attention largely addressed to Carolina affairs. The Representation of the case of the Dissenters in South Carolina," made by John Ashe, had been supplemented by DeFoe's "Party Tyranny in Carolina," and public interest had been awakened in the grievances of the distant colonists. Boone, from South Carolina, had secured the co-operation of merchants dealing with the province, and their petition to the House of Lords had led that body to address the queen, setting forth the illegality of the proceedings at Charleston, and the queen in council had thereupon declared the church legislation of Governor Johnson null and void, and had directed steps to be taken to declare the charter forfeited; and besides, the church dignitaries had expressed their strong disapproval of the measures by which the Church party in South Carolina had sought to carry out their political purposes.

Gordon's
letter,
C. R., I,
708-715

C. R., II, 891

C. R., I, 634

C. R., I, 643

Under these circumstances John Porter's mission could hardly fail of success. He obtained substantial redress, and after lingering a year in England, returned, in October, 1707, bearing an instrument of writing, or commission, for the settling of the government, by which the laws imposing oaths were suspended; and he also brought an order suspending Colonel Cary as governor, and vesting the powers of that officer in the president of the council, to be chosen by that body, according to the custom before Daniel's time.

C. R., I, 709
Oct. 1707

He also obtained new deputations from the Lords Proprietors appointing other deputies, a majority of whom it

1707 is stated were Quakers. Thus equipped, his aim seemed accomplished; but difficulties, however, apparently arose in the performance of his programme.

New
element
in the
controversy
MSS.
Records
Off. Sec.
State
C. R., I, 710 On his return, in the fall of 1707, Porter found Governor Cary still absent and William Glover conducting the administration as president of the council. This arrangement he did not disturb. Indeed, it appears that Glover was then chosen president of the council, and for some time remained

May, 1708 at the head of the government with the sanction of all parties But later Glover refused to admit the Quaker deputies unless they would take the oaths. Discontent at once was manifested by many of the people, and it became so prevalent

Hawks, II,
381 that on May 13, 1708, Cary, who had then returned, Porter Foster, and Pollock, representing the various factions, united

C. R., I, 727 in a proclamation commanding the people's obedience to the existing government.

But hardly had this proclamation been issued before a new element entered to breed further disturbance.

C. R., I,
689, 732
Hawks, II,
310 Mr. Adams and Mr. Gordon, two ministers sent out by the Society for the Propagation of the Gospel in Foreign Parts, arrived in the colony about that time, and their coming set the Quakers and Presbyterians and all opposed to the church law in violent commotion. Glover writes to the

C. R., I, 689 Bishop of London, September 25, 1708, that "time had slipped away while I was engaged in the unhappy trouble which the enemy, alarmed at the coming over of these worthy gentlemen, has raised against me."

Mr. Adams wrote in October, 1709, that when Gordon and himself came over (April, 1708) "we found the government

C. R., I, 720 in the hands of such persons as were promoted for God's service and good order and from whom we met with all reasonable encouragement. But now the case is sadly altered for the Quakers, alarmed at our arrival," etc. And Glover himself two years later wrote to the Society: "Although the

C. R., I, 732 trouble and confusion this unhappy country has labored under ever since the arrival of your Lordship's missionaries has compelled me to retire from all public employment," etc

It was evidently the arrival of the two ministers that changed the aspect of affairs.

Porter breaks with Glover

While these commotions were agitating the colony, some time between May 13th and July 24th, it would seem that Porter found it expedient to break with Glover, and confessing the disappointment he had experienced at his hands, to establish the authority of the new council without waiting for the Assembly. To this end the new council was called together, and on July 24th it chose as president Colonel Cary, who doubtless agreed to conform his actions to the expressed will of the Lords Proprietors and to carry out the letter and spirit of the commission for settling the colony, which he perhaps found less hesitation in doing now that Granville was dead and the motive for siding with the Church party was no longer so apparent.

July 24, 1708
C. R., I, 793

C. R., I, 688, 710

What took place during that long, hot summer is not recorded, save only in a general way that the colony was the scene of great disturbances and that the Church party lost ground and fell into a pitiable minority.

Disturb-ances, 1708

On September 18, 1708, Mr. Adams, who remained in the colony after his coadjutor, Mr. Gordon, had withdrawn from the commotion, writes concerning the troubles: "Besides, we shall be engaged in perpetual broils as we now are at present, for our old worthy patriots who have for many years borne rule in the government with great applause cannot without concern and indignation think of their being turned out of the council and places of trust for no other reason but because they are members of the Church of England, and that shoemakers and other mechanics should be appointed in their room merely because they are Quaker preachers," etc.

C. R., I, 687

Two governments contending

But Glover was not content to be displaced in that manner, and still claimed the power and authority of the gov-

1708

ernor's office. And so there were two governments, each claiming to be regular and lawful, each with its adherents who loudly proclaimed their opponents to be rebels and traitors.

Both call the Assembly October, 1708

The whole colony became involved, and both sides being determined, the drift was to open rupture. Colonel Jennings of Virginia, wrote to the Lords Proprietors on September 20th that the Quakers had the cunning to set all the

Pollock's Letter Book

country in a flame and all but themselves in arms against one another, and there had already been one man killed in

Hawks, II, 380

the fray. There was no hope of peace save by submitting the matter to the legislature. Under these circumstances

C. R., I, 696-698

Colonel Pollock, on behalf of Glover, made an agreement with Cary to submit the claims of the two rival presidents to an assembly to be elected, and so Cary and Glover each issued separate writs for an election of an assembly to be held on October 3, 1708.

This election was quietly held in six precincts, but the result in Chowan was contested. The assembly consisted of twenty-six members, five from each of the four precincts of Albemarle and two from each of the three precincts in Bath County.

The Cary party carried Bath County and Perquimans and Pasquotank. In Chowan there was a contested election.

Oct. 11, 1708

Currituck alone stood faithful to the losing cause of President Glover.

Eight days later the Assembly met. The outlook was gloomy indeed for Glover. Moseley and the other Cary contestants from Chowan were seated without delay, and Moseley himself was elected speaker of the Assembly.

Glover departs to Virginia

C. R., I, 698

The commission to settle the government brought over by Porter was read and the Assembly determined that by that instrument the Lords Proprietors had suspended the laws made both in Governor Daniel's time and in Governor Cary's

1708
Pollock's
Letter Book

time relative to qualifying by taking oaths of office. Colonel Pollock insisted, however, that the former law was not so much as mentioned in the writing—but such was the decision of the Assembly. Glover protested that he would not be bound by the action of the body, although elected under his own writ, along with the writ of Cary. He insisted that they should be sworn—or, in other words, purged of the Quaker members—before he would abide by his agreement. His protest was treated with scant courtesy. He had appealed to the people. He had agreed to abide by the popular verdict; and now that the people had spoken, now that a large majority of the legislature was against him, he sought to reverse that judgment, and to that end invoked the same method of suppression that had been lately practised— at variance with the fundamental constitution of the colony as well as repugnant to the particular commission of the Lords Proprietors. But his efforts were without avail. Withdrawing from his agreement to submit his claims to the decision of the Assembly, he left the colony and took refuge in Virginia. In this voluntary exile Colonel Pollock accompanied him, and Gale, the presiding judge of the general court, went to England, and it was not until two years afterward, when Hyde entered upon the administration as president of the council, that they returned.

The Cary government was thus left in undisturbed possession. The council consisted of Cary, the president; Foster, Porter and the Quakers. One of the first measures of the new administration was to declare void all acts done by the Glover government during the preceding nine months, thus stigmatizing the retention of power by the old council through the exclusion of the new deputies as in the nature of rebellion.

But although all the machinery of government was in Cary's hands, there remained a large faction disappointed, sullen and antagonistic—and it was this faction that contained the men who had been trained in the management of public concerns. Changes were made in the local officers.

The Cary
government

1708   The old set gave place to the adherents of the new administration.

Emanuel Lowe, Archdale's Quaker son-in-law, was appointed to the land office, and other Quakers, Presbyterians
and Independents were given public employment. The
courts were open; suits were begun and prosecuted to judgment and execution; wills probated and administration
granted. The public lands were opened to entry and
patents granted, and all the branches of government appear
C. R., I, 684   to have been administered in due form; and particularly
is it noteworthy that the vestry act was maintained in opera-
C. R., I, 690   tion; and further that the Virginia government complained
of the large emigration of Virginians into North Carolina.

In December, 1708, the Proprietors appointed Edward
Tynte governor of Carolina, and expected him to appoint
Edward Hyde deputy-governor of North Carolina; but until
Hyde should arrive Cary was left unmolested in the administration of affairs. In March, 1709, the Proprietors appointed Lawson and Moseley, the speaker of Cary's house,
to settle the disputed line between Virginia and North Carolina; and in September, 1709, they appointed Christopher
Gale receiver-general in the colony and Lawson surveyor-
general, both of these being then in London. The Proprietors signified no particular displeasure at the situation of
affairs in North Carolina, but in after years the period of
Cary's administration was known as "Cary's usurpation."

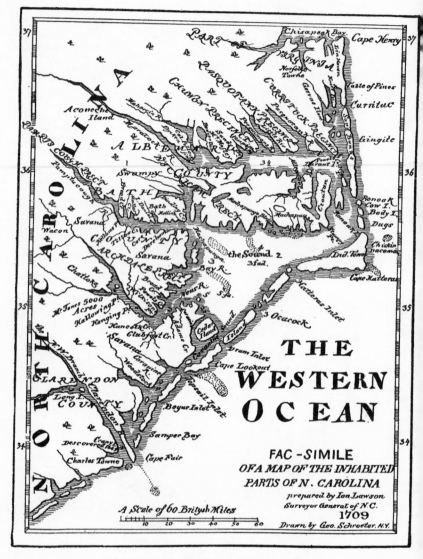

LAWSON'S MAP OF NORTH CAROLINA, 1709

CHAPTER XIV

The Cary Rebellion

The Palatines.—Their sufferings at sea.—They march through the forest.—De Graffenried's Swiss.—New Bern founded.—Hyde arrives in Virginia.—Invited to Carolina.—Glover's influence.—The Quakers excluded.—His authority denied.—The new Assembly.—Hyde succeeds.—The Cary administration declared a usurpation.—Partisan legislation.—Hyde embodies men.—Cary prepared.—Roach aids Cary.—The people divide.—Governor Spotswood seeks to mediate.—His agent threatens Cary.—Cary prepares to engage, but fails.—Hyde's moderation.—Cary and Porter sent to England.

The Palatines

It was during the time while Lawson was in England and was preparing his History for publication that arrangements were made for the settlement of a considerable number of colonists on the Trent, in Archdale Precinct, near where the French had settled and where Lawson had a large tract of land. Great numbers of Protestants had been expelled from the Palatinate, a fertile and populous country on the Rhine, now embraced in Baden and Bavaria, and many thousands, utterly impoverished and destitute, sought refuge in England. Their support had become a heavy tax on the public, the English people being at that time themselves in great distress, and efforts were made to disperse them throughout the kingdom and the American colonies. Baron De Graffenried, a Swiss nobleman, being in negotiation with the Lords Proprietors for land in Carolina for a Swiss colony, was induced to take charge of a number of these poor Palatines. The queen assumed the expense of their transportation and made a donation of £4,000 for their benefit, while a committee of lords supervised the agreement with the Proprietors and inspected the vessels before the final embarkation. Six hundred and fifty of the most robust of the Palatines were selected by De Graffenried, who placed them under the direction of Christopher Gale, John Lawson and a third associate; and ample provision being made for

1710

German Protestants

1710

The
Palatines
sail

their sustenance, at length, in January, 1710, after religious services by their pastor and other demonstrations of interest, the two transports sailed from Gravesend, accompanied for protection by a squadron of naval vessels commanded by an admiral.

Hardly had the voyage begun, however, before storms arose and impeded the progress of the vessels, and the voyage was protracted to more than three months. Unhappy, indeed, was the fate of these poor exiles driven from their prosperous homes by cruel religious persecution. During their long voyage more than one-half succumbed to disease on shipboard, while the sufferings of the others impaired their strength and vitality. Finally, in April, they reached the Chesapeake, but as they were entering that friendly harbor a French vessel captured one of the transports and plundered it of everything valuable, depriving the miserable immigrants of even their clothing.

April, 1710

C. R., I, 718

After landing, their numbers were still further diminished by fever and disease before they were able to set out through the forests for their march to the Chowan. Eventually the remnant reached the plantation of Colonel Pollock, who provided for their necessities and transported them in boats to the Trent, where they finally arrived in horrible plight, finding no preparations made to receive them, although Lawson was engaged until August in locating them. Gale, the receiver-general, had been a member of the general court in North Carolina from 1703 until the overthrow of Glover's administration, when he went to

Lawson
locates the
Palatines

England. He now returned with Lawson, and was, as chief justice, destined to play an important part in the affairs of the colony. He had brought instructions from the Proprietors to use such of the public revenues as could be spared for the support of the Palatines; but Cary having received the public funds, withheld them from Gale, and inadequate provision was made for the colonists, who found themselves driven to the necessity of selling even their clothes to the neighboring settlers for meat and bread.

The Swiss
June, 1710

Six months after the departure of the Palatines, De Graffenried, who had been created a landgrave by the Lords Proprietors, followed with his colony of Swiss. Their voyage

1710
was more fortunate, and after a few weeks they landed in excellent spirits on the banks of the James and likewise came by land to Colonel Pollock's, reaching the Trent in September, where they found the unhappy Palatines in miserable plight.

Being a landgrave, De Graffenried had official prominence in the province, and he used every effort to ameliorate the condition of his colonists, and addressed himself to the work of building a town, which he named New Bern. Many planters now occupied the lands on the Pamlico; the French colony had been increased by accessions from Virginia; lands along the shore, even between North River and Core River (near the present town of Beaufort), were taken up in 1709, and the settlements were extending southward along the coast. So it happened that the period of Cary's administration was marked by a considerable expansion and development of the province, but yet the administration was not efficient. The new men appointed to office were not trained in official duties, grave complaints were rife, and the government lost some of the prestige it had acquired on the withdrawal of Glover and his adherents to Virginia.

New Bern founded 1710

The Cary administration

Records Carteret County

Hyde arrives in Virginia

Such was the condition when Colonel Edward Hyde, who had been selected by the Proprietors as deputy-governor of North Carolina, reached Virginia, in August, 1710, where, however, he failed to receive his commission as he had expected, for Edward Tynte, the governor of Carolina, who was to have sent it to him from Charleston, died without doing so. Hyde's coming had been anxiously expected by the Glover faction, who hastened to make their court to him; but being without a commission, he prudently remained in Virginia and awaited developments. Being the first cousin of the queen, the "awful respect" due to his family drew public sentiment toward him; and there being no question that the Proprietors had designated him for appointment as deputy-governor, Cary was persuaded to join in an invitation that Hyde should come to Carolina and enter upon the administration as president of the council.

In January, 1711, this invitation was accepted, and Hyde

August,1710

C. R., I, 731, 733

Jan., 1711

Hyde's
administra-
tion

C. R., I,
768, 781, 784

Glover's
influence

Opposition
arises

coming to Carolina, settled himself in Chowan, near Colonel
Pollock's, who, as well as Glover, had returned about that
time to his Carolina home.   But although the new president came in by common consent, he was met at the outset
with the same practical question that had so largely entered
into the politics of the colony during the preceding decade.
Should Quakers be admitted to office?   Should they be
allowed to enter into office without qualifying themselves
by taking an oath?   This question could not be avoided.   It
met the new administration face to face and demanded an
unequivocal answer.

Hyde might perhaps have determined the matter in accordance with the practice of the preceding administration
and agreeably to the fundamental constitution of the colony
had it not been for the influence exerted by the adherents
of Glover, who had suffered no little because of their fidelity
to the cause they represented.   They prided themselves that
it was the cause of the legitimate, lawful and regular government no less than the cause of the Church and of true
religion, and they sought, not without avail, to impress the
new governor with the correctness of their views, and doubtless he espoused them the more readily since they were in
conformity with the prevailing notions in England in regard
to the Quakers.

Urmstone, who had succeeded Mr. Adams as the solitary
clergyman in the colony, wrote that "after long debates
Hyde persists in Mr. Glover's opinion of not suffering
the Quakers, who had deputations, either forged or granted
by those who were not Proprietors, to be of the council, or
have anything to do in the administration," which meant that
the Quakers were excluded from the council, as in Glover's
time.   And again Pollock wrote to the Lords Proprietors, in
September, 1712, that "the Quakers are not permitted to sit
in the Assembly."

This decision on the part of Hyde opened afresh all the
old sores, and threw into the opposition a strong party, who,
having lately enjoyed the powers of government, were easily
led to make another stand for the principles they had so
ardently maintained.   The leaders of that party coming to
understand that Hyde's administration would be in the

nature of a return of the Glover faction, whose temper was very bitter and hostile, sought to weaken it by withdrawing their adherence and declaring that Hyde, having no commission, was not a legal governor.

The new Assembly

The Cary officers, it is said, falling in with these suggestions, retained their records, seals and other muniments of office and would not surrender them to Hyde's appointees. Such was the situation when, in March, 1711, the Assembly, *March, 1711* called by Hyde, met at Colonel Pollock's residence in Chowan. Of that Assembly Urmstone writes: "With much difficulty we had the majority. . . . The Assembly was made up of a strange mixture of men of various opinions and *C. R., I, 768* inclinations: a few Churchmen, many Presbyterians, Independents, but most anythingarians—some out of principle, others out of hopes of power and authority in the government to the end that they might lord it over their neighbors, all conspired to act answerably to the desire of the president and council." The Quakers being excluded, the Assembly was sufficiently manageable.

The rising sun was too strong for those who were deemed *Hyde succeeds* to be on the wane. Hyde triumphed over the opposition. The "awful respect" of his great name was heavy weight in his favor, and "the Presbyterians, Independents and anythingarians" of the Assembly were drawn to his side in hopes of favors to come, and also because three months before he had been brought in as governor by common consent; while *Partisan legislation* Cary's administration had fallen into disrepute because of inefficiency, and he himself had either squandered or had not collected the quit rents due the Lords Proprietors. Whatever were the influences working the change, the *Cary and Porter impeached* Assembly was quite as severe against the Cary party as the former Assembly had, in October, 1708, been against its Glover opponents. It declared that Cary and Porter had failed to attend with Hyde as members of his council, that they had been guilty of sedition and had sought to overturn Hyde's government, and they impeached them for high crimes and misdemeanors and committed them to the custody of the provost marshal.

1711
C. R., I, 785
Proceedings
in the courts
annulled
It petitioned the Lords Proprietors to remove Cary, Porter and Moseley from any share in the government; and as Cary's government had declared void all proceedings had nine months before it came in, so this Assembly declared void all proceeding, save certain exceptions, that had been in Cary's courts, land offices, etc., during the space of two entire years.

C. R., I,
785, 786
It further re-enacted the former law in regard to the qualification of all officers by oaths according to the strictness of the English laws, and enacted that all laws made for the establishment of the Church in England should be in force in the colony.

C. R., I, 780
And various sundry other enactments were made in the first flush of victory by those who had been under the ban for three years, of such a character as to draw even from Cary's
usurpation Spotswood, "that they added some other clauses perhaps too severe to be justified, wherein it must be confessed they showed more their resentment of their ill-usage during Mr. Cary's usurpation (as they call it) than their prudence to reconcile the distractions of the country."

C. R., I, 791
Particularly was an act passed directing Cary to account with Hyde for all funds that he had collected for the Lords Proprietors, and upon his failing to do so within two months, Hyde was authorized to issue execution against his property. Truly, Cary had fallen from his high estate, and the Glover party, animated by a fierce resentment of their injuries, were pursuing him with a strong hand. Having disrobed him of power, they sought to press him to the wall. But as Spotswood wrote, their measures were beyond their power to enforce them. By their want of moderation they threw the whole opposition into violent antagonism.

Hyde
embodies
men
Both Cary and Porter escaped from the custody of the provost marshal and regained their liberty, and two months having elapsed without the former having accounted for the money of the Lords Proprietors, Hyde embodied a force May, 1711 to go and take him. On Sunday, May 26th, Hyde, with some secrecy, collected about eighty men at his own house in Chowan, and on Monday crossed the sound and went twelve miles up the river, where his force was increased to one hundred and fifty men. Hastening through the wilder-

ness, on the 28th they reached Cary's house at Pamlico, but he having received notice of their approach, made his escape to Governor Daniel's house, a few miles farther down the river.

1711
Dennis's
Narrative,
C. R., I, 803

The next day Hyde pursued, but found that his delay had been disastrous. Cary had called around him some forty followers and had so fortified himself that it was hazardous to attack him.

On June 1st the forces of the disappointed governor withdrew, having only their trouble for their pains, and having by an accident lost one of their own men, a kinsman of the governor, who unfortunately was killed during the expedition. So ended Hyde's fiasco, and well indeed had it terminated there! Whatever else may have been the disposition of Cary, he was not a man to shun danger, no matter in what form it came. He was as resolute as he was violent, and as audacious as implacable.

He at once infused into the people of Pamlico that the Assembly was not called by proper authority, that it was not duly elected, that Hyde was not governor, having no commission sent him, and therefore that he could not comply with this demand to account with Hyde for money belonging to the Lords Proprietors. Nor did his efforts end in words. He erected his standard and gathered his forces.

And just then Captain Roach, an agent of Dawson, one of the Lords Proprietors, brought his vessel into Pamlico, there being among his cargo several cannon and a quantity of small arms and ammunition. Roach vigorously espoused the side of Cary, and strengthened his cause as well by declaring that the Proprietors did not intend that Hyde should be governor, as by furnishing the munitions and sinews of war. A brigantine belonging to Emanuel Lowe was armed with cannon and a barco-longo was also equipped for active service.

Roach aids
Cary
C. R., I, 804

All was activity among the Presbyterians and Independents of Bath. And so with Hyde and his supporters in Chowan.

Pasquotank and Perquimans and Currituck seem not to have been involved, the Quakers remaining quiet and the

1711

other citizens of those counties responding but slowly to the call of the governor for active support. Indeed so slowly did they respond that Hyde early realized the superior strength of his adversary, and at once applied for aid to the governor of Virginia.

Spotswood seeks to mediate June, 1711

On June 13th Spotswood, in response to the demand, determined to send a mediator to seek a suspension of military operations until the differences of the contestants could be laid before the Lords Proprietors. To that end, on June 20th he wrote letters to each, Hyde and Cary, which he sent by Mr. Clayton, saying to Cary that he had ever advised Hyde to moderation and to endeavor to reconcile and unite both parties, and that it was on this basis that he now proposed mediation.

C. R., I, 760

On June 25th Clayton reached Pollock's residence, which was situated somewhat west of the site of Edenton, and on the next day delivered the letter to Cary, whose well-manned brigantine and barco-longo were then sailing off some twelve miles from Pollock's in the sound.

C. R., I, 795

Cary agreed to the proposition to meet Hyde the next day at an appointed place, and that in the meantime the forces should remain where they were. But Hyde, upon consideration, found the appointed place too inconvenient, and suggested two other points for a conference to be held on the 28th. But this proposition, says Hyde himself, did not reach Cary in time, because of bad weather, and negotiations thereupon were broken off.

Clayton again visited Cary and delivered a second letter from Spotswood, withheld at first, threatening Cary with his own armed interference if he should not come to terms.

Cary threatens Hyde with Parke's fate

Cary now declared he would make no terms, but that he would seize Hyde and his council, and that Hyde might expect the same fate that Colonel Parke had at Antigua.

This threat produced a great commotion among the friends of Governor Hyde, for two years before Colonel Parke, the governor of the island of Antigua, one of the British Isles in the Caribbean Sea, had after three years of tyranny and despotic oppression been seized by the outraged people, and had been torn limb from limb; a tragic fate, well known in Virginia, where one of Governor Parke's daugh-

ers had married Colonel Custis, and was thus allied to some
of the first people in that colony.

But Cary's threats were impotent. His men were not
qual to the occasion. On the morning of June 30th, he de-
ermined to make the attempt to seize Hyde, and approach-
ng Pollock's house that lay near the water, he fired two can-
on from his brig and, throwing a force into two boats,
nade a dash for the land.

But Hyde was prepared, and returning shot for shot,
truck the mast of the brig, and deployed his men along the
hore ready for the assault. Such an unexpected show of
orce struck terror into the hearts of Cary's men, who quickly
eturned to their vessel and sought to draw off.* Hyde in
urn manned some boats and gave pursuit. And now Cary's
orce thought only of escape. The brig was hastily run
shore, and the men fled into the woods. When Hyde's
oats approached, the brig, armed with six cannon, fell into
heir hands, along with her owner, Emanuel Lowe, and three
ailors, who composed her crew.

Being favored by this good fortune, Hyde issued a procla-
nation pardoning all who had been led into acts of violence,
xcept the chief movers, which, together with the loss of
restige incident to the miscarriage of the attempt to seize
Hyde, tended to draw the people away from Cary, whose
orces rapidly dispersed. Roach, however, fortified himself
t Pamlico, and it was said that John Porter went among the
ndians and endeavored to persuade them to fall upon the
eople on the western shores of Chowan, the inhabitants
here having espoused the cause of Hyde. The Indians, how-
ver, declined the invitation, if any were indeed made to them.
n the meantime, Hyde, flushed with his success in capturing
he armed brigantine, hastily threw on board of the vessel
. force of his own and sailed off to Pamlico to make an end
f the matter by capturing Cary at Roach's house, the place
where he had fortified; but again did the governor find dis-
retion the better part of valor. Cary was too strongly en-

1711

C. R., I,
762, 795

June 30

De Graffen-
ried's Narra-
tive, C. R.,
I, 918

Hyde's
moderation

C. R., I, 795

*This sudden flight was probably due to the appearance among
Hyde's followers of Baron De Graffenried's servant, in his yellow
oat, which led to the impression that some of the queen's troops
vere present, it being treason to make war on them.

1711
trenched; no attack was made, and the expedition returned without result. But Spotswood having on the application of Hyde sent some marines to his assistance, the appearance of these on Pamlico, about July 10th, being troops of the queen, accomplished the final dispersion of the Cary forces.

Cary and Porter sent to England July 31
Colonel Cary and several of his most active supporters hastily proceeded to Virginia to take shipping for England, but were there seized by Spotswood, and, on July 31st, were sent to England on board a man-of-war under charges of rebellion and sedition. They arrived in London on September 25th, but there being no evidence produced against them, they were discharged.

Porter's will Off. Sec. State
On November 20th, within a month after his arrival, we find Cary before the Lords Proprietors obtaining copies of the charges made against him by Hyde. A year later he had returned to Carolina, Hyde having been instructed by the Lords Proprietors not to proceed to the punishment of any of the parties engaged against him. John Porter remained in England and died at Bridgewater during the spring or summer of 1713.

C. R., I, 750
On the death of Governor Tynte, the Lords Proprietors appointed Hyde governor of North Carolina in his own right, and a recent act of Parliament requiring the approval of the Crown, the royal assent was given, and on May 9, 1712, he received his appointment, bearing date Jan-

Final separation of North and South Carolina
uary 24th. Taking the oaths, he became Governor of North Carolina, being the first appointed by the Lords Proprietors since Ludwell's time, and this appointment was the beginning of the entire separation of the government of North Carolina from that of the southern colony.

CHAPTER XV

The Tuscarora War

The Indians disquieted.—Lawson's activities.—Lawson executed.—
The cause of the Indian war.—The massacre.—Preparations for
defence.—Active war.—Gale's mission successful.—Barnwell acts
vigorously.—War measures.—Barnwell makes a truce.—Barnwell's
Indians return to South Carolina.—Hostilities renewed.—The death
of Hyde.—Pollock's truce with King Blount.—James Moore arrives.
—He takes Fort Nohoroco.—Many Tuscaroras depart for New York.
—Major Maurice Moore arrives.—Effects on the settlers.—Harmony
in the colony.—Governor Eden.—South Carolina imperilled.—Aid
sent.—The Cores renew hostilities.

The Indians disquieted

In the dissensions of the colony, the Pamlico section adhered to Cary, and the Indians of that region were led by the
execrations of the neighboring whites to regard the new governor as a person to be detested by them, while the rapid
extension of the settlements to the southward and along the
waters of the Pamlico and Neuse raised apprehensions lest
they should be forced back and utterly expelled from their
old hunting grounds. At this time the tribes at the north
had dwindled into insignificance; they were the Meherrins,
the Nottoways, and the Chowans on Bennett's Creek and
the Pasquotank, some of whom had already fallen into the
habits of the whites, wore clothes and had cattle, making
butter for sale. On the western frontier, beginning in Virginia and extending nearly to the Neuse, were the Tuscaroras, a warlike tribe of northern origin. They occupied
fifteen towns and numbered altogether 1200 fighting men.
Adjoining them were the Woccoons, about one-tenth their
number; and a few miles distant were the Pamlicos, once an
important tribe, who had, however, been swept away by a
fearful epidemic some fifteen years before, and now could
boast only fifty braves. The Neuse and the Chautauquas,
who occupied the region allotted to De Graffenried's colony,

were likewise weak; but the tribes farther to the eastward on Bear River and Core Sound, were more populous. Near Bath was a small tribe of Pungos, and on the sounds to the south were found the Coranines; while at Hatteras lived the remnant of a tribe now reduced to sixteen braves, who claimed that some of their ancestors were white, and valued themselves extremely on their kinship to the English, and were very friendly. In confirmation of this claim, in effect that they were descended from Raleigh's Lost Colony, Lawson declares that some of them had grey eyes, a circumstance not observed among any other Indians.

In the distant interior, on the Eno, had been the Occoneechees, and nearby the Schoccories and the Keiauwees, and farther south the Saponas and the Toteros; but these a few years earlier had consolidated and had removed from Carolina into Virginia, settling at Christianna, ten miles

Byrd's Div.
Line, 89
north of the Roanoke. After remaining there some twenty-five years, however, they returned to Carolina and dwelt with the Catawbas. In all, there were some 1500 braves bordering on the south and west of the settlements; but the Indians to the northward, nearer the Virginia line, did not sympathize in the apprehensions felt by the lower towns concerning the encroachments made on the Pamlico and Neuse and were not inclined to be inimical to the whites.

Lawson's
work
Lawson had projected an interior road from the southern settlement to Virginia, and with a view to locating it he had made a progress through the region inhabited by the Indians; he had also as surveyor been conspicuous in establishing the Palatines and the Swiss, and in laying off plantations, and indeed himself had a large grant located on the Neuse; and thus he became an object of particular resentment among the discontented Indians.

Sept. 8, 1711
Such was the feeling early in September, some two months after the dispersion of Cary's forces and the flight of his principal adherents from the colony, when Lawson and Christopher Gale and Baron De Graffenried arranged for an expedition up the Neuse and to make a progress through the Indian towns with a view of locating the proposed road. Gale was fortunately detained, but the baron and Lawson, accompanied by two negroes, on September 8th, set out from

1711

Hawks, II, 389;
De Graffen-ried's Narra-tive, C. R., I,
925
Sept., 1711

New Bern by boat on the exploration, taking fifteen days' provision with them. On the evening of the second day, the Indians, discovering them, became alarmed, and mistaking the baron for Governor Hyde, seized them and hurried them in great haste to their king's town, on Cotechney, where a council of Indian chiefs was speedily assembled, by whom both the baron and Lawson were condemned to instant death.

Lawson
executed

De Graffenried, however, with great address, saved himself by asserting that he was not an Englishman, but a king and a friend of the queen of England, who would certainly punish them for any violence done to him. Reprieving him, on Lawson they reaped their vengeance by a summary execution; an unhappy fate, in strange contrast with the humane and friendly sentiments he had expressed in his History in regard to the proper treatment and the welfare and happiness of these original inhabitants of the Carolina territory. The day following the trial and execution of Lawson, the Indian chieftains informed De Graffenried that they had determined to make war on the English, and that the particular objects of their enmity were the people on the Neuse, Pamlico and Trent rivers and on Core Sound, for settlers had established themselves even in that locality.

The cause
of the
Indian war

Governor Pollock, writing to Governor Spotswood some nine months after the outbreak, gives this account of the origin of the war: "Our own divisions, chiefly occasioned by the Quakers and some few other evil-disposed persons, hath been the cause of all our trouble. For the Indians being informed by some of the traders that the people that lived here were only a few vagabond persons that had run away out of other governments and had settled here of their own head, without any authority, so if they were cut off there would be none to help them; this, with the seeing our own differences rise to such a height that we, consisting of only two counties, were in arms against each other, encouraged them to fall on the county of Bath, not expecting that they would have any assistance from this county or any other English plantation. This is the chief cause that moved the Indians to rise against us so far as I can understand."

Hawks, II,
434

This internecine strife and bitterness doubtless led the

Indians to consider that a favorable time and opportunity; but the cause, the reason of their enmity, was quite another thing. If some of Hyde's adherents are to be believed, they had during the Cary troubles declined to attack the whites, although invited to do so; and it was only after quiet had been restored and Cary and Porter had been absent two months that hostilities began. In July some of Hyde's adherents alleged that at the time of the dispersal of Cary's forces, John Porter had gone among the Tuscaroras and sought to incite them to cut off the inhabitants on the Chowan who were adherents of Hyde, but they had refused to be drawn into such an enterprise. In the massacre now resolved on, the upper towns of the Tuscaroras again declined to participate; but the Cotechneys, the Woccoons, the Pamlicos, the Cores and the Neuse Indians were the chief promoters of the murderous work, and the victims were the settlers who had located on the frontier and who had been Cary's supporters. The outbreak was evidently an effort of the southern tribes to preserve their hunting grounds, which the settlers were now fast occupying.

Cary's adherents the sufferers

The massacre

Five hundred warriors, consisting of Indians from every tribe on the southern frontier, having congregated at Hancock's town on the Cotechney, formed into small bands and dispersed themselves as if in a friendly way throughout the new settlements. On the morning of September 22d, about sunrise, they fell upon the unsuspecting planters in their isolated homes and began a fearful massacre. In two hours one hundred and thirty persons fell beneath their bloody blows. On some plantations all, men, women and children alike, were ruthlessly and barbarously murdered; at others, the men only were slain, and the women and children were spared to be held, however, as slaves. In savage wrath, they slew and burned and pillaged, and the entire region south of the Albemarle was a horrid scene of brutal murder and desolation. The French settlers on the Pamlico suffered heavily, eighty of De Graffenried's colonists fell victims, and the outlying districts were depopulated.

Sept. 22, 1711

De Graffenried's Narrative, C. R., I, 933

In those hours of fearful calamity, those who fortunately escaped the first fury of the savages fled in dismay to convenient points of refuge. They collected at Bath and at ten other places, where they hurriedly fortified themselves against attack.

Many incidents of the butchery were heart-rending, and some of the escapes heroic. At the house of John Porter, Jr., his wife, Sarah Lillington, seeing an Indian in the act of dashing her infant's brains out against a tree, rushed upon him and rescued her child from his clutches. Captain Maule being present, he and Colonel Porter seized their guns and covering the flight of the females, successfully beat off the savages until they had reached the landing, where taking a boat they pushed out into the broad river and escaped, beholding in the distance their home enveloped in flames.

For two days the murderous bands glutted themselves with blood and revelled in spoil, but on the third day, the plantations being deserted, laden with booty and carrying eighty women and children preserved as captives, they returned to their fort on the Cotechney. The dead lay unburied in that hot September sun, food for the vultures, the dogs and wolves. Many bodies were shockingly mutilated, and others fancifully arranged by the savages in their wild and merry glee. Mr. Nevill, an old gentleman, was laid on his floor with a clean pillow beneath his head, which was ornamented with his wife's head-dress, and his body decently covered with new linen; while Mrs. Nevill was set upon her knees in the chimney corner, her hands lifted up as if in prayer; and a son was laid out in the yard with a pillow under his head and a bunch of rosemary at his nose.

C. R., I, 826

Fugitives from their homes, with their butchered friends unburied, the air polluted from their decomposing remains, the survivors of Bath County kept watch and ward at the asylums they had gained, in momentary dread of the reappearance of the foe, while the other settlements were paralyzed with fear lest the whole colony should be destroyed.

Although a blow so sudden and unexpected, so terrible and shocking, at first staggered even the most resolute, Governor Hyde and the leaders in Albemarle speedily took such measures of safety as were open to them. Since the Quakers would not bear arms, but little aid could be expected from them, while the inhabitants west of the Chowan being themselves apprehensive of attack, assembled in strongholds for

Effects of the massacre

1711 their own protection. But factions were hushed and former opponents vied with each other in patriotic efforts for the common weal. Information was hurriedly despatched to Governor Spotswood, who caused some of the Virginia militia to collect near the Tuscarora towns bordering on the Virginia line, and sought to enlist the upper Tuscaroras in C. R., I, 815 the suppression of the hostile Indians. As an inducement to engage their assistance, he offered six blankets for the head of every enemy they would bring him and "the usual price for the women and children as slaves." These towns, Oct. 15, 1711 however, asked for a month to consider the proposal, and then determined to remain neutral; but fearful of their defection, the hostile tribes sent their women and children toward the Cape Fear, leaving only the warriors in their own territory; and then they again began to roam throughout the Pamlico region, and collisions between their bands and the inhabitants were of frequent occurrence.

Active war
C. R., I, 828 Indeed, with the opening of October, companies having been organized and equipped, active warfare was inaugurated; and scouting parties sent out from the forts were ambushed and often sustained heavy losses. A company of fifty C. R., I, 826 men approached one of the Indian strongholds and was repulsed by three hundred braves. Early in that month Captain Brice, who commanded at Bath, sent off some fifty men for special service, and the Indians fell upon them in the woods, and for three days a desultory battle was maintained, the whites eventually being driven in with considerable loss.

Taking advantage of the absence of this detachment, the garrison then being reduced to only a hundred men, another force of Indians attacked it, while a number of Indian prisoners within the fort rose and took the whites in the rear. The males of the latter, however, were quickly despatched and the women and children secured, and then the assault was successfully repulsed. Of the captives within the fort, thirty-nine women and children were then sent abroad and sold as slaves.

Gale's
mission
successful
C. R., I, 828 Christopher Gale, the receiver-general, having been sent to Charleston by sea to solicit aid, the South Carolina Assembly promptly responded with assistance. Colonel Hugh Grange, with others, was elected to secure the neces-

sary supplies, and Colonel John Barnwell was appointed to 1711
the command. Gale hastened back on his return voyage
from Charleston, bringing a considerable supply of ammunition, but he was taken prisoner by the French and was
detained for several months. In the interval during his
absence, the North Carolina government receiving no information from him relative to the result of his mission, again
sent a despatch boat to Charleston asking aid, and Barnwell's force, largely drawn from friendly Indians, was hurried forward.

North Carolina was the dividing ground between the
northern and southern Indians, and there was no affinity
between the Indians of South Carolina, who had originally
come from beyond the Mississippi River, and those of eastern North Carolina, who had at some previous time migrated
from the northward; and the southern Indians were not
averse to availing themselves of this opportunity of attacking the Tuscaroras and the neighboring tribes, expecting
to make profit from the sale of their prisoners as slaves.

Barnwell, his troops consisting of fifty whites and some
Cherokees and Creeks, passed along the Santee to the Congarees, then up the Wateree River to the vicinity of the
Catawbas, near where Charlotte is, embodying detachments
of all these tribes in his force. He then came east to the McCrady's South Carolina, I, 499 1712
Yadkin and crossed the Cape Fear below the junction of
the Haw and Deep and then pursued a northeast course,
striking the Cotechney at an Indian town called Torhunte,
eventually arriving on the lower Neuse on January 28th.*
He seemed to have followed a trading path used by the
Indians and traders leading from Torhunte to the Catawbas,
a shorter course than that generally taken by the Virginia
traders, who, crossing the Roanoke higher up, came by a
route near Oxford and Hillsboro to the trading ford near
Salisbury and then down to the Catawbas. But his progress
through the wilderness was difficult and attended with much
delay and suffering for the want of provisions.

*He had 218 Cherokees under Captains Harford and Turstons,
79 Creeks under Captain Hastings, 41 Catawbas under Cautey, and
28 Yamassees under Captain Pierce.

Barnwell acts vigorously

On reaching New Bern, Barnwell acted with great vigor, and immediately fell upon the hostiles some twenty miles above New Bern, killing three hundred and taking more than a hundred prisoners. But as soon as this victory was won, half of his force, satisfied with their booty, deserted him and returned to South Carolina, carrying their prisoners, who were shipped to the West Indies to be sold into slavery. Notwithstanding his force was now much reduced, Barnwell pursued the enemy until they retired into a stronghold which they had fortified on a high and inaccessible bluff overlooking the river, which could not be attacked with advantage. Withdrawing from that section, he led his Indians some thirty miles to the east of New Bern, where he encountered the Cores and drove them from their towns, and pursued them with such fury that a great many were slain. On his return he was reinforced by two hundred and fifty whites, under Captains Brice, Boyd, and Mitchell, and together they assaulted Fort Cotechney, or Hancock's Fort, near the site of Snow Hill, but were driven off. Nevertheless, the people felt so relieved by his presence, and were so elated from their former despondency by the result of his movements, that when the Assembly met it adopted an address to the Lords Proprietors in high praise of him.

To carry on the war heavy duties had been laid on both exportations and importations, and now the legislature authorized the issue of £4,000 of paper currency, the first of such currency issued by the colony; and urgent application was made to Virginia for two hundred white soldiers from that province. Governor Spotswood undertook to raise such a force, but ascertaining that the North Carolina authorities had made no provision either for their pay or their maintenance, and meeting with obstacles because of opposition in the Virginia Assembly, he found it impracticable to proceed. Under the circumstances, as the expenditure would be for the Lords Proprietors, he suggested that the territory north of the Albemarle should be mortgaged to secure the repayment of the money that would have to be advanced for the purpose, but since the Assembly had no

authority to enter into such an agreement, those terms could
not be accepted by it, and the desired assistance was not furnished by Virginia.

In April, Barnwell proposed to make another attack on
Fort Cotechney, and at the suggestion of De Graffenried,
who, having been released, was now again in the settlement,
some cannon were carried through the forest, borne on long
shafts with a horse in front and one behind, and these were
well placed to bombard the stronghold. When all was in
readiness for the assault the cannon were discharged and
hand grenades were thrown into the fort; and these unaccustomed instruments of warfare so terrified the Indians
that they begged for a truce. A council of war was held
by Barnwell and his officers, and since it was feared that
the large number of women and children held prisoners by
the Indians would be massacred in the mêlée if the fort were
carried by assault, a truce was granted upon the condition
that all the white prisoners should be immediately released,
and with the expectation that it would eventually be followed by a lasting peace.

This failure to press the Indians to an extremity at that
favorable time created dissatisfaction on the part of the
governor and his council with Barnwell, who nevertheless
justified it by in turn complaining that his troops were not
furnished with provision and that a cessation of the siege
was desirable on that account.

Deplorable indeed was the condition of the unfortunate
captives now restored to freedom, being bereft of husbands
and fathers and their homes destroyed by the barbarous
savages; widows and orphans, they were helpless dependents upon the charity of people whose own necessities were
great, but for the moment they were transported with joy
at their happy deliverance from impending death, and with
grateful hearts blessed those who had rescued them from a
fearful fate.

Barnwell's Indians were disappointed at the truce and ces-
sation of operations, as they had hoped to take more prisoners and to profit by their sale; but he withdrew to New Bern,
where provisions could be had; and after a few weeks, under
the pretence of a good peace, he lured the eastern Indians

1712

to the vicinity of Core village, where his savages fell upon them unawares and took prisoners many women and children.

Barnwell
leaves
North
Carolina
C. R., I 904

The South Carolina Indians now hurried home with their captives, leaving Barnwell and the companies raised in Albemarle to carry on the hostilities which this breach of faith naturally engendered. On July 5th Barnwell himself was wounded, and taking shipping, he returned to Charleston, promising, however, to use his best endeavors to have other assistance sent.

Hostilities renewed

As long as Barnwell's force was on the Pamlico the enemy had been held in check, but now that the country was clear, furious at the treacherous breach of the truce, the hostile Indians became very active, and again was the region south of the Albemarle a scene of bitter warfare. The farms were deserted, the crops abandoned, and the inhabitants again assembled in their garrisons for mutual protection; while around those places of refuge hostile bands incessantly prowled, scalping all who fell into their hands. A small number of Yamassees, however, had remained, and under Captain Mackay did good service near Bath; but the savages roamed at will throughout the country at large, devastating the plantations and confining the people to their forts; and so another summer was passed with no crops made and the Pamlico and new settlements in a state of siege.

Summer of
1712

A call to
arms *en
masse*
C. R., I, 877

Fully aroused to the necessity of decisive action, the Assembly now made a draft of the entire fighting population to subdue the enemy, and all who would not enroll themselves as soldiers were to forfeit £5 for the maintenance of the struggle. In addition to the garrisoned plantations, two considerable forts were now erected, one at Core Point, on the sound, in the vicinity of the Core Indians, and one at Reading's plantation, on the Tar River, in the section open to the Cotechneys. But although the emergency was so great, many were discontented at the strenuous measures of the administration, and some of the inhabitants left their homes and fled to Virginia.

Forts
erected

In the midst of these difficulties the yellow fever broke out in the colony, and Colonel Hyde, who had received his commission as governor only that May, was taken with a violent fever and died on September 8th, after a week's illness. Fortunately, Colonel Pollock was ready to continue the administration as president of the council, for he had large experience and great ability, and could command the confidence not only of the inhabitants, but of the authorities in Virginia and of South Carolina. A packet ship had been employed to ply between the province and Charleston, and Governor Craven had already agreed to send an additional force of friendly Indians, the charges to be paid in North Carolina bills, and President Pollock sought to infuse into the people confidence and hope, although at the moment affairs seemed desperate. Captain Byrd, who had been sent on an expedition, fell into an ambuscade, and he himself was killed and many of his men slain; and in September Colonel Mitchell and Colonel Mackay, who had with them one hundred and forty men, were defeated and compelled to abandon the enterprise they had undertaken.

There was unexpected delay in starting the expedition from South Carolina, but Governor Craven hurried on some barrels of powder and shot and twenty guns, which were supplied to the forces then at Coretown Fort, who were awaiting the arrival of reinforcements before again proceeding to assault Fort Cotechney. In the meanwhile the Indians had attacked Fort Reading, on the Tar, and also had made an assault on the garrison at Colonel Jones's plantation, near the mouth of the Pamlico, but were successfully repulsed in both instances.

Pollock's truce with King Blount

But while preparing for a protracted struggle, Colonel Pollock had wisely renewed negotiations with Tom Blount, the king of the Upper Tuscaroras, and toward the end of September succeeded in arranging with him to seize Hancock, the chief of the Cotechney Indians, and bring him in alive with a view to making peace. Indeed, the hostiles themselves were in distress for the want of food; and at length, through King Blount, a truce was agreed on to last

1712
The death of
Hyde, Sept 8
C. R., I, 869

Pollock
succeeds

Losses

Sept., 1712

C. R., I, 882

C. R., I,
880, 883

1712

until January 1st, and in the interval the Tuscaroras were to cut off all those who had participated in the massacre and were to surrender a number of the chief men from each of the six Indian forts as hostages for the good behavior of the hostile tribes.

James
Moore
arrives
Dec. 1, 1712

C. R., I, 892

Before the truce had expired, the new army from South Carolina, consisting of thirty-three whites and a thousand friendly Indians under Colonel James Moore arrived on the Neuse, and moved to the Chowan for convenience in obtaining needed provisions until it was seen whether the Indians would surrender the hostages as agreed on. This they failed to do, and preparations were made to strike a blow that would break their power.

1713

Indian forts

The facilities for reaching the Pamlico and Neuse and even Core Fort by water transportation had been of great advantage during the war, and now the necessary supplies were sent forward by boat, and on January 17th Colonel Moore marched from Chowan, but a heavy snow falling, he was obliged to remain inactive at Fort Reading on the Tar until February. In the meantime, the Indians had fortified themselves in two strongholds, one, Cohunche, which was Hancock's fort on the Cotechney, and the other called Fort Nohoroco.

He takes
Fort
Nohoroco

March 23,
1713

At length, all being in readiness and his army being reinforced by a considerable number of whites raised in the colony, among them a company under Captain Maule, on March 20th Colonel Moore invested Fort Nohoroco, and after three days' hot fighting took it. His loss was 46 whites and 91 friendly Indians, while he took 392 prisoners and 192 "scalps," and reported 200 others killed and burned within the fort and 166 killed and taken outside of the fort in a scout. In all, the Indian loss was about 800. This was perhaps the severest battle ever fought with the Indians up to that time. It broke the power of the Tuscaroras, and although there were emissaries from the New York Indians, urging them to persist in hostilities, they now made peace, surrendering all of their prisoners and delivering up twenty of their chief men to Colonel Moore.

C. R., II,
19, 27-29

Indian
power
broken

The
Tuscaroras
move north

Soon afterward, the greater part of this powerful tribe, including those in Fort Cohunche, retired up the Roanoke

1713

and removed to New York and became the sixth nation there. Hardly had the fort been taken, before many of the South Carolina Indians hurried home to sell their prisoners; so that Colonel Moore was left with only one hundred and eighty of those who came with him. These scouted the woods, seeking other prisoners until June, when Colonel Moore collected them and marched against the Mattamuskeets, who had fallen on the inhabitants of Croatan and of Roanoke Island, and on the planters of Alligator River and had butchered forty-five of them. On the approach of Colonel Moore, these savages quickly dispersed in the swamps of Hyde, but Moore pursued them with vigor and broke them up.

C. R., II, 30

C. R., II, 39, 45

In the meantime another detachment of friendly Indians, under Major Maurice Moore, hoping to take more prisoners, had started from South Carolina; but Colonel Pollock stopped them and sent them back; and in September Colonel Moore himself returned home, having won high praise for his bravery and wisdom, and leaving many grateful hearts among those he had rescued from captivity and saved from death. His brother Maurice, however, remained, and having married Mrs. Swann, the widow of Colonel Swann, became the brother-in-law of Edward Moseley, and being allied with the strongest family connection in the province, for a generation exerted a large influence in its affairs.

Maurice Moore arrives

During these perilous times many of the Huguenots who had established themselves on the exposed frontier accompanied their pastor, Philippe de Richebourg, and joined their brethren on the Santee; while De Graffenried, who after a six weeks' detention with the Indians had been released through the efforts of Governor Spotswood, but who had for himself and his colonists made a treaty of neutrality with the hostile Indians, now sought to protect his colonists, and later intended to remove them to the Potomac; but a series of misfortunes interfered, and after mortgaging the land he had obtained from the Lords Proprietors to Colonel Pollock to secure the advances made for his people, in the spring of 1713 he sailed from New York for England. His Swiss and Palatines remained, and, indeed, the pacification of

De Graffenried returns to England

1713

MSS.
Records
Carteret
County

Harmony
in the
colony
C. R., II,
145
De Graffen-
ried's Narra-
tive

the hostile Indians was followed by a quick expansion of the settlements to the southward. On Core Sound and North River lands patented "during Cary's usurpation" were now occupied; and in October, 1713, the town of Beaufort was laid off into lots, which were sold to purchasers. The following February tracts of land were taken up on Bogue Sound. To the northward, in November, 1713, a grant was issued to John Porter for 7000 acres between Drum Inlet and Topsail Inlet, including Point Lookout. It was recited that this land had been surveyed before the instructions prohibiting such grants.

All the inhabitants being concerned in the common defence a spirit of harmony and co-operation was fostered, and Colonel Pollock bore testimony that the Quakers had contributed more aid than he had expected from them; but he never became reconciled to Moseley, attributing to his influence the previous internecine trouble of the colony, and ascribing to him a purpose to cause Barnwell to be appointed governor in place of Hyde, and alleging that Barnwell's truce with the Indians was a movement to that end. This appears, however, to be only another illustration of the distorted views which personal antagonisms and animosities were responsible for in that period of our history; and indeed Governor Spotswood took occasion to recommend to Pollock that he should abate somewhat his enmity to Moseley.

After Colonel Hyde was established in the government, the proceedings of the Cary courts were declared void, and doubtless the justices were superseded by other appointments. William Glover, who would naturally have been designated as the presiding justice, was dead in October, 1711, and the court was then presided over by Nathaniel Chevin, one of the oldest of the councillors. On the return of Christopher Gale to the province after his capture by the French on his way from his mission to South Carolina for aid, he was appointed colonel of the militia of Bath County, and in July, 1712, he began to execute the office of chief justice, and in March, 1713, used that title. In January, 1716, he received his commission as chief justice from

March, 1713

1. St. Thomas's Church, Bath
2. Philip Ludwell   3. Christopher Gale
4. Book-Plate and Autograph of Edward Moseley

the Lords Proprietors. As far as appears, he was the first chief justice of the province.*

Charles Eden governor

On learning of the death of Governor Hyde, the Lords Proprietors appointed Charles Eden to succeed him, and the new governor arrived in the colony and took the oath of office in May, 1714. Although all was quiet at that time, shortly thereafter about thirty braves of the Cores and other neighboring tribes, who had suffered so heavily during the war, in revenge for their losses, began a systematic course of irregular warfare. One day they would massacre in one vicinity, and a few days later they would appear many miles away and cut off unsuspecting families. And soon their numbers increased until they were estimated at two hundred

Cores on the war path

*Dr. Hawks mentions that Edward Moseley was chief justice from 1707 to 1711. The writer has been unable to find that there was any chief justice in the province before 1713. Major Sam Swann was the senior justice of the general court, after the governor ceased presiding over the court, from 1697 until his retirement in 1703. Then William Glover, who was next in commission, was the senior justice until 1706, when, on the departure of Governor Cary from the colony, Glover became president of the Council, and Christopher Gale, who had been a justice of the court from 1703, became the presiding justice. He presided during the year 1707, and perhaps until the overthrow of the Glover government in the summer of 1708, when with Pollock and Glover he probably left the colony. On the accession to power of the Cary faction, in 1708, all court proceedings for nine months were annulled and declared void; and on the incoming of Hyde, three years later, the court proceedings for the two years of Cary's administration were likewise annulled. Moseley may have been chief justice during Cary's administration, but the writer has found nothing to indicate it. He was not licensed to practise until 1714. In 1711 the court was held by Nathaniel Chevin, Francis de la Mere, and Jonathan Jacocks. At the general court held July 29, 1712, the justices were Christopher Gale, William de la Mere, Thomas Relfe, and Thomas Garrett. There was no chief justice. At the general court, March, 1713, Gale presided under the title of chief justice. Somewhat earlier, perhaps, the receiver-general had instructions from England to pay £60 for the support of the chief justice, and in April, 1713, the council resolved that Gale was entitled to this compensation, "as he had executed that office from July 1, 1712." He executed the office, but probably held no appointment as chief justice. It seems that because of this provision of £60 for the support of the chief justice, Gale was appointed to that office in the spring of 1713. In 1715 the Lords Proprietors commissioned him as chief justice, and he was sworn in January 21, 1716.

Hawks, II, 139

Proceedings annulled

C. R., II, 34, 80, 217

1715

hostiles. Again alarm seized the people, and some determined on flight to Virginia. To prevent that exodus, a proclamation was issued forbidding such removals; and Governor Spotswood gave orders for the arrest of any who should come into that province without a passport from the North Carolina authorities. Garrisons were again posted on the southern frontier, and parties of whites and friendly Indians were sent out to suppress the enemy; but at length

Feb. 11, 1715

on February 11, 1715, a treaty was made with the Cores and their allies by which they were to observe peace, and territory on Mattamuskeet was assigned them for occupancy.

South
Carolina
imperilled

Hardly had this peace been concluded before information was received of a very extensive uprising of the Indians in South Carolina, threatening the utter destruction of that colony. The Yamassees near the Savannah River having been instigated by the Spaniards, to the number of 6000, suddenly fell on the planters, and killed 400 whites, while 650 braves of the Catawbas and Cherokees came down the Santee, driving those who escaped into Charleston for safety. Governor Craven's energy and determined spirit alone saved them. Enrolling every man into the militia, he drove the

C. R., II,
180

Yamassees back beyond their old territory and expelled them from Carolina. Toward the last of May, the North Carolina council ordered that ten men should be drawn from each of the three companies, forming the "Governor's Own Regiment," and that Colonel Theophilus Hastings should proceed with them by water to Charleston; and also that fifty men should be sent by land under Colonel Maurice Moore.

Colonel
Maurice
Moore's
expedition

The route taken by Colonel Maurice Moore was by New Bern down the coast to Old Town, then along the coast by land to the vicinity of Charleston, where he was largely reinforced. He then proceeded to Fort Moore, on the Savannah, seventy-five miles north of Augusta, and from there to the northwest, through Rabun Gap, against the Cherokee Indians.

Colonel Moore and his force were fortunate in rendering such valuable service in South Carolina that the General Assembly of that province invited him to its floor and thanked him in person for his aid; to Colonel Hastings they afterward paid £250 for his services, and to Colonel Moore they made a gift of £100. Indeed, the situation in South Carolina became so critical that application was made at London for troops and munitions to be sent from England, and the Lords Proprietors admitting their inability to protect their Carolina possessions, the matter of·their purchase was considered by the Crown, but no definite action was then taken.

In the fall of that year, the Cores broke their peace and killed some settlers, and the council resolved that that tribe should be exterminated; and again companies were raised to carry on hostilities, generally composed of ten whites and some auxiliary Indians, who made profit in taking the hostiles alive and selling them as slaves. This desultory warfare continued for about three years, rangers being required to clear the woods and protect the settlers from massacre. How terrible and murderous was the war may be inferred from the number of infants, more than fourscore, that fell victims, besides the older children and mature persons.

The Cores renew hostility C. R., II, 200

1715-18

By agreement with the Tuscaroras, they were to occupy a territory between the Pamlico and Neuse, but in fear of the hostile Indians of South Carolina, in the summer of 1717, they desired to be placed in a more protected section, and were assigned a region for occupancy north of the Roanoke.

CHAPTER XVI

Eden's Administration, 1714-22

The Assembly of 1715.—The Church of England established in the colony.—Other laws.—The precincts.—Partisan disagreements.—"Blackbeard" harbors in Pamlico Sound.—Complicity of Knight.—Moseley and Moore search the records.—Knight exonerated, resigns and dies.—Moseley punished.—Revolution in South Carolina.—The dividing line.—Colonel Pollock president.—William Reed succeeds him.—Edenton.—Carteret Precinct.—A blow at nepotism.

The Assembly of 1715

Nov. 13, 1715

The Assembly that first met Governor Eden in 1715 was a notable one, convening just after the Indian war, and following the dissensions that had marked Governor Hyde's administration. Moseley, always at the head of the Popular party, was the speaker, and although differences between the council and administration on the one hand and the Assembly on the other again found expression, some of the greater questions that had agitated the colony had been finally settled by the course of events. The rights claimed for the Quakers under the concessions were now denied them. The sentiment that prevailed in England found a full voice in Albemarle. Liberty of conscience was declared; but Quakers were rendered ineligible to office; nor were they allowed to give evidence in any criminal case; nor could they serve on juries, but their affirmation was to be taken as a substitute for an oath in those cases in which their testimony was admissible.

C. R., II, 207

All officers, including members of the Assembly, were required to take the test oath as well as the oaths of office.

The Church of England established in the colony

The Church of England, being the only one which under the charter could have public encouragement, was declared the established church. The two counties were divided into nine parishes, for each of which vestrymen were selected, with the duty of providing a minister at a stipend not exceeding £50, and to build a church and a chapel in each parish; and to meet those expenses, they were to collect all fines and forfeitures imposed by law; and were empowered to lay a poll tax not exceeding five shillings per annum on the poll. It was also enacted that every person appointed a vestryman who neglected to qualify for one month was to forfeit his place, and unless he were a dissenter, should also forfeit £3. So if a dissenter were selected as a vestryman, he need not have qualified. But while these provisions were made for the employment of ministers, they were not put in operation. No pastors were regularly settled in the colony; only missionaries came, being sent out by the Society for the Propagation of the Gospel. In 1711, John Urmstone, a missionary, came to Chowan, and he remained in the colony about ten years. Rev. Mr. Rainsford came in 1712, but removed to Virginia in about twelve months. In 1718 Rev. Mr. Taylor came, but died after a residence of two years. In 1723, Thomas Bailey was in the colony as a missionary, and Rev. John Blacknall for awhile. These appear to have been all. The vestry act does not seem to have been carried into effective operation in any precinct, but at Edenton there was generally a missionary. In 1732 there was no minister of the Church of England in the entire colony.

Magistrates who by a former law were empowered to perform the marriage ceremony were forbidden to exercise that function in any place where a minister resided.

The Assembly fixed the price at which skins, hides, furs and produce were to be received in payment of debts, including quit rents and public dues. It re-enacted laws that had long been in force, including those based on the Fundamental Constitutions which had been adopted and carried into operation as nearly as circumstances permitted. Among these was that which has been known as the biennial act, which, conformably to the 73d and 75th articles of the Constitutions, provided that in September of every second year, the people were to choose assemblymen, who were to convene in session the next November, thus making provision for the regular meeting of the people's representatives indepen-

1715

Parishes erected

The Church established

Missionaries

Other laws
C. R., II.,
213

1715

The new
precincts
C. R., II,
214

C. R.,III 453

Acts of
Assembly
1715

The revisal
of 1715

C. R., II,
217

dently of any action on the part of the governor and council; although the right to alter the time and place of meeting was allowed to the Palatine's Court; and the powers vested in the Lords Proprietors by the Crown were not denied.

At that time, Bath County was divided into three precincts, now named Beaufort, Hyde* and Craven. The inhabitants of Craven Precinct were to vote at Swift's plantation, at the mouth of Hancock Creek, while those of the town of New Bern were to vote in that town; the inhabitants of Beaufort were to meet at Bath Town, and those of Hyde at Websterson's plantation on the west side of Matchapungo River. The Albemarle precincts were to return five members; those of Bath County only two each. The inequality was doubtless because the new precincts were so sparsely settled. Under the original constitution, each of the precincts of Albemarle County was entitled to five members, but that provision was held not to apply to Bath County. The Assembly also provided for another issue of paper currency, elected a public treasurer, levied a tax to retire the currency, and arranged to pay its indebtedness to South Carolina. Also provision was made for the appointment of a register in each precinct to register deeds and record all births, deaths and marriages, as had long been the law and was required by the Constitutions. In fact, all the laws were revised and re-enacted at this session, and the common law of England was declared in force in North Carolina.

When the acts were submitted to the Lords Proprietors, they disapproved of the provision requiring the receiver of quit rents to receive the provincial bills for dues to the Proprietors, and they further informed the Assembly, "we have resolved that no more land shall be sold in the province, but only in England," and they reminded the Assembly that no act thereafter passed would be valid for a longer time than two years unless it received their approval.

In the fall of 1715 they appointed Christopher Gale chief justice, and he was sworn in January 24, 1716.

*The territory embracing Mattamuskeet Lake was attached to Currituck Precinct, and so remained until 1745, when it was annexed to Hyde.

The journals of the house contained several resolutions, as having been adopted, but which the governor and council declared had not been passed; the first was a declaration against impressments by the governor and council, as being a great infringement of the liberties of the people; another was in condemnation of the treatment of the Core Indians; another, in condemnation of those who refused to take the public bills as paper currency in payment of fees, was evidently aimed at some of the administrative officers. Not content with mere resolutions, the Assembly appointed a committee to represent the deplorable circumstances of the colony to the Lords Proprietors. Evidently the former factions were not entirely hushed. On the contrary, the differences springing from diverse interests now became the basis of two parties, one adhering to the officials who represented the Proprietors, and the other composed of those inhabitants who sought the general welfare, which may well be called the Popular party.

Nor was the governor antagonized by only the People's party. He had some enemies closer at hand. In the summer of 1717, Christopher Gale sailed for London, with the purpose, as alleged by Parson Urmstone, himself a very erratic character, of accomplishing Governor Eden's downfall, and with the hope of supplanting him. This none too pious missionary introduces us to both the parties without evincing much partiality. The complaints against the governor, he asserts, were not groundless: "His honor has acted toward all men very arbitrarily, not to say unjustly." He is declared "to be a strange, unaccountable man." But of Gale, the parson entertained no better opinion.

The result of Gale's mission, however, was not hurtful to Eden; on the contrary, at the same meeting of the Lords Proprietors at which Gale was reappointed chief justice, Eden was made a landgrave. But Gale, whether smarting from his disappointments, or for other reasons, did not return to Carolina for several years. And another affair occurred that stirred the colony and involved the administration.

1715
Partisan
disagree-
ments
C. R., II,
243, 244

C. R., II,
299

1718

Thack harbors in Pamlico Sound

Among the pirates who infested the Atlantic coast, having their rendezvous in the Bahamas, was Thack, or Thatch, or Teach, his name being written in several ways, familiarly known as "Blackbeard." One of his lieutenants was Major Steed Bonnett, a man of gentle birth and of education. These sometimes came into the sounds of North Carolina; and they had friends there, as in Virginia and South Carolina. But among the better class of people, there was indignation that pirates should be tolerated by the officers.

C. R., II, 320, 335

When the king offered pardon to all pirates who should surrender and reform, Thack availed himself of the terms and came in and promised to lead an honest life; but after a month he was again on the high seas. At length Captain Woodes Rogers, who had saved Alexander Selkirk from his desert island, was sent to break up the nest of pirates in the Bahamas. While he was successful in capturing many, Bonnett and Thack were not taken, and found a refuge in the inlets of North Carolina.

Shortly afterward Thack sailed from the Pamlico and soon returned with a cargo of oranges and other fruit, sugar and spices, taken from a French vessel, which he had captured on August 22d, near the Bermudas, and then burned off the coast of Carolina. Some of this plunder he stored

C. R., II, 325

in the barn of Tobias Knight, an Englishman who had come over with Eden and who was secretary of the colony; and in the absence of the chief justice, Gale, had been appointed to that high position. Information was sent by some of the inhabitants to Governor Spotswood, who, deeming himself clothed with authority, determined to capture the pirate.

Spotswood acts

There were two British men-of-war in the harbor; but there was so much sympathy for the pirates in Virginia, that Governor Spotswood would not hazard communicating his purpose even to any member of his council. Obtaining two sloops, and fitting them out secretly with men supplied from the men-of-war, he sent them under the command of Lieutenant Maynard in search of Thack's vessel, the *Adventure,*

Nov. 22, 1718

which on November 22, 1718, was discovered near Ocracoke Inlet. A desperate battle followed. Knowing the shoals of the sound, Thack had some advantage; but at last,

1718

hard pressed, the *Adventure* was stranded. As Maynard's sloop now approached the pirate ship, Thack poured into it a murderous broadside that swept off many of the crew. But Maynard, ordering his men below, steered directly for the *Adventure,* and as the vessels closed, Thack and his crew sprang upon the deck of the sloop and, animated by a desperate courage, hoped to take possession and make their escape. But Maynard's men rushed from below, and in the hand-to-hand encounter that ensued the pirates were overcome. The *Adventure* carried 8 cannon; and of the crew of 18 men, 9 besides Thack were killed outright, and 9, some desperately wounded, were taken prisoners; of the king's men, 12 were killed and 22 wounded. The prisoners who survived were taken to Virginia, tried and convicted of piracy.

C. R., II, 325

Upon the capture of Thack's vessel, Governor Spotswood sent Captain Brand of the British Navy to obtain the stolen merchandise. Colonel Maurice Moore and Jeremiah Vail accompanied him to Pamlico, and the goods were found, some being discovered in the barn of Tobias Knight. Immediately the governor and some of his council remonstrated at the action of Governor Spotswood, claiming that these proceedings were unlawful and improper. Separating Colonel Pollock and Governor Eden from Tobias Knight, it appears that the governor regarded that it was an invasion of his government for Governor Spotswood to send a force into North Carolina waters even for the purpose of capturing a pirate; and he keenly felt and warmly remonstrated against Captain Brand's taking possession of the sugars and removing them to Virginia, to be disposed of by the court of admiralty. Colonel Pollock doubted the strict legality of Governor Spotswood's action, but advised Governor Eden to make no point about it. While the council stood by Knight, Eden's action is hardly consistent with innocence as to the alleged complicity with the pirate, and he certainly did not give expression to any great satisfaction at Thack's destruction. Still if Eden had any association with Thack, it was less open and notorious than the bearing of some of the governors of other colonies toward the pirates.

Complicity of Knight

C. R., II, 319

C. R., II, 341, 346, 349

The public records according to the instructions of the

1718
Moseley and
Moore
search the
records
Lords Proprietors were to be open to public inspection; but in the absence of any public buildings, they were kept in rooms of private houses. The records of the secretary's office were deposited in a private house at Sandy Point, near Edenton; and Maurice Moore and Edward Moseley, being determined to search the records for incriminating evidence regarding improper dealings between the authorities and Thack, on December 27th broke into that room, barred the door and proceeded to make an investigation. For this alleged trespass and misdemeanor, the governor issued a warrant for their arrest, and sent a considerable body of men to apprehend them. Indignant at such a posse being sent to take him, Moseley exclaimed that "the governor could find men enough to arrest peaceable citizens, but none to arrest thieves and robbers." The intimation was plain, that the governor was willing to shield the pirate, and the allegation was *scandalum magnatum*. Moseley and Moore were bound over to court, and an indictment followed as a matter of course. At the trial of the pirates before the admiralty court in Virginia, the evidence implicated Tobias Knight as being in complicity with Thack, and a copy of the testimony was sent by Governor Spotswood to Governor Eden. At a meeting of the council, about the opening of April, this testimony was considered and an order was passed to serve a copy of it on Knight, who was not in attendance. At the next meeting in May, Knight filed a statement in explanation. While making sweeping denials, alleging that he was pursued "by Moore and Vail and that family," he declared that he had not sought to conceal the fact that the sugars were stored on his premises; and he alleged that they were lodged there at the request of Thack only until a more convenient store could be procured by the governor for the whole cargo. This apparently connected the governor with the transaction, and would necessarily involve him if Knight were found implicated in any illicit dealings regarding these goods. The governor himself made no particular explanation, but the result of the investigation could not be doubtful.

C. R., II,
344

The council hastened to declare that Knight was not guilty, and ought to be acquitted of the crimes laid to his

1718
The council
exonerates
Knight, but
he resigns
and dies

charge. Still of Knight's complicity there is no question, while his explanation that seemed to involve Governor Eden may well be entirely disregarded. The circumstances are inconsistent with his innocence. Thack, being a notorious pirate, had accepted the king's offer of pardon; had then returned to his trade; had again surrendered and made application for a second pardon; and while the application was still pending, he had sallied out with his vessel armed with eight cannon and manned by a crew of desperadoes, and having taken a French merchantman and transferred the cargo to his own ship, had burned his prize off the North Carolina coast; and then coming in, devised the story not likely to impose on the credulity of any one, that he had found a wreck on the high seas and had saved the cargo. A part of his stores was conveyed at the dead of night to the barn of the chief justice of the colony and concealed beneath the fodder. When Knight was first questioned by Captain Brand, he positively denied that any such goods had been concealed on his premises. The denial being ignored and he being informed that a memorandum found on the person of the dead pirate attested the facts, he reluctantly made the admission. Also in Thack's possession was discovered a letter from Knight of recent date, beginning, "My friend," and containing friendly advice, in itself being full proof of the intimate connection and guilty association. Against these facts, the exoneration by the governor and council carried no weight. Knight resigned as chief justice, Colonel Frederick Jones becoming his successor, and then he died before the summer had ended. Such was the termination of the career of that English adventurer, who, like many others sent over by the Proprietors to hold important office, sought to win fortune at the expense of honor and character, and was utterly indifferent to the good fame and material welfare of the inhabitants of the province. He was doubtless quite right in ascribing to the Swann and Lillington connection a purpose to uncover his nefarious dealings. The gentlemen of that family had a patriotic interest in removing from their settlement the reproach of harboring pirates, as their action in searching the records sufficiently indicates.

For their offences Moore and Moseley were tried at the

C. R., II,
344

1719
C. R., II,
366, 368
general court in October, 1719. To the indictment for break--
ing into the secretary's office, they with Thomas Luten and
Henry Clayton pleaded guilty; and a fine of £5 was imposed
on Moore, and of five shillings on Moseley. But the case
against Moseley, for his scandalous words, was regarded as
more serious. The jury rendered a special verdict—that
Moseley had uttered the words, and "if the law be for the
king, then he was guilty." After several days' delay, the
court ruled that he was guilty; and it being considered that
his action was in the nature of stirring up sedition, he was
sentenced to pay a fine of £100, and to be incapable of holding

C. R., II,
368
any office or place of trust in the colony for three years. His
practice, however, was large and important, and as he was
silenced as a lawyer, the business of the court was so impeded
that the chief justice, Jones, requested that his disabilities
as an attorney might be removed; and in view of the allegation that he had intended to raise sedition, perhaps also because of the recent revolution in South Carolina, Moseley was
led to state, in a petition to the council, that his words were
not uttered with such a sinister design, but only through
heat and passion; and he asked to be relieved of the sentence. But the governor, perhaps, felt that there was too
much truth in what Moseley had so bluntly alleged for the
offence to be forgiven, and the only concession he made was
that Moseley might bring to an end such litigation as had
been committed to him before the sentence was imposed, but
should take no new cases. So for three years the leader of
the Popular party and the most influential citizen of the
province was excluded from all public employment and forbidden to practise law.

Revolution in South Carolina

While these matters were in progress in North Carolina,
the condition in South Carolina had become so intolerable
under the inefficient government of the Lords Proprietors,
that the people having determined on a revolution, following
the methods practised in England, formed an association to
stand by each other; and the Assembly which convened on
November 28, 1719, resolved itself into a convention, and
threw off the authority of the Lords Proprietors, offering the

administration to Governor Johnson, who had succeeded
Craven, if he would continue to act as governor and hold the
province for the king. This Governor Johnson properly refused to do, and the people then elected James Moore governor, and applied to the king to receive South Carolina as
a royal province.

A revolution so complete and successful cast dismay
among the Proprietors and their officers in North Carolina,
and raised anew in England the question of the Crown's
resuming possession of the entire territory of Carolina. It
also led to the consideration of the dividing line between
the two governments.

The South Carolina authorities claimed the Cape Fear River
as a boundary, and asserted that their government had issued
grants for land on that river; but in the earlier days the
Santee had been the northern limit of South Carolina, and
more lately, after Clarendon County had ceased to exist, the
territory north and east of Cape Fear was assigned to the
North Carolina government. As there were no settlements
in the Cape Fear region, the question had not been of importance, and before the boundary was marked North Carolina had occupied the southern bank of the Cape Fear River
as a portion of Bath County.

Conditions in North Carolina

As painful and devastating as the Indian war had been,
its sacrifices were not without compensation. Although the
trade in furs largely ceased the colony received a greater
benefit from quieting all apprehensions of Indian outbreaks.
The savages being suppressed, the extension of the plantations proceeded without interruption and population continued to flow in, the settlements progressing to the southward as well as to the westward along the navigable streams.

In January, 1670, the Assembly had passed an act restricting grants of land in any one survey to six hundred and sixty
acres in order to remedy the evil of large tracts or plantations being insufficiently cultivated; and the Proprietors
in 1694 had authorized Governor Archdale to sell land in
Albemarle in fee for what he could reasonably obtain for it;
however, not under £10 for a thousand acres, and reserving
an annual rent of not less than five shillings to a thousand

Land
patents

acres. Later the Proprietors, understanding that advantage was being taken of them by the issue of patents for thousands of acres in a body which was not seated, but thus withdrawn from other purchasers while yielding no rents, in their instructions to Governor Hyde forbade the issue of any patents whatsoever. They also forbade the survey of any lands within twenty miles of the Cape Fear River. In January, 1712, however, at Governor Hyde's instance, they modified these directions so that he was allowed to issue patents not to exceed six hundred and forty acres in a body, requiring a cash payment of twenty shillings for every hundred acres, and an annual rent of one shilling sterling money of Great Britain per acre. These terms necessarily applied only to the lands in Bath, for those in Albemarle were held under the Great Deed. The council represented in 1718 that these orders relating to the sale of land imposing such hard terms were inconsistent with the settlement of the province, and it unavailingly asked that they might be revoked. At that time there were about one million acres held subject to quit rents, and there were about two thousand tithables in the colony; and despite the orders, the people were spreading out in Craven and up the Neuse and along the Roanoke. Indeed, the province was making rapid strides in importance when, in March, 1722, Governor Eden died.

Eden dies
March, 1722

Colonel
Pollock
president

So far as the internal affairs of the colony were concerned, during the latter years of Eden's administration at least, the people enjoyed a period of repose. Except for the irritation that may have incidentally grown out of its attitude toward Moseley, his administration was apparently quiet and pleasant, although the desultory depredations of the Indians added somewhat to the cares of his official life. On his death, Colonel Pollock was again chosen president; but that valuable citizen, who for twenty years had been one of the most prominent and influential, as he was doubtless the richest, of the inhabitants, did not long survive this last accession of power. In all the contests that had divided the people he had taken sides against the party to which Moseley adhered. When the latter stood for popular rights, Pollock threw his influence toward maintaining the authority

His death,
August 30,
1722, and
character

of the administrative officers; but of his sterling worth, ability and character there is no question.

1722

On his death, toward the last of August, he was succeeded by William Reed, who was in no wise comparable to him, either in social position or in respectability of character.

William Reed succeeds him

Chief Justice Gale, after an absence of nearly four years, returned to the province just as Governor Eden expired, and resumed his official functions, and he also took his seat at the council board as a deputy of James Bertie, one of the Lords Proprietors.

A hamlet had sprung up on Queen Anne's Creek and Governor Eden had made his residence there, and the council and general court met at that place. It was now incorporated as a town under the name of Edenton, and became the established seat of government. An Assembly was held here in October, 1722. The previous Assembly was presided over by William Swann, but Moseley's disabilities having now expired by the passage of three years, he was chosen speaker of the new body. Among its acts was one establishing seats of government in the several precincts and settling the courts and court-houses. And because the territory west of the Chowan had become so populous, a new precinct was laid off in that territory named Bertie, doubtless in compliment of the Proprietor.

Edenton

S.R., XXIII, 102

Bertie Precinct

In August, 1722, the council had established Carteret Precinct, extending southward indefinitely to the bounds of the government, including all the settlements in that direction; and the town of Beaufort was incorporated into a seaport, entitled to a collector of customs; and a road was directed to be opened from Core Point to New Bern. The growth of the province had been retarded for the want of commercial facilities, and to improve navigation an act was passed to encourage a settlement at Ocracoke Inlet, because of the good anchorage and harbor there.

Carteret Precinct C. R., II, 458, 459

Another act had for its object to discourage the influx of official adventurers by prescribing a qualification for officers that would exclude such persons as any new governor might bring over as satellites in his train; it prohibited the governor from granting any office to any British subject who had not resided three years in the province.

Official adventurers discouraged

CHAPTER XVII

Administrations of Burrington and Everard, 1724-31

Governor Burrington explores the Cape Fear.—Opposition to him.
—Burrington displaced.—Sir Richard Everard.—Antagonism be-
tween Assembly and governor.—Altercations of Burrington and the
governor.—The ministers.—The settlement of the Cape Fear.—The
Assembly sustains Burrington.—He appeals to the Proprietors.—
Personal controversies.—The dividing line with Virginia.—Purchase
by the Crown.—Carteret retains his share.—Everard breaks with
Gale.—The lords of trade.—The currency act.—The end of the
Proprietary government.—Conditions in North Carolina.—No public
schools.—Few ministers.—The Baptists.—Industries.—Population.—
Social conditions.

Governor Burrington

1724

To fill the vacancy caused by the death of Eden the Lords
Proprietors proposed to appoint George Burrington, of
Devon, governor of North Carolina, and on February 26,
1723, the king gave his assent; but it was not until the
succeeding January that Burrington reached Edenton and

Jan., 1724

took the oaths of office. The new governor had held office
under the Crown in every reign since the revolution of
1688, and must have had considerable official experience.
He was a man of violent temper, firm and resolute, and one
who could brook no opposition. Thomas Jones, a son of
Chief Justice Jones, had intermarried with Miss Swann, the
stepdaughter of Moore, and had thus connected his father
with the Moseley and Moore faction; while by the death of
Colonel Pollock Chief Justice Gale was left the most respectable and influential member of the opposition. On Burrington's arrival he not unnaturally allied himself with the
dominant party, that contained not merely the numerical
majority controlling the Assembly, but almost all the influential men in the province. Moseley himself was now of
the council,* and the power of the administration was with

*To fill a vacancy in the council, the other councillors could
temporarily elect.

his friends. The Assembly met three months later and formally begged that the instructions of the Lords Proprietors
prohibiting the sale of lands in Bath might be disregarded
until an address could be sent to them in England. It was
asserted that, the land office being closed, persons coming
into the colony to locate could obtain no grants and were
forced to go elsewhere, and that the welfare of the province
demanded a change in regard to these matters. Burrington
entered heartily into the measure. There was a particular
prohibition against making any grant on the Cape Fear
River, but he obtained by purchase an old patent issued by
Governor Hyde in 1711 to Thomas Harvey, calling for five
thousand acres, and he determined to locate it on that river.
There were other such patents for lands bearing that date
eventually located on the Cape Fear, but whether they were
issued pursuant to a purpose to make a settlement in that
region at that time, or whether they were issued in blank
and originally intended for a different locality, is a question
not now possible to determine. With a view to opening up
that region to settlers, Burrington undertook to make a
thorough exploration of it. He visited it in person, and
underwent much hardship, privation, exposure and danger
in exploring its streams, its swamps and wildernesses. If
he was not persuaded to this resolution by Maurice Moore,
he was at least seconded and encouraged in it by him.

Moore, who had traversed that country in going to the
aid of South Carolina in 1716, determined to form a colony
and settle there, and to this end he interested his brothers
and friends in South Carolina and his family connections
in Albemarle and Bath counties, who agreed to join him in
making a new settlement.

But while these matters were in progress, Burrington's
unfortunate temper threw him into personal antagonism
with the chief justice and other officials. In addition to
his salary as governor, the Lords Proprietors had granted
him and two associates a lease of the exclusive right of the
whale fisheries along the coast; and whether from some
incident springing from that lease or from some dereliction
of duty on the part of the naval officer at the port of Roanoke, and of the collector of customs, the governor in the

1724
C. R., II,
528

Explores the
Cape Fear
C.R., II, 569

C. R., III,
502

C. R., II,
569

Opposition
to
Burrington

1724
C. R., II,
561

summer of 1724 threatened violence to one and imprisonment to the other. Chief Justice Gale, who was also a collector of a port, sustained his brother officials, and toward the chief justice Burrington was abusive and violent, Gale even declaring that the governor had come to his residence at night and threatened to kill him and to burn his house over his head. Burrington had been affable to the people and had so ingratiated himself that he was popular among the rich as well as the poor; and now the assemblymen stood by him, while the councillors generally supported Gale. The chief justice speedily left the colony and sailed for England, bearing a representation, signed by seven of the council, complaining of the governor's violence and arbitrary conduct.

C. R., II, 559

Everard
appointed
governor
Jan., 1725

Arriving at London, Gale hastened to inform the commissioners of customs, under whom he held his office as collector of the port at Beaufort, of the illegal action of Burrington, and declared that, believing his life in danger, he had been obliged to flee from the province, and that he could not return but at the hazard of his life. In addition, Gale appears to have impressed the Lords Proprietors with the belief that Burrington was preparing to lead a revolution, as James Moore had done in South Carolina, and throw off the authority of the Proprietors. Evidence of this, according to his enemies, was afforded by his association with Maurice Moore, his visits to South Carolina, his appointment of Moseley to administer the government during his temporary absence, his arrangement for the settlement of the Cape Fear, notwithstanding the prohibition of the Proprietors, and his courting popularity among the people and his friendly alliance with the leading inhabitants. In this mission Gale was more successful than in his alleged attempt to overthrow Eden. The fears of the Proprietors were at once aroused, and apprehending that they might lose their province either through revolution or by the king taking possession because of the illegal conduct of their governor, in haste they appointed Sir Richard Everard to supplant Burrington, and in July, 1725, Everard reached Edenton and took the oaths of office. Gale accompanied the new governor, who not unnaturally looked to him for

C. R., II, 562

Everard
reaches
Edenton,
July, 1725

advice and counsel, and being a weak man, fell entirely under his influence.

According to the biennial act, an Assembly was to be elected in September, and as the time approached, Burrington became very active in managing to secure the election of members who were friendly to him. He visited all the precincts and stirred his friends to zeal and activity. By law the Assembly was to meet in November, but Gale advising that there was no need for an Assembly at that time, the governor in October issued a proclamation proroguing it until April. On the other hand, it was declared that under the fundamental constitution of the province the governor had no power to postpone the meeting of the Assembly, and, in disregard of the proclamation, the members convened at Edenton on the day fixed by law, Burrington being a member, and the body chose Moore as speaker.

The Assembly was entirely in sympathy with the deposed governor, and having resolved that the prorogation was an infringement of their liberties and a breach of the privileges of the people, they declared that at their next meeting they would proceed to no business until their lawful privileges were confirmed. The governor and council refused to recognize that the house was in session, but nevertheless, the house adjourned from day to day, and the next day adopted an address to the Lords Proprietors in which they represented that the great happiness which the province had enjoyed under the administration of Burrington had been "much disturbed by the unexpected change made through many false and malicious calumnies raised against that gentleman by persons of the most vile character and desperate fortunes"; and they solemnly denied that there was any disposition or design on the part of Burrington or any one else to cause such a revolution as had taken place in South Carolina; and they represented that great evils were apprehended from the vile administration which the province was threatened with from a governor "entirely influenced by a few persons of the most irreligious and immoral character."

Antagonism between Assembly and governor Nov., 1725

C. R., II, 577

C. R., II, 577, 578

Having given expression to these sentiments, the house adjourned to the first Tuesday in April, the day set by the

1725

governor for its meeting. Burrington, strengthened by the support the house gave him, felt no restraint in making evident his contempt for Everard. Announcing that in nine months he would be restored to the office of governor, he promised places to his friends who had been dismissed by the new administration, and he carried himself very defiantly toward the governor, in utter disregard of law and order.

C. R., II, 648

Proclaiming that Sir Richard was an ape, a noodle, and no more fit to be a governor than Sancho Panza, he sought to disparage him with the people, and going to Sir Richard's residence at Edenton in the night, he called him out and threatened him and abused him with great opprobrium.

Altercations of Burrington and the governor C. R., II, 651

In one of these violent demonstrations, a night attack on the governor's house, he was accompanied, among others, by Cornelius Harnett, an Irishman who had recently come into the colony with several thousand pounds' worth of merchandise and had established himself as a merchant. Indeed, on the night of December 2, 1725, after their assault on the governor, they broke open the doors of the house of the constable and beat that officer furiously; and James Potter coming to his neighbor's aid, they violently assaulted him; and then forcing the door of Thomas Panis's residence, they assaulted him and drove his family out of the house. The governor himself was disorderly, but not quite so violent in his demonstrations as Burrington. But together they caused about Edenton a discreditable uproar, and the greater part of the province was more or less interested in their bitter antagonism, Gale's friends in the council gathering around Everard, while the assemblymen were of Burrington's faction. Even the only two ministers in the province took different sides. Rev. Mr. Bailey, a missionary, was of the Burrington faction, and received no courtesy but hard usage from Everard; while Rev. Mr. Blacknall, who had come over with the new governor, and sided with him, was

The ministers, C. R., II, 604

represented by Sir Richard to the Bishop of London as a very good preacher, a gentleman, perfectly sober, and beloved by all but Mr. Burrington's party. This Mr. Blacknall, who was of a highly respectable connection in England, perhaps in ignorance of the provincial law, was led soon after his arrival to perform the marriage service between a white man and a mulatto woman. On the same day, perhaps ascertaining that he had committed an offence, he went before the chief justice and made an affidavit of the fact. Being subject by law to a penalty, one-half of which was for the use of the informer, he claimed his half, which lessened his fine to that extent. Doubtless he erred through ignorance. There was nothing to his personal advantage in his delinquency, and he lost no time in acknowledging his violation of the law and in evoking its operation. But he did not remain long in the province, soon going to Maryland.

This factional disturbance in Albemarle perhaps rather hastened than delayed the settlement of the Cape Fear. Bath County extended from Albemarle Sound down to the undefined southern limits of the province; and when Carteret Precinct was established it included the entire unsettled region, embracing the Cape Fear and down to the South Carolina line. The first known grant in that wilderness was issued to Maurice Moore on June 3, 1725, for fifteen hundred acres on the west bank of the river, sixteen miles below the present town of Wilmington, where he laid out a town which he called Brunswick, in honor of the reigning house, and invited settlers to locate there. His brothers, Roger* and Nathaniel, and other friends came from South Carolina, and Maurice Moore and a large part of the Lillington connection also prepared to remove from Albemarle. The former took up lands on the lower Cape Fear, while the Albemarle contingent located their grants on the northeast branch, where Burrington also took his five thousand acres, by grant dated June 25, 1725;† and other accessions being made, at last there was reason to hope that the advantage of a good port and harbor would be obtained for the province.

At the March term of the court Burrington and Harnett

The settlement of the Cape Fear

Carteret Co Records

Stag Park

---

*Roger Moore, because of his wealth and large number of slaves, was called "King Roger." There is a tradition on the Cape Fear that he and his slaves had a battle with the Indians at the "Sugar Loaf," nearly opposite the town of Brunswick. Governor Tryon, forty years later, mentioned that the last battle with the Indians was when driving them from the Cape Fear in 1725. The tradition would seem to be well founded.

†Some of the names bestowed on localities by Hilton in 1663 are yet retained: Stag Park, Rocky Point, etc.

1726
C. R., II,
698

April, 1726

C. R., II,
608

C R , II,619

were indicted for their violent trespasses and assaults, and the latter left Albemarle, and going to the Cape Fear, conducted a ferry across the river at the new town of Brunswick, which at the March term of the general court at Edenton in 1727 was duly established and legalized. Burrington was in his seat as a member of the Assembly which met pursuant to the prorogation on April 1st. That body remained steadfast to his interests and manfully stood by him, notwithstanding his disorderly conduct. John Baptista Ashe, with whom Burrington had established very cordial relations, having been acquainted with several members of his family in England, was, in the absence of Moore, chosen speaker, and he strongly supported the ex-governor. Sir Richard opened the proceedings with an address appealing for love and charity, and that all breaches should be healed, that the country should flourish and all be happy.

The house met this tender of the olive branch with a resolution that all its debates should be secret, and that any member who should disclose the purport of any debate should be expelled. After a week's delay an answer was adopted to the governor's address, detailing at large the alleged grievances of the people, and aimed at the administrative and court officers, who were denounced as vile and base characters; and they called on the governor to heal the breaches by bringing them to punishment. The governor was, however, reported to be dangerously ill, and the address could not be presented. The house next delivered an address to Burrington, full of compliments, and thanking him for his many services and the advantages received under his mild administration; and then an address to the Lords Proprietors was adopted, declaring that they would esteem it one of the greatest favors if the Proprietors would restore Burrington to the office of governor. Called to the governor's dwelling, because he was too ill to attend at the council chamber, the house presented its address and asked for an answer to their grievances; but instead of a reply, the secretary announced that the governor and council had agreed on a prorogation, and the governor verbally pronounced a prorogation, which the house on its return to its chamber declared illegal; but nevertheless, it adjourned to the day appointed. Burrington forwarded the resolutions in his favor to the Lords Proprietors, and addressed to them a memorial relative to his administration. He mentioned that because of mighty storms in August before his arrival the crops had been destroyed and there was almost a famine, yet a thousand families came to live in the province during his administration, and more would have come had not provisions been so scarce; that he had reorganized the militia; and finding that the magistrates were of no respectability, he had prevailed on Colonel Moseley, Colonel Harvey, Colonel Swann, Colonel Maule and other gentlemen to preside over the precinct courts, which had borne excellent fruits in establishing the courts in the confidence and respect of the people; that he had purposed being of use to Governor Everard, and he took occasion to warn him against the advice of Gale, Lovick, and Little, but unavailingly; that great improvements had been effected through his own efforts, and that he had remained in Carolina expecting to learn from them the nature of the complaints against him, but was still in ignorance; and that he would take the first opportunity to clear his character, if sullied.

In the meantime the prosecutions against him were continued on the docket, no particular efforts being made to arrest him and bring him to trial. He did not leave the province, but established himself on the Cape Fear, at Governor's Creek, five miles below Brunswick, where he remained until 1728. Yet he was quiet. Edmund Porter, who had recently returned to Carolina after an absence of some ten years, was almost as violent toward the officers as the deposed governor had been, and there was generally in progress a sharp controversy between some private person and either the governor or the chief justice or the attorney-general, apparently of a personal nature; but in the course of the proceedings they were made to bear the character of sedition and rebellion. In this remote and sparsely settled country doubtless the officers frequently acted arbitrarily, while occasionally some citizen, not sufficiently respecting the government, manifested a spirit of excessive freedom and independence and was guilty of disorderly offences.

1726

Burrington appeals to the Proprietors

C.R., III, 28

Personal controversies

1728

C. R., II, 733

The dividing line

After years of delay, in 1728 the dividing line between Virginia and Carolina was established. Governor Eden and Governor Spotswood had agreed on a compromise of the vexed questions involved, which had been accepted by the authorities in England, but the king delayed authorizing the actual survey to be made, so the matter lay in abeyance until, in 1727, the governor of Virginia informed Sir Richard that he had received instructions to appoint surveyors on the part of the Crown. The line was to run from the north shore of Currituck Inlet due west to the Chowan; if it struck the Chowan between the mouths of Nottoway and Wiccons Creek it was to continue west to the mountains. But if it struck to the south of Wiccons Creek it was to follow the Chowan to that creek and then due west; and if that line struck the Blackwater River to the northward of Nottoway River it was to come down the Blackwater to the Nottoway and then west to the mountains. On the part of North Carolina, Christopher Gale, John Smith, Edward Moseley, and William Little were appointed the commissioners, and William Byrd, Richard Fitzwilliam, and W. Dandridge were to act for Virginia, representing the interest of the Crown. On March 7th a cedar post was fixed on the seashore as the beginning of the line. Four days later they struck the land "formerly belonging to Governor Gibbs," now to Mr. Bladen, one of the Lords of Trade, which was found to lie in North Carolina. The line cut the Blackwater above the mouth of the Nottoway, and so the surveyors followed the stream down to the point, the report saying that the former Virginia commissioners had been in error twenty-one and one-half miles. So there were thrown into Carolina a great quantity of land and many families that had formerly been claimed by Virginia, computed at a hundred thousand acres of land and three hundred tithables. It is also noted that when the surveyors struck Dismal Swamp the Virginia surveyors went around it, but the North Carolina surveyors boldly essayed the attempt and passed through it. The first one to come out on the west side was young Sam Swann, a nephew of Moseley, whose vigor, energy and learning subsequently

1728

Swann passes the Dismal Swamp. C. R., II, 755

1728

led to his taking a prominent part in the affairs of the colony. On April 5th the commissioners suspended the work, which was resumed on September 25th, and a week later the Roanoke was reached.

On October 6th, when Hycootte Creek was reached, one hundred and sixty-eight miles from the inlet and forty-five miles west of the Roanoke River, the North Carolina commissioners resolved that they had gone far enough for the present, it being fifty miles beyond any inhabitants. The Virginia surveyors, however, preferred going on, and ran the line about seventy-two miles farther west, being altogether a distance of two hundred and forty-one miles from the sea, reaching the hills of the present county of Stokes.

C. R., II,776

C. R., II, 815

Purchase by the Crown

There had been some movement looking to the purchase of the Carolinas by the Crown, which perhaps was interrupted by the sudden death of the king in 1727, but in January, 1728, a number of the Lords Proprietors united in a memorial offering to surrender their interests; and an agreement for the surrender being reached, an act of Parliament was prepared authorizing and establishing the agreement, and the conveyance was made. At that time the eight shares were held and owned by the following Proprietors: That of Clarendon by James Bertie; that of Albemarle by the Duke of Beaufort; that of Craven by Lord Craven; that of Colleton by Sir John Colleton; that of Carteret by Lord John Carteret; that of Ashley by a minor, John Cotton; that of Sir John Berkeley by Joseph Blake; and that of Sir William Berkeley by Mary Dawson, widow of John Dawson, or Elizabeth Moore or Henry Bertie, there being a legal controversy to determine their rights.

C. R., III,; The last Proprietors

All joined in the conveyance except Lord John Carteret, who was at that time lieutenant-general and governor of the Kingdom of Ireland, and his share was reserved to him.

By the agreement, each of the seven shares was to be purchased at the price of £2,500, being £17,500 in all; and the payment was to be made and the conveyance executed in June, 1729. There was, however, a considerable amount

Sale completed, June, 1729

1728
Carteret
retains
his share
of quit rents due to the Proprietors, and to satisfy their claim for rents the king allowed them an additional sum of £5,000.

Everard
breaks with
Gale

C. R., III, 2
Notice of the proposed sale was, in December, 1728, conveyed to the governor and council, and the council addressed a memorial to the king manifesting their happiness in the transfer of the province to the protection of the Crown, and then they continued: "That it was with the greatest sorrow that they felt obliged to make remonstrance against the character of Sir Richard Everard, whose incapacity, weakness, disregard of law, wickedness, and violence" they proceeded to set out with great particularity.

C. R., III, 5
On the other hand, some three weeks later Sir Richard published a declaration to convince mankind, and in particular the inhabitants of the province, that all the unhappy misunderstandings and dissensions between him and the Assembly and other gentlemen of good note were owing to the calumnies and false information given him by Chief Justice Gale, John Lovick and William Little, who he declared were the only enemies to the repose and quiet of the people.

The Lords
of Trade
Burrington appears to have been at that time at his plantation on the Cape Fear, but he soon departed for London. There, in August, he had the satisfaction of presenting to the authorities this declaration of Sir Richard's, which was a tardy vindication of his own character from the former C. R., III,63 representations of both Gale and the governor. The Board of Trade, to whom was committed the affairs of the colony, now had before them the statement of the council reflecting on Everard and the proclamation of Everard denouncing Gale and Little; while another paper was received by them, ostensibly the remonstrance of the inhabitants of North Carolina against the appointment of Burrington as governor. In the meanwhile, the administration of the province was not interfered with, and Everard, Gale and their associates remained in undisturbed possession of their respective offices.

The
currency act
C. R., III,
145
After the execution of the deed transferring the province, and probably with information of it, but before official notification, at its session of 1729 the Assembly passed a very

important act relating to the currency, making Sir Richard a present of £500 in consideration of his assenting to it. Dr. Hawks, with a copy of the act before him, says that it was passed in 1727, and was to go into effect in 1728; but in that he was mistaken: perhaps such a bill was prepared for the Assembly of 1727, and the copy he saw was a bill drawn up two years before it was enacted into a law.

By that act five commissioners were appointed to prepare and issue bills to the amount of £40,000. One-fourth was to be delivered to the treasurer to redeem the old bills, which if not redeemed were to become valueless within a fixed time. A treasurer was appointed for each precinct, and the residue of the bills was to be apportioned among the precincts according to their several needs and lent out by the precinct treasurers to citizens on mortgages of unencumbered real estate of twice the value of the loan. The loans were to be repaid in fifteen years, one-fifteenth and the interest being paid each year, the rate of interest being 6¼ per cent. The loan feature of the act had been in use in South Carolina and in other colonies and had proved a beneficent governmental operation, and doubtless was of much advantage to the people of North Carolina. While it was provided that twenty shillings of the bills were to be held as being worth fifteen pennyworth of silver as current in Virginia, yet as they might alter in value, it was provided that each succeeding legislature should periodically revise this arrangement and declare the value in silver of twenty shillings in bills according to the then situation. Contracts specifically made to be paid in sterling money or in gold and silver were not at all affected by this act.

This law took effect, and there being about £10,000 of the former issue of bills outstanding, they were retired; and the currency of the province was this new paper money when the king's officers came into authority, and so continued for many years, for although the validity of the act was questioned, it was never repealed.

The end of the proprietary government had now come, and with it passed away the distinctive features of administration founded on the Fundamental Constitutions. Until then the office of Palatine had survived, and landgraves and caciques—the orders of Carolina nobility. With the end of the proprietary system these all necessarily fell. But other than that the transfer to the Crown worked but little change in the general system of government.

Influence of the transfer

For two-thirds of a century the colony had been under the general management of the Proprietors; but left largely to itself, it had developed on its own lines. The grant to Charles's courtiers of an immense territory in the wilds of an unsettled continent could not have been expected to bring them speedy fortune. It entailed some considerable outlay at first, and the development being slow, no riches had been amassed at the expense of the settlers. Still, one-eighth of Carolina was a noble patrimony, and had the Proprietors been able to retain their shares for another generation, and had acceptable agents to represent their interests after population had thickened, they would have enjoyed a princely inheritance.

Conditions in North Carolina

Growth slow

Naturally the growth of North Carolina had been particularly slow. The situation was much less favorable than in the settlements to the north, or even in South Carolina. To the first plantations, situated on Albemarle Sound, access was difficult and dangerous. Roanoke Inlet was not only shallow, but beset with treacherous and shifting shoals; and Ocracoke, though bolder, was not well known, while the storms of Hatteras were a perpetual menace to adventurous merchantmen. The absence of a good port and harbor tended to stifle the growth of the colony, while more favored and attractive localities drew elsewhere the enterprising emigrants from Europe who sought new homes in America.

Education

Life was easy and pleasant, but the population was so sparsely seated that social advantages and the benefits that attend the gathering together of many families into a compact community were deplorably lacking. There were no public schools. There were doubtless some schools and also some tutors employed on the plantations, but no academies for the improvement of the young had been established in the colony. But notwithstanding the absence of schools, education was not entirely neglected. A will of that period con-

1729

tains this direction: "I will that my slaves be kept at work on my lands, that my estate may be managed to the best advantage, so as my sons may have as liberal an education as the profits thereof will afford. And in their education I pray my executors to observe this method: Let them be taught to read and write, and be introduced into the practical part of arithmetic, not too hastily hurrying them to Latin or grammar; but after they are pretty well versed in these, let them be taught Latin and Greek. I propose this may be done in Virginia, after which let them learn French. Perhaps some Frenchman at Santee will undertake this. When they are arrived to years of discretion let them study the mathematics. I will that my daughter be taught to write and read and some feminine accomplishment which may render her agreeable, and that she be not kept ignorant as to what appertains to a good housewife in the management of household affairs."

Ashe's will, Off. Sec. State

There was but little organized religion among the inhabitants, except alone the Society of Friends. Efforts to build churches and engage pastors of the established Church of England had not been effective. There was generally a missionary or two in the vicinity of Edenton, but sometimes not one was resident in the whole province. An effort had been made to found a library at Bath, and Edward Moseley, whose liberal views had thrown him on the side of the Quakers in what was known as the "troublesome time" of 1708 to 1711, and who was ever among the foremost in patriotic works, had presented a well-selected library to be kept at Edenton, setting an excellent example of practical philanthropy, which, however, neither Pollock nor Eden nor Gale nor any of his wealthy antagonists was inclined to follow.

Few ministers

Libraries, C.R., II, 583

Dr. Brickell, writing in 1731, says: "The want of Protestant clergy is generally supplied by some schoolmaster, who reads the liturgy and then a sermon. Next to the Quakers the Presbyterians are the most numerous. They have had a minister of their own for many years, chiefly along the Neuse"; while still earlier there had been some independent preachers, who claimed neither holy orders nor affiliation

Denominations

1729

The
Baptists
N. C. Bapt.
Hist. Papers

C. R., III,
48

Industries

C. R., II, 241

Population
C. R., III,
433

Social
conditions

with any organized church. Mostly around Bath clustered the Roman Catholics, who had a clergyman of their own.

The first Baptist congregation was organized about the time when the proprietary rule was drawing to its close. "In 1727 the Baptists organized a single church, now known as Shiloh, in Camden County." Two years later Everard, writing to the Bishop of London, said that when he first came over, in 1725, there were no dissenters except Quakers in the government; but now Paul Palmer, the Baptist teacher, had gained hundreds; and he asserted that the Quakers and Baptists were then flourishing among the North Carolinians. He mentions that there was at that time not a single clergyman in the province, meaning of the Church of England, while the Quakers and Baptists were very busy making proselytes and holding meetings daily in every part of the government. There was no ground for any friction among the people on the score of religious differences.*

The industries were very limited. Besides farm work, there was some shipbuilding, for early in the settlement a colony from the Bermudas had begun that as an occupation, and it had been continued without interruption. Mention was made of a young man being brought from Virginia to be apprenticed in Albemarle to learn the shipbuilding trade, and Matthew Rowan came from Ireland to build a ship or two for some persons in Dublin. The building of ships was one of the established industries of the colony.

In the whole province there were in 1729 about 30,000 inhabitants; for four years later, in 1733, allowing for about 1000 immigrants coming in subsequent to his own arrival, Governor Burrington estimated the whites at 30,000, the negroes at 6000 and the Indians at 800.

With such a small population, many very poor and expending their energies in clearing fields and in building cabins for temporary abode, each family measurably dependent on its own labor and resources, as hired help must necessarily have been scarce, there could be but little expectation of those social conditions that are developed in a

---

*In 1729 an act was passed that apparently gave to the freeholders in each parish the right of electing the vestrymen.

ong-settled and concentrated community. But the colony was on the eve of a fuller development at the very time that the Proprietors conveyed their interest to the Crown. The opening of the Cape Fear River to settlement, giving a very fair port to the colony, was followed by a considerable immigration to that section, which soon became of greater importance commercially and industrially than the more northern portion of the province.

Dr. Brickell, in his "Natural History of North Carolina," written about 1731, mentions incidentally that New Bern has but few houses or inhabitants; Hancock Town, on the northwest branch of Neuse River, about two hundred miles from its mouth, formerly an Indian town, and where they had a fort in time of war; Beaufort is small and thinly inhabited; Brunswick has a great trade, a number of merchants and rich planters." Of the Indians he gives some account. Those that lived near the settlement numbered not over fifteen hundred or sixteen hundred, including women and children. There were three kings—King Blount, King Durant, King Highter. "They pay tribute once or twice a year. The women make the corn, the men hunt. They live in wigwams, except the civilized kings, who have houses. The Indians, being of several nations, have different customs. Some are civilized and are very serviceable to the planters, hunt and fowl for them, make weirs, assist in planting corn, etc. Many also speak English. There was formerly a nation called the Pasquotanks, who kept cattle and made butter, but at present none have cattle." He mentions that there were "no Muchapungoes or Coranines to be met with at this day, 1731. The Saponas live on the west branch of the Cape Fear; the Toteros are neighbors to them; the Keyawees live on a branch of the Cape Fear that lies to the northwest." He also states that "the Indians have a great aversion to the negroes, and kill them when they find them in the woods." He made an extended journey to the western part of North Carolina on an embassy to the Indians inhabiting there. Two or three years later Burrington mentioned that the smaller tribes, who had resided near the settlements, had entirely disappeared.

CHAPTER XVIII

Burrington's Second Administration, 1731-34

The Board of Trade.—The seal.—Everard's enemies.—Burrington appointed governor.—The province during the interim.—Burrington arrives.—Opposition to the royal instructions.—The first royal Assembly.—Matters of controversy.—Currency act declared void.—The quit rents.—Fees of officers.—The Assembly affronted.—The basis of political action.—Burrington's instructions.—He dispenses with the Assembly.—Appoints new councillors.—Schoolmasters.—The general court.—The governor erects new precincts.—His action disregarded.—New conflicts.—Burrington's arbitrary conduct —He is removed.—The second Assembly.—Chief Justice Little arraigned.—The governor addresses the house.—The third Assembly.—Burrington attempts to vindicate himself.—He rules without council or Assembly.—The difficulties of the situation.—Altered patents.—His opinion of the people.—Controversial documents.—His progressive action.—Dividing line between the Carolinas.—Landgrave Smith's grant.—Questions settled and unsettled.—The province grows.—Religious conditions.—The last Assembly to meet Burrington.—No act passed during his administration.

The Board of Trade

1729

South Carolina had been a royal province several years when, upon the transfer of seven of the proprietary shares of Carolina to the king, the administration of public affairs in North Carolina was likewise assumed by the Crown. The management of the province now fell to the care of the commissioners for trade and plantations, a board of the Privy Council restored, after a lapse of twenty years, in 1696, and at this time composed of the Earl of Westmoreland, P. Dominique, Thomas Pelham, Edward Ashe, Martin Bladen, W. Cary, Sir Oliver Bridgman, and Sir Thomas Frankland. To this board was committed the determination of all administrative questions relating to the colonies.

C. R., III,
20, 25

the governors being appointed on its recommendation by the king and council, and the chief officers, although designated by it, also being commissioned by the Crown.

The original seal of the county of Albemarle had been continued in use as the seal of North Carolina, while the Lords Proprietors had the great seal of their province of Carolina at London. This seal, adopted shortly after the royal grant was made, bore on one side of it a scroll, on which were sketched two well-filled cornucopias supported by two Indians, together with legends and heraldic ornamentation. Upon the transfer of dominion to the Crown, a new seal becoming necessary, the commissioners adopted one similar to that of the Lords Proprietors; the two figures and the cornucopias were preserved, but now the devices represented Liberty presenting Plenty to the king; and this seal, with some slight alterations, has continued to be the great seal of the State of North Carolina.

The seal
C. R., III,
79, 119

Notwithstanding the sale, Sir Richard Everard might have been retained as governor; but if there was a disposition to continue him in the administration his enemies succeeded in rendering it impossible. The contest between them was a bitter one. Everard, perhaps in view of the change, had broken with Gale and his son-in-law, William Little, and throwing himself into the arms of the popular party, had ascribed all of his delinquencies to the bad advice of those men, his former friends, whom he now denounced in unmeasured terms. They, on the other hand, hastened to make representations and prefer charges against him that destroyed the possibility of his retention. They alleged that he was a party to frauds in the issuing of land grants to the disadvantage of the king; that he was arbitrary, tyrannical and violent in his conduct; and, moreover, that he was disaffected toward the reigning house—that he had hailed the death of George I in 1727 with joy, declaring, "Now farewell to the house of Hanover"; and especially that he had been concerned in the Preston rebellion, the rising at Preston in favor of the Pretender in 1715. Before this last allegation was made public in the colony, Edmond Porter, who had returned to North Carolina in 1725 and was now judge of admiralty, was industrious in befriending

Everard's
enemies
C. R., III, 5

C. R., III,
2-4, 31

1729

Everard; and particularly he represented to the Secretar
of State, the Duke of Newcastle, that Everard, upon learn
ing of the purchase by the Crown, had given written order
that no more patents for land should be issued until new

C. R., III,
18, 49

instructions should be received; but that Lovick, the secre
tary, and Moseley, the surveyor, were disobedient and had
utterly disregarded the governor's positive orders. But
Porter himself had been accused of having participated in
the same rising, after he had fled from Albemarle on the
suppression of Cary's adherents, and when this charge was
made against the governor Porter quickly withdrew his
support. Indeed, as soon as Everard's loyalty was called
in question every friend fell away from him, and the charge
proved fatal to his hopes.

Burrington appointed governor

Burrington, who had continued to reside on his Cape
Fear plantations, now hastened to England to press his own
claim; and with all the documents with him, he was able
to clear himself of the defamatory allegations Gale and his
party had formerly made against him, and he succeeded

C. R., III,
66

in securing the prize. In the fall of 1729 it was decided
that he should be appointed governor, and the next Jan
uary his commission was signed; but his instructions were
not finally prepared until December, 1730, when he took his
departure for Carolina.

C. R., III,
85

Being directed to recommend officers, he desired that the
following persons should be of his council: James Jenoure
surveyor; Robert Halton, Edmond Porter, John Baptista
Ashe, Eleazar Allen, Matthew Rowan, Cornelius Harnett,
and John Porter; also James Stallard and Richard Evans,

1730

who, however, never came to Carolina. Burrington would
make no recommendation for chief justice and secretary,
leaving their selection to Colonel Bladen, who designated
for chief justice William Smith, a young barrister of Lon
don; and for secretary, Nathaniel Rice, his own son-in-law;
while John Montgomery was later appointed attorney-
general.

The
province
during the
interim

When information was received in the colony of the pur
chase by the Crown, in the absence of particular directions,

1729

there was some cessation of the exercise of governmental functions. The legislature held its session as usual in November, 1729, and with Everard's assent passed several acts, particularly one for the issue of £40,000 of paper currency; and presently there was unusual activity in locating blank patents, which had long since been issued, and some of them without the payment of any purchase money. But the chief justice ceased to hold courts and the members of the council did not attend the governor when he called a meeting of the board. So it happened that for two years previous to Burrington's return no general court was held, nor any Assembly for eighteen months, while some of the precinct courts had likewise suspended their sessions, and there was a general arrest of the operations of government. The condition was one tending to anarchy, but the people were busy and there were no riots nor serious disturbances. Still it was desirable to re-establish at once the regular and orderly administration of justice and to have the Assembly convene to meet the new governor and recognize the changes produced by the purchase and prescribed in his instructions.

C. R., III, 145

C. R., III, 142

On reaching Edenton toward the end of February, Burrington, together with several of his new councillors, took the oaths of office and immediately issued writs for the election by the freeholders of an Assembly, which was called to meet on April 13th, and ordered a general court to be held at Edenton on April 1st. When the court met the grand jurors for the entire province made a loyal address to his Majesty the king, reciting that as it was the first court held since the purchase, they took the earliest opportunity to express their devotion to his Majesty; and then they thanked the king for the appointment of Burrington as their governor.

1731 Burrington arrives C. R., III, 134, 142

It is to be observed that neither Moore, Moseley nor Swann had any share in the administration. It is said that Burrington had quarrelled with Moore about the location of his patent for five thousand acres of land, he proposing to locate it on the rich lime lands at Rocky Point on the northwest branch of the Cape Fear; but Moore had preceded him and had taken up those lands himself, so that Burrington, disappointed and angry, was obliged to content himself with

Opposition to the royal instructions

1731

lands at Stag Park, several miles higher up that river. This, together with other causes of difference, led to personal antagonism between Burrington and Moore's connections; but there was no opposition manifested to him immediately on his arrival. Doubtless the leading inhabitants felt a keen interest in the changes that would probably attend the purchase by the king, and they waited developments with anxiety. Just before the Assembly was to convene, in April, Ashe arrived at Edenton from the Cape Fear to attend the council, and the tenor of Burrington's instructions became known. Until then all had been agreeable at the council board; but Ashe immediately began to oppose the governor, and endeavored by "false reasoning and fallacious argument"

C. R., III, 331

to impose upon the judgment of the other councillors. Unsuccessful at first, he soon gained the chief justice and Edmond Porter to join him. And after the Assembly met, it was not long before the members of that body were also earnestly co-operating with him.

The first royal Assembly

Moseley was the speaker. The governor at the opening of the session presented a written address, for the kind terms of which the Assembly resolved to return him thanks; and then they began the consideration of the matters called to their attention in the address. Among these recommendations was one to appoint an agent to look after the affairs of the province in England, which later was acted on by a subsequent Assembly, and this channel of communication

C. R., III, 287, 296

with the authorities at London eventually became highly important; another was to prevent the depreciation of paper currency, and still another to establish a new town on the Cape Fear, and to appoint commissioners for that purpose. This last proposition ignored the town of Brunswick, which Moore had laid out in 1725, and which had become a mart of commerce and had been made two years before the seat of government for New Hanover Precinct; and it was a direct blow aimed by Burrington at Moore's interests.

Matters of controversy
C. R., III, 268, 331

Three days later Speaker Moseley and some other leading members of the house waited on the governor and asked him if he would not ratify the currency act and some other laws whose validity was in doubt, as they had been assented to by Governor Everard after the news had been received of the purchase by the Crown. This Burrington not only refused to do, but he declared the currency act was a nullity; and to show that he disregarded it he appointed William Smith, the new chief justice, treasurer of the province in the room of Edward Moseley, who was appointed treasurer in that act. This the Assembly resented, and it hotly represented that the province already had a treasurer with whose ability and integrity they were very well satisfied; and who, having been appointed in an act of Assembly by the governor, council and Assembly, could not be removed but by the like power. The governor, a majority of the council adhering to him, replied that Moseley was indeed a person of sufficient ability, "and we heartily wish that his integrity was equal to it"; and as to his appointment they said "the act of 1729, by which he was appointed, is void," that being the act under which all the paper money then current in the province had been issued. This attack on the speaker, involving also the validity of the currency, led to a declaration by the Assembly that Moseley's "integrity was equal to his abilities," and that the act of 1729 was not void; and even if it should be disallowed by the king, Moseley's appointment was also under previous acts, whose validity was unquestioned. C. R., III, 268, 302

In Burrington's instructions reference was made to the large amounts of quit rents that were many years in arrears in Carolina at the time of the purchase, and the king offered to remit those arrearages if the Assembly, in an act on that subject, would require all grants to be recorded in the office of the receiver or auditor, so that a perfect rent roll could be made out, and would further require the payment of rents to be in proclamation money, and that fees should be paid in proclamation money also—that is, in current specie of foreign coinage the value of which was ascertained and fixed in sterling money by proclamation of the Crown. Currency act declared void

Referring to this offer, the Assembly informed the governor that while the rents were largely in arrears in South Carolina, they had been regularly paid in this province, and that the king's offer was of no interest to the inhabitants Quit rents C. R., III, 294 of North Carolina; yet it passed a bill requiring all future grants to be recorded in the receiver's office, and offered to pay the quit rents in tobacco or other products or in bills at some small discount; but the Assembly would not agree to make payment in specie at all. The governor insisted that the rents were payable in sterling money, and that he and his council were authorized to regulate the fees.

Fees of
officers
C. R., III,
297, 308

These fees had, by an act of Assembly, for twenty years been payable in paper currency at its face value, but the governor, basing his action on his alleged instructions, had already ordered that the officers should not be required to receive the bills unless at the rate of four for one, a change that increased the fees fourfold. To this matter the Assembly now adverted, declaring the practice of exacting "four for one" illegal and an extortion, and asked the governor to issue a proclamation forbidding it.

Burrington was a man of very strong characteristics, doing nothing by halves. He was vain, proud, arbitrary and violent, intemperate in his conduct, and entirely self-reliant. Indifferent to others, when aroused he worked his will with passion, and, heedless of consequences, struck his

C. R., III,
300

opponents with a strong hand. He himself had authorized this practice which the house characterized as extortion; and full of indignation, he sent a message to the house: "For my own part, I cannot refrain from telling you that whoever the person was who formed the said paper of complaint, I compare him to a thief that hides himself in a house to rob it, and, fearing to be discovered, fires the house

C. R., III,
265

and makes his escape in the smoke." Thereupon the house replied that "the complaint was the unanimous voice of the whole house, no member dissenting, and that they regarded that such treatment of any member was a great indignity and contempt put upon the whole house, and a breach of privilege."

And now the breach between the governor and the assembly was beyond healing; he had not only insulted the speaker, but had affronted the house. Whatever chance there had been to lead the Assembly to observe his instructions had been destroyed by his ill-temper, and his opponents had triumphed. Divergence of views might have been expected, but mere differences might to some extent have been reconciled by a conciliatory policy, while now adjustment had become impracticable.

The position of the leading men in the province was substantially that the purchase by the king of the proprietary shares carried with it only the rights of the several Proprietors and worked neither alteration in the constitution of the province nor in the rights and powers which the people and the Assembly had immemorially enjoyed, and the house was resolved to maintain its privileges. Still there was an inclination, in so far as it might be proposed, to put the Assembly on the footing of Parliament, and to concur in changes tending to that end. But Burrington could not brook opposition, and at length, on May 17th, after a stormy session of five weeks, during which no bill carrying out any of the governor's instructions was passed, he wearied of the contest and prorogued the Assembly until September. Thus ended the first session, with Burrington baffled and the opponents of any constitutional changes brought somewhat into harmonious action. At the first, the situation being novel and the ground untried, the leaders in the council as well as in the house had to feel their way and carefully weld their associates into an organized opposition; but before the house separated they had reached safe ground, and the position of the leaders came to be well understood and sustained by the people.

Burrington's instructions

Among Burrington's instructions was one limiting suffrage to freeholders, whereas before all freemen could vote. Another was that in all acts for levying money express mention should be made that the money was granted to the king; and no money was to be levied which was not liable to be accounted for to the king. Others were that all officers were to be appointed by the governor and council, and this the governor held to embrace the treasurer; that all quit rents and fees should be paid in proclamation money; that the governor should not assent to any bill providing for the issue of paper currency unless it contained a clause declaring that it should not take effect until approved by

1731

The basis of political action

C. R., III, 262, 264

May, 1731
C. R., III, 324

C. R., III, 93, 100, 103

the king; and that no public money should be disposed of except by the governor's warrant approved by the council, the right of the Assembly to direct payment without the governor's consent being denied.

There were other instructions relating to the quantity of land that might be taken up and to the payment of quit rents, at variance with the Great Deed of grant; and that old instrument, which had been authenticated by Governor Archdale in 1695 and then recorded, and which had been delivered to Richard Sanderson for safe keeping, was produced in the house and committed for preservation to the care of the speaker; and a direction was made that it should be formally brought to the attention of his Majesty the king, with the hope that he would not disregard it.

Schoolmasters

Among other instructions that, however, were not germane to the antagonisms then raised was one in regard to schoolmasters: "And we do further direct that no schoolmaster be henceforth permitted to come from this kingdom and to keep school in that our said province without the license of our Lord Bishop of London, and that no other person now there, or that shall come from other parts, shall be admitted to keep school in North Carolina without your license first obtained." And another, that touched the king's private purse, was for the particular benefit and advantage of the Royal African Company, "who were to bring in a constant and sufficient supply of merchantable negroes at moderate rates."

C. R., III, 116

The general court

C. R., III, 237, 310, 322

C. R., III, 241

To hold the general court in April the governor had appointed three assistants to sit with the chief justice, as had been the custom in proprietary times, and when the Assembly was considering a court bill requiring that a general court should be held four times a year in each of the counties, apparently there being a proposition to erect a third county, inquiry was made by the house as to the judicial power of these assistants, and the governor and council replied that they had no judicial power whatever; but a few days later the governor changed his opinion and held that they had an equal voice in determining all questions with the chief justice, a position that seemed at variance with the powers and rights conferred in the commission of the chief justice, signed by the king himself, and which was so derogatory to the authority and station of the chief justice that Smith regarded it as a personal affront, and three days after the Assembly was prorogued he resigned his seat in the council, and a bitter feud sprang up between him and the governor. A few days later, after conferences with the leading members of the Assembly, in which he undertook to represent their grievances to the Crown, he left for England, declaring that he was going to have Burrington displaced; and, because of his absence, John Palin was appointed chief justice by the governor and council, the councillors present being only John Lovick and Edmond Gale, whom the governor appointed that day for this special purpose.

1731

C. R., III, 239

Burrington dispenses with the Assembly

In November, an election having been held under the biennial act in September, a new Assembly met at Edenton, but the governor at once prorogued it to meet in March, saying that he had made representations to his Majesty about the obstructive conduct of the last Assembly, and had asked for further instructions, and until they were received he himself would take care that the business of the province was transacted.

1731

C. R., III, 253

When he realized that his old friends were alienated and that he could not control even the majority of those councillors who were in the province, Burrington cast about to strengthen himself by attaching the other faction to him. In July he called a council at Edenton, which because of the distance from the Cape Fear was attended only by Surveyor-General Jenoure and Edmond Porter, some of the other councillors not being in the province. The situation did not, according to the terms of his instructions, warrant his appointing new councillors; but he was animated by a purpose to strengthen himself and to weaken the opposition, and with this view, he appointed John Lovick and Edmond Gale councillors, persons whom he had previously denounced as being utterly unworthy of any public station; and these being facile, he began to oust those councillors who were disagreeable to him.

Appoints new councillors

July, 1731

Beginning with Edmond Porter, who had formerly been

1731
C. R., III,
412
his close friend, but who was now not only in the opposition, but was at bitter enmity with Gale and Little, he heard charges brought against him by Little and suspended him as judge of admiralty, and turned him out of the council; and he appointed Gale to the vacant judicial position. He next cited Cornelius Harnett to answer because of a debt Harnett and Rev. Mr. Marsden owed to the captain of a vessel which had been wrecked, and whose damaged

C. R., III,
332
cargo they had bought; and he succeeded in forcing Harnett to resign. With Ashe, who the governor declared "was altogether bent on mischief," he had more trouble. Ashe would not resign, and a notable conflict ensued between them. But for a time Burrington had entrenched himself securely in the council and could control the appointment to vacancies.

The governor erects new precincts

Nov., 1731
The governor and council assuming the power to lay off precincts, their authority to do so was strongly contested. However, they erected the precinct of Onslow and that of Edgecombe, extending from Roanoke River to the northeast branch of the Cape Fear; and also, in November, 1732, Bladen, although at that time it was said that there were

May, 1732

C. R., III,
417, 450
not three freeholders nor thirty families in Bladen, and not many more in Onslow. That such a power resided in the governor and council was denied as being a derogation of the rights of the Assembly, and not only a violation of the Fundamental Constitutions, which it was asserted had been accepted by the people of North Carolina in 1669 and also in 1698, but against all the laws and established precedents; for though at different times the governor and council had

C. R., III,
439, 450, 451
laid off precincts, such as New Hanover, in 1729, yet the legislature had afterward passed acts establishing them and fixing their representation.

His action
disregarded
Not only were those who proposed to maintain the vested rights of the people antagonistic to this claim of authority by the governor and council, but they paid no attention to his instructions and proclamations that only freeholders should vote for members of the Assembly, and, in utter dis-

regard of his directions, all freemen were allowed to vote as formerly.

New conflicts

Constantly circumstances brought about some new occasion for either personal or official conflict between the governor and his adversaries. The chief justice, Smith, had already gone to England threatening to obtain his removal, and Burrington apprehended that Colonel Bladen was aiding and fostering this design with the hope of securing the appointment of his own son-in-law, Rice, as his successor. About twenty men from South Carolina had settled on the Cape Fear, among them three brothers of a noted family named Moore, all of the set known as the Goose Creek faction, "always very troublesome in that government," who the governor had been told would expend a great sum to get him turned out; and between them and Moseley on the Chowan messengers were constantly passing. However, notwithstanding all menaces, he was not terrified, "but acted with such resolution and firmness that the province was soon put in a quiet condition and has so continued without any imprisonments or persecutions." Such was Burrington's declaration a year after his arrival; but his unwisdom raised him enemies in London, while his arbitrary course embittered his opponents in Carolina. Eight months after he assumed the government he wrote to the Board of Trade that Ashe had intended to go to England to cooperate with Smith for his removal, but as he had not gone "Baby Smith will be quite lost, having nothing but a few lies to support his cause, unless he can obtain an instructor from a gentleman in Hanover Square." The following June the Board asked him to explain that reference, and he avowed in a rambling letter that it was meant for Colonel Bladen. The compliment paid to Colonel Bladen by naming a precinct in his honor was hardly sufficient to atone for such an indignity.

C. R., III, 338

C. R., III, 370

And if in February Burrington could applaud himself for not having resorted "to imprisonment and persecution," by March his mild behavior had given way to more arbitrary inclinations. He had issued a direction that no one should be allowed to practise law unless licensed by himself; and doubtless an attorney's oath was exacted of all who applied

Burrington's arbitrary conduct
C. R., III, 356, 375, 504

for a license. Moseley had been licensed to practise in 1714, and was a lawyer of twenty years' standing, although in late years he had retired from the business. However, in March, 1732, he did appear for Edmond Porter; and while with his hand on the book to take the oath, the governor in a great rage ordered his arrest and threw him into prison, presumably for appearing as an attorney without the governor's license. At the next term of the court, in July, Moseley hazarded a remark on a legal question to the chief justice in court; whereupon the governor again ordered the sheriff to commit him to jail. On habeas corpus before the chief justice and full court an order was quickly made for his release; but the governor was indignant at the proceeding, claiming that the court ought not to release within twenty-four hours any one whom he had ordered to prison; and he so abused Palin, the chief justice, whom he himself had but recently appointed, that that officer resigned, and

William Little, Gale's son-in-law, was appointed to the position; and all the associate judges resigned and a new set was appointed. Palin's resignation, however, did not deter the governor from again pressing the court to do duty in his behalf. On Old Town Creek, a few miles above Brunswick, Ashe had a plantation, while Burrington had one on Governor's Creek, lower down. There was a question as to the ownership of two mares which Burrington's servants had, under his orders, branded with his mark and taken into possession. Ashe brought an information before the general court at Edenton and claimed the mares as his property, and also claimed the penalty which the law prescribed for

branding stock belonging to another. Burrington thereupon had him arrested for his "scurrilous libel," and caused the warrant to be returned before himself and Judge Owen, who exacted the bond Burrington suggested, being £1,000, which Ashe deemed excessive and would not give. On habeas corpus before the chief justice, Little refused to examine into the cause of the commitment, but the bond was reduced one-half, even that being a heavy bond; and it was alleged that these proceedings were contrived to prevent Ashe's departure for England, where, at the request of many, he was going to secure a redress of grievances.

In the meantime representations had been made to the
Board of Trade of Burrington's oppressive and lawless conduct, and before he had been in office two years his removal
was determined on, and in March, 1733, Gabriel Johnston
was commissioned by the king as his successor.

1733
C. R., III,
534

The second Assembly

Not realizing that the Board of Trade might be persuaded to disregard his representations, and conscious of
his purpose to rule well if not wisely, Burrington did not
deviate from the course he had marked out for himself with
reference to those who did not sustain his administration.
Brave, bold and self-reliant, he was always candid. There
was in his disposition no element of craft or dissimulation.
He thought he knew what would best promote the development of the province, and he sought to carry into effect
his views regardless of opposition. He thought he knew
what his instructions required of him, and he resolutely
undertook to obey their tenor. Finding the Assembly at
points with him about the payment of quit rents and fees,
he applied for additional instructions, and avowed his purpose to have no Assembly until those instructions were received. Eventually, toward the end of March, 1733, the
long delayed answer came to his request, and he at once
ordered an election to be held in May for assemblymen to
meet in July. When the body convened he explained that
his new instructions were similar to the first he had received. Moseley was again the speaker, and in his reply
to the governor's speech he dwelt on the impracticability of
paying the quit rents in specie, and denied that they were
payable in sterling money, as now claimed. Originally he
asserted they were payable in produce, and when paper
money was issued a law was passed that this paper currency
should be good for all payments except alone for the purchase of land, for as to that the Lords Proprietors had
always exacted specie. The lands in Albemarle were never
sold, while some in Bath County were granted on quit rents
alone and others were sold for specie. reserving a much
lower quit rent in addition to the purchase price; and the
house insisted that the Assembly of 1731 had offered to his

July, 1733

C. R., III,
561

Quit rents

1733

Majesty all they could do in regard to the payment of rents. As for the disuse of the Assembly, it said there were other matters requiring the attention of the governor than the quit rents; among them not merely exorbitant fees taken by the officers, but the perversion of justice by evil and wicked officers, especially by Chief Justice Little and his associates on the bench.

Chief
Justice
Little
arraigned
C. R., III,
587

This grave charge against the chief justice at once brought a reply. Little in a long and caustic letter petitioned the governor and council that since they could not try him as a court, they would examine into any charges made against him and ascertain whether or not he were unfit to be a councillor; for he admitted that if he were guilty of perverting justice he ought to be removed from the council board. This paper being communicated to the house, it was referred to a committee, and the house temporarily proceeded with its other business. There were several new points on which quarrels now arose with the governor. The house would not recognize the new precincts of Bladen, Onslow, and Edgecombe, erected by the governor and council, and would not admit the members elected in them. It had some of the officers appointed by the governor arrested and brought to its bar for misconduct; and finally it cited several officers, among them the chief justice, before it to answer why they had exacted in payment of their fees four times the amount in currency which the law had fixed.

C. R., III,
562

The
governor
addresses
the house
C. R., III,
598, 603, 604

At length, on the fourteenth day of the session, the committee on Little's petition reported that it contained scandalous expressions reflecting on the dignity of the house, and he was ordered into custody to answer for affronting the house. Matters had now reached a serious pass, and the governor intervened to protect his officer. He sent an address to the house sustaining Little, assuming that the particular charge against him was taking fees at four for one, which the governor himself had directed and which had been done by Chief Justice Smith prior to Little, and who, having just returned from England, had been gratefully thanked by the Assembly for his services abroad.

This assumption of the governor that the only charge against Little was the taking of improper fees led to a fierce

1733

arraignment of the judicial action of the chief justice while on the bench, and brought forward the governor's own conduct in regard to the imprisonment of Ashe and with reference to Porter. The governor in his turn gave a loose rein to his anger and vehemently defended himself and assailed the house; and then, not a single law having been passed, he dissolved the Assembly.

July, 1733
C. R., III,
608, 611

The third Assembly dissolved

The regular election for an Assembly was held in September, and in November the house met at Edenton; but there was no quorum of councillors to make another house, so after waiting several days, the governor had the members to attend him and dissolved the Assembly. But before parting with them, however, he read a long paper in vindication of his conduct from the aspersions of his enemies. In June he had applied for leave to return to England, having doubtless heard that a successor had been appointed to his office, and feeling that there was no longer any occasion to fight the battles of a government that did not sustain him. The address he now made was therefore couched in very different terms from any of his former productions. It was a manly, sensible address, and his moderation must have disarmed enmity and won him friendly sympathy. It put many of the complaints against him in a different light from what the circumstances were made to bear when pressed by his adversaries; and it rather sustained his opinion that some at least among those whose bitter hostility and antagonism he had aroused "were subtle and crafty to admiration."

Nov., 1733

C. R., III,
613-622

Change of
tone

For nearly a year ensuing Burrington conducted public affairs with neither an Assembly nor a council. He himself had a long and dangerous illness, some of the council died and others left the province. Rice, who at one time when Burrington was absent from the province, being the senior and ranking member of the council, was sworn in as president of the council, was suspended by the governor on his return, because of "villainies," as was also Montgomery, another "villain." Halton neglected to attend for two years, and Ashe, who died in the fall of 1734, had not attended for more than twelve months. Everard also was dead, and so

Oct., 1734
C. R., III,
627, 628

1734

was Chief Justice Little. To succeed Little, Daniel Hanmer was appointed, notwithstanding Smith had returned from England and was ready to resume the functions of his office. At length a collision took place, the final result of which produced unexpected consequences. The details of it are obscure. Burrington claimed that Smith, Rice, Montgomery and some of their confederates attempted to assassinate him by shooting at him with pistols, and that he would have been murdered if some courageous men had not come to his assistance and rescued him. Bills of indictment were at once found against these councillors in Hanmer's court, and they fled by night to Virginia, where they continued until Governor Johnston landed in North Carolina. These proceedings threw the province into new confusion and disorder during the last months of Burrington's administration.

The plot against his life C. R., IV, 165

It was Burrington's misfortune to have been the first governor appointed to establish in the province those changes which the Board of Trade deemed necessary upon the purchase by the Crown. In an attempt to carry out their directions any one would have met with embarrassment and been confronted with all the opposition that the popular leaders could lawfully make; but more than that, Burrington had troubles that another person of a different temperament might have avoided. He was embroiled personally with the Moores and their kindred, with Moseley, Porter and Swann, because of conflicting interests and disputes about land; and many of his personal difficulties grew out of his antagonism with those men.

Altered patents

Without doubt there had been some abuses in regard to the issuing of patents and the location of blank warrants. For instance, Edmond Porter alleged that Burrington himself in 1725 obtained a warrant issued in 1711 for six hundred and forty acres of land in Albemarle, charged with a quit rent of two shillings sixpence, and altered it to a Bath County purchase warrant for five thousand acres at sixpence quit rent, and located it at Burgaw. The grant, which is recorded at Beaufort, seems at least in part to sustain Porter's assertion, for it is based on a warrant issued in 1711, when grants for five thousand acres were not allowed, and when no entries were permitted on the Cape Fear at all.

C. R., III, 502

Other such warrants, bearing internal evidence of having been issued in 1711, located on the Cape Fear, might well lead to an erroneous impression that there had been an attempted settlement on that river about that time. The use of blank patents had been general in all sections of Bath County, and any attempt to destroy the validity of titles based on them would necessarily lead to violent antagonism; and later Governor Burrington himself successfully argued before the Board of Trade that these grants were not to be disturbed.

As for the various affairs in which Burrington was made to appear at a disadvantage, there were probably two sides to most of them—as in his conflict with Ashe about branding the mares, which presents quite a different appearance when Burrington gives his version of the circumstances.

C. R., III, 617

His own opinion of the people, expressed in a letter to the Board of Trade a year after his arrival, was that "the inhabitants of North Carolina are not industrious, but subtle and crafty to admiration; always behaved insolently to their governors; some they have imprisoned, drove others out of the country; at other times, set up two or three supported by men under arms. All the governors that were ever in this province lived in fear of the people (except myself) and dreaded their assemblies. The people are neither to be cajoled, nor outwitted. Whenever a governor attempts anything by these means he will lose his labor and show his ignorance. They never gave the governor any present except Sir Richard Everard. With him they agreed for £500 in bills to pass the pretended laws in 1729, in the name of the Proprietors, when he was shown the act of Parliament of the king's purchase. It must be allowed, were these acts valid, the assemblymen made a good bargain for the people they represented."

His opinion of the people
C. R., III, 338

These ideas of the characteristics of the people furnish some key to Burrington's conduct. The crafty people seem to have withstood him, but he had the resolution not to quail before them. There was, indeed, no duplicity in his actions, either in his private quarrels or his public controversies; and had it not been for his infirmity of temper, notwithstanding the zeal of the popular leaders to prevent unconstitutional alterations in their government, his relations with them might have been on a more pleasant footing. Still contests must have necessarily arisen, for he candidly avowed that the people should be curbed, and he urged a repeal of the biennial act, saying that "that act must be repealed before the people of this country can be brought into a good subjection"; and also the repeal of the act appointing treasurers to the precincts, who he claimed had the local influence to control the assemblymen; and the necessity of taking the power of the purse away from ' the Assembly.

Controversial documents
C. R., III, 325, 356, 375, 450-457

His position on these subjects alone was quite sufficient to array the people strongly against him. As these and other such questions involved the constitution of the province, their discussion led to historical research of much interest, and the papers written on those subjects not only throw much light on the obscure history of the province, but are highly creditable to the authors. Particularly noteworthy is that of Rice and Ashe on the constitution of the province, while those that relate to Moseley and Porter, some written by Burrington himself, are often strong and full of interest.

If this first administration of a royal governor was a period of violent antagonism, it was also one of patriotic fervor, although the personal controversies were so intermixed with political action that it is difficult to separate them. The basis of it all was a resolute purpose on the part of the leading inhabitants to preserve the constitutional rights of the province; and the contest then begun continued in one shape or another until the connection with the Crown was brought to a close by the Revolution of 1776.

Burrington's progressive action

Still, in many respects Burrington's career gives indisputable proof that he sought to promote the progress of the province. He made journeys to every part of the inhabited country, examined the roads, urged the construction of bridges, sought to organize the militia on a good footing and to raise the standard of the precinct courts; and he urged

C. R., III, 372, 435

an extension of the general courts. He explored the harbors and caused charts to be made of Ocracoke, Beaufort, and Cape Fear inlets, the only ones of use to the commerce of the province, and he otherwise endeavored to render his administration serviceable to the inhabitants; but perhaps the best service he rendered was in deferring the running of the line as proposed between North and South Carolina, which, if once established, would have given to South Carolina a large part of our interior territory, which the South Carolinians coveted, for the directions at that time were to run the dividing line thirty miles distant from the Cape Fear River up to the head of that stream and then a due west course.

1734

C. R., III, 244, 372, 435

The South Carolina authorities claimed that the Cape Fear River itself was the dividing line, and in support of that view they asserted that grants issued by that government had been located on that river. It does appear from a deed made by Schinking Moore to Richard Eagles, March 14, 1763, recorded in the register's office of New Hanover County, that a grant of 48,000 acres of land was issued May 13, 1691, to Landgrave Thomas Smith, and that said Smith and wife Mary conveyed to William Watters 700 acres thereof located on the northeast branch of the Cape Fear River, just above the dividing of said rivers; and on April 21, 1736, Maurice Moore conveyed to Colonel Thomas Merrick a tract of land lying at a place called the Haulover, on the east side of the Cape Fear River, "beginning at Landgrave Smith's corner tree," etc.

Landgrave Smith's grant C. R., III, 125, 154

Book E, New Han. Co Records, 35, 313

From these conveyances it would seem that Landgrave Smith's tract was located on the Cape Fear River, and its bounds were recognized after the permanent settlement. Roger Moore, who came to the Cape Fear about 1725, married a daughter of the Landgrave, and perhaps the fact that that particular grant was located on the Cape Fear may have in some degree influenced the removal of the Moores, resulting in the permanent settlement of the Cape Fear, which by some of the older residents was spoken of as the third attempt to settle that river.

Many of the questions raised by Burrington in the course of his administration were not settled at that time. At London they were referred to the law officers of the Crown, good lawyers and fair men, who made a thorough examination before delivering an opinion; and often there was long

Questions settled and unsettled

delay before the facts could be definitely ascertained warranting a decision. In regard to the validity of the Great Deed, the law office was apparently misled by Mr. Shelton, the secretary of the Lords Proprietors, who declared that it had never been recognized at all by the Lords Proprietors, and it therefore held that the instrument was intended to have only a temporary effect. When this opinion was communicated to Burrington he replied with considerable vigor, urging the same view which the Assembly entertained—that it was a valid grant and contract and could not lawfully be ignored.

In regard to the validity of the currency act passed in 1729, it was held that all acts passed before Governor Everard had notice of the sale to the king were valid; any passed after such notice were null. But that act being in operation, it was never disallowed or annulled, and the paper currency authorized by it continued to be the chief money used in the province. Other questions remained undetermined; but it appearing that the governor had sat with the councillors when the legislature was in session and had taken part in the discussion and in the consideration of bills, he was rebuked and reminded that as he represented the king, his sole function was to allow or disallow bills that passed the two houses, and that he must not meddle with the Assembly. Such was the custom in England, and the purpose was to conform the province to the customs at home. One of his instructions was, "You shall take care that the members of the Assembly be elected only by freeholders, as being more agreeable to the custom of the kingdom, to which you are as near as may be to conform yourself in all particulars." That idea eventually commended itself to the people, and subsequently they sought to model their legislature after Parliament.

In the meantime the province received accessions in population and made progress in importance. While the northern section had grown more populous, requiring the erection of Edgecombe Precinct, there being twenty families on the Tar River alone, the opening up of the Cape Fear proved of still greater consequence. Settlers were locating on both branches of the river; the wealthy South Carolina planters, who had removed to the lower portions of the river, had begun the cultivation of rice, while saw-mills were erected and the forests yielded for export tar, pitch, turpentine, staves and plank. Bladen was being settled as well as Onslow. John Maultsby had taken out, about 1731, a warrant for six hundred and forty acres of land opposite the confluence of the two branches of the Cape Fear; and John Watson located a similar warrant adjoining and below that tract; and in 1732 a few enterprising men had for trade settled on Maultsby's entry and called the place New Liverpool, and the next spring Michael Higgins, Joshua Granger, James Wimble and John Watson joined in laying off a town, called New Town or Newton, on the Watson entry, which soon became a rival of Brunswick. Roads had been opened from the Cape Fear to South Carolina, and two roads led to the northward, one by the coast to New Bern and one by Rocky Point to Edenton; while there was easy communication by water with Charleston, with the great sounds and with Norfolk. During one year forty-two vessels had sailed from Brunswick well laden with valuable cargoes. The products had so increased that in addition to those of the forests, and of grain and tobacco, much live stock was sold abroad, many cattle and at least fifty thousand fat hogs being yearly driven to Virginia. Although there had been no great change in the way of church privileges, yet there had been some important ones. John La Pierre, a Frenchman, who had come to South Carolina in 1708, and had officiated on the Santee, had about the year 1727 come to the Cape Fear, where he remained several years. In 1732 Dr. Richard Marsden, who had cast his fortune with the Cape Fear people some four years earlier, had a charge at New River, which Burrington was seeking to promote and develop, and where about one hundred families had settled. For a time Rev. Bevin Granville officiated at Edenton and the surrounding country, where he baptized over one thousand children. In Albemarle there was one Presbyterian minister with a congregation and there were four meeting houses of the Friends. In 1735 John Boyd was employed in the Northwest parish, where he claims to have likewise baptized one thousand infants. In that section he reported "no sects," but lower down the

Religious conditions

C. R., III 48

country there were a great many Quakers and Baptists; for Paul Palmer's work was indeed progressing.

Burrington had applied for permission to return to England, and in expectation of receiving it in October, he filled up the council board by the appointment of a number of new members and called an Assembly to meet him at Edenton on November 6th. When the Assembly met Moseley was again chosen speaker; but former antagonisms seem to have largely subsided.

The last Assembly to meet Burrington

The governor addressed the Assembly in a conciliatory speech complimenting the members, and "not doubting that they would promote the passing of such acts as are recommended or required in the king's instructions." Moseley, as speaker, returned hearty thanks for his kind speech, and added: "That we are very glad you have conceived so good an opinion of our understanding and capacity to serve this province." In his reply the governor accepted "your answer to my speech very kindly," and assured them that the good opinion he entertained of the wisdom and good intentions of the members was grounded on the real merit he knew they were possessed of; and he wanted them to so act that "this country may have reason to thank us at the end of this session, and their posterity not only to remember us with gratitude, but to bless our memories." As the temper of the governor seemed to be not so arbitrary, the house itself became more complacent. On the second day of the session it ordered a bill to be prepared declaring that only freeholders should vote, agreeably to the king's directions; and

they ordered other bills to be brought in establishing the three new precincts, Edgecombe, Onslow, and Bladen; and were proceeding on a line that must have been very acceptable to Governor Burrington when, on November 13th, it was

certified by proclamation that Governor Johnston had published his commission on the Cape Fear in open council. Burrington's administration immediately closed. The house proceeded no further in business, but stood dissolved, there having been no act of Assembly passed during the whole period that Burrington was governor.

CHAPTER XIX

JOHNSTON'S ADMINISTRATION, 1734-52

Governor Johnston arrives

On the arrival of Governor Gabriel Johnston at Cape Nov., 1734 Fear he was met with great cordiality by the gentlemen of the vicinity, and he lost no time in assuming the reins of government. There had been no change in the list of councillors originally appointed by Governor Burrington, except that on Burrington's recommendation Roger Moore and Cullen Pollock had been selected to fill vacancies, and now Edward Moseley and Matthew Rowan were added to the board. The suspensions and appointments made by Burrington a few months earlier were unknown in London, and were a surprise to Johnston when informed of them. On November 2, 1734, Johnston opened his commission at Brunswick in the presence of the gentlemen of the town and

1754

C. R., IV, 1 of councillors Robert Halton, Eleazar Allen and Roger Moore, who had not attended Burrington's board then in session with the Assembly at Edenton. Being informed that Burrington had supplanted many officers illegally, the governor on the day he qualified issued a proclamation commanding all officers, civil or military, who had been removed or suspended to resume their offices and enter again on the discharge of their duties; and Smith, the chief justice; Rice, the secretary; Halton and Edmond Porter at once took their places at the council board.

Burring-
ton's
enemies in
the
ascendant
C. R., IV,
77, 81 Hanmer, lately appointed chief justice, and Burrington's other appointees were now roundly and freely characterized as base tools to work Burrington's arbitrary will on deserving gentlemen who had the manhood to disagree with him. The tables were indeed completely turned; and the late governor's enemies being in control of the Assembly as well as of the council, those who had fled the province, ostensibly in fear of their lives, returned in triumph.

Burrington
goes to
England

C. R., IV,
45 Adverting to the disorders that prevailed, Governor Johnston ordered a court of oyer and terminer to be held at Edenton on December 2d, and issued writs for the election of an Assembly, which was to meet on January 15th. His prompt and strenuous action, at once ignoring all courtesy that might have been due to his predecessor and reversing the whole course of the administration, was a bitter humiliation to Burrington, who now left the province with his family and returned to England, where he, however, continued to interest himself in North Carolina affairs.

Johnston
cordially
received About the middle of January the governor in great state made his journey through the counties from Brunswick to Edenton, where he met the Assembly, being received with every manifestation of cordial approbation; and, indeed, the Assembly, generally so parsimonious, made an appropriation of £1,300 to pay the expenses of his equipage on that occasion.

Jan., 1735 Moseley being in the upper house, as the council was now called when acting as a part of a law-making power, in conformity with the disposition to assimilate the Assembly to Parliament, William Downing was chosen speaker of the lower house; and there was a continuation of the same influ-

1735

ences that formerly controlled the action of that body, and the zeal of the representatives to maintain the rights of the people was unabated.

On one point at least the governor, the council and the house were agreed: they found a common ground in their denunciation of Burrington and his appointees. Smith, the oldest councillor, presided over the upper house; and he and Porter and Rice, along with Moseley and Moore, were fierce in their arraignment of the deposed governor and of his profligate tools and accomplices, alleging that they had persecuted and expelled from the province his Majesty's officers, whose lives were in danger, and were only preserved by timely and hasty flight; and the Assembly and Governor Johnston heartily joined in the general condemnation. C. R., IV, 81

In its first flush of patriotic ardor the Assembly made an allowance to the king of £1,300 for the service of the public in the province, and ordered bills to the amount of £10,000 to be struck off; and passed an act to call in the outstanding paper money, which had been largely counterfeited, and to issue £40,000 of new bills in exchange; also acts limiting suffrage to freeholders, according to the instructions of the governor to conform the Assembly to Parliament; and for establishing the precincts of Onslow and Bladen, allowing them representatives in the house. But notwithstanding this disposition to be on friendly terms with the governor, the old points of controversy again arose to disturb the harmony; and especially was the house settled in its purposes that the quit rents should be paid either in current paper money or in produce on the farms, while the governor, who was sustained by a majority of the council, held that they were payable in specie. The Assembly and the governor

C. R., IV, 150, 154, 155 S.R., XXIII, 117

Onslow and Bladen

Disagreement over the quit rents

When Chief Justice Smith was in England he learned that the Lords Proprietors had ordered all enactments of the Assembly to be certified to them, and such as were not confirmed by them were to expire at the end of two years; and as the practice of certifying the acts to the Proprietors for confirmation had fallen into desuetude, he ascertained that of the whole body of laws in the province only six had been C. R., IV, 201, 290

1735

confirmed, and therefore he considered that all others had ceased to have legal effect. So impressed was he with this view that he submitted the matter to the law officers of the Crown with a request for instruction; but no decision was reached and no instruction was given at that time on the points he raised.

Governor Johnston, however, had no hesitation in agreeing with Smith, and made this view the basis of his position in discussing the quit-rent subject with the Assembly; and a majority of the council also sustained the chief justice and Colonel Halton, to whom the matter of the rents had

C. R., IV, 94

been referred as a committee, in holding in effect that payments were to be made in silver, and that his Majesty could collect his rents without asking the consent of the Assembly; and, indeed, the conduct of the chief justice was such that in a controversy between him and Moseley, in the presence

C. R., IV, 33

of the speaker and other members of the house, Moseley, giving way to his indignation, struck him, and was bound over to the general court to answer for the assault.

Quit rents

The governor, who relied on the rents to pay his salary, being sustained by the chief justice and a majority of the council, also took the advanced position that two years after

The Great Deed

the Great Deed was signed the Lords Proprietors, by their action, revoked it, and it was therefore a nullity; and insisting that the laws which had formerly been confirmed were no longer operative, he declared that he would proceed to collect the rents in silver, and that those who were not content to make the payments he demanded could settle up arrears and move out of the province, abandoning their

C. R., IV, 20, 112

homes and the lands they had improved. This suggestion but added fuel to the flames; and Moseley, to whose custody the Great Deed had been committed by the previous Assembly, now formally presented it to Speaker Downing for safe keeping. Being unable to move the house from its position, Johnston on March 1st made a great show of indignation and prorogued the Assembly.

Undeterred by opposition, the governor asserted his purpose to proceed; and notwithstanding the general opinion that there must be an act of Assembly providing for the collection of the rents, he assumed that his personal views should necessarily control, and he determined to make it plain that he was master of the situation, and issued a proclamation requiring all rents to be at once paid to the receiver-general. However, he so far yielded to the circumstances of the inhabitants as to assent that the rents might be paid in paper currency instead of silver, but at the rate of seven for one; and if not voluntarily paid, the receiver was to distrain; and in that case eight for one was to be exacted; and he proceeded to erect a court of exchequer, with Smith as chief baron, the particular business of the court being to enforce the collection of the rents. There was, however, no receiver in the province, the king's receiver-general, John Hamerton, being a resident of South Carolina; so to facilitate the collections Eleazar Allen was appointed receiver for North Carolina, a proceeding which so angered Hamerton that he issued a proclamation warning the people not to make any payment to Allen. But this only served to rouse the governor's spirit, and he ordered that assistant receivers should be appointed to attend at every precinct court house and make distress if need be. Some rumors of discontent were heard because of this new turn of affairs, and the governor was astute in selecting and appointing militia officers who would sustain his administration. He did not propose to brook opposition to his methods, and was ready to enforce his will at every hazard.

Nearly all of the councillors then resided on the Cape Fear, and the growing importance of that region, together with its fine navigable river, led the governor at first to make that his residence instead of Edenton.

He was, however, at points with the Moores because of their landholdings, some of their lands having been obtained under old blank patents, which they had bought, and which the governor considered as in fraud of the rights of the king; and he viewed the town of Newton with more favor than he did Brunswick, and perhaps determined to locate there.

Wilmington incorporated

Immediately on his return from Edenton, in 1735, doubtless at his instance, an application was made to the council

C. R.. IV, 67

C. R., IV, 15

C. R., IV, 8

March, 1735
C. R., IV, 43

1735

to incorporate that rival of the older settlement in which the Moores were interested, but the councillors apprehended that they had not the power.

However, he proceeded to give signal proofs of his favor to Newton. He ordered that on May 13th a land office should be opened there; also on the same day a court of oyer and terminer was appointed to be held there; also the court of exchequer, of which William Forbes and James Innes were designated as assistant barons; and likewise the council. Truly, that May 13, 1735, was a gala day for the little village, which had already made progress in its struggle for trade and importance against the established seat of local government lower down. The governor, realizing its advantageous situation, threw all of his influence to secure its ascendancy. He bought land there, as did also Colonel Halton, Captain Innes, Captain Rowan and Woodward, the surveyor-general, and James Murray, who came to be a close friend to the governor; and the next year an act was introduced to incorporate the town under the name of Wilmington, in honor of the governor's patron at Court; but the Moores were able to defeat the measure in the house. However, a session or two later the bill was brought forward again. The council was composed of eight members. The presiding officer, Chief Justice Smith, voted for the bill, making a tie; and he then voted a second time to break the tie; and the bill being hurried to the house, was put through before the Moores had time to oppose its passage. This occasioned a strong remonstrance from those interested in Brunswick, who protested that it was illegal for a member of the council to cast two votes. At the next session the house again passed the bill to cure this alleged defect.

C. R., IV, 44, 45

Wilmington incorporated

Immigrants

Attention now began to be attracted to North Carolina, and particularly to the region drained by the Cape Fear River, as a home for settlers, and Governor Johnston stimulated interest among his friends in Great Britain by his letters and representations. Before he had been in the government a year he was in communication with Mr. Dobbs and some other gentlemen of distinction in Ireland, and

C. R., IV, 72-74

with Henry McCulloh, a kinsman of his and a merchant in
London, relative to their sending over families; and Captain
Woodward, as their attorney, selected a tract on Black River,
in New Hanover, of sixty thousand acres for them; and in
January, 1736, McCulloh petitioned the Board of Trade for
two other tracts, one at the head of the Northeast and the
other at the head of the Northwest River, which were
allowed him. Simultaneously with this movement, Governor
Burrington, then in London, and Mr. Jenner proposed to
settle a colony of Swiss between the Neuse and the Cape
Fear rivers, and asked that a new precinct should be laid
off in that region for them; but later the location desired
was changed to one nearer the mountains. However, this
proposed colony seems eventually to have been merged in
McCulloh's undertaking. This enterprising gentleman was
appointed by Governor Johnston his agent in England, and
he also secured an appointment as inspector-general of the
grants and revenues of the king in South and North Carolina; and a few months later, having associated two merchants, Huey and Crymble, and some other gentlemen with
him, he obtained an order for twelve tracts of land of one
hundred thousand acres each, not to be at a greater distance from each other, however, than ten miles, and each
tract to be subdivided into eight equal parts. For these tracts
the grantees were not to begin to pay quit rents until the
expiration of ten years, having that time for settlement. The
grants were ordered to be located on the head waters of
Neuse, Peedee and Cape Fear rivers, and they were the
basis of the immense land interest subsequently held by
McCulloh in North Carolina.

To induce the immigration of settlers, it was urged that
the climate on the Cape Fear was as good as that of England;
that living was cheap; that fortunes were easily made; that
those who came early and took up land would find that its
value was doubled yearly, as had been the case on the lower
part of that river. These inducements appealed strongly to
enterprising young men to leave the well-occupied marts of
Britain and seek their fortunes in a country where hope
promised them such advantages. Captain Innes, a man of
unusual merit, seems to have accompanied the governor when

Marginal notes:
1735
C. R., IV, 73

C. R., IV, 685, *et seq.*

C. R., IV, 156, 157

McCulloh's grants

C. R., IV, 668

Letters of a Loyalist

1736

he arrived, and among those who were induced through the influence of the governor to come over in the fall of 1735 was James Murray, a young Scotchman, then resident at London, who brought with him a stock of goods, and arrived

James
Murray

on the Cape Fear January 1, 1736. Not being able to obtain a house at Newton as he had intended, he opened his store at Brunswick, where he found ready sale for all of his merchandise except "wigs." These fashionable ornaments of dress, much to Murray's disgust, he was unable to dispose of, either at Charleston or on the Cape Fear.

Free Masons

But if the people would not wear wigs, they nevertheless brought with them the ideas and habits of the people at home. In 1735 they made application to the Grand Lodge of England for a charter of a Free Mason's lodge, which was granted under the name of Solomon Lodge; and one of the first buildings erected in the village of Wilmington was a Mason's lodge.

Swiss, Irish
and Scotch
C. R., IV,
685-687

The first considerable number of families coming together were Swiss, who arrived about the end of 1736, and a colony of Irish, who were settled on the upper waters of the Northeast; among the latter being Colonel Sampson, the Owens,* Kenans and Walkers; and in September, 1739, the McNeals, Duncan Campbell, Colonel McAlister and several other Scotch gentlemen brought over three hundred and fifty Scotch people, who settled in the western part of Bladen Precinct. Earlier a colony of Welsh settled in the upper part of New Hanover County, on what has since been known as the "Welsh Tract."† To encourage such colonies the Assembly exempted from taxation for ten years all bodies of Protestants settling in the province numbering forty persons, and in particular appropriated £1,000 for the benefit of the Scotch settlers.

The South
Carolina
dividing
line

Governor Burrington having fortunately postponed settling the boundary line of South Carolina, Governor Johnston appointed commissioners for that purpose, one of

---

*The Holmes family appears to have located at first in Edgecombe and then to have removed to Duplin.

Records
New
Hanover
County,1737

†In March, 1737, the Welsh Tract extended from Burgaw Creek to Widow Moore's on Black River, and then to the bounds of the precinct, embracing Duplin and Sampson counties.

1735

whom was Eleazar Allen. The commissioners met at Allen's residence, Lilliput, near Brunswick, on April 23, 1735, and agreed that a due west line should be run from Cape Fear along the seacoast for thirty miles, and then proceed northwest to the thirty-fifth degree of north latitude, and then run west. A week later they ran the line to Little River, and in September continued it seventy miles to the northwest; and two years later it was extended in the same direction twenty-two miles. There the work was discontinued until 1764, when the line was run west to the vicinity of Catawba River. S. R., XI, 149

When the receivers first began to collect the rents, which were then several years in arrears, many persons paid, and the governor was much gratified at the success of his plan of proceeding without the sanction of the Assembly; but at length, on rents being demanded in Chowan, Moseley refused to give his countenance to a proceeding he deemed illegal and subversive of the rights of the people. He declined to pay, and others thereupon stood with him, and collections almost wholly ceased. C R., IV, 246

While his officers were meeting with success the governor had had no use for an Assembly, and being determined to set his face against the biennial act, under which elections were held without his writs, he dissolved the Assembly so chosen in September, 1735, without permitting it to convene. The next year he issued his writs for a special election of assemblymen, and convened the Assembly in September, 1736. In his address to that body he urged that the interests of the people and of the province would be best subserved by promoting religion and education, and asked that provision should be made for public worship, and that at least one school should be established in the province. The house at that time, however, had more pressing matters to consider than the academic promotion of virtue, and called the attention of the governor to the unlawful action of those who were collecting rents under his orders, and declared that their conduct was an intolerable grievance. Nevertheless, the house passed a fee bill, which the governor rejected, and also a bill providing for a rent roll and for the collection of rents, and for quieting possessions, by the provisions of which all blank patents were declared valid, the validity of The new Assembly Sept., 1736 C. R., IV, 225, 226

1736

C. R., IV,
241, 272

the Great Deed reaffirmed and the rents declared payable in
commodities, rated at specified values; and the value of th
paper money was to be annually fixed by a commission com
posed of the governor, four members of the council and th
speaker and six members of the Assembly, to be chosen by
the house. This bill was so clogged with provisions which
in the opinion of a majority of the council, were detrimenta
to his Majesty's interest, that the upper house rejected it
and the governor, having twice unavailingly called the hous
to attend him, prorogued the obstinate Assembly unti
March; and when it then met, the house having ordered
into custody the officers who had been collecting the rent
from unwilling citizens under compulsion from fear o
distraint, the governor promptly dissolved it.

The
governor
appeals for
instructions

C. R., IV,
250

C. R., IV,
267

In the meantime Governor Johnston had immediately afte
the adjournment of the first Assembly made a full representa
tion to the Board of Trade of the differences between th
people and himself. He had urged that the Great Deed hac
been revoked by the Lords Proprietors; that except six un
important laws the former legislative enactments had neve
been confirmed and were now nullities; that especially th
biennial act ought to be repealed; that the blank patent
ought to be set aside; and he asked instructions as to thes
matters as well as in regard to the Assembly's contentior
about the rents. But the Board of Trade took no heed anc
his appeals for direction were in vain. No instruction
having been received in reply to his request, Governor
Johnston now advised the Crown officers at home that unles
the old laws were annulled his Majesty would have very
little to do in his province, for the people had taken especia
care to make themselves independent both of the Crown anc
of the Lords Proprietors; and he asked that a company o
troops, that would not be under the direction of the Assembly
might be sent to the province and he be commissioned as
captain of it. Evidently the governor was minded to carry
out his will and purposes even by force if necessary; and
perhaps there was some occasion for troops, for when at
the general court a man was imprisoned for insulting the
marshal of the court, the people of Bertie and Edgecombe
understanding that his offence was non-payment of quit

1736

rents, rose to the number of five hundred and approached Edenton with the purpose of rescuing him, cursing the king, and with their hearts full of rebellion. While it was only in these two precincts that the people openly embodied, yet the seeds of insurrection were widely disseminated, and the governor hastened to advise McCulloh that the biennial act should at once be repealed and that the people should be warned and commanded by a royal proclamation to obey the governor. With this spur, the Board of Trade during C. R., IV, 251 July, 1737 the summer obtained from the king an order repealing that law; and conformably thereto, in November Governor Johnston issued a proclamation giving notice of its repeal. Biennial Act repealed Such was the ending of one of the muniments of liberty and safeguards of freedom which Shaftesbury had embodied in his celebrated Fundamental Constitutions in the early days of the settlement.

At an Assembly held in New Bern in March, 1739, the dis- Precincts converted into counties S. R., XXIII, 129 position to fashion the province after the model of England had its effect, and an act was passed converting the precincts into counties, and for appointing sheriffs in each of them, but as that necessarily supplanted the official functions of the marshal, that office was abolished, and Colonel Halton was allowed a money consideration for his damages. Provision was also made for holding circuit courts, and at an adjourned session a month later the struggle over the quit-rent trouble, which had lasted so many years, was adjusted by a compromise, which was very agreeable to the governor, provision being made for a rent roll and the rents to be paid in a Rent roll prepared limited number of commodities, such only as the governor approved—tobacco, hemp, flax, deer skins and beeswax; and the value of the provincial currency was to be fixed by a commission as in the bill formerly rejected by the council. One of the considerations for the passage of this bill by the Assembly was that it confirmed the blank patents, in which nearly all of the chief men of the province were in some measure interested, and it gave an assurance of title to lands which they had improved, in some instances at great expense.

On the other hand, the governor and his officers had for some time been without compensation for their services, and

1739

as this arrangement opened the way for the payment of their salaries, it was very gratifying to his Excellency, who hastened to send the act to England with his approval and urgent request for its confirmation. In the meanwhile, not doubting that it would be confirmed, he put it into operation, and that cause of disagreement between the administration and the opposition was regarded as entirely removed. Still, the antagonism between the governor and the Moores, who were spoken of by the administration as "the family," remained;* but this cause of difference being settled, Eleazar Allen abandoned the governor and joined "the family," which put the administration in the minority in the council. This unexpected defection of Allen led the governor to immediately appoint as councillor James Murray, on whose fidelity he could rely.

Progress in the colony

The exports of the Cape Fear River had now become relatively considerable. The vast pine forests were filled with light wood, being the heart of the resinous pine after the body of the fallen tree had decayed many years before, and the business of making tar engaged a large part of the population; indeed, so much of this staple article of commerce was speedily produced that the markets of the world soon

Products

became overstocked. The Moores and their friends, who together had brought some twelve hundred slaves to the settlement, began in 1735 the culture of rice, of which large crops were now being produced for export; and in 1738 George Lillington reported to the Assembly that he had brought the culture of indigo to perfection; while particular efforts were made in various parts of the province to grow hemp and flax. The silkworm was also introduced, sawmills had been erected, bricks were burned, and much progress was made in comfortable living as well as in profitable commerce.

Chief Justice Smith impeached

There had been constant accessions to population, and the chief matters of difference between the people at large and the administration having been settled, an era of good will was ushered in, and there was a period of quietude and of steady growth. Still the chief justice did not give satisfaction in his courts. In some measure he seems to have

*Murray's "Letters of a Loyalist."

1740

justified the opinion expressed of him by Burrington, and there were many complaints of his irregular proceedings. At length, in 1739, matters reached a crisis, and there was a determination to impeach him. The Assembly was to have met in New Bern in November, but because of adverse winds C. R., IV, 351, 352 the members from Albemarle, who were coming by water, were delayed, and only twenty-six members at first appeared. That number was sufficient for a quorum and the body might have been organized. But the chief justice had been very useful to the governor, and it was alleged that in order to protect this officer, with the governor's connivance, resort was had to management, and Smith procured four members to take to the bushes and absent themselves, thus preventing an organization. After waiting two or three days, a majority of the council advised a dissolution—advice which the governor hastened to follow, and the impending impeachment was thus avoided. From the method pursued to break the quorum that Assembly became known among the people as the "Bush Assembly." A new election was, however, at once Feb., 1740 C. R., IV, 468, 500, 5c ordered, and when the body met Smith managed to secure the good will of a majority by promising to have passed a certain bill allowing some additional commodities to be received in payment of taxes and in discharge of debts, the rating of these commodities to be at a very high value. Sir Richard Everard, the son of the former governor, however, presented and pressed the resolution of impeachment, setting out in detail some eighteen impeachable offences; but a majority of the house, being thus won over to the cause of the chief justice, cut short the time for bringing forward the testimony, and by a preponderance of six votes held that the evidence presented was insufficient to justify the proceeding. So Smith not only thus avoided the blow, but, indeed, during the year found an opportunity of dealing one to his old enemy, Hanmer, who had been used by Burrington to keep him out of his office. Hanmer was charged with perjury and tried before Smith and convicted. He begged for mercy, but Smith was obdurate, and imposed on him such a heavy punishment that in 1743 Hanmer, being then released from prison, petitioned the Crown for relief against the chief justice, who, he alleged, had persecuted him and destroyed

1740

his fortune and wrecked his health. Smith, however, did not survive long enough to engage in this new controversy. In 1744 he died, and John Montgomery succeeded him as chief justice; himself surviving only a few months, when Edward Moseley was appointed to the position.

Moseley
chief
justice

For years there had been a constant disregard by the English traders of the commercial regulations which Spain had thrown around the commerce of her American colonies with a view of excluding foreign trade and maintaining an exclusive dealing with the mother country. The contract of the English for the importation of negroes, known as the Asiento, increased their facilities for smuggling and maintaining an illicit trade with the Spanish colonies, which was carried on with great gain, particularly by the merchants of Jamaica. There were besides other causes of differences between England and Spain, which, however, in the spring of 1739 had been amicably settled by a convention; but the convention was not promptly carried into effect, and the English traders, fearing that their trade would be cut off by it, were clamorous in demanding a "free sea" even in the Spanish Main.* To please them war was declared with Spain on a point that was of unusual interest to the English colonies in America, as it related to unrestrained commercial intercourse with the Spanish settlements to the southward.

The
Spanish war

1740

In view of these hostilities, in the summer of 1740 Governor Johnston received instructions to raise such troops as could be obtained in the province, and he called a special session of the Assembly to make provision for them. The members were zealous in their patriotic ardor, and with notable unanimity appropriated £12,000 sterling for the maintenance of the levies; and the governor hired four vessels at Edenton, three companies of a hundred men each being raised in the northern counties, and one vessel at Wilmington, where a hundred men enlisted, to convey them on the expedition. So ready were the people to go that many

C. R , IV,
421

---

*While the merchants were clamoring, one Jenkins, a sailor, appeared before Parliament and exhibited one of his ears that had been cut off by the Spaniards. This turned the scale against Walpole's peace policy, and the war became known as "the war of Jenkins's ear."

more companies could have been obtained had adequate provision been made for them.

These troops were originally intended to operate with the
expedition under General Oglethorpe against St. Augustine,
and some of them were despatched on that service. That
expedition having failed, they sailed for Jamaica, where the
British forces were concentrated. Captain Innes commanded
one company, and with him were Lieutenant Pringle and
Lieutenant Douglass, who appear to have come from England. They sailed from Wilmington on November 26, 1740,
and were actively engaged in the West Indies. Later these
forces were in Admiral Vernon's expedition against Cartagena, where, after meeting with some successes, the want
of co-operation between the army and the navy worked their
ruin. Not only were there great losses on the land, but
after the troops were driven to re-embark a fever broke out
among them and nine out of ten of the colonial contingent
succumbed to disease, the entire loss in the expedition being
over 20,000 men. But few of the North Carolina troops
returned. That they bore an honorable part in the operations may be gathered from the fact that Lieutenant Pringle
was wounded at the siege of Boca-Chica, while Captain
Innes won such distinction and his merit was so thoroughly
recognized that in 1756 he was appointed commander-in-chief
of the Virginia forces. Colonel Washington was glad to
serve under him.

Expedition to Cartagena

The decision of the Board of Trade

After the act relating to the rents had been in operation
some two years the governor was humiliated at receiving
information that it had been disallowed by the king. The
passage of the act had been obtained by him after a long
conflict with the Assembly, and it happily settled many contentions; but the half dozen merchants in London trading
to North Carolina protested against the provision which
allowed a commission to fix the value of the currency; and
for that reason the entire settlement of the vexed questions
was annulled. It is no wonder that the governor's patience
was taxed beyond measure by this untoward and unwise
action. But that was not his only disappointment; the other

1741

Quit-rent law disallowed

1741
C. R., IV,
287
questions submitted by him were all decided practically adverse to the positions he had taken. In February, 1738, the law officers made their adverse report, but it was held up three years at London and not communicated to Governor Johnston until 1741, notwithstanding his anxious solicitude

The Great Deed for decisive instructions. In regard to the Great Deed, it was held that that instrument was revocable, but that its revocation could not affect grants made while it was in operation; and whether it was revoked by the commission and instructions to Governor Sayle in 1669, as contended by Johnston and McCulloh, depended on whether Albemarle was within Sayle's territory—which, indeed, had been limited to "south and west of Cape Carteret"; and even were it within that territory, the board considered that a long and quiet enjoyment of land would cure all defects of title.

The quit rents The greater question was as to the payment of the quit rents, and its decision was entirely in conflict with the governor's views and sustained Moseley and the Assembly at all points in the controversy. It was held that the rents were not payable in specie, but might be paid in commodities at the market value, and that the place of payment was on the farms.

C. R., IV,
291
Concerning Johnston's contention that the whole body of the laws were a nullity, it was decided that as they had been

Laws confirmed in use among the people and acquiesced in by the Proprietors they were not void and could not be repealed by the Crown; still they made an exception in regard to the biennial act, and held that it was in the province of the king to repeal and annul that for special reasons, as had been done.

Blank patents After a full examination into the matter of blank patents, the nature of which was fully explained to them by Governor Burrington, the law officers decided that notwithstanding the Lords Proprietors had ordered their land office to be closed, yet the patents were good if the Proprietors were made privy to them, or had afterward received the consideration money; but those issued after notice of the king's purchase were not good; and they held that the circumstance
C. R., IV,
322
that the patents were blank as to boundaries was not of itself sufficient to avoid them; and if any of the patents were voidable, the proper course to annul them was by infor-

mation in the courts. These decisions, however, were not for three years communicated to the governor, who in ignorance of them had maintained his position on the matters involved with partisan loyalty and devoted zeal in behalf of what he regarded were the legal rights of his sovereign. Disheartened in the extreme, for the only gratification he had enjoyed was in the repeal of the biennial act, the governor, receiving no salary whatever, nevertheless continued to apply unavailingly for new instructions, until at length, in 1747, the humiliating answer came that he had better try to get a new act passed for the collection of rents not containing the objectionable feature of a commission to fix the value of the currency that had caused the rejection of the former act. He had asked for bread and they gave him a stone.

But notwithstanding this ill-usage, Governor Johnston would abate nothing from the tenor of his original instructions, and the receivers of rents would not settle them for commodities, and now rated the provincial currency at only one-tenth the value of specie. As great as was this rate of depreciation, it was equaled in the neighboring province of South Carolina, where for three-quarters of a century the currency was never at a less discount than 700 per cent.; and where twenty-eight of the merchants of Charleston having, in 1722, presented a memorial complaining of broken pledges in not retiring the currency, the Assembly ordered them all into the custody of its officers.

The people of North Carolina, however, were not content with having their currency rated so low, and abstained from paying their rents; and so little money was collected that the governor's salary remained unpaid; and especially was this the case after the northern part of the province had been set apart to Earl Granville, the rents in arrears as well as those annually to accrue in that territory after 1744 being the individual property of that Proprietor, while those accruing in the lower portion of the province, which had not been so long settled, were of comparatively insignificant value.

Embarrassed by his pecuniary condition, other matters bore equally hard on the governor. Civil war was raging in his

Margin notes:
1744

C. R., IV, 583

Currency ten for one

Governor's salary unpaid

1744

native country,* where the young Stuart prince had erected the standard of his father and had gathered around him his zealous Highlanders, while the low-country Scotch, being Presbyterians and followers of John Knox, adhered to the Protestant house of Hanover. The situation of his kindred and friends gave him much concern; and because of the war with Spain and then with France, the seacoast of the province was opened to easy assault, and its defenceless condition was the occasion of much uneasiness; forts should be built and a militia organized; assemblies and general courts had been constantly held at Edenton, which was too

Matters in dispute settled

inaccessible as a seat of government, and a more convenient location was desired, where the officers should reside and the public records be kept; the acts of the Assembly were in confusion and a codification indispensable; the time for which the provincial bills were to run was about to expire, and provision should be made for renewing them; while other subjects of almost equally grave importance claimed attention. Yet assemblies would meet, and because of jealousy between the houses or disagreements with the governor, little or nothing was accomplished. Still, one by one these subjects were considered, and occasionally some would be acted upon, except alone that establishing a seat of government; as to that there was an irreconcilable difference between the houses, the northern members of the Assembly insisting on Bath, the governor and the council, of whom a majority resided on the Cape Fear, proposing New Bern; so there could be no agreement.

Westward expansion

Granville and Johnston counties 1746 C. R., IV, 831, 834

But whatever were the perplexities of government, the province continued to grow in population and importance. Virginians from the beginning had flocked across the border. After the old precincts at Albemarle were well occupied, these immigrants from the adjoining province possessed themselves of Bertie, and there the population became so numerous that in 1741 the new county of Northampton had to be erected. Five years later the first settlement that the Virginians had made on the Tar had so expanded that Edge-

*It is said that Governor Johnston's brothers were in this rising.

combe had to be divided, and Granville was portioned off on the western frontier; while in like manner Johnston County (first proposed to be named Essex) was formed from the western part of Craven, extending up the course of the Neuse.

In New Hanover 22,000 acres of land had been surveyed for McCulloh between the Northeast and Black rivers, and 50,000 acres were located for him a little higher up, which were under the care of Dr. William Houston, near Soracte and the Golden Grove, where the Irish and Swiss settlers had been established in 1736. In 1736 George Vaughan, a barrister of Dublin, Ireland, purchased of a Mr. Hewitt 12,000 acres of land situated in this territory and apparently a part of the 50,000 acres laid off for McCulloh and his associates; and the next year, 1737, John Sampson, a nephew of Vaughan, settled on the tract as agent. Three years later Vaughan resolved to appropriate the land, together with one hundred slaves, to the purpose of Christianizing five Indian tribes* then said to be in the vicinity; and under an arrangement Sampson sought to carry out these general purposes, but for some reason the plan appears to have miscarried. Indeed, the settlement of upper New Hanover prospered so well that in 1749 a new county was formed out of that territory, at first proposed to be called "Donegal," or Fane, but on consideration was named Duplin, in honor of Lord Dupplin, one of the Board of Trade.

And even a still more interesting movement was witnessed on the other branch of the Cape Fear. Some Scotchmen had been induced, perhaps through the influence of Governor Johnston, to come to that region shortly after his appointment, and later there were large accessions of the same population. In 1739 Colonel McAlister arrived with three hundred and fifty Scotchmen in one body. After the disaster at Culloden the adherents of Charles Edward were put to the sword and threatened with extermination. The chieftains and more prominent leaders were quickly despatched, while the humbler people were hunted like wild animals in a chase and butchered without compunction of conscience. The

1746

S.R., XXIII
248, 249

Court
Records,
New
Hanover
County
C. R., IV,
1064

Duplin
County

C. R., IV,
viii

The Scotch
migration

*Indian relics are still found widely scattered throughout Duplin and Sampson counties.

1746

Culloden

Highlanders
in Cumber-
land, 1746

Vass, Hist.
New Bern
Presby.
Church

Anson
County
C. R., IV,
888, 1064

bloody work was, however, at length arrested by a tardy proclamation of mercy, and a pardon was issued under the great seal exempting from the death penalty nineteen out of twenty who had escaped the terrible slaughter. To determine who should be the victims of this melancholy fate, there was resort to the haphazard chance of casting the lot. Those undefended by fortune perished, the other nineteen being adjudged to suffer only expatriation—a merciful boon, perpetual exile. The removal of entire clans was enforced, and hundreds who, not being involved in the trouble, might have remained in their desolated country preferred to abandon their beloved mountains and share the fortunes of their compatriots rather than remain in their deserted homes. Indeed, the feudal tenures of the olden time were then destroyed, and the ties that bound the clansmen to their chiefs passed away, introducing new conditions that were intolerable to the Highlanders. Some influences turned the tide of migration to the upper Cape Fear, where a number of their Highland companions had already located. So that in 1746 the vicinity of the present town of Fayetteville was occupied by a considerable colony of these unhappy Scotchmen, and shipload after shipload of these unfortunate people disembarked at Wilmington and then penetrated far into the wilderness of the interior. In 1749 Neal McNeal at one time brought over five hundred with him, and they scattered through Bladen, Anson and what is now Cumberland counties. Five years later the stream began to flow again, and from that time onward there were constant arrivals from the Highlands of Scotland, until a vast territory was occupied by them. Beliol, of Jura, one of the Hebrides Islands, found employment for a vessel regularly engaged in bringing in annually Scotch emigrants, who were reared almost within hail of classic Iona, the hallowed home of primitive Presbyterianism. Even as late as in 1775 a colony of three hundred and fifty arrived, and joined their kindred on the upper Cape Fear.

From South Carolina other colonists had pushed up the Peedee, taking possession of the fine lands along that river far to the west of the Bladen settlements, so that in September, 1748, they besought the council for the benefit of a new

1746

S. R., XXIII
343

C. R., IV,
811

:ounty, saying that there were between two hundred and
hree hundred white tithables in the Peedee country a hun-
lred miles distant from the court-house; and in answer to
heir prayer a county was established called Anson, in honor
)f the brave commodore whose fame at that time was
·esounding throughout the world. Indeed, so rapid had been
he progress of settlement that when, in 1746, Moseley and
he other commissioners for running the Granville line
·eached the Saxapahaw, at the present southeast corner of
Chatham County, they found settlers and houses already
here, though the country was but sparsely occupied, and
he region to the west was as yet uninhabited.

Granville's
territory

Sir John Carteret, who held high office at Court, perhaps
inimated by an ambition to be the sole possessor of immense
:erritories in the New World, had, in 1729, declined to dis-
)ose of his share on the purchase by the Crown of Carolina,
ind by the king's command his portion was set apart to him
n severalty adjoining Virginia, and the dividing line was
igreed to be the parallel of latitude 35° and 34', by which
ibout two-thirds of the province became his individual prop-
!rty. Carteret, by the death of his mother, had just then
succeeded to the title of Lord Granville. He had the year
)efore overthrown the Walpole administration, and was sec-
·etary of state; and he had uncontrolled ascendancy over the
cing, and was "not only the most brilliant debater, but the
iblest statesman of his time."

His line run

In the winter of 1743 his line was run from Hatteras to
3ath, and in the spring of 1746 it was continued to Saxapahaw, passing near the present towns of Snow Hill and
Princeton; and when extended farther west it became
?ventually the southern boundary of the counties of Chatham,
Randolph, Davidson, and Rowan. From the time it was
run all the interest of the Crown ceased in the rents within
that extensive territory, they belonging exclusively to Granville, who appointed Moseley and Halton his agents for collecting the rents and making grants in his name.

This division of the province between the king and Granville, and the conflicting interests of the northern and
southern counties, and the desire of the governor to establish a seat of government in New Bern, led to one of the

most strenuous struggles that marked the course of public
affairs.

The unarmed rebellion

The Assembly was composed of fifty-four members, o
whom, as the northern counties had five each while th
southern counties had but two, the majority always lay wit
Albemarle; so to compass his purpose with regard to estab
lishing a seat of government the governor skilfully resorte
Nov., 1746
C. R., IV,
870
to management. An Assembly having met in New Bern i
June, 1746, and the houses having disagreed as between Bat
and New Bern, the governor prorogued the body to meet a
Wilmington in November, at a time when the northern mem
bers would be engaged in sending their cattle and hogs t
Virginia for sale, and could not conveniently attend at s
remote a place. The Albemarle representatives, relying o
their power to break a quorum by remaining away, agree
on that course and did not go to the Cape Fear. In forme
years the result would have answered their expectations; bu
with the growing importance of the Cape Fear region an
the divergence of interests that had arisen between the sec
tions new conditions had come to defeat these calculations
C. R., IV,
838, 843
When the house assembled, there being eight old member
and seven newly elected, fifteen in all, in attendance, th
speaker, Sam Swann, calling to his aid the rule of the Britis
Parliament by which 40 members out of 556 constituted
quorum, declared a quorum present, and the house proceede
to business. Only two bills were passed, but these were o
great importance. By one of them the seat of governmen
was fixed permanently at New Bern, where public paper
were required to be kept, instead of at the private residence
of the officers in the different parts of the province, a
had been the practice; and circuit courts were establishe
to be held throughout the province; while the othe
was intended to destroy the inequality of representation b
allowing to each county in the province two representative
and no more. This was a direct blow at the northern coun
ties, which the Albemarle people furiously resented. The
declared that by the constitution of the province the origina
Albemarle counties had a right to five members, of whic

they could not be deprived; and that a quorum of the house
consisted of a majority of all the members, and that a less
number could not lawfully pass a bill. They asserted that
the governor had by artifice and trick devised this proceeding,
and as they had fallen into the trap, they now prepared to
meet the emergency by a counter-plot. By agreement, they
were to abstain from attending future sessions; and their
declaration that the act establishing the seat of government
and appointing commissioners to erect the public building at
New Bern was a nullity raised an obstacle in the way of
giving effect to that law which could not be overcome, and
the buildings were not erected. The governor issued writs
for a new Assembly to meet in February, ordering the
sheriffs to return but two members from any county, but
the Albemarle people disregarded these instructions and
voted for five members as formerly. Throughout the whole
region there was concert of action, and the entire section
was united as one man to preserve their constitutional rights.
When the Assembly met the elections in those counties were
held void, and new writs were issued for another election,
but the people to a man abstained from voting. There were
no elections held. The northern counties would not be represented by less than five members. Both sides, however,
appealed to the higher authority of the Crown; but the law
officers in England, who during the whole colonial period
acted on a high plane and sought to be fair and impartial,
would not decide except on a full hearing, and required
testimony to be taken in the province as to the disputed facts.
This delay brought no harmony to the province, and as
months passed the interests of the sections conflicted more
and more. The public men who had formerly acted in unison
drifted apart; faction and party spirit ran high, and the province became divided into two sectional parties, whose antagonism constantly grew in bitterness.

The governor did not choose to risk another Assembly, or
perhaps deemed it ill-advised to disturb existing conditions,
so year after year the Assembly elected in February, 1747,
continued to meet under successive prorogations. Having
no representatives, the northern counties refused to obey the
laws enacted by the Rump; they did not recognize the new

The two
repudiated
acts
C. R., IV,
855, 864
Feb., 1747

Northern
counties not
represented

They refuse
obedience

1747
C. R., IV,
1312
circuit courts, and especially they would pay no taxes to support a government in which they had no share; and as the northern inhabitants would pay no taxes, after a while neither would the southern, who would not bear the burden of government alone. The house eventually became like the Long Parliament in England, a body exercising the functions of government, but no longer representative of its constituents. While its enactments had the force of law in the southern counties, in the northern they were utterly disregarded.

The Spanish invasions

S. R.,XXII,
403
Notwithstanding the defection of the northern members, the Assembly had to deal with matters of general interest. Particularly did the defenceless condition of the coast give great concern. In 1741 several Spanish privateers took possession of Ocracoke Inlet, and seized the vessels arriving S. R.,XXII,
262, 278 there. They also landed and carried off the cattle of the inhabitants. Eventually they were driven away, but their depredations were so great that provisions had to be supplied to the distressed people at a cost to the province of more than £10,000.

Aug., 1747
Again in 1744 they harassed the coast; and in 1747 boldly entered the harbor of Beaufort. Major Enoch Ward hastily gathered some militia and held them at bay until August 26th, when they succeeded in gaining possession of the town itself. In a few days, however, Colonel Thomas Lovick and Captain Charles Cogdell came to the rescue with a sufficient Beaufort
Taken
S. R., XXII,
263 force, and early in September the Spaniards were expelled, suffering considerable loss. At least ten of the invaders were captured. But so successful were these forays that the next summer they were continued, and the coast was ravaged. Early in July some of the Spanish ships lay in the harbor of 1748 the lower Cape Fear, while a company of militia held the S. R.,XXII,
286 shore against them.

At that time six of the Spaniards were captured, and they withdrew, only, however, to return in heavier force about the beginning of September. On the 4th of that month the alarm was given at Wilmington that they were ascending the river, and the militia companies hurried in detachments to the scene. The general defence had been committed to Eleazar Allen, Roger Moore, Edward Moseley and William Forbes, as commissioners; while Major John Swann was in immediate command. Among the companies participating in the defence were those commanded by Captain William Dry, Captain John Ashe and Captain John Sampson. These alone numbered more than 300 troops. The Spaniards quickly took possession of Brunswick, and for four days, from the 6th to the 10th, hostilities were active. At length, on the 10th, one of the Spanish vessels was blown up, and the others were driven off. All that day Colonel Dry was employed burying dead Spaniards, and two days later he was getting the guns, anchors and other valuables ashore from the wreck. It was from this destroyed vessel that the painting was obtained which is still preserved in the vestry-room of St. James's Church at Wilmington. The spoils from the wreck were appropriated for the use of the churches at Brunswick and Wilmington. A considerable number of the Spaniards were killed and wounded; while at least twenty-nine fell into the hands of the inhabitants. The alarm occasioned by these attacks aroused the people, and the Assembly readily yielded to the suggestion of the governor to make preparations for defence. A bill was passed to issue new currency to the amount of £6,000 sterling for the purpose of erecting two large forts, one at Cape Fear and the other at Ocracoke, while smaller ones were to be built at Core Sound and Bear Inlet; but only the one at Cape Fear was ever completed. The governor, however, had been particularly instructed not to assent to a new issue of currency, and in violating these directions he imposed terms which he hoped would shield him from blame for his disobedience. He required that the Assembly should agree that the use of commodities in the payment of taxes should cease, and that all public payments should be made in proclamation money. This was a point gained which the governor had long had very much at heart, and from his standpoint it was cheaply bought.

Sept. 10

Brunswick attacked, Sept. 6-10, 1748

R. S., XXII, 271-286

S. R., XXIII 292

1748

Effort to displace Johnston

The passage of this currency bill and the disturbed con
dition of affairs in the province, however, led the London
merchants and McCulloh to make an effort for Johnston
C. R., IV,
936
removal. Toward the end of 1748 John Morris, Franci
Corbin, Arthur Dobbs and others began proceedings agains
him, which J. A. Abercromby, who had just been appointe
agent for the province by the Assembly, very skilfull
delayed, and then McCulloh filed a memorial in his ow
behalf complaining of alleged misconduct on the part of th
governor, which later seems to have been sufficientl
No reports
answered. One of the allegations against Governor John
ston was that he had ceased making any reports to th
officials at home, but while the Board of Trade stated tha
for five years, between 1741 and 1746, they had received n
communications from him, it appeared that letters and pack
ages had been sent by the captains of the merchant vessels
who had not delivered them. Doubtless the governor was
however, negligent, for he was receiving no salary and a
his efforts to procure an adjustment of controversies tha
might result in his collecting rents sufficient to pay salarie
had been defeated by the non-action of the home governmen

Local
differences
At length, in 1748, the Assembly having passed the cur
rency bill with his concurrence, the next year they passe
two others that afforded him great satisfaction: one pro
viding for a codification of the laws and the other to prepar
a rent roll, requiring that all grants and deeds should b
recorded for that purpose. The northern counties wer
opposed to all of these measures. Trading to Virginia, the
naturally wanted a currency of equal value with the Virgini
currency, and were opposed to any depreciation of Nort
Carolina money; and being now in Granville's territory, thei
pecuniary interest was no longer identified with that o
the southern counties. Quite an uproar was raised in th
province in 1749, and the governor in his address to th
Assembly, now composed exclusively of southern members
sought to strengthen them in their position and prevent them
from yielding to the clamor of their former associates o
C. R., IV,
972
the Albemarle section. "Go on, therefore, gentlemen," h
said, "and continue in the same good cause you have begun

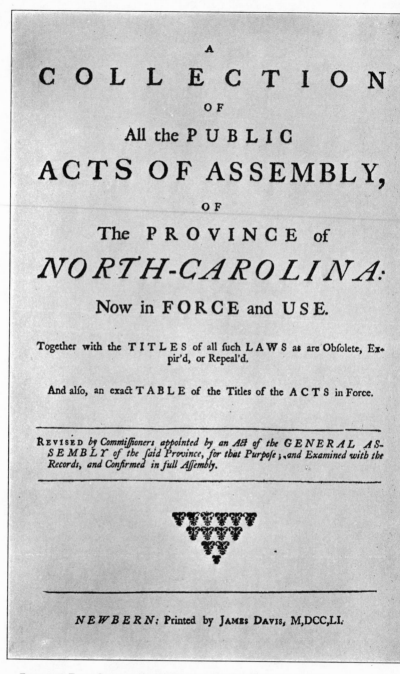

A

COLLECTION

OF

All the PUBLIC

ACTS OF ASSEMBLY,

OF

The PROVINCE of

NORTH-CAROLINA:

Now in FORCE and USE.

Together with the TITLES of all such LAWS as are Obsolete, Expir'd, or Repeal'd.

And also, an exact TABLE of the Titles of the ACTS in Force.

REVISED *by Commissioners appointed by an Act of the GENERAL AS-SEMBLY of the said Province, for that Purpose; and Examined with the Records, and Confirmed in full Assembly.*

NEWBERN: Printed by JAMES DAVIS, M,DCC,LI.

FACSIMILE TITLE PAGE OF THE FIRST PRINTED NORTH CAROLINA REVISAL, REDUCED

Nothing adds a greater lustre to virtuous and public-spirited action than a steady, undaunted perseverance. Let no vain, clamorous boasting, no monstrous calumnies and forgeries, industriously spread among ignorant people, no petulant and noisy behavior in private conversation, the constant attendant of a bad and desperate cause, deter or dishearten you." But if the governor was firm, so were the leaders of the Albemarle people; the northern counties were immovable; still the Assembly continued its sessions without regard to the vacant seats in the hall, and session after session it passed acts of public importance.

Early in 1749 it appointed an agent to represent the province at London; and it passed an act to encourage James Davis to set up a printing office in the province, and accordingly in that year the first printing press was put in operation in North Carolina, and after that the laws were printed at the end of the sessions when they were passed and distributed among the counties. There had been a school kept at Brunswick in 1745, and now the legislature passed an act to establish a free school, of which John Starkey was the author, but which, however, did not become effectual; and it also established new counties, and, indeed, conducted legislation as if there were no opposition to their enactments within the province.

First printing press C. R., IV, 980

C. R., IV, 990

Samuel Swann and Edward Moseley had been appointed commissioners to revise the laws of the province, and the revisal having been made, it was reported to the Assembly on April 14, 1749. Subsequently this revisal was printed, and was known from its sheepskin binding as "Yellow Jacket."

"Yellow Jacket"

It was in 1748 that we have a last view of the poor Palatines as a distinct body. The land on which they had located was originally granted to De Graffenried, who to obtain needed supplies for his people had mortgaged it to Colonel Pollock. In the next generation the mortgage was foreclosed and the Palatines lost their homes. On their petition to the king, Governor Johnston was directed in March, 1748, to allot to them an equivalent in lands elsewhere, and to exempt them from any rent for ten years. Two years later Governor Johnston gave them lands in what are now Craven, Jones, Onslow, and Duplin counties, where their descendants

Palatines

are still to be found—many of their names, however, having in the passage of time been anglicized, as has also been the case with the Germans of the interior.

Wreck of
Spanish
fleet
    About two years after the attack on Brunswick, in a great storm on August 18, 1750, five vessels of the Spanish mercantile fleet were cast ashore on the coast; one was lost at Currituck Inlet, one was sunk at Cape Hatteras, one was beached at Ocracoke, one at Drum Head Inlet and one near Topsail. The cargoes were all valuable, that of the vessel wrecked at Ocracoke being worth a million dollars. Its commander, Don Bonilla, made no application for aid, but for some weeks was carrying on futile negotiations with the neighboring bankers for small vessels to carry off his cargo. Eventually, however, Governor Johnston sent Colonel Innes there to give security and protection to the shipwrecked mariners and the valuable merchandise. On arrival he found that the Spanish captain had loaded his silver on two small sloops, one of which slipped away, carrying off a hundred chests of silver, but the other Colonel Innes was able to secure, and eventually the property was returned to its owners.

The contest between the counties

It was long before the Crown officers took action in the matter in dispute between the old and the new counties; but eventually they directed depositions to be taken touching the facts underlying the respective contentions. On the part of the governor and new counties it was asserted that the right of the old counties to five representatives was founded on the biennial act, which had been repealed by
C. R., IV,
1152-1225
the king. On the other hand, the old counties traced back the privilege to the Fundamental Constitutions, under which Albemarle was divided into four precincts, each allowed five representatives; and although it was admitted that the Fundamental Constitutions had long ceased to be operative, yet it was claimed that rights under it had been sanctioned by usage. Wyriott Ormond and Thomas Barker were appointed the agents to manage the affair, and they conducted it with great skill, while all the other leaders and

public men of the northern counties zealously co-operated with them.

Yet the southern counties were also active, and when the Assembly met in March, 1752, holding its eleventh session, there were high hopes that these differences would be speedily determined conformably to the wishes of the governor. These expectations, however, were not realized, and the evil conditions continued to prevail. How evil they were may be gathered from the testimony of Bishop Spangenberg. "In the older counties," wrote the bishop from Edenton in September, 1752, "there is perfect anarchy. As a result, crimes are frequently occurring, such as murder and robbery. The criminals cannot be brought to justice. The citizens do not appear as jurors, and if court is held to decide such criminal matters no one is present. If any one is imprisoned the prison is broken open and no justice is administered. In short, such matters are decided by blows. Still the county courts are held regularly, and what belongs to their jurisdiction receives the customary attention." The condition, however, was not altogether bad, for while the people would not recognize the new courts organized under laws passed since they were denied representation, yet they maintained in full vigor the old county courts held under the long established laws of the province. Local government was thus maintained despite the unarmed rebellion and the apparent anarchy and confusion, and the progress and development of the province was not materially interrupted.

But Governor Johnston did not live to see the end of the controversy. On July 17, 1752, death terminated his long and stormy administration. Save the era of good-will, ushered in by the passage of the currency act of 1736, which was disallowed by the king, there were always contentions that disturbed the province while he was governor. Many of these sprang from his own action. Ardently desiring to promote the welfare of the inhabitants, he was anxious to establish a permanent capital, to have the laws codified and courts provided for, while the payment of his salary depended on the collections of rents and the preparation of a rent-roll. In seeking to accomplish these purposes he resorted to management and methods that resulted in the unarmed rebellion and the great confusion that prevailed in the northern counties. Still he left the province much more populous than when he arrived. Precincts were converted into counties, court-houses built, the southern boundary in part established, and the vexed matter of rents and the currency question settled; and the laws were codified, a better court system inaugurated, and considerable advances made in government.

During his administration, in 1748, the office of treasurer of the northern counties was created, and Thomas Barker was appointed to it, and Edward Moseley was appointed treasurer of the southern counties. On Moseley's death, Eleazar Allen succeeded him, and when Allen died, in 1750, a controversy arose over the exclusive right of the lower house to designate the treasurers. After some unavailing contention the upper house concurred in the appointment of John Starkey. By an act of 1754 Barker and Starkey were again appointed, but whenever a new appointment was to be made the upper house asserted a right to participate in the election, always, however, in the end relinquishing its pretension and concurring in the appointment made by the lower house. The period of Johnston's administration is, moreover, remarkable for the rapid settlement of the western part of the province.

The growth of the west

Population increases

While Virginians continued to cross the line into the upper portions of Granville County, the more remote interior came to be occupied by an influx of unexpected settlers. The north of Ireland had in Charles I's time been settled by Scotch Presbyterians, who were now removing in large numbers to the New World. Some came to Charleston, and pushed into the up-country from that point, but still greater numbers landed at Philadelphia, and having made some settlements in Pennsylvania, turned southward, and by 1739 reached the Valley of Virginia. Others pressed still further to the south, and by 1745 made settlements in that well-watered district between the Catawba and the Yadkin, which has been called a veritable Mesopotamia. These were soon followed by another stream of immigrants known as the

1752

The
Germans
and the
Scotch-Irish
C. R., IV,
xxi

Pennsylvania Dutch—Germans who had previously located in Pennsylvania.* These settlers made "the great wagon road from the Yadkin River through Virginia to Philadelphia, distant four hundred and thirty-five miles," of which a map is preserved in the Library of Congress. It ran "through Lancaster and York to Winchéster, thence up the Shenandoah Valley, crossing the Fluvanna River at Looney's Ferry; thence to Staunton River and down the river through the Blue Ridge, thence southward crossing the Dan River below the mouth of Mayo," and on near Salem to the mouth of Reedy Creek. Other settlers from Virginia and the north came farther east, by the old Red House in Caswell County, and then followed the Indian trail across the Haw to Trading Ford, near Salisbury. In 1746 Matthew Rowan was in the western region, and estimated that there were not above one hundred fighting men in the entire section between Virginia and South Carolina. Seven years later he thought that there were then thirty times as many, and said their numbers were increasing daily. These immigrants, coming in bodies, settled in neighborhoods to themselves, forming respectively German and Irish communities, scattered here and there throughout the wilderness, and maintaining their customs and manners as well as speech and characteristics, and largely transmitting them to their posterity.

C. R., V, 24

Similarly, Quakers from Virginia and Pennsylvania in 1750, or earlier, located at Cane Creek and at New Garden; and from time to time their numbers were increased by accessions until the Society of Friends gave a particular cast to the inhabitants of that section.

Weeks's
Southern
Quakers
and Slavery,
102–105

The territory north of Granville's line being withdrawn from the king's domain, and about sixteen hundred square miles between the Catawba and the Uwharrie having been set aside for McCulloh, and the line dividing the province from South Carolina not having been run beyond the Peedee, the

Orange
County
1752

*Pennsylvania was dominated by the Quakers, who lived chiefly in the eastern part of that province, and would make no preparations for defence against the Indians. When the Indians became hostile, through the influence of the French, the settlers on the frontier, getting no protection from the Quaker government, sought more secure homes in western Carolina.

1752

administrative officers paid but slight attention to these interior settlements that were growing so rapidly, almost without their knowledge and entirely independently of their influence. Still the extension of population westward from the seacoast counties was realized, and by 1752 the upper parts of Bladen, Johnston, and Granville becoming well populated, a new county, called Orange, was erected, beginning at the Virginia line, near Hyco Creek, running south to where Granville's line crosses the Cape Fear, and then west with Granville's line to the Anson line, and with the Anson line north to Virginia.

In the fall and winter of that year, 1752, Bishop Spangenberg made an extensive journey throughout the western region to locate one hundred thousand acres of land purchased from Lord Granville for the Moravians. Setting out from Edenton in September, on November 12th he camped on the Catawba near what he called the "Indian Pass." The nearest settlement was that of Jonathan Weiss, or Perrot, a hunter, twenty miles distant. He found many hunters about there who lived like Indians, and whose purpose was to secure skins and furs for sale. A week later the bishop was near Quaker Meadows, about two miles from the site of the present town of Morganton. Here he thought himself fifty miles beyond the settlements. The whole woods were full of Cherokee Indians pursuing game. Higher up the Middle Little River he found the remains of an Indian fort, where apparently the Indians had lived some fifty years earlier, and other indications of Indians having inhabited that region were met with later. It was in that vicinity that Lederer stopped in his explorations, 1670, and Dr. Brickell found Indians there in 1731.

Entering the mountains by mistake, on December 3d the bishop reached a branch of New River at an old Indian field, and followed that river to within fifteen miles of the Virginia line. Then turning southward, he reached the head waters of the Yadkin, and coursing down a very rapid stream, eventually got out of the Blue Ridge Mountains and returned to the Yadkin, where he found a Welshman, Owen, who had settled on that stream the preceding spring. This was four miles above an old Indian settlement, known as Mulberry

C. R., IV, 1348

Explorations by Spangenberg, 1752

C. R., IV, 1 14 et seq.

Owen

Fields, not far from Wilkesboro. But except Owen's, the bishop understood there was no other habitation within sixty miles. Later the Moravians found seventy-three thousand acres in one body, one hundred and fifty miles from a landing on the Cape Fear and three hundred and fifty miles from Edenton, and there they made their settlement.

CHAPTER XX

Dobbs's Administration—1754-65

Dobbs's visit to Point Lookout.—President Rowan.—County of
Rowan.—Old style abolished.—The French claim.—Christopher Gist.
—The French invasion.—Innes's regiment.—Innes commander-in-
chief.—Decision of vexed questions.—Dobbs appointed governor.—
Instructions to Governor Dobbs.—The constitution reformed.—
Dobbs reaches New Bern.—The growth of the province.—The Indian
inhabitants.—The Croatans.—The old counties elect their five mem-
bers.—The new Assembly.—Tower Hill.—The French and Indian
War.—The frontier settlements.—Fort Dobbs.—The first news-
paper.—North Carolina troops in the war.—Major Hugh Waddell.
—Fort Duquesne taken.—McCulloh's grant.—Internal matters.—
Dobbs County.—The governor arbitrary.—The king's bounty.—
Causes of difference.—The house outwitted.—The Enfield riots.—
The Assembly protests.—The governor not sustained.—The court law
annulled.—No courts held.—A new Assembly.—The Assembly resolute.—The secret session.—The governor makes terms.—Courts re-
established.—The Cherokee war.—The western counties desolated.—
Fort Dobbs attacked.—Bethabara threatened.—Walnut Cove surrounded.—Conditions more peaceful.—King George III.—Some
differences reconciled.—At the end of the war.—The council declares
its patriotism.—Population.—The Indians.—Abortive efforts for free
schools.—The courts.—Religious conditions.—Republicanism rife.—
British views with reference to America.—The right to tax claimed.
—The Assembly of 1764.—The *Weekly Post Boy* at Wilmington.—
Tryon appointed to relieve Dobbs.—The public agitated.—The firm
stand of the Assembly.—Claims exclusive privilege of imposing taxes.
—The Assembly concurs with Massachusetts.

Extracts from Governor Dobbs to the Board of Trade

1755

DOBBS'S VISIT TO POINT LOOKOUT

I set out from New Bern April 9, 1755, to view the River Neuse,
and proceeded up it near one hundred miles to the falls to see
what proper situations were upon that river for the seat of government, as being the most central and convenient for the whole
province. The most convenient place is at Stringer's Ferry, on the
north side of the river, about four hundred yards from it, upon a
gentle rising ground near forty feet higher than the river. It is
about forty-two miles by land from New Bern to it.

I arrived here [Portsmouth Harbor] last night from Edenton
by water in a sloop. We passed through Albemarle Sound, Roanoke

or Croatan, and Pamlico Sounds, and so over the swash to Occacock Island; and from thence to this road near Core Banks, where
I summoned the commissioners to meet me to fix upon a place to
erect a fort or battery to protect the ships in the harbor, out of
which they were taken by privateers last war. The storms, they
tell me, for some years past have made vast havoc among these sandy
islands. The opening of Occacock Inlet, betwixt this and that inlet,
is enlarged from two to four miles. Beacon Island, which lays
betwixt them, within the entrance, is one-half washed away, and
become only a dry sand at low water. . . . A town is laid out
called Portsmouth, where the merchants propose to erect warehouses
to lodge their goods in and load all their goods in large ships here
by lighters from the several towns of Edenton, Bathtown and New
Bern. The company sailed hence to Virginia about three weeks
ago. We hope they are now near their rendezvous. I proceed from
this to view the harbor at Cape Lookout and Topsail Inlet. . . .
Of Cape Lookout, he says, I have gone up in a canoe within Core
Sound, and no vessel being in the harbor, I had no boat to sound it;
but all agreed to the depth laid down, and that the French and
Spanish privateers had known it of late years, brought in their
prizes there, wooded, watered and heaved down their vessels, and
sent ashore and killed the cattle and furnished themselves with fresh
provisions and excellent fish. . . . This I fixed upon as the only
proper place to build a fort upon, but as this harbor is the best,
although small, of any harbor from Boston to Georgia, and may be
of the utmost consequence to the trade and navigation of England,
where all our cruisers can ride in safety, as in a mill- pond, and
warp out at any time in an hour; where they can wood, water and
clean, and be at sea in a few hours; where the whale fishers of the
northward have a considerable fishery from Christmas to April, when
the whales return to the northward; and where our trading ships
may have always a safe harbor upon easterly storms; and the
whole bay without, a safe road against all but southwesterly winds,
when they can run into the harbor; and since in time of war it has
been and will be a place of safety for French and Spanish privateers,
to infest the whole coast, I think it should be made a station for our
guardships or cruisers.

Rowan's administration

On the death of Governor Johnston, Nathaniel Rice,* who
was the ranking councillor, took the oaths of office as presi-

---

*Rice was secretary of the province, and Henry McCulloh was
appointed to succeed him in that office.

1753

C. R., V, 38
dent, but he himself did not long survive his accession to this dignity. He expired in the following January, Matthew Rowan succeeding him in the administration. Rowan was one of Burrington's councillors, and had for twenty years been of the council and was highly esteemed in the province.

Rowan
County
C. R., V, 76
The old Assembly, which had now dwindled away to about sixteen members, continued to meet, one session being held in the spring of 1753, when, among other acts, it passed one recognizing the large immigration to the western section, establishing the county of Rowan, composed of that part of Anson which lay north of Granville's line. This Assembly held its first session in February, 1747; but at that time the year began on March 25th, so that the record in its journal states that it was begun in February, 1746. By a British statute passed in 1750 "the old style" was abolished, and the year thereafter was to commence on January 1st; and two years later eleven days, being those from September 3d to the 13th, inclusive, were omitted from the reckoning in order to readjust and reform the calendar.*

New Style

The French invasion

Hardly had President Rowan been qualified before matters of great importance claimed his attention. In view of probable encroachments by the French in the interior, the king had directed the governors of the American colonies to be prepared for such an emergency. In possession of Louisiana and of Canada, the French claimed the whole intervening territory, and upon their first movement toward taking possession along the western slope of the Alleghanies, the Ohio Company in 1750 sent to North Carolina for Christopher Gist, then at his home on the banks of the Yadkin, where it approaches the Virginia line, and employed him to visit the Ohio region and make friends of the Indians. Crossing the mountains on the head waters of the Potomac, he went far into the Indian country, breaking the hold of the French upon the tribes there, and the next year he went again to the same region and established the first English settlement

*The shortest day in the year had fallen on December 10th; now by this rectification of the calendar it became December 21st. March 25th was, centuries earlier, the date of the vernal equinox, and hence was originally made the beginning of the new year.

across the mountains. Governor Dinwiddie now proposed 1754 an embassy to the lakes, and a party was formed consisting of George Washington, an interpreter, two Indian guides, and Gist. On the return, Washington, taking Gist as his sole companion, separated himself from the others and successfully completed the journey that made him famous, even at that early age. But the French were not to be deterred from C. R., V, 392 their purpose, and speedily invaded western Virginia. To meet them, Governor Dinwiddie proceeded to organize an army, and North Carolina was called on to assist. In March the Assembly voted an aid to the king of £40,000, of which £12,000 was for the purpose of organizing a regiment of seven hundred and fifty men for service in Virginia; several thousand for the construction of forts, and £6,000 for Starkey's public school; and under this act £22,000 of paper money was struck off. At the moment it was thought that Virginia would provide the supplies for these troops, but that province would not furnish the needed provisions, so in view of the larger expense than was at first contemplated the number of men to be enrolled was reduced to two hundred and fifty. President Rowan appointed Innes to the command Innes' regiment of the regiment; and the other officers were Caleb Granger, 1754 lieutenant-colonel; Robert Rowan, major; and captains Thomas Arbuthnot, Edward Vail, Alexander Woodrow, Hugh Waddell, Thomas McManus, and Moses John DeRosset. At that early period North Carolina learned the lesson that war is largely a question of finance. The northern counties would not circulate the new currency, as they did not recognize the legality of the Assembly, nor would they pay the taxes laid to meet these bills. This currency would C. R., V, 313 not, therefore, pass in Virginia; so without specie, and our currency being at a great discount abroad, in order to supply these troops the Carolinians drove beef cattle and hogs to Virginia, where they had to be sold at a sacrifice.

Governor Dinwiddie, knowing the capabilities of Colonel C. R., V, 125 Innes Innes, on June 3d tendered him the appointment of com- commander-in-chief mander-in-chief of all the forces to be employed against the French. At that time Colonel Innes was in North Carolina superintending the departure of his regiment, but he hastened to the front, and two days after the Great Meadows disaster

1754

reached Winchester, and hurrying on to Wills Creek, took formal command. After that reverse it appeared to Governor Dinwiddie that the available force was not sufficient to attack the French, who had fifteen hundred men, while Innes had but seven hundred and fifty; and because it was not thought well to advance for the want of provisions, Governor Dinwiddie suggested that the troops be scattered, some being sent to Alexandria and some stationed at Winchester. The supplies for the North Carolina troops becoming exhausted, and Virginia being unwilling to furnish any, on August 11th, at Winchester, the North Carolina regiment was disbanded and sent home, leaving for defence only about one hundred and fifty troops, which Virginia had at the front. Colonel Innes remained in command until October, 1754, when he was superseded by Governor Sharpe, of Maryland, who had been particularly designated by the king to be the commander-in-chief; but although superseded, Innes continued in service as camp master general, completed the construction of Fort Cumberland, made treaties with the Indians, and organized the forces.

C. R., V, 130-133

Decision of the vexed question

While these matters were in progress North Carolina affairs had received attention in London. Upon being informed of the death of Governor Johnston, the king, on January 25, 1753, appointed Arthur Dobbs to succeed him.

C. R., IV, 73

Governor Dobbs had apparently been interested in North Carolina matters as early as 1733, and in 1735 had a grant of twelve thousand five hundred acres on Deep River and one for sixty thousand acres on Black River, in New Hanover Precinct. He also had a grant for a large territory between Salisbury and the Catawba Indians, and on these tracts in 1757 there were some seven hundred inhabitants. His interest in North Carolina was so active that in 1749 he had co-operated in the movement to have Johnston removed.

Following his appointment, the Board of Trade being directed to prepare instructions, were confronted with the various undecided questions relating to the province that had been so long before them, and which they now took steps to have determined.

C. R., V, 81, 108, 113-116

The whole constitution and all the laws of the province were at their instance subjected to a very close examination.

1. St. Paul's Church, Edenton
2. Arthur Dobbs   3. Hugh Waddell
4. Court House, Edenton

1754

The law officers thought that the usage which had prevailed, by which the old counties had five representatives, was not shown to be illegal; but they considered that fifteen might properly be a quorum of the Assembly. In their opinion the king's prerogative extended to the establishment of counties and the incorporation of towns, and fixing their right of representation, and they held that those matters were not within the cognizance of the legislature. C. R., V, 81, 108, 113–116

Since fifteen was held a quorum, the Assembly of 1747, which was still in existence, was a legal body, and all its acts were valid until repealed. But the act depriving the northern counties of their five members, it was considered, had been passed by management, precipitation and surprise, and that, together with the act fixing the seat of government and establishing the circuit court was for that reason declared inoperative. In conformity with the recommendation of the law officers, instructions to Governor Dobbs were drawn, directing the repeal of all laws establishing counties, and ordering him to issue charters for counties and for towns and to fix their representation in the Assembly; and also to repeal all laws establishing places for holding the courts and for a seat of government. Likewise the acts relating to quit rents were repealed, and the rents were again declared to be payable only in money; and also many other laws that had long been in use in the province were now annulled by the king. Indeed, the whole constitution was reformed and the Assembly was shorn of many of the powers it had exercised. Still, the exclusive right to levy taxes remained to that body, and the power now claimed by the Crown to fix the seat of government and establish courts could avail but little if the Assembly would not provide the means to make it effective. Since the acts establishing counties and allowing representation were annulled and no longer in force, the governor was directed to issue his writ for the election of an Assembly to consist of sixty members, each county having the particular representation which the Crown had fixed and allowed it, being, however, exactly the same as before the act of 1747, except that some counties and towns were overlooked and inadvertently omitted. Instructions to Governor Dobbs C. R., V. 1107

About the end of July, 1754, Governor Dobbs sailed from

1754
England, and reached Virginia after a voyage of ten weeks
For more than a month he was engaged in arranging with
Governor Dinwiddie and Governor Sharpe of Maryland th
details of a plan of campaign against the French, and h
reached New Bern only at the close of October. Immedi
ately on arriving he proceeded to make himself acquainte
with the affairs of the province, and called for a militi

C. R., V, 161
Population

return. As indicating the extension of population at tha
time, Bertie reported 720 men for military duty; Northamp
ton, 737 men, which was thought to be 200 short; Edge
combe, 1317; Granville, 734; Orange, 490; Anson, 790; and
Rowan, 996. At Wilmington, Governor Dobbs found
seventy families and at Brunswick twenty. There were six
teen vessels in the Cape Fear River, while it was estimated

C. R., V, 158

that one hundred came in annually. Eighteen feet of water
was reported at the bar. At Wilmington a good town house
had been built, and a brick church stood ready for the roof
while at Brunswick the church, also of brick, was not quite
so far advanced. Forts had been begun below Brunswick
at Ocracoke and at Beaufort.

The Indian
inhabitants
C. R., V,
161, 321

The Indian war being in progress,* particular inquiries
were made as to the location of Indians in North Carolina
In Bertie County there were reported a hundred warriors
of the Tuscaroras and two hundred women and children
In Chowan, two men and three women and two children. In
Granville County there were the Saponas, with fourteen men
and fourteen women. The Meherrins had seven or eight
fighting men in Northampton. The report concludes: "These
are all the Indians except about eight or ten Mattamuskeet
Indians, and as many on the islands or banks, a total of
twenty." The reports of the colonel of Bladen County and
of Captain William Davis, who had a troop of light horse, both
said "no Indians" in that county. Colonel Rutherford of that
county, who was also the receiver-general, added this memorandum: "Drowning Creek, on the head of Little Peedee,
fifty families, a mixed crew, a lawless people, possess the

---

*At the first session of the general court for the southern counties,
including Rowan, after the arrival of Governor Dobbs, the grand
jury, in an address to him, stated that seventeen persons had been
murdered and ten carried off by the Indian enemy.

1754

lands without patent or paying quit rents; shot a surveyor for coming to view vacant lands, being enclosed in great swamps. Quakers to attend musters or pay as in the northern counties." These reports show that there were no Indians there, but that some fifty families of mixed blood had settled themselves on Drowning Creek. These doubtless were the same people who in more recent times have been called Croatan Indians. Their origin is obscure, but probably they came up from South Carolina—"a mixed crew." Quakers had settled at Carver's Creek as early as 1740.

The Croatans

Governor Dobbs on his arrival issued a proclamation dissolving the Assembly of 1747, and calling for the election of new members. His writs were directed to all the counties conformably to his instructions, and five members were once more returned from the northern counties. Thus the end had come of the "Long Assembly," and the northern counties rejoiced in their right to send five representatives, while the new counties had but two.

The unarmed rebellion successful

When the new Assembly convened, in December, 1754, the animosities that had so long existed between the sections had not subsided, and for speaker there was a tie vote, the candidates being Sam Swann, the speaker of the last Assembly, and John Campbell, who respectively represented the warring factions. Some of the northern members had not then come in, while Swann had no hope of any considerable accessions to his supporters, and so, realizing his defeat, he withdrew from the contest and Campbell was unanimously chosen. In their reply to the governor's address the Assembly said: "We shall endeavor to obliterate the remembrance of our former contests and the ill consequences that attended them;" and in an address to his Majesty they returned their sincere thanks that he had been pleased "to examine the constitution of the province and to repeal several laws repugnant thereto, whereby the people, by your Majesty's favor, are restored to their ancient rights and privileges, and the contests which subsisted among us are happily terminated."

C. R., V, 154

Campbell speaker

After Governor Burrington's time the governors had kept their instructions private, except such as were particularly intended to be made public. Governor Dobbs now laid before

C. R., V, 213, 249, 254

1754
the Assembly his instructions claiming for the king the right
to select a place for the seat of government and to designate
the places at which courts should be held. Although this
was in derogation of the long-established power of the legislature, the Assembly without making any point of it conformed its action to the king's command, and when considering a bill establishing supreme courts of justice, requested
the governor to designate the several places where he would
appoint the courts to be held. The governor designated
New Bern and Edenton for the counties near those towns;
Enfield for Northampton, Edgecombe and Granville; Salisbury for Rowan, Orange and Anson, and Wilmington for the
Cape Fear counties. Thus a new court law was passed
in 1754.

Court law

In regard to the repeal of the acts establishing counties,
the Assembly requested the governor to solicit the king not
to repeal them because of the many inconveniences that
would ensue, and further, that he would allow the Assembly
to continue to establish new counties, reserving to the king
the power of granting charters to towns, establishing fairs
and appointing places for holding courts of justice. Agreeably to this request, the governor recommended to the Board
of Trade that the desire of the Assembly should be complied
with, and in June, 1755, additional instructions were given,
allowing the Assembly to re-enact all laws establishing
counties and towns, provided that they should contain no
clause allowing representation, as that was to be the exclusive
right of the king.

Counties and
towns re-
established

C. R., V, 406

For the seat of government the governor selected a site
at Tower Hill, near Stringer's Ferry, on the Neuse, but he
had been instructed not to definitely locate it except after
consultation with the Assembly. In 1756 he brought that
site to the attention of the legislature, and a committee was
appointed to examine and report upon it, which they did
favorably.

C. R., V,
342
Tower Hill
as site for
capitol

Governor Dobbs also communicated to the Assembly a
proposition from George Vaughan, of Lisbon, Ireland, who
had called his nephew, John Sampson, home from
Duplin County and arranged the details of a plan to transport immigrants to that county, and had purchased a ship

for that purpose, and also to engage in trade, with a view of creating a fund for the establishment of a seminary, with the expectation that the Assembly would lay a tax on all the negroes in the province to increase it; but the Assembly did not act upon the subject of the seminary. On the contrary, the £6,000 then in hand to establish a public school was diverted for purposes of defence.

The war had been conducted with but ill success, and now a company of one hundred men was raised to serve at the north for a year and ten months, and fifty men were enlisted to defend the western part of the province. Of the former, the governor's son, Edward Brice Dobbs, an officer of the British army who had accompanied his father, was appointed the captain, and that company joined the army in Virginia, then under the command of General Braddock. General Braddock was sent from England with several British regiments and was invested with supreme command of military affairs in the colonies. He led his forces into the mountains near Fort Duquesne, where on July 9th he suffered a terrible defeat, himself being killed. Captain Dobbs's company was fortunately not in this disastrous engagement, being with Colonel Dunbar, at that time scouting in the woods. After this defeat, Colonel Dunbar, who succeeded to the command, precipitately withdrew to Philadelphia, leaving Colonel Innes in command at Wills Creek, and the North Carolina company remained there with him on the frontier. However, during the summer Colonel Innes, being very much dissatisfied with his situation and the management of affairs, resigned and returned home.

On our own western frontier some of the Indians had become hostile, in one settlement having slain some fifteen persons and carried off captive about an equal number. They ranged at will through the frontier settlements and caused much apprehension in the western districts. To arrest them, Captain Waddell, with a company of frontiersmen, scouted along the mountains.

In the summer of that year, 1755, Governor Dobbs visited the western part of the province, passing through Salisbury, which then consisted of seven or eight log houses and the court-house. He viewed his extensive tract of land in that

1755
C. R., V,
355, 356
Dobbs visits
the West
vicinity, lying on Rocky River and its branches, which had
been patented in 1746, and he found seventy-five families
located on it.   He visited between thirty and forty of them,
each having from five to ten children, who went barefooted
and with a single garment in warm weather; while no woman
wore more than two thin garments.   They were Scotch-Irish
Presbyterians, who had settled together in order to have a
teacher of their own opinions and choice.   Besides, there
were twenty-two families of Germans or Swiss, all industrious.   They raised horses, cows, hogs and sheep; Indian corn,
C. R., V,
357
wheat, barley, rye and oats; made good butter and tolerable
cheese, and had made good success with indigo.   Captain
Waddell was then on the frontier, and Governor Dobbs
selected an eminence with good springs on Third Creek for
a fort of refuge for the settlers, which was afterward begun
by the people and finished by direction of the Assembly.   It
was named Fort Dobbs in his honor.   The southern Indians,
however, remained faithful to the whites, and the troubles
at that time were soon quieted.

1753
Moravians
In November, 1753, the Moravians, coming by way of
Winchester and Saura Gap, made their first settlement on the
land Bishop Spangenberg had purchased on the Yadkin,
calling it Bethabara.   The hostile Indians at the north now
C. R., V,
1148
drove many settlers from Pennsylvania to North Carolina,
where they located on Muddy Creek, South Fork, and neighboring streams.   Many also stopped at Bethabara.   For protection against the Indians the Moravians enclosed their mill
and settlement with palisades, but they were not interfered
Clewell,
Hist. of
Wachovia
with.   In 1758, many Cherokees and Catawbas, going north
to aid the English, passed through the Moravian settlement,
being well provided there with provisions and otherwise
Weeks, Press
of North
Carolina in
Eighteenth
Century, 16
kindly treated.   It was during this period of war, when information of passing events was eagerly sought, that the
first newspaper was published in the province.   Franklin,
the postmaster-general for the colonies, in the summer of
1755 appointed James Davis, the printer, postmaster at New
Bern; and the following October the Assembly authorized
a post to be run every fifteen days between Suffolk and
Wilmington, Davis undertaking to send the messengers; and
he also conveyed at stated periods letters and packages to

THURSDAY, OCTOBER 18, 1759. [Numb. 200.]

THE

NO. CAROLINA GAZETTE.

With the Freſheſt Advices, Foreign and Domeſtic.

VENICE, May 17.

THE Plague having broke out in the ſeveral Places of the Morea, and alſo in the adjacent Parts of Rumelia, the Officers of Health have taken into Conſideration the Danger of Infection from thence ariſing to Corfu, Zante, Zephalonia, Santa-Maura, Preveza and Vonizza, and from thoſe Iſlands to this Capital; and have reſolved that the ordinary Quarantine of 28 Days, which Ships coming from the ſaid Iſlands perform here, ſhall be increaſed to 40 Days complete, and printed Orders are accordingly publiſhed for that Purpoſe.

Paris, June 15. On the 6th, as the Pleyade and Oiſeau Frigates were returning from Marſeilles to Toulon, they were diſcovered by the Engliſh Fleet; and 3 Ships of the Line, and 20 Boats, were ſent to give them Chace. After exchanging ſome Broadſides, the Wind

other Hand, we are told that they are in Want of all Neceſſaries, and that they would not begin their March from Poſen till the latter End of next Month; and, if we true what we hear, that a large Army of Pruſſians hath entered Poland, going to attack them, an unhappy Blow may deſtroy all our Hopes, and fruſtrate our Plan of Operation. The People here in general are very uneaſy, our Affairs being but in a very indifferent ſituation.

Hanover, June 19. Our Regency aſſembled, and it was reſolved to ſend a Deputation to intreat Prince Ferdinand to reinforce the Garriſon of this, and ſome other Towns of greateſt Importance. Juſt as the Deputies were ſetting out, Advice came of the Retreat of the French, who drew back to join M. de Contades, and advance with their whole Force againſt the Allies. Accounts differ as to their Strength: Some make their Number to be about 74 or 75,000; but others, who appear to be better informed

June 30. The Muskets made at Vincennes, which weigh only 9 Pounds, carry a Ball 900 Paces, and fire 15 Times in a Minute, were invented by one Bordier, who died lately *a l'Anglois*, shooting himself through the Head, to be freed from the Chagrin of his private Affairs; however he left behind him his Secret: In such a War as the present, in which the Liberty of Europe is at Stake, the Powers that are forced to act on the Defensive, are authorized to employ against their Enemies the most destructive Weapons. At a Time, when Extent of Empire was the Point in Contest, Cardinal Mazarin shut up in the Bastile an able Engineer, with his terrible Secret of making Bombs, each of which he said would destroy 500 Men.

The Ministers and general Officers employed in preparing for the Expedition, seem insensible of the presumptive Security affected by the English, and continue their Dispositions with as great an Ardour as ever. The Comptroller-General wrote on the 23d to M. de Maziere, Farmer General, to assist in forwarding to Brittany 400 Boxes of that alimentary Powder which is prepared at the Hôtel Royale des Invalides, and of which a small Quantity is sufficient to subsist a Man for 1 Day. Six Hundred Boxes more set out the Day before Yesterday, for Havre-de-Grace.

Vienna, June 16. Of late there has been a Coolness between our Court and that of Versailles; and, what is more remarkable, we have had no Minister from France for some Time past: And, it is said, our Minister has left France. As to our good Allies the Russians, we cannot tell what to think of them: Indeed, it is said, they have already penetrated into Silesia; but, on the

that after would be cut off, and that the Enemy would enter this Electorate; but we are informed that he hath deceived the French, and by a masterly Stroke of Generalship hath entered the County of Ridberg, without the Enemy's daring to molest his Rear. The Letters from the Army are so full of the Praises of Prince Ferdinand, that we are now almost as easy as if we had no Enemy in the Field; nevertheless, we are taken the necessary Precautions to guard against a Surprize, the rather as there is a Want of Harmony amongst the Generals, of which wise People fear the Consequences.

Toulon, June 23. The English have no Reason to be pleased with their Attack on our Batteries the 6th: It is said, that the Captain of the *Jersey* was killed; several dead Bodies have been thrown ashore, amongst which we can distinguish some Officers; we have recovered three Anchors, and three Cables, which they were obliged to cut away that Day; 2 of them weigh 68 Cwt. and the other 64 Cwt. They have on them the Names of the *Jersey* and *Guernsey* of 70 Guns, and the *Conqueror* of 60. They have been carried to our Arsenal. The English Fleet, to the Number of 21 Sail, has appeared again.

July 10. They write from Silesia, that the King of Prussia is at last in Motion; and that Marshal Daun, on the first Advice thereof, thought proper to retire.

Paris, June 30. Our Advices from the East Indies are very favourable; and indeed we have Need of some good News, to take off a little of the Bitterness of such as we have received from the West-Indies: We have lost Guardaloupe as unfortunately as the Isle Royale; our Disgraces are brought upon us by Fatalities which have puzzical Causes, and which it behoves the Government to probe to the Bottom,

FACSIMILE OF NORTH CAROLINA GAZETTE, 1759. EXACT SIZE OF ORIGINAL

every county in the province. This opened the way for Davis to issue a newspaper, and probably in December, 1755, he began the publication of the *North Carolina Gazette*. The *Gazette* continued to furnish its readers with "the freshest advices, foreign and domestic," at the price of sixteen shillings per annum, for six years, when, perhaps because unremunerative, the publication ceased.

At the third session of the Assembly, which met on September 30, 1756, Speaker Campbell was unable to attend because of ill health, and Sam Swann was chosen speaker. The necessity of maintaining a force in the field was now thoroughly appreciated by the Assembly, and strenuous efforts were made to co-operate with Governor Dobbs. £4,000 were appropriated for the erection of the fort at the west, and another company, under Captain Andrew Bailey, was employed in that quarter.

C. R., V, 688, 717

Fort Dobbs

In the spring of 1757 South Carolina was threatened by the Indians on her frontier, and two-thirds of the militia of the lower counties were ordered to be held in readiness to march to the assistance of that province. To supplement the forces in Virginia, especially in their scouting operations, bands of Indians from the Meherrins and Tuscaroras, as well as the Catawbas, were sent northward to join the army now under the command of General Forbes. Captain Dobbs's company, as well as Captain Caleb Granger's and Captain Arbuthnot's (with whom were Lieutenant Henry Johnston, Lieutenant Ferguson and Ensign David Rogers), and also Captain McManus's company (John Payne being one of the lieutenants), after serving in Virginia, were formed into a battalion and sent to New York under the command of Captain Dobbs, who was now promoted to be major. There Captain Granger's company served in the Crown Point campaign. On the return of Lieutenant Payne, he was promoted to be captain, and later he marched his company to South Carolina.

C. R., V, xxv *et seq.* C. R., V, 967 Haywood, Beginning of Freemasonry in North Carolina, 4

Service at the North

In 1758 two other companies were raised, one for Fort Johnston, under Captain James Moore, who also led his company to South Carolina; and one for Fort Granville, on the coast, under Captain Charles McNair. During that year 300 men were sent to join General Forbes; 200 went by sea,

C. R., V, 967

1758

and 100, taken from the western frontier, passed up the Valley of Virginia, and with these troops were a number of Cherokee Indians, the whole battalion being under the command of Major Hugh Waddell, who had won great fame for his courage and capacity.

William Pitt was now at the helm of affairs in England, and was prosecuting the war with great vigor. The disasters of the previous campaign were to be succeeded by strenuous endeavors for victory. In Virginia, General Forbes pushed forward toward Fort Duquesne; but winter set in while he was still forty miles from his destination. In that mountainous wilderness, without information, and ill prepared for a siege of the fort or to pass the winter in that desolate region, the general was in such sore straits that he offered a reward of £50 to any one who would capture an Indian from whom information could be obtained. Sergeant John Rogers, of Waddell's command, fortunately succeeded in taking an Indian alive, and because of the information gained from him the general, who was contemplating a retreat, discarded that purpose, continued his advance, made a forced march, and found that the enemy had on his approach abandoned their stronghold. Passing into the hands of the English, Duquesne was at once named Fort Pitt, in honor of the great war minister; and the Indians came in and made treaties of peace, which secured a cessation of hostilities along that frontier.

Waddell,
A Colonial
Officer, 61

C. R., VI,
284

Nov. 25,
1758

McCulloh's
grants
C. R., V,
xxxiii, 1106

During this period of the war and unrest the controversy between Henry McCulloh and Granville, within whose territory some of the McCulloh grants had been located, was brought to a conclusion by an agreement that McCulloh was to become Granville's tenant, and in lieu of all other rents he was to pay an annual sum of £400 from 1757 until 1760, after which date he was to pay four shillings for every hundred acres of land retained by him, but he was to reconvey and surrender to Granville all lands not then settled. As the period for settling McCulloh's grants in the king's domain was about to expire, in 1756 he petitioned that because of the wars and difficulties he be allowed three years' additional time, and accordingly the time for settlement was extended for him until 1760, when he was to surrender his grants, retaining only two hundred acres of land for each white person settled by him in the province.

At first Governor Dobbs appears to have gotten on quite well with the Assembly. The matter of quit rents was not so interesting to the people as formerly, not only because half of the province had been conveyed to Granville, but on the growth and development of the colony, the thickening of population and the general advancement in prosperity it was not so essential that the rents should be paid in farm produce, and the determination of the Crown that they should be paid in money no longer met with serious resistance. But the instructions of the Crown officers limiting the powers of Assembly caused some dismay among the leaders both at the north and at the south; and there was evidently a spirit among them to come together again. Indeed, neither side could boast a complete triumph over the other, for the action of the Assembly in 1747 fixing a quorum at fifteen and proceeding with legislation in the absence of a majority was upheld, and while the two important acts which the northern members protested against were annulled, that action was not taken on their ground and their position was not sustained; and the subject-matters of those acts were taken entirely from under the power of the Assembly and declared to be within the prerogative of the Crown. Necessarily, there were personal antagonisms which only time could heal. The defeat of Swann at the opening of the new Assembly was to have been expected, and his election as speaker at the third session indicates that progress had been made in the direction of restored fraternal relations. The general desire to co-operate in measures of defence appealing to their patriotism doubtless also conduced to healing the breaches.

At the session of November, 1758, the Assembly complimented the governor by locating the capital at Tower Hill, and by creating a new county, embracing the seat of government, which was called Dobbs in his honor; and it also laid a tax to pay the salaries of the chief justice and attorney-general.

But notwithstanding this disposition on the part of the Assembly to be complaisant, there was a divergence between the Assembly and the governor, who seems to have developed

1758
an arbitrary and exacting spirit and would brook no opposition to his purposes. Old, self-willed and petulant, he
appears to have regarded himself as a ruler rather than as a
mere executive officer, and he sought to constrain rather than
to influence.

The king's bounty

It was known that to reimburse the colonies for their war
expenditures the Crown proposed to allow £200,000 for distribution among all of them, and £50,000 was to be given
to the southern colonies exclusively. The control of that part
of these funds which would be allotted to North Carolina
now became a subject of difference between the Assembly
and the governor. The governor asserted his prerogative to
dispose of the money, while the Assembly claimed the right
to use it in their own discretion; and also the right to appoint
an agent for the province and to select the committee to
correspond with him and give him directions. The governor

Causes of difference C. R., VI, 1-3

very emphatically denied all these claims. In the bill locating
the seat of government at Tower Hill no appropriation had
been made for the construction of the public buildings; but in
a second bill granting an aid to the king and providing
for the equipment of three companies to consist of one
hundred men each there were embodied provisions appropriating out of the expected funds £4,500 for the erection of

C. R., V, 1087

the government houses, and also appointing James Abercromby agent for the province, and designating Sam Swann,
Thomas Barker, John Starkey, George Moore and John Ashe
as a committee of correspondence. The governor objected
to this bill, as it was in conflict with his notions of the rights
of the Assembly, and determining to defeat it, he resorted
to what he called *finesse*. Going among his friends in the
council, he suggested to them not to oppose either of the
two bills and to let the objectionable aid bill go to the third
reading, excepting some trifling matters of amendment.
Thus a bill locating the seat of government was passed; but
when the aid bill came up the governor procured the council
to postpone it for some days, and in the meantime he prorogued the Assembly. He himself described the result:

The house outwitted C. R., VI, 3

"Upon this disappointment the lower house were all in a
flame, the managers being greatly disappointed, and represented to me that there must be a dissolution unless the

1759
C. R., V,
1094
Dec., 1758
Free Schools
John Ashe's
address

pper house would resume the bill." It ended, however, in
he house appointing Abercromby their own agent for two
ears and appointing their own committee of correspondence,
nd in their making an address to the Crown praying
hat a part of the sum allowed North Carolina should be
aid out in purchasing glebes and establishing free schools in
ach county. By the governor's action the aid bill was
efeated, and no provision was made for raising troops for
efence at that time. Spring was not over, however, before
he need of more forces at the north resulted in pressing calls
n Governor Dobbs for additional troops, and he was driven
o the necessity of hastily summoning the Assembly to meet
t New Bern. The house convened on May 8, 1759, and pro-
eeded to pass an aid bill exactly similar to the one that the
overnor had succeeded in defeating by his boasted *finesse*.
he upper house, however, amended it by striking out all
he sections not pertinent to the raising of troops, to which
he Assembly not agreeing, it was prorogued, and the session
nded without the adoption of any measure whatsoever.
Necessarily these causes of difference led to much irrita-
ion, which was emphasized by the governor's non-action in
egard to disturbances in the interior of the province.

May, 1759
C. R., VI,
40

On January 24, 1759, there were riots in Granville's terri-
ory, and a number of citizens who were discontented at the
rauds practised by Granville's agents and their entry takers
nd surveyors forcibly took possession at night of the house
f Francis Corbin, the chief agent, and seized him and carried
im off some seventy miles, and held him in duress until
e gave a bond. And Robert Jones,* then attorney-general,
made affidavit that the rioters intended to silence him, or
"to pull deponent by the nose and also abuse the court," and
unless they were suppressed "there would be no safety in the
ounties in which they lived."

The Enfield
riots

C. R., V,
vii

Because of this lawlessness the Assembly addressed the
governor and pointed out that no steps had been taken to
punish the offenders and requested that the chief justice and
other justices and other officers should be required to exert
themselves and bring the guilty parties to punishment; and
also requesting that if it should be necessary the regiments of

The
Assembly
protests
C. R., VI,
105, 106

*The father of Willie and Allen Jones.

1759

militia in the several counties might be called out to assist th
civil powers, cause obedience to the laws and restore peac
and order; and the Assembly loudly complained that the gov
ernor had taken no action in this matter, but, on the contrary
had seemed to lend it his countenance by appointing mer
engaged in the riots to be magistrates and to hold other posi
tions under the government.

The
governor not
sustained

During the summer the Board of Trade at London re
ceived from the governor his letter enclosing the rejecter
aid bill, together with his reasons for not allowing it to pass
which he put on the ground that the bill diminished hi

C. R., VI,
55

Majesty's prerogative. In their reply the Board said tha
the proposed act did not appear to them to have that effec
"to such an extent as you seem to apprehend." They sus
tained the Assembly in their claim to have the right to appro
priate the funds allowed them by the king; and also in thei
right to appoint an agent, and they asserted that they saw
no ground to disapprove the aid bill in its abstract principle
still they concurred in the view that separate matters em
braced in the measure ought not to have been incorporater
in one act; and they also thought that the committee o
correspondence, while properly appointed by the legislature
ought to have included some members of each house
Although urged by the governor to repeal the act of 1754
by which the Assembly had appointed the treasurers, the
Board peremptorily refused to do so, saying that the practice
of appointing treasurers by the legislature, and even o
making them responsible to only one house, had prevailed so
long that it would be improper to interfere with it. It woulc
seem that these decisions so adverse to the positions taker
by the governor, and so clearly sustaining the Assembly ir
its view of these matters, might have led to some abatement
of Governor Dobbs's arbitrary conduct, but having once
assumed a position antagonistic to the popular leaders, he
became more strenuous in his opposition rather than com
plaisant.

The court
law annulled

About that time there came over instructions repealing the
act fixing the seat of government at Tower Hill, for the
Board said that it was only intended that the Assembly should
recommend a location, not definitely fix the place; and also

repealing the act of 1754 establishing supreme courts and enlarging the jurisdiction of the county courts. By that act the office of associate justice had been created, the appointees to hold during good behavior, and in the absence of the chief justice they were to exercise full jurisdiction. As a qualification for appointment they were to have been barristers of five years' practice in England or attorneys of seven years' practice in this or an adjoining province. These features were objectionable to the Board of Trade, for they restricted the power of the king to select, thus encroaching on his prerogative, and they also rendered the justices independent of the Crown. The bill therefore had been annulled by the king, while the former court law of 1746 had been repealed by the Assembly. So the province was to be left without any court system whatever. Under these circumstances the governor deemed it prudent to withhold the announcement until the next session of the Assembly, which was to convene in December. When the Assembly met, in view of these new instructions, the lower house prepared another bill to establish courts that would be free from the particular defects that had led to the repeal of the original act; but this new measure was not agreeable to the governor and council, who objected to the manner in which the judges were to be paid and to the judicial power conferred on the associate justices provided for in the bill, and it failed to pass the upper house. So for a time—eight months in 1759 and 1760—there was a cessation of the courts in the province.

C. R., VI, 56
180

No courts

The governor had received among other instructions one forbidding him to assent to any act making paper money a legal tender; he was also informed that he might call a new election for assemblymen if he should choose to do so. Thereupon he dissolved the Assembly, it having already held nine sessions, and issued writs for the election of assemblymen to meet on April 22, 1760. The differences between the governor and the leaders now came to an acute issue, and the year 1760 is notable for its conflicts. It is also notable as the beginning of the practice of passing temporary court laws.

Currency

One of the reasons why the governor had not previously dissolved the Assembly was that he did not know how to apportion the representation. Most of the counties and towns had applied for charters of incorporation, but some had not. In issuing his writs for the election he omitted Tyrrell and other counties and some of the towns. Where elections were held, however, the Assembly admitted the members without regard to the writs, falling back on the old constitution of the colony and ignoring the claim set up by the Crown that it had a right to apportion representation at its will. Thus originated another cause of conflict with the governor.

The particular object the governor had in view in calling the Assembly was to have passed an aid bill, as great military efforts were in contemplation for the ensuing campaign. But riots and disorders had continued in Edgecombe, Halifax and Granville counties, and the Assembly was in illhumor at the governor's conduct in not seeking to suppress them. It adverted to the scenes of violence that had disturbed the peace of the province, and dwelt on the fact that there were no courts in existence to curb and restrain the lawless people; and it declared it would pass no aid bill until the superior court bill was assented to. The governor, on the other hand, was firm in his purpose to come to no terms with the popular leaders and would not assent to the court

Secret
session
May, 1760

bill. Finally, after some heated controversy, on May 23, 1760, the house, animated by a spirit of defiance, took bold action. It resolved itself into a committee of the whole, and warning the members that if any one should divulge what might be said in the debate he should be dismissed from the house, spent five hours in considering the action of the governor, and adopted a series of twenty resolutions aimed against him, and declaratory of his arbitrary conduct, and also prepared a long address to the king complaining very bitterly of his Excellency, which was to be presented by the agent of the province and was not to pass through the governor's hands at all. This resolute action apparently made some impression on the governor, who then proposed to come to terms, offering to prorogue the Assembly for three

The
governor
makes terms
C. R., VI,
410-414

days, and agreeing that if they would pass an aid bill, and also the court bill, with a clause limiting its operation to two years unless ratified by the king, he would assent to it in that form. This gave some hope of the establishment of courts and of correcting the disorders that threatened the peace and prosperity of the province, and so the leaders of the Assembly assented to the proposition and a court bill was passed similar to the previous one—the associate justices were to be skilled lawyers and were to hold during good behavior. With this beginning, for a period of more than ten years it became the practice to pass a court bill in that form, by which the duration of the courts became subject to a limitation of two years. Also under the agreement the house passed an aid bill, but the governor now had changed his mind as to the aid bill, and as he did not like some of its provisions, especially deeming the bounty offered for enlistments too small, and as he considered that the pressing necessity for raising troops no longer existed, he chose not to assent to it. At that time there was also a divergence between the two houses, for the upper house would not pass the bill appointing Abercromby the agent, so the house passed another appointing Mr. Bacon, which, however, shared the same fate. The clash involved matters of right and power and the privileges of the respective bodies, the lower house claiming the exclusive right of designating the agent, and also of selecting the committee of correspondence, which the upper house would not assent to. The house then by solemn resolution appointed Bacon agent of the Assembly, not of the province. In the midst of the turmoil the governor prorogued the Assembly until September 1st.

1760
C. R., VI,
420, 426, 437

C. R., VI,
437

The western counties desolated

While the governor and Assembly were engaged in their controversies conditions in the western part of the province became deplorable. In October, 1759, the people who had made their homes on the waters of the Yadkin and Catawba heard with dismay that the Creeks and Cherokees, theretofore friendly, had declared war against the English. Bands of Indians began to pass the defiles of the mountains and roam along the foothills. A reign of terror set in. Accounts of atrocities and butcheries and of destroyed homes came thick and fast to Salisbury and Bethabara. They were intensely

Clewell,
Hist.
Wachovia

harrowing, while some of the escapes were marvellous. Many brave men, reluctant to abandon their homes, fortified them with palisades, and forts or stronghouses were erected where neighboring families could assemble for safety. The men slept with their rifles at hand, and the most resolute were in dread of stealthy attack, of ambush and of having their houses burned at night. It was then that Fort Defiance and other forts in that region were hastily constructed by the people.

The narratives of those who escaped massacre were heart-rending, while many men, women and children fell victims to the cruel tomahawk of the merciless foe. Few particular accounts of these individual experiences have been preserved; but all the section west of the Catawba and of the upper Yadkin was desolated. Fort Dobbs, where Colonel Waddell was stationed, was, on February 27, 1760, unsuccessfully assailed by the hostiles; and information came through the "Little Carpenter" that Bethabara would be attacked, and preparations were made for the defence. At length a large body of Cherokees stealthily surrounded the town; but hearing the village bell ring, they supposed themselves discovered and retired. Again they approached just as the night watchman blew his trumpet, and they withdrew, and then desisted, although during that spring they remained for six weeks in the vicinity devastating the country. Among those who found refuge at Bethabara was a farmer named Fish and his son, who had escaped from their home on the Yadkin. Anxious to see if their house had been burned, they prevailed on another refugee, a stranger, to return with them to ascertain. On the way they were ambushed. Fish and his son fell, while the stranger was pierced by several arrows, one of which, passing through his body, protruded from his back. However, he escaped the Indians, and seeking to return, forded the Yadkin, where he soon saw another company of savages approaching. Again plunging into the river, he crossed and succeeded in eluding them. A storm set in, and he wandered all night in a pelting rain, suffering torture from his wounds, and in dread of being overtaken. Thus passed twenty-four hours, when at length he reached Bethabara, where the arrows were skilfully extracted by the good

Dr. Bonn. Unfortunately the name of this man was not recorded.

A detachment of soldiers marched out to give burial to the bodies of Fish and his son. On their way they found a farmer besieged and defending his home, which the savages had already succeeded in setting on fire. They quickly drove the hostiles off and saved the farmer and his children. The next day, March 12th, came an appeal for help from Walnut Cove, which was surrounded by the Indians. A company hastened to their rescue and brought in the survivors. A farmer, Robinson, had constructed a palisade around his house and resolutely made defence. Eventually he was driven from it into his log house, where he continued the struggle. At length his last load of powder was exhausted and he and his wife and children fell victims to the bloody tomahawk. Soon, however, sufficient soldiers arrived to secure protection, and on Easter Sunday, 1760, as many as four hundred soldiers attended the church services at Bethabara.

Walnut Cove desolated

The Assembly had been prorogued until September, but on receiving information of a general uprising of the Indians, and learning that the militia had refused to march beyond the limits of the province, Governor Dobbs convened the houses again on June 30th. All were now of one mind. An aid was at once voted to the king; a force of three hundred men was raised for service, the militia was organized, and authority was given to embody them for defence.

June, 1760

C. R., VI, 439

At a subsequent session held in November, 1760, there was a purpose to send five hundred men to co-operate with Virginia and South Carolina against the Cherokees; but in the aid bill then passed the Assembly had named the agent at London, whom the governor disapproved of, and for this reason he rejected the bill and prorogued the Assembly, which reconvened in its fifth session on December 5th to reconsider its action; but the house was firm in resisting the blandishments of the governor, who then dissolved it. The tide of war had rolled away from the borders of the province and the necessity for harmonious action had passed.

C. R., VI, 513

In February, 1761, information being received of the accession to the throne of the young king, George III, he was

1761 King George III

C. R., VI, 520

1761
proclaimed with great enthusiasm amid the firing of cannon on the Cape Fear, and writs for a new election of assembly-men were at once issued, and the body convened on March 31st.

When the Assembly met it lost no time in upbraiding the governor with his defeat of the aid bill, and because he had called the Assembly together at Wilmington instead of at some more convenient point, and the disagreement was pro-nounced. Rev. Mr. Moir wrote April 13th, while the Assembly was in session: "The misunderstanding between the governor and leading men of this province still subsisting, we are as unhappy as ever." But in the end the Assembly became more complaisant; a committee of correspondence was appointed embracing members of both houses, and a new agent was named, probably not objectionable to the gov-ernor—these, as at the previous session, being features of the aid bill, which the governor now approved. At the same session the tax to pay the salaries of the chief justice and attorney-general was increased.

In the meanwhile the Board of Trade had written to Gov-ernor Dobbs that he had no right to interfere with the appointment of the agent by the Assembly, but that he should urge the house to conform to the instructions of the Crown and recognize fifteen members as constituting a quorum, and to pursue the same method in regard to paying out moneys and auditing accounts that was in use at home.

A new election was called, the Assembly meeting in April, 1762. At that session Sam Swann, who had since 1743, with a single interruption, been the speaker, retired from that office, and his nephew, John Ashe, succeeded him. In all the controversies with Johnston and Dobbs, Swann had been the great leader. Indeed, on one occasion Johnston had silenced him as a lawyer, and Dobbs felicitated himself that as extreme as had been his own action he had never gone to that length.

Differences between the Assembly and council, whose mem-bership since the purchase by the Crown thirty years before had been changed only on the death of its members, and which was now composed of Hasell, Rutherford, DeRosset, Spaight, Sampson and McCulloh, led those gentlemen to say

C. R., VI, 552

C. R., VI, 539

The Assembly sustained

Ashe speaker

The council

to the Assembly: "We apprehend ourselves as nearly concerned in the blessings of liberty and property as any other inhabitants of this province, and shall ever with cheerfulness concur with you in every measure that to us shall appear conducive to the securing of these most valuable blessings." A new court law was passed that year, in which provision was made for an associate justice at Salisbury.

In conformity with political and religious conditions, it was considered that efforts should be made to maintain the Church of England as the national church in the province. From 1701 there had been parishes and vestrymen and some provision made for supporting clergymen of the established church. But so little effort was made to carry the law into effect that often there were only one or two clergymen in the province. As the province grew and the policy was introduced to fashion the government on the model of the mother country, renewed efforts were made in this respect. The vestry act of 1760 being repealed by the king, in 1762 another act was passed, which, however, was also disallowed because the appointment or employment of the ministers was conferred on the vestry and not allowed as a privilege of the Crown, although under that act all ministers employed had to hold the license of the Bishop of London. Thus it happened that in the autumn of 1762 all the vestries in the province were dissolved and the entire church system disorganized. Two years later, however, a new act was passed, in which the vestries were given power to levy a ten-shilling tax toward building churches, maintaining the poor, paying the readers and encouraging schools in each county.

The vestry act

S.R.,XXIII 605

Under Pitt's able administration the war had been so vigorously and successfully pressed that in the fall of 1760 Canada was conquered and the Indians brought into peaceful relations with the English. Three years later a treaty of peace was signed, by which the British Empire extended from the Gulf of Mexico to Hudson Bay and from the Atlantic to the Mississippi; and the colonists, now freed from fears of foreign foes, could devote themselves more exclusively to home affairs. The tide of immigration that ten years earlier was setting so strongly to western Carolina was, however, checked because of the Indian war. Yet at the conclusion

Peace of Paris,

C. R., VI, 1027, 1040

of peace North Carolina had a population of about 100,000 whites and more than 10,000 negroes. On the Cape Fear were forty saw-mills producing some 30,000,000 feet of lumber annually, and there were exported from that river 36,000 barrels of naval stores.

The Indian aborigines had nearly disappeared. On a reservation of ten thousand acres on the Roanoke were congregated all that remained of the Tuscaroras, the Saponas, and Meherrins. Of the first there were one hundred braves, of the last two only twenty each. The Catawbas had numbered three hundred warriors, but in 1761 so many were swept off by smallpox that only sixty braves remained, an equal number of women and hardly more than one child to each pair.

The remnants of the Hatteras Indians appear to have joined the Mattamuskeets on their reservation in Hyde, where were only some seven or eight Indian men. Originally it was said that the Indians had a violent antipathy to the negro, but in time that repugnance seems to have subsided, and there was some admixture of the two races.

Educational facilities in the province were limited. In 1749 John Starkey introduced a bill making an appropriation of £6,000 for a free school, but in 1754 that money was used for other purposes. Another appropriation of £6,000 was, however, then made. But there was some objection in England to this bill and it was disallowed. Four years later the Assembly prayed the king that a part of the sum allowed the province by the Crown in return for its aids might be used to establish churches and a free school in each county; but there was always an objection. Frequent applications were made for this permission, and as late as 1763 the request and denial continued, the Board of Trade merely saying that until the Assembly should be sufficiently compliant as to remove the original objections it would not consider the subject. Eventually, in 1765, Governor Tryon, probing the matter, could get no light on the subject otherwise, and formally asked the Assembly what the cause of difference was, receiving the answer that the Assembly did not know, as the objection had never been communicated to that body. On again representing the matter to the Board of Trade he was advised that "some complaints had been made against the original act by some merchants." And so because of Governor Dobbs's wilfulness in not communicating to the Assembly those objections in order that they might be removed or answered, "the complaints of some merchants" resulted in depriving the province of the benefit of free schools. Such was one of the results of the colonial system of government. 1762

The court system provided for a superior court, with a chief justice appointed in England, and three associates, who, in 1761, were Marmaduke Jones, William Charlton and Stephen Dewey—all good lawyers; but in 1762 the new act divided the province into five districts, in each of which, except the Salisbury district, an associate justice was appointed, who in the absence of the chief justice had jurisdiction to hear and determine all cases, except mere matters of law. For the Salisbury district an assistant judge was appointed. He was to be a learned lawyer and his jurisdiction was as ample as that of the chief justice himself. These court laws were to endure only for two years unless approved by the king, so there were constant re-enactments. S. R., XXIII 550 C. R., VI, 621 The Judicial System

Notwithstanding the provision made for the maintenance of an orthodox parochial clergy, there were in 1764 not more than six established clergymen in the province, and only three or four churches then finished. But the Presbyterians had their ministers, and the Quakers had again become flourishing. The Baptists also were numerous. Parochial clergy C. R., VI, 1039

Paul Palmer in 1727 gathered together a congregation of Baptists in the Albemarle section, and about 1742 William Sojourner settled on .Kehukee Creek, where later the Kehukee Baptist Association was formed, and early in 1755 Shubeal Stearns, a native of Boston, settled on Sandy Creek, where he soon drew into his communion more than six hundred members; and these churches became mother churches of the Baptist associations in North Carolina. Baptists

A new sect, too, had sprung up, calling themselves Methodists, zealous and enthusiastic religionists, but disclaimed by Mr. Whitefield, then on his passage through the province, as the followers of Wesley and himself, yet doubtless owing their origin to Whitefield's teachings in New England. C. R., VI, 1061 Methodists

Governor Dobbs was loud in his denunciation of all oppo-

1763

Republican-
ism rife
C. R., VI,
304-309

C. R., VI, 32

British
views with
reference to
America

McCulloh

C. R., VI,
1021

The right to
tax claimed

sition to his measures and schemes, and ascribed the antagonism of the leaders in the Assembly to a spirit of republicanism, which he declared was more rife in this province than in any other. He insisted that Speaker Swann, his two nephews, John Ashe and George Moore, and John Starkey, who formed the committee of correspondence, composed a junto, whose object was to lessen the prerogatives of the Crown and absorb the administration into their own hands and extend the power of the Assembly. That the Assembly under its leaders was ever determined in the assertion of its right to hold the purse and maintain the freedom of the people as subjects of Great Britain is sufficiently plain. How far any of the inhabitants were disaffected toward the monarchical system does not appear. Proud of their birthright as British subjects, they never contemplated the relinquishment of self-government under the constitution of the province; but they were loyal to their king and had no expectation of any change until at length, to their dismay, changes came.

The colonies had cheerfully made great appropriations to aid the king in the prosecution of his wars and to relieve the necessities of the Crown. But these were voluntary offerings. In England it was held that the general government of the mother country had a right to something more—to exact by law a fund for the purposes of the Empire. The regiments stationed in America were to be supported by the American colonies. The colonial governments were to be reformed and a surer provision made for the compensation of the governors and other officers. Quickly following the treaty of peace, these and other matters of similar import were discussed in England, and on October 10, 1763, Henry McCulloh, who for thirty years had been concerned with the American colonies, proposed a stamp act to raise the necessary funds. In January, 1764, Governor Dobbs wrote to the Board of Trade: "I apprehend the British Parliament may lay duties upon goods imported into the several colonies to support the troops necessary to secure our great acquisitions on this continent, as also to support the additional officers of the revenue." Such was the drift of official sentiment.

The Assembly of 1764

At the session of the Assembly held in Wilmington in February, 1764, that town began to be regarded as the seat of government for the province. Andrew Steuart, a printer located there, was employed to publish the laws. Brunswick and Bute counties were erected. An act was passed for building a school-house and a residence for a schoolmaster in New Bern, and John Starkey and Joseph Montfort were appointed the public treasurers for the term of three years. John Ashe was again elected speaker of the Assembly.

The early newspapers

Perhaps the conflicting interests of New Bern and Wilmington, or the more personal ambitions of two printers, in the summer of 1764 led to the revival of Davis' newspaper, now under the name *The North Carolina Magazine, or Universal Intelligencer.* And in September Andrew Steuart began at Wilmington the publication of *The North Carolina Gazette and Weekly Post Boy.* The *Post Boy,* however, was short-lived, and ceased to exist in 1767, being succeeded two years later by *The Cape Fear Mercury,* published by Adam Boyd.

Tryon appointed to relieve Dobbs

Governor Dobbs, who was now nearly fourscore years of age and very infirm, asked leave to return to England; and to relieve him, William Tryon, a young officer of the Queen's Guards, was, on April 26, 1764, appointed lieutenant-governor, and in July received his final instructions. On October 10th he arrived at Brunswick, expecting to enter at once on his duties; but to his disappointment he found that Governor Dobbs would not depart until the coming spring.

It was expected that there would be warm disputes when the General Assembly should meet in October, 1764. In the previous March the suggestion of McCulloh had been acted on and a resolution had passed Parliament, without question,

1764

that it was expedient to lay stamp duties on the colonies, and the public mind was greatly agitated. For a century England had restricted and regulated the commerce of her colonies, and in recent years Parliament had exacted heavy duties on trade with the adjacent French and Spanish settlements, while no manufactured goods could be imported except alone from English ports. But that had been for the expansion and regulation of commerce. Now a different interest was to be subserved, and Parliament proposed to tax the colonies for purposes of revenue. In England no one disputed the right; in America it was a question so novel and so momentous that at first public opinion was not pronounced. The omnipotence of Parliament had never been disputed. But on the passage of the resolution in March came an examination into the subject. The illumination was gradual. The power to tax was the power to destroy, and America became enshrouded in a turmoil of anxious thought. Such were the conditions when the Assembly met in October.

The power to tax

The firm stand of the Assembly Oct., 1764

As if to emphasize the spirit of the house, the governor and council having appointed a printer "under the sounding appellation of his Majesty's printer," the house declared it knew of no such office, and it resolved that James Davis should print the laws; and when the governor claimed for himself as a representative of the Crown, in conjunction with the king's councillors, the right to direct payment out of the funds allowed the province by the king, the house resolved "that the treasurers do not pay any money out of any fund by order of the governor and council without the concurrence or direction of this house." It proposed to hold the purse strings.

C. R., VI, 1314-1318

And in reply to the opening address of the governor the house said: "It is with the utmost concern we observe our commerce circumscribed in its most beneficial branches, diverted from its natural channel, and burdened with new taxes and impositions laid on us without our privity and consent, and against what we esteem our inherent right and exclusive privilege of imposing our own taxes."

Claims the exclusive privilege of imposing taxes C. R., VI, 1261

As yet no other Assembly in any other colony had made so positive a declaration. Incidentally the power of Parliament was flatly denied. Massachusetts had addressed a cir-

Assembly concurs with Massachusetts Bancroft, V, 204

cular letter to the other colonies asking concert of action in making a representation to the Crown and desiring "their united assistance." The speaker, John Ashe, on November 17th laid this letter before the house, and it was resolved that "Mr. Speaker, Mr. Starkey, Mr. McGuire and Mr. Harnett and Mr. Maurice Moore be a committee to answer the above letter," and "to express their concurrence with the sentiments of the House of Representatives of Massachusetts." Such was the first movement on the surface of the troubled waters. The house asserted its exclusive right to lay taxes, and to direct payment out of the public funds, and it sent to Massachusetts its concurrence in the proposed remonstrance.

1764

C. R., VI, 1296

Martin, North Carolina, II, 188

THE FIFTH EPOCH—1765-75

CONTROVERSIES WITH THE MOTHER COUNTRY

CHAPTER XXI

TRYON'S ADMINISTRATION—1765-71 : THE STAMP ACT

Governor Tryon's administration.—Unrest in Mecklenburg.— The cause of complaint in Orange.—The Assembly of May, 1765. —The vestry act.—The stamp act passed.—Desire for independence imputed to the colonists.—Popular ferment.—Speaker Ashe declares the people will resist to blood.—The Assembly prorogued.—Patrick Henry in Virginia.—Barré's speech in Parliament. —Sons of Liberty.—An American congress called.—Dr. Houston stamp-master.—North Carolina not represented.—Famine and disease in the province.—The people set up looms.—Action at Wilmington.—Liberty not dead.—Dr. Houston resigns.—Governor Tryon feels the people.—Deprecates independence.—The reply.—Desire for independence disclaimed.—The act not observed.—Non-importation. —The people united.—Conditions in England.—British merchants and manufacturers clamor for repeal.—Pitt.—Camden.—Conditions in America.—No business transacted.—The West settled.—In Granville's territory.—Judge Berry commits suicide.—The rising on the Cape Fear.—The people form an association.—They choose directors. —Fort Johnston seized.—Tryon's house invaded.—The act annulled. —Business resumed.—The Assembly prorogued.—The stamps stored. —The act repealed.—London rejoices.—America grateful.—Mayor DeRosset's manly sentiments.—Judge Moore suspended.

Governor Tryon

On March 28, 1765, Governor Dobbs, who was then preparing to depart for England, died at his villa at Brunswick, and William Tryon assumed the reins of government as lieutenant-governor, he having qualified as such in the preceding November. An officer of the army and a cultured gentleman, just turned thirty-six years of age and in the flush of vigorous manhood, and in many respects a masterful man, he at once gained the esteem of the people. To the Assembly on its meeting he promised his best endeavors to render acceptable service to the province, and declared that

e should ever deem it equally his duty "to preserve the
eople in their constitutional liberty as to maintain inviolable
ae just and necessary rights of the Crown"; and to the
ower house in particular he said: "In the integrity of my
eart I must declare I look for neither happiness nor satis-
action in this country but in proportion to the assistance
meet with in my endeavors to promote the prosperity of
s inhabitants." Events, however, were happening that
orely perplexed him. A condition of unrest pervaded the
rovince. In Mecklenburg County, where Selwyn had large C. R., VII, 37
acts of land obtained from McCulloh, many settlers had
ocated without deeds and would not acknowledge his claim Riot in Mecklen-burg
f ownership, and when his agent undertook to survey a
act for widow Alexander a mob assembled under the leader-
aip of Thomas Polk and severely whipped and abused the
arveyor, John Frohock, Abraham Alexander, and several
chers who were running the line, destroyed the compass, and
areatened young Henry Eustace McCulloh with death.

Toward the northern frontier there was trouble brewing Martin, North Carolina, II, 191
f a different character. After the adjournment of the
ssembly in November, 1764, reports reached Governor
obbs of serious disturbances in the county of Orange result- Unrest in Orange
ag from the exactions of the county officers, and Governor
obbs issued a proclamation forbidding any officer from
king illegal fees. But this did not arrest the evil, and the
gitation soon extended to Granville. "A Serious Address
o the Inhabitants" of that county was issued in June, 1765.
a it the authors declared that "they were not quarrelling
ith the form of government, nor yet with the body of
aeir laws, but with the malpractices of their county officers C. R., VII, 89
ad the abuses of those who managed their public affairs."
While the frontier settlements were thus agitated over their
ocal matters, on the seaboard the people were disquieted
acause of the purpose of Parliament to tax the colonies.

Immediately on entering upon his duties Governor **Tryon** Tryon's action
aconvened the Assembly, the meeting being held at New
ern on May 3, 1765. He urged that body to institute a C. R., VII, 41 *et seq.*
rict examination into the condition of the public funds,
ad recommended the re-enactment of the vestry act free
om the objections made to it; but in doing so he professed

1765
C. R., VII,
41 *et seq.*

C. R., VII,
205

himself the warm advocate of toleration as well as of prog
ress. Among other improvements, he suggested the estab
lishment of a post route from Suffolk to Wilmington, wher
it would connect with one to Charleston. In 1763 provision
had been made for one year for a post between Suffolk and
Wilmington. Now, at the instance of the governor, the
Assembly raised a committee to make this post route perma
nent, but for some cause the committee was not progressive
and did not carry out the purpose.

Agreeably to the governor's suggestions, a new vestry ac
was passed. The selection of ministers of the established
church was to be no longer with the vestries, but with the
governor, who also had the power to suspend them. On his
appointment the ministers were to be received into their
parishes as incumbents. The vestry were to pay the salary
and lay the taxes for that purpose. At this session contest
again arose between the two houses.

In 1759 the Board of Trade had instructed Governo
Dobbs that the committee of correspondence ought to consis
of members of both houses, which the lower house would
not agree to. In 1765 the council asked that all correspond
ence should be submitted to it, and the house hotly denied

Agent
suspended

the request. Referring to this episode, Governor Tryon
represented to the Board of Trade that if the house persisted
in that course the agent ought not to be recognized. The
house, nevertheless, maintained its right; so the agent was
suspended and was not recognized by the Board; and it was
not until 1768 that a new agent was appointed.

There was another contest over the appointment of a
treasurer. John Starkey having died, the lower house nom
inated Richard Caswell, while the upper house desired Louis
Henry DeRosset, one of the councillors. Their disagree
ment was not composed when, on the morning of May 18th
the Assembly was suddenly prorogued.

The stamp act

In England

A year had elapsed since Parliament had passed the reso
lution that it was expedient to tax the colonies. At length,
in February, 1765, the bill prepared by the ministry was
introduced in the House of Commons, where some oppo-

sition was encountered, fifty votes being cast in the negative; but in the House of Lords there was no division. On March 25th the bill received the royal assent.* To the petitions of the colonies in opposition to the measure it was constantly replied that their antagonism was founded in a desire to sever their connection with the mother country, and that the issue should then be met and the dissatisfied Americans should be reduced to submission. This, however, was not the spirit that animated the colonies. Indeed, while remonstrating, there was no other thought but of acquiescence. In April New York was still tranquil and Massachusetts was not aroused. Otis, the Boston leader, indignantly repelled the imputation that America was about to become insurgent, and declared it to be "the duty of all humbly and silently to acquiesce in all the decisions of the supreme legislature." No one will "ever once entertain a thought but of submission." "They undoubtedly have the right to levy internal taxes on the colonies"; and he solemnly declared, "From my soul I detest and abhor the thought of making a question of jurisdiction." *In America*

Bancroft, V, 271

The colonial agents in England, while vigorously opposing the passage of the act, had no other idea but that it would be carried into successful operation. Ingersoll returned to Connecticut as the stamp master, and Franklin recommended to his friends to apply for the places. In Virginia Richard Henry Lee sought the appointment. Still, when the event was imminent and news came in May that the act was passed, the people fell into a ferment. It was a matter of feeling rather than of cold reason. The popular heart was moved without regard to those in public station.

The Assembly of North Carolina had on the last day of October, 1764, declared that "we esteem it our inherent right and exclusive privilege to impose our own taxes." Virginia a fortnight later had less positively asserted the right, and had argued that the people of that province "cannot now be deprived of a right they have so long enjoyed"; but neither Massachusetts nor any of the other colonies, had *C. R., VI, 1261*

---

*This act not only required the payment of stamp taxes but provided for the trial of offenders against the act out of the province and without a jury.

1765
C. R., VII, i.
Martin,
North
Carolina,
II, 195

claimed exemption from parliamentary taxation. But the public mind now became agitated, and Governor Tryon, seeing
the trend of affairs, asked the speaker of the house what the
people would do. "Resist unto blood and death," was the
emphatic answer of Ashe. Apprehensive that the lower
house was about to take some action, the governor, on Saturday, May 18th, after the house had adjourned, suddenly

C. R., VII,
88

prorogued the Assembly till November, the business of the
Assembly being unfinished and not at all rounded up.

Near a fortnight later the session of the Virginia Assembly
was drawing to its close without any action having been
taken on the stamp act, when Patrick Henry, who had been
elected to fill a vacancy, took his seat as a member. At
once, on May 28th, he offered a series of resolutions on
the subject and sustained them in an impassioned speech.
"Cæsar had his Brutus; Charles I his Cromwell, and
George III"—"Treason! Treason!" was echoed throughout the hall—"may profit by their example."

Wirt, Life
Patrick
Henry, 75
et seq.

Opposed by the speaker, by Pendleton, Bland, Wythe, and
the Randolphs, the resolutions were adopted by a majority of
but a single vote; and the next day the last of the resolutions—the one asserting that "the colony had the sole right
and power to lay taxes"—was expunged from the record.

When the bill was before the House of Commons Colonel
Isaac Barré, who had served with Wolfe in Canada, made
an eloquent defence of the colonies, saying: "They planted
by your care! No; your oppressions planted them in
America. They fled from your tyranny. They nurtured by
your indulgence! They grew by your neglect of them. As
soon as you began to care for them, that care was exercised
by sending persons to rule them—men whose behavior on

Sons of
Liberty

many occasions caused the blood of those Sons of Liberty to
recoil within them." A copy of Barré's speech was hurried
to New York, and there, in June, was printed and distributed
by the thousands, while the startling words of Henry were
being echoed throughout America. The people became
greatly inflamed and aroused, and the expression "Sons of
Liberty" was treasured from Massachusetts to Georgia. Still
as yet the only thought was to secure relief by petition and
remonstrance. The Massachusetts Assembly, being then in

session, called for an American congress, which should consist of committees appointed in the several colonies by the representatives of the people, to meet in New York in October "to consider of a united representation to secure relief," and even then the question of exclusive right to tax the colonies was carefully avoided. The people watched and waited, hugging the delusion that their English friends would not drive them to despair. The Congress

In England there was no thought of retreat. The stamps were prepared and stamp masters were appointed for every colony. On July 11th the commissioners of the treasury appointed Dr. William Houston, of Duplin, stamp master for North Carolina. He did not apply for the position, and it is probable that he was appointed at the instance of McCulloh, for he appeared in North Carolina in 1735 as McCulloh's agent for settling his grants on the northeast branch of the Cape Fear, and for many years remained in that employment. The act was to go into operation on November 1st, and the stamps were early sent to the northern colonies. In October the Congress met. North Carolina, Virginia, Georgia, and some other colonies were not represented, as their assemblies could not meet to send deputies. It formulated a remonstrance and petition. Houston, stamp master

That summer was the hottest ever known in North Carolina in the memory of the inhabitants. There was a general failure of crops; and such was the extreme scarcity of provisions that the slaves were fed on "cattle and apples" until the potato crop matured in the fall. The following June vessels were prohibited from carrying out any breadstuffs, except for the necessary supply of the crews, and the Assembly was prorogued in April because of the scarcity of food. The yellow fever broke out in New Bern, and Governor Tryon himself was seized by a malarial fever that confined him until late in November. Yet notwithstanding their other distresses, the stamp act held the first place in the minds of the people. At Edenton and New Bern, as well as at Wilmington, the inhabitants adopted strong resolutions expressing their utter abhorrence of the odious act, and to manifest their indignation and purpose "the people of North Carolina set up looms for weaving their own clothes." C. R., VII. 154

1765
North
Carolina
Gazette
Nov. 20, 1765
Nor did their demonstrations stop there. On October 19th "near five hundred people assembled at Wilmington and exhibited the effigy of a certain honorable gentleman; and after letting it hang by the neck for some time near the court-house, they made a large bonfire with a number of tar barrels and committed it to the flames. The reason assigned for the people's dislike to that gentleman was from being informed of his having several times expressed himself much in favor of the stamp duty. After the effigy was consumed they went to every house in town and brought all the gentlemen to the bonfire, and insisted upon their drinking, 'Liberty, property, and no stamp duty, and confusion to Lord Bute and all his adherents,' giving three huzzas at the conclusion of each toast." This assemblage probably marked the formation of the Sons of Liberty on the Cape Fear, and was composed of the people of New Hanover and the adjoining counties.

C. R., VII,
123-125

Proceedings
at
Wilmington

"On October 31st another great number of people assembled at Wilmington, and produced an effigy of Liberty, which they put into a coffin, and marched in solemn procession with it to the churchyard, a drum in mourning beating before them, and the town bell, muffled, ringing a doleful knell at the same time; but before they committed the body to the ground they thought it advisable to feel its pulse, and when finding some remains of life they returned back to a bonfire ready prepared, placed the effigy before it in a large two-armed chair, and concluded the evening with great rejoicings on finding that Liberty had still an existence in the colonies."

Houston
resigns

Dr. Houston, on November 16th, came to Wilmington, and the people, three or four hundred in number, immediately gathered together with drums beating and colors flying and carried him into the court-house, where he signed a resignation, which was followed by great demonstrations; and in the evening "a large bonfire was made and no person appeared in the streets without having 'Liberty' in large capital letters in his hat; and they drank in great form all the favorite American toasts, giving three cheers at the conclusion of each." In Cumberland, at New Bern, and at his own home in Duplin, the people made similar demonstrations and hung Dr. Houston in effigy and then burned the effigy.

Governor Tryon, who was now somewhat recovered from his protracted illness, seeing the determination of the people, sent out circular letters to about fifty of the principal inhabitants, requesting their presence at dinner with him on November 18th. In his interview with these gentlemen the governor expressed his "hope that no violence would be attempted in case the stamps should at any time arrive in the province"; and also he hoped "that none in this province were desirous of destroying the dependence on the mother country." He mentioned "the impossibility of the stamp act operating in all its parts in this province, where the whole cash of the country would scarcely pay a single year of the tax," and declared his intention of making such representations that, whether the act were repealed or not, there would be a favorable indulgence and exemption of this colony; and as an inducement for allowing the act to have effect in part, he "generously offered to pay himself the whole duty arising on" certain instruments.

C. R., VII, 127-130

The next morning the gentlemen waited on the governor with their reply, saying: "We cannot but applaud the happy distinction of this province, which has a governor so studious of promoting and so well satisfied to prosecute its advantages and prosperity." They disclaimed "any desire to interrupt or weaken the connection between Great Britain and her colonies," but declared that "we cannot assent to the payment of the smaller stamps; an admission of part would put it out of our power to refuse with any propriety a submission to the whole; and as we can never consent to be deprived of the invaluable privilege of a trial by jury, which is one part of that act, we think it more consistent as well as securer conduct to prevent to the utmost of our power the operation of it." The governor in his reply regretted that his intentions of service to the province at this junction had so little prospect of success, and lamented the consequences he apprehended from the resolution the gentlemen had adopted.

The people refuse his overtures C. R., VII. 129

Such was the spirit of the Cape Fear gentlemen, openly

1765

C. R., VII,
143

avowing their purpose not to permit the operation of the act in any particular; and all the counties of the province were in full sympathy with them. Ten days after the dinner, and after Houston had resigned, some stamps arrived at Brunswick on the sloop-of-war *Diligence,* but because of the situation of affairs they remained on board that vessel until her departure in the spring.

Contemporaneously with these proceedings in North Carolina, the merchants of New York City entered into a resolution not to import any goods until the stamp act was repealed. Elsewhere their example was followed; and the people organized themselves into associations, taking the name applied to them by Colonel Barré in Parliament, "Sons of Liberty." A patriotic fervor possessed the people, and even before importations had ceased they discarded clothing of British manufacture and began to wear the homespun of the country. Rich and poor, those of the highest social and political station as well as the humblest citizens, joined in the cry of "Liberty, property, and no stamps." Never were the people so united; there was but one voice—to resist. In December Gadsden, of South Carolina, wrote: "The whole force of North Carolina was ready to join in protecting the rights of the continent," and in January the Sons of Liberty in New York resolved "that they would march to the relief of those in danger of the stamp act." Such was the sentiment that prevailed throughout the colonies.

In England other matters of serious import stirred the court and divided the people, and changes in the ministry were frequent. But at length the attitude of the colonists arrested attention; and merchants and manufacturers, aghast at the possible consequences to their business, united their clamors with those of the Americans for repeal. The king, nevertheless, was resolute, and when Parliament opened on January 14th he informed it that "orders had been issued for the support of lawful authority." Pitt, however, declared emphatically that Parliament had no right to tax the colonies, and like a clap of thunder he startled the house when he exclaimed, "I rejoice that America has resisted." In the House of Lords Camden spoke with equal strength. But

The spirit
of America

The king
resolute

Jan., 1766
Pitt

Camden

at first they were overborne. The purpose to maintain the omnipotence of Parliament was fixed. But politics were in a turmoil, and changes in the ministry suddenly occurred. A month after the session began Conway, now in the ministry, moved for leave to bring in a bill to repeal the act. He declared that it had interrupted British commerce and destroyed one-third of the manufactures of Manchester—had thrown thousands of poor out of employment, and that to assist the Americans, France and Spain would engage in war with Britain. Amid great excitement, despite the opposition of the king, leave was given by a vote of 275 to 167. The first step to repeal was taken.

The new year opened in America with all in a state of suppressed excitement. The act had not been operative. The courts were either closed or transacted little business. Newspapers were published on unstamped paper and ships sailed without legal clearances. It was a condition of unarmed rebellion.

Open rebellion on the Cape Fear

In North Carolina, Tryon having received his commission as full governor, on December 21st dissolved the Assembly and issued writs for the election of new members. The election was held in the midst of excitement on February 11th, and the legislature was to convene April 22d. Writing in January from New Bern, Rev. Mr. Reed said: "The people here are peaceable and quiet, yet they seem very uneasy, discontented and dejected. The courts of justice are in a great measure shut up, and it is expected that in a few weeks there will be a total stagnation of trade." On Christmas Tryon wrote home: "The obstruction to the stamp act . . . has been as general in this province as in any colony on the continent. . . . No business is transacted in the courts . . . though . . . regularly opened, and all civil government is now at a stand." Such was the situation in the east. At the west not a man favored the stamp act; but that matter was not so interesting on the frontier as in the marts of trade. Ten years of peace had brought renewed immigration from the north. A settlement from New Jersey was made on the Yadkin. The Moravians received accessions,

1766

and had engaged in manufactures. "They have mills, forges, furnaces, potteries, foundries, all trades and things in and among themselves." They drew copper from the neighbor-

C. R., VII, 285

ing mines. "They are all bees, not a drone suffered in the hive; what they do not consume they sell in the adjacent territory," receiving for their products furs and peltry, which they send off to Virginia and into South Carolina, obtaining in return rum, sugar, linen and woollen goods, pewter and tin wares and other necessaries. While this development was being made at Bethabara, Rowan and Mecklenburg counties were being occupied. During the fall and winter of 1765 a thousand wagons passed through Salisbury, and the people were clearing the forests seventy miles west of Fort Dobbs and forty miles beyond the Catawba.

In Granville's territory

In Granville's territory the land offices were closed on the death of Lord Granville in 1763, and his heir and successor had not yet opened them again. Some of the occupants of his lands dreaded the expected reopening, because of the abuses of his agents; while others were discontented because they could not obtain titles to the premises they had improved. The grievances of the people in the back country continuing, the movement for redress progressed, securing

C. R., VII, 144

the adherence of many of the inhabitants. Specie was very scarce, and while even the merchants estimated that because of the great growth of the province £200,000 of paper currency was needed, the amount outstanding was only £75,000. Necessarily there was great pecuniary distress. Such was the general condition of the province—unrest at the west, insufficient currency, civil government at a stand, and the Sons of Liberty holding together, not knowing what a day might bring forth.

Another event added to the gloom on the Cape Fear— the suicide of Chief Justice Berry. On March 18, 1765, a duel occurred between Lieutenant Whitehurst and Alexander Simpson, master, both of the British sloop *Viper*, the cause

C. R., VII, 94

of which was said to have been some woman. Simpson was wounded and Whitehurst killed. Simpson was apprehended, but the night before Governor Dobbs died he made his escape from jail and fled to Virginia. He was subsequently taken and put on trial at New Bern, where Chief Justice Berry held the court. The case was tried before the arrival of all of the witnesses for the prosecution, and Simpson was acquitted, at which the governor manifested much displeasure. When, on December 20th, the governor called a council at Wilmington to qualify under his new commission, Judge Berry, on being notified to attend, conceived that the council was called for the purpose of suspending him, and was so impressed with the belief that he at once shot himself in the head, and after lingering eight days died. The melancholy affair was greatly regretted. To succeed Berry, Governor Tryon commissioned James Hasell as chief justice. He was the senior member of the council and had at different times filled the office of chief justice for seven years. At the same time, in January, 1766, he appointed Robert Howe an associate judge.

Thus far Tryon had managed so astutely that there had been no clashing with the people. But it could not be averted.

In January two merchant vessels, the *Dobbs* and the *Patience,* came into the Cape Fear and were seized because their clearance papers were not duly stamped, and were held by the British men-of-war, the *Diligence* and the *Viper.* At once the patriots of that region were aroused and demand was made for their release. The matter was referred to the attorney-general, Robert Jones, who was at his home on the Roanoke, and during the delay the leaders of the people arranged their plans. The mayor of Wilmington resigned and Moses John DeRosset, a strenuous opposer of the act, was elected in his place. The people of Onslow, Duplin, and Bladen were brought together at Wilmington to meet those of New Hanover and Brunswick, and they entered into an association. "Detesting rebellion, yet preferring death to slavery, . . . we hereby mutually and solemnly plight our faith and honor that we will at any risk whatever, and whenever called upon, unite and truly and faithfully assist each other to the best of our power in preventing entirely the operation of the stamp act." On the next day, February 18th, the people chose John Ashe the speaker, Alexander Lillington and Colonel Thomas Lloyd "directors to direct the movement." General Hugh Waddell was appointed to marshal and command the citizen soldiery, of whom six hundred were

1766

Death of Judge Berry

C. R., VII, 160

C. R., VII, 168 *et seq.*

North Carolina Gazette, Feb. 26, 1766

Ashe and Waddell lead in oper rebellion

The Association

The Directory

1766
armed, while there were one hundred of the people unarmed. The purpose was to secure the liberation of the detained vessels, and they resolved to march to Brunswick and require their release and prevent the operation of the stamp act in any particular. It was an orderly movement of the people, organized under civil authority of their own appointment, with the military subordinate to the directory, at the head of

C. R., VII,
172 et seq.
which was the speaker of the Assembly. Accompanying the directors were the mayor and corporation of Wilmington, and gathered around them were all the gentlemen of the Cape Fear—a cavalcade of patriots intent on a high purpose and

The
Diligence
and the
Viper
defied
full of high resolve. As a measure of this incipient war the inhabitants of Wilmington determined that no provisions should be furnished to the British cruisers, and when the contractors' boat came to the town for supplies they seized the crew and threw them into jail, and with a great demonstration hauled the boat through the town in triumphal procession.

C. R., VII,
178
The directors sent by Harnett and Moore a letter notifying Governor Tryon, who, after Dobbs's death, resided at Brunswick, that they proposed him no personal harm, but were coming to right their wrongs; and forward the companies marched, Waddell's patriotic soul flaming high as he resolutely led them on to their act of treason and flagrant rebellion.

Fort
Johnston
seized
C. R., VII,
186
Quickly a detachment seized Fort Johnston; quickly the public offices were invaded and the papers of the detained vessels obtained. But yet the vessels were held by the men-of-war. Recognizing that a crisis was reached, the king's officers determined to stand by the colors of his Majesty to the last. There was to be no yielding to the insurgents.

The council
At noon on the 20th a council was held, attended by the governor and all of the British officers; and Captain Lobb, the senior naval officer, declared his unalterable purpose to hold the ship *Patience* and to require a return of her papers, which the insurgents had taken. And so it was agreed by the governor and all. But in the afternoon a party of the insurgents—doubtless the directors, Waddell, Harnett, James and Maurice Moore, Mayor DeRosset and the corporation of Wilmington—boarded the ship of war *Diligence,* and

here, under the royal flag, surrounded by his Majesty's officers, they made demand upon Captain Lobb to surrender the vessels and abandon any purpose to sustain the stamp act. What passed is not recorded; but in the evening Captain Phipps, of the *Viper,* came on shore and reported to the governor that "all was settled." The vessels were released. The people had redressed their grievances. The stamp act was not to be enforced in any particular. The governor was indignant, disgusted, but powerless.

The collector, the comptroller, the clerks, and other provincial officers, one of them, William Pennington, being taken by Harnett from the residence of Governor Tryon, were now brought with great formality all together, at the centre of a circle formed by the people, and there were constrained to make public oath never to perform any duty with regard to the stamps. The stamp act being thus annulled in North Carolina, in triumph the people returned to their homes victors over the governor and the king's forces.

The effect of this bold and determined movement, that had no exact parallel in any other colony—for first the people ordained a government with authority to direct and secondly they organized a military force subordinate to the directory—resulting in the full accomplishment of the purpose designed, must have been lasting on the minds of the people. It established the leaders still more in public confidence, for successful achievements appeal strongly to the popular heart. It also brought home to the people the value of organized resistance and prepared them to take resolute action when at a later day their rights and liberties were again invaded. With this experience, under the same chieftains, they were the more easily marshalled to sustain the measures of 1775 in open revolt from the dominion of the mother country. The submission of Tryon and of the king's naval forces to their power, the remembrance of that glorious triumph easily paved the way for their formation of military companies in March, 1775, for the destruction of Fort Johnston, and the expulsion of Governor Martin from the soil of the province.

After that no attempt was ever made to observe the stamp act in North Carolina. The governor and all public officers abandoned the contest. Vessels sailed in and out as before

1766

C. R., VII,
188

Houston
gives up his
documents

In
Parliament

The act
repealed

Rejoicing in
London

the act was passed. The business of the courts was resumed, and the act was entirely disregarded.

But as the Assembly was to meet in April, on February 26th the governor prorogued it till November, and he declared his purpose not to allow any Assembly to meet until he had received further instructions from the king. On April 15th Dr. Houston again appeared at Wilmington, and there he was forced to surrender to Mayor DeRosset his commission and his instructions. The *Diligence* having been ordered to depart, the boxes of stamps were transferred at the end of March to the *Viper,* and later were deposited in Fort Johnston, where they remained until sent back to England.

Proceedings similar to those in North Carolina took place in all the colonies, but nowhere else was there equal boldness and resolution in action; yet in every province the law had been entirely annulled by popular resistance. Still the issue was undetermined, and America, in an attitude of defiance, waited with anxiety for news from England.

Although the House of Commons, responsive to the demands of British trade and commerce, had expressed a willingness to repeal the stamp act, yet Parliament was by no means ready to abandon its alleged right to tax the colonies. *Pari passu* with Conway's bill for repeal, another, declaring the absolute power of Parliament to bind the colonies in all cases whatsoever, was rushed through the two houses; and in the House of Lords the repeal bill met with strenuous opposition and protests, but finally, on March 18th, it received the unwilling and sullen assent of the king. The multitude, however, applauded. There was great rejoicing in London, the vessels on the Thames displayed all their colors, the church bells rang out joyous peals, and at night the city was illuminated with bonfires, and all the principal houses were lighted from within. The swiftest vessels hurried the news across the Atlantic, where it was received with public demonstrations of universal gladness and heartfelt patriotism. So sudden a popular revulsion from apprehension and defiance to gratitude and loyalty is without a parallel in history. The colonists at once rescinded their resolves of non-importation, gave their homespun clothes to

1766

he poor, and turned their attention once more to their local concerns. Throughout North Carolina there was great rejoicing. At New Bern the gentlemen met at the court-house to celebrate the event. An elegant dinner was served in common-hall, Cornell presiding. Many toasts "were drank under a display of colors and other ensigns of Liberty, among them, toasts to Camden, Pitt Conway and Barré; 'the Liberty of the Press'; 'the Governor and the Province'; the whole conducted with great good order, decency and decorum." The day concluded with a ball in the court-house "and the evening was most happily and agreeably spent." At length on June 13th Governor Tryon received official intelligence of the repeal, and a week later Moses John DeRosset, mayor of Wilmington, on behalf of the corporation, addressed formal congratulations to the governor. In the course of subsequent correspondence DeRosset and the other gentlemen at Wilmington declared that they were well assured that the governor's conduct had always been regulated by no other motive than a generous concern for the public good. Still there was no abatement of manly expression, and in regard to their own action they pointedly said: 'Moderation ceases to be a virtue when the liberty of British subjects is in danger." Thus in the general rejoicing, while there was no admixture of bitterness for Tryon, there was asserted a resolution to maintain the rights of the people as British subjects; and Governor Tryon afterward mentioned that only one person connected with the uprising on the Cape Fear ever expressed any regret at his action, and he was not a native of the province.

While all of the gentlemen of the Cape Fear had taken a pronounced part in these stamp act proceedings, the governor manifested his displeasure at the action of Maurice Moore alone. He was assistant judge for the district of Salisbury, and because of his intemperate zeal and conduct in opposition to the act the governor suspended him, and on March 7th appointed Edmund Fanning to the vacancy. In addition to his personal participation in the expedition to Brunswick, Moore had published a pamphlet showing that the colonists "are constitutionally entitled to be taxed only by their own consent."

The colonists grateful

S.C. Gazette Aug. 5, 1776

C. R., Vii, 242

CHAPTER XXII

Tryon's Administration, 1765-71 : The Regulation

Murmurs from the west.—The governor's proclamation.—The reform movement.—The general polity of the province.—Tryon's action.—Purpose of the reformers.—Removal of the Tuscaroras.—The Assembly meets—November, 1766.—The burden too heavy to bear.— The address to the king.—The southern treasurer.—No provincial agent.—The governor's palace.—The seat of government —Presbyterian ministers to perform marriage ceremony.—The Cherokee line.—The Watauga settlement.—The need of currency.—New legislation.—The speakers to be gowned.—Tryon joins in asking for currency.—New custom duties proposed.—The Assembly prorogued.—The Regulators associate.—The meetings.—Oath-bound. —Hillsboro raided.—Consternation of the officers.—Rev. George Micklejohn the peacemaker.—The governor advises an appeal to the Assembly.—Fanning seizes Husband.—The people aroused.—A petition to the Assembly.—Presented to the governor.—His reply —He reaches Hillsboro.—Sends Harris to collect taxes.—Harris's report.—Hillsboro threatened.—Disturbing rumors.—The agreement. —The voice of Anson.—Trouble in Johnston.—The governor's demands.—The army of 1768.—The Presbyterian ministers support the governor.—The march to Hillsboro.—The Regulators embody. —The governor's terms.—The malcontents disperse.—The court held.—Tryon desires to leave.—Regulators' address.—Resolve of Assembly.—Remedial legislation proposed.—Hillsboro riots.—Riot act.—Alamance.—The battle.—The trials and executions.

Murmurs from the west

1766

On June 25, 1766, Governor Tryon, happy at the turn of affairs, issued a proclamation announcing the repeal of the stamp act and on the same day, in pursuance of particular instructions received from the Crown, he issued a proclamation in the king's name, stating that complaints had been made that exorbitant fees have been demanded and taken, to the great dishonor of the king's service and the prejudice of the public interest; and all public officers whatever in their respective stations throughout the province were forbidden "to receive any other fees than those established by proper authority on pain of being removed from their offices and prosecuted with the utmost severity of the law." On the

C. R., VII, 138, 231, 232

1. NORTH CAROLINA CURRENCY, 1748   2. NORTH CAROLINA CURRENCY, 1776
3. EDMUND FANNING
4. MONUMENT TO THE REGULATORS

1766

ame day, because of the extraordinary want of provisions 1 the province, it was determined that the General Assembly should not then be convened, but should stand pro-ogued until October.

C. R., VII, 249, 250

While the eastern part of the province now returned to a appy quietude, the disturbed conditions at the west were ot allayed. In August the leaders of the reform movement 1 the county of Orange issued an advertisement, referring o the success of the Sons of Liberty in withstanding the ords of Parliament, and proposing that each neighbor-ood throughout the county should meet and appoint one r more men to attend a general meeting at Maddock's Mills, at which meeting let it be judiciously inquired whether the ree men of this country labor under any abuses of power," nd proposing to call upon all persons in office to give an account of their stewardship, a proceeding similar to the town-hip meetings immemorially held in Massachusetts. On)ctober 10th such a meeting was held, but none of the fficers appeared as requested. Disappointed in this first ttempt, both at the lukewarmness of the people and the on-attendance of the officers, the leaders proposed that an-ther conference should be called, and the practice be maintained, believing that "on further matured deliberation the inhabitants will more generally see the necessity of it and the umber increase in favor of it to be continued yearly."

Reform movement at the west

1766

The complaints of these people were because of the administration of local affairs. The general polity of the province vas the outcome of circumstances. The king appointed the governor, the chief justice and the attorney-general, the irst two of whom being sent from England while the last 1ad been appointed from among the citizens. The council vas a continuing body, appointed by the Crown, and, as none 1ad ever been removed, holding for life. From Burrington's administration appointments had been made only to fill vacancies caused by death or removal from the province. When a vacancy occurred, the governor made a temporary appointment until the Crown could act. A part of the ex-enses of the administration was paid by the quit rents; out generally the needs of government were met by taxes issessed by the Assembly. There was no tax on land or

The general polity of the province C. R., VII, 472 *et seq.*

property, only on the poll and on some minor subjects c
taxation. As the expenses increased, the poll taxes wer
multiplied and became grievous, especially in the frontie
counties, where the people were without market for thei
produce and had no currency and many of them were poor.

There were five judicial districts, for each of which a
associate judge was appointed by the governor; and whil
the associate for the Salisbury District alone was require
to be a lawyer by profession, yet all of these associates wer
lawyers. To each district court there were two clerks, on
for civil causes appointed by the chief justice, the other th
clerk of the Crown for criminal cases, appointed by th
secretary of the province.

There was a court for each county, pleas and quarte
sessions, held by the justices of the peace, and to each o
these courts there were likewise two clerks, one for civi
causes and the other the clerk of the Crown. The appoint
ment of the first was with an officer of the province, denominated "The clerk of the pleas"; the clerks of the Crown wer
appointed by the secretary of the province. Oftentimes one
person filled both offices. The sheriffs of the different
counties were annually appointed by the governor, but he
was confined to select from among three persons recommended by the justices of the peace; and the register of
deeds was likewise appointed by the governor to hold during his pleasure. The fees of all officers were fixed by law,
and a part of the compensation of the chief justice also
consisted of fees incident to his court. The influence of
these local officers was felt in the election of members of
the Assembly and in perpetuating their own power, and they
became dominant factors in the management of public
affairs. The attorneys-at-law were also potent influences,
and of these there were forty-five practising in the province.
Convinced of the abuses that these conditions led to, Governor Tryon sought to mitigate them, and among other
things announced that no county court clerk or practicing attorney should be appointed a justice of the peace—the justices
of the peace being appointed by the governor with the sanction of the council, to hold at his pleasure. All local affairs
were within the administration of these justices, who, sitting

as the court of the county, primarily passed on all complaints of exorbitant fees or charges of maladministration by the county officers, had cognizance of county matters, laid county taxes and settled with county officers. Under that system there was no responsibility to the people. The justices of the court annually recommended the sheriff for appointment and they influenced the election of assemblymen. They were appointed by the governor on the recommendation of the Assembly. Thus they became a part of a self-perpetuating circle, composed of officers, lawyers, justices and their dependents, controlling local affairs, and with interests widely different from those of the people at large. Popular discontent could not make itself felt in legal and accustomed channels; and this seems to have been the fundamental reason for the innovation proposed by the reformers to introduce county meetings of the inhabitants annually to consider the action of their officials and all public matters, and such at first was the extent of the demand.

No responsibility to the people

During the summer of 1766 the sachem of the Tuscaroras, who had moved to New York fifty years before, came to the province, and after spending some time with the Indians on the reservation, arranged for the removal of more of that tribe to join the Six Nations. The funds for their removal were supplied by Robin Jones, attorney-general, who had long manifested a particular kindness toward those isolated and almost friendless Indians. A part of the reserve was conveyed to him as security, and one hundred and thirty Tuscaroras in August marched north, leaving only one hundred and four of that tribe, including women and children, remaining in North Carolina.

Removal of Tuscaroras

C. R., VII, 431

The Assembly meets

C. R., VII, 343

On November 3d the legislature convened at New Bern, being the first meeting of the representatives of the people since May, 1765. During the intervening eighteen months the public voice had been stifled by the astuteness of the governor, and now harmony and good understanding subsisted throughout the province. On the first day of the session, November 3d, John Harvey of Perquimans was unanimously elected speaker, and it was not until November 7th that

Harvey speaker

John Ashe, the speaker of the former house, appeared and took his seat as a member. The temper of the house while kindly was not subservient. The committee to prepare a response to the governor's opening address were Elmsly Maurice Moore, Sam Johnston, Cornelius Harnett, Edmund Fanning, Robert Howe and Joseph Hewes. In it they said "This house is truly sorry that any reason whatever should have prevented your meeting this Assembly till this time. The alarming tendency of the stamp act and the reproachful names of rioters and rebels which were liberally bestowed on his Majesty's faithful subjects of North America rendered it in our opinion highly expedient that this house should have been assembled some months sooner." Continuing, they said: "It is our duty to acknowledge in the most grateful manner the moderation and goodness of his Majesty and the justice of his Parliament in removing from us a burden much too heavy for us to bear." A similar tone of fine manhood pervaded the address, yet they manifested a kindliness toward the governor himself, and congratulated him "on a peculiar mark of the royal favor to this province, manifested to us in your appointment to this government; and be assured we will cheerfully take all occasions to render your administration easy and happy."

C. R., VII, 347-350

The tone of the Assembly

The council took great exception to the strictures of the Assembly, but the governor carefully suppressed his own sentiments, merely declaring that he was "an utter stranger to the reproachful and detestable title of rebel; that such an opprobrious title never found place in my breast; nor am I conscious of having ever misrepresented or aggravated any part of the disturbances in the colonies, either general or particular."

On November 22d the house appointed Messrs. Ashe, Fanning and Howe a committee to prepare an address of thanks to the king "on the happy event of the repeal of the stamp act;" and on the 26th Ashe, the central figure in the stamp act proceedings, submitted the address to the house. It was strong and manly as well as patriotic. There was no wavering; no apology. The language used to the governor was now repeated to the king. The stamp act was "a burden much too heavy for us to bear," but they

GATCHEL & MANNING
PHILA.

GOVERNOR'S PALACE, NEW BERN

1766

spoke of their "cordial and natural attachment to the mother country, and love and duty to his Majesty's royal person."

Because of the failure to elect a treasurer for the southern district at the last session the governor had appointed as temporary treasurer Samuel Swann, and now the lower house proposed to appoint John Ashe. The upper house, however, again asserted its right to participate in the election, and inserted the name of Louis DeRosset, as on the former occasion. But on the lower house standing firm the council proposed to amicably settle the difference by joining in and making the same nomination, without abandoning its claim of participation; and Ashe was thereupon elected. The restoration of good feeling between the Assembly and the Crown was signalized by the passage of an act appropriating £5,000 for the building of a residence for the governor at New Bern, virtually making that the seat of government; and taxes were laid for the purpose of paying the cost of construction. To the governor himself was given power to design the building and to contract for its completion. Governor Tryon soon found that the amount appropriated was not sufficient to complete a building according to the plans adopted, but nevertheless he proceeded in the erection of a magnificent structure, surpassing any other building in the colonies, having reason to believe that the Assembly would make an additional appropriation.

C. R., VII, 324
S. R., XXIII, 664

New Bern the Capital

At this session the act concerning marriages, passed in 1741, was amended, much to the gratification of the Presbyterians. By that act the justices of the peace where there were no established ministers were authorized to perform the marriage ceremony. These justices in the western counties were for the most part Presbyterians, as the great mass of the inhabitants were, and now the law was changed, extending the privilege of performing this service to Presbyterian ministers; but the fee for the service was reserved to the ministers of the established church in the parishes where one was settled; and the marriage license was to be granted by the governor, who furnished a supply in blank, and signed by him, to the county clerks. On December 2d, with very amicable relations existing between the

S. R., XXIII, 672
Marriage Act

1766
C. R., VII, 675

1767
governor and the Assembly, the session was brought to its close.

The Cherokee line

In the progress of settlement the colonists were encroaching on the hunting grounds of the Indians, and there was more or less friction along the whole frontier from Canada to Georgia. The king and ministry were anxious to prevent hostilities, and some of the Cherokee chieftains had visited England and been assured by the king of his purpose to protect them. Dividing lines were ordered to be run that should mark the hunting grounds of the Indians and the limits of the territory open to settlers. Such a line had been run from McGowan's Ford, on the Savannah, northeastwardly to Reedy River, leaving a considerable territory east of the mountains in South Carolina as Indian lands; and Governor Tryon was ordered to have that line continued through western North Carolina. The Indians had in October agreed that the line should run from Reedy River north to the mountains, and then to Chiswell's lead mines on the New River or the Kanahwa. Now some chiefs contended that it should be run direct from Reedy River to the mines. Governor Tryon was desirous that the change should not be made, but that the North Carolina boundary should be the mountains. In order to effect his purpose he proposed to attend the meeting of the Indians and surveyors. It is to be observed that the dividing line between North and South Carolina had been marked out only to the Catawba nation, and to the westward of the Catawba River it had not been established at all; but in any event North Carolina was interested in running the Indian boundary north from Reedy River to the mountains, for that left no Indian hunting grounds east of the mountains. Many Indian chieftains were to be present and locate the line. On May 6th the governor left Brunswick, and on the 21st, with an escort of fifty men and a considerable number of surveyors and woodsmen, he took up his march from Salisbury for Reedy River, where he was to meet the Indians. On June 4th, with their sanction, Governor Tryon directed the line to be run a north course to the mountains. He favorably im-

C. R., VII.
245, 460, 470

1767

1767

pressed the Indian chieftains, one of whom was the Wolf of the Keowee, the others having similar names; and they complimented him, after their fashion, by conferring on him the title of "The Great Wolf." The line was run fifty-three miles north, where it struck a mountain, which the surveyors named Tryon, now in Polk County, on the dividing line between the Carolinas, but then supposed to be well within the limits of North Carolina, in fact located on the map of that period as being in the Brushy Mountains, so little was then known of the western portion of the province.

C. R., VII, 508
Great Wolf of Carolina

On his return the governor issued a proclamation forbidding any purchase of land from the Indians and any issuing of grants for land within one mile of the boundary line.

Some years earlier adventurous hunters had begun to pass the mountains in search of game. Of these Daniel Boone was perhaps the boldest. He crossed the valley of the Holstein, passed through Cumberland Gap, and visited Kentucky. At length, about 1768, settlements began to be made on the Watauga, the first to erect a cabin and to move his family, it is said, being William Bean, removing from some North Carolina settlement. Others soon followed. Thus began the occupation of that region, which later received large accessions from the inhabitants of the western counties.

Boone

Watauga

On December 5th the legislature again met. It made provision for paying the cost of running the Indian boundary, amounting to about £400, expressed its sense of high obligation to the governor for superintending it in person, thanked him for his care in erecting the governor's house and for calling attention to abuses in the collection of taxes by the sheriffs, and referred to the harmony and industry that prevailed in the province, but called attention to the distress, almost ruin, that seems "to be our inevitable lot from the great want of a sufficient quantity of circulating currency."

C. R., VII, 565

New legislation

The two years for which the court law had been enacted being about to expire, a new law, establishing six judicial districts, was enacted to continue in force for five years and until the end of the next session of Assembly thereafter. These courts were to be held by the chief justice and two

S. R., XXIII, 688

1768
associate justices, and in case of the absence of the chief justice or either of the others, it was lawful for one to hold the court. Maurice Moore and Richard Henderson were appointed the associates.

S. R.,
XXIII, 711,
723
An additional £10,000 was granted for finishing the governor's house and a poll tax of 2s. 6d. was imposed for three years for that purpose. A stringent law was enacted with regard to the accounting of sheriffs, and members of the Assembly were declared ineligible to the sheriffalty. Public warehouses were established for tobacco at Campbellton, at Tarboro, Kinston, Halifax, and seven other points in the northern part of the province, inspectors to give receipts for the same, their receipts or notes being transferable in the course of trade; and similar warehouses were established at Campbellton and Halifax for the storage of hemp and flax.

Commissioners were appointed to construct a public road from the frontier in Mecklenburg County—that then extended to the mountains—through Rowan, Anson and Bladen, to Wilmington. The design was to connect the back country with the seaports of the province, the people of Mecklenburg and Rowan having theretofore established trade relations with Charleston.

Under Governor Tryon's influence and the progress of events, there was a disposition to depart from the simplicity of former years, illustrated by the construction of the governor's palace, and the Assembly determined that the speaker and other officers of the two houses should appear in robes appropriate to their offices, and the governor was requested to procure them at the public expense. On January 16, 1768, the business of the session being well finished, the Assembly was prorogued until May.

Tryon joins
in asking for
currency
Because of the general distress incident to insufficient currency, acknowledged by the governor and merchants as well as by the people, a petition to the king was drawn by the Assembly, praying leave to issue £100,000 in paper currency, and promising not to make any currency lawful tender for any indebtedness to the Crown or to any merchant or C. R., VII,
681 others residing in Great Britain. The inference was that this paper currency would be made legal tender for debts within the province. Governor Tryon strongly urged that

this request should be granted. He dwelt on the great need for currency in the province, representing that there was not enough for the payment of taxes, and that indeed he thought that the ability of the people to raise the funds for the governor's mansion depended on this proposed issue of currency. He therefore had a personal interest in the matter. But the petition was denied on the ground that legal tender paper currency led to frauds, and that no consideration of local inconvenience would induce the ministry to ask Parliament to depart from the principles of the act it had passed in 1764 forbidding the issue of legal tender paper money. Later Tryon again urged that this favor be granted to the people, for the public distress was augmented by the new taxes laid for the mansion, for the judges and other officers, and for other expenses that had been incurred at his instance. Much to his mortification he was curtly answered by the Earl of Hillsborough that the subject had been disposed of and could not be reconsidered.

Pursuant to the declaratory act of March, 1766, new cus- tom duties had been imposed on the colonies by act of Parliament and a board of customs officers was appointed. This proceeding led to the publication of "Letters from a Pennsylvania Farmer" that again aroused the colonists, and the Assembly of Massachusetts in February, 1768, issued a circular letter to the other colonies, asking for "a united and dutiful supplication" to the Crown, but the apprehension was expressed that they would be considered "factious and disloyal, and having a desire to make themselves independent of the mother country." This letter was received by Speaker Harvey on the first day of April; and at the end of that month the governor prorogued the Assembly till the middle of June. In the meantime the burgesses of Virginia had made a similar address. Soon afterward Governor Tryon received directions from the Earl of Hillsborough that if the Assembly of North Carolina should indicate any purpose to take action on the subject, he should prorogue or dissolve it, and in conformity with these instructions he prorogued the Assembly.

1768

The Regulators associate

While continental matters were thus again claiming public attention, the people in the back parts of North Carolina were continuing their efforts to redress their local grievances. The initial proceedings of this movement had been directed from Sandy Creek, a tributary of the Deep (now in the eastern part of Randolph County), where Hermon Husband* resided. In the same vicinity lived his brother-in-law, James Pugh; William Butler, the Coxes, Hendrys, Fudges, and other active men. Farther north was the residence of James Hunter, the first cousin of James and Alexander Martin, a man of parts and a strong speaker. Rednap Howell, another agitator, was a schoolmaster, and a maker of rhymes, whose point and wit, rather than their musical cadences, appealed to the popular heart. The greatest interest was manifested by the people west of the Haw. In February, March and April meetings were held at various points, and it was resolved that they should be held regularly every three months. The officers had not attended, as required, to give an account of their stewardships. The demands of the people were unsatisfied. Under the direction of their leaders they proposed to press forward, and a new character was imparted to the movement. An oath-bound association was entered into, binding the subscribers to pay no taxes until they were satisfied that the levies were agreeable to law; and to pay no officer any more fees than the law allows; and they desired "that the sheriffs will not come this way to collect the levy, for we will pay none before there is a settlement to our satisfaction," and they asked that their assemblymen and vestrymen should appoint a time to settle with them. Hitherto the inhabitants engaged in these proceedings had assumed no name, and were spoken of as "the mob," or "the country;" now they began to be known as "the Regulators."

The Sons of Liberty had vetoed the power of Parliament to tax America. The Regulators of Sandy Creek, not questioning the power of their county courts and Assembly to

1768
C. R., VII,
713 *et seq.*

C. R., VII,
671, 726

C. R., VII,
699, 726 *et seq*

---

*While this name has been generally spelled Husbands there is no question that the true spelling is Husband. See facsimile autograph in Weeks, Southern Quakers and Slavery, 178.

1768

lay taxes, vetoed the collection of the levies until they themselves should have passed on the propriety of payment.

The grievances they sought to remedy were general, all The oath-bound association
persons except the officers being affected, and they had the
sympathy of even those who had not subscribed the association. By April they were assured of the coöperation of
many in the adjoining counties of Rowan and Anson, and
they were strengthened in their purposes by these accessions.
It was not long before an occasion arose for determined action. On April 8th Sheriff Harris of Orange distrained a
horse for a levy. The people were quick to resist. A hun- C. R., VII, 705, 710 *et seq.*
dred armed men appeared in Hillsboro, then a hamlet of two
stores, a few straggling log dwellings, a framed building or
two, and a small wooden court-house. They seized the sheriff Hillsboro raided
and tied him, took possession of the horse, treated several
of the inhabitants roughly, and being provoked by some one
at the residence of Colonel Edmund Fanning, shot several
bullets through the house, but without wounding any one.
Colonel Fanning was an attorney and was absent, attending
the court at Halifax. He was a representative of the county
in the Assembly, colonel of the militia and register of deeds,
by the appointment of the governor, in whose regard and
esteem he stood very high. He was the leading officer of the
county, and had now become the chief object of popular resentment.

This outbreak caused consternation among the officers of
the county. They had long been threatened; now threats
had become action. John Gray, the lieutenant-colonel of the
militia, hastened to consult with Major Lloyd, proposing to
call out the militia men, and he despatched information to
Colonel Fanning. Fanning immediately ordered the captains C. R., VII, 713 *et seq.*
of the militia to raise their companies; but the defection was
so prevalent that to the astonishment of the officers, only
one hundred and twenty men responded. Indeed Adjutant
Francis Nash, who was also the clerk of the court, reported
that such was the universal dissatisfaction with the officers
and leading men, that one hundred and fifty men could not be
raised in the whole county to oppose the Regulators. Fanning hurried to Hillsboro and found that the people in
every part and corner of the county were confederating by

1768

solemn oath and with open violence to refuse payment of taxes and prevent the execution of the law, threatening death and destruction to himself and others. He reported to Governor Tryon that he learned that on May 3d they were to environ the town with fifteen hundred men and execute their vengeance on him; and if not satisfied to their desire

C. R., VII, 716

they were to lay the town in ashes. Great was the excitement, and panic prevailed. On April 25th the Regulators held a general conference, and on that occasion the minister

Micklejohn counsels moderation

of the parish, Rev. George Micklejohn, attended and persuaded them from going to Hillsboro in a body, but to appoint twelve men to be there on May 11th and have a settlement with the officers in accordance with instructions then agreed on.

C. R., VII, 718, 720

Governor Tryon, on being informed of the riotous proceedings of April 9th, ordered the militia of Bute and six neighboring counties to hold themselves in readiness to march to Fanning's assistance; and wrote advising that if there were any grievances, the people should appeal to the Assembly; and he declared that every matter founded in equity and justice would have his support, on condition, however, that the people would disperse and that order and tranquillity should be restored. These despatches were borne by his secretary, Mr. Edwards. But Fanning had not been content to await developments. He proposed to act with reso-

Husband and Butler arrested

lution. On Sunday night, May 1st, having caused warrants to be issued for the arrest of Husband and William Butler, Fanning with twenty-seven men dashed out to Sandy Creek and early Monday morning made the arrests, and hurried back to Hillsboro, where an order was prepared to incar-

C. R., VII, 743

cerate the prisoners in the New Bern jail. The news flew through the country and a prodigious enthusiasm aroused the people; they hurried with their arms to Hillsboro, but in the early morning as some seven hundred men were approaching the town, they were, to their astonishment, met by Husband. As quick as Fanning had been, popular action

The people in arms

had been equally as speedy. The country was in arms, and the prisoners could not be conveyed to New Bern without rescue, and so, constrained by the uprising of the people,

1768

Fanning caused them to be released on bail. Thus Husband was unexpectedly restored in safety to his friends.

Later in the morning Secretary Edwards came out to meet C. R., VII, 733, 758, 767 the people. He read to them the governor's proclamation, and promised in the governor's name, if they would return to their homes and be quiet, he would seek to secure a redress of their grievances and would lay the matter before the Assembly. To this they agreed, saying that that was all they wanted. Such a petition was drawn for signature. While it was being circulated among the people there were a few days of repose. Ralph McNair, a warm friend of Their petition Fanning, had lately spent some days with Husband, who had conferred with him as to the criminal offences that mobs might commit, and on McNair's return to Hillsboro he addressed a long letter to Husband more fully explaining these criminal matters, and urging him to come and confer with Fanning, bringing with him other men of his neighborhood, such as William Butler, John Lowe and James Hunter; and he enclosed a petition which he suggested should be adopted and signed by the Regulators. But that petition did not meet their views, and at a general meeting, held on May 21st, it was resolved to hold by the first draft that had then been signed by about four hundred and fifty men, and a committee was appointed to prepare an address to the governor, giving a full narrative of the grievances of the people, and of their action from the beginning. This paper is exceedingly C. R., VII, 759 *et seq.* well written and reflects much credit on its author. It was signed by John Lowe, James Hunter, Rednap Howell, Harmon Cox, John Marshel, William Cox, William Moffitt and George Hendry, one of whom probably wrote it. It was drawn with candor, and in some measure it bears testimony of the esteem in which Governor Tryon was held even by the Regulators themselves. At a meeting of the committee C. R., VII, 766 on May 30th, held at Cox's Mill on Deep River, they directed James Hunter and Rednap Howell to lay this address, the petition, and all the accompanying papers before the governor and council. This duty was performed on June 20th, and the next day the governor, with the concurrence of the council, wrote his reply addressed to "the inhabitants on the south side of the Haw." While calling on

1768

C. R., VII,
792, 794
Tryon's
answer

the people to desist from any further meetings and to abandon all title of Regulators or associators, and to allow the sheriffs and other officers to execute their duties, the governor promised to "listen to the voice of distress and the just complaints" of the people and "the hardships they may groan under," and to give orders for the prosecution of every officer who had been guilty of extortion or illegal practices. At their request the governor also informed them that the provincial tax for 1767 was seven shillings, to which were to be added the county and parish taxes. The Regulators, however, concluded that some of the provincial taxes laid for a particular object had long since answered the purpose of their creation, and that the public funds should be in a very different situation from that reported by the Assembly and the treasurers. They also saw that the proclamation of the governor against the taking of illegal fees had had no effect, for the register, they said, had raised his fees rather than reduced them.

Tryon reaches Hillsboro

On July 6th Governor Tryon, who resided during the summer months in the up country, arrived with his family at Hillsboro. Days passed, and no answer was received to his letter, but he learned that the Regulators were continuing

C. R., VII,
796

their meetings. A difficult situation was presented. Large numbers of the inhabitants, not actuated by any vicious propensity, had joined themselves together in an oath-bound association to nullify the law. That the grievances they complained of were not merely imaginary, the governor had reason to believe. Thus far he had treated them with consideration, courtesy and respect. He had received their communications from their representatives and had answered while firmly, yet neither arrogantly, defiantly nor unkindly. As a representative of the king and the chief officer of government, he could do not less than require submission to the constituted authorities, but apparently he sought conciliation. The time coming on for the appointment of sheriffs, he did not reappoint the sheriffs of Orange and Rowan, but substituted Lea for Harris in Orange and appointed a new sheriff for Rowan. Still Harris had to collect the back taxes,

C. R., VII,
799, 821

and the governor on August 1st, being determined to assert the authority of the province, sent Harris among the Regulators to make collections and advise them that he expected them to obey the laws of the country according to his letter of June 21st.

Two days later the sheriff returned and reported that he found assembled at the meeting at George Sally's nearly four hundred men, who unanimously refused to pay any taxes and declared they would kill any man who should dare to distrain for their levies. Other unavailing intercourse ensued between the governor and the Regulators, and the flame of discontent was constantly fanned. By August 9th five hundred men assembled at Peeds, and information was brought to Hillsboro that if the insurgents' demands were not complied with they would burn the town. The next day they approached to within twenty miles of Hillsboro, and matters wore a serious aspect. But Tryon was not dismayed. He ordered out all the militia, two hundred and fifty of whom obeyed the call, and proceeded to fortify the town. On the evening of the 12th eight of the principal insurgents sought an interview with the governor to arrive at an understanding.

One of the wild rumors that flew among the people was that the governor was to bring down the Indians on them, and that he was raising the militia to harry their settlements. It was this that inflamed them. At this interview the governor made denial of such purposes; Colonel Fanning and Mr. Nash agreed to submit the differences between the people and themselves to the judgment of the supreme court; and it was further agreed that the accounts of the sheriffs and other officers, after being examined and approved, should be posted at the court-house, and that the sheriff should make no collections until after the approaching superior court in September. At the same time the governor gave directions that the Regulators should meet on August 17th at George Sally's, where the sheriffs should attend with their settlement and give satisfaction to the people. These terms satisfied the leaders, and the Regulators dispersed and returned to their homes. But the governor was not at all satisfied. By show of force the people had gained a point; and unless

The Regulators determined

C. R., VII, 819 et seq.

They approach Hillsboro

C. R., VII, 804

Tryon orders out militia

They disperse

1768

C. R., VII,
724, 766

In Anson

C. R., VII,
807

In Johnston
C. R., VII,
885

C. R., VII,
706

the powers of government were asserted, they would persist
in having their own way. The extension of the movement
had become formidable. Already their general meeting was
spoken of by their committeemen as their "General Assembly." From Anson, where in May the inferior court
had been broken up, came an address to the governor from the malcontents, informing him that they to
the number of five hundred had resolved if nothing happened to their succor to defend their "cause in the disagreeable manner of a force, and to have persisted
unto blood." In August also came the disturbing information that a body of eighty men had assembled at
Johnston County court with the intention of turning the
justices off the bench. It was the very first day of the term.
The justices adjourned court for the term, and rallying the
friends of government attacked the insurgents, and after a
smart skirmish drove them out of the field. It seemed
to the governor, if the movements were not arrested,
that civil government in most of the counties would be over-
turned, and that the insurgents would abolish all taxes and
debts, and all laws for the enforcement of order. The trial
of Butler and Husband was to be at the September term of
court, and grave apprehensions were felt that the Regulators
would rescue their leaders if convicted. Against such an
event the governor took pains to guard. On August 13th,
with the concurrence of the council, he required that twelve
of the principal men should wait on him at Salisbury and
give bond as security that no rescue should be made of Butler
and Husband; and he determined to call on the people not
involved in the defection to rally for the support of government. He proposed to embody the militia of the western
counties to protect the court and enforce its judgments.

The army of 1768

Aug., 1768

On the very day that Sheriff Lea was to meet the people
at George Sally's by the governor's own appointment, Governor Tryon left Hillsboro for Salisbury, where he arrived
the next evening. He issued orders for the review of the
Rowan regiment on the 26th, and then hastened on to Mecklenburg, where he found emissaries from Orange arousing

the people. The purpose of the governor was to collect a 1768
force of volunteers through the militia organizations to sus-
tain the court and curb the Regulators. On the 23d nine C. R., VII, 809 *et seq.*
hundred militiamen were reviewed at Colonel Polk's, and The governor seeks aid
an association oath to "maintain the government and laws
against all persons whatsoever who shall attempt to alter,
obstruct or prevent the due administration of the laws or
disturb the peace and tranquillity of the province," was tendered them, but it being objected to, the call for volunteers
was postponed. Subsequently a large number volunteered.

Reaching Salisbury on the 25th, the governor found that
the Regulators, while declaring that they had no intention
to release the prisoners, declined to give the bonds required.
But if disappointed by this denial, the governor had the C. R., VII, 814
satisfaction of receiving assurances from another quarter.
The four Presbyterian ministers in the western counties sent The Presbyterian ministers
him an address, enclosing the pastoral letter they had writ-
ten to their flocks, urging the Presbyterians to be steadfast in
support of government. He also found much gratification
in the result of the review of the militia at Salisbury. So
prompt and unanimous was the Rowan regiment to respond
to his call for volunteers that the governor with great formality presented the king's colors to the Rowan regiment,
and requested that Captain Dobbins' company, which was
the first to volunteer, should bear them. Returning to Meck- C. R., VII, 823
lenburg, he directed the volunteers from that county to
assemble on September 12th, and issued orders for the
Rowan regiment to join him at Salisbury on the 13th. On
the night of the 13th the two battalions encamped on the
Yadkin, having with them two pieces of artillery, nine
wagons and accompanied by droves of beeves. *En route* to C. R., VII, 828
Hillsboro this little army passed for three days through the
very heart of the disaffected district. Orders had been issued
for the Orange and Granville militia to assemble, and on the
21st all the forces were united at Hillsboro. Here, too, the
governor was joined by a number of gentlemen from the
east and a company of cavalry. But the insurgent leaders The Regulators embody
had not been inactive. They had collected a force of some
eight hundred men, and at daybreak of the 22d took post
within less than a mile of the town. However, instead of

1768
C. R., VII,
841

making any attack, they opened negotiations for a settlement of differences. Governor Tryon had been ill for several days, an illness that confined him for some five weeks. He convened a council of his officers and required that the Regulators should deliver up their arms, surrender five of their chiefs for trial, and should also declare that they would pay all taxes assessed against them. Not relishing these terms, the malcontents deemed it best to disperse. Thirty of them, however, delivered up their arms. The superior court opened its session on September 22d. It was presided over by Martin Howard, the new chief justice, who had been appointed by the king and now displaced Hasell. He was a lawyer of Rhode Island, where, because of his loyalty in stamp act times, he had been hung in effigy, and his house and property destroyed by the outraged people. Leaving Rhode Island, he had in the intervening years resided in England. With him on the bench were Maurice Moore and Richard Henderson, the associate justices; while McGuire, a fine lawyer, was the prosecuting officer, and John Cooke, appointed by the chief justice, clerk of the court. Husband was indicted and tried for being concerned in the riot, but was acquitted. Fanning was indicted in many cases for extortion, found guilty, and in each case was fined a penny and costs. His defence was that he had submitted the question to the inferior court as to what fees he was entitled to, and he had in every instance taken less than the court had adjudged would be his due. William Butler was indicted for rescue of goods and also for a riot, and John Philip Hartso was likewise indicted for a riot. These were convicted. Butler was fined £50 and sentenced to six months' imprisonment. Hartso's sentence was lighter. Francis Nash appears to have been indicted for extortion, but his case was not tried, and he was bound over till the next term of the court. An indictment against James Hunter, Hamilton and others was found a true bill by the grand jury, but was quashed for irregularity; another indictment against James Hunter and others was also quashed; and still another. From these proceedings it would appear that the court held the scales of justice with an even and impartial hand. Immediately at its close Governor Tryon issued a proclamation, "out of com-

They retire

Martin
Howard

The court
held

C. R., VII,
843 *et seq.*

Trials of
1768

1768

passion to the misguided multitude, and being much more inclined to prevent than punish crimes of so high a nature," granting pardon to all concerned in the disturbance of the public peace, except Hunter, Husband and eleven others; and he released the prisoners and suspended the payment of their fines for six months, and later asked the king to extend pardon to all, both as to persons and fines, except alone as to Husband; and he represented to the king that "to say that these insurgents had not a color for their showing a dissatisfaction at the conduct of their public officers would be doing them an injustice, for both the register and clerk of the county of Orange were found guilty of taking too high fees." Colonel Fanning on conviction immediately resigned as register.*

The governor's attitude

Quiet was now restored to the province, and the Assembly, being convened on November 3d, on the 7th a quorum appeared, and the governor made a report of his proceedings against the Regulators. The house expressed to Governor Tryon its fullest conviction of the necessity for marching troops to Hillsboro, and its detestation of the riotous and illegal proceedings of the insurgents, and gratefully thanked him for his action. It also thanked him for his efforts to secure an emission of paper currency as a legal tender, and again declared that it was "the only remedy of saving this province from ruin." It concurred in the governor's opinion that the interior policy of the country was never more an object of serious concern than at that juncture, and the house added that it was happy in supporting his actions, and that it most sincerely wished that he should long continue to preside over the province.

Nov., 1768 Governor thanked by Assembly

C. R., VII 931

Tryon desires to leave

Toward the close of 1768 it had doubtless come to be understood that Governor Tryon was desirous of relinquishing his position as governor. His relations with the Earl of Hillsborough, who was the minister in charge of the colonies, were close, and to him probably Tryon confided his wishes. Not only did he see loom up before him the contest with the people growing out of their resolute purpose not to submit to

*In England the law officers held Fanning blameless. (C. R. VIII, 33.)

1768

the exactions of Parliament, but the particular conditions in North Carolina must have been a source of annoyance as having been in some measure the result of his own action in fastening taxes on the people beyond their ability to pay, and thus inflaming the discontent which required force to

S. R., XI,
219
Mercer,
lt.-gov.

suppress. Besides, he had suffered grievously in his health, and so in December, 1768, George Mercer was appointed lieutenant-governor. Mercer was a Virginian, and had served with Washington in the French and Indian War. He had been stamp distributor in 1765, and had suffered for his loyalty. Like Martin Howard, he had taken up his residence in England, and now it was proposed to provide for him, as had been done for Howard, in North Carolina. He waited in England expecting to take Tryon's place when he should leave. A little later, an infant son having died in March, and perhaps urged by his wife, Tryon made a formal request to be restored to his regiment, or to be employed at court.

He had so managed as to avoid issues and disputes with the Assembly, and at this session his personal influence was

In other
colonies

still a factor. There had been clashing elsewhere. In Massachusetts the opposition to the collection of the custom duties had led to orders for troops and armed vessels to be stationed at Boston. On receiving information of this movement the people of that city, much excited, requested the governor to convene the Assembly, and when he refused the towns and districts appointed deputies to hold a convention.

Nov., 1768

This body, the first of the kind, met and issued an address on the subject of the people's grievances. In other colonies public ardor was also aroused. When the North Carolina Assembly convened, Speaker Harvey presented the two letters from Massachusetts and Virginia that had been received in

C. R., VII,
928

the spring. There was evidently a division of sentiment, but moderation prevailed. The speaker was verbally directed to make reply to the letters; and then local affairs engaged the attention of the body. Among the acts passed was one prohibiting that the two offices, clerk of the superior court and clerk of the inferior court, should be held by the same person.

Tryon
County

A new county was set off on the frontier of Mecklenburg and named Tryon in honor of the governor. Disappointed

in its hopes of being allowed to issue legal tender currency, 1768
the Assembly, to pay the indebtedness of the province, now S. R.,
XXIII, 759
et seq.
directed promissory notes to be issued to the amount of
£20,000, and it authorized the sheriffs to receive in
payment of all taxes, except those for the sinking fund, these
notes and the promissory notes and receipts given by the inspectors at the public warehouses for tobacco, hemp, rice,
indigo, wax, tallow and deer skins. Such were the best
measures the Assembly could devise to relieve the financial
stringency and to make easy the payment of taxes. To
lighten taxation the house also adopted a resolution that a
tax of a shilling per poll imposed in 1760, and one of two
shillings imposed in 1761 had had their effect and ought not
thereafter to be collected; and although the governor could
not give his assent to the resolution, the direction of the
Assembly was obeyed by the treasurers, sheriffs and people. C. R., VII,
983
Governor Tryon, however, again offered to lay before the
Crown an impartial statement of the situation, and to urge
that permission be granted to emit legal tender paper currency.

The obstacle to the appointment of a provincial agent C. R., VII,
877, 973;
VIII, 9
H. E.
McCulloh,
agent
continuing, the house by resolution appointed as its agent
Henry Eustace McCulloh, who, though a member of the
council, was in England on leave, and was a correspondent
of Speaker Harvey; and it adopted a remonstrance and address to the Crown, expressing "their concern and anxiety
because of the acts of Parliament in regard to taxation" and
declaring that "free men cannot be legally taxed but by
themselves or their representatives," and praying the king's
"interposition in favor of the distressed and oppressed people in the colony." Its tone, however, was submissive rather
than obstructive. It did not please Sam Johnston,
who denounced it as "great pusillanimity." On the other
hand Tryon felicitated himself on the temper and moderation of the Assembly. Doubtless there was a motive to
seek favor abroad and, through the good offices of Governor
Tryon, to secure if possible permission to issue legal tender
currency, which was deemed so vitally necessary to the peace
and happiness of the people. The chief obstacle in the way
of accomplishing this purpose was Lord Hillsborough, and

1769

C. R., VII,
973

C. R., VIII,
39, 58-60

March, 1769
C. R., VIII,
32

with him Tryon was supposed to have a particular influence. Having adopted its address and appointed an agent to present it, the house now appointed a committee of that body to conduct the correspondence. Among those appointed were Samuel Johnston and Joseph Hewes, but they declined the service, Johnston saying that the proceedings "were so inconsistent with his sentiments" that he refused to join in the address. The address was well received by the king, and Lord Hillsborough at once indicated that while he could not assent to the issue of a legal tender currency, yet if the Assembly would ask to issue a paper currency founded on credit, similar to that of New England and Maryland, every indulgence would be allowed.

In England there was much diversity of views in regard to America. Parliament in February urged the king to action, and that he should have offenders against the law transported to England and tried there; but McCulloh wrote to Harvey: "I have it from authority to acquaint you that the acts complained of are to be repealed—their proud stomachs here must come down—our politics are a scene of confusion. Men's minds seem greatly inflamed. The ministry most cordially hated." Hillsborough himself wrote to Tryon that "in the opinion of the present ministry it was inexpedient to tax America; that instead of other taxes, at the next session the ministry is to propose to take off the duties on glass, paper and colors."

Six months had now passed with no notable disturbance among the people. At March term James Hunter was tried at Hillsboro and, although convicted, was awarded a new trial. Husband, who was also then tried, was acquitted. Sheriff Lea, when attempting to arrest some of the former insurgents, was seized by their friends and severely whipped; but the governor, who seemed inclined not to be too quick to raise a quarrel with the people, said that the act did not meet with the general approbation of the Regulators, and the people were quiet; yet the council recommended that the prosecution of the offenders should be conducted with the utmost rigor of the law. On May 6th, Governor Tryon, announcing that he had qualified under his commission as governor, dissolved the Assembly and issued his writ for an election of new members, to be held July 18th.

In view of this election the Regulators issued an address to the inhabitants of the province, hoping to change the personnel of the Assembly. In it it was declared that the causes of the commotions were the misapplication of the public money to the enriching of individuals without defraying the public expenses; pillaging the people by exorbitant and unlawful fees of public officers; limiting the jurisdiction of the inferior courts, dragging the people into the superior courts, adding greatly to the necessary expenses and cost of litigation. Especially was stress laid on the enormous increase of the provincial tax, and with fine art it was said: "Many are accusing the legislative body as the source of all these woeful calamities. These, it must be confessed, are the instrumental cause." But the address bluntly laid the trouble at the door of the people, and asserted that "the original, principal cause is our own blind, stupid conduct in choosing persons to represent us who would sacrifice the true interests of their country to avarice or ambition." It was declared that "the majority of our Assembly is composed of lawyers, clerks and others in connection with them, while by our own voice we have excluded the planter." It was a strong address. It had its effect in Orange, Granville and Anson. In Anson, Spencer was rejected by the people; in Granville, Tom Person and Howell Lewis were elected. Orange sent Husband and Pryor instead of Edmund Fanning and Thomas Lloyd. Mecklenburg and Rowan, however, stood firm. In the latter Rutherford was again returned, but Frohock, then under grave charges, gave place to Sheriff Locke. While there were other changes in several counties, they do not seem to have been due to these influences. However, the Regulators were not content to rest there. In August a committee was raised to attend the Salisbury court, and to bring to justice those officers who had broken the law; but their efforts were without avail, for in every case they presented the grand jury ignored the bills. Yet they had this satisfaction—that the governor, having received authority from the king, now issued his proclamation pardoning

1769
C. R., VIII, 38
Wheeler, Hist. North Carolina, II, 325

The causes of complaint

Husband's book

C. R., VIII, 106

C. R., VIII, 67

1769

James Hunter and all other persons who had been concerned in the disturbances of the previous year. The ordeal of the courts had been stood. No punishment had resulted.

Storm at New Bern

On September 7th a great disaster befell New Bern and the eastern part of the province. The severest storm ever known devastated that section. The tide rose in a few hours at New Bern twelve feet higher than ever before, and the wind blew so violently that nothing could stand before it. Every vessel and boat was driven up into the woods. One entire street, with its houses, storehouses and wharves, was swept away, and several of the inhabitants were carried off in the flood. Bridges and ferryboats were destroyed, and the roads were impassable for weeks because of the fallen

C. R., VIII, 71, 159
The new Assembly

trees. For the most part the crops were lost and there was great suffering in all that region. In the midst of this wreckage the Assembly met in October at New Bern, Harvey again being the speaker. The situation was somewhat different from that at the previous session. In May the Virginia Assembly had adopted vigorous resolutions against the acts of Parliament, and George Washington was about to present resolutions again recommending the non-importation of British goods, when Lord Botetourt, the governor, hastily

Oct., 1769

dissolved the Assembly. But the members were not to be

The meeting at Raleigh Tavern

thus outdone. They immediately convened as a sort of convention at Raleigh Tavern and adopted Washington's resolutions and communicated their action to the other colonies, and once more non-importation agreements were entered into by the people in all the provinces.

Similar sentiments dominated in North Carolina, and to allay them Governor Tryon in his address to the Assembly

C. R., VIII, 88

urged that: "The weighty concerns that will fall under your consideration this session require all possible temper and moderation;" and he had the happiness to inform the body that the ministry, instead of laying further taxes, had the intention to propose to Parliament to take off the duties on glass, paper and colors; and he besought their prudence and candor and a confidence that would remove the prejudices that had been excited against the mother country.

The house proceeds to business

Petitions were presented to the Assembly by many inhabitants of Anson County, and also by inhabitants of Orange and Rowan, setting forth the grievances of which the Regulators complained, and urging remedies. These papers, like the address to the governor of May, 1768, were admirably drawn. Especially were the remedies recommended in the Anson petition worthy of the earnest consideration of the Assembly. They proposed reforms that in the progress of events had become necessary in the administration of public affairs. The house first, with the concurrence of the governor, appointed an agent for the colony, McCulloh being continued in that employment. Then, when it had hardly entered on the business of the session, Speaker Harvey presented the resolutions transmitted by the House of Burgesses in Virginia.

Nothing now was to be gained by moderation. The appeals of the governor were disregarded and the Assembly at once unanimously adopted similar resolutions and also

"RESOLVED, That the sole right of imposing taxes on the inhabitants of this his Majesty's colony in North Carolina is now and ever hath been legally and constitutionally vested in the house of Assembly, etc.

"RESOLVED, That all trials for treason or crime whatsoever committed in said colony by any person residing therein ought of right to be had and conducted in and before his Majesty's courts held within said colony," etc.

In the address to the king the Assembly said: "We cannot without horror think of the new, unusual, and permit us to add unconstitutional and illegal mode recommended to your Majesty of seizing and carrying beyond seas the inhabitants of America suspected of any crime," etc.

An address to the king was adopted which the committee of correspondence was to transmit to McCulloh "with directions to cause the same to be presented to his Majesty and afterward to be published in the English papers." This measure, as violent as it was unexpected, was a blow in the face to the governor. As a salve to his wounded pride, the house, however, assured him of its steadfast confidence in

Nov., 1769
Petitions for
new counties

C. R., VIII,
75-81, 151

C. R., VIII,
122
The
Assembly
defiant

C. R., VIII,
135

1769

Nov. 6-7,
1769

S. C. Gaz-
ette, Dec. 8,
1769

Non-im-
portation

his good purposes and intentions, and of its unalloyed esteem and attachment; but its action required him under his
instructions to dissolve the Assembly, and this he did with
some show of mortification rather than of anger. But the
members, notwithstanding the dissolution, immediately repaired to the court-house, organized by electing John Harvey
moderator, and prepared an association paper which they
signed, pledging themselves to non-importation and not to
use goods of British manufacture.

C. R., VIII,
169, 170

Writing to Lord Hillsborough in January, Tryon referred to his application to be relieved as governor, and remarked that the proceedings of the Assembly wounded his
sensibilities—the more because he was dangerously ill at the
time. He had no expectation of re-establishing cordial relations. "Confidence, my lord," said he, "that delicate polish
in public transactions, has received an ugly scratch, and I
fear we have no artists here who can restore it to its original
perfection." He would have been glad to leave the province
at once, but until the building at New Bern should be completed and his accounts should be passed on, he felt it necessary to remain; but he ardently requested leave to return to
England in the spring of 1771. Hillsborough about the same
time directed him to call a new election of representatives,
and urged that he should be cautious in his speech; for indeed the governor's address to the last house, "pledging the
faith of the Crown for the repeal of some taxes," had been
brought into Parliament, and a motion made there that "it
was derogatory to his Majesty's honor, and to the freedom
of parliamentary deliberation." But Hillsborough was able
to protect him, and the proposed rebuke failed to pass.

Martin,
Hist. North
Carolina,
II, 253

The wishes
of the
people

Before the dissolution the house had entered zealously on
business. The petitions of the inhabitants of the different
western counties were read to the Assembly by Husband, one
of the representatives of Orange. Apparently they were not
drawn by the same hand. One from Orange, signed by
Francis Nash and other officers of the government, asked
that there should be established at Hillsboro a public inspection of tobacco and hemp, and other commodities; one

C. R., VIII,
75-80

from Anson County particularly desired that Presbyterian
ministers might be allowed to celebrate marriage with pub-

ication of banns. The grievances complained of by the Regulators were set forth in petitions from Anson and from Orange and Rowan. The state of the sinking fund was particularly commented on. A division of Orange and Rowan was asked for. It was proposed as remedies for existing evils the use of tickets and ballots at elections; imposing taxes on estates; not collecting taxes in money until there was more currency; abolishing fees and perquisites for the chief justice, paying him by a salary; giving to a single justice the power to enter final judgment without appeal and without lawyers on small debts; restricting the fees of clerks and lawyers, and relieving defendants of costs on indictments when not found guilty by the jury. The Assembly was also requested to send a remonstrance to the king on the conduct of the receiver of quit rents, and also in regard to the action of the governor and council in granting warrants for lands. And the Assembly was asked to establish warehouses on the Peedee, on the Catawba, at Campbellton, and at some point in Tryon County; and finally that every denomination of people might marry according to their respective ceremonies. Some of these proposed reforms had in the progress of events become necessary in the administration of public affairs, and were worthy of the earnest consideration of the Assembly.

Reforms

Agreeably to these petitions the Assembly had at once begun to devise remedial legislation. A bill allowing a single justice to try cases involving only £5 passed all of its several readings, except the third in the council, when the dissolution occurred, and it fell. Another, to limit the fees taxed for attorneys, met with a similar fate. The Assembly was pressing forward in the consideration of such measures when it was notified of the impending dissolution; and then in its last moments, with the hope and expectation of beneficial results, it passed some resolutions intended on the one hand to remove grievances and on the other to curb popular demonstrations. It resolved that the public accounts, beginning with the year 1748, should be examined and stated by Mr. John Burgwin, confessedly a very competent accountant, who was required to make his report at the next session; and it resolved that if any public officer exacted illegal fees, on

C. R., VIII, 101
The Assembly responsive

C. R., VIII, 139
Public accounts

1769 conviction he should receive the highest punishment the house could inflict. But opposition to sheriffs being prevalent and peace within the province being of the greatest moment, the house declared that all persons who opposed sheriffs in the execution of their office should be regarded as enemies of their country and deserving of the highest punishment.

The failure of remedial enactments because of the unexpected dissolution was a great disappointment to those members of the Assembly who sympathized with the Regulators. A similar disappointment was felt generally by the people at the west. They had counted much on their appeal to the Assembly, and now the Assembly had passed without result.

Feb., 1770 In February the governor issued a proclamation for a new election of assemblymen. In view of this election the leaders of the Regulators at once entered on an active campaign to gain members favorable to their interest. Large parties visited the counties in the upper districts, and even ill-treated those who refused to join their standard. As yet they had not paid their taxes. For the year 1766 the sheriff C. R., VIII, 156, 192, 195 of Rowan reported 1833 of them delinquent. For the year 1768 only 205 paid taxes in that county, not being one in ten of the inhabitants. On March 13th, the day after the election, Judge Moore, who was holding court at Salisbury, wrote to the governor that "there is no such thing as collecting the public tax or levying a private debt," and that civil process could not be executed among the Regulators. Early in April the governor therefore issued a proclamation commanding the enforcement of the law and requiring that all sheriffs obstructed in their office should attend at the next meeting of the Assembly.

The Sons of Liberty Active The rebellious action of the late Assembly, however, determined the governor to postpone the meeting, and he prorogued the Assembly until November. But proroguing the Assembly did not deter the people. At a general meeting of the Sons of Liberty of the six Cape Fear counties, held at Wilmington on July 5th, Cornelius Harnett being the chairman, it was resolved to adhere to non-importation; and as South Carolina Gazette, July 26, 1770 Rhode Island had violated her faith, they resolved to have no mercantile dealings with Rhode Island, and that "all mer-hants who will not comply with the non-importation agreement are declared enemies to their country." And it was asserted that not only the inhabitants of the six counties, but of every county in the colony, were "firmly resolved to stand or fall with them in support of the common cause of American liberty." The temper of the people was firm and fixed to maintain their rights and to resist British aggression; and Governor Tryon saw with uneasiness on the one hand the resolute Sons of Liberty, and on the other the discontented inhabitants of the interior agitating for desirable local reforms and for a mitigation of local grievances which he was powerless to remedy.

Early in June the palace was so near completion that the governor removed from Brunswick and took up his residence in it.

The superior court broken up

When the superior court was to meet at Hillsboro in September, Chief Justice Howard was absent. Judge Richard Henderson opened the court on Saturday, September 22d. On taking his seat a petition, addressed to the chief justice and associate justices, was presented by James Hunter, in which it was declared that the juries were illegally drawn and were prejudiced, and that the county justices were parties to the delinquencies of the sheriffs and other officers; that the officers still took illegal fees; that the sheriffs would not settle, and their bondsmen were insolvent; that justice was not administered in the courts, and that they had determined to obtain redress, but in a legal and lawful way. On receiving this address Judge Henderson promised to make an answer to it on Monday; but on the opening of the court on that day some one hundred and fifty Regulators, at the head of whom were Husband, Hunter, Howell, Butler, Hamilton and Jeremiah Fields, came into the courthouse armed with clubs and whips. Fields, addressing the court, declared that the Regulators did not propose to have the cases against their leaders postponed, but that the trials should proceed at once; and as they objected to the jurymen drawn for that court, they would have others appointed who would not be prejudiced against their own party. The judge undertook to reason with

Hillsboro,
Sept., 1770
C. R., VIII,
235, 245

Cause of
discontent

the crowd and addressed them, whereupon they with drew, but immediately fell on John Williams, an attorney who was coming into court, in such a furious manner that it was with great difficulty his life was saved by his escaping into a storehouse. Their blood being now up, they seized Colonel Fanning, who had sought shelter on the bench, and dragged him by the heels out of the door of the court-house, and were dealing him furious blows when he, too, succeeded in escaping and took refuge in a store, which the mob then attacked, demolishing the windows with stones and bricks, trying to force him from his shelter. During the uproar several approached the judge on the bench, telling him with great oaths that his "turn should be next;" but Hunter and others soon informed the judge that he should not be hurt if he would proceed to hold the court till the end of the term, requiring, however, that no lawyer should be allowed to attend except alone the prosecuting officer, and saying that "they would stay and see justice impartially done." In the meantime Thomas Hart, Alexander Martin, Michael Holt and many others had been severely whipped, and Colonel Gray, Major Lloyd, Francis Nash, John Cooke, Tyree Harris and others fled for safety. The judge did not disdain to resort to artifice. He agreed to hold the court as required; but after four or five hours, the rage of the crowd having subsided a little, they permitted him to adjourn the court for the day, and conducted him with great parade to his lodgings. At ten o'clock that night the judge, thinking discretion the better part of valor, escaped by a back way, gained the woods and fled to his home in Granville.

Fanning, having surrendered to them, was allowed to return to his home on his word of honor to attend them the next day. They decreed his death, but more humane counsels prevailed, and he was permitted to take to his heels and run until he should get out of their sight. They then destroyed his residence and household effects. For two days the riot continued, the merchants and inhabitants being run out into the country, expecting their stores and houses to be pillaged and laid waste. But besides breaking the windows of most of the houses, not much substantial damage was done, except to Fanning's dwelling.

1770
C. R., VIII,
253, 254

Judge Henderson hastened to make a report of these proceedings to the governor, who convened his council; and on
October 18th the governor issued his proclamation requiring the justices to make diligent inquiry into the offences
committed and transmit the depositions of witnesses to be
laid before the next General Assembly. Judge Henderson's
broken faith in not continuing to hold his court met with
severe retribution. On the night of November 12th his barns
and stables were destroyed, several horses being burned in
the conflagration, and two nights afterward his dwelling
house was set on fire and consumed. Contemporaneously C. R., VIII, 258-264
with the news of this destruction came the disquieting information to the governor that the Regulators proposed to come
down to New Bern to intimidate and overawe the Assembly,
then about to meet or to prevent Colonel Fanning from taking his seat as a member. In the meantime some of the in- The Redressers
habitants at the west, seeking self-preservation, entered into C. R., VIII, 274
a sworn association under the name of Redressers to assist
and protect each other. Among those thus associated were
Edmund Fanning, Francis Nash, Adlai Osborn, Alexander
Martin, Jesse Benton, John Hogan, Thomas Hart, James
Murphey, Will Mebane and others afterward prominent as
citizens in that region.

On December 5th the Assembly met. There was no great Dec., 1770
change in membership. Hillsboro having been created a
borough town, Fanning was returned as its member.

John Harvey, who had been speaker during the last two
assemblies, was now ill at home, and in his absence Samuel
Johnston proposed for speaker Richard Caswell, who was
unanimously chosen. The governor received the Assembly in
the new mansion, which was then finished; and considering
New Bern as the established seat of government he later, at
the request of the Assembly, ordered the secretary to remove
all the papers of the secretary's office from Wilmington to
that town.

The governor in his address again repeated his earnest C. R., VIII 282 et seq.
recommendation for a new system of keeping the public ac-
counts and inveighed strongly against the loose methods that
had always been in vogue in the province. He also urged
the most scrupulous inquiries into the complaints against

1770

public officers, and that a clear statement should be made of the fees to which they were legally entitled. Animadverting with great indignation on the mob who in contempt of the resolve of the last house had torn "justice from her tribunal and renounced all legislative authority," he urged the raising of a sufficient body of men to protect the magistrates and civil officers in the execution of the laws. He nevertheless directed particular attention to the desirability of establishing a public seminary in the back country, and otherwise recommended that there should be general coöperation in measures for the public good.

Tryon transferred to New York

The Earl of Hillsborough had some months before mentioned to the governor that he had had an opportunity of having him transferred to New York and would have done so had he thought that Governor Tryon desired it. The governor expressed regret that the position had not been offered him. He now informed the Assembly that he had received leave of absence, but hoped that before his departure he would be able to give stability to the interior police of the country, and restore to the province the blessings of peace. At the very time he was making this communication to the Assembly, arrangements were being made in England for his transfer to New York, and on December 12th he was appointed governor of that province. In view of his expected departure for England, and there being no friction at the moment over continental affairs, the relations between the governor and the Assembly were most cordial. The Assembly warmly expressed its gratification and appreciation of his valuable services as governor and their confidence in the sincerity of his efforts to promote its prosperity and welfare, and he repeatedly declared his unchangeable purpose to use his influence under all circumstances to advance the peculiar

C. R., VIII, 317

interests of the province. "Neither time nor distance can ever efface from my mind," said he, "the just sense of the obligations I owe you for your favorable opinion of my public services." On all sides there was a purpose to enter at once on the consideration of the remedial legislation which had been interrupted by the dissolution of the previous Assembly. Edmund Fanning, a close friend of the governor and the greatest sufferer at the hands of the Regulators,

Fanning active

was among the foremost in this important work. He presented petitions from the Presbyterians asking that their clergy might be authorized to perform the marriage ceremony according to their own rites, also petitions for the division of Orange County, and he otherwise sought to promote the wishes of the people. A committee was raised to consider the amendment of existing laws, and Mr. Fanning from that committee reported that the laws establishing fees of the various officers should be made more clear; that the Presbyterian clergy should be allowed to solemnize the rite of marriage by a license, without any fee to the established clergy; that the law relative to the inferior courts should be amended, and their jurisdiction and that of single magistrates should be enlarged; and he suggested that the committee should be continued during recess. Colonel Rutherford was similarly active, and introduced several bills for the erection of new counties, which the people by their petitions requested. The counties of Wake, Guilford, Chatham and Surry were thus established. The fees of officers were regulated, and the charges of attorneys-at-law were fixed according to the service rendered. The amount in every case was to be included in the bill of costs, and nothing more than the law allowed was to be demanded by them; yet any client was permitted the privilege of paying more after the matter was concluded if he felt so disposed; and if any lawyer neglected his case the court was to direct that he should pay the costs.

Because of the scarcity of money sheriffs were forbidden to sell property for less than two-thirds of the appraised value. The fees of clerks were regulated, and those theretofore allowed by law to the chief justice were abolished, and an adequate salary was provided for him. To encourage immigration, all persons who should come into the province directly from Europe were exempted from the payment of taxes for four years. In order to promote education Governor Tryon in his address had recommended the establishment of a public school in the western part of the province, and Fanning brought in a bill for that purpose; and an act was passed incorporating Queen's College at Charlotte, a hamlet in Mecklenburg, so called in honor of her Majesty.

1770

C. R., VIII, 322

The new counties

S. R., XXIII, 789

S. R., XXIII, 782 *et seq.*

Queen's College

1771

These and various other acts were intended and calculated to remove and redress the grievances of which the Regulators had complained.

The riot act

Jan., 1771

But the Assembly was not willing to stop there. It proposed that the peace of the province should not be disturbed. It passed an act introduced by Samuel Johnston to prevent

C. R., VIII, 481

tumultuous and riotous assemblies. It enacted that if ten or more persons, being unlawfully, tumultuously and riotously assembled together, to the disturbance of the public peace, after being openly commanded by any justice or sheriff to disperse, should notwithstanding remain together one hour thereafter, they should be adjudged guilty of felony and suffer death. And it was made the duty of such justice or sheriff and such persons as should be commanded to assist to apprehend the rioters; and if any of them in resisting should be killed the officers should not be held liable; and it was enacted that the prosecutions under that law might be in any superior court in the province, and not necessarily in the county or district where the offence was committed; and also if any bill of indictment was found for an offence under that act, it was lawful for the judges of the superior court to issue a proclamation to be put up at the court-house and at

Johnston's bloody bill

each church or chapel of the county where the crime was committed, commanding the indicted person to surrender himself to the sheriff within sixty days; and if the person did not surrender himself according to the proclamation he was to be deemed guilty of the offence as if he had been convicted; and it was made lawful for any one to slay such outlaw.

Drafts ordered

In anticipation of further riots and insurrections the governor was authorized to order out drafts from the different regiments of militia, who were to be paid for their services, and he was authorized to draw his warrant for the payment of such sums of money as should be necessary, which the treasurers were required to honor. And if any number of men should in an armed and hostile manner oppose the military force raised under the act, they were to be considered as traitors and treated accordingly.

Such was the measure of repression to vindicate "the honor of government." "Your absence," wrote Iredell to Harvey, "at so critical a period is much to be regretted." "This bill, I believe, you would have thought expedient, though severe; but desperate diseases must have desperate remedies."

It was indeed a severe penal act, but was to remain in force for only one year and no longer, and during that period it was to be read by the justices at the court-house door in every county on the second day of court, and by the minister, clerk or reader at their place of public worship immediately after divine service once every three months.

By it the Assembly proposed to maintain the authority of government, to prevent riots and suppress insurrections even at the cost of blood.

It had been said that the Regulators proposed to embody and forcibly prevent Edmund Fanning from taking his seat. Because of these threats the governor was so apprehensive that he caused a ditch to be dug from Neuse to Trent River enclosing the inhabited part of the town; and the militia of the neighboring counties were directed to oppose the insurgents should they come. During the sitting of the Assembly James Hunter published a letter addressed to Judge Maurice Moore in the New Bern *Gazette,* which was deemed slanderous. Moore was a member of the house, and the house took notice of it, and it being understood that Hermon Husband, also a member of the house, had caused it to be printed a committee was appointed to investigate the matter. After an examination the house resolved that Husband was guilty of gross prevarication and falsehood; and as he had insinuated in conversation that, in case he should be confined by order of the house, he expected down a number of people to release him, he was adjudged in contempt of the house, and was immediately expelled. The governor at once convened the council, the chief justice being one of the body, and it being considered that if Husband should rejoin the Regulators fatal consequences might ensue, they unanimously requested the chief justice to take depositions and issue his warrant for apprehending Husband, who was committed to jail and confined until he could be tried.

Margin notes:

1771
C. R., VIII, 270

New Bern fortified

C. R., VIII, 269, 331

Husband arrested

1771
C. R., VIII.
495
On January 15, 1771, the riot act was passed. A week later the governor informed the Assembly that he had received intelligence that led him to apprehend that the insurgents were preparing for some speedy act of violence—the liberation of Husband by force. All now was in a flutter, and an appropriation was made to enable the governor to withstand the expected assault. The public business was hurried to an end, and on the 26th the Assembly was prorogued to meet on May 10th. Governor Tryon apparently had a disposition to try conclusions with the Regulators. He did not wish to leave the province at the end of his term in a state of anarchy and confusion, and so he rather courted a situation that would result in the speedy suppression of disaffection. C. R., VIII, 490 The legislation of the session was calculated to disarm opposition, and he hoped that it would disorganize the adherents of the Regulator chieftains. After Husband had been in jail a month reports were received that the people of Orange were assembling, and on January 19th the governor appointed a special court under the riot act to be held by the chief justice on February 2d for the trial of Husband and Militia
moves other alleged criminals. In anticipation of an attempt at rescue, the governor ordered the militia of the neighboring counties to be in readiness to repulse the insurgent C. R., VIII, 498 force. The Wake regiment assembled at Colonel Hunter's; that of Johnston County at Smithfield, while Colonel Caswell held the Dobbs militia at Kingston. It was reported that the march on New Bern would begin on the 11th, and a proclamation was issued prohibiting for a reasonable time the sale of firearms and ammunition, lest they should come Husband
discharged into the hands of the mob. On February 8th, however, the grand jury of the special court, having considered the bill preferred against Hermon Husband for libel, found it not a true bill and Husband was discharged. Being now free, he C. R., VIII, 500-509 leisurely returned to the back country. In the meantime the Regulators had been active, and having embodied a large force, crossed the Haw River, and proceeded to the eastward. With that detachment were thirteen wagons, while four wagons had not yet crossed the river, when Husband reached Hunter's Lodge in Wake County, where the Wake regiment was assembled, and wrote assuring his friends of his

release and safety. William Butler having received this
communication from Husband, hastened to the Regulator
camp and, the object being accomplished, the insurgents retired. The danger being passed, on February 17th Colonel
Hinton discharged the Wake militia, and the other regiments
were likewise disbanded. There was a temporary lull; but,
nevertheless, the governor and council thought it prudent
to perfect the defences at New Bern, where another term of
court was to be held early in March.

Notwithstanding the remedial acts so lately passed, the
Regulators were not at all content. They were inflamed by
the passage of the riot act. The power of government had
ceased to be feared, and the tyrannical and bloody features
of that act, instead of constraining obedience and restoring
quiet, only served to arouse their indignation and excite
their ire. Rednap Howell, a maker of popular ballads,
had moved much among the people, and his rhymes
doubtless contributed largely to give them good heart and
prepare them for action. There were at least some forty
of these popular pieces, although only a few have been
preserved. They were indeed well calculated to stir the disaffected and warm them up to patriotic ardor. On the return of the Regulators from their intended expedition to
release Husband, their purpose was announced to attend the
Salisbury court, then about to be held, and on March 6th
some five hundred of them encamped in the woods on the
banks of the Yadkin River, where were the Hamiltons,
Hunter, James Graham, Teague, Gillespie and other leaders
in command. Having arrested Waightstill Avery, a young
lawyer of that region, they carried him to their camp, and
declared their purpose of flogging Judge Moore, and of
killing all the clerks and lawyers. But such vaporings were
probably only vain boastings. On the same day Colonel
Alexander Martin and John Frohock, who had been officers
of Rowan, and who with others were charged with having
taken illegal fees, went to their camp and desired to know
their designs and purposes. To them they answered that
they had no intention to disturb the court or to injure any
person; and that they were armed only to defend themselves
if assaulted. On being informed that their late behavior to

Adjustment
agreed on

the judges had been such that no court would be held, they seemed greatly concerned. A plan was then proposed for accommodating matters between the people and the officers of Rowan against whom they complained. The matters in dispute were to be left to arbitrators, the Regulators appointing Husband, Graham, Hunter and Thomas Person to act for them; Martin and Frohock chose Matthew Locke, John Kerr, Samuel Young and James Smith on their part. The meeting of the arbitrators was fixed for the third Tuesday in May, and the settlement was to extend not only to the officers of Rowan County but to all those who would voluntarily join in the arbitration. The Regulators, evidently pleased at this proposed adjustment, gave three cheers and returned to their homes. Well had it been had this path to peace been pursued, and by this settlement out of court the tranquillity of the province been restored. But circumstances were no longer favorable to such negotiations.

Alamance

March, 1771
C. R., VIII,
528-531
Indictments

On March 11th another special court convened at New Bern attended by the chief justice and Judges Moore and Henderson. The grand jury on the 15th presented the insurgents as being enemies to government, and to the liberty, happiness and tranquillity of the inhabitants of the province. True bills were found against Husband, Hunter, Butler, the Hamiltons, James Few, Rednap Howell and many other leaders of the Regulators, there being thirty-one persons indicted, and the witnesses were recognized to attend on May 11th, when the cases were to be tried. On March 18th, two days after the court adjourned, the governor came into possession of a letter written by Rednap Howell a month earlier, from which it appeared that he had been sent to Halifax to "raise the country," and that he had "animated the people to join the Regulation," and he declared "if it once takes a start here it will run into the neighboring counties of Edgecombe,

C. R., VIII,
536-539

Bute and Northampton." At the same time the governor received a letter from the judges expressing their opinion that they could not attend the superior court at Hillsboro on March 22d with any hope of transacting the business of the court, or indeed with any prospect of personal safety to

themselves. The governor submitted these matters to the
council, and it was agreed with their advice to raise a sufficient force to maintain order and reduce the insurgents to
obedience to the laws. The courts were to be held and the
administration of justice was not to cease.

Fearing the extension of the Regulation movement among
the inhabitants of the eastern section, an association paper
was printed and circulated through the counties for signature, in which those who signed it bound themselves to stand
with the government against the Regulators until the tranquillity of the province should be restored; and the governor
at once issued orders for the militia to assemble, and called
for volunteers and drafts to form a force that would suppress the insurgents. From each county a number was
required, aggregating in all 2250 men. The governor
hastened to Wilmington and appointed General Waddell
general of the forces to be raised, with directions to march
through the western counties by way of Salisbury to Orange,
while he himself with the eastern militia would march direct
to Hillsboro. The governor's authority for this movement
was founded on a clause of the riot act; and he was upheld
by all of the gentlemen of the east.

Many of them at once volunteered to accompany him on
his intended expedition and none held back. Caswell was a
colonel, Ashe a general, Harnett was particularly active,
while John Harvey was detained by his continued illness.
His son, a member of the Assembly, was, like him, esteemed
by the governor. On March 19th, the day Governor Tryon
issued his orders to the colonels to collect their men, he enclosed a copy to Harvey, saying: "If you . . . can procure from the counties of Pasquotank and Perquimans, with
the assistance of Colonel Taylor, a company of fifty men,
. . . and contrive so as they might be at Hillsboro
the sixth day of May, I should be glad to take them under
my command. I take this opportunity to thank you for
your kind present to me last winter. . . . I wish your
son could command the company." But the Albemarle section was so remote from the scene of disturbance and had so
little intercourse with that part of the State that the people
took but little interest in the Regulation, and in a general

The
governor
acts
C. R., VIII,
540-549

C. R., VIII,
548

Waddell in
command

C. R., VIII,
698

1771

way many of the inhabitants sympathized with the Regulators in their distresses. Joseph Montfort, the northern
treasurer, had no money of the contingent fund in hand,
which under the riot act alone could be used to pay bounties
and the expenses of the troops, and so he did not honor the
C. R., VIII, drafts made by Governor Tryon for bounties, and but few
650
volunteers from the Albemarle section participated in the
expedition.

C. R., VIII,   The southern treasurer, John Ashe, on the other hand, not
651
only paid out what public moneys he had, but issued notes
to the amount of six thousand pounds to meet the expenses
of the expedition; and so the same difficulty did not arise in
embodying and moving troops from the lower counties.

Frohock and Martin having communicated to the governor their agreement for settlement with the insurgents, the
arrangement was denounced by him as "unconstitutional, dishonorable to government, and introductive of a practice most
C. R., VIII, dangerous to the peace and happiness of society." Yet he
545, 701
asserted his abhorrence of the conduct of any man who was
guilty of extortion, and declared it to be their duty to give
satisfaction and make restitution if they had abused their
trust.

Tryon   Earlier the governor might have rejoiced at this proposed
courts the
struggle   settlement of differences, but to his mind the situation no
longer admitted such an adjustment. The leaders of the
Regulators had gone too far. The power of the insurgents
to overturn government was too apparent. The day for
temporizing had passed. The authority of the law was now
to be asserted. While the responses of the eastern militia
were far from general, yet a considerable force collected at
the call of the governor. Perhaps his greatest disappointment was the action of the Bute militia, some eight hundred
of whom assembled, but when invited to volunteer they declined to a man, saying that they favored the Regulators.
Almost equal was the attitude of the Wake militia, although
after some delay, with considerable efforts, Colonel Hinton
secured by draft fifty recruits from that county. Indeed
throughout the territory west of Smithfield the great bulk of
the inhabitants sympathized with the disaffected element. A
considerable proportion of those farther west had but recently

come into the province, were unacquainted with the laws and the system of government, had no association with the eastern people, and knew but little of the leading men who had habitually controlled public affairs. In a word, many of them had so recently become inhabitants and were so unsettled in their new homes, and were so cut off and secluded in the frontier settlements that they were virtually strangers within the commonwealth.

General Waddell in his progress to the west was joined by a detachment of the Anson militia and parts of the regiments of Mecklenburg and Tryon under their respective colonels, and some companies from Rowan. Colonel Frohock, who should have commanded the Rowan militia, was rather sarcastically excused from attending by Governor Tryon because of his negotiations with the Regulators. Accompanying Waddell's force also was a detachment of artillery under Colonel Robert Schaw of Cumberland. On May 5th General Waddell with nearly three hundred men crossed the Yadkin near Salisbury, and went into camp on Pott's Creek. There, finding himself confronted by a considerable number of insurgents, he halted and threw up entrenchments. On May 10th, at a council of war, under the advice of Colonel Rutherford and his other officers, it was resolved that it was too hazardous to engage the enemy, who were reported by Captain Alexander of Mecklenburg, to extend a quarter of a mile, seven or eight deep, with a large body of horsemen, extending one hundred and twenty yards, twelve or fourteen deep. Nor was this formidable force the only peril that threatened General Waddell, for it was apprehended that many of his own troops would not fight the Regulators, but rather, in case of a conflict, would join them. Under these adverse circumstances General Waddell prudently retreated across the Yadkin and took post near Salisbury, where he strongly fortified himself and remained until May 28th. In the meantime he had suffered a severe loss in the destruction of a supply of powder and other munitions of war that were being transported from Charleston for the use of the army. A small band of Regulators under the direction of Major James White and his brothers, William and John White, having blackened their faces, from which they became known as

C. R., VIII, 601, 701

General Waddell

C. R., VIII, 608

C. R., VIII, 610

C. R., VIII, 623
The Black Boys

1771

the "Black Boys," came up with the wagons midway between Charlotte and Salisbury (near the site of the present town of Concord), and, having taken possession of them, destroyed the blankets and fired the ammunition, making a tremendous explosion of the powder. Such animosity toward government was now the general feeling that pervaded all that region, and General Waddell found himself hemmed in by forces too powerful to contend with.

C. R., VIII, 574

Governor Tryon was more fortunate. Leaving New Bern on April 23d, accompanied by the militia of Carteret, Craven and adjoining counties, and two swivel guns mounted on carriages, he moved toward Smithfield, where he was joined by detachments from New Hanover, Dobbs and Johnston. On May 4th he marched to Hunter's Lodge in Wake, where he remained four days awaiting other detachments and organizing his forces.

On the 9th he encamped on the Enoe. Accompanying him were volunteer detachments of horse from Bute and other counties, and many of the leading gentlemen of the east, among them Robert Howe, Alexander Lillington, John Ashe,

Supporters of Tryon

James Moore, Richard Caswell, Abner Nash, Willie Jones, John Harvey, Jr., and others distinguished in the military and civil annals of North Carolina; while in like manner with General Waddell were Moses Alexander, Thomas Polk, Samuel Spencer, Griffith Rutherford, William Lindsay, Adlai Osborn and many in later times honored for their devoted patriotism.

In the meantime, while the forces of the government were being thus collected, the disaffected inhabitants at the west were all astir. The leaders gave information of the points where they were to assemble. Every highway and byway was filled with men hurrying to the front. Great crowds passed rapidly from the extreme west through the quiet settlement of Wachovia, and the men of Anson met those of Surry and from the foothills of the mountains at the ren-

Feeling of the Regulators

dezvous between the Haw and the Deep. So often had these men assembled, so often had they met and boldly made declaration of their purpose to right their wrongs, defying the power of government, that now with enthusiasm they responded to the call of their leaders, and hastened to assert

their manhood. They were manly men, animated by a purpose to fearlessly resist oppression, and were not to be overawed by a show of power. Probably no one thought of sub-
verting government; no one thought of wresting the province from the dominion of the British Empire; they only
thought that they would stand up openly and with their own
strong hand prevent the operation of laws passed by the
Assembly, which, under the circumstance of their situation
and lives, they deemed unjust and found oppressive. With
little currency among them, lawful taxes bore hard and illegal taxes they would not pay; and, smarting under the
exactions of greedy officials, which even the governor, the
courts and the Assembly had found to be illegal, they were
imbued with the determination to protect themselves from
the power of a government whose authority sat lightly on
them. Unawed by the reported march of the militia, they
themselves would assemble and once more assert their own
mastery. Many came unarmed, and but few probably realized that there was really impending a conflict involving
life and death. They gathered in force between the Haw and
the Deep, and learning of the governor's approach, went
forth to meet him. Tryon, hearing of their advance, on C. R., VIII,
May 11th marched from Hillsboro, crossed the Haw, and 582
on the night of the 13th encamped on the Great Alamance.
There he prepared for battle. On the 13th the governor
had received an express from General Waddell informing
him that he was surrounded by about two thousand Regulators and had been forced to retire; and he also learned that
their rendezvous was to be at Hunter's plantation on Sandy
Creek with the view of obstructing the junction of the two
government detachments, and later came the disquieting intelligence that they were preparing to attack his camp. In- C. R., VIII,
stead, however, of an attack, about six o'clock in the evening 640
the governor received, at the hands of James Hunter and
Benjamin Merrill, a communication from them desiring to
know if he would hear their petition for a redress of their
grievances. He laid this letter before a council of war,
and informed the Regulators that he would return an
answer by twelve o'clock the next day. That night S. R., XIX,
Captain John Walker and Lieutenant John Baptista Ashe, 845

1771

who had been sent out to reconnoitre, were captured by the insurgents, tied to trees, severely whipped, and detained as prisoners. When the governor's messenger was conveying his answer to the camp of the Regulators they gave him such insults that he returned without delivering it. Early on the morning of the 16th, the two forces being about five miles apart, the governor moved forward, and about ten o'clock came within a half mile of the Regulator encampment, and there formed a line of battle. He then sent forward Captain Malcolm, one of his aides, and the sheriff of Orange with his letter, requiring them to lay down their arms, surrender up their outlawed leaders, and submit to the laws of the prov-

C. R., VIII, 642

ince. These terms were rejected with disdain, and gradually the two lines approached until the government forces occupied the ground which the van of the Regulators had first occupied, but from which it had fallen back to their main body. Some communications now passed for the exchange of Walker and Ashe for seven of the Regulators who had been captured by the militia, and the proposition was agreed to. The insurgents delayed and sent word that they would comply within an hour. The governor, suspecting that the delay was intended to enable the enemy to outflank him, determined to wait no longer.

The battle begins, May 16, 1771

May 16, 1771

The governor sent word by his aide, Captain Philemon Hawkins, that he would immediately give the signal for action, and cautioned the Regulators to take care of themselves; that if they did not directly lay down their arms they would be fired on. "Fire and be d——d!" was the an-

Martin, Hist. North Carolina, II, 282

swer. The governor thereupon gave the order, which, not being immediately obeyed, rising in his stirrups and turning to his men, he called out: "Fire! fire on them or on me!" Accordingly, the artillery began the fire, which was followed by a discharge from the whole first line, and the action almost instantly became general.

C. R., VIII, 647, 648

Of the militia there were about 1100. The number of the Regulators has been variously estimated at between 2000 and 4000; but a considerable portion of them were unarmed, and probably but few expected to engage in a battle. They

vere not marshalled in organized companies; had no trained 1771
S. R., XIX, 846
:aptains to command; and were a concourse of resolute citi-
:ens rather than an army in battle array. Their chief commander was James Hunter.

At the first fire many left the field, among them being
Hermon Husband. After the conflict had lasted half an hour
he Regulators occupied a piece of woods and fought from
>ehind the trees, as in Indian warfare. To dislodge them
Tryon advanced his first line and drove them from cover, The woods fired
>ursuing them half a mile beyond their camp. In one ac-
:ount of the battle preserved in the Moravian records, it is
;aid that "many had taken refuge in the woods, whereupon
he governor ordered the woods to be set afire, and in con-
;equence some of the wounded were 'roasted alive.'" It is
o be observed, however, that in the middle of May a woods
ire progresses but slowly, even if it burns at all.

In the earlier stages of the battle, Robert Thompson, a
Regulator, who had been taken prisoner, defying the power
of his captors, undertook to make his escape, and it is said
:hat Governor Tryon shot him down with his own hand. C. R., VIII, 520
Thompson had been a strenuous agitator, and doubtless Thompson slain
was a bold, determined man. For slaying him Governor
Tryon was criticised. If no other means to prevent escape
was at the moment available, any soldier would have
been justified in taking a prisoner's life, otherwise not.
While in the heat of battle one's actions are not to be too
nicely weighed, life is never to be taken unnecessarily.

The loss of the militia was reported as nine killed and The losses
sixty-one wounded. A detachment from Beaufort County
under Captain John Patten, being a part of the regiment C. R., VIII, 634
commanded by Colonel William Thompson, of Carteret, suffered the greatest proportionate loss, fifteen killed and
wounded out of thirty. Those of the insurgents who participated in the action stood up manfully. They were not
dismayed by the artillery, and indeed held their ground at
such short range that they silenced the artillery, requiring
particular efforts to dislodge them by advancing riflemen for
that purpose. Their loss was, according to one account, nine
killed and thirty missing, and according to another upwards
of twenty were killed. Their conduct under fire was as C. R., VIII, 585

spirited as it was bold, and for two hours they protracted the unequal conflict with the trained militia despite the severe losses they suffered. The insurgents being driven from the field, the militia advanced some little distance, but finding the enemy dispersed, withdrew to their original encampment. Thus closed that fateful and unhappy day. The wounded on both sides were humanely cared for, and the next evening the dead were interred, and there were prayers and thanksgivings for the victory.

Few hanged May 17th

The ceremonies of the day were concluded by the hanging of James Few, a prisoner—a proceeding that has attached well-merited odium to the name of Governor Tryon.

Caruthers, Life of Caldwell, 158

Haywood, Life of Tryon, 133

Of Few it has been said "That he was of a fanatical turn of mind, and believed himself raised up by the hand of God to liberate his country." "That he was sent by Heaven to relieve the world from oppression, and that he was to begin in North Carolina." An account of his execution given in the Community Diary of the Moravians a week later says:

Clewell, Hist. of Wachovia

"A certain young man, a fine young fellow, had been captured, and when given the alternative of taking the oath or being hanged he chose the latter. The governor wished to spare his life, and twice urged him to submit. But the young man refused. The messenger described how, with the rope around his neck, he was urged to yield but refused, and the governor turned aside with tears in his eyes as the young man was swung into eternity."

Few had been indicted for felony at the special court held at New Bern on March 11, 1771. He was one of those

C. R., VIII, 532

who refused to surrender themselves within the time limited by the riot act. Under that act he was deemed guilty of the offence charged as if he had been convicted thereof by due course of law, and it was made lawful for any one to take his life, but this outlawry was dependent on the required publications of the proclamation, a fact not ascertained as to Few. But of this Governor Tryon seems not to have been advised. He regarded Few, Hunter, Husband as outlaws. Still, the

C. R., VIII, 651

contingency had not then arisen when Few could have been lawfully slain as an outlaw, nor was Governor Tryon justified in dealing so summarily with a prisoner. He sought to extenuate his needless act by saying: "This gave great

satisfaction to the men, and at this time it was a necessary
sacrifice to appease the murmurings of the troops, who were
importunate that public justice should be immediately executed against some of the outlaws that were taken in the action, and in opposing of whom they had braved so many dangers and suffered such loss of lives and blood, and without
which satisfaction some refused to march forward while
others declared they would give no quarter for the future."
Such might well have been the feelings of some of the
eastern militia, but it was not the part of a commanding officer to be swerved from his own sense of duty by the
intemperate passion of his soldiers. He was there to assert
the majesty of the law and to maintain the authority of
established government—not to blazon the power of successful arms by a needless act of butchery.

1771
Tryon's
apology

S. R., XIX,
845

Subsequent movements

The next day the wounded were sent to the plantation of
Michael Holt with a surgeon and medicines, and the main
army proceeded to Lewis's mill, three miles beyond the field
of battle, where a detachment under Colonel Ashe that had
been advanced was surrounded by about three hundred of
the Regulators. Immediately after the battle a proclamation
had been issued granting pardon to all who should come
into camp, surrender up their arms, take an oath of allegiance to the king and an oath of obligation to pay their
taxes, and to support and defend the laws of the land.* Exceptions, however, were made of the outlaws and prisoners
taken and some fourteen others. Many now accepted these
terms and submitted. The army the next day marched to
James Hunter's and destroyed his dwelling and outhouse,
and then took possession of Hermon Husband's plantation,
finding there "a large parcel of treasonable papers;" and,
the inhabitants continuing to come in, submitting themselves
to government, the proclamation of pardon was renewed and
the time extended; but the exceptions now embraced the

C. R., VIII,
649

Pardons and
exceptions

*Governor Martin spoke of this "oath as one of allegiance, etc.,
etc." Atticus described it as "your new coined oath to be obedient
to the laws of the province, and to pay the public taxes." To that
description the governor himself added, "to support and defend the
laws of the land," as in the text.

1771

"Black Boys" and some others at first omitted, among them being Thomas Person. The outlaws named were Husband, Hunter, Howell and Butler, and on their heads a price was set. Heavy rains, which had begun on May 20th and continued until the 28th, added much to the discomfort of the men, many of whom were seized with pleurisies.

The army remained a week in Sandy Creek, then passed to Deep River, and on June 1st was in the Jersey settlement. On June 4th, on Reedy Creek, General Waddell's forces joined the main army, and they marched to Wachovia, where they remained several days, and at Salem on June 6th they celebrated the king's birthday and the victory of the 16th.

C. R., VIII, 651

During this march the houses and plantations of those who were outlawed were laid waste and destroyed, and their owners fled from the province.

The insurgents having been quieted on the Deep and the Haw, and information being received that they were rising to the south and west, General Waddell was detached on June 8th with some five hundred men and artillery to move into that section and suppress them; and on the same day Governor Tryon began his return movement.

The army reached Hillsboro on the 14th, where the cattle and horses were turned on the plantation of William Few, the father of James Few, who was said to have been "very

S. R., XIX, 852

active in promoting the disturbance of the country." Having taken some prisoners on May 13th, Governor Tryon ordered that a special term of court under the riot act should

C R., VIII, 712

be opened at Hillsboro on the 30th of that month, but the governor had kept the prisoners along with the army with the view of parading them before the country, and the court had been kept open awaiting their arrival for trial.

The trials

The trials began on June 14th and lasted until the 18th, when twelve prisoners were sentenced to death on the charge of high treason. Six of these were immediately executed. The record of the court has not been preserved. Four of those executed were Benjamin Merrill, Robert Matear, Cap-

The victims

tain Messer and James Pugh. The names of two are unknown. Six were reprieved: Forrester Mercer, James Stewart, James Emerson, Herman Cox, William Brown and James Copeland, and later they were pardoned by the king. The melancholy spectacle of the execution was accompanied by a military parade,* and its terrors were augmented by the impressiveness of the scene. The governor attended with the entire army, and caused all of the prisoners to be brought out to witness it.

The people, utterly subdued, their leaders fled or taken, The people submit had continued to come in and ask for pardon, so that by June 19th more than three thousand had submitted to the government and taken the oath to pay their taxes and obey the laws which Governor Tryon had exacted of them. When, later, General Waddell had made his report, giving C. R., IX, 78 the result of his excursion into the southwestern part of the province, the entire number who had taken the oath aggregated 6409, and about 800 guns had been turned into the government by the malcontents. Apparently then the western counties were disarmed and thoroughly subjugated. But the people were not pacified, and many moved from the province, some passing the mountains and finding homes in the forests of the Holstein settlement.

Governor Tryon, having on June 13th received informa- Tryon departs tion that he had been appointed governor of New York, and from the province having instructions to repair without loss of time to that C. R., VIII, province, communicated to the army that he would march 675 to the southward immediately after the executions, and that he would leave the army under the command of Colonel Ashe, he himself hastening to New Bern. On June 30th he embarked for New York, where he arrived on July 7th and assumed the administration. He carried with him the June, 1771 C. R., IX esteem and good-will of the leading men of the eastern part 9, 142 of the province, who commended his bravery and courage, and approved his administration in the difficult circumstances that attended it.

*A gruesome memorial of this event is preserved in State Records, XXII, 465:
"The Public to Thomas Donaldson, Dr.—19th June, 1771. To hanging six men at Hillsboro Court of Oyer, etc., five pounds each— thirty pounds. P'r Thomas Donaldson."

1771

As the disturbances incident to the Regulation movement were a marked feature of affairs during that period, so the efforts of the government to suppress them were also unusual and remarkable. The riot act, passed by the Assembly, of which Caswell was speaker, and Harnett, Johnston, Hewes, Howe, the Moores and many others who led in the revolutionary movement three years later, were members, and which received the approval of the governor, was such a stringent measure as to challenge criticism. That clause of it which required indicted persons, after proclamation, to surrender themselves within sixty days and stand trial on pain of being deemed guilty and of being held outlaws subject to being killed by any one, was considered by the Crown officers as "irreconcilable to the principles of the constitution," "full of danger in its operation" and "unfit for any part of the British Empire;" although they mentioned that "the circumstances of the province may excuse inserting such clause in this act." It was certainly a fierce and bloody expedient, resorted to because the persons accused could not be arrested. Other than that, the act received the approval of the Crown, and inasmuch as its operation was limited to a single year, it was allowed to stand until its expiration. James Few was the only person who suffered death under it, as an outlaw, if indeed the governor justified even his execution by that sanction.

The riot
act in
England
C. R., IX,
285, 286
S. R., XI,
240

The army, after Tryon's departure from Hillsboro, proceeded to Colonel Bryan's in Johnston County and there the detachments separated, marching to their respective counties, where they were disbanded. The cost of the expedition, about £60,000, had in part been met by notes issued by Treasurer Ashe, which he announced would be received by him in payment of taxes. These notes circulated as currency, and in some measure gave relief to the people in the scarcity of a circulating medium.

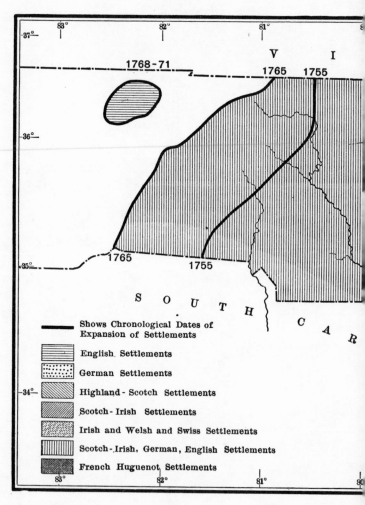

83° 82° 81°
−37°−

V   I

1768-71   1765   1755

−36°−

−35°−   1765   1755

S   O   U   T   H   C   A   R

━━━ Shows Chronological Dates of
     Expansion of Settlements

▭▭▭ English Settlements

▦▦▦ German Settlements

−34°− ▨▨▨ Highland - Scotch Settlements

▩▩▩ Scotch - Irish Settlements

▒▒▒ Irish and Welsh and Swiss Settlements

▥▥▥ Scotch - Irish, German, English Settlements

▓▓▓ French Huguenot Settlements

83°   82°   81°   80

MAP OF NORTH CAR
L

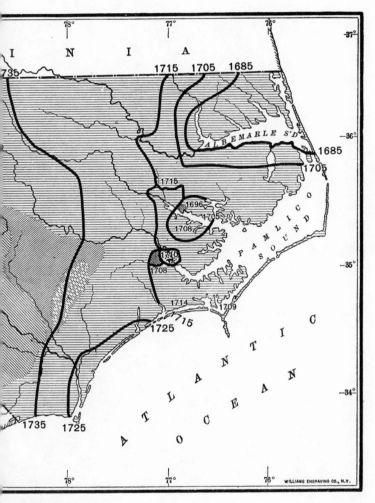

78°　　　　　77°　　　　　76°　　　　　-37°

I　N　I　A
735　　1715　1705　1685

-36°
ALBEMARLE S'D
1685
1705

1715
1696
1705
1708

PAMLICO
SOUND

1740
1708
-35°

1714　　1709
1715
1725

ATLANTIC

O　C　E　A　N
-34°

1735　1725

78°　　　　　77°　　　　　76°　　WILLIAMS ENGRAVING CO., N.Y.

CHAPTER XXIII

In the homes of the people

McRee, in his "Life of Iredell," has given an admirable
portrayal of two communities in the province about the time
of Martin's administration. Of the region of which Edenton was the centre, he says:

1772
McRee's
Iredell, I,
31-34

It was of such remarkable fertility that it might well have been
styled the granary of the province; it was also the place of concen-
tration and market-town for the opulent planters of a large district
of country. . . . The climate was humid and unhealthy, but soft
and luxurious. Game and fish were abundant, and cattle and sheep
and swine throve and multiplied upon the spontaneous fruits of the
earth. If there was little of the parade and pomp of older communities, if many of the appliances of luxury were wanting, ease
and abundance were the reward of but a slight degree of frugality
and industry. No palatial dwellings existed—tapestry and plate were
wanting; but the homes of the planters were comfortable and ample
for all the purposes of hospitality, while their tables groaned beneath
dainties beyond the reach of wealth on the other side of the Atlantic.
He who supposes them an untutored people is grossly deceived. The
letters that will appear in the course of the narrative will demonstrate that they were equal in cultivation, ability, and patriotism to
any of their contemporaries. The men were bold, frank, generous,
and intelligent; the females, tender and kind and polite. The
strength of the former was developed by manly labors. The taste of
the latter was improved and their imaginations exalted by the varied
forms of beauty that surrounded them. . . . In 1769 the town of
Edenton was the court end of the province. Within its limits and
in its immediate vicinity there was, in proportion to its population, a

greater number of men eminent for ability, virtue, and erudition than in any other part of America. Colonel Richard Buncombe was a native of St. Kitts. He was educated in England and possessed a large fortune. Of "Lawyer Pearson, an English gentleman," little is known save that he married the mother of Sir Nathaniel Dukinfield, and thus became master of large estates. Colonel John Dawson (a lawyer who married the daughter of Governor Gabriel Johnston) resided at Eden House, noted for its splendid hospitality and the refined society generally assembled there. Dr. Cathcart was a gentleman of extraordinarily fine sense and great reading. His two daughters "were possessed of the three greatest motives to be courted: beauty, wit and prudence, and money; great fortunes, and toasted in most parts of the province."

And so McRee continues with brief accounts of Joseph Hewes, Thomas Barker, Thomas Jones, Jasper Carlton, Stephen Cabarrus, Robert Smith, Charles Johnson, William Cumming, Sir Nathaniel Dukinfield, the Harveys and the Johnstons, who "possessed talents and attainments that, when combined, not only enabled them to determine the politics of their district, but gave them a potent influence in the province."

Of the lower Cape Fear he likewise says:

Mr. Hooper was a native of Boston and a graduate of Cambridge, Mass. After studying law with James Otis, he became a citizen of Wilmington. That town and its vicinity was noted for its unbounded hospitality and the elegance of its society. Men of rare talents, fortune, and attainment united to render it the home of politeness and ease and enjoyment. Though the footprint of the Indian had as yet scarcely been effaced, the higher civilization of the Old World had been transplanted there and had taken vigorous root. There were Colonel John Ashe, the great popular leader, whose address was consummate, and whose quickness of apprehension seemed intuition, the very Rupert of debate; Samuel Ashe, of stalwart frame, endowed with practical good sense and a profound knowledge of human nature; Harnett, "who could boast a genius for music and taste for letters," the representative man of the Cape Fear; Dr. John Eustace, "who united wit, and genius, and learning, and science"; Colonel Thomas Lloyd, "gifted with talents and adorned with classical literature"; Howe, "whose imagination fascinated, whose repartee overpowered, and whose conversation was enlivened by strains of exquisite raillery"; Dr. John Fergus, of stately presence, with velvet coat, cocked hat, and gold-headed cane, a graduate of Edinburgh and an excellent Latin and Greek scholar; William Pennington, afterward master of the ceremonies at Bath, "an elegant writer, admired for his wit and his highly polished urbanity"; Judge Maurice Moore, of versatile talents, and possessed of extensive information; as a wit, always prompt in reply; as an orator, always daring the mercy of chance; Maclaine, irascible but intellectual, who trod the paths of honor nearly *pari passu* with Iredell and Hooper and Johnston, and "whose criticisms on Shakespeare would, if they were published, give him fame and rank in the republic of letters."

Social conditions

And he continues to portray the social characteristics of the Hills, Lillingtons, DeRossets, Moores, and others who then adorned the Cape Fear region.

New Bern, as well, was a centre where refinement and elegance abounded. It was the residence of the governor; an emporium of trade, with wealthy merchants, enterprising citizens and cultivated society. Originally settled by the Huguenots, Palatines, and Swiss, by industrious Germans as well as by Welsh and Englishmen, the region of which it was the social metropolis was inhabited by a population notable for their thrift, politeness and fine characteristics. There the first academy had been established and maintained; there the first printing press was erected, and there the first newspaper, the *North Carolina Gazette,* was published—in December, 1755—followed, at length, by another at Wilmington, in September, 1764.

Weeks, Press of North Carolina in Eighteenth Century, 18, 29, 58

Among the earliest publications of Davis's press, other than provincial laws, was a sermon preached before the General Assembly by Rev. James Reid, in 1762, "Recommending the Establishing Public Schools for the Education of Youth," printed by the Assembly, that "the same might be dispersed in the several counties within this province."

Halifax had also become a nucleus of elegant society, with rich planters and cultured citizens; while at Hillsboro, where the governors spent their summers, the simplicity of backwoods life was giving place to the refining influences of advanced social conditions. In all the counties were men like Willie and Allen Jones, the Kenans, Dicksons, Battles, Holmes, Hawkins, Haywoods, Harts, Alstons, Rowans, Lloyds, Osborns, Polks—too numerous to specify, men of education and culture, many of whom were native and "to the

1771

At the west

C. R., VIII, 630

Immigrants

The marts of trade

manor born," while others, like Caswell, Hooper, Hewes, Avery, the Sumners, Martins and McDowells, had but recently come from other communities, well educated, energetic, enterprising, vigorous in mind and in body.

Along the Virginia border the people were chiefly of colonial descent; but on the upper waters of the Cape Fear were congregated thousands of Highlanders, many of whom were well educated. At Wachovia the Moravians had been prosperous, had erected mills and had grown in importance; while the Scotch-Irish, who occupied the fertile regions watered by the Catawba and tributaries of the Yadkin, were interspersed with Germans, of whom there were some three thousand families, likewise accompanied by their pastors, men of learning, who taught the young while ministering to their congregations.

And in their new homes the Scotch, Scotch-Irish and the Germans preserved their former manners and customs and their racial characteristics, and these have in some measure been perpetuated so that after the lapse of a century and a half their respective settlements can still be distinguished. Similarly a settlement of Quakers, coming from Nantucket, who located at New Garden, has preserved its peculiar characteristics, while the Jersey settlement on the Yadkin near Salisbury, so called because made by emigrants from New Jersey, has retained its original appellation.

Facilities of communication were scant. This was a particular hardship with the settlers at the far west who, coming from the north, located at a considerable distance beyond the frontier settlements extending from the coast. There was a wide breadth of forest intervening between the inhabitants of Sandy Creek, Wachovia, Salisbury and the Catawba, and the marts of trade on the lower Cape Fear. Easier roads led to the towns of Virginia and of South Carolina, and those became the markets of the western counties. There was no specie in the province, while the amount of paper currency became entirely insufficient as the population was rapidly augmented.

At the east both saw-mills and grist-mills had long been established; at the west the new settlers quickly began to erect them on the streams where they located; and these became important points in their social and business life.

Felling the forests, clearing the fields, building houses, opening roads, constructing mills—in a word, making their homes habitable in those secluded regions—called forth the best exertions of those new settlers; and fortunate was it for them that their winters were mild, the summers temperate, while their fields yielded rich harvests, and the bright sunshine brought buoyant hope, health and happiness. Many of the families, observed Governor Dobbs, have ten children in them, and experience has long since proved that the natural increment of population in that favored region is nowhere exceeded in the world.*

The state church

It was contemplated in the original grant to the Lords Proprietors that there might be a state church and presumably that it would be conformable to the usage in England. The first effort in that direction was made in 1701, when each precinct was declared to be a parish, for which a vestry was appointed, and the vestry was empowered to employ ministers and to lay a tax of not more than five shillings on the poll for parish purposes, which included looking after the poor as well as providing a place of worship. Ten years later, when Governor Hyde met his first assembly, an act of Parliament having been passed declaring the province a

C. R., I, 789, 790

*In 1810 the editor of the Raleigh *Star* received many communications from intelligent men residing in every part of the State, throwing light on the commencement and progress of settlements in North Carolina. This mass of manuscripts was subsequently deposited in the library at Chapel Hill, but now cannot be found. Mr. Caruthers, who examined it, said: "From it we learn that Edgecomb began to be settled in 1726 by people from Virginia, who came there for the sake of living at their ease, as the climate was mild, the range good, and game in abundance; Wayne in 1735, but made little progress until 1750; Caswell in 1750, but had not more than ten families until 1755, when the Leas, Graves, Kimbros, Pattersons and others came from Orange and Culpepper counties in Virginia; Rockingham in 1750, by hunters, who were soon followed by a more substantial population; and Guilford about the same time, as appears from the deeds of land obtained by the Nottingham company. That company, by agents sent out for the purpose, purchased 33 surveys, or 21,120 acres, on the waters of North Buffalo and Reedy Fork; and one of their deeds, which is now before me, is dated December 3, 1753." (Caruthers' Life of Caldwell, 93.)

1771

member of the Crown of England, the Assembly enacted tha
the laws of England "are the laws of this government so fa
as they are compatible with our way of living"; and that a
the statute laws of England made for the establishment o
the Church and for the indulgence to Protestant dissenter
were in force in the province. This enactment firmly established the Church of England as the state church, and pu
in force the Act of Toleration, which remitted all penaltie
for non-conformity in the case of Protestant dissenters wh
did not deny the doctrine of the Trinity.

S.R.,XXIII,
187

In 1729 apparently each parish was invested with the righ
to elect its own vestrymen, who still had the privilege o
employing their ministers, being members of the establishe
church. Up to that time there had been in the province n
other ordained ministers of any denomination; but abou
that time Paul Palmer and Joseph Parker organized Baptist churches in the Albemarle section. In 1741 the vestry
law was amended requiring vestrymen to declare that they
"would not oppose the liturgy of the Church of England.'
They still had the right to lay a tax on the poll for parish
purposes, and by a two-thirds vote they could withdraw the
stipend agreed to be paid to any minister. At that period
there were only four ministers of the established church in
the province, perhaps an equal number of Baptist ministers
and none of the Presbyterian faith. There was but little

The rite of
marriage

room for clashing among the ministers. Later some differences arose in regard to the right of Presbyterian ministers
to perform the marriage service. Originally in 1666 certain
civil officers were empowered to perform the marriage ceremony, and "the persons violating this marriage shall be punished as if they had been married by a minister according to
the rites . . . of England." The Quakers married according
to their own rites. In 1715 it was again enacted that magistrates might perform the marriage service in parishes where
no minister was resident; but in all cases a license or the

S.R.,XXIII,
10, 158

publication of banns was required. The law remained unchanged until 1741, when it was again enacted that no minister or justice should celebrate the rite of marriage without
license or banns; and that the parish minister, if one, should
be entitled to the fee unless he neglected or refused to per-

1771

orm the service. There were still no Presbyterian ministers
ettled in the province and but very few Baptist ministers,
nd it was nowhere the practice for Baptist ministers at that
ime to perform the marriage service. About 1755 Hugh
McAden and James Campbell established themselves respec-
ively in Duplin and Cumberland counties, where they organized Presbyterian congregations. These were regularly
ordained ministers of that faith. A little later Rev. Henry
Pattillo, James Criswell, David Caldwell, Joseph Alexander
and Hezekiah Balch had charges of the same communion
further in the interior. In their respective settlements there
were but few adherents of the Church of England. Now,
however, some clashing because of religious differences became observable.

Originally introduced in 1701 in an effort to secure some
religious services for the colony, at a later period the state
church was fostered by influences emanating from Great
Britain. It was a survival of former usages, and was not
then so inharmonious with the times as it subsequently became. In every European country religion was the care of
the state; and in England the established church was at
once the mainstay of the Crown and the support of the ruling dynasty, while it had long been the bulwark protecting
Protestantism from the domination of Catholicism. When
the province became attached to the Crown, the king being
at the head of affairs, ecclesiastical as well as civil, and all
provincial laws requiring his concurrence, his officers sought
to strengthen and promote the state church, and such was
the tenor of the instructions given to the governors. Par-

S.R.,XXIII,
679-823

ticular effort was to be made to that end—even schoolmasters being required to be members of the established
church. Such was one of the results of the domination
of the Crown, of the close connection of the province
with the mother country. North Carolina was to be

New Bern
and Edenton
academies

fashioned after England—a consequence not so intolerable, for all the inhabitants were British subjects, reared
under existing institutions, and regarding their king as the
fountain of all honor and justice.

The freeholders of the east dominated the Assembly, and
they were largely in sympathy with the Church of England.

1771
The parish
taxes

Weeks,
Church and
State in
North
Carolina, 51
Legislation therefore conformed to the wishes of the Crown
Yet it was by no means onerous. But while the burdens im
posed were not heavy, nevertheless the principle of taxation
for church purposes was offensive to many of the dissenting
inhabitants. How slight the tax was may be gathered from
the report of Quaker sufferings made annually "to th
Meeting for Sufferings" in London; "in 1756, chiefly for th
maintenance 'of an hireling priest,' " £10 14s. 5d.; two year
later, £14 17s. 6d.; 1759, £85; 1760, £23; 1761, no sufferings
nor in 1762, nor 1765. In 1768 fines were reported amount
ing to £5 4s., "being for priests' wages and repairing thei
houses, called churches." In 1772, 30s., church rates; non
in 1773 nor 1774.

The amount of tithes collected here, says Dr. Weeks, i
ridiculously small; but in this small sum was wrapped th
whole principle of liberty of conscience.

At the west the Presbyterians concerned themselves bu
little with the vestry laws. They either did not elect vestry
men, or chose those who carried into operation only the pro
visions relating to the poor of the parish, not providing any
stipend for "an orthodox minister." Yet certainly some of
the incidents of the state church bore hard on the follow
ers of Knox, as on the Baptists.

Since the assemblymen, North Carolinians, enacted the
laws, there was no infringement of any liberty of worship
there was no persecution. "There was no opportunity for
it under the existing laws, and the dissenters were aggres
sive and powerful. The manuscript records of the Friends
show perfectly conclusively that while they suffered distraint
for tithes and military levies, they were not imprisoned.
They suffered no bodily violence." "There was more re
ligious liberty at the beginning than at the close of the
colonial life of North Carolina, but there is no well-authen
ticated case of bodily persecution in our annals, unless we
Weeks,
Church and
State in
North
Carolina, 48
count the imprisonment of the Quakers who refused to bear
arms in 1680 as such, and this seems to have been more
political than religious in its character."

Yet the effort to maintain the state church system in a
province where so many were indisposed to support it was a
source of irritation, without any compensating advantages,

1771

while fundamentally erroneous in principle. The established church as a state institution was out of place in America, where the people, bursting the bonds of the past, had emerged into a new life, with greater freedom of thought and action nurtured by their close contact with nature; and one of the chief objects in view, strengthening the Crown, was defeated by its rendering the Crown antagonistic to the dissenters in that relation of life which was dearest to the people, their church affiliations. In 1762 provision was made "for an orthodox clergy," by which the salary of clergymen was fixed at £133, and, as formerly, a fee for marrying was allowed, although performed by another. The vestry still had the right to select the clergyman, who, however, was required to have a certificate from the bishop of London that he had been ordained in the Church of England. In case of bad conduct he could be removed by the governor and council. This last provision was objectionable to the authorities in England, and for that reason the act was not allowed. Three years later a similar act was passed, the freeholders in every parish being required to elect twelve vestrymen, and if they elected a dissenter who refused to qualify he was fined. The vestry could levy a tax of ten shillings on the poll for church purposes, for encouraging schools, maintaining the poor, etc. To meet the objection raised to the former act it was now provided that while clergymen might be suspended by the governor for misconduct, the suspension should be only until the bishop of London passed on the cause.* The churches of that communion in all the colonies were under the supervision of the bishop of London.

The Vestry Act

S. R., XXIII, 956

Governor Tryon, with great connections, was very anxious apparently to commend himself to the authorities at home, and yet he declared that he was a zealous advocate of the principles of toleration. It seems that the Presbyterian ministers in the settlements at the west had performed the marriage ceremony without either license or publication of banns, contrary to the law in England, and in the province since 1711. When the act of 1762 was on its passage, the council proposed an amendment, "that no dissenting minister of any

C. R., VI, 881

*This act was re-enacted in 1768, and again in 1774 for ten years.

1771

The
Presbyterian
ministers
denomination whatever shall presume on any pretence to marry any persons under the penalty of forfeiting £50 proclamation money for every such offence." The house rejected that proposed amendment, and the act was passed without such a provision. This action was doubtless considered as impliedly confirming the right of the Presbyterian ministers to perform the marriage service, the Assembly having pointedly declined to concur in a provision declaring it unlawful. Still any marriage without license or banns was irregular under the existing law. One of the first acts passed in Governor Tryon's time, reciting this irregularity, made valid all such marriages and made it lawful for Presbyterian ministers, regularly called to any congregation, to celebrate the rite of marriage in their usual and accustomed manner, as any lawful magistrate might do, there having been issued

S. R.,
XXIII, 672
a license for the same. The fee for such service was, however, reserved to the minister of the Church of England in that parish, if one, unless he refused to do the service. This act did not allow Presbyterian ministers to marry by the publication of banns, and therefore it was not agreeable to the Presbyterian communities, and they made bitter complaints. To remedy this, at the session of December, 1770, an act was passed allowing these ministers to perform the service with publication. Governor Tryon was eager to please the Presbyterians, but Lord Dartmouth caused the act to be disallowed, saying that he could not approve of the dissenters in

S. R.,
XXIII, 826
C. R., VIII,
527; IX, 682
North Carolina having any greater privileges than allowed to them in England, and that he was not at liberty to admit a different mode of marriage in the colonies than required by the act of Parliament. Such was one of the effects of colonial dependence on the mother country—a Presbyterian minister could perform the marriage ceremony only as allowed by act of Parliament.

The
Episcopal
clergy
Under Tryon's active management the clergy of the Church of England in the province increased from five to eighteen. These were distributed chiefly throughout the eastern and northern counties. Some were supported solely by the stipend received from the Society for the Propagation of the Gospel and the voluntary offerings of the people; others, being established in parishes, received the allowance

made for them by law. There was, however, but little friction between them and the Presbyterians, who were settled
chiefly at the west and dominated that entire section. In
1766, Rev. Andrew Morton, being sent from England as a
missionary to minister in Mecklenburg County, ascertained
when he reached Brunswick that that county was settled
by Presbyterians, and did not go there. In Rowan there
were some of the established church who asked for a minister, and about 1770 Rev. Theodorus Drage was assigned to
that parish and undertook to have a vestry elected; but the
Presbyterian element was too strong for him to contend
with, and after a year or two he gave up his charge.

From an early date there had been adherents of the Baptist faith in the province. When in 1711 religious affairs became governed by the laws prevailing in England, the Toleration Act came into force. By this all penalties were re- The test oath
mitted for non-conformity in the case of Protestant dissenters
who did not deny the doctrine of the Trinity upon their taking the oaths of allegiance and the test oath, declaring that
"I do believe that there is not any transubstantiation in the
sacrament of the Lord's Supper or in the elements of bread
and wine at or after the consecration thereof by any person
whatsoever." It required, however, that their places of worship should be registered in the county courts, and that the
doors of their place of meeting should be open during the
time of worship;* and their ministers were to subscribe
the thirty-nine articles of religion, except those relating to
ecclesiastical government and infant baptism. At the time The Toleration Act
of the adoption of this act of toleration, on the accession of
William and Mary to the throne and the expulsion of the
Stuart kings, it was understood that it relieved from penalties
all except alone the Roman Catholics and Unitarians. Every
other denomination was content with it. In North Carolina,
under that act, the Baptists as well as the Presbyterians were
required to register their churches, although probably the
requirement was not always observed. In 1770 the Pres- C. R., VIII, 227, 507
byterians of Rowan registered two of their churches.

The first churches organized by the Baptists were Shiloh The Baptists
and Meherrin; the next, in 1742, Kehukee; Sandy Run, 1750;

*These requirements were aimed at the Catholics.

1771

1739

Fishing Creek, 1755; also Reedy Creek, Sandy Creek in Randolph and Grassy Creek in Granville. After that others followed fast, so that by 1771 there were twenty-two distinct congregations, besides the branches springing from those parent churches which they supplied. At the September term of the county court of Edgecombe, "Jonathan Thomas, a nonconforming preacher, produced an ordination writing signed by George Graham and John Moore, the pastors of the Baptists, ordaining him to go forth and preach the Gospel according to the tenets of that church; and he therefore took the oaths of allegiance and subscribed the test appointed for that purpose." A similar proceeding was had at the June session of 1740 of the county court of Craven, and the applicants were given liberty to build a house of worship. It seems, however, that some of them were accused of having violated the Toleration Act and they were bound over to appear at the next term of the general court.*

The
Methodists

The present Methodist organization was not then in existence. Rev. Mr. Whitefield passed through the province in 1739 and again in 1764, and preached at Wilmington, New Bern and perhaps elsewhere, but still regarded himself as a minister of the Church of England. It was not till 1772 that Joseph Pilmoor, the first Methodist minister in North Carolina, began his ministrations. The year following the first society was formed by Robert Williams; the first circuit was formed in 1776. The next year John King, John Dickens, LeRoy Cole and Edward Pride were appointed to the North Carolina Circuit, and at the close of the year they reported nine hundred and thirty members. King resided near Louisburg, and later ten miles west of Raleigh. The first conference was held near Louisburg on April 20th, 1785, at which Bishops Asbury and Coke were present.

Education and schools

Educational facilities in Albemarle were from the beginning greatly lacking. If there were schools and schoolmasters in the earlier years no mention was made of them; yet as many of the inhabitants, born and bred in Albemarle, evi-

*A verbatim copy of the minutes of that court is to be found in Vass's "History of the New Bern Presbyterian Church."

'771

dently received some training in their youth, there must have been teachers among them. When the ministers of the established church began to come in, about the opening of the eighteenth century, there are traces of some local schools. Charles Griffin was a school-teacher in Pasquotank, as well as lay reader. There was a school taught by Mr. Mashburn at Sarum, thought to be near Bandon, and about three miles from Ballard's Bridge. Perhaps there were others employed as lay readers who also taught school.

School-masters to be licensed

When the province passed under the immediate control of the king and its institutions were in a measure conformed to those of the mother country, Governor Burrington was instructed in 1731 that no schoolmaster should be permitted to come from England to North Carolina to keep school without the license of the bishop of London; and "that no other person now there or that shall come from other parts shall be admitted to keep school in North Carolina without your license first obtained."* This instruction was in aid of the general purpose to promote the established church, to train children in that faith, and strengthen the hold of the Crown on the people. Its natural effect must have been to discourage educational work in the province. We hear of no more schools except one taught about 1745 at Brunswick and the act of 1745 to build a school-house at Edenton. In 1749 John Starkey, himself it is said an ordained Episcopal clergyman, introduced a bill in the legislature to establish a public school, but the act did not become operative. Later, in Governor Dobbs's time, it was proposed to have a free school in every county; but that effort also miscarried.

1758 C. R., V, 1074

Notwithstanding the instructions given to Burrington were repeated to all later governors, it appears that the Scotch-Irish and other settlers in the interior had their local schools soon after coming to the province, as Governor Dobbs indicated when on a visit to his lands in Rowan and

*In 1714, an act known as the Schism Act was passed by Parliament forbidding any person to teach school who was not a member of the established church; this act was, however, repealed in 1719, under the administration of the Whig party, which continued for nearly sixty years. Apparently, the governor could license a teacher who was not of the established church, if so disposed.

Mecklenburg counties. They were probably not licensed by him. Although Wilmington had no organized Presbyterian church, Rev. James Tate, a Presbyterian minister, came from Ireland about 1760 and opened a classical school there, the first ever taught in that place. In the same year Crowfield Academy was established at Bellemont, near the site of Davidson College.

In 1764 it was proposed to erect a schoolhouse on some church property in New Bern, Thomas Tomlinson, on the first of January of that year, having opened a school there.

The school building was probably completed in 1766, when an act of the Assembly incorporated the trustees, provided a tax on rum to raise a salary of £20 per annum, and required the admittance of ten poor pupils, tuition free; and the license of the governor was required. In 1770 an act was passed reciting that the inhabitants of Edenton had erected a convenient schoolhouse. Trustees were

appointed to conduct the school, and the master, as in the case of the school at New Bern, was required to be a member of the established church, recommended by a majority of the trustees and licensed by the governor. These two academies at New Bern and Edenton afforded educational advantages that were of great benefit, extending through many years, to the people of the eastern counties.

In 1767 Dr. David Caldwell opened a classical school in Guilford County that became famous, a large number of eminent men receiving their education there. A year or two

later Rev. Henry Pattillo began to teach in Granville. One of his pupils, Charles Pettigrew, then of the Presbyterian faith, in 1773 became the principal of the Edenton Academy. A little later Rev. Daniel Earl, who had been the minister at Edenton, established a classical school in Bertie.

In 1771 the Lutherans on Second Creek, Rowan County, sent Rintelmann and Layrle to Europe to obtain "help to support a minister and school-teacher." Their efforts resulted in the establishment of Godfrey Arndt as the schoolmaster of that settlement.

In 1768 Joseph Alexander succeeded Mr. Craighead as pastor of Sugar Creek; "a fine scholar, he, in connection with Mr. Benedict, taught a classical school of high excellence and usefulness." Indeed, there was probably a school 1771 kept open in most of the seven Presbyterian settlements in Mecklenburg County.

There was a grammar school at Charlotte before 1770, and S. R., XXV, 519*d* in that year Edmund Fanning introduced a bill to establish a seminary of learning there under the name of Queen's Queen's College College. Fanning, Pattillo, Abner Nash and other trustees were directed to meet at the grammar school and elect a president and tutors. The college was to have the right to confer degrees. The president was to be of the established church, and licensed by the governor, but that was not required as to the trustees or tutors. To endow the college, a tax of sixpence was laid on all liquors brought into the county of Mecklenburg for ten years. The trustees met and elected Fanning the president. Fanning, however, left the province, along with Governor Tryon, in the summer S. R., XXV, 520 of 1771, and at the next session of the Assembly, in December, 1771, the charter was amended, enabling degrees to be conferred in his absence.

The original act having been sent to England, the Board of Trade reported "that this college, if allowed to be incorporated, will in effect operate as a seminary for the education and instruction of youth in the principles of the Presbyterian Church," and the Board doubted whether the king should give that encouragement to the Presbyterians in North Carolina. The Board also objected to the looseness of the C. R., IX, 250, 251 wording of the tax clause; but in particular it recommended that the king should disallow the act because it came under the description of those unusual and important acts which were not to be passed without a suspending clause; that is, such acts were not to go into effect until the king had assented to them. The king disallowed the act in April, 1772, but the college seems to have been continued; and in April, 1773, the amendment being disallowed, a proclamation was issued by Governor Martin in June declaring that C. R., IX, 596, 597 the amendment was of no effect. The school was maintained, Graham, Life of Gen. Jos. Graham, 18-25 apparently without interruption, under the name of Queen's Museum, and in 1777 the state legislature incorporated it as S. R., XXIV, 30 Liberty Hall, that act of Assembly then declaring that a number of youths there taught had since completed their education at various colleges in different parts of America.

That there were other schools at that period in other settlements cannot be doubted; while for higher education the colleges of William and Mary, Harvard, Yale, Princeton, in America, were patronized, and some of the youths from the seacoast counties at least were educated in England.

Taxation

In those early days, when wealth found investment only in lands and in negro property, the subjects of taxation were few, and for general purposes the exclusive tax was on the poll. The expenses of government had from the first been cast on the Lords Proprietors, at least to a great degree. The salaries of officers were paid from the quit rents by the *Land tax* receiver-general and by fees. In 1715, however, a tax was laid of 2s. 6d. on every one hundred acres of land, in addition to fifteen shillings tax on the poll; but the land tax was for that year only.

After the transfer to the Crown the same system was continued, and the Crown officers and provincial officers were paid from the quit rents* and by fees. Many years passed before the Assembly could be induced to make some little provision for a salary for the chief justice and the attorney-general. The chief current expense was in connection with the assemblies.

Poll tax As soon as Governor Johnston came in the Assembly granted an aid to the king, striking off currency for that purpose, and laying a tax on the poll to retire that currency. From time to time similar action was taken, provision being made to pay the provincial notes by a poll tax.

S. R., XXIII, 190 Similarly there was a county tax for bridges, court-houses, jails, etc., which generally ran about one shilling on the poll; and there was a parish tax usually applied to the care of the poor, and similar local purposes—and in some parishes a part of the fund going for the minister's salary, chapels, glebes, etc. This tax was limited to ten shillings, and seems to have run from one to three shillings generally. In 1768 the provincial tax aggregated seven shillings per poll. One

*All grants of land up to the Revolution were made subject to the quit rent.

shilling was still being collected to sink the aid to the king granted twenty years earlier, and five shillings of the entire tax was because of these aids. There was a tax for contingent expenses of government—to pay the chief justice, attorney-general, the expenses of the Assembly, etc. In that year there was a further tax of eight pence, which had been laid for two years to pay for the erection of the governor's palace. The county tax that year in Orange County was one shilling and the parish tax three shillings. The poll tax was levied on all male whites over sixteen years of age and on all slaves, female as well as male, over twelve years of age. By this distribution, property paid a tax, for as the lands were held by quit rents, most of the accumulated wealth was represented by slaves. For special purposes, some other taxes were imposed. A tonnage tax on vessels was collected for a fund to purchase powder. A tax on rum and liquors was sometimes laid for a local purpose—as for the New Bern Academy and Queen's College.

Quit rents

In order to have the commodities marketed in a merchantable condition, there were laws regulating how they should be put up for the market; and there were many places specified where these articles of commerce could be inspected by an officer appointed for that purpose, and they were not to be shipped out of the province unless inspected. Public warehouses for the inspection of tobacco were established at Edenton, at a point on the Chowan and at Hertford; at Jones's and Pitts's Landing, in Northampton; at Tarboro, Halifax, Campbellton; at Dixon's, Kingston, and Shepherd's, in Dobbs County. The inspectors at these warehouses, on receiving commodities, gave inspectors' notes for the same; and these notes or receipts were receivable in payment of public taxes at the following rates: Tobacco, at fifteen shillings per hundredweight; hemp, forty shillings; rice, twelve shillings; indigo, four shillings a pound; beeswax, one shilling; myrtle-wax, eight pence; tallow, six pence; Indian-dressed deer skins, two shillings, six pence. Thus it took rather more than a pound of tallow to pay the tax that was levied to build the governor's mansion, and fifty pounds of tobacco paid the entire provincial tax of 1767-68.

Inspectors' notes

S. R., XXIII, 782

1771

S. R.,
XXIII, 788

Lawyers

The lawyers were regulated, and by act of 1770 they were not allowed to charge more than ten shillings for any advice in a matter before the inferior court, where no suit was brought; nor more than £1 for advice in a matter cognizable in the superior court. In suits for land they could charge no more than £5. In no other suit in the superior court could they charge more than £2 10s., and in the inferior court their fee was just one-half of that. They were to be fined £50 if S. R.,
XXIII, 789 they demanded any larger compensation. Their fee was embraced in the bill of costs in the suit, and if the attorney neglected his case the court could order him to pay all costs occasioned by his neglect. After any case was determined, any client could, however, make further compensation, if he chose to do so, to his lawyer.

Quakers and the militia

Quakers had been subject to a fine for not mustering; in 1770 they were excused from mustering, but still they were required to render military duty in time of peril. It was provided that the colonel of the county should make a list of all male Quakers between the ages of sixteen and sixty, who should be under the command of some officer appointed by the governor. In time of invasion or insurrection a proportionate number of this Quaker force might be called into service, but could provide substitutes or could pay £10 instead.

Servants and slaves

Negro slavery was introduced into the colony at an early date, and servants by indenture was an English institution of long standing. Many persons came to America, paying their way by an agreement to render service for a definite period of time, these being called redemptionists. There were but few redemptionists brought to North Carolina, but apparently there was a considerable number of indented servants. The law forbade the emancipation of negroes except for meritorious services, to be passed on and allowed by the justice's court for the precinct or county. In 1723 such a considerable number of free negroes, mulattoes, and other persons of mixed blood came into the colony, several of whom intermarried with the whites against the law, that a particular act was passed expelling them; and no negro set free was allowed to remain in the province longer than six months.

In 1741 a further act was passed on the subject of Christian servants, by which indented servants were meant, and of negro slaves, regulating their correction and punishment, their diet, lodging, etc.; these matters being under the supervision of the county justices. In case any Christian servant should, during the time of his servitude, become diseased, the church wardens had to see that he was cared for.

If any person should import a slave who had been free in any Christian country, such slave was to be returned to the country from which he was brought, and a penalty was fixed for the offence. Slaves were required to remain on the plantation, and only one of them was allowed to have a gun to hunt for his master.

In the trial of slaves other slaves could give evidence, but in no other cases.

CHAPTER XXIV

Martin's Administration, 1771-75

Martin's administration.—The Regulator chieftains.—Pardon asked.—The Assembly meets.—Act of oblivion recommended.—The line between the Carolinas.—The quarrel with the governor.—The Assembly dissolved.—Sarah Wilson.—Purchase of Granville's territory proposed.—Governor Martin proposes reforms.—He confers with the Regulators.—The province tranquil.—Martin's view of the commotion.—The house objects to the South Carolina line.—Disagreement of the houses over James Hunter.—Fanning's losses.—Changes at the west.—The court bill.—The attachment clause.—The house resolute.—It is dissolved.—Courts by prerogative.—Quincy's visit.—Martin to become Granville's agent.—Colonial affairs.—Committee of Correspondence.—The act of oblivion again fails.—The house affronts the governor.—The courts cease.—The governor seeks conciliation.—Temporary courts of oyer.—The one shilling tax.—Harvey urges a convention.—Continental affairs.—Tea destroyed at Boston.—Parliament closes the port of Boston.—The McDonalds come to the Cape Fear.

Martin's administration

1771

After the hasty departure of Governor Tryon from the province, at a meeting of the council held in New Bern on July 1, 1771, James Hasell, the eldest councillor and the president of the board, assumed the administration, requiring all officials to qualify again, as if he had been appointed

August, 1771

governor. It was not until August 11th that Josiah Martin, the new governor, who had been detained in New York by illness, arrived at New Bern and entered on the discharge of his duties. Governor Martin, like Tryon, had been a lieu-

C. R., X, 47

tenant-colonel of the British army, but had two years earlier sold his commission and left the army because of ill health. He was just thirty-four years of age, an accomplished gentleman, a man of education, having strong connections in England. He had enjoyed the advantage of consultation with Governor Tryon at New York, receiving from him much information in regard to the local affairs of the province. His purpose seems to have been to continue in the same line of conduct that Tryon had pursued. Pleased with

President Hasell, he took early occasion to recommend him 1771 C. R., IX, 50, 277 for the position of lieutenant-governor in place of Lieutenant-Governor Mercer, who, it was rumored, had been appointed to a new government erected on the Ohio, but this proved to be an error, for Lieutenant-Governor Mercer still remained in England, enjoying the honors if not the emoluments of his office.

Applications were speedily made for the pardon of many of the leading Regulators. Husband had fled to Maryland, and later located in Pennsylvania. Howell also took refuge in Maryland, then moved to Virginia, but finally returned to the home of his youth in New Jersey. Hunter, who had strong connections in North Carolina, after some months' sojourn in Maryland, returned and took up his abode among his people. The Assembly favored him, as well as the county C. R., IX, 268, 269 courts, much to the disgust of the governor. His friends asked for his pardon, but it was never formally granted, yet he remained undisturbed and was later regarded as a supporter of Governor Martin's administration. William Butler made his petition for pardon, saying: "It is with the utmost abhorrence that I reflect on the proceedings of the people formerly called Regulators, being fully convinced that the principles which they had espoused were erroneous, and therefore most sincerely promise never to do the like again." The friends of the "Black Boys" in like manner petitioned C. R., IX, 57, 99 for mercy for them. Later the six convicted Regulators were pardoned by the king, and no other proceedings were instituted, although unavailing efforts were made to capture Husband in his hiding place in western Maryland.

Governor Martin convened the Assembly on November 19th, being the second session of the body elected in 1770. 1771 Husband had been expelled, and John Pryor, the other member from Orange, being dead, McNair and Nash were elected in their stead. Thomas Person, although excluded from pardon by the proclamation of Governor Tryon shortly after the battle of Alamance, appeared and took his seat, but C. R, IX, 136 Benjamin Person, one of the members from Bute, had died. General Waddell had been elected from Bladen County to fill a vacancy. There were no other notable changes in the body.

1771

November

C. R., IX,
269

Jan., 1771
Fire in
Wilmington,
South
Carolina
Gazette

Governor Martin's opening address was very satisfactory to the Assembly, and Maurice Moore, Samuel Johnston and Abner Nash were appointed a committee to prepare an answer to it. Their address was reported to the house by Judge Moore, and it is notable in that it contains but little of the laudation lavished by the council on Governor Tryon although it declared that "his spirited conduct and the bravery of the troops in the expedition against the insurgents deserve the acknowledgments of the whole country." Indeed, Judge Moore seems to have been at points with the late governor, shortly after whose departure there appeared a letter signed "Atticus," attributed to Judge Moore,* roughly handling him and holding him up to ridicule. The house urged the governor to grant a general pardon to all persons concerned in the insurrection except Husband, Howell and Butler. The omission of Hunter from this excepted list is remarkable, since he was the general of the insurgent forces. Governor Martin, however, thought it beyond his power to grant pardons, and replied that he had already offered such a measure for the consideration of the king, and at a subsequent session he informed the house that the king recommended it to pass a general act of pardon and oblivion.

The house proceeded to address itself to local affairs, passing bills to establish new counties at the west, to construct a public road from the western counties to Campbellton, to amend the act in relation to fees for officers, and other legislation calculated to promote the welfare of the people. Wilmington had suffered by a heavy fire, and an act was passed regulating the affairs of that town, particularly in view of possible conflagrations. A two-shilling tax was laid to retire debenture bills to the amount of £60,000, directed to be issued because of the expenses incurred in the Alamance campaign.

The line between the Carolinas

South Carolina had desired the line between the provinces to be so established as to give her a large territory at the west. On the other hand, Governor Tryon had urged that the line from the Yadkin River should be extended direct

---

*Also attributed to Abner Nash. Perhaps it was their joint work.

1771

to the Indian boundary, which he thought it would reach somewhere near Reedy River. But South Carolina, claiming that the original division before Brunswick was settled had been the Cape Fear River and that when the line was run to the Yadkin the surveyors had erroneously allowed North Carolina eleven miles too much, now insisted that the boundary should be the Catawba River to its source in the mountains. The king, however, decreed that the line should follow the boundaries of the reservation allotted to the Catawba Indians, and then up the Catawba River to its forks, and from there a due west course. Such were the instructions given to Governor Martin, who asked for an appropriation to carry them into effect. The Assembly demurred, **The line not satisfactory** replying that it had no funds for the purpose, and with some indignation it petitioned the king not to insist on that line. After adjournment, however, Governor Martin ran that line, much to the dissatisfaction of North Carolina. It deprived the province of a wide breadth of valuable territory well settled, for population had now extended to the mountains; but notwithstanding all remonstrances, it never was altered. While the western part of the province was receiving these accessions of population, immigrants were continually arriving at the ports, and in the winter of 1771 no less than one **C. R., IX, 259** thousand Highlanders disembarked on the Cape Fear.

The clashing over the sinking fund tax

Among other business that the Assembly undertook was the passage of a new court law. But the session was brought to an unexpected close with that and much other business unfinished. Besides the act for the issue of £60,000 of **Dec., 1771** debenture notes, both houses passed a bill to issue £120,000 of proclamation money, which the governor considered repugnant to the act of Parliament prohibiting the issue of paper currency of legal tender, and did not assent to. On the same day, Saturday, December 21st, a bill was **The shilling tax discontinued** passed to discontinue a tax of one shilling for the sinking fund, which appeared to have had full operation. The governor was determined not to assent to that, saying that it was a measure teeming with fraud and inconsistent with the public faith; but the leaders in the Assembly were equally

1771
The
Assembly
firm

determined in their resolution to relieve the people of what they regarded an unnecessary burden. Despite the antagonism of the governor, they proposed to proceed. In view of the fact that he would not ratify the act, the house passed a resolution that the tax had accomplished its purpose and should no longer be collected; and that it would indemnify the sheriffs in not collecting it. This was similar action to that taken in 1768, to which Governor Tryon objected, but which, notwithstanding his objection, was successfully made

C. R., IX,
230, 233

The
Assembly
dissolved

effective. On learning that this resolution had been adopted by the house, Governor Martin hastily commanded their attendance, and before it could be entered on their journal of proceedings he immediately dissolved the Assembly. Treasurer Ashe was a member of the body, as well as Treasurer Montfort, who had been elected at a bye-election as the representative of the town of Halifax, and pursuant to the resolution, they omitted that tax from the sheriffs' lists.

C. R., IX,
234

The governor at once wrote to the treasurers, insisting that they direct the sheriffs to collect the tax as usual. While the treasurer of the northern district complied, the southern treasurer refused and obeyed the mandate of the Assembly. Thereupon the governor issued a proclamation commanding the sheriffs to make the collection, but his order was not generally obeyed. Thus came a breach between the new governor and the people, on a local matter, which Governor Tryon always had the address to avoid.

Sarah
Wilson

During the course of the winter an accomplished woman, calling herself Lady Susanna Carolina Matilda, sister to the queen of Great Britain, travelled through Virginia, being entertained at the houses of the gentlemen, and many had the honor of kissing her hand. To some she promised governments, to others regiments or promotions of different kinds in the treasury, army and navy, acting her part so adroitly as to levy heavy contributions on persons of the highest rank. At New Bern she received marked attention from Governor Martin and his wife, and at Wilmington she

Martin,
Hist. of
North
Carolina,
II, 292

was also received with every distinction. Eventually, at Charleston, where much attention was paid her, her masquerade was discovered, and she was apprehended. Her name was Sarah Wilson. She had been a maid of honor.

Having access to the royal apartments, she rifled a cabinet of many valuable jewels, for which she was tried and condemned to death. By an act of grace her sentence was softened into transportation, and she had been landed in Maryland during the preceding fall, where, as a convict, she was purchased by a Mr. Duval. Shortly afterward she effected her escape from her master, and when at a prudent distance, assumed the name of the queen's sister, and for a brief season wore her borrowed plumage with fine effect.

Governor Martin proposes reforms

Governor Martin, in considering the situation of affairs in the province, became greatly impressed with the desirability of the Crown's purchasing Earl Granville's territory, which was then offered for sale at a price between £60,000 and £80,000 sterling. The quit rents in 1766 exceeded £6,000 proclamation money. After that time the land office was closed, but so many settlers had seated themselves without grants in that domain that in 1772 it was estimated the rents would yield half as much more, and could titles be obtained it was thought that very shortly the rents would amount to £12,000. Such had been the great progress of settlement. But as no quit rents had been paid for five or six years, and the accumulation of indebtedness was heavy, the tenants, even those who had no titles, were very apprehensive concerning the day of payment, and there was a great ferment among them, ready to break out with violence when payment should be exacted. For these reasons the governor urged the purchase by the king, and the Assembly held the same view, for at the next session they solicited that the purchase should be made.

The governor had been instructed to request for the Crown the power of appointing the six clerks of the superior court, theretofore vested in the chief justice, and he now urged that the thirty-four clerks of the counties, the appointment of whom was vested in the clerk of the pleas, Mr. Strudwick, should likewise be appointed by the Crown. These clerkships yielded the incumbents from £50 to £500 per year, and they paid an annual rent running from £4 to £40 to Mr. Strudwick, who thus received £560 per annum,

Quit rents

C. R., IX, 262

The clerks

C. R., IX, 264-266

a handsome income from this sinecure. Besides, Mr. Strudwick was also secretary of the province, which yielded a fine income. Governor Martin dwelt on the evils of this system, by which these clerkships were bestowed on the best bidders, not persons chosen for loyalty, integrity or ability, who were led to extortion upon the people to indemnify themselves for that part of the profits which they had to pay for the appointment. With adroitness they managed the magistrates, who became confederated with them, and thus arose oppression and shameless conduct among those who ought to have been ministers of justice. In addition, he called attention to the facility with which the clerks found their way into the Assembly, and, being independent of the administration, opposed and embarrassed designs for the public good. He therefore urged most strongly an improvement in the polity of the province by the changes he recommended.

The governor at the west

Following the example of Governor Tryon, Governor Martin proposed to pass the summer at Hillsboro. Departing from New Bern on June 21st, with twenty persons accompanying him, forming quite a cavalcade, he was more than ten days in making the journey, and when he approached Wake Court House was met by a number of gentlemen, who rode out from Hillsboro to escort him to his residence. That summer proved so dry and the drought was so prevalent that there was a notable failure of crops, not only in western North Carolina, but in South Carolina, as well as to the northward; and the demand for breadstuffs elsewhere was so great that it became necessary for the governor by proclamation to forbid the removal of any grain from the province.

At Hillsboro, the governor was waited on by many of the Regulators, and then for the first time he comprehended that the outlawed chiefs were so only by virtue of the riot act, which had then expired—and that, besides, it had not been ascertained by law that the proclamations had been published in conformity with the act, and therefore it was uncertain whether they were outlaws or not. He made a

1772

our to Salisbury and the Moravian settlement, and when in Guilford County had a conference with large numbers of the Regulators, among them James Hunter. They all expressed contrition, and the governor came to entertain very different views concerning the regulation movement. He extended his journey to the eastward as far as Halifax, remarking the great superiority of the inhabitants of Granville and Bute in wealth and refinement over those to the westward. In the course of his journey he reviewed the militia of Orange, Guilford, and Chatham, bringing together the people that he might reprehend them for their past offences and exhort them to good behavior. C. R., IX, 329 Martin's views C. R., IX, 349

He submitted legal questions concerning the Regulators to the judges and attorney-general, with a view of ascertaining their status. In the opinion of the judges, the riot act having expired, the people who had participated in former disturbances were liable only under the previous law. Anticipating that there would be a general act of pardon passed by the Assembly, he directed that the outlaws and others should come into court and give their recognizances, which they accordingly did, and he had the satisfaction of reporting to the Earl of Hillsborough that all confusion and disorder had passed away and that peace and tranquillity reigned supreme. He also reported that the commotions were provoked by the insolence and cruel advantages taken by mercenary, tricky attorneys, clerks and other little officers, who practised every sort of rapine and extortion, bringing upon themselves the just resentment of the outraged people; and that they, by artful misrepresentations that the vengeance which the wretched people aimed at them was directed against the constitution, begat a prejudice against them, which was craftily worked up until the people were driven to acts of desperation. C. R., IX, 332 *et seq.* C. R., IX, 348 C. R., IX, 330

That the governor's heart was softened toward those who had been associated as Regulators was apparent, and his sympathies were so enlisted that he gained their good will, and at a later period they were easily moulded to his purposes.

Letter from James Hunter to William Butler

Morehead's
James
Hunter,
2d ed., 44, 45

"November 6, 1772.

"DEAR FRIEND: Sorry I am that I have not the good fortune to see you. . . . I took this journey into Maryland with no other view but to see you, Harman and Howell, as I reckoned you were afraid to come and see me; but have had the bad fortune to see none of you— only Howell, whom I saw in Augusta County, on the head of James River. I expect you have seen Harman by this time, as he had gone with his family to the Red Stone. But I would not have you publish it.

"Things have taken a mighty turn in our unfortunate country. This summer our new governor has been up with us and given us every satisfaction we could expect of him, and has had our public tax settled and has found our gentry behind in our, the public, tax, 66,443-9 shillings, besides the parish and county tax; and I think our officers hate him as bad as we hated Tryon, only they don't speak so free. He has turned Colonel McGee out of commission for making complaint against outlawed men—and he has turned out every officer that any complaint has been supported against. In short, I think he has determined to purge the country of them. We petitioned him as soon as he came, and when he received our petition he came up amongst us and sent for all the outlawed men to meet him at William Field's, told us it was out of his power to pardon us at that time because he had submitted it to the king, and the king's instruction was to leave it to the governor, council and Assembly to pardon whom they saw fit. But assured us he had given strict orders no man should be hurt or meddled with on that account, which made us wish for you all back again. Though some are of opinion Harman will not be pardoned, I am of a different mind. The country petitioned for you—upward of 3000 signers; his answer was that he would recommend it to the Assembly, and freely gave his consent that nothing might be left to keep up the quarrel. He came to see us the second time, and advised, for fear of ill-designing fellows, to go to Hillsboro and enter into recognizance till the Assembly met, which eleven of us did. He bemoaned our case and regretted that the indemnifying act had put it out of his power to give us full redress. Our enemies, I believe, would be glad to see you three pardoned, for some of them have gotten severely whipped about your being kept away, and I think the country is as much master now as ever. The outlawed men since they came home are very ill-natured and whip them wherever they find them, and the governor thinks it no wonder they do not take the law of them. There is a great deal of private mischief done. The people want you back, and I think you would be quite safe, though we can be

The out-
lawed men

better assured when the Assembly breaks up; it sits December 10th,
when it is allowed that an indemnifying act will pass on all sides.*
Our governor has got Fanning to forgive the pulling down of his
house, and he has published it in print advertisements all over the
country. The governor has published a statement of the public
accounts at every church and court-house in the province for seventeen years back, in print, with the sheriffs' names and the sum they
have in hand for each year, and a great many of their extortionate
actions—a thing we never expected—to the great grief and shame of
our gentry. If you should go to that far country, I wish you would
come and see us first; and let me assure you, you need not go on
that account. Morriss Moore and Abner Nash have been up to see
me, to try to get me in favor again, and promised to do all they
could for you, and I think they are more afraid than ever. I have
now some good news to tell you, which I heard since I left home.
I met John Husbands on his way to Maryland to prove his father's
debt, which the governor told him, if he would, in order to prove
that Harman was in his debt, he should have all his losses made up,
and told me that McCollough was come and was in our settlement,
and was to have a meeting at my house the next Monday by a
message from the king. Jeremiah Fields and others had been with
him to know what it was, but he refused to tell them; he came to
my house, only said that he had tidings of the gospel of peace to
preach to us all; and was much concerned that I was not at home,
for he had particular business with me. I am much troubled, dear
brother, that I had not the good fortune to communicate my thoughts
to you by word of mouth, for I have so much to tell you that I could
not write it in two days. The outlawed all live on their places
again, and, I think, as free from want as ever. I came home in ten
months after the battle, entered a piece of vacant land adjoining my
old place, and rented out my old place. I add no more, but subscribe
myself your loving friend and brother sufferer.

"JAMES HUNTER.

"P.S.—Your friends are all well and desire to be remembered
to you."

John Harvey speaker

A new Assembly, the members of which had been elected
in the spring, was prorogued to December, and then to
January 18th following, but the attendance being small, the
session did not begin until the 25th. Because of Speaker
Caswell's action in relation to the resolve forbidding the

*C. R., IX, 877. Act of indemnity disallowed by home govern-
ment.

1773

collection of the one shilling tax, Earl Hillsborough had directed Governor Martin not to assent to Caswell's election as speaker, should the house again elect him. But now John Harvey was once more in his seat, and at Caswell's instance he was unanimously chosen speaker, Caswell himself having fixed his eye on the southern treasuryship. The session opened with every appearance of good will between the governor and the Assembly, and at once the house addressed itself to the passage of a large number of necessary bills. During the session the robes for the speakers and the maces having arrived, the treasurers were directed to provide suitable robes for the doorkeepers and mace bearers; and there was some disposition to have triennial assemblies, conformably to the law in England.

The governor communicated to the Assembly the cost of running the line from the Catawba nation to the mountains, but that body refused to pay it, saying that the line was C. R., IX, very objectionable; that it was run in the interest of South 211, 563, 578 Carolina, and that this province would bear no part of the expense. It was declared that a million acres of land had been taken from the province, on which were located many settlers; that a large part of Tryon County had been thrown into South Carolina, and the sheriff of Tryon County had to be relieved because of the arrears of the taxes which he had not collected. Notwithstanding the indignant remonstrance of the last house, the governor now communicated that any respectful petition would be considered by the king, and the house directed its Committee of Correspondence to require the agent to urge another line on the king's attention.

Act of oblivion defeated

There were echoes of the regulation movement. Many were the applications for allowances because of the expense suffered in connection with Tryon's march. Among those allowed by the house was the payment of £37 to William C. R., IX, Few for the destruction of his wheat and rye field by 433, 547 Tryon's horses and cattle. An act of oblivion being proposed, among those excepted from its operation in the council were James Hunter, Samuel Devinny, and Ninian Bell

Hamilton. In the house these names were omitted from the excepted list, and the bill fell because the council would not concur with the house in granting pardon to Hunter.

Edmund Fanning had left the province and returned to New York. His attorneys had been directed to institute suit against those who had destroyed his house and property. But Governor Martin, fearing that this proceeding would revive animosities and produce some disturbance, prevailed on Fanning to abandon his actions at law and rely on the justice of the Assembly. His claim was for £1,500. The amount was moderate, but the house refused to pay it, saying that it could not appropriate public funds for private purposes; and although some discontent might arise from his suits, it would be local, while the inhabitants of the whole province would object to having the public money used that way.

Fanning

C. R., II, 548, 561

This being the session for the election of treasurers, Montfort was re-elected for the northern district, but by means which Ashe's friends hotly denounced as unjust, he was defeated by Caswell.

C. R., IX, 1054

Changes at the west

The development of the western section led to efforts to furnish the inhabitants of the interior needed facilities for transportation. At the little village of Charlotte, Queen's College had been established, although the act was disallowed because it vested in the trustees the right of appointing the master. Now a bill was passed to make it the county seat of Mecklenburg, but this, too, was rejected, as it contained provisions relating to other subjects of legislation. But in view of its growing importance, a highway was ordered to be built from Charlotte to Bladen.

Charlotte

On the Cape Fear, the hamlet of Cross Creek found a rival in Campbellton, less than a mile distant. Campbellton had become the mart of the northwestern counties, and a road was directed to be constructed from it to Dan River; also, in the superior court bill, it was proposed to discontinue the court at Hillsboro and attach Orange and Granville to the Halifax district, while Chatham and other counties were grouped in a new circuit, the court to be held at Campbellton.

Campbellton

1773
February

The court bill

The Assembly, in committee of the whole, directed that a new court bill be drawn, providing for both superior and inferior courts; for the retention by the chief justice of the power to appoint the superior court clerks; and prohibiting the clerk of the pleas from selling or disposing of any county clerkship for any gratuity or reward whatsoever, and making any clerk who should give any gratuity or reward for his clerkship incapable of holding the office.

C. R., IX, 477

The sale of clerkships

The council sought to amend this bill in various particulars. While agreeing that there should be no sale of a clerkship, it proposed to allow the clerk of the pleas to reserve a proportion of the fees to himself; and especially, because of the king's commands, it desired an amendment that in all cases of attachment, where the defendant resided in Europe, the proceedings should be stayed one year. The house refused to concur, and the council finally passed the bill, but with a clause suspending its operation until it should be approved by the king. The old court laws, however, were about to expire, and some immediate provision for maintaining a judicial system was imperatively necessary. Under this stress, two other bills were at once introduced, with the view of continuing the former laws in force for six months, and until the next session of the assembly. In the council both of these bills were so amended as to exempt from attachment the landed property of persons who were not residents of the province, and requiring twelve months' notice to the debtor. This was an innovation in the law and usage which had ever prevailed in the province, and as it would be attended with great inconvenience, often resulting in the defeat of justice, the house refused to concur. The action of the council was, however, in conformity with the governor's instructions, and in the contest much heat was evolved. Finally the council, content with defeating the superior court bill, passed that continuing the inferior courts; but the governor was not so complacent, and he refused his assent even to that measure. Thus neither bill became a law, while the general act, passed earlier in the session, could have no operation until the king had given his assent. And so it was that

S. R.,
XXIII, 872

The attachment clause

C. R., IX, 558

The bills defeated

C. R., IX, 600

1773

the contingency had arrived upon which on the adjournment of the Assembly the entire judicial system of the province was to fall. With hot animosity, the house, appealing to the judgment of mankind, passed a resolution that there should be published in the gazettes copies of the governor's instructions and of the various communications between the two houses, so that their conduct could be fully understood.

No courts C. R., IX, 581

On the day this action was taken, March 6th, the governor having rejected the inferior court bill and sixteen others of less importance, prorogued the Assembly until the 9th, hoping by this act of discipline to bring the members into a frame of mind more compliant with his wishes. But the members had equal resolution, and, upon the prorogation, most of them returned to their homes; and although fifteen, with the speaker, appeared on the 9th, and the governor and council urged that, under the royal instruction given twenty years earlier, fifteen constituted a quorum, Speaker Harvey communicated to the governor that the members present would not make a house unless there should be a majority in attendance; and that he not only had no expectation of the arrival of other members, but those then at New Bern were preparing to depart. The house had refused to obey the governor. Nothing was left but its immediate dissolution, and writs were at once issued for the election of new members, the Assembly to be held on May 1st.

March, 1773

The Assembly firm C. R., IX, 599

C. R., IX, 595

Prerogative courts

Without any laws providing for courts or juries, or directing how jurors should be drawn, with at least the ordinary number of criminals in jail, and a necessity existing to enforce the criminal laws for the preservation of peace and order, Governor Martin now bethought himself of his authority, under the king's prerogative, to establish courts of oyer and terminer, and on March 16th appointed Maurice Moore and Richard Caswell commissioners, together with the chief justice, to hold such courts. During the summer they were held in several of the counties under the order of the governor.

C. R., IX, 607

1773

Governor Martin having the previous year visited the western counties, now spent some time in the Albemarle section, and likewise in the counties bordering on South Carolina; and in his report of these journeys he spoke favorably of the fertility of the soil and the prosperous condition of the people.

Quincy's visit

The policy of the ministry and of Parliament in regard to the colonies had been a source of continual irritation, especially with the more commercial communities of the north; and in their plans for resistance the Massachusetts leaders deemed it expedient to have the united support of all the inhabitants of America. To this end, early in 1773, Josiah Quincy passed through North Carolina, seeking to establish a plan of continental correspondence, which the Virginia Assembly had recommended. At Wilmington he dined with about twenty persons at Mr. William Hooper's, and spent the night with Cornelius Harnett, whom he characterized as "the Samuel Adams of North Carolina." He mentioned in his diary: "Robert Howe, Harnett and myself made the social triumvirate of the evening. The plan of continental correspondence, highly relished, much wished for and resolved upon as proper to be pursued." He was surprised to find that "the present state of North Carolina is really curious; there are but five provincial laws in force through the colony, and no courts at all in being."

C. R., IX, 610

Granville's land office opened

Earl Granville being now desirous of having his territory cared for, offered to make Governor Martin his agent, and the governor submitted the matter to Earl Hillsborough and received permission to undertake that employment in addition to his other duties. Granville's land office had been closed for several years.

During the summer the governor received instructions from the king disallowing the court law passed at the last session, but allowing attachments in a modified form. He had determined not to convene the Assembly until he had received these instructions, and prorogued it from time to time until the last of November, when the new house met, again electing Harvey as speaker.

Colonial affairs

1773

Immediately on its assembling, Speaker Harvey laid C. R., IX, 737, 740 Nov., 1773 before the house resolutions received from other colonies, and a committee, composed of Johnston, Howe, and Harnett, was appointed to prepare appropriate answers. Among these resolutions were those of the Virginia Assembly of March 12th proposing a Committee of Correspondence, in C R., IX, 741 which the house concurred, and it appointed eight members as a standing Committee of Correspondence, with directions to obtain the most early and authentic intelligence of the ministry's plans that related to the colonies; and, particularly were they required to report on a court of inquiry lately held in Rhode Island, with powers to transmit persons accused of offences to places beyond seas for trial. This action—the appointment of committees of correspondence— was the first step in the path that led to the union of the colonies. It was significant of a purpose of co-operation, and as time passed and event followed event, the bands of union were forged and the colonies became welded together in an indissoluble confederacy.

The house informed Governor Martin that in its opinion Prerogative courts overthrown he could not erect courts of oyer and terminer without the concurrence of the legislature, and that it would make no provision for defraying the expenses of the courts he had instituted. Samuel Johnston was the leading spirit in the C. R., X, 401 Assembly. He was pronounced against courts of prerogative and the house was unanimous in its action. Necessarily the system fell and the courts ceased. New bills were brought in for the establishment of courts, and for pardon and oblivion for the Regulators, and to discontinue the poll tax of one shilling. The council, however, objected to the first, insisting that it should be drawn conformably to the king's instructions, to which the house would not agree; nor did it act on the other measures.

The act of oblivion again fails

On December 21st the governor sent a verbal message requiring the immediate attendance of the house at his palace. Before complying, the house hastily passed a resolution appointing a committee, composed of the speaker and seven

1774
The aid of
Tryon
asked
C. R., IX,
787

other members, to prepare an address to the king on the subject of the court law, particularly relative to attachments, and to address Governor Tryon requesting him to convey the same to his Majesty, and "support our earnest solicitations with his interest and influence, and that he will accept of this important trust as testimony of the great affection this colony bears him, and the entire confidence they repose in him." Governor Martin having found the temper of the Assembly so firm in its opposition to his measures, prorogued it until March 1st, and the session closed without the passage of a single act.

C. R., IX,
800

When the governor learned of the address to Governor Tryon, of New York, his mortification was unbounded, his pride having received a severe blow, which he considered extremely undeserved; but he suppressed his anger and still pursued a persuasive policy.

No courts
in the
province
C. R., IX,
831
March, 1774

The governor's prerogative courts having suddenly fallen, there were in March, when the Assembly met again, neither criminal nor civil courts in existence. The governor made another earnest appeal for conciliation, and it was proposed as a temporary measure of relief that there should be three acts passed, one establishing courts of justice, one relating to foreign attachments, and one relating to the fee bill of 1748. On these measures, for the first time, the yeas and nays were entered on the house journals. The house refused to assent by large majorities, all the leading members voting in the negative.

C. R., IX,
930

The house having again passed a court bill, which the governor felt it his duty to reject, temporary acts were passed to establish courts of oyer and terminer and inferior courts, to last for one year, and then until the next session of the Assembly, to which he gave a reluctant assent. The friction between the Assembly and the governor was indeed pronounced, for the assemblymen were immovable, and notwithstanding Governor Martin was conciliatory to the last degree, yet he was bound by his positive instructions and could not meet the views of the popular leaders. On March 24th he prorogued the body until May 25th. But before its adjournment the house again resolved that the one shilling tax should not be collected. This was more

S. R.,
XXIII, 931

Temporary
court law

1an the spirit of the governor could brook, and now giving 1774
2in to his wrath and indignation, he immediately issued his C. R., IX, 946
roclamation dissolving the Assembly with marks of his
2nsure and disapprobation. The original act having been The Assembly dissolved
1assed by the three several constituents composing the legis-
1tive body, the governor held that the house "had assumed
1e dangerous power of dispensing with the positive laws of
1e country, and that it was a political enormity to abrogate
1 solemn and important law by its single veto." The session, Courts of oyer and
1owever, was not without avail, for provision was made for terminer
1stablishing inferior courts and criminal courts; of the latter,
1lexander Martin and Francis Nash were the judges of the
1alisbury and Hillsboro districts, respectively. So much at
1ast had been accomplished.

But this very important act was defective. It was cer- S. R., XXIII, 945
1ainly badly drawn. Governor Martin assented to it with
1reat reluctance, and always spoke of it contemptuously. C. R., IX, 1060
1Jnder his instructions he could not assent to such a general
1ourt law as the Assembly insisted on, but because of the
1eplorable situation, in the absence of any courts of criminal
1urisdiction, he gave his assent to this temporary act, which
1ad been hastily passed by the Assembly. It authorized the
1overnor to commission the chief justice to hold courts of
1yer and terminer and general jail delivery, and to appoint
1wo other persons resident in each district to hold the courts
1f their districts in the absence of the chief justice, but by
1nadvertence the powers conferred on these judges were not
1hose probably intended, the draftsmen being unskilled.
1hief Justice Howard left North Carolina for the summer,
1nd James Hasell was appointed chief justice in his stead.
1he summer terms were to be held in June and July and the
1winter terms in December and January. When the court Moore attacks the
1onvened at Wilmington, at the close of July, Maurice Moore courts, July, 1774
1aised objections because of the defects in the act and in the
1commission of the judge. Moore had been on the bench in
1Governor Tryon's time, and had been appointed by Gov-
1ernor Martin one of the judges of his prerogative courts,
1which the Assembly had repudiated as being illegal and
1unconstitutional. The destruction by the Assembly of the
1court of which he was a judge on the score of illegality and

1774
McRee's
Iredell, I,
201
unconstitutionality seems to have inflamed the depose
jurist, who had held his honors by the appointment of th
governor, and now with zest he made his legal exception
to the constitution of the Assembly's court, "very indecent
reflecting upon the legislature, happy in the weakness
the judge." Because of his strictures, the court adjourne

C. R., X, 1
Nevertheless, these courts continued to be held, at least
some if not all the districts, until the summer of 1775.

Harvey urges a convention

The condition of the province, although in the absence
courts there were fewer disorders than might have bee
anticipated, was, in 1774, a fruitful source of grave alarm
to thoughtful citizens. Something, they said, must be don
to save the country from anarchy. Biggleston, the gov
ernor's secretary, mentioned to Speaker Harvey that th
governor did not intend to convene another Assembly unt
he saw some chance of a better one than the last. Promptl
Harvey replied that the people then would convene one them
April, 1774
selves. On the night of April 4, 1774, a week after th
dissolution of the Assembly, Harvey and Johnston passe
the night with Colonel Buncombe, and Harvey was "in
very violent mood, and declared he was for assembling
C. R., IX,
968
convention independent of the governor, and urged upon u
to co-operate with him." He declared that he would lea
the way and "issue hand-bills under his own name, and tha
the Committee of Correspondence ought to go to work a
once." Such a proceeding was not unknown. It had bee
resorted to once, years before, in Massachusetts, but now
was a revolutionary movement and was a bold departure
Harvey had already spoken of it to Willie Jones, who prom
ised to exert himself in its favor, and now Johnston wrote t
Hooper on the subject, and asked him to speak to Harnet
and Ashe and other leaders on the Cape Fear.

Continental affairs

But not only were the affairs of the province then acute
continental matters also were agitating the people. Th
agreement of the colonies not to give their assent to an
law taxing America had led to the disuse of taxed tea
large quantities of which lay stored in the English ware

ouses of the East India Company. To counteract this, arliament allowed the export of teas from England without the former export duty, so that the teas, even after aying the American tax, could be sold at a cheaper price. With the hope of speedy sales, the East India Company hipped cargoes to New York, Philadelphia, Charleston and Boston. Those for the two former ports were returned to London. At Charleston the tea was unloaded, but stowed way in cellars unsold. At Boston, where a considerable llicit trade in tea was carried on by Hancock and other merchants, which they did not wish interfered with, the government insisted that the tea should be landed and sold. To revent this, a number of the inhabitants, disguised as Indians, on the night of December 18th boarded the ships, roke open the chests and emptied the tea into the harbor. nformation of this proceeding caused great excitement in England. American affairs engrossed the attention of Parliament. Four acts were passed. By the first the port of Boston was closed, to take effect on June 4th, the custom ouse being transferred to Salem. By the second the charter f Massachusetts was abrogated and town meetings, except or elections, declared unlawful. By the third all officers f the Crown, in case of indictment, were to be sent to England for trial. The fourth related to the quartering of oldiers on the colonies. While these measures, aimed directly at the old colonies, excited indignation, a fifth, respecting the government of the new province of Quebec, occasioned even greater apprehension. In that, every limi- ation of the constitution was disregarded. The legislative ower was vested in a council appointed by the Crown. Roman Catholicism was established as the state religion. Roman Catholics were eligible to office. There was to be no writ of habeas corpus. The French civil law, without ury trials, was ordained; and the bounds of the province were extended south to the Ohio and west to the Mississippi, hedging in the northern colonies. If charters could be abrogated, government by general assemblies abolished, Protestantism supplanted by Catholicism and the writ of habeas corpus ignored, America owed her liberties only to the sufferance of her masters.

1774

Under the changing condition there was to be a conflic between the colonies and the mother country was apparent and in view of it the king regarded with apprehension the wonderful growth of the colonies, and sought to check the removal of his subjects from Great Britain to his American dominions. Thus, in 1772, after James McDonald and his associates of the Isle of Skye, proposing to settle in North Carolina, had petitioned for an allotment of forty thousand acres of land, the request was refused on the ground that too many British subjects were removing to the colonies. Mc Donald was the head of that large and influential connection of which Flora McDonald was a member—that admirable woman whose picturesque career has given her a unique distinction among her sex. Notwithstanding this refusal, the McDonalds did not relinquish their purpose but continued their preparations to join the stream of Scotchmen who were migrating to the Cape Fear. In the spring of 1774 three hundred families came from the Highlands; and although the king in February of that year gave instructions which virtually closed his land offices and withdrew his land from entry, yet in the following winter some eight hundred other Scotchmen disembarked at Wilmington. Among them were the McDonalds. Flora and her husband, Allan, after a brief sojourn at Cross Creek, resided temporarily at Cameron Hill, near Barbecue Church, some twenty miles to the northward of Campbellton, and then located in Anson County.*

C. R., IX, 303

Arrival of Highlanders

C. R., IX, 1020

*At Wilmington the inhabitants gave Flora McDonald a public reception and ball; she was received at Cross Creek with great demonstration, martial music and the strains of the pibroch.

CHAPTER XXV

MARTIN'S ADMINISTRATION, 1771-75—*Continued*.

Organized resistance.—The Committee of Correspondence.—William Hooper.—The Wilmington meeting.—The cause of Boston the cause of all.—Parker Quince.—The first convention.—The counties organize.—Governor Martin's proclamation.—The convention held.—The resolution.—Non-importations.—Tea not to be used. —The revolutionary government.—Committees of Safety.—Instructions to delegates.—Governor Martin's attitude.—Goes to New York.—The Continental Congress.—The revolution progresses.—Cornelius Harnett.—The Edenton tea party.—Governor Martin returns.—The Transylvania colony.—The second convention called.—Proceedings on the Cape Fear.—John Ashe.—Robert Howe. —The Regulators disaffected.—The Highlanders.—Enrolled Loyalists.—The Assembly and the Convention.—John Harvey presides.— The American Association signed.—The governor's address.—The house replies resolutely.—The Assembly dissolved.—The last appearance of Harvey.—North Carolina at court.—Thomas Barker.— Governor Tryon.—North Carolina favored.—The battle of Lexington.—Martial spirit aroused.—The governor questioned by Nash. —He is alarmed.—The negro insurrection.—He seeks refuge at Fort Johnston.

Organized resistance

1774

To the dissatisfied colonists was imputed by the advisers of the king, from the very beginning of the controversy, a purpose to sever their connection with the mother country; but while that idea doubtless occurred to the minds of philosophic students as a remote possibility, it was not at all entertained by the people at large, who, born British subjects, had neither inclination nor purpose to change that relation. Among those who were casting their eye to the future was C. R., IX, William Hooper. Writing April 26, 1774, to James Iredell, 985 he said: "The colonies are striding fast to independence, and ere long will build an empire upon the ruins of Great Britain," but yet he was not agitating for a separation at that time.

The plan proposed by Harvey for the people to convene an assembly did not at once materialize; but when the port

1774

of Boston was closed, in North Carolina as in every other part of America, there was a storm of indignation; and the proposition was revived.

S. R., XI, 245, 246

June

On June 9th the Committee of Correspondence received sundry letters and papers from the northern colonies respecting the oppressive proceedings against Boston. These, the next day, they sent forward to the committee of South Carolina, saying that they could only express their individual sentiments, but believed that the inhabitants of the whole province concurred with them; that they thought that the province ought to consider the cause of Boston as the cause of America; that they should concur and co-operate in measures agreed on by their sister colonies; that it was expedient that deputies should be appointed to adopt measures; and that if assemblies could not meet, they should pursue the laudable example of the house of burgesses in Virginia—meet and form associations and put a stop to all commercial intercourse with Great Britain.

The cause of Boston the cause of all

Some ten days later, on June 21st, the committee replied to the communication from Virginia, expressing the same sentiments as in their letter to South Carolina. Agreeing to the call of a general congress, they said: "As this cannot be effected but by a convention of the representatives of the several provinces, we think that the conduct pursued by the late representatives of Virginia is worthy of imitation when the governors shall decline to convene the people in their legislative capacity. . . . Should not our Assembly meet on July 26th, to which time it now stands prorogued, we shall endeavor in some other manner to collect the representatives of the people." These communications were signed by John Harvey, Edward Vail, Robert Howe, John Ashe, Joseph Hewes, Sam Johnston, Cornelius Harnett and William Hooper.

Movement for a convention

Hooper was especially concerned for the distresses of his kinspeople and friends, among whom he had been reared at Boston, and doubtless was a moving spirit in subsequent proceedings; but the general sentiment that the time had come for action was shared by Harvey and the other members of the Committee of Correspondence, and doubtless by the inhabitants generally.

Governor Martin, having on March 30th dissolved the Assembly, the next day issued writs for an election of new members, but informed the Earl of Dartmouth that he did not propose another meeting of the Assembly until the fall. And so the contingency arose requiring action by the people in their own behalf. On July 21st the inhabitants of the district of Wilmington held a general meeting, at which William Hooper presided as chairman, the purpose being to prepare the way for a convention of the people.* At that meeting a resolution was adopted appointing eight gentlemen of the Cape Fear to prepare a circular letter to the counties of the province, urging that deputies should be sent to attend a general convention at Johnston Court House on August 20th to adopt measures that would avert the miseries threatening the colonies; and a resolution was adopted expressing concurrence in holding a continental congress on September 20th. The voice of the meeting was "that we consider the cause of the town of Boston the common cause of British America." C. R., IX, 1016 A convention called

Already the distresses of the indigent inhabitants of the closed port, whose business and industries were arrested and whose workmen were without employment, had appealed to the sympathies of the people of the Cape Fear, and liberal contributions of money and provisions had been made; the ladies equally with the men manifesting their sympathy by generous donations. Parker Quince, a patriotic merchant, tendered his vessel to transport these contributions, himself going to deliver them. And now the meeting suggested that other communities should make a similar demonstration of their sympathetic and patriotic interest. Contributions sent to Boston

At once North Carolina resounded again with the cry of "Liberty and Property." Meetings were held in various communities and provisions, contributed alike on the seaboard and in the interior, were sent to Boston by Edenton, Wilmington and New Bern; and the counties responded with ardor to the circular letter of the Wilmington committee. The meeting was finally fixed to be at New Bern on August 25th. Every county except Edgecombe, Guilford,

*Governor Swain, in Appleton's Cyclopedia, attributed this movement largely to John Ashe.

1774

Hertford, Surry, and Wake was represented by deputies selected at meetings of freeholders, the members of the Assembly being for the most part chosen as representatives in the convention. At these county meetings patriotic resolutions were adopted and committees of correspondence were appointed, which became the first nucleus of the power and authority of the respective communities in the management of local affairs in antagonism with the established government.

The voices of the counties

The discussions by James Iredell, Judge Moore and others, in the public prints and elsewhere, of the constitutionality of the courts by prerogative, which had been repudiated by the Assembly that spring, had brought forward anew the basic principles of the constitution, which now found expression in the declarations of the counties. The people of Pitt resolved "that as the constitutional assembly of this colony are prevented from exercising their rights of providing for the security of the liberties of the people, that right again reverts to the people as the foundation from whence all power and legislation flow." A clearer declaration of the sovereignty of the people and the sanction of government had not theretofore been made. Echoes of the same fundamental principles are to be found in most of the proceedings, and generally it was declared "that it is the first law of legislation and of the British constitution that no man be taxed but by his own consent, expressed by himself or by his legal representatives."

C. R., IX, 1030

The resolves of Rowan contained a further sentiment: "That the African trade is injurious to this colony, obstructs the population of it by freemen, prevents manufacturers and other useful emigrants from Europe from settling among us and occasions an annual increase of the balance of trade against the colonists;" and "that to be clothed in manufactures fabricated in the colonies ought to be considered as a badge and distinction of respect and true patriotism."

C. R., IX, 1026

The freeholders of Granville resolved: "That those absolute rights we are entitled to as men, by the immutable laws of nature, are antecedent to all social and relative duties whatsoever;" and "that by the civil contract subsisting between our king and his people, allegiance is the right of

C. R., IX, 1034

the first magistrate and protection the right of the people; that a violation of this compact would rescind the civil institution binding both king and people together." The very frame and foundation of civil government had been examined and was then declared. The common sentiment found expression in the Granville resolutions: "Blessed with freedom, we will cheerfully knee the throne erected by our fathers, and kiss the sceptre they taught us to reverence," yet "as freemen we can be bound by no law but such as we assent to, either by ourselves or our representatives. That we derive a right from our charters to enact laws for the regulation of our internal policy of government, which reason and justice confirm to us, as we must know what civil institutions are best suited to our state and circumstances."

The springs of patriotism were yielding now the first streams that, uniting and swelling, in the course of time became the mighty current that swept America into the stormy seas of revolution.

On August 12th Governor Martin, greatly concerned at the proposed revolutionary congress, convened his council and issued his proclamation enjoining all of his Majesty's subjects from attending any illegal meetings, and commanding every officer in the province to aid and assist in discouraging and preventing them; and especially in preventing the proposed meeting of deputies at New Bern. But nevertheless the convention was held, and the governor had the mortification of observing that all the members of his council except James Hasell freely mixed with the members, giving them aid and countenance, and apparently being in full sympathy with them. C. R., IX, 1029

C. R., IX, 1056

At the meeting of August 25th* John Harvey was chosen moderator. Hewes, one of the standing Committee of Correspondence appointed by the last Assembly, presented letters received by that committee from the other colonies, and it was thereupon resolved to appoint three delegates to attend the general congress to be held at Philadelphia. There was much rivalry among some of the members to secure these appointments. William Hooper, who was one of the leading members and to whose pen the resolutions adopted by the Aug. 25, 1774

C. R., IX, 1063

*A similar convention was held by Virginia on August 1st.

convention are attributed, was the first selected, and with him were Joseph Hewes and Richard Caswell.

The delegates to the Continental Congress

Perhaps remembering how Parliament had yielded to the demands of the colonists and their friends in Great Britain eight years earlier, the provincial leaders may have conceived that now similar influences would again prevail, and that the mission of deputy to the general congress would be only a temporary employment. Thus it may be that for personal reasons this honorable post was particularly sought by those selected—Hooper, deeply interested on behalf of his Boston kindred; Hewes, largely concerned in his mercantile firm at Philadelphia; and Caswell, desirous of revisiting his old home in Maryland wearing the high honors he had won

C. R., IX, 1061

in Carolina. But in any aspect, the selections were well made. They were among the foremost men of the province, possessing abilities equal to the station. Of the lofty devotion of Hooper and Hewes there could be no doubt; and although Governor Martin conceived the idea that Caswell was going with the current against his inclinations and judgment, yet he, too, gave every pledge of devotion and zeal, urging his son to take his musket and, exposing the secrets of his heart, declared that he would shed his last blood "in

C. R., IX, 1250

support of the liberties of my country." That Caswell sprang at once into the group of the most influential leaders and made a lasting impression on his associates in the Continental Congress is beyond question. Indeed, it is to be doubted whether any other colony sent a delegation of superior merit to that body, whose amazing excellence extorted the admiration of the world!

The intolerable acts

Declaring themselves "his Majesty's most dutiful and loyal subjects," the deputies entered into resolutions of the most positive character. They asserted that any act of Parliament imposing a tax on the colonies was illegal and unconstitutional; that the Boston port act was a cruel infringement of the rights of the people; that the act regulating that province was an infringement of the charter; that the bill empowering governors to send persons to Great Britain for trial will tend to produce frequent bloodshed. And in the way of enforcing a redress of grievances, the convention resolved that after January 1, 1775, they would import or

buy neither East India goods nor goods of British manu- 1774
facture; nor would they export any products of the country; Non-importation
nor should any slaves be imported or brought into the province; and after September 10th they would not suffer any
East India tea to be used in their families, but would consider
all persons not complying with this resolve as enemies of the Retaliatory
measures
country.

The revolutionary government

The convention then laid the foundation for a revolutionary government by providing that at every future meeting
the counties and towns shall be represented, and recommended that a committee of five should be chosen in each C. R., IX,
1047
county to take care that the resolves of the congress should
be properly observed, and to act as a committee of correspondence. These later became known as Committees of
Safety.

The convention gave directions to the deputies to the general congress based on an unchangeable purpose to defend
their persons and property against all unconstitutional encroachments, and authorized them to enter into an agreement that until there should be an explicit declaration and
acknowledgment of colonial rights, there should be a cessation of all imports and exports; and to concur with the deputies from other colonies in any regulation or remonstrance
that a majority might deem necessary measures for promoting a redress of grievances.

In view of the precarious health of Colonel Harvey, Samuel Johnston was empowered to convene the deputies of the
province at such time and place as he should think proper.
And so a positive step was taken toward the revolution that
was impending, provision being made for the orderly assembling of deputies who should represent the people and exercise the power of government over those who would assent
to be controlled by the resolutions of congress.

Governor Martin's attitude

The position of Governor Martin was now delicate in the
extreme. He realized that the power of government had
largely passed into the hands of the committees of corre-

spondence and the provincial Assembly, and was greatly
mortified at the falling away from his support of the members of his council and other gentlemen whom he thought
bound by the ties of duty and obligation to oppose the revolutionary faction. He, however, ascribed the condition of
affairs in North Carolina to the personal ambition of
aspirants for the treasuryship rather than to a more patriotic
design. At the election for treasurers in 1772 Johnston had
been defeated by Montfort and Ashe supplanted by Caswell.
Caswell had been one of his judges appointed by prerogative,
and the opposition to that court the governor attributed to a
purpose to render Caswell unpopular in the interests of a
combination between Johnston and Ashe—a conjunction
which he regarded as extremely formidable to the interests of
the country and productive of further and worse consequences. The convention having adjourned, and there being
no other movement of the people on foot, Governor Martin,
in September, because of ill health, left the province for New
York; doubtless also he wished to confer with Governor
Tryon. In his absence the administration devolved on James
Hasell.

margin note: C. R., IX, 1053

The Continental Congress

The action of the general congress was substantially on
the lines indicated by the resolutions of the Provincial Convention of North Carolina. There were adopted resolutions
of non-importation and non-exportation, which, being signed
by the members on behalf of themselves and their constituents, became an association paper, which they agreed "to observe by the sacred ties of virtue, honor, and love of country." It was recommended that committees should be chosen
in every county and town to see to the observance of the
association by the people, and that the committees of correspondence should be active in disseminating information.

margin note: The Association, Sept. 10th

The post of deputy was one of honor, but also one of
danger. On the adjournment of the congress, Hewes wrote
to Iredell: "Our friends are under apprehension that administration will endeavor to lay hold of as many delegates as
possible, and have them carried to England and tried as
rebels; this induced the congress to enter into a resolve in

margin note: McRee's Iredell, I 227

such cases to make a reprisal. I have no fears on that head;
but should it be my lot, no man on earth could be better
spared. Were I to suffer in the cause of American liberty,
should I not be translated immediately to heaven as Enoch
was of old?" Such was the general feeling—a spirit of sacrifice and self-immolation. The fires of patriotism were
indeed lighted, and an ardor to maintain the rights of
America animated the inhabitants of every province.

The revolution progresses

During the fall and early winter local committees convened the freeholders in the several counties of North Carolina, and, conformably to the resolutions of the provincial
and continental congresses, standing committees of safety
were appointed. The earliest proceedings of any committee
that have been preserved are those of Rowan County. On
September 23d the people there took action, led by William
Kennon and Adlai Osborn, and doubtless the inhabitants of
Mecklenburg County were equally forward under the influence of Tom Polk, the Alexanders and Brevards. On October 4th the freeholders of Pitt met, and on the same day
there was a general muster of Colonel Bryan's regiment of
militia in Johnston. At Halifax, Willie Jones, Samuel Weldon and their associates on the committee in December declared Andrew Miller, a merchant of Halifax, under the ban
for refusing to sign the association. In the Albemarle
region, Johnston, Hewes, and Harvey directed events, while
Richard Cogdell, Abner Nash, Alexander Gaston and other
patriots took strong and zealous action at New Bern.

The freeholders of Wilmington having appointed their
Committee of Safety, on November 23d that body immediately began to exert authority. Captain Foster informed the
committee that a quantity of teas had been imported in the
brig *Sally* by himself, Messrs. Ancrum, Brice, Hill and
others, and the importers did not know how to dispose of it,
and they desired the advice of the committee.* A letter was

Tea at
Wilmington

*Extract from Letter Book of William Hill:
                          "BRUNSWICK, July 26, 1774.
"Messrs. KELLY & Co., London, England:
  "The tea, though repeatedly written for, is not come at all, but
I need not find fault or make any objections now; for the flame into

addressed to Mr. Hill, making inquiry whether the tea might not be regularly re-exported in the same vessel. To this inquiry Hill replied that, in the absence of the collector and the comptroller, he could not answer what they would determine; but, said he, "The safety of the people is, or ought to be, the supreme law; the gentlemen of the committee will judge whether this law or an act of Parliament should, at this particular time, operate in North Carolina. I believe every tea importer will cheerfully submit to their determination." Such was the sentiment that pervaded every breast—

which this whole continent is thrown by the operation of the Boston port bill will presently show itself in a universal stop to all intercourse between Great Britain and the colonies. . . . Though the want of the tea has for some time past been a serious hurt to me, yet 'tis now a lucky omission, as I am very doubtful our committee would have ordered it back. But I hate politics, and your papers are by this time filled with the resolutions of the different provinces, towns, etc., in America. It may not be amiss to say that they are sending large contributions from every port on the continent to Boston for the relief of the suffering poor," etc., etc.

"BRUNSWICK, August 17, 1774.

"The tea I am as much surprised to see now as I have been disappointed in the want of it these eleven months past. Had it come agreeably to my request, in July, 1773, it would have afforded a profitable sale; but it is now too late to be received in America. If I were ever so willing to take it, the people would not suffer it to be landed. Poison would be as acceptable. I hope you will not be surprised, therefore, to receive it again by the same ship. By this you will easily perceive how vastly mistaken your correspondents have been, in their opinion of disunion among the American provinces; and I can venture to assure you that North Carolina will not be behind any of her sister colonies in virtue and a steady adherence to such resolves as the Continental Congress now sitting at Philadelphia shall adopt."

Mr. Hill added that he would "decline, until the present difficulties are happily over, further intercourse with Great Britain."

"BRUNSWICK, December 1, 1774.

"GENTLEMEN:

"The *Mary* luckily arrived two days before the importation limit expired; for, from and after this day, all goods imported from Great Britain are to be vendued—the first cost and charges to be paid to the importer; the profit, if any, to go to the relief of the sufferers by the Boston port bill.

"The tea of Ancrum & Company and Hewes & Smith was inadvertently landed; but they delivered it to the collector for the duties, and it is now lodged in the custom house."

"BRUNSWICK, June 3, 1775.

"The whole continent seems determined, to a man, to die rather than give up taxation to those over whom they can have no constitutional check."

that the safety of the people was the supreme law, and that 1774 November the committees were to determine how far any act of Parliament was to be operative. The people were asserting the supremacy of their will over the authority of the mother country.

At Wilmington the committee put a stop to horse racing, Rule of Safety Committees to parties of entertainment, to the importation of negroes, requiring them to be returned to the countries from which they had been shipped; forbade any increase in the price of goods, sold the cargoes of merchandise that were imported, paying the profit for the benefit of the Boston sufferers, and particularly took action to secure a supply of powder. Its leading spirit was Cornelius Harnett; but with him were associated not only the gentlemen of the country, but most of the merchants of the town. Throughout every part of the province there was similar action. The patriots were resolute. The merchants refused to receive any more tea shipped to them; locked up their stock, never to be sold, and one even threw his stock into the river. Nor were the women indiffer- S. C. Gazette, April 3, 1775 ent spectators of passing events. They sympathized with the ardor of their fathers, husbands and brothers, and were willing to make every sacrifice the situation demanded. At Wilmington they had contributed most generously for the Spirit of the women Boston sufferers, and doubtless in every community they were imbued with the same patriotism.

The Edenton tea party

The Edenton ladies, shortly after the adjournment of the convention, held a meeting on October 25th, and declared that they could not be indifferent to whatever affected the peace and happiness of their country; and that since the members of the convention had entered into the particular resolves adopted by that body, they themselves proposed to adhere to the same resolves, and they therefore subscribed an association paper as a witness of their solemn determination to do so. From that time East India tea was discarded by the ladies of Edenton.*

*In the earlier stages of the disagreement between the colonies and the mother country the sympathies of a large part of the English people were with the colonies, whose cause was strongly supported by many newspapers and by leading cartoonists. The following

Governor Martin returns

On December 7th Governor Martin began his return journey from New York by land, reaching New Bern on January 15th. He observed the inhabitants everywhere greatly
aroused, and committees carrying into execution the measures
of the general congress. At Annapolis he saw with horror
his former companion in arms, General Charles Lee, then
a British half-pay officer, drilling the people; while in North
Carolina he realized that the committees were completely
exercising the functions of government. To his distress at
the political situation there was to be added a sore personal
affliction, the loss of a little son, the third child of whom
he had been bereaved since his arrival in Carolina. He
found awaiting him at New Bern his appointment as agent

extracts are taken from a volume entitled "The Boston Port Bill as
Pictured by a Contemporary London Cartoonist," by R. T. H.
Halsey, published by the Grolier Club, 1904:
"An account of a meeting of a society of patriotic ladies at Edenton, in North Carolina, appeared in various English papers about the
middle of January, 1775. Possibly the imposing list of signatures
attached to the resolutions passed at this gathering caused our cartoonist to select this incident as one fairly representative of the
moral and physical support the women of the colonies were contributing to the common cause. No reader of English newspapers,
during the long protracted dispute between the king and the colonies,
could have remained ignorant of the political activities of the
colonial women. . . .
"The above citations from the English press of the frugality, industry and cheerful abstinence from many of the comforts of life
displayed by the women of the American colonies, have been quoted
to demonstrate that the political activities of the colonial women
were well known to the public on whom our cartoonist depended
for a market for the sale of his prints. The especial incident, the
action of a society of patriotic ladies at Edenton, in North Carolina,
which he had selected as being typical of the attitude of the women
in the colonies, was described in several London papers about the
middle of January, 1775.
"The following extract from the *Morning Chronicle and London
Advertiser* (of January 16, 1775) tells of the association formed by
the women of Edenton, in their endeavors to assist in carrying out
the resolutions taken by the men of North Carolina, and furnished
the cartoonist for his illustration—extract of a letter from North
Carolina, October 27th (1774)—'The provincial deputies of North
Carolina, having resolved not to drink any more tea, nor wear any
more British cloth, etc., many ladies of this province have determined to give a memorable proof of their patriotism, and have accordingly entered into the following honorable and spirited association. I send it to you to show your fair countrywomen how zealously
and faithfully American ladies follow the laudable example of their

nd attorney of Granville; and there was at once need for is action.

The Transylvania colony

Richard Henderson, an eminent attorney, who had served n the bench a few years earlier, had arranged for the pur-hase from the Cherokee Indians of a large portion of their unting grounds in Kentucky and Tennessee, and was pre-aring to occupy that wilderness with a colony. This was articularly in contravention of the king's proclamation, and f the acts of Virginia and of North Carolina. The territory, xtending from the Ohio southward, lay partly in the king's lomain and partly within the lines of Lord Granville. Gov-

usbands, and what opposition your *matchless* ministers may expect o receive from a people, thus firmly united against them':

"EDENTON, NORTH CAROLINA, October 25 (1774).

"As we cannot be indifferent on any occasion that appears nearly o affect the peace and happiness of our country, and as it has been hought necessary, for the public good, to enter into several par-icular resolves by a meeting of members deputed from the whole rovince, it is a duty which we owe, not only to our near and dear onnections, who have concurred in them, but to ourselves, who are ssentially interested in their welfare, to do everything, as far as ies in our power, to testify our sincere adherence to the same; and ve do therefore accordingly subscribe this paper as a witness of our ixed intention and solemn determination to do so:

Abagail Charlton,	Sarah Beasley,	Sarah Valentine,
Elizabeth Creacy,	Grace Clayton,	Mary Bonner,
Anne Johnstone,	Mary Jones,	Mary Ramsey,
Mary Woolard,	Mary Creacy,	Lydia Bennett,
Jean Blair,	Anne Hall,	Tresia Cunningham,
Frances Hall,	Sarah Littlejohn,	Anne Haughton,
Mary Creacy,	Sarah Hoskins,	Elizabeth Roberts,
Mary Blount,	M. Payne,	Ruth Benbury,
Margaret Cathcart,	Elizabeth Cricket,	Penelope Barker,
Jane Wellwood,	Lydia Bonner,	Mary Littledle,
Penelope Dawson,	Anne Horniblow,	Elizabeth Johnstone,
Susanna Vail,	Marion Wells,	Elizabeth Green,
Elizabeth Vail,	Sarah Mathews,	Sarah Howe,
Elizabeth Vail,	Elizabeth Roberts,	Mary Hunter,
J. Johnstone,	Rebecca Bondfield,	Anne Anderson,
Elizabeth Patterson,	Sarah Howcott,	Elizabeth Bearsley,
Margaret Pearson,	Elizabeth P. Ormond,	Elizabeth Roberts.

" . . . Our cartoonist has pictured in the closing cartoon of the series a living room of a colonial home, filled with women, both of high and lowly station, matrons and maidens, all clothed in gar-ments the materials of which bore no trace of having emanated from the looms of Manchester or Birmingham."

1775

ernor Martin hastened to issue a strong proclamation for
bidding the proposed settlement from being made, and declar
ing that all who should enter into any agreement with th
Indians would expose themselves to the severest penaltie
Still Henderson did not remit his exertions to carry h
design into execution. Daniel Boone blazed the way, an
a colony was successfully established on the dark and blood
ground of Kentucky.

Proceedings on the Cape Fear

The general congress recommended that another should b
convened on May 10th; and early in February Colone
Harvey gave notice to the committees of safety to have elec
tions of deputies to attend another provincial convention. O
the 20th of that month the New Hanover committee in
vited co-operation with that of Duplin, indicating that o

March 6,
1775
Troops
organized

March 6th there would be several matters of much concer
to American welfare agitated.   John Ashe, who had lon
been colonel of New Hanover County, had declined to accep

C. R., X,
48, 149

a new commission from Governor Martin, thus disassociatin
himself from the military organization of the constitute
authorities; and the people of New Hanover had met an
chosen field officers for a regiment, he becoming the colone

C. R., IX,
1149-1157
March, 1775

Similar action was taken in Brunswick, and Colonel Rober
Howe was training the people to arms.   On March 6th a
association paper was agreed to by the New Hanover com
mittee and recommended to the committees of the adjacen
counties, by which the subscribers "most solemnly engag
by the most sacred ties of honor, virtue, and love of country"
to observe every part of the association recommended b

C. R., X, 38

the Continental Congress.   At the same time it appears tha
there was a proposition to seize Fort Johnston, but it wa
thought not advisable.   Some of the inhabitants of Wilming
ton were reluctant to sign the association paper, and Colone
Ashe appeared in the town at the head of some five hundred
of his regiment and menaced the people "with military execu

C. R., X, 48

tions if they did not immediately subscribe."   Without doubt
being now an active leader in the throes of a revolution, Ashe
used every influence that could be exerted to infuse zea
among the people, to fix the wavering and to overawe those

who were disinclined to cast their fortunes with the revolutionists. The commanding figure on the Cape Fear, he was at once stalwart, bold and determined. With him were his kinsmen, and Harnett and Howe, Moore and Lillington; unhappily, DeRosset and Waddell, leaders in the stamp act times, had passed away. For their resolute action, Harnett, Ashe, Howe, and Abner Nash were particularly marked out by the governor as proper objects of proscription, because they stand foremost among the patrons of revolt and anarchy." C. R., X, 98

The disaffected in the interior

But amid these evidences of defection the governor found some comfort. The Regulators had never been pardoned, and were still fearful of punishment. From time to time, as apprehensions arose, others would follow those who had earlier removed from the province; and many of the former insurgents were yet uneasy. The king had recommended to the Assembly to pass an act of oblivion, but session succeeded session without bringing the comforting assurance that there were to be no more prosecutions. Now some of the Regulators presented addresses to the governor, much to his satisfaction. Some two hundred inhabitants of Rowan and Surry assured him of their determination to continue his Majesty's loyal subjects. More than one hundred residents of Guilford, "being before an unhappy people, lying under the reflection of the late unhappy insurrection," declared that they held a firm attachment to his Majesty. From Anson came the assurance from more than two hundred to continue steadfast in the support of government. The governor speedily took measures to attach these people to him, giving them every encouragement; and so hopeful was he of their united support that on March 16th he wrote to General Gage, at Boston, asking for arms and a good store of ammunition, and promising, with the aid of the Regulators and Highlanders, to maintain the king's sovereignty in North Carolina. He had indeed ascertained that many of the Highlanders who had so recently settled in the province, and others being, like the Regulators, oath bound, would enroll themselves beneath his banner; and he sent emissaries among

C. R., IX, 1160 *et seq.*

C. R., IX, 1167

them and association papers for them to sign. To strengther this movement, he caused the several addresses received by him to be published in the *North Carolina Gazette,* and soor had the satisfaction of finding that some fifteen hundred men were enrolled in his support.

The Assembly and the Convention

C. R., IX, 1178

The Provincial Convention or congress was to meet at New Bern on April 3d and the Assembly on the 4th, the two bodies being composed substantially of the same members. Or April 2d Governor Martin issued a proclamation forbidding the convention to be held, and exhorting members to withdraw themselves and desist from such illegal proceedings Nevertheless the convention met, chose Harvey moderator and proceeded to business; and on the 4th the house met, Harvey being chosen speaker. On the following day the governor issued another proclamation, commanding all his Majesty's subjects to break up the illegal convention, but his warnings were disregarded. Indeed, on that very day, the Assembly being in session and Harvey in the chair as speaker, the members of the convention who were not assemblymen, and there were about twenty more of the former than of the latter in attendance, took their seats in the house, which was then converted into the convention; and the body proceeded to the transaction of business as such, later the business of the house being resumed. On information of this proceeding, Governor Martin's wrath knew no bounds, and quickly changing the upper house of the legislature into a council, he brought the subject before them, but was advised that it was inexpedient to take notice of it. The convention signed the association adopted by the general congress, thanked Hooper, Hewes, and Caswell for their services as deputies and reelected them to attend the next congress, to be held on May 10th, and invested them with power to bind the province in honor by any act that they might do. It recommended the encouragement of arts and manufactures, and that premiums should be offered by the local committees to promote industries throughout the province. It declared that his Majesty's subjects have a right to meet and petition the throne and to appoint delegates for that purpose, and that

The two bodies sit together

C. R., IX, 1213

The Association signed

the governor's proclamations commanding the convention to disperse was a wanton and arbitrary exercise of power.

To the house the governor made a long and heated address, inveighing against the illegal convention, pointing out that it was dishonorable to the Assembly for such a body to meet, and warning them of the dangerous precipice on which they who had solemnly sworn allegiance to the king then stood, and informing them of the satisfaction he had received in the assurance of support by the inhabitants of the interior.

The reply of the house was spirited and bold. It declared that the members, with minds superior to private dissensions, had determined calmly, unitedly, and faithfully to discharge the sacred trust reposed in them by their constituents; acknowledging their allegiance to the king, they declared that the same constitution which established that allegiance bound his Majesty under as solemn obligations to protect his subjects, making each reciprocally dependent. Asserting that the king had no subjects more faithful than the inhabitants of North Carolina, or more ready, at the expense of their lives and fortunes, to protect and support his person, crown, and dignity, they expressed their warm attachment to their sister colonies and heartfelt compassion for Boston, and declared the fixed and determined resolution of the colony to unite with the other colonies to retain their just rights as British subjects. They reiterated what the convention had affirmed with regard to the legality of that body, approved the proceedings of the Continental Congress, and resolved to exert every influence to induce the inhabitants of North Carolina to observe the rules it had recommended. They thanked the North Carolina deputies for their faithful conduct, and approved of their re-election by the convention. The governor, on the evening of Friday, the 7th, having obtained information of the nature of the Assembly's address to him, early the next morning dissolved the body.

Although later Governor Martin called for the election of new members to be held on June 23d, this was the last Assembly ever convened under royal authority. It was also the last appearance in public affairs of that sterling patriot, John Harvey, whose health had long been delicate; and now,

C. R., IX, 1198, 1201

Reciprocal duties declared

April, 1775 The Assembly dissolved

1775

wasted by disease, he bade farewell to those associates who had given him so many evidences of their esteem and confidence, and who, under his guidance, had entered upon that determined action which subsequently led to the independence of the colony. About the middle of May he fell from his horse and died, lamented by his compatriots.

Death of Harvey

North Carolina at Court

In England some conciliatory measures had been proposed that, however, did not at all appeal to the colonists. Thomas Barker, who twenty years earlier had been a lawyer of influence in the Albemarle section, and once treasurer, was now in England, and Alexander Elmsly, who also had been a member of the Assembly and a man of influence in that section, being also in London, to them it was given in charge by the Assembly of 1774 to present the address of the province to the Crown. They took the liberty of suppressing that address as adopted by the Assembly and of writing another, which was received with favor by the Board of Trade; and Governor Tryon, being also at London, exerted himself in behalf of North Carolina; so that when, about the middle of February, a bill was introduced into Parliament forbidding trade with the colonists, North Carolina and New York were excepted. This was regarded in the province as an unenviable distinction, and was ascribed to a purpose to detach North Carolina from the common cause, while at the same time leaving open communications by which Great Britain could continue to receive needed supplies of naval stores so essential for naval operations. This tender was at once rejected by the inhabitants with disdain, and North Carolina, paying no attention to it, remained faithful to the common cause. To the northward military companies were forming, and the Virginia Assembly provided for the raising of a company in each county. Such a proposition was brought forward in the North Carolina convention, but was then deemed inexpedient.

Barker and Elmsly suppress address to king

C. R., IX, 1208 North Carolina excepted

C. R., IX, 1214

The battle of Lexington

But all hopes that the peace would not be broken quickly vanished. On April 19th the first clash of arms occurred at Lexington, and information of that battle was hurried from Boston by successive couriers to Charleston. On May 3d the courier from Nansemond reached Edenton; on May 6th, New Bern; two days later, Wilmington and Brunswick. On May 9th, Montfort, at Halifax, despatched the news to Burke at Hillsboro, and it spread rapidly throughout the province. It created great excitement. The people were stirred as never before. A new phase was now imparted to public affairs, the people feeling that they must fight. Independent military companies at once began to be organized. It was the same throughout all America. Toward the end of April Caswell and Hewes left the province to attend the Congress. In Virginia and Maryland they were escorted through the several counties by the military companies, and on reaching Philadelphia they found twenty-eight companies organized and 2000 men drilling morning and evening, and only martial music could be heard in the streets. The change had been electrical.

On May 16th Nash and others had begun the formation of companies at New Bern. The governor, fearing that some mounted cannon on the palace grounds would be seized and carried off, on May 23d caused them to be dismounted; and when Nash and a committee of citizens waited on him to ascertain the cause of this action, the governor said that the carriages were unsafe, and he was making preparations to celebrate the king's birthday; but while he was indignant at being called to account by the people, he was also alarmed and prevaricated in order to quiet them.

Governor Martin seeks safety

A day or two later an emissary arrived from New York and informed Governor Martin that General Gage was about to send him the arms and munitions desired, and there was reason to suppose that the shipment had been discovered. A report also had been propagated that the governor had formed a design of arming the negroes and proclaiming freedom to those who should resort to the king's standard, and the public mind was much inflamed against him. Indeed, there was then brewing a plot for a negro insurrection in

Margin notes:
1775
C. R., IX, 1234, 1239

May, 1775

C. R., IX, 1248

C. R., IX, 1256; X, 41, 43

The governor questioned

Martin, Hist. of North Carolina, II, 353

the region near Tar River. By timely good fortune, on July 7th the plot was discovered.

C. R., X, 94
Negro
insurrection
planned

On the following night the negroes were to rise and murder the whites, moving from plantation to plantation, and then, having embodied, they were to march to the west, where they expected to be received and protected by the inhabitants who were still attached to the king. Companies of light horse scoured the country, and the negroes were speedily suppressed, but apparently not without some of them being killed.

The purpose was avowed in some of the colonies to seize the royal governors and detain them, and Governor Martin, fearing the discovery of the shipment of arms, especially in connection with his alleged design to arm the negroes, be-

C. R., X, 41

came very apprehensive for his personal safety. The military companies formed at New Bern were a menace, and, separated from the king's forces, he had no friends to pro-

Martin
leaves
New Bern,
May 31, 1775

tect him. He hurried his private secretary to Ocracoke to stop any vessel bringing in arms, ordering it to proceed to Fort Johnston. The same night he despatched his wife and family to New York, bearing letters to General Gage, and he asked that a royal standard should be furnished him. Being now entirely alone, on the last day of May he locked the palace, left the key with a servant, and took his departure southward. Giving out that he was going to visit Chief Justice Hasell, he took flight for Fort Johnston, where he

C. R., X, 44

safely arrived on June 2d. His flight perhaps gave a new impulse to the popular movement, strengthening the hands of Nash, Cogdell, and Gaston; and on June 8th the association was being signed in every part of the county, and the militia were forming into companies and choosing their own officers.

C. R., X, 45
The last
election

Elections were held for assemblymen on June 23d, and a considerable number of inhabitants gathering at New Bern on that occasion, they went to the deserted palace and took possession of the six cannon there, and removed them to the court-house.

CHAPTER XXVI

THE MECKLENBURG RESOLVES, MAY 31, 1775

The Mecklenburg declaration.—Historical statement.—Documents and observations.—Conditions in May.—Mecklenburg aroused.—The great meeting at Charlotte.—Colonel Polk proclaims the resolves.—Independence declared.—The old government annulled.—The leaders in Mecklenburg.—The effect elsewhere.—At Salisbury.—At New Bern. — Bethania. — Reconciliation still desired. — Apprehensions.— Thomas Jefferson.—The Regulators.—The patriots in the interior.—The clashing in Anson.—New Hanover acts.—Governor Martin's plans.—McDonald arrives.—New Hanover impatient.—Fort Johnston burned.—The Revolution progresses.—Dunn and Boote confined.

In May, 1775, the condition of public affairs was alarming. Boston was occupied by a hostile British army, and "the cause of Boston was felt to be the cause of all." The situation having been discussed by some of the leading citizens of Mecklenburg County, and several local meetings having been held at different points in the county, Colonel Thomas Polk called for the election of two delegates from each of the militia districts of the county "to take into consideration the state of the c⌐untry, and to adopt such measures as to them seemed best to secure their lives, liberties, and property from the storm which was gathering and had burst on their fellow-citizens to the eastward by a British army" (statement of G. Graham and others). The delegates, having been chosen, met at Charlotte. The news of the battle of Lexington had arrived and the people were much excited (*ibid.*). Resolutions were adopted that were with great formality read by Colonel Polk to a large concourse of citizens, composed of nearly one-half of the men of the county, drawn together by their interest in the occasion (*ibid.*).

The manuscript records of these proceedings appear to have been in the possession of John McKnitt Alexander until the year 1800. In 1794 he sent a copy of them to Dr. Hugh Williamson. In April, 1800, his residence was destroyed by fire and these original records were then burnt.

Subsequently John McKnitt Alexander sought to reproduce the burnt records. Apparently he made some rough notes as a basis for reproduction on a half sheet of paper, which he preserved. Attached to that half sheet, when discovered after his death in 1817, was a full sheet in a handwriting unknown to his son, Dr. Joseph McKnitt Alexander, which contained an account of the proceedings in Mecklenburg, including a series of resolutions which has since been known as "The Declaration of May 20th."

In September, 1800, a copy of this "full sheet" was sent by John McKnitt Alexander to General William R. Davie with the following certificate appended to it:

"It may be worthy of notice here to observe that the foregoing statement, though fundamentally correct, yet may not literally correspond with the original record of the transactions of said delegation and Court of Inquiry, as all those records and papers were burned, with the house, on April 6, 1800; but previous to that time
of 1800, a full copy of said records, at the request of Dr. Hugh Williamson, then of New York, but formerly a representative in Congress from this State, was forwarded to him by Colonel William Polk, in order that those early transactions might fill their proper place in a history of this State then writing by said Dr. Williams (*sic*) in New York.

"Certified to the best of my recollection and belief this 3d day of September, 1800, by

"J. McK. ALEXANDER,
"Mecklenburg County, N. C."

This certificate fixes the character of "the full sheet" and of the "Davie copy" to which it was annexed. They were not copies of any record. In like manner, it is to be said of all other copies of the resolutions purporting to have been adopted at Charlotte on May 20th, that they have only this origin and source, and are copies of the Alexander document of 1800.

The remembrance of Mecklenburg's patriotic action was cherished locally, but no contemporaneous publication of the proceedings seems to have been preserved in that county; nor was the copy sent to Dr. Williamson ever published; nor did General Davie give publicity to the paper sent him.

John McKnitt Alexander died on July 10, 1817, and after his death his son, Dr. Joseph McKnitt Alexander, found in his mansion house a bundle of old pamphlets, and with them the "half sheet" and the "full sheet" of manuscripts above mentioned. In 1818 inquiry was made concerning the proceedings in Mecklenburg, and Dr. Joseph McKnitt Alexander sent a copy of the "full sheet" to Hon. William Davidson, then a member of Congress. On the 30th of April, 1819, the following publication appeared in the *Raleigh Register:*

"It is not probably known to many of our readers that the citizens of Mecklenburg County, in this State, made a declaration of

independence more than a year before Congress made theirs. The
following document on the subject has lately come to the hands
of the editor from unquestionable authority, and is published that
it may go down to posterity:

NORTH CAROLINA, MECKLENBURG COUNTY, May 20, 1775.

In the spring of 1775, the leading characters of Mecklenburg
County, stimulated by that enthusiastic patriotism which elevates
the mind above considerations of individual aggrandizement, and
scorning to shelter themselves from the impending storm by submission to lawless power, etc., held several detached meetings,
in each of which the individual sentiments were, "that the cause
of Boston was the cause of all; that their destinies were indissolubly
connected with those of their Eastern fellow-citizens—and that they
must either submit to all the impositions which an unprincipled, and
to them an unrepresented, parliament might impose—or support
their brethren who were doomed to sustain the first shock of that
power, which, if successful there, would ultimately overwhelm all in
the common calamity." Conformably to these principles, Colonel
Adam Alexander, through solicitation, issued an order to each captain's company in the county of Mecklenburg (then comprising the
present county of Cabarrus), directing each militia company to elect
two persons, and delegate to them ample power to devise ways and
means to aid and assist their suffering brethren in Boston, and also
generally to adopt measures to extricate themselves from the impending storm, and to secure unimpaired their inalienable rights,
privileges and liberties, from the dominant grasp of British imposi-
tion and tyrannny.

In conforming to said order, on May 19, 1775, the said delegation met in Charlotte, vested with unlimited powers; at which time
official news, by express, arrived of the battle of Lexington on that
day of the preceding month. Every delegate felt the value and
importance of the prize, and the awful and solemn crisis which
had arrived—every bosom swelled with indignation at the malice,
inveteracy, and insatiable revenge, developed in the late attack at
Lexington. The universal sentiment was: let us not flatter ourselves that popular harangues or resolves, that popular vapor will
avert the storm, or vanquish our common enemy—let us deliberate
—let us calculate the issue—the probable result; and then let us
act with energy, as brethren leagued to preserve our property—
our lives—and what is still more endearing, the liberties of America.
Abraham Alexander was then elected chairman, and John McKnitt
Alexander, clerk. After a free and full discusssion of the various
objects for which the delegation had been convened, it was unanimously ordained:

1. *Resolved,* That whoever directly or indirectly abetted, or in any way, form, or manner, countenanced the unchartered and dangerous invasion of our rights, as claimed by Great Britain, is an enemy to this country—to America—and to the inherent and inalienable rights of man.

2. *Resolved,* That we, the citizens of Mecklenburg County, do hereby dissolve the political bands which have connected us to the mother country, and hereby absolve ourselves from all allegiance to the British Crown, and abjure all political connection, contract or association with that nation, who have wantonly trampled on our rights and liberties—and inhumanly shed the innocent blood of American patriots at Lexington.

3. *Resolved,* That we do hereby declare ourselves a free and independent people, are, and of right ought to be, a sovereign and self governing association, under the control of no power other than that of our God and the general government of the congress; to the maintenance of which independence we solemnly pledge to each other our mutual co-operation, our lives, our fortunes, and our most sacred honor.

4. *Resolved,* That as we now acknowledge the existence and control of no law or legal officer, civil or military, within this county we do hereby ordain and adopt, as a rule of life, all, each and every of our former laws, wherein, nevertheless, the Crown of Great Britain never can be considered as holding rights, privileges, immunities, or authority therein.

5. *Resolved,* That it is also further decreed, that all, each and every military officer in this county is hereby reinstated to his former command and authority, he acting conformably to these regulations. And that every member present of this delegation shall henceforth be a civil officer, viz., a justice of the peace, in the character of a *committeeman,* to issue process, hear and determine all matter of controversy, according to said adopted laws, and to preserve peace, and union, and harmony, in said county, and to use every exertion to spread the love of country and fire of freedom throughout America, until a more general and organized government be established in this province.

A number of by-laws were also added, merely to protect the association from confusion, and to regulate their general conduct as citizens. After sitting in the court-house all night, neither sleepy hungry, nor fatigued, and after discussing every paragraph, they were all passed, sanctioned, and declared, *unanimously,* about 2 A.M. May 20th. In a few days, a deputation of said delegation convened, when Captain James Jack, of Charlotte, was deputed as express to the congress at Philadelphia, with a copy of said Resolves and Proceedings, together with a letter addressed to our three representatives there, viz., Richard Caswell, William Hooper and Joseph Hughes—under express injunction, personally, and through the State representation, to use all possible means to have said proceedings sanctioned and approved by the general congress. On the return of Captain Jack, the delegation learned that their proceedings were individually approved by the members of congress, but that it was deemed premature to lay them before the house. A joint letter from said three members of congress was also received, complimentary of the zeal in the common cause, and recommending perseverance, order and energy.

The subsequent harmony, unanimity, and exertion in the cause of liberty and independence, evidently resulting from these regulations and the continued exertion of said delegation, apparently tranquillized this section of the State, and met with the concurrence and high approbation of the Council of Safety, who held their sessions at New Bern and Wilmington, alternately, and who confirmed the nomination and acts of the delegation in their official capacity.

From this delegation originated the Court of Enquiry of this county, who constituted and held their first session in Charlotte—they then held their meetings regularly at Charlotte, at Colonel James Harris's, and at Colonel Phifer's, alternately, one week at each place. It was a civil court founded on military process. Before this judicature, all suspicious persons were made to appear, who were formally tried and banished, or continued under guard. Its jurisdiction was as unlimited as toryism, and its decrees as final as the confidence and patriotism of the county. Several were arrested and brought before them from Lincoln, Rowan and the adjacent counties.

[The foregoing is a true copy of the papers on the above subject, left in my hands by John McKnitt Alexander, deceased. I find it mentioned on file that the original book was burned April, 1800. That a copy of the proceedings was sent to Hugh Williamson, in New York, then writing a "History of North Carolina," and that a copy was sent to General W. R. Davie.   *J. McKnitt.*"]*

Shortly after the publication of this document in the *Register,* in 1819, Colonel William Polk, being interested, obtained certificates from General George Graham, William Hutchison, Jonas Clark, Robert Robinson and others, residents of Mecklenburg, corroborative of its authenticity, and further certifying that within a few days after the adoption of the Resolves Captain Jack went as a messenger to bear them to the Continental Congress.

*Dr. Joseph McKnitt Alexander, son of John McKnitt Alexander, used this signature.

They certified on honor that:

"We were present in the town of Charlotte, in the said county of Mecklenburg, on May 19, 1775, when two persons elected from each captain's company in said county appeared as delegates, to take into consideration the state of the country, and to adopt such measures as to them seem best. . . .

George
Graham
and others

"The order for the election of delegates was given by Colonel Thomas Polk, the commanding officer of the militia of the county, with a request that their powers should be ample, touching any measure that should be proposed. We do further certify and declare that to the best of our recollection and belief, the delegation was complete from every company, and that the meeting took place in the court-house about 12 o'clock on the said day of May 19, 1775, when Abraham Alexander was chosen chairman, and Dr. Ephraim Brevard, secretary. That the delegates continued in session until in the night of that day; that on the 20th they again met, when a committee, under the direction of the delegates, had formed several Resolves, which were read, and which went to declare themselves, and the people of Mecklenburg County, free and independent of the king and Parliament of Great Britain—and from that day thenceforth all allegiance and political relation was absolved between the good people of Mecklenburg and the king of Great Britain; which Declaration was signed by every member of the delegation, under the shouts and huzzas of a very large assembly of the people of the county, who had come to know the issue of the meeting."

The
protracted
meeting

The public
meeting

Captain
Jack

On December 7, 1819, Captain Jack made the following affidavit:

"Having seen in the newspapers some pieces respecting the Declaration of Independence by the people of Mecklenburg County, in the State of North Carolina in May, 1775, and being solicited to state what I know of that transaction: I would observe that for sometime previous to and at the time those resolutions were agreed upon, I resided in the town of Charlotte, Mecklenburg County; was privy to a number of meetings of some of the most influential and leading characters of that county on the subject, before the final adoption of the resolutions—and at the time they were adopted; among those who appeared to take the lead may be mentioned Hezekiah Alexander, who generally acted as chairman; John McKnitt Alexander, as secretary; Abraham Alexander, Adam Alexander, Major John Davidson, Major (afterward General) William Davidson, Colonel Thomas Polk, Ezekiel Polk, Dr. Ephraim Brevard, Samuel Martin, Duncan Ochletree, William Willson, Robert Irvin.

"When the Resolutions were finally agreed on, they were publicly proclaimed from the court-house door in the town of Charlotte, and were received with every demonstration of joy by the inhabitants.

"I was then solicited to be the bearer of the proceedings to congress. I set out the following month, say June, and in passing through Salisbury, the general court was sitting. At the request of the court I handed a copy of the Resolutions to Colonel Kennon, an attorney, and they were read aloud in open court. Major William Davidson and Mr. Avery, an attorney, called on me at my lodging the evening after, and observed they had heard of but one person (a Mr. Beard), but approved of them.

"I then proceeded on to Philadelphia and delivered the Mecklenburg Declaration of Independence of May, 1775, to Richard Caswell and William Hooper, the delegates to congress from the State of North Carolina."

Other statements were made by men of the highest character, all confirming the fact that there were proceedings in Mecklenburg in May, 1775, relating to independence, and some giving the details with great particularity.

On January 20, 1820, John Simeson wrote to Colonel William Polk: "I have conversed with many of my old friends and others, and all agree in the point, but few can state the particulars. . . . Yourself, sir, in your eighteenth year and on the spot, your worthy father, the most popular and influential character in the county, and yet you cannot state much from recollection. Your father, as commanding officer of the county, issued orders to the captains to appoint two men from each company to represent them in the committee. It was done. Neill Morrison, John Flennigan, from this company; Charles Alexander, John McKnitt Alexander, Hezekiah Alexander, Abraham Alexander, Esq., John Phifer, David Reese, Adam Alexander, Dickey Barry, John Queary, with others whose names I cannot obtain. As to the names of those who drew up the Declaration, I am inclined to think Dr. Brevard was the principal, from his known talents in composition. It was, however, in substance and form like that great National Act agreed on thirteen months after. Ours was toward the close of May, 1775. In addition to what I have said, the same committee appointed three men to secure all the military stores for the county's use—Thomas Polk, John Phifer, and Joseph Kennedy. I was under arms near the head of the line, near Colonel Polk, and heard him distinctly read a long string of grievances, the Declaration and military order above."*

Simeson

*The accuracy of the memory of this witness, Mr. Simeson, in one particular at least is remarkable. By the last of the resolves of May 31st, Colonel Thomas Polk and Dr. Joseph Kennedy were appointed to purchase ammunition, as the witness recollected after the lapse of forty-five years.

1775
Cummins
Francis Cummins wrote in 1819 to Mr. Macon: "At length, in the same year, 1775, I think—at least positively before July 4, 1776—the males generally of that county met on a certain day at Charlotte, and from the head of the court-house door proclaimed independence on English government, by their herald, Colonel Thomas Polk. I was present and saw and heard it."

Davie copy
In November, 1820, General Davie died, and there was found among his papers a manuscript copy of the proceedings at Charlotte, in the handwriting of John McKnitt Alexander, to which was appended the note above printed to the effect that "the foregoing statement, though fundamentally correct, yet may not literally correspond with the original records, as all those records and papers were burned with the house on April 6, 1800."

This "Davie copy" was then sent to the son, Dr. Joseph McKnitt Alexander, who preserved it. It was the same as the document published in the *Raleigh Register* except some slight verbal differences.

The resolutions thus presented to the public as those adopted at Charlotte in May, 1775, were without hesitation accepted in North Carolina as authentic and genuine. But Mr. Jefferson and Mr. Adams denied their authenticity. Therefore, other affidavits and certificates were procured, and a committee of the General Assembly was appointed "to examine, collate and arrange such documents as relate to the Mecklenburg Declaration of Independence"; and at the session of 1830-31 it reported that "by the publication of these papers it will be fully verified that as early as the month of May, 1775, a portion of the people of North Carolina . . . did by a public and solemn act declare the dissolution of the ties which bound them to the Crown and people of Great Britain, and did establish an independent, though temporary government for their own control and direction." Their report was directed to be published by the State.

The State
Pamphlet
The original documents found by Dr. Joseph McKnitt (Alexander) were submitted to this committee, passed into the hands of the state authorities for a time, appear to have been returned, but subsequently came into the possession of Governor David L. Swain. They consisted of a torn half-sheet of paper, on which were written some notes in the handwriting of John McKnitt Alexander, being apparently rough first attempts to reproduce statements and resolutions: this half-sheet being stitched to a full sheet (containing substantially the paper published in the *Raleigh Register*, and also furnished to General Davie), which was in an unknown handwriting. These papers were accompanied by a certificate as follows: "The sheet and torn half-sheet to which this is attached (the sheet is evidently corrected in two places by John McKnitt Alexander, as marked on

Joseph
McKnitt
Alexander's
certificate,
Hoyt, 135

—the half-sheet is in his own handwriting) were found after the death of John McKnitt Alexander in his old mansion-house in the centre of a roll of old pamphlets, viz.: 'an address on public liberty, printed Philadelphia, 1774'; one 'on the disputes with G. Britain, printed 1775'; one 'on State affairs, printed at Hillsboro, 1788'; and an address on Federal policy to the citizens of N. C., a 1788'; and the 'Journal of the Provincial Congress of N. C., a held at Hallifax, the 4 of April, 1776,' which papers have been in my possession ever since.

"Certified November 25, 1830.

"J. McKNITT."*

Among the certificates then published was one from Samuel Wilson: "I do hereby certify that in May, 1775, a committee or delegation from the different militia companies in this county met in Charlotte, and after consulting together they publicly declared their independence on Great Britain and on her government. This was done before a large collection of people who highly approved of it. I was then and there present and heard it read from the court-house door." Wilson

John Davidson on October 5, 1830, wrote: "As I am perhaps the only person living who was a member of that convention, and being far advanced in years, and not having my mind frequently directed to that circumstance for some years, I can give you but a very succinct history of that transaction. There were two men chosen from each captain's company to meet in Charlotte to take the subject into consideration. John McKnitt Alexander and myself were chosen from one company; and many other members were there that I now recollect whose names I deem unnecessary to mention. When the members met and were perfectly organized for business, a motion was made to declare ourselves independent of the Crown of Great Britain, which was carried by a large majority. Dr. Ephraim Brevard was then appointed to give us a sketch of the Declaration of Independence, which he did. James Jack was appointed to take it on to the American Congress. . . . When Jack returned he stated that the Declaration was presented to Congress, and the reply was that they highly esteemed the patriotism of the citizens of Mecklenburg, but they thought the measure too premature. I am confident that the Declaration of Independence by the people of Mecklenburg was made public at least twelve months before that of the Congress of the United States." Davidson

*W. H. Hoyt's work on "The Mecklenburg Declaration of Independence," 1907, where both the notes on the half sheet and the writing on the full sheet are reproduced from the Bancroft manuscripts.

1775
Joseph
Graham

General Joseph Graham wrote October 4, 1830: "Agreeably to you request I will give you the details of the Mecklenburg Declaration of Independence on May 20, 1775, as well as I can recollect after lapse of fifty-five years. I was then a lad about half grown, was present on that occasion (a looker on).

The public
meeting

"During the winter and spring preceding that event, several popular meetings of the people were held in Charlotte, two of which I attended. Papers were read, grievances stated and public measures discussed. . . . On May 20, 1775, besides the two persons elected from each militia company (usually called committee-men), a much larger number of citizens attended in Charlotte than at any former meeting—perhaps half the men in the county. The news of the battle of Lexington, April 19th preceding, had arrived. There appeared among the people much excitement. The committee were organized in the court-house by appointing Abraham Alexander, Esq., chairman and John McKnitt Alexander, Esq., clerk, or secretary to the meeting. After reading a number of papers as usual, and much animated discussion, the question was taken, and they resolved to declare themselves independent.

Out of
protection

"One among other reasons offered, that the king or ministry had by proclamation or some edict, declared the colonies out of the protection of the British crown; they ought, therefore, to declare themselves out of his protection and resolve on independence. That their proceedings might be in due form, a sub-committee, consisting of Dr. Ephraim Brevard, a Mr. Kennon, an attorney, and a third person whom I do not recollect, were appointed to draft their declaration. . . . The sub-committee appointed to draft the resolution returned, and Dr. Ephraim Brevard read their report, as near as I can recollect, in the very words we have since seen them several

The public
meeting

times in print. It was unanimously adopted, and shortly afterward it was moved and seconded to have proclamation made, and the people collected, that the proceedings be read at the court-house door, in order that all might hear them. It was done and they were received with enthusiasm. It was then proposed by some one aloud, to give three cheers and throw up their hats. It was immediately adopted and the hats thrown. . . ."

Hunter's
statement

In a memoir of his life Rev. Humphrey Hunter,* who was present at the meeting in Charlotte, being then twenty years of age, and deeply interested, says: "Orders were presently issued by Colonel

*"This memoir is dated in 1827 and appears to be a response to a request made by Dr. Alexander (Joseph McKnitt), and thus loses, in some degree, the authority to which it might otherwise have been entitled had it been a contemporaneous production." (Address of R. M. Saunders, 1852.) Hunter was then seventy-two years of age. He died August 21, 1827.

'hos. Polk to the several militia companies, that two men, selected
rom each corps, should meet at the court-house on May 19, 1775,
n order to consult with each other upon such measures as might
e thought best to be pursued. Accordingly on said day a far larger
umber than two out of each company were present. . . . Then a
ull, a free, and dispassionate discussion obtained on the various
ubjects for which the delegation had been convened, and the fol-
owing resolutions were unanimously adopted: [Resolutions like
hose published in the *Register*.] . . . Then a select committee was
ppointed to report on the ensuing day a full and definite statement
•f grievances, together with a more correct and formal draft of
he Declaration of Independence. These proceedings having been
hus arranged and somewhat in readiness for promulgation, the
lelegates then adjourned until to-morrow, at 12 o'clock. May 20th,
t 12 o'clock, the delegation, as above, had convened. The select
ommittee were also present and reported agreeably to instructions,
riz.: a statement of grievances and formal draft of the Declaration
of Independence, written by Ephraim Brevard, chairman of the said
ommittee, and read by him to the delegation. The resolves, by-
aws and regulations were read by John McKnitt Alexander. . . .
There was not a dissenting voice. Finally, the whole proceedings
vere read distinctly and audibly at the court-house door, by Colonel
Thomas Polk, to a large, respectable and approving assemblage of
itizens who were present and gave sanction to the business of the
lay."

The accuracy of the statements made in the manuscripts found
oy Dr. Joseph McKnitt Alexander was for a generation unquestioned
n North Carolina. It was only after the discovery of the contemporaneous publication of other resolutions, adopted at Charlotte on
May 31, 1775, of similar import, that any suggestion of inaccuracy
arose.

In 1838 a Pennsylvania newspaper of 1775 was found containing
several resolutions adopted at Charlotte on May 31, 1775; and in
1847, a copy of the *South Carolina Gazette and Country Journal,*
published at Charleston, of the date of June 16, 1775, was found.
It contained a full series of resolutions adopted at Charlotte, May
31, 1775. Later other papers were found containing, in part, the
same resolutions. No contemporaneous reference to any other resolutions than those of May 31st has ever been discovered.

After the Resolves of May 31st were brought to light in 1847
many persons believed that they were the only ones adopted at
Charlotte, while others adhered to their belief in the genuineness
of the "Declaration of May 20th." The subject has been ably discussed by some of the most eminent of our citizens. The original

papers, the half sheet in the handwriting of John McKnitt Alexan
der, the full sheet in the unknown handwriting, the Davie cop
with its certificate, and other documents connected with the subje
passed into the hands of Governor D. L. Swain, but are now lo

Recently a copy of the *North Carolina Gazette,* published at Ne
Bern June 16, 1775, was found, containing the Resolves of May 31
and a transcript of the same Resolves, published in the *Cape Fe
Mercury,* probably in the issue of June 23, 1775, sent to England
Governor Josiah Martin, has been found and published. It is
be observed that at the period of the first publication there w
no question as to the particular details, and the witnesses gave test
mony concerning the general subject that in May, 1775, there we
proceedings in Mecklenburg declaring independence.

Hoyt,
The
Mecklen-
burg Dec. of
Ind., 276

Some described the public meeting at which the resolutions we
proclaimed by Colonel Polk; others did not mention that meetin
The Alexander document of 1800 states that the delegates met o
May 19th and continued in session until 2 o'clock on the mornin
of the 20th, when the resolutions were adopted, and makes n
reference to any public meeting. Rev. Humphrey Hunter state
that the meeting was on the 19th, and on the 20th there was th
public proclamation. General George Graham and several othe
testify, to the best of their recollection and belief, that the meetin
was on the 19th and that there was a public meeting on the 20t
General Joseph Graham says that the delegates met on the 20t
and that the resolutions were adopted, and shortly afterward we
proclaimed. Other witnesses give an account of the public meetin
Many merely say that the proceedings were in May, 1775.

The Resolves of
May 31st fit
the
description
The evidence shows that there were some meetings of the leadin
citizens; that Colonel Polk caused the election of two men fro
each militia district, who met in Charlotte in May; that there wa
a protracted meeting extending into the night; that the next day th
resolutions having been adopted were proclaimed at a large publi
meeting by Colonel Polk and were received with enthusiasm.

General Joseph Graham says: "One among other reasons offere
was that the king or ministry had by proclamation or some edi
declared the colonies out of the protection of the British Crown.
That idea finds expression in the preamble to the Resolves of Ma
31st published at the time, and is not referred to in the Alexand
document of 1800.

Mr. Simeson says: "In addition to what I have said, the sam
committee appointed three men to secure all the military stores fo
the county's use—Thomas Polk, John Phifer and Joseph Kenned
I was under arms near the head of the line, near Colonel Polk, an
heard him distinctly read a long string of grievances, the declara

on, and military order above." The resolution appointing Colonel Polk and Dr. Joseph Kennedy a committee to get ammunition, is recalled by the witness, is the last of the Resolves of May 31st, and is not a part of the document of 1800. The testimony of General Graham and Mr. Simeson connects the public meeting with the Resolves of May 31st.

These and other circumstances lead to the belief that inasmuch as none of the witnesses speak of two public meetings, at which Colonel Polk proclaimed independence, there was but one such meeting; and the Resolutions which he read were those of May 31st, published on June 13th in Charleston; June 16th in New Bern and June 23d at Wilmington, and in part, in the northern papers. If there was any other public meeting, it is not mentioned by any one. If there were any other Resolutions ever adopted and proclaimed, no copy was preserved. What the evidence proves

Governor Swain thus speaks of the Davie copy: "It was not taken from the record; it is not shown to be a copy of a copy, or that there was a copy extant in September, 1800."

The author in seeking to give effect to all statements as far as they can be made to consist, follows those witnesses who state that the delegates convened on the day previous to the public meeting.

He follows those who give an account of the public meeting, and he accepts the contemporaneous publication of the proceedings as fixing the day, and as containing the resolutions, or action taken, that being the only contemporaneous evidence.

Variations in recollection, after the passage of forty or fifty years, may be expected; and no witness, after forty years had passed, would probably undertake to repeat from memory a set of Resolutions of which he had never seen a written copy.

The great leading fact is the public meeting and its incidents, the Resolves adopted and ratified by the people and published to the world as the action of Mecklenburg.

With reference to the difference in dates, it may be observed that Rev. Mr. Hunter, who, when writing his memoirs, appears to have copied from Alexander's document of 1800, putting the meeting on the 19th of May, states that on that memorable day he was twenty years and fourteen days of age; and he also states that he was born on the 14th day of May, 1755. That would seem to make the date the 28th day of May. The day not then in question

If when the Alexander document was being prepared, the date was not ascertained from any record, but was calculated, and the calculation was based on the birthday of a person born previous to 1752, perhaps the eleven days' difference between the Old and New Style may account for Alexander's variation from the true date stated in the contemporaneous publications. Some of the wit nesses appear to have followed the Alexander document as to the date—a matter then of minor importance.

It is further to be noted that while the Alexander document differs from the published resolutions in language, yet it embraces the same subject matter, and the purpose seems to have been to give an account of the same transaction and event.

The preamble of the resolutions of May 31st, "To provide in some degree for the exigencies of the county in the present alarming period," accords with the purposes of the election of the delegates stated by the witnesses as leading to the meeting.

THE RESOLVES OF MAY 31ST.

(From the *North Carolina Gazette,* June 16, 1775. Published at New Bern.)

CHARLOTTE TOWN, MECKLENBURG COUNTY, May 31st.

The action taken at the public meeting

This day the committee met, and passed the following Resolves:

Whereas, By an address presented to his Majesty by both houses of Parliament in February last, the American colonies are declared to be in a state of actual rebellion, we conceive that all laws and commissions confirmed by, or derived from, the authority of the king or Parliament are annulled and vacated, and the former civil constitution of these colonies for the present wholly suspended. To provide in some degree for the exigencies of this county in the present alarming period, we deem it proper and necessary to pass the following Resolves, viz.:

I. That all commissions, civil and military, heretofore granted by the Crown to be exercised in these colonies, are null and void, and the constitution of each particular colony wholly suspended.

II. That the provincial congress of each province, under the direction of the great continental congress, is invested with all legislative and executive powers within their respective provinces, and that no other legislative or executive power does or can exist at this time in any of these colonies.

III. As all former laws are now suspended in this province, and the congress has not yet provided others, we judge it necessary for the better preservation of good order, to form certain rules and regulations for the internal government of this county, until laws shall be provided for us by the congress.

IV. That the inhabitants of this county do meet on a certain day appointed by this committee, and having formed themselves into nine companies (to wit: eight for the county, and one for the town of Charlotte), do choose a colonel and other military officers, who all hold and exercise their several powers by virtue of this choice, and independent of Great Britain, and former constitution of this province.

V. That for the better preservation of the peace and administration of justice, each of those companies do choose from their own body two discreet freeholders, who shall be empowered each by himself, and singly, to decide and determine all matters of controversy arising within the said company, under the sum of twenty shillings, and jointly and together all controversies under the sum of forty shillings, yet so as their decisions may admit of appeal to the convention of the select men of the whole county; and also, that any one of these shall have power to examine and commit to confinement persons accused of petit larceny.

VI. That those two select men, thus chosen, do, jointly and together, choose from the body of their particular company two persons, properly qualified to serve as constables, who may assist them in the execution of their office.

VII. That upon the complaint of any persons to either of these select men, he do issue his warrant, directed to the constable, commanding him to bring the aggressor before him or them to answer the said complaint.

VIII. That these select eighteen select men thus appointed do meet every third Tuesday in January, April, July, and October, at the court-house in Charlotte, to hear and determine all matters of controversy for sums exceeding forty shillings, also appeals; and in cases of felony, to commit the person or persons convicted thereof to close confinement until the provincial congress shall provide and establish laws and modes of proceeding in such cases.

IX. That these eighteen select men, thus convened, do choose a clerk, to record the transactions of the said convention; and that the said clerk, upon the application of any person or persons aggrieved, do issue his warrant to one of the constables to summons and warn the said offender to appear before the convention at their next sitting, to answer the aforesaid complaint.

X. That any person making complaint, upon oath, to the clerk, or any member of the convention, that he has reason to suspect that any person or persons indebted to him in a sum above forty shillings do intend clandestinely to withdraw from the county without paying the debt; the clerk, or such member, shall issue his warrant to the constable, commanding him to take the said person or persons into safe custody, until the next sitting of the convention.

XI. That when a debtor for a sum above forty shillings shall abscond and leave the county, the warrant granted as aforesaid shall extend to any goods or chattels of the said debtor as may be found, and such goods or chattels be seized and held in custody by the constable for the space of thirty days, in which term, if the debtor fail to return and discharge the debt, the constable shall return the warrant to one of the select men of the company where the goods were found, who shall issue orders to the constable to sell such a part of the said goods as shall amount to the sum due; that when the debt exceeds forty shillings, the return shall be made to the convention, who shall issue the orders for sale.

XII. That receivers and collectors for quit rents, public and county taxes, do pay the same into the hands of the chairman of this committee, to be by them disbursed as the public exigencies may require. And that such receivers and collectors proceed no further in their office until they be approved of by, and have given to this committee good and sufficient security for a faithful return of such moneys when collected.

XIII. That the committee be accountable to the county for the application of all moneys received from such officers.

XIV. That all these officers hold their commissions during the pleasure of their respective constituents.

XV. That this committee will sustain all damages that may ever hereafter accrue to all or any of these officers thus appointed, and thus acting, on account of their obedience and conformity to these Resolves.

XVI. *That whatever person shall hereafter receive a commission from the Crown, or attempt to exercise any such commission heretofore received, shall be deemed an enemy to his country;* and upon information being made to the captain of the company where he resides, the said captain shall cause him to be apprehended and conveyed before the two select men of the said company, who, upon proof of the fact, shall commit him the said offender into safe custody, until the next sitting of the convention, who shall deal with him as prudence may direct.

XVII. That any person refusing to yield obedience to the above Resolves shall be deemed equally criminal, and liable to the same punishment, as the offenders above last mentioned.

XVIII. That these Resolves be in full force and virtue until instructions from the general congress of this province, regulating the jurisprudence of this province, shall provide otherwise, or the legislative body of Great Britain resign its unjust and arbitrary pretensions with respect to America.

XIX. That the several militia companies in this county do provide themselves with proper arms and accoutrements, and hold themselves in constant readiness to execute the commands and directions of the provincial congress, and of this committee.

1775

XX. That this committee do appoint Colonel Thomas Polk and Dr. Joseph Kennedy to purchase 300 pounds of powder, 600 pounds of lead, and 1000 flints; and deposit the same in some safe place hereafter to be appointed by the committee.

Signed by order of the committee,

EPH. BREVARD,
Clerk of the committee.

Extract from Report of Historical Manuscripts Commission, Fourteenth Annual Report, Appendix, part X (1895); Presented to both Houses of Parliament by Command of her Majesty.

(Manuscripts Earl of Dartmouth, vol. II., Amer. Papers, p. 323:)

North Carolina

N. D. (May 31, 1775) resolutions (20) of a committee of the county of Mecklenburg in North Carolina, signed at Charlotte Town, by order of the committee, Ephraim Brevard. Suspending all laws and commissions given by the Crown, and proposing measures to establish a government for the province.

Four folio pages.

Endorsed: In Governor Martin's of June 30, 1775. No. 34.

W. H. Hoyt, "The Mecklenburg Declaration," at page 276, gives a copy of these Resolves, transmitted by Governor Martin. They are the Resolves of May 31, 1775.

The copy sent by Governor Martin

Extracts from the records of Mecklenburg County

April, 1775, North Carolina, Mecklenburg County.	At an Inferior Court of Pleas and Quarter Sessions begun and held for the county of Mecklenburg, on the third Tuesday in April, 1775.

Present the Worshipful

Robert Harris,
Hezekiah Alexander, } Esqrs.
Robert Irwin.

July, 1775, North Carolina, Mecklenburg County.	At an Inferior Court of Pleas and Quarter Sessions begun and held in the said county, on the third Tuesday in July, 1775.

The king's justices in Mecklenburg

Present the Worshipful

Robert Harris,
Abraham Alexander, } Esqrs.
Robert Irwin.

October, 1775, 3d Tuesday.	Same as above.
January, 1776, 3d Tuesday.	Same as above.
April, 1776, 3d Tuesday.	Same as above.

Conditions in May

At Philadelphia the North Carolina deputies were carried away by the enthusiasm that pervaded the northern colonies. Hooper wrote to Harnett and to Sam Johnston urging the necessity of having a provincial convention immediately after the adjournment of the general congress, and apprehensions were expressed lest North Carolina should delay too long the organization of troops. But even then companies were being formed throughout the province, and in Rowan, Mecklenburg, Tryon and in other counties public action emanated from the militia districts.

Mecklenburg declares independence

Indeed, so far from the people of North Carolina being indifferent or supine, a step forward was now taken in Mecklenburg County that was far in advance of the desires of either Hooper, Hewes, or Caswell, or their associates in congress. It was a declaration of independence, In March and April there had been many meetings of the Committee of Safety in Mecklenburg. The occupation of Boston by a hostile British army was a thorn in the flesh. The inhabitants of that town were suffering from their adherence to the rights of America, and again the cry rang throughout Mecklenburg that the cause of Boston was the cause of all. In May came the exciting news that Parliament in its address to the king had declared the colonies in rebellion, and therefore out of the protection of the law. The leaders felt that a storm was about to burst on the heads of the patriotic people. It was determined to prepare for it. Public meetings were held in various parts of the country, and the prevailing sentiment was found to be one of resolution. After conference, Colonel Thomas Polk, the commanding officer of the county, called for an election of two representatives from each of the nine militia districts of

he county to take into consideration the state of the country
and to adopt such measures as seemed necessary to safeguard their liberties. The election was held and amid great
excitement the delegates convened at Charlotte, and with
them came their friends and neighbors, so that nearly one-
half of all the arms-bearing men of the county assembled in
that little hamlet. As great as was the occasion, the excitement was largely increased by the arrival of the news of the
battle of Lexington, which had swept through the country
like a whirlwind, stirring the people to the profoundest
depths. To the meeting came all the leading inhabitants,
the Polks, Alexanders, Brevards, Davidsons, and all who
were leaders in thought and action. They met on the 30th
day of May, in the court-house, and Abraham Alexander
was called to the chair. A number of papers were read.
Stress was laid on the action of Parliament declaring the
colonies in rebellion. As they were held to be rebels, the
leaders urged that they should renounce their allegiance
and declare themselves independent. An objection was
made: If we resolve on independence, how shall we be
absolved from the oath of allegiance we took after the Regulation battle? With hot indignation the answer came—
That allegiance and protection were reciprocal; when protection was withdrawn, allegiance ceased. Independence
was resolved on, and a committee composed of Dr.
Ephraim Brevard and others was appointed to prepare the
resolutions. The discussion continued far into the night,
and then the delegates adjourned to reassemble at noon.
At twelve o'clock the following day, the delegates again met
and the resolutions prepared by Dr. Brevard were read and
adopted.

It was resolved that all commissions granted by the
Crown were null and void; that no other authority than that
of the Continental Congress and the provincial congresses
existed in any of the colonies; that military officers should
be elected who should hold their offices independent of Great
Britain, and an independent local government was provided
for.

These bold resolutions having been adopted by the delegates, it was determined that the action taken should be

Statement
of Graham;
Preamble of
Resolves

The great
meeting

Statement
of General
Graham

May 31st,
Wednesday

Independ-
ence

1775

May

Statements
of Simeson,
Cummins,
Graham,
Hunter

The
independent
government

proclaimed at the court-house door, and be formally announced to the people, who, animated by ardor, patriotism
and excitement, had come together in great numbers to participate in the proceedings of the day. Colonel Polk, the
leader in the measure, standing on the high steps of the
court-house, read the resolutions to the eager crowd; and the
people with much enthusiasm approved and endorsed this
first assertion of independence. As a manifestation of their
approval cheers were given, hats were thrown into the air,
and with enthusiastic applause the people ratified the great
action taken by the delegates. Mecklenburg thus first gave
expression to that spirit of independence which later
developed elsewhere, finally leading to a total abandonment
of all desire for reconciliation with the mother country.

By these Resolves all laws and commissions emanating
from the royal government were annulled, and the former
civil constitutions of the colonies were declared wholly suspended; and also it was declared that no other power existed
in any of the provinces but the provincial congresses under
the direction of the Continental Congress.

It being decreed that all laws, commissions, and authority
were abrogated, there was established a new government to
replace the old one. The plan provided that the inhabitants
of the county should form themselves into nine military companies, and choose a colonel and other military officers, who
should hold their power by virtue of the people's choice, and
independent of the Crown and of the former constitution of
the province; that each of these companies should appoint
two freeholders to exercise judicial functions under the
name of "selectmen"; that these eighteen "selectmen" should
hold a court for the county, and should meet at Charlotte
quarterly for that purpose.

It was further decreed that any person thereafter receiving any commission from the Crown, or attempting to exercise any commission theretofore received, should be deemed
an enemy to the country and should be apprehended. All
public moneys collected were to be paid to the chairman of
the Committee of Safety; the military companies were to
hold themselves in readiness to execute the commands of the
general congress and of the committee of the county, and

Colonel Thomas Polk and Dr. Joseph Kennedy were directed to purchase a supply of ammunition.

Those who appeared to take the lead in the proceedings resulting in this action, according to the recollection of James Jack, were Hezekiah Alexander, who generally acted as chairman; John McKnitt Alexander, as secretary; Abraham Alexander, Adam Alexander, Major John Davidson, Major William Davidson, Colonel Thomas Polk, Ezekiel Polk, Dr. Ephraim Brevard, Samuel Martin, Duncan Ochletree, William Willson, and Robert Irvin. Others mentioned were Waightstill Avery, William Kennon, William Graham, John Flenniken, James Harris and David Reece.

Statement of Simeson; Resolution XX

The actors

These Resolutions of the people of Mecklenburg completely overthrowing the colonial government and establishing a free and independent government founded on the will of the people, were published on June 16, 1775, at New Bern, in the *North Carolina Gazette,* and on June 13th in the newspaper at Charleston, and in the *Cape Fear Mercury,* published at Wilmington, probably in its issue of June 23d. Their publication produced a profound impression. The action at Mecklenburg, indeed, stirred the hearts of the patriot leaders and awoke enthusiasm in the breasts of their associates throughout the colony, while they aroused the ire of Governor Martin and caused dismay among the adherents of the Crown.

Wright, the royal governor of Georgia, hastened, June 20th, to transmit a copy of the Charleston paper to England, and Governor Martin forwarded the *Cape Fear Mercury,* saying: "I daily see indignantly the sacred majesty of my royal master insulted, . . . his government set at naught . . . and the whole constitution unhinged and prostrate, and I live, alas! ingloriously only to deplore it. The Resolves of the committee of Mecklenburg, which your Lordship will find in the enclosed newspaper, surpass all the horrid and treasonable publications that the inflammatory spirits of this continent have yet produced. . . . A copy of these Resolves, I am informed, were sent off by express to the congress at Philadelphia as soon as they were passed in the committee." And on June 25th, two days after the publication at Wilmington, and as soon as he could convene the

C. R., X, 47, 48

1775
C. R., X, 38
June
council at Fort Johnston, he brought to its attention "the late most treasonable publication of a committee in the county of Mecklenburg, explicitly renouncing obedience to his Majesty's government and all lawful authority whatsoever"; and on August 8th, in a proclamation, he said: "I have also seen a most infamous publication in the *Cape Fear Mercury* importing to be resolves of a set of people styling themselves a committee for the county of Mecklenburg most traitorously declaring the entire dissolution of the laws, govern-
C. R., X, 144
ment, and constitution of this country, and setting up a system of rule and regulation repugnant to the laws and subversive of his Majesty's government."

The Mecklenburg committee, conscious of the important advance they had made, determined to send a messenger post haste with their resolutions to the congress at Philadelphia. James Jack, young and vigorous, and a determined patriot, undertook the task. At Salisbury, on Thursday, June 1st, Colonel Alexander Martin, who had been appointed by Governor Martin a judge under the temporary act creating courts of oyer and terminer, opened a term of his court.* Colonel Martin was a deputy from Guilford to the second provincial convention, which had recently adjourned, was an earnest patriot, and, together with the other delegates, had signed the association of the Continental Congress. On the same day the Committee of Safety of Rowan also met at
C. R., X, 1-11
Salisbury. Rowan differed from Mecklenburg, as a much larger proportion of its inhabitants had been Regulators and were bound by the oath imposed by Governor Tryon, and the Rowan committee sought by moderate resolutions to

---

*The charge of Judge Alexander Martin at this term of the court has been preserved (the *South Carolina Gazette and Country Journal* of July 11, 1775). In it he extolled the right of trial by jury, "which our glorious ancestors waded through seas of blood to obtain, and compelled even majesty to ratify by that sacred paladium of British liberties, the Grand Charter. This, with other peculiar rights and privileges, the sovereigns of Britain through a long series of ages have plighted their faith by a most solemn oath to maintain; and for this kingly protection the subject has bound himself by as solemn a tie to hold allegiance and obedience to them so long as they shall continue to hold forth, secure and defend these choice, incalculable blessings to their people; this is that great, that reciprocal union between the king and the people." The judge inveighed against popish recusants. "Let me dismiss you, then, gentlemen," he said, "with this serious injunction: to support and defend, as far

induce the co-operation of those not inclined to adhere to the 1775
cause of the colonies. The committee, not yet having infor- June 1st,
C. R., X, 11
mation of any proceedings at Charlotte, wrote an elaborate
address to the committee of Mecklenburg requesting an account of their proceedings, promising a like return on their
part, and beseeching them by the ties of their common Protestant religion to exert themselves for the maintenance of
their chartered rights. But before the court had ended, and
it adjourned on Tuesday, June 6th, Captain Jack reached
Salisbury on his way to Philadelphia. At the request of
the court, he handed a copy of the Resolutions to Colonel
Kennon, and they were read aloud in open court. That Captain
Jack's
evening Major William Davidson and Waightstill Avery statement
called at the lodgings of Captain Jack and informed him that
they had heard of but one person, Mr. Beard, a prominent
attorney and a cautious man, who did not approve of them.
Captain Jack proceeded to Philadelphia and delivered the
Resolutions to Caswell and Hooper, North Carolina delegates
in congress.

On the publication of the Resolves at New Bern, Richard
Cogdell, the chairman of the Committee of Safety, forwarded the newspaper to Caswell, at Philadelphia, saying : Letters at
"You will observe the Mecklenburg Resolves exceed all other Hayes
committees or the congress itself." About a week later, on
June 27th, Samuel Johnston, on whom rested the mantle of
the lamented Harvey, wrote to Joseph Hewes, at Philadelphia : "Tom Polk, too, is raising a very pretty spirit in the
back country (see the newspapers). He has gone a little
farther than I would choose to have gone, but perhaps no
farther than necessary." That it was generally understood
that these Resolves constituted a declaration of independence,
while establishing a new government, is evident from the
records of the Moravian Church at Bethania of events
occurring during the year 1775. "I cannot but remark at

as in you lies, the constitution and the laws of your country, the
just prerogatives of the Crown and the declared rights of the people.
This is liberty, this is loyalty ; do you thus, loyal gentlemen, and you
will be free." The address, while asserting loyalty, touched on those
points that were particularly a cause of excitement among the Presbyterians of the west, and gave prominence to the idea of a reciprocal
union between the king and the people, which if broken on one side,
freed the other from allegiance.

1775
Moravian
annalist the end of the 1775th year," wrote the annalist, "during the summer of this year, that in the month of May or June the county of Mecklenburg, in North Carolina, declared itself free and independent of England, and made such arrangements for the administration of justice, which proceeding the Continental Congress at this time considered premature; afterward, however, the Continental Congress later extended same over the whole country."*

The Mecklenburg Resolves carried to Philadelphia were not officially brought to the attention of congress, and no reference was made to them in the proceedings of that body. † The congress was not prepared for the step taken. As yet the government of king and Parliament was recognized as lawfully subsisting, and congress, the provincial assemblies and conventions were still protesting in solemn form unswerving allegiance, as faithful subjects, to their king and country.

The avowed purpose was still complete reconciliation; and this was not yet a forlorn hope, for America was not without friends in England. As congress saw it on one side stood the deceived monarch, his irate "ministers of state, the profligate part of the nobility, and the corrupt majority

In England of the House of Commons; these drag an army to blow up the blaze of civil war." On the other, a prince of the blood, the most illustrious among the nobility, the most eloquent and virtuous commoners, the city of London and the body of the English nation—these being the affectionate friends

C. R., X, 57 of America and of liberty. Distinguished officers retired from the army rather than lift a hand to crush liberty in America, saying the result must needs be the destruction

---

*Translation from the diary of Bethany Church, written in German, furnished the author by Rev. J. H. Clewell, principal of Salem Female Academy. The statement made, that the Continental Congerss extended same over the whole country, must have reference to the establishment of local government by committees independent of the Crown, unless the annalist wrote after 1776. Miss Fries, of Salem, who has investigated the subject, asserts that he wrote in 1782.

†Although the newspapers at Philadelphia were strongly for the Whigs, they did not reproduce the Mecklenburg resolves from the Carolina newspapers, while other papers at the north did. This leads to the belief that Congress sought their suppression as being out of harmony with its purposes. (Hoyt's "The Mecklenburg Declaration," 80.)

of liberty in Britain and the establishment of tyranny and despotism on the ruins of the British constitution. The mayor and aldermen of London presented a remonstrance to the king, expressing their abhorrence of the measures being pursued to the oppression of their fellow-subjects in America; but his Majesty rolled under his tongue the word "rebellion"—for the Parliament had declared that the colonies were in a state of rebellion—and the royal purpose was to crush them into submission.

Yet congress still hoped by the aid of friends in England to secure a restoration of former conditions with a recognition of the traditional rights of the American colonies. On July 8th, after a dutiful address to his Majesty, reasserting their allegiance, congress issued an address to the inhabitants of Great Britain: "We are accused of aiming at independence. . . . Give us leave most solemnly to assure you that we have not yet lost sight of the object we have ever had in view—a reconciliation with you on constitutional principles. . . . We have . . . again presented an humble and dutiful petition to our sovereign, and, to remove every imputation of obstinacy, have requested his Majesty to direct some mode by which the united applications of his faithful colonists may be improved into a happy and permanent reconciliation."

The voice of Mecklenburg was thus out of harmony with the solemn declarations of congress, and no notice was taken of that first advance into the realm of independence—the annulling of the old constitution and of colonial laws and the ordaining of an independent government by the people themselves as the only source of power and sovereignty.

But while congress hoped for peace, it was to be on terms satisfactory to America. To wring concessions from the imperious ministry, a bold and defiant front was necessary.

The North Carolina delegates in congress, fearing that the people at home were too supine, on June 19th united in a stirring address, which they sent to the committees of all the counties: "We conjure you by the ties of religion, virtue, and love of country to follow the example of your sister colonies and form yourselves into a militia. The election of the officers . . . must depend on yourselves. Study

Margin notes:

1775

June

Reconciliation hoped for, July 8th

C. R., X, 75-83

Apprehensions

C. R., X, 20

the art of military with the utmost attention; view it as a science upon which your future security depends."

Daily it became more and more evident that the contest was to be decided on the battlefield. The men in arms at Boston were local minute men, drawn together from the adjoining provinces, commanded by their local officers. On June 15th congress made a great step forward, and adopted that army and placed it on a continental footing. Washington was chosen commander-in-chief. On the 20th he received his commission, and the next day he departed from Philadelphia for the seat of war. But while all eyes were centred on Boston, congress, in view of Governor Martin's activity, became apprehensive for the safety of North Carolina, and, like the delegates, urged the people to embody as militia under proper officers; and on June 26th it resolved that if the provincial convention should think it necessary, it might raise a thousand men in North Carolina, and congress would consider that force a part of the American army, and take it into the pay of the continent.

Thomas Jefferson

On June 21, 1775, while Captain Jack was still lingering at Philadelphia, after presenting the Mecklenburg Resolves declaring independence and establishing an independent government for that community, Thomas Jefferson, a newly appointed delegate from Virginia, arrived and for the first time took his seat in the Continental Congress. He had just achieved fame as the author of the Virginia resolutions rejecting the conciliatory proposition of Lord North. The ink was hardly dry with which he had penned his earnest appeal "to the even-handed justice of that Being who doth no wrong, that we may again see reunited the blessings of liberty and prosperity and the most permanent harmony with Great Britain." Like John Adams, Hancock, and all the other members of the congress, Jefferson was expecting to remain a British subject, and desired the "most permanent harmony with Great Britain"; and if he then heard of the Mecklenburg Resolves, if he then knew of the mission of Captain Jack to the congress, his thoughts were so far out of harmony with the proceedings at Mecklenburg that he dismissed them from his mind and forgot them; he and his associates were not yet in favor of such revolutionary action.*

The Regulators

Toward the end of June Caswell set off from Philadelphia to attend the convention, which was to convene on July 12th. After his departure congress received copies of General Gage's letter to Governor Martin, promising to send forward ammunition, and of Governor Martin's letter asking for a king's standard, and Hooper and Hewes became still more alarmed because of the situation in North Carolina. The reliance of Governor Martin was not only on the co-operation of the Highlanders, but on expected aid from the Regulators in the interior. From Dan River to the South Carolina line, from the forks of the Yadkin to the Haw and the Deep, there were thousands of inhabitants who had never been pardoned and who still called themselves "an unhappy people," subject to the penalties of their former insurrection. It seemed necessary to remove their grounds of apprehension—to place before them considerations why they should assist in maintaining the rights of the people as British subjects, and to assure them that the movement was not a rebellion with the object of seeking independence. To accomplish this purpose, Hooper and Hewes enlisted the aid of the Presbyterian ministers at Philadelphia and also of the German Lutherans and Calvinists. The Presbyterian ministers joined in an address to the Presbyterian congregations in North Carolina, declaring that "there was no desire to separate from the parent state. Believe no man that dares to say that we desire to be independent of our mother country."

C. R., IX, 1161, 1228

C. R., X, 86, 227 July, 1775

*In the correspondence of Adams and Jefferson in 1819 referring to the Mecklenburg declaration both say in substance: "Would not every advocate of independence have rung the glories of Mecklenburg in North Carolina in the ears of the doubting Dickensons who hung so heavily on us?" They evidently had in mind a subsequent period—when they themselves were advocating independence; not the summer of 1775, when they were still seeking reconciliation with the mother country. The Mecklenburg Resolves appear to have been suppressed in Philadelphia, not being admitted to publication there, while published in whole or in part by papers at other points at the north.

1775

August

The advices from Philadelphia and the efforts made to reconcile the disaffected element in the interior of the province and to bring them to a support of the common cause were calculated to arrest for a time the influences that attended the action at Charlotte. The pendulum swung backward.* Allegiance was not disavowed, although the people prepared for war. Court proceedings continued to be held in the name of the king, and notwithstanding on August 1st the Rowan committee resolved "that one thousand volunteers be immediately embodied in this county, elect their staff officers and be ready at the shortest notice to march out to action," and an earnest address was issued calling on the people to "rouse like one man in defence of our religion from popery, our liberty from slavery, and our lives from tormenting death," yet on the same day the inferior court of Rowan County met and "his majesty's commission of the peace was publicly read," and John Oliphant, W. T. Coles, and William McBride, Esqs., took the oaths prescribed by law, and proceeded to business; and Waightstill Avery, Esq., was appointed attorney for the Crown in the absence of John Dunn, Esq., deputy attorney. Farther to the west, however, the profession of loyalty was conditional. The committee of Tryon County, at its meeting on August 14th, adopted an association, which was also to be signed by the other inhabitants of that county, "uniting under the most sacred ties of religion, honor, and love of country, and engaging to take up arms and risk our lives and fortunes in maintaining the freedom of our country," and arranged to obtain powder and ball for the companies of that county; but resolving unanimously "that we will continue to profess all loyalty and attachment to our sovereign lord, King George III, his crown and dignity, so

At the west

C. R., X,
134, 135, 139

C. R., X,
163

---

*In Mecklenburg the inferior court of pleas and quarter sessions continued to be held by the magistrates theretofore appointed by Governor Martin, meeting on the third Tuesday in July, 1775, and the third Tuesday in October, and so on quarterly, the record showing as "present the Worshipful Robert Harris, Abraham Alexander, Robert Irwin, Esqrs.," the proceedings continuing regularly from April, 1775, till July, 1776, without interruption. On one occasion, however, an acting magistrate was taken from the Bench and sent to prison by order of the chairman of the committee.—Simeson's Statement.

ong as he secures to us those rights and liberties which he principles of our constitution require."

Elsewhere the action was not different—protesting loyalty, but getting ready a supply of powder and ball. On July 1st the committee of Pitt County resolved that, "We will pay all due allegiance to his Majesty, King George III; . . . at the same time, we are determined to assert our rights, . . . and that, under God, the preservation of them depends on a firm union of the inhabitants and a sturdy, spirited observation of the resolutions of the general congress." "We do hereby agree and associate under all ties of religion, honor, and regard for posterity." And the captains of the different companies were directed to call their men together to choose officers.

The clashing in Anson

In Anson, where there had been many Regulators, Colonel James Cotton, the lieutenant-colonel of the county, remained loyal to the government, and the people were much divided. Under his influence the Loyalists signed a protest against the proceedings of the Continental Congress, but the Committee of Safety and their friends were zealous. On May 25th they began to seize some of the leading men among the disaffected, confining them as prisoners and endeavoring to persuade them to abandon their allegiance. Early in June Colonel Spencer was urging the people to sign the association, saying that the king had broken his coronation oath, and the people were absolved by his example. On the second Tuesday of July about thirty of the committee met at the court-house and elected Colonel Spencer captaingeneral, and Thomas Wade and David Love and others were chosen captains of their companies. Both sides were active, Colonel Cotton ordering out the militia companies under the officers who remained loyal, and maintaining communication with Governor Martin, and, on July 7th, sending him a petition signed by many of the inhabitants; while, on the other hand, there were great meetings of the people who stood by the Continental Congress, and large numbers enlisted on the side of liberty.

In Surry County the committee, as a prelude to their pro-

1775
July

Pitt County

C. R., X, 6:

Anson
County

C. R., X,
125-128

C. R., X,
228

ceedings, indited the legend on their record-book, "Liberty or death. God save the king!"

After the arrival of Governor Martin at Fort Johnston, that point became still more of a storm centre. The situation rapidly developed excitement and resolution. Captain Collett, in command of the fort, was inciting negroes to leave their masters and take refuge within his lines. He seized corn and other supplies, and, inflamed by his conduct, the people began to subscribe association papers, preparing for action. On June 16th the governor issued his proclamation, warning every one that by such conduct they would expose themselves not only to the forfeiture of their lands and properties, but to the loss of life and everything they
held dear and valuable. Three days after this proclamation, on June 19th, the inhabitants of New Hanover, by an asso-
ciation paper, "united themselves under every tie of religion and honor to go forth and be ready to sacrifice their lives and fortunes to secure the freedom and safety of their country."

And the next day, June 20th, committeemen of Duplin, Onslow, Bladen, Brunswick, and New Hanover assembled in general meeting. They adopted the New Hanover association, which they directed to be printed, with a recommendation to the inhabitants of the district to sign it as speedily as possible. It was signed in Cumberland by Robert Rowan and his associates, and doubtless by the other patriots of the district. A committee composed of Howe, Maclaine, and Sam Ashe was appointed to
answer the governor's proclamation. In the answer they declared that the resolution respecting America introduced by Lord North favoring North Carolina and New York, which Governor Martin had commended, added insult to the injury it intended; that by it it was hoped to divide the colonies, and, by breaking one link in their chain of union, render their subjugation more easy; that it was a base, flagitious, wicked attempt to entrap America into slavery, which ought to be rejected with the contempt it deserved; and it was a duty that the people owed to themselves, their country, and posterity by every effort, and at every risk, to maintain, support, and defend their liberties against any invasion or encroachment whatsoever. On the 25th Gov-

1775

rnor Martin brought these matters to the attention of the ᴐuncil, and it was agreed to strengthen the fort, and also ᴐ prorogue the Assembly, that had been called to meet on uly 12th, until September.

C. R., X, 38-40

In May he had informed the king that fourteen hundred ʀ fifteen hundred persons in the interior had signed dec- ᴀrations in favor of the government, and now he wrote that e could collect among the Highlanders three thousand ffective men, and still more in the interior counties, where, ᴇ declared, "the people are in general well affected and ɴuch attached to me—at least two-thirds of the fighting ɴen of the whole country, which may be computed, accord- ɴg to my best information, to exceed thirty thousand." Vith such views, he projected, after being furnished with ᴇn thousand stands of arms by General Gage, raising the ᴋing's standard and forming an army for the subjugation of ʜe province. He recommended Allan McDonald, the hus- ᴂand of Flora, for an appointment, and Alexander McLeod, ᴥf the marines, and Lieutenant Alexander McLean, also a ᴀalf-pay officer, and other influential Highlanders for ap- ᴐointments. For himself he begged the restoration of the ᴿank he held in the army in 1769, asking permission to ᴄommand a regiment of Highlanders. Expecting to take ʜe field, he again wrote for a king's standard and also for a ᴇnt and camp equipage for his own use. His hope of a ɴilitary commission was, however, disappointed, for the ᴋing had arranged differently. Determined to follow the ᴣovernor's recommendation to embody a force of High- ᴀnders, the king directed that they should be under the ᴄommand of Lieutenant-Colonel Alexander McLean; but ᴀbout the middle of July General McDonald and Major McLeod, bearing secret commissions, arrived at Ocracoke ʄrom New York and proceeded to New Bern. Johnston, ʟearning of their arrival, instructed the committee at New Bern to secure them, but they took an oath satisfactory to ʈhe inhabitants and were allowed to proceed to the interior.

C. R., IX, 1256; X, 45, 46

C. R., X, 46, 47

C. R., IX, 1174

C. R., X, 117

Emissaries were continually passing from the Loyalists to ʈhe fort, which was being strengthened by new works, so ᴀs to make its capture difficult. Under these circumstances ʈhe people of the Cape Fear clamored for a new convention;

1775

July
C. R., X, 92

and the committee wrote to Johnston that "some enterprising men wished to make an effort to take the fort, but were
afraid of having their conduct disavowed by the convention."
The committee thought that a number of men should be
raised and kept in pay for the defence of the country, and
that a convention alone could do that.

On May 31st, Howe, Harnett, and Ashe, knowing of the
death of Colonel Harvey, wrote urging Johnston to convene
a convention as soon as possible, and in this request the New
Bern committee concurred. But the Assembly was expected
to meet on July 12th, and Johnston deemed it best to wait.

C. R., IX,
1285
Johnston
calls the
convention

When the Assembly was prorogued, he delayed no longer,
and on July 10th issued a call for a convention to be held
at Hillsboro on August 20th; and he recommended a larger
representation of the people, not less than five, so that each
county elected at least five deputies, and the inequality
of representation which had so long been a matter of variance between the old and the new counties came to an end.
Elections were held for the convention, but the committee
at Wilmington could not wait for the body to assemble.

C. R., X,
114

They concluded that Captain Collett should not be suffered
to remain in the fort, and communicated that opinion to the
officers and committees of the neighboring counties. A great
many volunteers immediately collected. On July 15th
Colonel Robert Howe set out with a detachment for Fort
Johnston, and the committee resolved that as many men as
would voluntarily turn out should be despatched to join
them, and that the officers of the several companies in New

C. R., X, 93

Hanover should immediately equip those willing to go on
that service. On the 16th Colonel Ashe, in command, sailed
from Wilmington.

Martin
retires to the
Cruizer

Rumors of this intended movement led Captain Collett
hastily to evacuate the fort, the governor himself taking
refuge on the sloop-of-war *Cruizer,* and he directed the
stores, small arms and ammunition to be transferred to a
transport that lay in the harbor, the heavy guns to be dis-

C. R., X,
97, 102, 108,
132

mounted and the fort dismantled. On the same day Colonel
Ashe, in the name of the people, addressed a letter to Governor Martin, informing him of the purpose to carry the
cannon away from the fort. But Ashe also had another

purpose. The design to seize the arms and munitions at the
fort being defeated by the quick action of Governor Martin,
it was in contemplation by the use of fire-rafts to drive the
Cruizer and the transport from the river, or burn them, and
preparations were made to that end; but that design was
eventually abandoned.

The New Hanover detachment joining Howe at Brunswick, the entire force, amounting to some five hundred men,
proceeded to Fort Johnston, and on the night of July 18th
took possession of the fort, to which Ashe set fire, burning
it so far as it was destructible; and the next day he burned
the dwelling and outhouses belonging to Captain Collett,
who was so obnoxious because of his conduct, especially his
efforts to entice the negroes from their masters. The ringleaders of this savage and audacious mob, wrote Martin,
were Ashe and Harnett.

On the return of the men from the fort, they were met
by a detachment of some three hundred volunteers from
Bladen, who had turned out at a minute's warning. There
was no hesitation. All were equally resolved. But the
movement was hasty, and the fort speedily destroyed. Such
was the first positive act in the way of military operations in
the drama of the Revolution in North Carolina. The flames
of Fort Johnston cast a lurid light throughout the province,
and another impulse was given to popular action. From that
date Governor Martin, expelled from the soil of the province, remained on shipboard. From his vessel he beheld
with varying hopes and fears the progress of the Revolution. The action of Mecklenburg greatly disturbed him.
How far would the example be followed by other counties
in annulling British authority and establishing an independent government? He was anxious to hear from the interior, from the back country, where he hoped for so much
aid, and where he supposed the people were attached to
himself personally. He was disheartened by advices that
the "people of Bladen were pursuing the example of Mecklenburg," and that in the seacoast counties the people had
chosen military officers, and were frequently assembling in
arms. But a considerable body of Germans, settled in
Mecklenburg, gave him comfort by sending a loyal declara-

Margin notes:
1775
July

July 18, 1775

C. R., X,
109

The
Revolution
progresses

C. R., X,
106

1775
C. R., X,
231
July

tion "against the very extraordinary and traitorous resolves of the committee of that county." And the news from Anson was encouraging. There the clashing among the people was, even at that early date, so violent and bitter as to be incipient civil war, and Colonel Cotton continued to send assurances of the steadfast devotion of a large number of Loyalists.

From his first arrival at the fort, Governor Martin contrived to maintain some correspondence with the loyal element in the interior, and it being apprehended that he was organizing the Highlanders, the Wilmington committee early forbade any intercourse with him except by their permission. On July 3d, it being reported that Allan McDonald intended to raise troops to support the government, the committee addressed him on that subject, requiring him to desist; and Joseph Hewes wrote emphatically on July 8th:

C. R., X, 86 "If the governor attempts to do anything he ought to be seized and sent out of the colony; so should" Judge Howard.

Communications had been addressed by the governor to staunch friends in the interior to enroll loyal adherents and to sign association papers. Letters of that tenor had been

Dunn and
Boote

received by John Dunn and Benjamin Booth Boote, two influential Loyalists at Salisbury. On July 18th they were put under guard by the Rowan committee, were examined,

C. R., X,
93, 136, 184,
306, 673-679

arrested, and, under the orders of Colonel Alexander Martin (then judge), Adlai Osborn, Colonel Spencer and Colonel Polk, they were, at the close of July, conveyed by a detachment of light horse to South Carolina, where they were confined by the South Carolina authorities. A year later, while they were on parole, Boote took the oath as a supporter of the American cause, and Dunn became a good patriot. But in 1780 Boote joined Cornwallis's forces on the invasion of South Carolina.

At the time of the arrest of these men, August 1st, the Rowan committee ordered that one thousand volunteers be immediately embodied in that county, elect their staff officers and be ready at the shortest notice to march out to action.

C. R., X,
127

In Anson the zeal of Colonel Spencer, Wade and their associates was irresistible, and Colonel Cotton and his loyal militia were overpowered. Disheartened at the turn of affairs, Cotton, with several of his most devoted friends, set out to report to the governor, and reached the *Cruizer* on August 13th, bearing evil tidings of their discomfiture. On their attempted return they were apprehended by the vigilant committeemen in Bladen, and subsequently, under stress of circumstances, took the test oath and submitted themselves to the authority of the congress.

At the end of July, it being learned that the governor himself intended going into the back country, the Wilming-ton committee advised the committees of the different counties of his design, and requested them to keep a strict lookout and arrest him. The unremitting activity of the patriots, however, rendered such a movement too hazardous; but still it was the cherished purpose of Governor Martin to penetrate into the interior and marshal the Loyalists, and, confident of his military prowess, try conclusions with the rebels.

The governor to be arrested

C. R., X, 124

CHAPTER XXVII

The Provincial Council, 1775-76.

The spirit of resistance

1775

August, 1775

C. R., X, 86

In the meantime the spirit of resistance was nourished by men like Hewes, who declared that "the powers of government must soon be taken into the hands of the people." "The administration," said he, "has even tried to let loose the Indians on our frontier, to raise the negroes against us, . . . and have sent a formidable army to cut our throats, and then abuse us with the names of rebels and cowards." "I consider myself now over head and ears in what the ministry call rebellion. I feel no compunction for the part I have taken, nor for the number of our enemies lately slain in the battle at Bunker's Hill. I wish to be in the camp before Boston, though I fear I shall not be able to get there till next campaign."

Martin's proclamation

C. R., X, 145-150

On August 8th Governor Martin issued a manifesto denouncing the leaders of the sedition and treason, and warning the people against being seduced to their purposes. Particularly were Hooper, Hewes and Caswell, John Ashe and Robert Howe singled out for denunciation. His chief design was to appeal to the people to remain loyal. He

realized that the approaching convention was to be held at
Hillsboro with the view of influencing the inhabitants of
the interior, and this effect he sought to counteract by skilfully playing on the fears and hopes of the people. He
dwelt on the faithful loyalty of those in the western counties,
who had theretofore "resisted all the black artifices of falsehood, sedition, and treason," and who, upon his representation, had "received the king's most gracious approbation and
acceptance." Particularly he mentioned those in "Dobbs,
Cumberland, Anson, Orange, Guilford, Chatham, Rowan,
and Surry," who he declared had given him more "especial
and public testimonials of their loyalty, fidelity, and duty";
but he tendered to all his Majesty's most gracious pardon on
their return to their duty to their king; and he offered
ample reward and encouragement to any who should deliver
up to him the few principal persons who had seduced them
to treasonable outrages.

1775
August

C.R., X, 146

The Provincial Congress*

Indeed, the efforts of the two contending parties were
now anxiously directed to obtaining popular support. Samuel
Johnston had counted on the influence the convention might
exert, and to popularize that body he had urged the elec-

*The names Convention and Congress are often applied indiffer-
ently to these bodies. It is to be observed that those of August,
1774, and April, 1775, called themselves conventions and were presided over by a moderator. That of September, 1775, called itself a
congress and elected a president. The first two claimed to be lawful
meetings of the people, assembled for a legal purpose under the constitution. The object then was to remonstrate against an infringement of constitutional rights. By September, 1775, the character of
these bodies was changed. They were not mere lawful meetings of
the people to remonstrate. They were revolutionary bodies, ordaining government and exercising administrative and legislative powers.
Perhaps they took the name of congress to conform to a new American system—making a difference between the former government and
that then established. The authority of the British Government was
no longer respected—that of the Continental Congress had taken its
place. The people no longer claimed to be acting under the constitution of the British Empire.
The Congress differed from the Convention in the manner of
voting. In the Convention the members voted as in the Assembly,
each casting a vote. In the Congress the counties voted, each county
having a single vote, without regard to the number of deputies in
attendance. In the Continental Congress each colony had one vote;
in the Provincial Congress each county had a vote, and in the Provincial Council each district had a vote.

tion of an increased delegation from each county, the number not being limited. Bertie had sent eleven delegates, Chatham ten, Dobbs, Wake, Rowan, Guilford, seven each; Mecklenburg, Tryon, Bute, New Hanover, six each; and the other counties five; the entire membership numbering one hundred and eighty-four. This enlarged representation resulted in the attendance of many men of the first capacity, who had not theretofore been employed in legislative business.

Sunday, August 20th, opened with the straggling hamlet of Hillsboro aglow with unusual excitement. Several stores, an insufficient court room, a dozen widely separated residences, a church building and a small inn for the wayfaring traveller constituted the village, where now were assembling the representatives of the people. At noon those members who had arrived assembled in the church, but immediately adjourned until the next day. On Monday, the 21st, at ten o'clock, one hundred and eighty-four delegates answered to their names, and Richard Caswell, just from the Continental Congress, proposed Samuel Johnston for president of the body, and Rev. George Micklejohn opened the congress with prayer.

Events had moved rapidly since the last convention in April—the battles of Lexington and Bunker Hill, the destruction of Charlestown, the formation of independent companies, the organization of a continental army, the proceedings at Charlotte, the flight of the governor, the burning of Fort Johnston, and the expulsion of the royal governor from the soil of the province, and the cessation of the provincial legislature. The established government had ceased to exist. And so the convention was confronted with new conditions. No light was shed upon the pathway by past experience, but with resolution the members addressed themselves to the great questions presented for their consideration. It was the largest meeting of representative Carolinians that had ever assembled. The last convention was composed of but sixty-seven members; this was near three times as numerous. The two previous revolutionary bodies had been called conventions; this now assumed the name of the Provincial Congress. The others had not entered on legislative action; this pro-

posed to make laws to bind the people under the sanction
of legitimate power, and to exert the authority of established government.

The leaders

Although the thirteen counties that might be allotted to
the west sent some seventy deputies, the preponderance was
still with the east, and the vote was taken by counties. But
Person and Penn, the Martins, Polk, Avery and Spencer,
John McKnitt Alexander, Moses Winslow, Kennon and
Sharpe, Burke, the Williamses, Armstrong and Winston
were strong and mighty leaders, speaking the patriotic sentiments of the west. The northern counties and the eastern,
as well as the Cape Fear section, also sent their most trusted
and experienced men. Such a gathering of great North
Carolinians, forceful and determined, had never before
assembled to take counsel of their liberties. Although the
venerated form of John Harvey was missed, there were Sam
Johnston, the younger Harveys, the Nashes, Caswell, Howe,
Hewes, Harnett, Hooper, the Joneses, the Moores, the Ashes,
the Sumners, Kenan, Owen, Robeson, Guion, Bryan, Lamb,
Jarvis; and, indeed, all the giants of that generation gathered there to secure and maintain the freedom of their country. The future, full of personal peril, was veiled in obscurity, but their hearts were brave, their course determined, and
they had at least some light from the assembled wisdom of
the Continental Congress.

The conditions

As yet hope of reconciliation was still entertained, and
they were to make a last appeal for their rights as British
subjects, professing allegiance and disclaiming any desire for
separation.

But war was flagrant, and every preparation was to be
made for the inevitable conflict. Proclaimed rebels and
traitors seeking independence, they were to organize resistance to internal and external foes, while still asserting that
they sought only those chartered rights they had inherited
from their fathers as subjects of Great Britain. The old government having passed away, its head a fugitive, and the
Assembly suspended, the congress was to ordain some gov-

1775
August

ernment to preserve peace and order, to administer justic
and to conduct military operations.

The people were divided. Large bodies not conversan
with the causes of the revolt, strangers to the hopes and fear
of America, not in sympathy with North Carolina, had bu
recently located in her borders, while many thousands of th
older inhabitants held aloof, not comprehending that thei
liberties had been invaded and that the hour had struck t
resist British aggression. It was the computation of Gov
ernor Martin that two-thirds of the inhabitants were ye
loyal and would rally to the standard of the king. To seve
these ties it was the part of Congress to demonstrate the im
potency of the British Government and to manifest contemp
for the power and authority of its chief representative
C. R., X, 180 Among their first actions, therefore, was to denounce Gov
ernor Martin's recent proclamation and to order "that th
said paper be burned by the common hangman."

In like manner, to counteract the blandishments and th
threats of Governor Martin, who, through his emissaries
endeavored to persuade the Regulators that they remaine
liable to punishment unless pardoned by the king, and tha
their pardon could only be obtained by taking up arm
against those who were defending American liberty, th
congress at its first opening resolved that every one o
the late insurgents ought to be protected, and that it woul
protect them from any attempt to punish them for engagin
in the late insurrection; and a committee, composed of Mauric
C. R., X,
169 Moore, Caswell, Thomas Person, Kennon, Locke, Rev. M
Pattillo, Hunt, Burke, Penn, and others, was appointed t
confer with those inhabitants of the province who entertaine
any religious or political scruples, and to induce them t
heartily unite with congress for the protection of consti
tutional rights. This committee was to influence not merel
the Regulators, but the Quakers and others who had scruple
preventing their active co-operation. Person alone ha
affiliated with the Regulators, unless, indeed, Memucan Hun
had done so; but Penn, although he had but lately come int
the province, doubtless was a favorite with them; and Judg
Moore had in 1772 held as a judge that they were not liabl
to punishment under the riot act; as "Atticus," had severel

1775
August

denounced Governor Tryon for his "inhuman conduct" in relation to Few and the other Regulators; had visited James Hunter at his home and had sought "to get him into favor again, and had promised to do all that he could for William Butler"; and doubtless had been instrumental in inducing the Assembly to insist on embracing Hunter in the proposed act of oblivion, the contest between the council and the Assembly over his pardon leading to the failure of that measure. Locke, Kennon, Pattillo, and Burke were, in like manner, doubtless influential among those who were disaffected; while the addition of Caswell, Thomas Jones, and George Moore to the committee gave an assurance that the congress was not merely seeking to persuade, but that it would faithfully observe the obligations which it assumed to give every protection in its power to those who would co-operate with it.

C. R., X,
173, 174

A similar committee was appointed to confer with the Scotchmen who had so lately arrived in the province, of whom more than one thousand had reached the Cape Fear within the past few months, and explain to them the nature "of our unhappy controversy"; and still another committee, Judge Moore, Hooper, Caswell, Hewes, and Howe, was appointed to present the controversy in an easy, familiar style to the inhabitants of the province.

These efforts were not without avail. Quickly following the appointment of the committees, there was a conference held with the chiefs of the Regulators. They had some scruples about the oath administered to them by Governor Tryon; but some of them at once signed the test or associa-tion, others from time to time gave in their adherence, and others still agreed to neutrality, so that as early as September 9th apprehensions of danger from them were no longer entertained.

C. R., X,
243

By the middle of October Governor Martin realized the success of these endeavors, and wrote to the Earl of Dartmouth: "According to my information, a committee was appointed by this Provincial Congress to gain over the late insurgents in the western counties, who had heretofore made to me the strongest professions of their loyalty and duty to the king and of their resolution to support his Majesty's

C. R., X, 266

1775
C. R., X,
265, 266

government, as also to treat with the Cherokee Indians; and my intelligence runs that this committee received assurances from the former that they would observe a strict neutrality but I can learn nothing of its success with the Indians."

In like manner, the efforts to influence the Highlanders were attended with good results. Governor Martin continued "I have heard, too, . . . with infinitely greater surprise and concern, that the Scotch Highlanders, on whom I had such firm reliance, have declared themselves for neutrality"; and this result he attributed to Farquard Campbell, "who has been settled from his childhood in this country, is an old member of the Assembly, and has imbibed all the American popular principles and prejudices."

Nor was the pulpit silent. Ministers of the gospel urged their flocks to stand for their rights. In Guilford, David Caldwell, the leading Presbyterian of the province, from the pulpit raised a powerful voice for unity of purpose and co-operation in maintaining American liberty. Succinctly and graphically he portrayed existing conditions and eloquently urged the duties of patriotism.

Caruthers's
Caldwell,
283, 284

"We petitioned," said he, "his Majesty in a most humble manner to intercede with the Parliament on our behalf. Our petitions were rejected, while our grievances were increased by acts still more oppressive, and by schemes still more malicious, till we are reduced to the dreadful alternative either of immediate and unconditional submission or of resistance by force of arms. We have therefore come to that trying period in our history in which it is manifest that the Americans must either stoop under a load of the vilest slavery or resist their imperious and haughty oppressors; but what will follow must be of the utmost importance to every individual of these united colonies. . . . If we act like the sluggard, refuse, from the mere love of ease and self-indulgence, to make the sacrifices and efforts which the circumstances require, or, from cowardice or pusillanimity, shrink from dangers and hardships, we must continue in our present state of bondage and oppression . . . until life itself will become a burden; but if we stand up manfully and unitedly in defence of our rights, appalled by no dangers and shrinking from no toils or privations, we shall do valiantly.

1775
August

Our foes are powerful and determined on conquest; but our cause is good, and in the strength of the Lord, who is mightier than all, we shall prevail. . . . If I could portray to you . . . the results of your conduct in this great crisis in our political destiny; or if I could describe . . . the feelings which you will have of self-approbation, joy, and thankfulness, or of self-reproach, shame, and regret, according to the part you act—whether as men and as patriots, or as cowards and traitors—I should have no difficulty in persuading you to shake off your sloth and stand up manfully in a firm, united, and persevering defence of your liberties. . . . We expect that none of you will be wanting in the discharge of your duty, or prove unworthy of a cause which is so important in itself, and which every patriot and every Christian should value more than wealth, and hold as dear as his life."

Proceedings of the Provincial Congress

Realizing that the American colonies were embarked in a common cause, the congress resolved that the inhabitants of North Carolina should pay their full proportion of the expense of maintaining the army and conducting its operations; and recognizing that the former government had passed away, and that it was necessary to institute a new one for the province, a committee of fifty members was appointed to prepare a plan of government to meet the exigency of the occasion.

Mr. Hooper presented for the consideration of the congress articles of confederation, which had been framed for submission to the several provincial conventions, preliminary to their adoption by the Continental Congress. This instrument conferred on the general congress the power of making war and peace; of entering into alliances; of determining on reconciliation with Great Britain; of settling all disputes between colony and colony, and of making ordinances necessary to the general welfare. The proposed confederacy of the united colonies was to continue until the terms of reconciliation proposed by congress should be agreed to by Great Britain, until reparation should be made for the injury done to Boston and the expenses of the war

C. R., X, 175

1776
Proposed
articles of
confederacy
rejected
repaid, and until all British troops should be withdrawn from America. On the failure of these requirements, the confederacy was to be perpetual. It could not have been expected that these demands would ever be assented to by Great Britain; and thus, in effect, this proposition was to establish a perpetual union or confederacy, on the basis of independence. Such was the measure offered by William Hooper to the convention on August 24, 1775. It was taken into serious consideration.

McRee's
Iredell,
I, 263
Johnston, president of the convention, on September 5th wrote to Iredell: "I was much afraid the plan contained in it would have been adopted; but in a committee of the whole house, though they at first seemed inclined to receive it after hearing the reasons offered against it, it was almost unanimously rejected." By its provisions equality among the colonies was abolished and the smaller ones placed at the mercy of the larger; this doubtless caused its rejection When it was rejected, by the recommendation of Johnston himself, the congress declared that "the present association ought to be further relied on for bringing about a reconciliation, and that a new confederacy ought to be adopted only in case of the last necessity." Through Johnston's wisdom they had escaped a danger; and the delegates were instructed not to consent to any plan of confederation until it should be approved by the Provincial Congress.*

Independence not the object

C. R., X,
202
As yet independence was not the purpose of the patriot leaders, and the members of the congress signed a test professing their allegiance to the king, while declaring themselves bound by the acts of the continental and provincial congresses; and they issued an address to the inhabitants of the British Empire, saying: "We have been told that independence is our object; that we seek to shake off all connection with the parent state. Cruel suggestion! Do not all our professions, all our actions, uniformly contradict this?" They declared, in the presence of the Almighty

*This proposed constitution invested the Continental Congress with power to regulate commerce, post roads, and the currency. The representation was to be one delegate for every 5000 polls, and each delegate was to have a vote.

Being, who "knows our most secret intentions, that it is our most earnest wish and prayer to be restored . . . to the state in which we were placed before the year 1763." "This declaration we hold forth as a testimony of loyalty to our sovereign, and affection to our parent state, and as a sincere earnest of our present and future intentions."

In this the congress but followed the example of the general congress of the colonies at Philadelphia. There was to be no discord in the voice of America in seeking justice of friends and kindred in Great Britain.

The design of Governor Martin to embody the Loyalists was a constant peril, threatening the peace and repose of the province; while the Indians and negroes, aroused by British emissaries, might at any time fall upon the whites. Preparations to meet such contingencies were quickly made. The Continental Congress having agreed to receive a thousand men raised by the province as a part of the continental army, two regiments of continentals, of five hundred men each, were at once organized. Four hundred of them were to be stationed in the district of Wilmington, one hundred of these being located in the vicinity of Fort Johnston, two hundred near Salisbury, two hundred near New Bern, and two hundred near Edenton. Of the first regiment James Moore was chosen colonel, his competitor being John Ashe, who was defeated by a single vote; Francis Nash, lieutenant-colonel; and Thomas Clark, major. Robert Howe, Alexander Martin, and John Patten were the field officers of the second regiment. The captains, lieutenants and ensigns were also appointed, and these at once became active in raising their companies.

Continental battalions

C. R., X, 187

For an additional military force the province was divided into six districts, and a battalion consisting of ten companies of fifty men each was to be raised in each district. These were known as minute men, and as soon as the companies were filled the battalions were to be formed, and they were to be trained at once for fourteen days, and after that were to be mustered every fortnight in their counties. The colonels of the minute men were, for the Edenton district, Edward Vail; for that of Halifax, Nicholas Long; Salisbury, Thomas Wade; Hillsboro, James Thackston; New

Minute men

1775
C. R., X, 197
Bern, Richard Caswell; Wilmington, Alexander Lillington; and these officers were to take rank from the date of their commissions, which was to be determined by the organization of their respective battalions.

These minute men were to be enlisted for only six months, and a bounty was allowed them of twenty-five shillings "to buy a hunting shirt, leggings, or splatter-dashes, and black garters," which constituted their uniform. To promote the organization of the minute men and regulars, congress thought it well to disband the independent companies that had been formed in the various counties. The militia, too, was organized, field officers being appointed for each county.

The plan of government

C. R., X, 208
The plan of temporary government devised provided for town and county committees, elected by the freeholders; and that in each district there should be a Committee of Safety consisting of a president and twelve members, who should sit at least every three months, having a superintending power over the town and county committees, directing the operations of the militia, and censuring and punishing delinquents; and there was to be a Provincial Council of thirteen members, two selected from each district and one by the congress at large; this council to have full power to do all matters and things to defend the colony, but not to alter or suspend any resolution of the congress. The Provincial Council and committees of safety had judicial powers conferred on them and the right to give judgment for all demands not in excess of £20.

C. R., X, 211
It was further ordained that on the third Tuesday in October in every year the freeholders in each county were to choose committeemen and also five deputies to represent them in congress, and that there should be annually held on November 10th a Provincial Congress. Committees of secrecy, intelligence, and observation were to be chosen by the town and county committees, who had power to examine all suspected persons and send them to the district committees of safety.

The courts of oyer and terminer were held for the summer term of 1775, but then ceased.

1775
C. R., X,
216
August

The congress did not interfere with the organization of
he inferior courts, but recommended that the magistrates
ppointed by Governor Martin should qualify and act; how-
ver, it directed that after September 10th no suit should
e begun in any court or before any magistrate without
eave from the county committee. With the assent of the
ocal committees of public safety, judicial proceedings were
o continue, and the county courts were regularly held dur-
ng this chaotic period.

The test

The congress also adopted a test, which was required to
e taken by all delegates to the Provincial Congress; and
ater it was required to be subscribed by all persons holding
ny position of honor or trust; and, still later, by all the
nhabitants generally.*

C. R., X,
212

Hooper, Hewes, and Caswell were thanked for their ser-
ices in the Continental Congress, and were re-elected, and
hey were invested with such powers that all acts done by
hem not inconsistent with instructions should be obligatory
pon every inhabitant of the province; but Caswell and
ohnston being elected treasurers, as they had formerly been
oy the Assembly, Caswell declined to serve as a deputy.
Remaining in the province, besides being treasurer, he became a colonel of minute men. To fill that vacancy, John
Penn, who had come to North Carolina from Virginia about
a year earlier, was chosen. Some dissatisfaction had been
elt originally that the three deputies were from the eastern

---

*[Adopted September 9, 1775, required to be subscribed by all vestry-
men and others holding places of trust.]
We, the subscribers, professing our allegiance to the king and
acknowledging the constitutional executive power of government,
do solemnly profess, testify and declare, that we do absolutely be-
ieve that neither the Parliament of Great Britain, nor any member
or constituent branch thereof, hath a right to impose taxes upon
these colonies, or to regulate the internal police thereof, and that
all attempts by fraud or force to establish and exercise such claims
and powers are violations of the peace and security of the people,
and ought to be resisted to the utmost, and that the people of this
province, singly and collectively, are bound by the acts and resolutions of the continental and provincial congresses, because in both
they are freely represented by persons chosen by themselves; and
we do solemnly and sincerely promise and engage, under the sanction
of virtue, honor, and the sacred love of liberty and our country, to
maintain and support all and every the acts, resolutions and regulations of the said continental and provincial congresses to the utmost
of our power and abilities.

part of the province, and Penn was now taken probably as a western man and as a friend of Thomas Person, both being representatives of Granville County.

To provide means to sustain the new government, it was directed that a sum of $125,000 should be emitted in bills, the standard being the Spanish milled dollar, departing from the British currency of pounds and shillings for palpable reasons; and a tax of two shillings a year on every taxable person was laid, to be collected in 1777 and for nine years thereafter, to pay off this indebtedness; and the congress recommended that all public taxes due should be paid by the people; but, except the county and parish taxes, those laid by the old government to accrue in the future were not to be collected.

The congress took steps to obtain a supply of arms and ammunition, and, realizing the necessities of the situation because of the cessation of importations, it offered bounties for the manufacture of the most important articles. Among the commodities whose production it sought to stimulate were saltpetre, sulphur, and gunpowder, common salt, linen and woollen goods, hollow ironware, pins and needles, and wire for cotton cards and woollen cards; and a considerable bounty was offered for the erection of rolling mills for the production of nails, a furnace for the manufacture of steel and of pig iron, and for a mill making various kinds of paper. Not only were the needs of the army to be supplied, but the necessities of the people were to be provided for.

Congress adjourns

Its business being now well completed, on Sunday, September 10th, at six o'clock in the morning, the congress met in its last session. It had solved the momentous questions of that eventful day. It had established a system of government, and had provided for its perpetuation. It had raised troops for the defence of the province and created a public fund. It had appealed to the mother country for reconciliation, and had drawn to the support of the cause many who had been wavering. With brighter hopes and with greater confidence, and yet not without apprehension, the members now returned to their homes.

At once the many military officers, both continental and of the minute men, whose rank was to be determined by their promptness in the organization of their command, entered with zeal upon the work of securing enlistments. Throughout the province there was the greatest activity. Especially was this so on the lower Cape Fear. John Ashe, so long the military leader of his district, defeated in his aspirations, mortified at his enforced separation from his troops, determined not to be without a command. Governor Martin wrote in October: "It is possible also that the resentment of Mr. John Ashe, occasioned by his disappointment of the chief command of the military establishment formed by the Provincial Congress, will cause some division here, for it seems he and his friends are raising men of their own authority, in opposition to Mr. James Moore, his brother-in-law, who is appointed military chief under the congress."

Mr. George Hooper is quoted as saying "that he could never forget General Ashe's return from the convention of Hillsboro in September, 1775. He was in a state of prodigious excitement. His object was to raise a regiment, and he accomplished it. You cannot imagine what a commotion he stirred up. He kindled an enthusiasm in New Hanover and adjacent counties of which there is no parallel in the traditions of the State. He struck the chords of passion with a master hand. His words roused the soul like the roll of the drum or the roar of artillery at the commencement of an action. Every breast heaved, as if with the sentiment of the Athenian orator, 'Let us away! Let us arm! Let us march against Philip!'" Not only was Ashe's proposed regiment in conflict with Moore's regulars, but also with Lillington's minute men. Their respective friends were all activity. Wearing the legends on their hats, "Who will not follow where Ashe leads?" "Who will not follow where Lillington leads?" they dashed from community to community, from neighborhood to neighborhood, arousing the people and securing enlistments for their corps. At his own charges, Ashe raised a regiment, and for some time maintained it out of his private purse. The final organization of Lillington's battalion was perhaps delayed by this irreg-

Recruiting

C. R., X, 270

Hooper's Memoir of John Ashe, N. C. Univ. Mag., III, 371, (1854)

1775
ular proceeding. Moore was more successful, and soon had his continental regiment fully organized, two companies of which were stationed near Fort Johnston, where they were fired on by the British cruisers in the harbor.

C. R., X,
335, 336
The hostile demonstrations of these ships of war led the Wilmington committee to direct John Slingsby and others to procure necessary vessels and chains to sink in such part of the channel as they thought proper to prevent their ascent up the river.

Martin's
activity
It had been Governor Martin's expectation in July to receive a supply of arms and munitions, and with these he hoped to equip a sufficient force of Highlanders and Regulators not merely to subjugate the province, but also to hold South Carolina and Georgia. Later he realized that the time for

C. R., X,
306–308
that had passed, and, without aid from the British army, he would be unable to carry out his cherished design. At length his plan received the sanction of the ministry, and on September 22d an expedition was arranged to subdue the southern colonies. On November 7th Dartmouth wrote him that seven regiments might be expected to reach the Cape Fear about the time that letter would be received, and that he should lose no time in sending emissaries among the inhabitants with authority for raising and embodying as many men as could be procured, bringing down with them horses and wagons for the use of the army.

Arrival of
Highlanders
In the meantime Highlanders continued to arrive—about the middle of October one hundred and seventy-two, a little later another shipload, and early in December a shipload reached Norfolk, who desired permission, which was given, to pass by land to their destination in Carolina. On the upper Cape Fear Major McDonald, who had recently arrived, under the orders of General Gage, was forming a battalion of Highlanders to be commanded by Colonel McLean; and Allan McDonald and Alexander McLeod,

C. R., X,
325
each having commissions, were enrolling companies. Governor Martin also became more hopeful of aid from the Regulators on learning that many had become indignant with the action of congress at Hillsboro; and he was persuaded that the loyal subjects infinitely outnumbered the

editious throughout all the very populous counties of the west.

1775

In the presence of these threatened dangers, the Provincial Council held its first meeting at the court-house in Johnston County on October 18th. Cornelius Harnett was unanimously elected president, perhaps because it was his section of the province that was in peril, as well as because of his capacity and zealous activity. It took measures to perfect the defence of the province, exercising the high powers with which it was invested. Each district had one vote.

Provincial Council Oct., 1775

C. R., X, 283

The Indians placated

The Cherokee and Creek Indians, who had long been under the direction of a very competent British officer, John Stuart, were being influenced to take sides against the colonists, and the Continental Congress had appointed a commission, one of whom was Willie Jones, to secure their neutrality. In October the Creeks met two of these commissioners at Augusta, and in November Willie Jones and the other commissioners convened at Salisbury and sent a "talk to the beloved red men in Georgia," urging their neutrality and promising the usual gifts which were annually distributed among the Indians—powder, blankets, trinkets, etc., etc.

On the other hand, Stuart and his agent among the Indians, who had first also urged them to neutrality, now began to influence them to active hostility. "I found no argument," said Stuart, "prevail so much among the Indians as telling them that while the present disturbances continued they could not expect to be supplied with ammunition and other necessaries from Carolina and Georgia; and that it would be their own interest to join his Majesty's faithful subjects in restoring government and good order." He therefore recommended that all supplies should for the present be stopped. That, he thought, would determine the savages to engage on the side of the British.

Pursuant to the policy of congress, a supply of Indian goods, embracing some powder, was despatched through upper South Carolina as a present to the Indians. Several years before, during the same period when the Regulators

1775
December

were active in North Carolina, a movement somewhat similar had taken place in that part of South Carolina, society being disorganized by a social disturbance. Courts and lawyers having roused the animosity of the people, they undertook to regulate matters without regard to existing usages. Their chief leader was a man named Scovell, and they were generally known as Scovellites. After they were dispersed they were out of sympathy with the other inhabitants; indeed, there was a wide stretch of unoccupied territory intervening between their habitations and the seacoast counties. Most of them remained loyal to the king. It was among them that David Fanning had found a residence, he becoming, like them, an adherent of the Crown. Their leaders resolved to intercept the powder and goods being conveyed to the Indians under a small escort, and embodying a sufficient force, they seized the pack horses, declaring that the ammunition was being sent to the Indians to enable them to make war upon themselves. At once Major Williamson marched against them to recover the powder, but the Scovellites were too strong for his force, and he was compelled to retreat, taking refuge in a stockade fort at Ninety-six, where they besieged him. The patriot authorities, aroused to the necessities of action, called on their friends in western North Carolina for aid, and early in December Lieutenant-Colonel Alexander Martin, of the Second Continentals, who had in the Salisbury district two companies of continentals, one of the First Regiment, Captain George Davidson, and the other of the Second Regiment, Captain John Armstrong, proposed to march to their assistance. He was joined by 200 men from Rowan under Colonel Rutherford, 300 from Mecklenburg under Colonel Polk, and 100 from Tryon under Colonel Neal. This body of 700 North Carolinians reached General Richardson, of South Carolina, and Colonel Thompson, of the Third South Carolina Regiment, at Saluda River about December 16th, when the Scovellites hastily abandoned their efforts on Ninety-six, gave up the siege and returned to Saluda River. Unaware of the near approach of this new patriot force, they were surprised on December 22d and 400 of them taken prisoners. In the engagement Colonel Polk was wounded. The powder

The
Scovellites

C. R., X,
408

Colonel
Martin
marches to
aid South
Carolina

The Snow
Campaign

C. R., X,
340, 341

Graham's
Graham,
198

which they had seized again fell into the hands of its lawful
owners, and was conveyed to the Indians. The weather during this short but eventful campaign was so inclement and stormy, with such heavy snows, that it was known to history as the "Snow Campaign."

Still earlier than this expedition beyond the limits of the
State was a call from Virginia for aid in repelling British operations in the vicinity of Norfolk, where Lord Dunmore had begun a predatory warfare, burning houses, ravaging plantations and carrying off negroes. By proclamation, he
declared that all indented servants and negroes who would join his Majesty's forces should be free; and several hundred of the inhabitants, many of them negroes, repaired to his standard. Taking possession of Norfolk, Dunmore constructed a fort on the highway from the south for its protection; and Colonel Woodford, in command of the Virginia troops, fortified at Great Bridge, a few miles distant. The district committees of safety in North Carolina had power to call into active service the organized troops of the province. To assist the Virginians, the committee at Halifax hurried Colonel Long with the minute men of that district to Great Bridge, and on November 28th ordered
Major Jethro Sumner to raise what minute men and volunteers he could and follow Colonel Long with the utmost despatch; and Colonel Howe, whose chief command was at New Bern, was directed to lead his continentals also to Norfolk. On December 7th affairs at Great Bridge were reaching a crisis. Colonel Woodford wrote to Governor Henry: "As to the Carolina troops and cannon, they are by no means what I was made to expect; sixty of them are here and one hundred will be here to-morrow; more, it is said, will follow in a few days under Colonel Howe; badly armed, cannon not mounted, no furniture to them."

Two days later Captain Fordyce, commanding a force of British regulars and a detachment of sailors, assaulted the Virginia fortifications. He and many of his officers were killed, and the British were completely routed, with great loss, retreating at once into Norfolk. Colonel Howe arrived after Colonel Woodford had won this great victory. Woodford was not a continental officer, and cheerfully yielded the

Howe
commands
in Virginia

command to Howe, as being of superior rank, perhaps the more cheerfully as they had served together on the Holstein in the French and Indian War. From that time until March Howe continued to direct military operations in lower Virginia; the immediate command of his regiment devolving on Major Patten, Colonel Armstrong being in western North Carolina.

Pressing on after the battle of Great Bridge, Howe drove the British and the Tories from Norfolk and took possession of the town.

On December 30th Captain Bellew, commanding the British ships, notified Colonel Howe that he would not suffer men in arms against their sovereign to appear before his Majesty's ships, and he warned Colonel Howe that his sentinels must not be seen or the women and children might suffer—a plain intimation that he proposed to fire on the town unless the American sentinels should be withdrawn. Howe's reply was that he had given orders to his sentinels not to fire on any boat unless approaching the shore in a hostile manner. But Dunmore's mind was made up. He proposed to destroy Norfolk, even if it involved the slaughter of women and children. Without further warning, about three o'clock on the afternoon of the next day, a cannonade of one hundred pieces opened on the devoted town and continued without interruption until ten o'clock that night. Under cover of their guns, the British landed and set fire to the houses at several places near the water. They landed frequently, but were repulsed in every instance. Once, indeed, they reached the street with several field pieces, but were driven back with considerable loss. In the meantime the conflagration spread with amazing rapidity, and the women and children, seeking to escape, were subjected to the British fire and some of them were killed. For two days the fire raged, and nine-tenths of the town was destroyed before it was extinguished. A midshipman on board the British ship *Otter* thus describes the event: "The detested town of Norfolk is no more! Its destruction happened on New Year's Day. About four o'clock in the afternoon the signal was given from the *Liverpool,* when a dreadful cannonading began from the three ships, which lasted till

C. R., X,
372

Norfolk
burned

C. R., X,
381, 387, 395

Jan. 1, 1776

'twas too hot for the rebels to stand on their wharves. Our boats now landed and set fire to the town in several places. It burned fiercely all night and the next day; nor are the flames yet extinguished; but no more of Norfolk remains than about twelve houses, which escaped the flames."

A month later Colonel Howe, with the concurrence of his officers, visited the Virginia convention, then sitting at Williamsburg, and on his recommendation that body directed that the remaining houses, only twelve in number, should be destroyed. In Colonel Howe's encounters with the British, although his forces were under a long-protracted, heavy cannonade, he lost only five or six men wounded and none killed. It was his good fortune to bear himself so well that notwithstanding local jealousies, he won high applause and received the thanks of the Virginia convention, while gaining merited distinction for himself and his North Carolina troops.

Colonel Howe had with him some six hundred North Carolinians on this duty in Virginia, and the aid given so expeditiously and effectively at the same time against the Scovellites at the south and Dunmore at the north established for North Carolina an enviable reputation throughout America.

Measures for defence

On December 18th the Provincial Council met at the court-house of Johnston County in its second session.

C. R., X, 349

It was now known that the province was to be invaded; and as the inhabitants were not well supplied with arms and ammunition for defence, commissioners were appointed to make and repair guns and to purchase munitions of war; and the delegates in the Continental Congress were directed to send powder, drums, colors and fifes from Philadelphia for the use of the troops.

C. R., X, 355

Waightstill Avery, one of the members, was directed to repair to South Carolina and obtain twenty hundredweight of gunpowder, a supply of which had been received from abroad by that province. Powder and ammunition belonging to the British Government had also been seized in South Carolina, Georgia, and apparently Florida.

1775
C. R., X,
352, 362
December

Because of the necessity to continue importations and protect vessels engaged in such commerce, the council took steps to fit out three armed ships, one at Wilmington, one at New Bern, and one at Edenton, and gentlemen at each of those towns were appointed to charter one or more vessels, which they were to load with commodities and send abroad to procure arms and ammunition for the province. And renewed efforts were made to obtain at home an additional supply of arms and equipments. It was ordered that two battalions of minute men should be embodied in the district of Salisbury, one of them to be under Griffith Rutherford, as colonel, and the other to be commanded by Colonel Thomas Polk. It was also directed that the test adopted by the Provincial Congress should be signed by all the minute men and militiamen, and it was recommended that no person should be allowed any relief against a debtor unless ten days previous to his application he should have subscribed the continental association and the test.

*Importa-
tions*

*Progress of
events*

Early in September the address of the Continental Congress urging the king to point out some way for an accommodation was presented to the ministry by Governor Penn. Three days later Dartmouth replied that to it no answer would be given; while in a speech from the throne it was declared that the protestations of loyalty were meant only to deceive, the rebellious war being carried on for the purpose of establishing an independent empire. When information came of this closing of the door to all hope of accommodation the colonists were profoundly moved. So far there had been no purpose to separate. All that fall the chaplains in Washington's army were still leading their troops in prayer "for the king." In December, James Hogg, who was attending the Continental Congress seeking recognition for Transylvania, wrote that "the famous John and Sam Adams" presented this difficulty: "There seems to be an impropriety in embarrassing our reconciliation with anything new; and the taking under our protection a body of people who have acted in defiance of the king's proclamations will be looked on as a confirmation of that independent spirit with which we are daily reproached." As yet, even those aggressive delegates from Massachusetts were unwilling to give

*Hope of rec-
onciliation*

C. R., X,
373

color to the charge that they favored independence.* To make a reasonable explanation of the resort to arms while professing allegiance, the Whig leaders denounced the efforts to deprive the colonists of their constitutional rights as emanating from a profligate ministry, and stigmatized those who opposed the American cause as "tools of the ministers," and the British troops were known as "ministerial troops." It was sought to emphasize a distinction between the king and his ministry; but, indeed, the king was more determined than Lord North, an amiable man, who still hoped for some accommodation. George III was of an arbitrary disposition. Being intent to free himself from the great Whig leaders, who had governed ever since the house of Hanover came to the throne, he had placed at the head of affairs Lord North, who was a Tory, and the administration at this period was conducted by Tories. The Parliament was subservient, but the people were greatly divided. There were those who opposed the administration for political reasons and others who favored America for industrial and commercial purposes. Men like Horace Walpole considered that the constitution was in danger from the despotism of the king, and that the preservation of British liberty was involved in the struggle of the Americans for their rights as British subjects; the merchants and manufacturers realized that the prosperity of Great Britain required a cessation of the disturbance. About November 1, 1775, Walpole wrote: "The ministers have only provoked and united, not intimidated, wounded or divided, America. At this instant they are not sure that the king has a foot of dominion left on that continent." "It is certain that the campaign has answered none of the expectations of the administration. It seems to be the opinion now that they will think of pacific measures. They have even talked in Parliament of treating. The Parliament grants whatever is asked; and yet a great alteration has happened in the administration. The Duke

1775
The Tory ministry blamed

The Whigs in England

Walpole's Letters, I, 391, 392

*After the event John Adams claimed that he favored independence as early as the summer of 1775. The question in such cases is, when did he really begin by acts and measures to promote the cause? When did he seek to disseminate views favorable to the success of the cause? The above letter indicates that neither of the Adamses was promoting independence early in December, 1775.

of Grafton has changed sides, and was turned out last Friday. Lord Dartmouth has quitted the American province and taken the privy seal. Lord George Germaine is made secretary of state for America, and Lord Weymouth has taken the southern province. The town is impatient to see whether this change of men implies any change of measures. I do not see why it should, for none of the new ministers have ever inclined to the Americans; and I doubt whether the success of the latter will make them have a better disposition toward the present administration. They have felt their strength, and experienced how much less hurt we can do them than we imagined. If they have such ideas of independence as have been imputed to them, and as probably some ambitious men among them may have, we have done nothing to convince them that their plan is impracticable. . . . We must exhaust our men, money, navies and trade. These are the four trifling articles we pay to the old scheme of arbitrary power. When will the kings of England learn how great they may be by the constitution; how sure of ruin if they try to be despotic? Cannot the fate of the Stuarts teach even the house of Hanover to have common sense?"

Tories and Whigs

On December 24th the council resolved that, "Whereas, Governor Martin hath distributed great numbers of Tory pamphlets in the western parts of this province, where the people are not well informed," the delegates in congress be desired to secure the best pamphlets to counteract and frustrate the wicked and diabolical tools of a corrupt ministry. Anterior to this era there had been no political differences among the colonists. The king and the ministers had since 1688 been Whigs and the colonists were in full sympathy with the administration. But when George III broke with the Whigs and formed the first Tory ministry under Lord North, and the measures oppressive to America were devised, those who adhered to the ministry and allied themselves with the Tory party became Tories.

The other inhabitants, being in the opposition, naturally called themselves Whigs, for the Whigs in England violently pposed the administration. Thus these English party names vere, in 1775, applicable in America.

Once introduced they became fixed; and even after inde-endence and separation became the object of the struggle, he revolutionists still called themselves Whigs. Likewise he adherents of the Crown continued to be known as Tories, and the name Tory became a term of odium and reproach, ynonymous with detested enmity to the country: the Tories eing considered traitors and hated as men aiding to de-rive the people of their rights and liberties.

CHAPTER XXVIII

The Provincial Council, 1775-76—*Continued*

Martin prepares to act.—He sends commissions.—The rising.—The Western patriots.—Caswell marches.—At Wilmington.—At Cross Creek.—The Tories embody.—Moore at Rockfish.—McDonald marches.—Moore's Creek.—The battle.—Death of Grady.—The Spoils.—Trouble in Currituck.—The effects of the victory.—In Virginia.—In North Carolina.—Mary Slocumb's ride.—Reports of Caswell and Moore.

Martin prepares to act

1775

C. R., X, 407, 652, 653
Early in December Governor Martin sailed for Charleston, where he was detained a month, returning to the Cape Fear only in January. Doubtless his conferences there strengthened his purpose to embody the Loyalists in the interior. His original design had been to send a British battalion to Cumberland as a nucleus around which the Highlanders and Regulators should centre; but no British force had reached him, although he had been advised that a large expedition was now on the way to the Cape Fear. On his return from South Carolina some of the Loyalists C. R., X, 397, 487-489 of Brunswick County solicited him not to delay longer, representing "that the rebel troops were weak; that one-third of them had not been provided with arms; that they were equally deficient of ammunition, and that the people were sore under their new-fangled government and had a disposition to revolt; and that they would engage in a month's Plans to embody the Loyalists time to raise two or three thousand men." Major McLean had gone into the interior with instructions to ascertain the number of men that might be relied on; and now the anxious governor confided a commission to a confidential messenger, recommended by the Brunswick Loyalists, to establish the concert he proposed and to carry necessary instructions to the people of the more distant counties. At length Major McLean brought gratifying assurances that two or three thousand men, one-half of them well armed, would quickly respond to his call. This organization extended

1776

from Surry County to Brunswick, and the plan promised good hope of success. Again McLean was despatched with powers to proper persons to raise and embody men and with orders to press down to Brunswick by February 15th; and soon came a verbal message "that the Loyalists were in high spirits and very fast collecting; that they assured themselves of being six thousand strong, well furnished with wagons and horses; that they intended to post one thousand at Cross Creek, and with the rest would take possession of Wilmington by February 25th at farthest." By these emissaries commissions were conveyed to the McDonalds and other Scotch leaders in Cumberland and Anson; to John Pyle, of the county of Chatham; to William Fields, James Hunter, Saymore York, and others, of Guilford; Samuel Bryan and others, of Rowan; Gideon Wright and James Glyn, of Surry; Paul Barringer,* of Mecklenburg; Michael Holt, of Orange; and Philemon Hawkins, of Bute.* These and their associates were to erect the king's standard and array his Majesty's faithful subjects in their respective counties, forming them into companies of fifty men each, and with authority to commission the company officers. The preliminary arrangements having been secretly made, the Loyalists soon were all astir.

The Tory leaders

C. R., X, 441

Now the mission of Donald McDonald and Alexander McLeod, who had reached New Bern the previous June, became known. The first had an appointment as brigadier-general and the latter as colonel in the British army, and they had been sent by General Gage to organize not merely an insurrectionary force, but a division of Loyalists in the interior of North Carolina for service in any part of America. At this crisis General McDonald took the chief command, by virtue of his commission. Allan McDonald, the husband of Flora, was appointed by Governor Martin to a subordinate position, but the highest in his gift. He was a man of great influence and high station among his countrymen. As Boswell saw him on his native heath, just prior to his departure for America, he was the *beau ideal* of a Highland chieftain—of graceful mien and manly looks;

---

*Barringer and Hawkins did not accept these commissions, but were Whigs. Holt and Hunter later took the oath.

1776

Graham's
British
Invasion,
115

"he had his tartan plaid thrown about him, a large blue bonnet, with a knot of blue ribbons, . . . and brown coat, . . . and tartan waistcoat with gold buttons, . . . a bluish filibeg, and tartan hose; . . . jet black hair tied behind; . . . a large, stately man, with a steady, sensible countenance," then near fifty years of age; a man, indeed, who might well have swayed his countrymen to any enterprise.

Flora
McDonald

His wife, who beyond her romantic career had also a presence both notable and attractive, vied with her husband in manifestations of enthusiasm and devoted loyalty. She accompanied McDonald on horseback in arousing the Scotch to action, visiting the camp and exerting all of her persuasive powers in rallying the people to the standard.

Ibid., 111

The entire territory between the Cape Fear and Haw on the east and the waters of the Yadkin on the west, inhabited largely by the Highlanders and Regulators, was permeated by loyal influences, and a close association existed between the chieftains of the Scotchmen and the leaders of those whom Governor Martin distinguished as "the country people." Both responded with alacrity to the call of the governor, and there was general co-operation throughout

C. R., X,
594 *et seq.*
The rising

that entire region. The Tories of Bladen and Surry and Guilford as well as the Highlanders of Cumberland and Anson prepared for the march and were organized into companies by their local officers.

C. R., X,
443

At length, on February 5th, there having been a conference of the leaders, Donald McDonald issued his manifesto as the commanding general, inviting all to repair to his Majesty's royal standard to be erected at Cross Creek.

The movement then began. Secret at its inception, it now was open, and was at once discovered by vigilant Whigs. Messengers were immediately despatched to give warning to

C. R., X,
440

the patriot leaders. It was quickly known in Salisbury, where the district Committee of Safety met on February 6th and issued orders to the county committees to embody and send forward their minute men and militia.

The western patriots act

The committee of Rowan, meeting on the same day, urged the disaffected in the forks of the Yadkin to peace, now

t this time, "when the friends of American liberty in these 1776
C. R., X,
434
outhern colonies are determined, by the assistance of
almighty God, at the hazard of their lives and fortunes, to
quell an insurrection of the blackest nature, fomented and
supported by the arts of wicked and abandoned men in the
very bosom of this country"; and the committee "appointed
Monday, February 14th, as a day of public fasting, humilia- February
tion and prayer in this country, and recommended that it be
religiously observed."

Three days later the Tryon committee hastily convened, C. R., X
440
and, pursuant to the directions of the district committee,
resolved that each captain should detail one-third of the
effective men in his district and march to suppress the insurrection. In every part of the province the same zeal was
manifested. There was no hesitation. The action of the
Whigs was quick and determined. At the west they collected
at Charlotte, Salisbury, and Hillsboro.

Thomas Person wrote from Hillsboro on February 12th, C. R., X,
450
saying: "Things move very well in this place. The advocates for liberty seem very numerous, and by what we hear,
their enemies are likely to prove but few in number. In
short, we hear that they are mostly dispersed up ahead. . . .
'Tis said that the Scotch in Cumberland are making head.
. . . The forces will move from here, 'tis thought, to-morrow
for Chatham County, toward Cross Creek."

The Loyalists in Surry appear to have been speedily dispersed by the active Whigs of that county. In Guilford,
Colonel James Martin assembled the Whigs at the "Cross
Roads," but the Tories resolutely pressed on. A company Captain
Dent killed
of which Samuel Devinny, one of the former Regulators, was
the head, being opposed by Captain Dent, killed him. James
Lowe and Robert Adams were particularly charged with
firing the fatal shots. It thus appears that Captain Dent C. R., X,
560, 599
was the first North Carolinian to fall in the contest.

An express carrying intelligence that the Loyalists were The Whigs
in motion
embodying, and had on the 5th begun to march to Cross
Creek, was received by the district Committee of Safety of
New Bern on the 10th. The committee immediately directed C. R., X,
444
Colonel Caswell to march with his minute men to suppress
the insurrection, and the colonels of Dobbs, Johnston, Pitt,

1776
February
and Craven were ordered to raise the militia of those counties and join Caswell. Similarly, the patriot forces in Mecklenburg and Rowan, in Granville and Bute, in the Hillsboro district and on the Cape Fear, were put in rapid motion. The militia and minute men of Surry, Guilford, Orange, and Chatham, under Colonel Thackston, also hurried to the scene of operations.

C. R., X,
465 *et seq.*
At
Wilmington
On the 9th the express conveying the intelligence of the insurrection reached Wilmington. There the greatest activity prevailed. All vied in enthusiastic ardor. Colonel Moore issued orders to prepare for marching against the insurgents. The artillery was to be equipped, the companies armed, wagons supplied for transporting the provisions. For eighty hours there was severe, unremitting service, night and day, making preparations. At length, being ready, Colonel Moore, with his regulars and artillery, moved toward Cross Creek, being joined on his route by the Bladen militia. Four days later he was followed by the two companies of minute men of New Hanover under Colonel Lillington and Colonel Ashe's independent rangers, while Colonel Purviance remained with his militia for the defence of the town. On the 14th the *Cruizer* sloop-of-war with a tender passed Brunswick, and, fearing an attack, many inhabitants of Wilmington moved out, carrying the women and children, and breastworks were thrown up on the principal streets and wharves and on the hills above and below the town. Quickly there came Captain Clinton's company of minute men from Duplin, a minute company from Onslow, and a part of the militia from Onslow under Colonel Cray, and fifty men from Brunswick under Major Quince. These all assisted in completing the breastworks, mounting the swivels and preparing fire rafts. The *Cruizer,* however, made no attack on the town, but tried to pass up the Clarendon River into the Northwest, with the intention of meeting the Loyalists on their way down and protecting their provision boats from Cross Creek.

The attempt, however, was abortive. Riflemen on shore attacked the men from the *Cruizer* whenever they landed, and the water not being sufficient for the vessel to pass, she again fell below the island.

At Cross Creek

Cross Creek had for months been greatly disturbed. There a few sterling Whigs lived in the very midst of the Tory element. In the early stages of the movement Robert Rowan had formed an independent company, and patriotically sought to determine the action of the community. But there the Tory leaders held their meetings and resolved upon their course. The first rendezvous was appointed at **Cross Hill** Cross Hill, near Carthage, in Moore County, on February 5th; and thence the companies moved to Campbellton. Colonel Thomas Rutherford, who at the previous congress had been chosen colonel of the county, proved unfaithful, and gave in his adherence to the royal cause. He called for a general muster on the 12th. Many, however, would not obey. To arouse them, on the next day he issued a flaming **C. R., X,** manifesto, entreating, beseeching, and commanding the **429, 452, 491** people to join the king's army. On the 16th the converging **The royal standard erected** columns began to arrive, and Peter Hay bore the royal standard from Campbellton to Cross Creek, where it was formally erected. Now regiments came in from Anson, Chatham, Guilford, and Bladen, and companies from Orange and Rowan and other communities. The entire number of Loyalists then assembling at Cross Creek was variously estimated at between thirty-five hundred and five thousand men. Colonel Cotton, of Anson, and other leaders asserted that there would be five thousand of the Regulators in addition to the Highlanders. But it had been given out that Governor Martin was at Campbellton with a thousand British regulars to receive them, and this report had given an impetus to the movement. On approaching their encampment the state- **The** ment was found to be without foundation, and large num- **Regulators withdraw** bers abandoned the cause. Deceived in one matter, the Regulators lost confidence in all other representations made by their leaders, and hundreds retired.

General McDonald, who had fought at Culloden and at Bunker Hill, was, however, resolute, and, notwithstanding this defection, marshalled his forces, preparing to take up his route to the seacoast. There were two main roads, one on the south of the river to Brunswick and the other crossing Corbett's Ferry on the Black and leading to Wilmington.

McDonald moved forward some four miles on the former and rested, awaiting developments. On reaching the vicinity, Colonel Moore, understanding that the Loyalists would proceed by the former, took post at Rockfish Creek, four miles below McDonald's camp, and held that pass. There he was quickly joined by Rowan and sixty Whigs from Cross Creek, and later was reinforced by Lillington and Ashe and by Colonel Kenan with the Duplin militia, increasing his numbers to fifteen hundred. In the meanwhile Colonel Thackston and Colonel Martin were rapidly approaching from the west with still larger reinforcements. On February 19th General McDonald addressed a communication to Moore enclosing the governor's proclamation, offering free pardon and indemnity for all past transgressions if the colonel and his officers would lay down their arms and take the oath of allegiance, "otherwise he should consider them as traitors and take necessary steps to conquer and subdue them." Moore replied that he would give a more particular answer the next day, when he would perhaps have an opportunity of consulting with Colonel Martin,* then in the neighborhood. It appears that he sought to prolong the correspondence that Martin and Thackston might arrive. On the night of the 20th, the defection of the Loyalists continuing—indeed, two companies of Cotton's regiment deserted in a body and McDonald having information of Caswell's near approach from the east, the astute British general resolved to wait no longer, and under cover of darkness he crossed the river and took the upper road for Wilmington. At best he would have only Caswell to contend with, and he thought to easily overcome that detachment. Moore, on learning of the movement, directed Thackston and Martin to take possession of Cross Creek, and ordered Caswell to return and hold Corbett's Ferry over the Black, while Lillington and Ashe were hurried by a forced march to reinforce Caswell if possible, but if not, to take possession of Moore's Creek Bridge on the same road, but nearer to Wilmington. In the meantime, as it was apprehended that McDonald might attempt to pass through

*Lieutenant-Colonel Alexander Martin, of the Regulars. Lieutenant-Colonel James Martin, of the militia, was with Thackston.

Duplin, pursuing a route still farther to the eastward, the bridges in that county were partly demolished, Colonel Cray holding back Salter's company for that duty, and the inhabitants being ready to destroy the others if necessary to obstruct the march of the Tories. At Wilmington, Colonel Purviance was all activity, and to arrest their boats, should they descend the river, he threw a boom across the stream at Mount Misery, four miles above the town, and stationed one hundred and twenty men there, while with another detachment he held the pass of Heron's Bridge, ten miles out on the northeast branch. Having despatched his orders to intercept the progress of the Tory column, Moore hastened to Elizabethtown, hoping to strike McDonald on his route to Corbett's Ferry or to fall in his rear and surround him. McDonald was a very competent commander, resourceful, and determined. Failing to overtake Caswell, he departed from the regular road, raised a flat that had been sunk in Black River some five miles above Corbett's Ferry, quickly erected a bridge and passed that stream. Because of this movement, Moore ordered Caswell to retire to Moore's Creek, and himself hurried toward that point.

The battle of Moore's Creek Bridge

Lillington, unable to make a junction with Caswell, fell down the river in boats, and took post at Moore's Creek Bridge, and threw up some entrenchments near by; but later he abandoned that position, moved farther back, and erected other entrenchments, which he strengthened with a few pieces of light artillery. Toward the evening of February 26th Caswell also arrived at the bridge, and after he had crossed it the planks were removed. He placed his troops in a position farther off than that occupied by Lillington, who remained on the ground where he had entrenched. The Highlanders and some two hundred Regulators reached the same vicinity that night. General McDonald lay ill at a farmer's house, and in camp a council was held to determine whether an assault should be made or a detour attempted. McLeod, a trained soldier, who had left his bride (a daughter of Flora McDonald) at the altar in haste to do duty for his king, doubted; McLean, adventurous, spirited, a

Caswell's Report

Uni. Mag., II, 305 (1853)

veritable "spitfire," emphatically demanded courageous
action. "Well," exclaimed McLeod, as he closed the council

Feb. 27, 1776 "at dawn to-morrow we will prove who is the coward." In
the early morning their advance crossed the stream, and
observing the first entrenchments unoccupied, supposed the
road was open. Their commander, McLeod, loudly calling
on them to follow, dashed forward; but the artillery and
riflemen at once opened a murderous fire, and the unexpected
and destructive volley drove back the head of the column,
thirty falling on the ground and a number of others into
the stream. The gallant McLeod himself was pierced by
twenty balls. McLean survived, in after life sedate, sad-
dened by the unhappy fate of the bridegroom of an hour.

The victory A detachment was now thrown by Caswell, the commanding
officer, across the creek, and it resolutely attacked the disordered Tories, who, having lost their leaders, soon gave
way and fled. In a few moments the battle was over. A
great victory was won. The insurrection was suppressed
by one sharp blow and the peril that threatened the province
was averted. Happily, the patriot force escaped with but
little loss. Two men were wounded, one of them, however,
to the death—John Grady, of Duplin, the first North Carolinian recorded in history to yield his life on a contested
battlefield in the war for independence.

The spoils Routed, the Highlanders quickly dispersed, leaving their
general, then quite ill, in the hands of his enemies. Eight
hundred and fifty of the insurgents were captured, among
them many of their officers. Besides there fell into the
possession of the Whigs three hundred and fifty guns and
shot bags, one hundred and fifty swords and dirks, fifteen
hundred excellent rifles, two medicine chests, fresh from

C. R., X, England, one of them valued at £300 sterling; a box of
485, 559, 560, guineas, found secreted in a stable at Cross Creek, reported
595 to be worth £15,000 sterling, and thirteen wagons with their
horses—a fortunate addition to the slender supplies of the
provincial army. For some days detachments of the Whig
troops were occupied in scouring the country, arresting the
Loyalists and disarming them. Among those taken were
Colonel John Pyle, four of the Fields family, James Hunter,
Saymore York, Rev. George Micklejohn, Colonel Ruther-

ford, of Cumberland, and many of the leaders of the Regulators, as well as the McDonalds and other chiefs of the Highlanders.

The council in session

President Harnett, in view of the insurrection, had convened the Provincial Council at New Bern on February 27th, and the body was in session when information was received of the death blow given to the movement of the Loyalists. Colonel Caswell, being senior in rank to Colonel Lillington, despatched information of his victory, and Colonel Moore made a detailed report to President Harnett of the entire campaign. At once the council adopted resolutions returning thanks "to Colonel James Moore and all the brave officers and soldiers of every denomination for their late very important services rendered their country in effectually suppressing the late daring and dangerous insurrection of the Highlanders and Regulators." Equally good accounts being received of Howe's fine conduct in Virginia, the council, with just pride in the glorious achievements of North Carolinians, rendered thanks "in the fullest and most honorable terms to Colonel Howe and all the brave officers and soldiers under his command for their spirited conduct, having acquitted themselves greatly to the honor and good of their country." But in that hour of rejoicing there was also need for action. The scattered insurgents were to be apprehended, and all suspected of Toryism were required to take an oath that they would not under any pretence whatever oppose the measures of the continental or provincial congresses.

Almost simultaneously with the rising on the Cape Fear, disaffection manifested itself in Currituck, doubtless stimulated by the efforts of Governor Dunmore in Virginia. The militia of Bertie, Martin and some other counties were marched to suppress it; and the council on March 2d returned the warmest thanks to Colonel William Williams and the other gentlemen, officers, and soldiers from the counties of Martin and Bertie for their readiness and spirited conduct in marching against the enemies of their country; and the congress later made a considerable appropriation to

C. R., X, 469

Moore and Howe thanked

C. R., X, 472, 571

Rising in Currituck

1776

pay the militia of Bute, led by Colonel Hawkins against the insurgents during the "late Currituck expedition."

It being known that a British army was on its way to the South, the Continental Congress had recommended the Provincial Council to confer with the authorities of Virginia and of South Carolina to devise means of defence; and Sam Johnston, Thomas Jones, and Thomas Person were directed to go to Virginia, and Abner Nash and John Kinchen to Charleston, to consult on measures for the security of these colonies. As additional troops would certainly be needed, Colonel Polk and Major Phifer were directed to recruit seven hundred and fifty men to form a new continental regiment; and congress was called to meet at Halifax on April 2d.

The effects of the victory

Governor Martin was greatly disconcerted by this ending of the movement from which he had hoped so much; but he was not discouraged, and attributed the falling off of the country people from the enterprise to their disappointment in finding that a deception had been practised on them by the representation that he himself with one thousand regulars was at Cross Creek. He still expected that if such a force were to penetrate into the interior thousands of Loyalists would flock to his standard, and he represented to the ministry "that the little check the Loyalists have received will not have any extensive ill consequences. All is recoverable by a body of troops penetrating into the country."

And so, indeed, it was. The Loyalists, though disheartened, generally remained faithful to the Crown. Disarmed and deprived of their leaders, many of whom had been captured and confined, they had no heart to undertake any new movement, but thousands of them continued during the long years of the struggle unfriendly to the American cause and devoted adherents of Great Britain.

Frothingham, Rise of the Republic, 503

On the Whigs the victory had a potent effect. It animated them with hope, established confidence in their prowess, and added fuel to the fires of patriotism. Their spirit ran high. "You never knew the like in your life for true patriotism," wrote a North Carolinian to his correspondent in Philadel-

.hia, and the newspapers teemed with the details of the
.rilliant victory. Another Carolinian, writing to the
Remembrancer, said:

It is inconceivable to imagine what joy this event has diffused
through this province; the importance of which is heightened by
Clinton and Lord William Campbell's being now in Cape Fear. . . .
How amazingly mortified must they prove in finding that . . . in
.ss than fifteen days [we] could turn out more than ten thousand
independent gentlemen volunteers. . . . Since I was born I never
heard of so universal an ardor for fighting prevailing, and so per-
ect a union among all degrees of men. . . . I think the province
will and ought to call for hostages from the Regulators and High-
anders to be safely kept in some other province, beyond the possi-
ility of a rescue, during the present commotions.

The spirit of the Whigs

S. R., XI, 286, 287

Independence

Ten months had passed since the clash of arms at Lexing-
on had roused the passion of the patriots, and now Moore's
Creek brought joy throughout the colonies.

The ease with which a well-devised and widely extended
insurrection had been quelled excited an ardor that stirred
the Revolutionists from the seaboard to the mountains. The
iron had entered into their souls in the time of peril, and
now in the exultation and rejoicing there was mingled a
higher resolve, and suddenly the nature of the contest
changed. Theretofore reconciliation had been desired; now,
.s if by magic, the watchword became independence, and
the thoughts and aspirations of the people were centred on
entire and final separation. No longer as British subjects,
but as American freemen, they dared the hazard of the
struggle.

The change in purpose

Similar experiences, perhaps, worked a like result in Virginia. In April a great change was noted in that province.
Whereas in March the Virginians were not favorable to
independence, in April they were almost unanimous for it.
A letter written from Halifax about the middle of April,
which may be attributed to Hooper, who had just arrived
rom Philadelphia, says:

Frothing-ham, Rise of the Republic, 503

I arrived here after a tedious journey. As I came through Vir-
inia, I found the inhabitants desirous to be independent from
.ritain. However, they were willing to submit their opinion on the

1776

N. C. Uni.
Mag., II,
157,158(1853)

subject to whatever the general congress should determine. *Nort.
Carolina by far exceeds them,* occasioned by the great fatigue
trouble and danger the people here have undergone for some time
past. Gentlemen of the first fortune in the province have marched
as common soldiers, and, to encourage and give spirit to the men
have footed it the whole time. Lord Cornwallis with seven regiment
is expected to visit us every day. Clinton is now in Cape Fear with
Governor Martin, who has about forty sail of vessels, armed and un
armed, waiting his arrival. The Highlanders and Regulators are
not to be trusted. Governor Martin has coaxed a number of slave
to leave their masters in the lower parts; everything base an
wicked is practised by him. These things have wholly change
the temper and disposition of the inhabitants, that are friends t
liberty. All regard or fondness for the king or nation of Britain i
gone; a total separation is what they want. Independence is th
word most used. They ask if it is possible that any colony, afte
what has passed, can wish for a reconciliation. The Conventio
have tried to get the opinion of the people at large. I am told tha
in many counties there is not one dissenting voice.*

Mary Slocumb's ride

Mrs. Ellet's
Women of
Am. Rev.,
II, 361

There is recorded a picturesque narrative that illustrate
the furor which pervaded the entire Whig section when th
fathers, husbands, and brothers of the families hurried ou
to meet the Tories in February, 1776. War had never be
fore visited that section, but now was at their very doors
Its unknown terrors inflamed the imagination and disturbe
every household. Anxiety pervaded every heart. The men
courageously marched to the front, the women suffere
dreadful solicitude. Mrs. Mary Slocumb, the wife o
Captain Ezekiel Slocumb, gave this account of the experi
ence that befell her. Their residence was on Neuse River
in what is now Wayne County: "The men all left on Sunda
morning. More than eighty went from this house with m
husband. . . . They got off in high spirits, every man step
ping high and light. And I slept soundly and quietly tha
night, and worked hard all the next day; but I kept thinkin
where they had got to—how far, where, and how man
Regulators and Tories they would meet; and I could no
keep myself from the study. I went to bed at the usua

*The name of the writer of this letter is not stated, but fror
internal evidence the author attributes it, without doubt, to Hooper.

me. . . . As I lay—whether waking or sleeping I know
ot—I had a dream, yet it was not all a dream. I saw dis-
nctly a body wrapped in my husband's guard cloak, bloody,
ead, and others dead and wounded on the ground. . . . I
aw them plainly and distinctly. I uttered a cry and sprang
o my feet on the floor; and so strong was the impression on
ay mind that I rushed in the direction the vision appeared.
. . The fire in the room gave little light, and I gazed in
very direction to catch another glimpse of the scene. . . .
f ever I felt fear it was at that moment. Seated on the bed,
reflected . . . and said aloud, 'I must go to him.' . . . I
vent to the stable, saddled my mare—as fleet and easy a nag
s ever travelled—and in one minute we were tearing down
he road at full speed. . . . I knew the general route our
ttle army expected to take, and had followed them without
iesitation." All night long she rode through the piney for-
sts of Duplin and New Hanover counties. Then continuing,
he said: "About sunrise I came upon a group of women
nd children standing and sitting by the roadside, each one
of them showing the same anxiety of mind I felt. . . .
Again was I skimming over the ground through a country
hinly settled, and very poor and swampy, . . . when I
eard a sound like thunder, which I knew must be cannon.
t was the first time I ever heard a cannon. I stopped still,
vhen presently the cannon thundered again. The battle
vas then fighting. . . . I could hear muskets; I could hear
ifles; I could hear shouting. I spoke to my mare, and
lashed on in the direction of the firing and the shouts, now
ouder than ever. . . . A few yards from the road, under a
cluster of trees, were lying perhaps twenty men. They were
che wounded. I knew the spot, the very trees, and the position of the men I knew as if I had seen it a thousand times.
I had seen it all night. I saw all at once; but in an instant
my whole soul was centred in one spot, for there, wrapped
in his bloody guard cloak, was my husband's body! How
I passed the few yards from my saddle to the place I never
knew. I remember uncovering his head and seeing a face
clotted with gore from a dreadful wound across the temple.
I put my hand on the bloody face; 'twas warm, and an unknown voice begged for water . . . it was Frank Cogdell.

. . . Just then I looked up, and my husband, as bloody as
butcher and as muddy as a ditcher, stood before me."
is said that Slocumb's company was of the detachment tha
forded the creek and, penetrating the swamp, made th
furious charge on the Tory rear that decided the fate o
the day.

Colonel Caswell's report to President Harnett:

CAMP AT LONG CREEK, Feb. 29, 1776.

SIR: I have the pleasure to acquaint you that we had an engageme
with the Tories, at Widow Moore's Creek Bridge,* on the 27th cu
rent. Our army was about one thousand strong, consisting of th
New Bern battalion of minute men, the militia from Craven, Joh
ston, Dobbs and Wake, and a detachment of the Wilmington battalic
of minute men, which we found encamped at Moore's Creek th
night before the battle, under the command of Colonel Lillingto
The Tories, by common report, were 3000; but General McDonal
whom we have a prisoner, says there were about fifteen or sixtee

Caswell,
the victor

hundred. He was unwell that day, and not in the battle. . .
The Tories were totally put to the route, and will certainly dispers
Colonel Moore arrived at our camp a few hours after the engageme
was over. His troops came up that evening, and are now encampe
on the ground where the battle was fought. And Colonel Marti
is at or near Cross Creek, with a large body of men. Those, I pre
sume, will be sufficient effectually to put a stop to any attempt t
embody again. I therefore, with Colonel Moore's consent, am re
turning to New Bern with the troops under my command, where
hope to receive your orders to dismiss them. There I intend carry
ing the general.† If the council should rise before my arrival, b
pleased to give order in what manner he shall be disposed of. Ou
officers and men behaved with the spirit and intrepidity becomin
freemen, contending for their dearest privileges. RICHARD CASWELL

Report of Colonel Moore to President Harnett:

WILMINGTON, March 2, 1776.

SIR: On the earliest intelligence that the Tories were collecting an
embodying at Cross Creek, which I received on February 9th, I pro

*"Widow Moore's," on Black River, was a well-known plantatio
as early as 1737. The line dividing the Welsh Tract from Rocky
Point began on Black River at "Widow Moore's." From there th
Welsh Tract district extended to the bounds of the precinct o
county. It was so called, apparently, because laid off by the Evanses
for a settlement of Welshmen. (Records of New Hanover, A.D
1737.)
†General McDonald.

eeded to take possession of Rockfish Bridge, within seven miles of Cross Creek, which I considered as an important post. This I effected on the 15th with my own regiment, five pieces of artillery, and a part of the Bladen militia; but as our numbers were by no means equal to that of the Tories, I thought it most advisable to entrench and fortify that pass, and wait for a re-enforcement. By the 19th was joined by Colonel Lillington with 150 of the Wilmington minute men, Colonel Kenan with 200 of the Duplin militia, and Colonel Ashe with about one hundred of the volunteer independent rangers, making our numbers, then, in the whole about eleven hundred; and from the best information I was able to procure the Tory army under command of General McDonald amounted to about fourteen or fifteen hundred. On the 20th they marched within four miles of us, and sent in by a flag of truce the governor's proclamation, a manifesto and letter from the general, copies of which, together with another letter and my answers, you have enclosed. I then waited only until Colonel Martin and Colonel Thackston, who I had certain intelligence were on their march, should get near enough to cut off their retreat, and then determined to avail myself of the first favorable opportunity of attacking them. However, conrary to my expectations, I learned on the 21st that they had the night before, and that morning, crossed the Northwest river at Campbellton with the whole army, sunk and destroyed all the boats, and taken their route the most direct way to Negro-head Point.* I then despatched an express to Colonel Caswell, who was on his march to join us with about eight hundred men, and directed him to return and take possession of Corbett's Ferry over Black River, and by every means to obstruct, harass and distress them in their march. At the same time I directed Colonel Martin and Colonel Thackston to take possession of Cross Creek, in order to prevent their return that way. Colonel Lillington and Colonel Ashe I ordered by a forced march to endeavor if possible to re-enforce Colonel Caswell; but if that could not be effected to take possession of Moore's Creek Bridge, while I proceeded back with the remainder of our army to cross the Northwest at Elizabethtown, so as either to meet them on their way to Corbett's Ferry, or fall in their rear and surround them there. On the 23d I crossed the river at Elizabethtown, where I was compelled to wait for a supply of provisions until the 24th at night, having learned that Colonel Caswell was almost entirely without. Just when I was prepared to march, I received an express from Colonel Caswell, informing me that the Tories had raised a flat which had been sunk in Black River, about

*The point opposite Wilmington between the two branches of the Cape Fear River.

five miles above him, and by erecting a bridge had passed it wit
the whole army. I then determined as a last expedient to procee
immediately in boats down the Northwest River to Dollerson's Land
ing, about sixty miles, and to take possession of Moore's Cree
Bridge, about ten miles from thence; at the same time acquaintin
Colonel Caswell of my intentions, and recommending to him t
retreat to Moore's Creek Bridge if possible, but if not to follow o

Moore's
campaign

in their rear. The next day by four o'clock we arrived at Dollerson
Landing, but as we could not possibly march that night, for th
want of horses for the artillery, I despatched an express to Moore
Creek Bridge to learn the situation of affairs there, and was in
formed that Colonel Lillington, who had the day before taken hi
stand at the bridge, was that afternoon reënforced by Colonel Cas
well, and that they had raised a small breastwork and destroyed
part of the bridge.

The next morning, the 27th, at break of day, an alarm gun wa
fired, immediately after which, scarce allowing our people a mo
ment to prepare, the Tory army, with Captain McLeod at the head
made their attack on Colonel Caswell and Colonel Lillington, an
finding a small entrenchment next the bridge, on our side, empty
concluded that our people had abandoned their post, and in the mos
furious manner advanced within thirty paces of our breastwork an
artillery, where they met a very proper reception. Captain McLeo
and Captain Campbell fell within a few paces of the breastwork
the former of whom received upward of twenty balls in his body
and in a very few minutes their whole army was put to flight, an
most shamefully abandoned their general, who was next day take
prisoner. The loss of the enemy in this action from the best ac
counts we have been able to learn, is about thirty killed an
wounded, but as numbers of them must have fallen into the creek
besides many more that were carried off, I suppose their loss ma
be estimated at about fifty. We had only two wounded, one o
whom died this day. . . .

In order to avoid as much as possible the heavy expense unavoid
ably incurred by this expedition, I sometime ago directed Colone
Martin to disband all the troops under his command, except on
thousand, including the regulars, and with those to secure the per
sons and estates of the insurgents, subject to your further orders
and then to proceed to this place, unless otherwise directed. However, as I do not think the service just now requires such a number
of men in arms, I shall immediately direct them to disband all except the regulars, and with those to remain in and about Cross
Creek until further orders, . . . etc.

JAMES MOORE.

THE SIXTH EPOCH—1775-83
THE WAR FOR INDEPENDENCE

CHAPTER XXIX

The Provincial Council, 1775-76—*Continued*

The Provincial Congress.—The spirit of independence.—In the Continental Congress.—At Halifax.—The committee.—The undaunted spirit to declare independence.—The delegates instructed. —North Carolina leads the way.—The captured Tories.—The drums and colors.—War measures.—On the water.—The Tories. —Four new battalions.—For defence of Cape Fear.—Militia drafts.—Civil affairs.—The members of the congress.

The Provincial Congress

1776

Called to meet on April 2d, it was not until Thursday, the 4th, that a majority of the members of the congress assembled at Halifax. Seldom has a body met under similar circumstances. April, C. R., X, 499 The insurrection of the Highlanders and Regulators and the movement of the Tories in many parts of the State were in themselves causes of inquietude. It The situation was evident that in many counties, indeed, in nearly every community, there was a considerable element of disaffected persons not only unwilling to sustain the revolutionary movement but so far attached to the royal cause as to take up arms against their neighbors. Besides, the province stood in the shadow of a great peril. It was well known that a large British force was on its way to the Cape Fear and had been detained only by protracted storms, and its arrival was now daily expected. Dunmore, from the Chesapeake, was also sending expeditions along the coast to harass the inhabitants, capture vessels, and interrupt commerce. Within and without there was cause for foreboding. The jail at Halifax was filled with officers of the insurgent force and promoters of the insurrection, of whom some disposition had to be made to render them harmless, while policy and

1776

wise statesmanship required that a conciliatory course should be pursued reconciling the Loyalists at least to an acquiescence in the measures of the congress. The period for which the minute men had been enrolled was expiring, and the great need for additional troops, for arms, ammunition and equipments was a cause of anxious solicitude, while the province was absolutely without funds. The condition of affairs, too, seemed to demand a more efficient system of government, one that could direct military operations and conduct the civil administration with more despatch than the temporary arrangement that had been adopted by the previous convention. Such a pressure of important matters demanding immediate consideration and prompt action had never before been experienced by North Carolina statesmen. But the courage of the congress rose equal to the occasion, and with brave hearts the patriots addressed themselves to devising measures required by the exigency of their novel situation.

The spirit of independence

Not only were they strengthened by their overwhelming and glorious victory, but now they were animated by the spirit of independence. In this they were unanimous. Sam Johnston, the wise, prudent, and cautious, the counsellor and guide, was again chosen president without dissent, and he joyfully wrote at once to his brother: "All our people here are up for independence." A fortnight later, when Hooper and Penn came from Philadelphia, they learned that "in many counties there was not a dissenting voice."

McRee's
Iredell, I,
275

The Continental Congress and the people of the other provinces were dilatory, dallying with a delusive hope of reconciliation. Early in January Paine had published in Philadelphia a pamphlet, "Common Sense," that arrested attention. Among the deputies it seems to have been regarded "as a curiosity." Save a few individual expressions in local papers, it was the first cry for independence since Mecklenburg had raised her voice in May, 1775. A month later Penn, always among the boldest, sent a copy to Person without comment; and Hewes forwarded one to Johnston, saying only: "It is a curiosity. We have not put up any

The
development
of the
purpose

C. R., X,
446, 447

1776
February
11th

go by the wagon,* not knowing how you might relish
dependency. The author is not known; some say Dr.
ranklin had a hand in it; he denies it." Hewes's spirit led
m to say: "All accounts from England seem to agree that
e shall have a dreadful storm bursting on our heads
rough all America in the spring. We must not shrink
om it; we ought not to show any symptoms of fear; the
earer it approaches and the greater the sound, the more
ortitude and calm, steady firmness we ought to possess. If
e mean to defend our liberties, our dearest rights and
rivileges against the power of Britain to the last extremity,
e ought to bring ourselves to such a temper of mind as to
tand unmoved at the bursting of an earthquake. Although
e storm thickens, I feel myself quite composed."

In the
Continental
Congress

At the close of October the king had from the throne
harged the colonies with levying war for the purpose of
stablishing an independent empire; but he proposed, while
mploying a hireling force from the continent to subdue
hem, to send commissioners with power to grant pardons
nd receive the submission of the several colonies. He would
ot, however, treat with the Continental Congress. That
vas resolutely determined. By two to one the Parliament
vas of the same mind. Such was the information that came
cross the seas early in January. And yet the congress and
he people waited—anxiously waited for the arrival of the
ommissioners. On February 14th Penn wrote to Person:

C. R., X,
455, 456

"Our dispute with Great Britain grows serious indeed.
Matters are drawing to a crisis. They seem determined to
persevere, and are forming alliances against us. Must we
ot do something of the like nature? Can we hope to carry
n a war without having trade or commerce somewhere?

Foreign
alliances

. . The consequence of making alliances is perhaps a total
eparation with Britain, and without something of that sort
we may not be able to provide what is necessary for our defence. My first wish is that America may be free; the
second, that we may be restored to peace and harmony with
Britain upon just and proper terms."

At Philadel-
phia

Two days later, on February 16th, it was proposed to open
the ports and renew commerce with all the world except

*For general distribution.

1776

Great Britain. In the discussion, Wythe, of Virginia, said "How, as subjects of Great Britain—as rebels? No; we must declare that the colonies have a right to contract alli ances with foreign powers!" The eloquent Virginian struc the same chord as Penn; but the question of opening th ports, involving this difficulty, was destined to remain unde cided for more than two months.

Later Hewes wrote to Johnston: "I see no prospec of a reconciliation; nothing is left now but to fight it ou Nor are we unanimous in our councils. Jealousies, ill natured observations, and recriminations take place o

S. R., XI, 289

reason and argument. Some among us urge strongly fo independency and eternal separation, others wish to wait little longer and to have the opinion of their constituents or that subject. You must give us the sentiments of your prov ince when your convention meets." And on March 1st, th North Carolina deputies wrote to the Provincial Congres asking directions concerning forming alliances.

C. R , X, 494, 495

At Halifax, April 4th

On the organization of the Provincial Congress, Johnsto was unanimously called to preside, and committees were a once appointed to map out the business of the body Now it was determined to arrange for at least one year o actual war, and a committee of ways and means was directec to devise measures for supporting troops to be raised fo that period. A committee of secrecy was appointed, o which Johnston was the head, to whom all intelligence wa; first submitted, and it was their province to determine wha should be imparted to the congress itself. And on the fourth day of the session, April 8th, a committee composec of Harnett, Allen Jones, Burke, Nash, Kinchen, Person, and Thomas Jones was appointed to take into consideration the usurpations and violences attempted and committed by the king and Parliament of Britain against America, and further measures to be taken for frustrating them and for the better defence of the province.

C. R., X, 504

The undaunted spirit

The congress—all the members—were unanimous for sep- aration, for declaring themselves no longer British sub- jects, but citizens of a new-born nationality. It was a mo- mentous matter. It would change the nature of the struggle. Not as subjects rebelling against the oppressions of Par-

.iament, but as freemen asserting the right of self-government, were they now to invoke the arbitrament of arms. The
congress took steps to sound the people. It was ascertained
that the popular heart was strong for independence. In
many counties there was not a dissenting voice. Ominous
was the war cloud now gathering and expected soon to
burst on the devoted province. Already forty sail had
anchored in the harbor of the Cape Fear. There Clinton
with his detachment from the north waited the arrival of
Cornwallis with his seven regiments to subjugate the people.
The prospect was full of peril. But the hearts of the
patriots did not quail. Under the lead of Johnston, Harnett,
Ashe and their associates their spirit rose to loftier heights
as dangers thickened.

On the night of April 12th the congress having received
some very important intelligence,* at once took up for consideration the letter of March 1st, from Hooper, Hewes and
Penn, asking instructions in regard to forming alliances.

Harnett's committee was resolute and ready to report;
short and vigorous was the conclusion of the matter. Whatever of doubt there had been was now cast aside. The
bonds binding the people to the past were to be broken, and
a new purpose, a new hope, that of independence, was to
animate them to action. The question Wythe had thundered at Philadelphia was answered by the congress at
Halifax.

1776
McRee's
Iredell, I.
276
C. R., X,
495

To declare independence

Early Saturday morning Johnston wrote to his brother:
"The house, in consequence of some very important intelligence received last night, have agreed to empower their
delegates at Philadelphia to concur with the other colonies
in entering into foreign alliances, and declaring an independence on Great Britain. I cannot be more particular."

On the night before, Friday, April 12th, the committee
brought in its report, reciting the acts of the British ministry and of the king and Parliament and authorizing the
delegates to the Continental Congress to concur in declaring
independence.

*Apparently from General Moore. (S. R., XI., 276.)

1776

C. R., X,
512

They reported as follows:

"It appears to your committee that pursuant to the plan concerted by the British ministry for subjugating America, the king and Parliament of Great Britain have usurped a power over the persons and properties of the people unlimited and un-controuled; and disregarding their humble petitions for peace, liberty, and safety, have made divers legislative acts, denouncing war, famine and every species of calamity against the continent in general: the British fleets and armies have been and still are daily employed in destroying the people and committing the most horrid devastations on the country: that governors in different colonies have declared protection to slaves who should imbrue their hands in the blood of their masters: that the ships belonging to America are declared prizes of war, and many of them have been violently seized and confiscated. In consequence of all which, multitudes of the people have been destroyed, and from easy circumstances reduced to the most lamentable distress.

"And whereas the moderation hitherto manifested by the united colonies and their sincere desire to be reconciled to the mother country on constitutional principles, have procured no mitigation of the aforesaid wrongs . . . and no hopes remain of obtaining re-dress by those means alone which have been hitherto tried, your committee are of opinion that the house should enter into the fol-lowing resolve, to wit:

To concur in declaring independ-ence

"*Resolved,* That the delegates of this colony in the continental congress be empowered to concur with the delegates of the other colonies in declaring independency, and forming foreign alliances, reserving to this colony the sole and exclusive right of forming a constitution and laws for this colony, and of appointing delegates from time to time (under the direction of a general representation thereof), to meet the delegates of the other colonies for such pur-poses as shall be hereafter pointed out."

Night had already closed in; but doubtless with burning words Harnett, accomplished and silver-tongued, urged the adoption of the resolution presented by the committee with all his powers. It was unanimously accepted as the voice of North Carolina. No other business was transacted, but the session of the day closed with this great performance. The next day President Johnston wrote to Hooper, Hewes, and Penn in great haste: "The congress have likewise taken under consideration that part of your letter* requiring their

*Of March 1st.

nstructions with respect to entering into foreign alliances, nd were unanimous in their concurrence with the enclosed esolve, confiding entirely in your discretion with regard to he exercise of the power with which you are invested."

But Hooper and Penn were then in Virginia on their oute to Halifax, where they arrived in time to take their eats on Monday, the 15th. They had the gratification of nding the congress responsive to the sentiment of the eople, pronounced for independence, and earnest and ealous for defence.

C. R., X, 516

The first action

Indeed, this resolution for independence was the first tterance for separation that had been made on behalf of any olony in America. Mecklenburg's voice and action in May, 775, annulling all the commissions and powers derived from he Crown and establishing an independent government, was hen premature and out of harmony with the spirit of the imes; even now the people "of the other colonies from New England to Virginia were in solid array against indepenlence." This first voice of any province leading the way gave heart to the patriots and strengthened the independent spirit which was beginning to manifest itself in other communities. "It was warmly welcomed by the patriots and commended for imitation." In Virginia the idea of indeependence was said to have been alarming in March, but was welcome in April; and a month after North Carolina had acted the Virginia convention met and adopted a similar resolution, directing its delegates in congress to propose ndependence and separation. But it is the crowning glory of North Carolina that her sons had the manhood and spirit to desire independence, the wisdom to perceive that the change in the purpose of the contest would add to the probabilities of a successful achievement and the boldness to lead he way.

*Frothing-
ham's
Rise of the
Republic,
504, 509*

*Virginia acts
in May*

The captured Tories

One of the first questions that claimed the attention of congress was the disposition of the prisoners taken at

1776

Moore's Creek. They had been confined in the Halifax jail
Because his health was suffering, General McDonald was
immediately paroled to the town, and a day or two later
Allan McDonald was also admitted to parole. A committee
was appointed to examine into the cases of the different
prisoners, about fifty of whom were paroled to return home
while some were directed to be removed to other communities within the province, being allowed reasonable time to
arrange their affairs at home, and with the privilege of
removing their families, as they should prefer. George
Micklejohn was paroled to Perquimans, and James Hunter
to Bute. James Lowe and Robert Adams, who shot Captain
Dent, were ordered to Halifax jail. Persons were appointed
in the several counties to look after the families of the insurgents at their old homes or in their new ones.

Care of the
prisoners

C. R., X,
560

Eventually, toward the end of April, it was determined
that fifty-three of the number, including General McDonald
and other influential Highlanders, should be removed to
Pennsylvania, and others to Virginia and Maryland, where
they were confined until exchanged or discharged by congress.* In view of the rigorous measures which the congress felt constrained to take with regard to these insurgents, on April 29th it issued a declaration lamenting the
necessities and hardships of the occasion, and declaring to
those who still remained in the State that, "We administer
this consolation—that they may rest assured that no wanton
acts of cruelty, no severity, shall be exercised to the prisoners. . . . We have their security in contemplation, not to
make them miserable. In our power, their errors claim our
pity, their situation disarms our resentment. We shall hail
their reformation with increasing pleasure, and receive them
to us with open arms, . . . and shall bless the day which
shall restore them to us friends to liberty, to the cause of
America, the cause of God and mankind. . . . Much depends upon the future demeanor of the friends of the insurgents who are left among us as to the treatment our prisoners may experience. Let them consider them as hostages
for their own good behavior, and by their own merits make
kind offices to their friends a tribute of duty as well as

Policy
towards the
Tories

C. R., X,
548, 549

*They were confined at Reading, Pa., and Staunton, Va.

humanity from us who have them in our power." The
declaration from which this is extracted was directed to be
translated into Erse, and the committees appointed in the
several counties to take care of the families of the insurgents
were directed to see that there was no suffering.

The drums and colors

On the day the convention met there arrived at Halifax McRee's Iredell, I, 275
the wagon sent by the delegates at Philadelphia with powder,
drums and colors, as ordered by the council in December.
Up to this time, as far as appears, the troops of the province
had used no colors. At Charleston a flag bearing a crescent
was in use. At Boston, the Massachusetts troops used a
flag with a pine tree, the pine tree having for a century been
the emblem of that colony. On the sea, the early flag bore a *The flag*
rattlesnake, with the legend, "Don't tread on me." The first
flag of the united colonies was made at Philadelphia and
sent to General Washington, who raised it on January 2,
1776, at his headquarters at Cambridge. This flag consisted
of seven red and six white bars or stripes and a field of
the king's colors, red and white crosses on a blue ground.
It has been said that until 1777 the snake flag was used by
the southern states; but as the colors received in April were *The red and*
sent by the North Carolina deputies from Philadelphia after *white bars*
the striped flag had been made and used by Washington as
the continental colors, it is surmised that they were of that
pattern.

To supply the money needed in the military operations, *War*
congress directed the issue of $1,000,000 in notes, and re- *measures*
solved that a tax should be laid on the poll, beginning in the
year 1780, to retire that issue; and appropriations were made
to pay all the soldiers, militia and others that had been in
the service of the province, and for arms and equipments.
Commissioners were also appointed to procure sulphur, saltpetre, and salt, and to establish ironworks and foundries on
Deep River.'

On the water

The Cape Fear and Chesapeake Bay being closed, and
Beaufort frequently visited by British cruisers, the importance of Ocracoke Inlet as a channel of commerce became

1776
C. R., X,
353, 636, 637,
640-642

Importa-
tions

greatly increased. The enterprising merchants of Edenton and New Bern and of the village of Washington on the Pamlico despatched vessel after vessel abroad, whose return cargoes of salt, powder, cannon and other munitions of war and necessaries contributed largely to supply the needs of the public. The firms of Hewes & Smith, at Edenton, and John Wright Stanly, at New Bern, took the lead in this hazardous enterprise. Their patriotism and unremitting activity proved of great advantage to the American cause. Others also engaged in the same work, and besides trading vessels, there were fitted out privateers to prey on British commerce, while the State itself constructed armed cruisers for the public service. At Wilmington the *George Washington* was built; at New Bern, the *Pennsylvania Farmer;* at Edenton, *King Tammany;* while the *Heart of Oak,* the *Polly* and other vessels were granted letters of marque as privateers.

C. R., X,
550

The war on
the water

In order to interrupt importations through Ocracoke, Dunmore sent two armed sloops, the *Lily* and the *Fincastle,* to seize such vessels as might be there; and on April 14th the *Lily* captured the schooner *Polly,* removed part of her cargo and left a prize crew in charge of her. But the patriots were not idle. Three days later a number of armed men, in five whaleboats, captured the *Lily* and retook the *Polly,* the Whigs showing as much enterprise and skill on the water as on the land.

Because considerable importations were made through this channel for the benefit of Virginia as well as for the Continental Congress, of which Hewes was one of the most efficient agents, it was thought that Virginia should aid in keeping Ocracoke open. Application was therefore made to that province to fit out two armed vessels to act in conjunction with those equipped by North Carolina. The suggestion was acted on promptly, and two large row-galleys were built at South Quay by Virginia, one of which afterward came into possession of North Carolina.

The Tories

C. R., X,
593, 594

In different parts of the province the disaffected element made manifestations of their Toryism. In Edgecombe a

1776

body was dispersed by a party of Whigs under John Johnston; and the Committee of Safety of Rowan thought it well to disarm some of the inhabitants of Muddy Creek. But, on the other hand, that committee was cheered by patriotic resolutions signed by a number of ladies of Rowan, as had been the committee of Mecklenburg by resolutions entered into somewhat earlier by the young ladies of that county, that they would not receive the addresses of young gentlemen except the brave volunteers who had served in the expedition against the Scovellites. The women of the west were as resolute as the men.

Foote, Sketches of North Carolina, 511

The difficulties of enrolling the militia who were to turn out and supplying them with arms was forcibly stated by Colonel William Bryan, of Johnston, who was almost in despair from the adverse circumstances that surrounded him. He added: "We have several obstinate persons in this county, and I believe they are great Tories in their hearts; they are constantly sowing sedition in the minds of the people. I should be glad if the light horse could be directed to take a turn through our county. I believe if there could be a few of the heads of them subdued it would be of great service to the county. I have so little dependence in the militia that I don't think convenient to undertake to subdue them that way."

C. R., X, 611

Four new battalions

In view of the pressing necessity for more troops, the congress now raised four additional continental regiments, assigning to their command Jethro Sumner, Thomas Polk, Edward Buncombe, and Alexander Lillington. The period for which the minute men were enlisted having expired, some of the officers of that organization were transferred to these new regiments, among them Colonel James Thackston becoming lieutenant-colonel under Colonel Polk. Three companies of light horse were also raised, commanded respectively by John Dickerson, Martin Phifer, and James Jones. An artillery company was directed to be organized by Captain John Vance. To protect the coast, five companies were embodied and stationed from Currituck to the Cape Fear. Two battalions of militia, seven hundred and fifty men

Additional requirements

1776

each, were directed to be raised in the eastern districts, one to be under the command of Colonel Thomas Brown and the other under Colonel Philemon Hawkins. These battalions, the Second Continental Regiment, and all the recruits enlisted for the new regiments were ordered to report immediately to General Moore on the Cape Fear.

A new system was devised for the militia. The companies of the militia in the several counties were to consist of not less than fifty men. Each company was divided into five divisions. One of these consisted of the aged and infirm, the other militiamen being apportioned to four divisions, that drew lots to ascertain when they should go on duty, and were severally known as number one, two, three, and four, accordingly. Each county had its militia field officers; and the province was divided into six military districts, a brigadier-general being appointed for each. In his own district the brigadier took rank of the others. The militia was not to be under continental officers, except when ordered by the civil power to join the continental troops, and then the continental officer of equal rank took command.

On May 6th, because of information from General Moore, the congress directed the generals of the province to call out their militia and hasten to join General Moore, and ordered General Ashe to take command of the re-enforcements upon their arrival in his district. The generals elected by the congress were Allen Jones, for the Halifax district; John Ashe, Wilmington; Edward Vail, Edenton; Griffith Rutherford, Salisbury; Thomas Person, Hillsboro; and William Bryan, New Bern.*

Notwithstanding the military matters that were pressing on the attention of congress that body realized the necessity of making provision for the civil life of the province. On May 1st it resolved that all vestries elected in every parish, having taken the test adopted on August 23, 1775, should proceed to parochial business, and where no election had taken place on Easter Monday, April 8th, the freeholders were directed to meet in July and elect vestrymen, who should qualify themselves by subscribing the test. Con-

C. R., X, 561

The militia

C. R., X, 563

The forces embody

C. R., X, 563

Vestrymen to take the test oath

C. R., X, 554

---

*Richard Caswell was at first chosen brigadier-general of the New Bern district, but did not serve.

formably to this resolution, the vestry of Edenton on June 19th met and signed the test, as probably did all the other vestrymen chosen throughout the province, and as all the committees and other officers were required to do. It was the duty of the vestrymen in every county or parish to look after the poor and attend to much business not of an ecclesiastical nature.

Members of the congress of April, 1776, that declared for independence, April 12, 1776

For Anson County—Daniel Love, Samuel Spencer, John Crawford, James Picket and John Childs.

Beaufort—Roger Ormond, Thomas Respis, Jr., and John Cowper.

Bladen—Nathaniel Richardson, Thomas Robeson, Maturan Colvill, James Council and Thomas Amis.

Bertie—John Campbell, John Johnston and Charles Jacocks.

Brunswick—

Bute—Green Hill, William Alston, William Person, Thomas Sherrod and Philemon Hawkins.

Craven—James Coor, Lemuel Hatch, John Bryan, William Bryan and Jacob Blount.

Carteret—William Thompson, Solomon Shepard and John Blackhouse.

Currituck—Samuel Jarvis, James White, James Ryan, Gideon Lamb and Solomon Perkins.

Chowan—Samuel Johnston, Thomas Benbury, Thomas Jones, John Bap. Beasly and Thomas Hunter.

Cumberland—David Smith, Alexander McAlister, Farquard Campbell, Thomas Rutherford and Alexander McCoy.

Chatham—Ambrose Ramsay, John Thompson, Joshua Rosser, Jeduthan Harper and Elisha Cain.

Duplin—Thomas Gray and William Dickson.

Dobbs—Richard Caswell, Abraham Sheppard, George Miller, Simon Bright and William McKinnie.

Edgecomb—William Haywood, Duncan Lemon, Elisha Battle, Henry Irwin and Nathaniel Boddie.

Granville—Thomas Person, John Penn, Memucan Hunt, John Taylor and Charles Eaton.

Guilford—Ransom Southerland, William Dent and Ralph Gorrill.

Hyde—Rotheas Latham, Joseph Hancock, John Jordan and Benjamin Parmele.

Hertford—Robert Sumner, Matthias Brickle, Laurence Baker, William Murfree.

Halifax—John Bradford, James Hogan, David Sumner, Joseph John Williams and Willis Alston.

Johnston—Samuel Smith, Jr., Needham Bryan, Jr., and Henry Rains.

Mecklenburg—John Phifer, Robert Irwin and John McKnitt Alexander.

Martin—William Williams, Whitmill Hill, Kenneth McKenzie, Thomas Wiggins and Edward Smythwick.

New Hanover—John Ashe, John Devane, Samuel Ashe, Sampson Moseley and John Hollingsworth.

Northampton—Allen Jones, Jeptha Atherton, Drury Gee, Samuel Lockhart and Howell Edmunds.

Onslow—George Mitchell, Benejah Doty, John Spicer, John King and John Norman.

Orange—John Kinchen, James Saunders, John Butler, Nathaniel Rochester and Thomas Burke.

Perquimans—Miles Harvey, William Skinner, Thomas Harvey, Charles Blount and Charles Moore.

Pasquotank—Thomas Boyd, Joseph Jones, William Cuming, Dempsey Burgess and Henry Abbott.

Pitt—John Simpson, Edward Salter and William Robson.

Rowan—Griffith Rutherford and Matthew Locke.

Surry—Joseph Williams, Joseph Winston, Charles Gordon.

Tyrrell—Archibald Corrie.

Tryon—Charles McLean, James Johnston.

Wake—Joel Lane, John Hinton, John Rand, William Hooper and Tignal Jones.

Town of Bath—William Brown.

New Bern—Abner Nash.

Edenton—Joseph Hewes.

Wilmington—Cornelius Harnett.

Brunswick—

Halifax—Willie Jones.

Hillsborough—William Johnston.

Salisbury—David Nisbet.

Cambellton—Arthur Council.

CHAPTER XXX

THE COUNCIL OF SAFETY, 1776

Attempt to frame the Constitution.—Fundamental principles.—The problems involved.—The temporary government.—Congress adjourns.—The first invasion.—General Lee.—Clinton's disappointment. —The fleet arrives.—The ardor of the Whigs.—Clinton offers pardon.—No hostile movement.—The descent on Brunswick.—The regiments land.—The fleet sails.—The Council of Safety.—The attack on Fort Moultrie.—North Carolina's gallant troops.—Affairs at home.—The Continentals.

Attempt to frame a constitution

On April 13th the congress, now flushed by the desire of independence, appointed a committee composed of Johnston, Harnett, Thomas Jones, Nash, Burke, Allen Jones, John Johnston, Thomas Person, Sam Ashe, Samuel Spencer and nine others to prepare a temporary civil government. The committee seems to have at once undertaken to cast a permanent constitution. A majority of the committee favored the establishment of a purely democratic form of government, the governor, judges, and all other officers being chosen by the people, and every freeman having the right of suffrage. They were probably led to urge this departure from the old system not merely from the advocacy of the "inherent and unalienable rights of man," but with the hope and expectation that it would gain for the new government the support of the landless Highlanders and of others not freeholders, and of the Regulators, who were dissatisfied with the colonial regulations that had proved so oppressive in their practical operation.

This desire to extend suffrage is said to have been the rock on which the public men split. As yet there was no curb to the will of the legislative body. Never had a court declared any legislative action a nullity. Once elected and in possession of power the Assembly could extend its sessions and

1776
C. R., X,
515

April

A pure
democracy
advocated

Jones's
Defence,
277, 278

exert arbitrary sway, ignoring all limitations and every restriction that might be embodied in the constitution; and it was apprehended that a judiciary dependent on the will of the people would lack that stability and independence which constitute the safeguard of personal rights and of

Divergencies

property. The fundamental principles on which the new government was to be founded thus became a matter of the gravest concern. Divergencies at once arose. There were those who proposed to give the fullest recognition to the rights of the people as a source of all power, and others who deemed it wiser and more prudent not to inaugurate such a change in the administration of affairs as this would necessarily involve. Theretofore suffrage had been limited to freeholders; and the judiciary was appointed. Samuel Johnston, who had been the most influential man in the

Apprehensions

province, felt that the despotism of a democracy was to be feared, and that a judiciary resting on the popular will, with the judges not independent, but courting popularity, would be intolerable; and he was determined in his opposition to the establishment of a government without any practical limitation to its powers, and with the tenure of all the great offices dependent on the favor of the inhabitants generally. In his view those who advocated this system were "already entering on the race for popularity," and he apprehended that the greatest evils would result from such a plan of government. Instead of a pure democracy, he urged the establishment of a representative republic, with annual elections to hold the legislature in check. Educated in New England, he was a thorough republican. But he agreed with John Adams, who had written a dissertation on government advising the establishment of new constitutions on

McRee's Iredell, I, 276

the very principles that Johnston advocated. He would not yield. On April 17th he wrote: "I must confess our prospects are at this time very gloomy. Our people are about forming a constitution. From what I can at present collect of their plan, it will be impossible for me to take any part in the execution of it."

Jones's Defence, 278, 279

Being overborne, on the 18th he withdrew from the committee; but the next day Thomas Jones, also a conservative, but not so avowed in his principles as Johnston, notified him that the disagreeable difficulty which had interrupted the harmony of the committee had been adjusted, and invited him to meet the other members that evening.

And again, on April 20th, Johnston wrote: "We have not yet been able to agree on a constitution. We have a meeting on it every evening, but can conclude on nothing; the great difficulty in our way is how to establish a check on the representatives of the people, to prevent their assuming more power than would be consistent with the liberties of the people, such as increasing the time of their duration, and such like. . . . Some have proposed that we should take up the plan of the Connecticut constitution for a groundwork, but with some amendments, such as that the great officers, instead of being appointed by the people at large, should be appointed by the Assembly; that the judges of our courts should hold their offices during good behavior. After all, it appears to me that there can be no check on the representatives of the people in a democracy but the people themselves; and in order that the check may be more efficient, I would have annual elections." McRee's Iredell, I, 276, 277

Up to that time there had been no new constitution adopted in any province except alone South Carolina. The people of Connecticut were then living, and continued to live until 1818, under the charter granted in 1662 by Charles II, by which the governor and twelve assistants and the general assembly were chosen by a majority of the freemen of the colony; but the governor and his assistants were empowered to erect courts and appoint judges and otherwise administer public affairs. On March 26th South Carolina had adopted a constitution to regulate the internal polity of the colony "until an accommodation of the unhappy differences between Great Britain and America can be obtained." By it the electors were to be the same as under the old laws, and they were to choose members of the general assembly, who were to select out of themselves a legislative council to form a separate and distinct house, with equal legislative power as the Assembly itself; and these two houses were to choose a president of the province and a council of state. A printed copy of this constitution was obtained by the North Carolina congress. On April 28th Thomas The constitution of South Carolina

1776
McRee's
Iredell, I,
277, 278

Jones wrote: "The constitution goes on but slowly. The outlines of it made their appearance in the house for the first time yesterday, and by the last of this week it probably may be finished. The plan as it now stands will be subject to many alterations; at present it is in the following manner:

The first outline

First, a house of the representatives of the people, all free householders of one year's standing to vote; and second, a legislative council, to consist of one member from each county in the province, to sit as an upper house; and these two houses are to be a check on each other, as no law can be made without the consent of both, and none but freeholders will have a right to vote for the members of this council. Next, an executive council, to consist of the president and six councillors, to be always sitting, to do all official business of government. . . . The president and council to be elected annually, as also the Assembly and legislative council." The judicial system apparently had not been agreed on.

The constitution postponed

Johnston had so far prevailed that there were to be annual elections of assemblymen; and at least one branch of the Assembly was to be elected by freeholders. For two days this outline was debated by the convention in committee of the whole, but the divergencies were pronounced and other matters required attention, so on April 30th the subject was postponed until November; and a new committee, composed, however, of some of the same members, was directed to report a temporary form of government until the end of the next congress. Although Johnston was not a member of the new committee, his relations with it were so close that on the second day after its appointment he wrote: "Affairs have

McRee's
Iredell, I,
279

taken a turn within a few days past. All ideas of forming a permanent constitution are at this time laid aside. It is now proposed for the present to establish a council to sit constantly, and county committees to sit at certain fixed

C. R., X,
579

periods, but nothing is concluded." Ten days elapsed before the report of the new committee was considered by the

The Council of Safety

house. Then, as Johnston had indicated, a Council of Safety was appointed to sit from day to day at such places as they should think prudent and proper. The Provincial Council and the district committees were abolished.

As before, the members from each district selected two members and the congress one. But now Willie Jones, a leader among those who differed with Johnston, was selected by the congress in his stead. The other changes were: Nash, Kinchen, Spencer, and Avery gave place to Simpson, Rand, Hezekiah Alexander, and William Sharpe, while J. J. Williams filled the vacancy for Halifax.

1776
C. R., X,
581

Having on May 12th made this provision for the administration of provincial affairs, two days later the congress adjourned. Although it was a reasonable inference that those who opposed the views of Samuel Johnston were in the majority in the body, yet when it became necessary for him to leave the chair, on May 2d, Allen Jones, also a conservative, was elected vice-president; and on its adjournment the congress, in tendering thanks to its president for his faithful discharge of his duties, was particular to add that he had "in that, as in all other stations, approved himself the firm and liberal patron of liberty and a wise and zealous friend and asserter of the rights of mankind." But when Johnston left the hall it was not to return as a representative until the differences of that period had faded from memory.

Samuel
Johnston

C. R., X,
590

The first invasion

Toward the end of January General Clinton was detached from the British army at Boston with a small command to conduct operations elsewhere. When his departure became known, General Charles Lee was directed to repair to New York, his supposed destination. They arrived at that point on the same day, February 4th, but Clinton openly avowed that his expedition was intended for North Carolina. Such an avowal was received with doubt. On his sailing from New York, the Continental Congress created the Southern Department, assigned the command to General Lee, and on March 1st, appointed Moore and Howe brigadier-generals. Lee hastening to Virginia reached Williamsburg simultaneously with Clinton's arrival in the Chesapeake. The British general lingered with Dunmore until early in April, when he joined Governor Martin below Brunswick; still it was apprehended that the real point of attack would be Virginia,

1776

Moore and
Howe briga-
diers

Lee joins
Howe in
Virginia

1776

and Lee remained there a month making preparations to meet it.

Already were there many vessels in the Cape Fear harbor, drawn together in connection with the intended invasion, but week after week passed without the arrival of Sir Peter Parker's fleet bringing Cornwallis and his seven regiments of regulars. A succession of disastrous storms had delayed the vessels. Nor was this the only disappointment of the British commander. Instead of the promised support from the interior, instead of an army of Loyalists ready to co-operate, he found a hostile force awaiting him, and that the unexpected catastrophe that had befallen McDonald necessitated an entire change of plans.

May

Lee, following Clinton, had himself started southward, preceded by General Howe, directing Howe's North Carolinians under Major Patten and Muhlenberg's Virginia regiment to follow. On May 2d Howe reached Halifax, and on the floor of the house, pursuant to a resolve of the congress, the president returned him thanks for his conduct during the whole of the late dangerous, important, and critical campaign, and more especially for the reputation the North Carolina troops acquired under his command. General Lee was then approaching the border, and Colonel Long was directed to receive him at the boundary with a detachment of troops and escort him to the congress. From Halifax the general passed on to New Bern, making himself acquainted with the condition of affairs in the province.

C. R., X, 556

Lee received at Halifax

The fleet arrives

At length, about May 1st, the grand fleet began to arrive in the harbor, and all doubt about its destination being now removed, Moore despatched the news to the congress at Halifax. That body at once ordered all the continental battalions to report to General Moore, and in addition to the battalion that had been raised for Colonel Brown, a draft of fifteen hundred more militia was made from the eastern districts, those from Halifax and Edenton being assigned to the command of Colonel Peter Dauge. No drafts were made from the western districts, because of a particular purpose of importance at that time, but the western regiments were to hold themselves in readiness. This doubtless was to have a reserve force near at hand to suppress

S. R., XI, 296

any further rising by the Tories. The Whigs of North Carolina now displayed a glorious ardor, and rushed with impetuosity to the scene of the expected conflict. Soon it was estimated that the patriot force collected on the Cape Fear numbered ninety-four hundred men, all but the continentals being under the command of General Ashe. The approaches to the town were fortified, and vessels were sunk in the channel a few miles below to prevent an attack by water. Every preparation was made for stubborn resistance.

It had been announced that the king, ignoring the Continental Congress, would send commissioners to treat with each province separately, and it was thought that these commissioners might come with the fleet. North Carolina, spurning the suggestion that she could be detached from the general cause of America, resolved that "if such commissioners should arrive in this province, unless with a commission to treat with the Continental Congress, they should be required to return immediately to their vessel; and if at any time thereafter they should be found on shore they should be seized and sent to congress." But these commissioners did not come with Sir Peter Parker. Later they landed at the north after independence was declared, but their errand was bootless.

After full consultation with Governor Martin, and, indeed, with Governor Tryon at New York, as to the best course to be pursued to detach the people from the revolutionary government in North Carolina, General Clinton on May 5th issued a proclamation inveighing against the tyranny of the congresses and committees and entreating the people to avoid the miseries attendant on civil war by a return to the blessings of a free government. He offered pardon to all who should submit to the laws except alone Cornelius Harnett and Robert Howe. Howe had given great offence to Martin by preparing the address to the king in 1774 and procuring it to be sent through Governor Tryon instead of Governor Martin; he had also been among the very first to form companies and train the people to arms, and had expelled Dunmore from the soil of Virginia as the previous year he had assisted in driving Martin from the soil of North Carolina. In this last enterprise Harnett also had been a conspicuous

1776

Pref. Notes, C. R., X, xiii

May

Preparations for defence

The king's commissioners

C. R., X, 591

Clinton's proclamation

Harnett and Howe excepted from pardon

1776

actor, and now he was the president of the State when congress was not in session and at the head of the revolutionary government. The exception of these two patriots

The badge of honor

from the tender of pardon served only as a badge of honorable distinction, endearing them still more to the patriots of North Carolina. Two days after issuing this proclamation Clinton landed two regiments and made a reconnoissance in force into the interior, without, however, bring-

Moore and Ashe ready

ing on any engagement. Moore and Ashe held their forces well in hand ready for any emergency. They prepared to contest any advance Clinton might make; but days passed without any hostile movement. Besides the direct route into the interior, there was another, which it was feared the British might take, and three hundred and fifty horsemen guarded that road to give warning of such a movement and to impede it should Clinton make the venture. A hundred vessels lay at the entrance of the harbor opposite Fort Johnston, and a detachment of continentals, a hundred and fifty men, under Major William Davis, of the First Battalion, was stationed near Brunswick to hold marauders in

Jones's Defence, 261

check. Their headquarters were established at the mill of the Orton plantation, in the vicinity of the town. On Sunday, May 12th, between two and three o'clock, Cornwallis hastily threw ashore nine hundred troops, with the purpose of surprising and capturing that post. Vigilant sentries, however, watched the enemy, and these resolutely opened fire, giving the alarm, and Major Davis removed his stores and provisions and withdrew his detachment by a timely movement. Cornwallis, nevertheless, lost one man killed, several wounded, and a sergeant of the Thirty-third Regi-

The burning of Orton mill

ment, who was taken prisoner. Foiled in his purpose, his lordship burned the empty mill, and after remaining some hours in the village of Brunswick, he ravaged the neighbor-

S. R., XI, 396, 398

ing plantation of General Howe, carrying off some twenty bullocks as the reward of his enterprise. Three days later five of the British regiments went into quarters at Fort

Martin, Hist. North Carolina, II, 390, 391

Johnston and one on Baldhead, leaving one on board the ships. The larger part of the American forces remained near Wilmington ready for any movement, while a considerable body was encamped some two or three miles from the

enemy near Fort Johnston.   Thus matters stood day after
day during that period of apprehension and anxiety, but
Clinton made no movement.

It being known that the Tories had been disarmed, no aid Operations
abandoned
was expected from them should a column be thrown into
the interior; and it was apprehended that any attempt at
subjugation would result in a protracted campaign, which
might not be terminated before the troops would be needed
for more important movements then in contemplation.   And C. R., X,
653
in that event the withdrawal of the force, with subjugation
not completed, would have the appearance of defeat, entail-
ing worse consequences than would attend making no immediate effort to subdue the inhabitants.   Influenced by these
considerations, General Clinton deemed it inadvisable to begin at that time operations in North Carolina, and determined to use the army in connection with the war vessels
to reduce Charleston.   So toward the end of May the fleet The fleet
sails
sailed, coming to anchor off that harbor on June 7th.

Governor Martin accompanied Clinton, but there were left
on the station several vessels, one of which, the *Jenny*, was The Jenny
the abiding place of a considerable number of Tories, who,
deserting their habitations, had sought protection with the
fleet.   Among these were persons instructed by the governor to maintain a correspondence with the Loyalists of
the interior and give them every possible encouragement
during his absence.   Governor Martin continued with Gen- C. R., X,
653, 654
eral Clinton during the siege of Charleston, and accompanied
him later on his return to the north.

The Council of Safety

While the British army was still in the harbor, it was C. R., X,
619
considered that the Council of Safety should convene at
Wilmington, and the members met there on June 5th, and
Cornelius Harnett was unanimously chosen president.*   The
immediate danger had then passed.   But affairs were in a

---

*Some writers have erroneously supposed because Sam Johnston
and Willie Jones were chosen to represent the province in the
Council of Safety that they presided in the council, but not so.
Harnett was chosen to preside over both bodies.   He was president of
the Sons of Liberty in the six counties of the Cape Fear in 1770, and
doubtless from their organization in 1765.

1776

C. R., X, 638

turmoil. There were some outlying malcontents, concerned in the insurrection, now in the swamps of Bladen, who sent information to General Ashe that they were desirous of submitting themselves to the council; and it was resolved that they would be allowed to return to their homes on taking an oath to fight when called on in the American cause.

To suppress dissatisfaction

Efforts to inflame the minds of the people in Edgecombe and Dobbs were so important that Colonel Sheppard was directed to call out as many of the militia as were necessary to arrest those who were endeavoring to dissuade the people from sustaining the congress; similar action was taken with regard to Johnston County, while in Cumberland two companies of light horse were placed under the control of Colonel Folsome to maintain the authority of the congress.

Coal and iron on Deep River

C. R., X, 649

The council continued its efforts to provide munitions of war, and also a supply of salt, so absolutely necessary for the soldiers as well as the inhabitants; and an arrangement was made for the use of Wilcox's bloomery and forge on Deep River, some thirty miles south of Hillsboro, where good iron was produced from ore beds. The presence of coal in the immediate vicinity and the great profusion of natural supplies led the commissioners to report: "Upon the whole, nature has poured out with a bountiful hand on that part of our country everything necessary for the establishment of an extensive iron manufactory."

Armed vessels fitted out

The brig *Pennsylvania Farmer,* which had been equipped under the orders of congress, lay then at New Bern, and the council directed that she should be armed with eight of the cannon lately imported; and Richard Ellis, of New Bern, applied for letters of marque and reprisal for his armed sloop, the *Heart of Oak,* of seventy tons burden; and George Dennison, the captain of the vessel, was given letters permitting him to act against the enemies of the thirteen united colonies; and Edward Tinker, captain of the armed schooner *Johnston,* belonging to John Green and others, of New Bern, was also given letters of marque. Vessels were constantly arriving through Ocracoke with arms and munitions, one, the *Little Thomas,* having brought in twenty pieces of cannon.

Several of the prisoners who had been sent to Philadelphia

1776
C. R., X,
631

Dr. Pyle
escapes

and Virginia having made their escape and returned to their homes, now began using their utmost influence to infect others with their Tory principles; among them were Dr. Pyle and his son John. Colonel Folsome, in command in Cumberland, was directed to march with a party of horse, with the utmost secrecy, and to arrest them again. There were many other evidences of disaffection, and to counteract those influences required prompt action on the part of the busy members of the council, who were under a great strain because of the public affairs, much being of a delicate nature, that pressed upon them.

The attack on Fort Moultrie

On the departure of the fleet from the Cape Fear, Lee hastened to Charleston, accompanied by Howe, where he arrived early in June. Moore remained at Wilmington, but two continental regiments under Nash and Martin reached Charleston on June 11th, followed later by the Virginia regiment and the Third and Fouth Continentals, not then needed at Cape Fear. A rifle regiment raised at the west likewise repaired to Charleston. Felix Walker, afterward long a member of congress from the Buncombe district, says in his "Autobiography": "I was appointed lieutenant in Captain Richardson's company in the rifle regiment. I returned to Watauga and recruited my full proportion of men and marched them to Charleston in May, 1776, joined the regiment, and was stationed on James Island."

June

North
Carolina
Continentals
at
Charleston

When the fleet dropped anchor off the bar the Charlestonians barricaded their streets and prepared to defend the wharves of the city, and soon troops were stationed on the outlying islands enclosing the harbor. Colonel Moultrie began working night and day constructing a fort on the end of Sullivan's Island by bolting palmetto logs together for walls, with sixteen feet of sand between them. Week after week passed and no attack was made, so that toward the end of June the front of his fort was well finished and thirty odd guns were mounted in it. But powder was scarce, and there were hardly twenty-five rounds of ammunition for the guns. On the northeast of that island lay Long Island, a naked sand bank, and there Clinton landed more than three

Fort
Moultrie
begun

Clark's
battalion

thousand troops, intending to cross the narrow intervening waters and thus gain possession of Sullivan Island. To resist his advance Colonel Thompson, of South Carolina, was stationed at that end of Sullivan's Island with three hundred of his own riflemen, two hundred of Clark's North Carolina regiment, two hundred more South Carolinians under Horry, and with some light pieces on his flank; while Nash, for whom Lee had conceived a high opinion, was placed to defend the rear of the fort, which was unfinished, and a post of great consequence.

June 28th,
Battle of
Fort
Moultrie

After much fortunate delay, in the early morning of June 28th the fleet approached the fort and the battle began. The British brought into action ten times the number of guns that Moultrie could use, but made no impression on the palmetto fort. A flag of blue with a white crescent emblazoned with the word "Liberty" proudly floated over the rampart. In the torrent of balls the staff that bore it was severed, but as it fell Sergeant Jasper heroically seized the standard and again raised it on the bastion next to the enemy. The attempt to pass from Long Island was no more successful than the attack on the water. The brave Americans drove the infantry back on two occasions, and the

A glorious
victory

assault both on land and sea was a signal failure. The slow and skilful fire of Moultrie drove off the fleet and destroyed several frigates, the *Bristol* losing 40 men killed and 71 wounded and the *Experiment* 23 killed and 56 wounded; while the American loss, after ten hours of incessant conflict, was but 11 killed and 26 wounded. Repulsed, defeated, the army re-embarked on the vessels and the contest was over. A more glorious victory was hardly ever won, and the tidings flew from colony to colony, reaching Philadelphia just after the deputies in congress had signed the Declaration of Independence, and causing great joy throughout America.

C. R., X,
618c

Conduct of
the North
Carolina
troops

While Moultrie's gunners were heroes the infantry likewise won great applause. Of the gallant conduct of Clark's North Carolinians, Lee expressed himself in the highest terms, saying: "I know not which corps I have the greatest reason to be pleased with, Muhlenberg's Virginians or the North Carolina troops; they are both equally alert, zealous, and spirited." Twice the enemy attempted to land, "and

twice they were repulsed by a Colonel Thompson, of the
South Carolina rangers, in conjunction with a body of North
Carolina regulars. Upon the whole, the South and North
Carolina troops and the Virginia rifle battalion we have here
are admirable soldiers."

The Council of Safety had directed the county committees
to call on every person suspected of Toryism to render an inventory of his estate, and in case of neglect, the commanding
officer of the county was ordered to bring the suspected person before the board. This order, contemporaneous with the
glorious news of the repulse of General Clinton at Charleston, which created wild enthusiasm among the Whigs, caused
a great commotion among the Loyalists, and they flocked in
to sign the test and association.

Tories dis-
mayed

C. R., X,
666

After the repulse of the British fleet by Fort Moultrie,
General Clinton still lingered at Charleston, threatening
Savannah, and it was apprehended he might yet return to
the original plan of subjugating North Carolina. Toward
the end of July, however, he abandoned his design against
the southern colonies and sailed northward. When this became known, early in August, General Ashe discharged the
militia brigade from the districts of New Bern, Halifax, and
Edenton, reserving only a part of the Wilmington brigade in
active service. A British force of fifteen vessels still occupied the lower harbor and held Baldhead, remaining there
all summer, watched, however, by General Moore and by the
continentals and the militia remaining in the service. Hardly
had Clinton departed before General Lee began to organize
an expedition into Florida, being accompanied by General
Howe, the Virginia regiment, the Third North Carolina
Continentals, and some companies of the First and Second
regiments. But in September, having been ordered north,
General Lee departed, leaving Howe in command. The
troops in lower Georgia suffering much from sickness, fourteen or fifteen men dying every day, Howe thought it best
to relinquish the enterprise, and returned to Charleston.
During the fall the other continental regiments were held
by General Moore on the North Carolina coast, and efforts
were made to complete the organization.

C. R., X,
858

CHAPTER XXXI

INDEPENDENCE

Independence declared.—Lee's resolution.—The declaration.—
The North Carolina deputies.—The declaration proclaimed.—The
address of the council.—Religious teachings in Anson.—James Hunter a patriot.—The Indians hostile.—Rutherford crosses the mountains.—Washington district annexed.—The movement against the
Indians.—Rutherford successful.—The Surry regiment.—Moore's
expedition.—The Tories active.—Salt-making.—The British abandon
Cape Fear.—A winter campaign threatened.

Independence declared

1776

Some three weeks after North Carolina had instructed
her deputies to concur in declaring independence the Virginia convention met, and on May 15th adopted a resolution
directing her deputies to propose independence.   On the
same day Boston and a majority of the other towns in
Massachusetts, in their town meetings, instructed their local
representatives to the same effect.   On May 27th Joseph
Hewes, then the only North Carolina deputy in attendance
on the Continental Congress, presented the North Carolina
resolution, and immediately the Virginia instructions were
also presented.   These resolves and the action of the Continental Congress on May 15th, declaring that it was irreconcilable with good conscience for the people to take oaths
to support government under the Crown, and that the powers
of government should be exerted under the authority of the
people, brought the subject ⌐f independence sharply to the
attention of the other colonies, and the leaven had begun
to work.   Yet nearly two weeks elapsed before there was
any movement.   Then, on June 7th, Richard Henry Lee
offered in congress a resolution "That these united colonies*
are and of right ought to be free and independent States."

May 27th, The North Carolina resolution presented

June 7th, Independence proposed

*The expression "hath, and of right ought to have," the original
of this phrase, is found in the reply which the English Commons
made to King James I when he communicated his unsatisfactory
answer to their "Remonstrance de droit."   Rushworth was studied
by the American leaders for precedents.

1. SAMUEL JOHNSTON
2. WILLIAM HOOPER
3. JOHN PENN
4. JOSEPH HEWES

his resolution, so fraught with momentous consequences, was not considered that day; but, postponed until the next morning, it was debated until the 10th. Hewes, speaking for North Carolina, was unalterably fixed and urgent in favor of immediate action.

June 10th,
Bancroft's
Hist. U. S.,
IV, 424

A bare majority of the colonies favored Lee's resolution. New York, New Jersey Pennsylvania, Delaware, Maryland, and South Carolina were not prepared to support it, and its further consideration was, by a vote of 7 to 5, postponed until July 1st, Hewes casting the vote of North Carolina against the postponement. By that date it was hoped that new instructions might be received from the provinces that still held back. To lose no time, a committee was appointed to prepare a declaration of independence, and another committee was directed to draft a plan of confederation, Hewes being a member of the latter.

Jefferson's
Works, I, 12
et seq.

Seventeen days slowly passed, and then, on June 28th, a draught of the Declaration was reported to the house, where it lay on the table awaiting the decision on Lee's resolution. At length July 1st arrived, and that resolution was again taken up for consideration. Maryland and New Jersey had in the meanwhile given in their adherence. From Delaware only two members were present, and they divided, so the voice of that colony could not be recorded. The delegates from New York, having no instructions, asked leave to retire. Pennsylvania and South Carolina alone voted in the negative. At the request of Rutledge, of South Carolina, hoping for unanimity, the decision was postponed until the next day.

July 1st,
Lee's
resolution

When the congress met the following morning a third member had arrived from Delaware, casting the vote of that province for the resolution; changes had been made in the Pennsylvania delegation with a like result, and the South Carolina delegates no longer withheld their assent. New York still preferred to remain silent awaiting instructions, which, however, were freely given on the 9th of that month.

July 2d,
Independence agreed
on

Thus on July 2d was finally determined, by virtually the unanimous voice of all the colonies, the great question which North Carolina had proposed on April 12th. At that time Penn, who had left Philadelphia early in April, had returned,

and voted with Hewes for independence, but **Hooper** wa
still detained in North Carolina.

The declaration

Jefferson's draught of a Declaration, which had lain on th
table since June 28th, awaiting the vote on Lee's resolutior
was now taken up for discussion. Every word of it was dul
weighed, and the instrument was perfected. Durin
July 2d, 3d, and until the afternoon of the 4th, the cor
sideration of the Declaration continued, and then the instru
ment was agreed to. Very considerable changes were mad
in the draught reported by the committee, among them bein,
the incorporation into the text of the words used by Le
that the united colonies "are, and of right ought to be, fre
and independent States."

The North Carolina delegates

As this glorious consummation was at the instance o
North Carolina, and was accomplished measurably througl
the cordial and zealous support of her delegation, so ther
was no time when her delegates were not fixed and forward
in the important work of the Continental Congress. Caswel
had been the soul of energy, and gained for himself th
high opinion of the body. Penn, who succeeded him, wa
equally active and zealous. Hooper had long since cast hi
philosophic eye to the future, and beheld America "fast
striding to independence." His sympathies, his sentiments
and his talents placed him in the front rank of its influentia
members. In April he gladly announced that he had found
the people of Virginia desirous of independence, and that
North Carolina far exceeded Virginia; that in many counties
there was no dissenting voice—a condition and situation so
harmonious with his own personal views that he hastened
to send the information back to Philadelphia, where it was
published.

Hewes differed from his colleagues in being a trained
business man and not having followed a professional career.
Yet he had been longer engaged in public affairs than either
of his associates, and for years had been one of those who

ad given direction to political events in North Carolina. Thoroughly acquainted with commerce, connected with a mercantile house at Philadelphia, as at Edenton, familiar with affairs of the seas, he was early assigned to the Marine Committee, of which he became the principal member, discharging practically the duties of a secretary of the navy; and his mercantile houses rendered efficient aid, not merely in the course of ordinary business but in making advances for the benefit of congress. His spirit was such that he wanted to take the field, to be in camp, but his work in congress was too important for him to use the good musket and bayonet with which he had provided himself. Four days after the Declaration was signed he wrote: "What has become of my friend Hooper? I expected to have seen him ere now. My friend Penn came time enough to give his vote for independence. I send you the Declaration of Independence enclosed. I had the weight of North Carolina on my shoulders within a day or two of three months. The service was too severe. I have sat some days from six in the morning till five or sometimes six in the afternoon without eating or drinking. Some of my friends thought that I should not be able to keep soul and body together to this time. Duty, inclination, and self-preservation call on me now to make a little excursion into the country to see my mother. This is a duty which I have not allowed myself time to perform during the almost nine months I have been here." And indeed it was time, for this devoted patriot had exhausted his strength and prepared the way for his early grave.

Hewes's great work

On March 28, 1813, John Adams in the course of a letter drew a picture in which Hewes was presented as changing his attitude toward independence. That, as related, was evidently founded on imagination, tinted by the passage of many years. The circumstances seem to show that the portrayal lacked reality. The matter of independence was not brought positively before congress until May 27th, and then by Hewes presenting the instructions of North Carolina to concur in declaring independence; and North Carolina, represented alone by him, consistently voted for indepen-

Adams in error

1776

dence from the time the subject was first introduced into congress.*

The delay in Congress

Probably when Hewes broke the monotony of congress by presenting the instructions of North Carolina, there was a great and startling sensation, for congress was by no means prepared to act on the measure. Later in the day the Virginia instruction was likewise presented; but so out of harmony was it with the prevailing sentiment that ten days elapsed before the Virginia delegates found resolution to obey their instruction; and then, against the voice of Hewes, the matter was again deferred for three weeks longer.

C. R., X, 494, 498

It appears that as early as March 1st, Hooper, Hewes, and Penn wrote to the Provincial Congress asking instructions with respect to entering into foreign alliances, and it does not appear that any other delegates had at that time made a similar application. They seem to have been the first to move the waters. Their application on this subject utterly negatives Mr. Jefferson's aspersion, made in his old age, "that we had not a greater Tory in congress than Hooper." Mr. Jefferson imputed to Mr. Adams a failure of memory, and confessed that his own was not to be relied on. In this doubt of his own accuracy he evidently was entirely correct.

Bancroft's Hist. U. S., IV, 316

Mr. Hooper proposed in the Provincial Congress of August, 1775, the articles of confederation, and, being overborne, in the Continental Congress, contrary to his own wishes, obeyed the instructions of North Carolina. That he favored independence in April, 1776, is evident. Writing to Johnston six months later, when affairs were very gloomy, he expresses the feelings of his inmost heart: "The successes of Howe have given a strange spring to Toryism. Men who have hitherto lurked in silence or neutrality seem willing to take a side in opposition to the liberties of their country. . . . Were I to choose a motto for a modern Whig it should be, 'Whatever is, is right,' and on the reverse, 'Nil desperandum.'" Such was Hooper's spirit, to sustain all measures, to be steadfast in hope and constant in effort.

Jones's Defence, 325, 326

*Adams must have had in mind Rutledge, of South Carolina, who changed on July 2d, deciding the measure, to the dismay of those members who still feared to take this final step.

ı the congress he, with Franklin, Morris and Lee, formed ıe Secret Committee of Foreign Intercourse elected by the ıffrages of the members. No higher testimonial of implicit ɔnfidence was afforded to any of his associates.

he declaration proclaimed

The council had thought it best to hold sessions at differ- ıt points in the province and from Wilmington it removed ɔ Dobbs County, and then proceeded to Halifax, opening s session there on July 21st. And now came the joyful ews that independence had been declared, and the colonies ˙ere free and independent states. The day following its ıeeting, a copy of the Declaration of Independence was ɛceived, and the council directed that it should be read on ıugust 1st in the town of Halifax, and that it should be ɾoclaimed by the committees of every town and county in ıe most public manner.

In North Carolina

C. R., X, 682, 688

When Thursday, August 1st, came, an immense concourse f people assembled at Halifax to witness the ceremony of a ublic proclamation of independence. The militia com- ›anies of the county were all drawn up in full array. At ıidday Cornelius Harnett, the president of the Council of ›afety, ascended a rostrum erected in front of the court- ıouse, and the enthusiasm of the vast crowd was mani- ɛsted with tremendous rejoicing. Harnett, who had ever ˙een among the foremost in leading the way to indepen- ˙ence, now "read the declaration to the mute and impas- ioned multitude with a solemnity of an appeal to heaven. Nhen he had finished all the people shouted with joy, and ˙annon after cannon . . . proclaimed the glorious tidings hat the thirteen colonies were now free and independent tates. The soldiers seized Harnett and bore him on their ˙houlders through the streets of the town, applauding him as heir champion, and swearing allegiance to the instrument ıe had read."

August 1st

Jones's Defence, 269

In Cumberland County the members of the Committee of ›afety had either retired from the province or had resigned ınd refused to act. In that county alone the order to read he declaration appears not to have been observed, so that ɔn August 6th the Council of Safety directed Colonel Fol-

August

1776

C. R., X, 694

some or Colonel David Smith to call a general meeting of the inhabitants of Cumberland and proclaim the declaration to the people and to the regiment stationed at Cross Creek

Elsewhere independence was proclaimed with great demonstrations of joy. As North Carolina had been the first colony to propose it, the people now hailed it with gladness It was the consummation of their earnest desire; and it imparted to the contest a new character. The leaders well knew that they had burned their bridges behind them; and the people, animated by a great hope, and determined to be free, with unbounded enthusiasm threw the banner of independence to the breeze.

Because the province was now declared a free and independent State, the test prescribed by the congress in August, 1775, was changed by omitting the profession of allegiance; and the oath to be taken by witnesses was amended so as to read, "Between the independent State of North Carolina

C. R., X, 704

and the prisoner to be tried." The council also issued an address to the inhabitants, saying that as the congress had declared the thirteen united colonies free and independent states, "it be recommended to the good people of this now independent State of North Carolina to pay the greatest attention to the election . . . of delegates to represent them in congress, and to have particularly in view this important consideration." Not only were laws to be made, but a constitution, the cornerstone of all law, and "according as it is

C. R., X, 696

well or ill ordered, it must tend in the first degree to promote the happiness or misery of the State."

The council had been sorely tried by the disaffection of the Regulators, who continued to regard themselves as a separate people not allied with their fellow-citizens. Now in Anson County this defection took a novel form. James Childs, a preacher of the New Light Baptist persuasion,

C. R., X, 699

clothed his disloyalty in the garb of religion. He declared that it was one of the tenets of his church not to bear arms, either offensively or defensively; and he preached this doctrine in all the churches of his communion, and inculcated it by the terrors of excommunication; and he refused to take an oath of allegiance to the State. Arrested in Anson and sent to the council, he stood firmly by his doctrine. There-pon the council resolved that he must be considered as an nemy to the State, and he was sent to Edenton on his parole.

In view of such religious teachings, General Person and oseph John Williams were directed, each of them, to agree vith a proper person to go among the inhabitants of Anson nd other western parts of the State and instruct them "in heir duty to Almighty God, and explain to them the justice nd necessity of the measures pursued by the United States s the only means under God of supporting and maintaining ur civil and religious liberties." The remedy, however, vas not entirely efficacious. In October James Perry, one f the same persuasion, having great influence among the eople, from being a preacher, had likewise to be arrested n the same county and conveyed to Halifax.

But while the council was in session at Salisbury early in September a favorable change was observed, and James Hunter and Joseph Dobson made their appearance, and sked the "privileges of free citizens," declaring that they vere willing to take an oath of allegiance to the State, and he council resolved that they should be considered as "free citizens and members of this State." So also Booth Boote, vho, with John Dunn, had been paroled to Salisbury, having aken the oath, was admitted to citizenship; and later Dr. John Pyle and other prominent malcontents took the oath f allegiance, among them Rev. George Micklejohn, who had been paroled to Perquimans. Other action was constantly taken in the way of arresting and putting under bond or confining Tories or having them released from durance on their submission to the state authorities.

James Hunter a patriot C. R., X, 793, 797, 826

The Indians become hostile

Governor Martin's plan for the subjugation of North Carolina contemplated aid from the Indians, and John Stuart, the Indian superintendent, spent several months in the spring of 1776 with the governor awaiting the arrival of General Clinton's troops. As yet he had had no instructions to employ the Indians on the frontier, but he was keeping them in readiness to act when required. Later he departed for Pensacola to be in close communication with them; and arrangements were in progress for all the tribes from the

1776 Ohio to Alabama to begin hostilities against the western borders.

The Indians in arms

Toward the end of June fifteen Shawnees, Delawares, and Mingoes brought the war belt to the Cherokees, and it was received by the young men against the wishes of the older chiefs. Before measures had been fully arranged, bands of Cherokees, inflamed by the encroachments of the whites on the Holstein and Nolachucky, and eager for spoils, began their forays.

C. R., X, 657 et seq.

While the council was still at Halifax this proposed incursion of the Indians became known. In the first week in July the Cherokees had fallen on the inhabitants in South Carolina, plundered houses, killed some settlers and carried off several prisoners. Others attacked the forts on the

S. R., XI, 333

Holstein and Watauga. Most of the settlers, however, escaped, having been warned by Nancy Ward, from Echota, she being the "beloved woman" of that Indian capital, and always, like her kinsman, Attakullakulla (the Little Car-

They cross the mountains

penter), friendly to the whites. Some twenty women and children were victims of the tomahawk. Only Mrs. Bean, perhaps the wife of William Bean, the first white man to erect a cabin in that wilderness, and a boy named Moore were taken alive. The latter was burned at the stake, and Mrs. Bean was also bound to the stake ready for the burning when Nancy Ward interfered and saved her life. Unsuccessful in their assault on the forts, the Indian warriors crossed the mountains and fell on the unsuspecting families on Crooked Creek (near Rutherfordton), and, coming up the Toe, invaded the frontier of Rowan. The unheralded appearance of these murderous bands caused great conster-

C. R., X, 662, 669

nation. On July 12th Rutherford wrote to the council that he had received an express the week before that forty Indians were ravaging Crooked Creek, and that appeals were made to him for relief. He pleaded for expedition. Before twenty-four hours had elapsed he despatched another express that the Indians were making great progress in destroying and murdering in Rowan. "Thirty-seven persons,"

The massacre on the Catawba, July 10-11

he said, "were killed last Wednesday and Thursday on the Catawba," and "I am also informed that Colonel McDowell and ten men more and one hundred and twenty women and

ildren are besieged in some kind of a fort, and the Indians
ound them; no help to them before yesterday, and they
re surrounded on Wednesday. I expect the next account
 hear is that they are all destroyed. . . . Three of our
ptains are killed and one wounded. This day I set out
th what men I can raise for the relief of the district."
Pray, gentlemen, consider our distress; send us plenty of
wder, and I hope under God we of Salisbury district are
le to stand them."

Rutherford acted with that energy that ever distinguished
m. Within a week he was on the frontier with near
renty-five hundred men, for the western Carolinians had
rung to arms at the first call, animated by a consuming
urpose to inflict heavy punishment upon their murderous
e. Among those with him were Colonel Adam Alexander
d the Mecklenburg regiment, protecting the settlers on the
atawba. Leaving the main body at Old Fort, then called
avidson's, on July 29th, with a detachment of five hundred
en Rutherford crossed the mountains and dislodged some
vo hundred braves, who had established themselves on the
olachucky.

On August 13th the council adjourned to meet at the
ouse of Mr. Joel Lane, in Wake County, where it con-
ened on the 21st. Cornelius Harnett being absent with
ave, Samuel Ashe was unanimously chosen president. A
etition was received from the settlements on the Watauga
nd Holstein, called by the inhabitants there "the Washing-
n district," setting forth that about six years earlier they
ad begun to locate in that territory, and finding themselves
utside of Virginia, had formed a court and adopted the
irginia laws, and had enlisted a company of riflemen under
aptain James Robertson, stationing them on the frontier
 guard against an attack by the Indians. They asked that
ney might be annexed to North Carolina, promising to be
overned by the council and to lack nothing in the glorious
use of America. This petition was signed by John Carter,
ohn Sevier, William Bean and others as a committee, and
 it were attached more than a hundred names of settlers
n the Watauga and Nolachucky, among them being David
rockett. The council directed that they should hold an

Rutherford
crosses the
mountains

S. R., XI,
338

Washington
district
annexed
C. R., X,
701, 708-711

1776

election on October 15th and choose five delegates to repre sent Washington district in the congress of the State, t meet at Halifax on November 10th.

The
movement
against the
Indians

President Rutledge, of South Carolina, had earlier sug gested a joint movement on the part of Virginia and North an South Carolina against the Indians. He proposed to sen Major Williamson with eleven hundred men against the lowe Cherokees, and that a force from North Carolina shoul attack the Middle towns, and, joining Williamson, shoul proceed against Valley River and the Hiwassee, while th Virginians should come down the Holstein and attack th

Colonel
Williams
on the
Holstein

Over-hill towns. The council agreed to this proposition, an directed the militia from the Hillsboro district and fror Surry County to join Rutherford, while a regiment of thre hundred men under Colonel Joe Williams was to cross th mountains and join Colonel Christian and his Virginian

C. R., X,
789

at Big Island, on the Holstein. On August 23d Genera Person was despatched to Rutherford's camp with par ticular directions, and on September 1st Rutherford, with

Sept. 1st,
Ruther-
ford's march

great cavalcade of horses bearing his provisions and ammu nition, entered Swannanoa Gap and pressed forward. H took with him two thousand privates and eighty light horse with supplies for forty days carried by fourteen hundre pack horses. To defend the frontier in his absence, h ordered three captains with a hundred and thirty men t range in Tryon, one hundred and seventy-five in Rowan and a hundred in Surry, that then extended to the India line in the mountains. Among those accompanying th expedition were Colonel Martin Armstrong, Colonel Adan Alexander, Captain Benjamin Cleveland, William Lenoir and William Gray. The Orange regiment, under Colone Joseph Taylor, had reached his camp, but its assistance no being needed, it returned home.

Biog. Hist.
N. C., II,
384

Rutherford's course lay down the Swannanoa and Frenc Broad and up Hominy Creek to Pigeon River, then to Rich land Creek, and over the dividing ridge to the head of Scott' Creek, which he followed to the Tuckaseegee. He move with such rapidity and secrecy that he passed fifty mile into the wilderness without being discovered by the Indians The journey through the mountains was an arduous an difficult performance. Without a road and sometimes without even an Indian trail, he led his army over tremendous mountains and across rapid streams, pursuing his way in momentary danger of ambuscade by his wily foe. But so sagacious were his movements that he had penetrated two-thirds of the distance into the forests without interruption. At length, when only thirty miles from the Middle Settlements on the Tuckaseegee, he detached a thousand men to surprise the Indians by a forced march. Soon, however, in their quiet but rapid journey, they came upon some thirty of the savages, who disputed their progress, and sent information to the settlement, which thus was evacuated when Rutherford reached it. Immediately he began the work of destruction, and speedily devastated the fields and burned every house. Then, with a detachment of nine hundred men and ten days' provisions, he hurried along the Little Tennessee and moved on towards Valley River and the Hiwassee.

C. R., X, 860

Indian settlements destroyed

Williamson was to have met him at Cowee, but after devastating the Indian towns at the foothills, the South Carolinians were detained, and Rutherford proceeded alone. Missing the usual trail through Waya Gap, he crossed the Nantahala at an unaccustomed place. Five hundred braves lay in ambush at Waya, hoping to destroy his force as twenty years before they had Montgomery's. While they awaited his coming, Rutherford, pressing on, reached the head waters of Valley River. Every town on that stream was destroyed in turn, and it was as if a besom of destruction had swept over those settlements, so sudden and rapid were his movements. He had the good fortune to avoid a pitched battle, killed but twelve Indians, and captured nine. He also took seven white men, with whom he got four negroes, much leather, about a hundredweight of gunpowder and a ton of lead, which they were conveying to Mobile. His own loss was but three men.

C. R., X, 712, 861

While in the midst of this devastation they encamped, on Sunday, September 15th, at Nuckesseytown (doubtless Tuckaseegee), and there, after a sermon by Rev. Mr. James Hall, they buried one of Captain Irwin's men with due solemnity. A fortnight after Rutherford had begun his

Hunter's Western North Carolina, 198

1776

march the Council of Safety, which had adjourned to Salisbury to be in proximity to the scene of operations, despatched Colonel Waightstill Avery, with an escort, with directions to the general to send, if possible, a detachment to aid Colonel Christian against the Over-hill towns, and on his return to cut a road through the mountains for future use. A juncture was made by Colonel Williamson on September 26th on the Hiwassee; but then Rutherford's work had been thoroughly done, and the Valley Settlement had been C. R., X, 882 obliterated.　It was deemed impracticable to cross the Smokies and assist Colonel Christian, and they turned their faces homeward.　The Indians, driven from their valleys, homeless refugees without food or raiment, sought the dark recesses of the Nantahala, some fleeing to the Over hills, but the greater number finding a temporary home with the Creeks on the Coosawatchee River.　Others made their painful way to their British allies in Florida, where five hundred of them were received and supplied with food during that winter.　Rutherford on his return marked his road through the mountains, which has since been known as Rutherford's Trace.　Within a month from his departure he returned to Old Fort, reaching Salisbury early in October.

The Surry regiment

Beyond the mountains the Surry regiment, under Colonel Joseph Williams, Colonel Love and Major Winston, having joined Colonel Christian, moved cautiously along the great Indian warpath until the Little Tennessee was reached, C. R., X, 837, 844, 892, 912 where town after town was destroyed.　So swift had been the action that the Indians, unable to resist, soon sought terms of peace.　Some of the Indian head men came into camp, agreed to surrender all prisoners and to cede to the whites all the territory occupied in the Tennessee settlements.　On their solemn promise that such a treaty should be made, Christian agreed to suspend hostilities.　An exception was made, however, as to two towns which had been concerned in burning the Moore boy, but the peace town of Echota was not disturbed.　Colonel Williams was not pleased with Colonel Christian's action, attributing his leniency to the Cherokees to a settled policy on the part of Virginia to absorb their trade; and he recommended to the council that as the frontiers of North Carolina were inhabited far beyond the colony line, commissioners should be appointed to run the line farther west. By treaties soon afterward made the lower Cherokees surrendered all their territory in South Carolina except a narrow strip, and the middle and upper Cherokees ceded all their possessions east of the Blue Ridge, together with the disputed territory on the Nolachucky, Watauga, and New rivers.

The Indian cession

After reaching Old Fort, General Rutherford, to destroy some towns not on his route, and perhaps to aid Colonel Christian, directed Captain William Moore and Captain Harden, with the light horse of Tryon County, a hundred in number, to return to the Indian country. Leaving Cathey's fort on October 29th, they penetrated to the towns on Cowee Mountain. A detachment, pursuing the fleeing Indians to Soco Creek, "crossed prodigious mountains, which were almost impassable, experiencing there a severe shock of an earthquake, reached Richland Creek Mountains, and then returned to Pigeon River."

Moore's expedition C. R., X, 895-898

The Tories active

Tory emissaries during the summer, and especially in August, were active, and seem to have expected that they would be joined by a great number of Indian allies. Rutherford could not take the second battalion from Rowan, "the current of Tories running strong in Guilford and Anson"; and Colonel Folsome wrote: "It is most certain they wish for nothing more . . . than an opportunity of making a head, . . . numbers would fly to join the Indians, as it is their professed declaration"; while in Bladen, there were a number of deserters from the regular troops, Tories and other disaffected persons collected, whose action was so threatening that General Ashe despatched two companies under Colonel Brown to disperse them. Before Brown reached their settlement they killed Captain Nathaniel Richardson and committed other outrages, and then many of them fled into South Carolina.

C. R., X, 725, 732, 744

1776

C. R., X,
704, 720, 724,
739, 798, 840

Salt making on the coast

Salt being such an indispensable necessity, unusual efforts were made to obtain a supply for the public, and Robert Williams was employed to set up salt works at Beaufort, where pans for that purpose were erected. Conferences were held with Dr. Franklin at Philadelphia as to the best process of manufacture, and salt pans were ordered from that city. All along the coast the inhabitants began with their pots and kettles to make a supply. Early in October Sam Ashe wrote from the Cape Fear: *"Te Deum Laudamus* we here at present joyfully chant forth. The vessels of war . . . took their departure a few days since, first burning two of their tenders. We have now an open port. . . . The humor of salt boiling seems to be taking place here. I have seen some boiled . . . the cleanest and whitest of any . . . I ever saw in my life; every old wife is now scouring her pint pot for the necessary operation. God send them good luck." The council gave directions for supplying the people. The quantity being limited, it was doled out. Conner Dowd was to sell salt in his possession "to the Whigs who bore arms on the late expedition against the Tories at Moore's Creek at ten shillings per bushel, not selling more than a half bushel to each man."

The British abandon Cape Fear

During the summer General Moore remained at Wilmington. There still lingered several British vessels in the lower harbor, while a detachment of their troops was in

C. R., X,
787, 824, 840

possession of Baldhead. Toward the last of August Moore took three hundred men and departed on a secret expedition, no one having the slightest conjecture what was his purpose, unless to attack the enemy on that island. The result of the expedition is not recorded; but a month later the vessels departed, burning their tenders and the British sloop *Cruizer,* which had been on that station for several years, was the refuge of Governor Martin when driven from Fort Johnston, and now was probably so unseaworthy that she could not be removed. The ship *Jenny,* where the Tories seeking protection had found a resting place, also

A Loyalist
regiment

sailed for New York; and as these Loyalists had been or-

anized into companies with officers by Governor Martin,
n their reaching New York they were assigned to a Loyalist
egiment then formed at the north.

Toward the end of September the council again convened
t Halifax, and in the absence of the president, Samuel
Ashe, Willie Jones was chosen to preside.

A winter campaign threatened

The Continental Congress having directed that two of the
ontinental regiments should be conducted by General Moore
o join General Washington, subsequently, in view of a
probable winter campaign at the south, left it in the discretion of the Council of Safety to retain them in the State.
The council thought it best that they should not go north at
hat time, and the order was countermanded.

It being believed that a southern campaign was in con-
emplation by the British commander, preparations were
made to meet it. It was considered that the invasion would
be either in Virginia or South Carolina, and North Carolina
would protect herself by aiding in the defence. General
Moore had with him in North Carolina five continental regiments, except about one hundred and fifty of the First and
Second, these companies and the Third Regiment being with
General Howe in Georgia. They were distributed at different points in the eastern part of the State, while a small
detachment of the Third was at Salisbury with Colonel
Martin.

CHAPTER XXXII

The Constitution of 1776

Making the constitution.—Divergencies.—The conservatives.—The results of the election.—Johnston burned in effigy.—The congress meets.—The committee moves slowly.—Proceedings in the convention.—Citizenship established.—The principles of government.—Sovereignty of the people.—The Orange instructions.—Those of Mecklenburg.—Hooper urges the Delaware plan.—In the committee room.—The draught reported.—The bill of rights.—The religious test.—Thoroughly considered.—The Virginia constitution.—A representative republic.—Public schools.—The religious test adopted —The instrument conservative.—A new administration installed.

1776

Making the constitution

Hardly had the Indians been subdued before the sombre shadow of a British invasion cast itself over the seaboard of the southern states, and toward the end of the year, as at its opening, the people of North Carolina looked to the future with painful forebodings of grave perils and devastation. In the midst of these disquieting anticipations they were now to ordain a constitution and government for the independent State and start out the new commonwealth on its voyage through unknown and uncertain seas. Happy would it be for themselves and for posterity were the foundations of the political edifice well and strongly laid; deplorable indeed if tyranny and despotism should find a crevice through which they might enter.

Divergencies

The first effort to frame a constitution made apparent in the summer pronounced divergencies among the public men. Johnston, Hewes, Hooper, Thomas Jones, Iredell, Allen Jones and probably Nash, Caswell and possibly Harnett and Sam Ashe might be ranked as conservatives, with varying shades of difference between them. Willie Jones, Person, Burke, Penn, Avery, the Alexanders, John Ashe, Polk, and Dr. Caldwell might be classed as advocates of a pure democracy. But there is so little on which to hazard a conjecture, except uncertain tradition, that one hesitates to assign many of those mentioned to either side. All realized that they were severed forever from the past and were to establish a government for themselves and posterity on a republican basis. The Conservatives, Johnston and others, believed that the general features of the British system, with which they were familiar, offered the best government, freer from possible evils than any other known to history. They preferred a stable and independent judiciary, controlled only by the principles of law established by the decisions of the courts; justices of the peace and court officers also to have a stable tenure; the great officers to be appointed by the Assembly rather than by popular election, and the Assembly itself kept within bounds by annual elections.

The other extreme view looked to uprooting every vestige of the old government and the establishment of a pure democracy, with annual election of judges, clerks, and justices of the peace by the freemen of the commonwealth. Between these two extremes there were many shades of opinion. In view of the necessity of framing a constitution, on August 9th the council had prepared an address to the people, recommending that each county should choose five delegates particularly suited to represent them in this great work. Davis, the printer, was dilatory in printing this address for distribution, and Harnett expressed himself as anxiously awaiting the copies. "The advice of the council to the inhabitants has not yet got abroad," he said. "Davis ought to be hurried." Evidently he had the matter much at heart.

The election was held on October 15th. While there does not appear to have been any attempt at the organization of parties, yet here and there throughout the province opposition was manifested to the election of particular persons. At New Bern, Tisdale unsuccessfully opposed Abner Nash. Hewes was returned from Edenton as usual; Penn was not elected from Granville, strange to say; while Hooper was returned from Perquimans, as well as from Wilmington. Hewes and Hooper stood on the same line as Johnston and Iredell, while Penn was an ultra-democrat, in line with Thomas Person. Harnett was so desirous of the election

1776
October

McRee's
Iredell, I,
334

C. R., X, 914

McRee's
Iredell, I,
335, 336

of Hooper that he himself stood in Brunswick County, surrendering his hold on the borough of Wilmington that Hooper might be assured of a seat in the congress. Samuel Spencer, a strong democrat, was not returned from Anson. Mecklenburg added to her delegation Waightstill Avery, and Guilford, David Caldwell. There was considerable change in the personnel of the deputies, but except the changes above mentioned there was only one other notable leader not returned—Samuel Johnston. Allen Jones, John Johnston, and Thomas Jones and all the other conservatives were elected. For some reason a great effort was made to defeat Johnston, who had always been unanimously chosen to preside over the previous congresses, was in strong sympathy with the Continental Congress, and an ardent promoter of every measure tending to sustain independence; no man was more fixed than he in his American principles. No means were spared to poison the minds of the people against him personally; "to inflame their prejudices, excite alarm, and sow in them by indefinite charges and vague whispers the seeds of distrust." There was a hot and spirited canvass, resulting in Johnston's defeat; and the triumph was celebrated with riot and debauchery, the orgies being concluded by burning Johnston in effigy. While Hewes was elected from the borough, and Thomas Benbury and Thomas Jones were returned from the county, James Blount, Luke Sumner, and Jacob Hunter replaced Sam Johnston, John B. Beasly, and Thomas Hunter. Apparently James Blount was the opponent of Johnston, and succeeded in displacing him. The election and its result in Chowan led to the characterization of Johnston's opponents by Mr. Iredell as "rioters," to whom he ascribed such principles as these: "I despise every man who differs from me. I am sure he must be a Tory. I think a man more liable to be a Tory who has hitherto been most earnest in the cause." "I impute to gentlemen all our present difficulties." "I am a sworn enemy to all gentlemen." "I believe it honorable and proper to persecute poor distressed individuals when we have them in our power, provided we want courage to prove in any other manner the alacrity of our zeal against those we suppose enemies of our country." This "creed of a rioter" would indicate that the principal charges against Johnston were personal, based on his wealth and lofty bearing and on some kindness to distressed persons, perhaps Tories, which was imputed to him as Toryism. There is found in it no trace of disagreement between him and his countrymen on the fundamental principles of government. The strenuous opposition to him has been attributed to Willie Jones and his friends, it being suggested that they desired to remove Johnston from his dominant position in public affairs, the more readily to secure the adoption of an ultra-democratic form of government, which he opposed; if so, his defeat was without avail.

1776
November

The congress meets

The congress met on November 12th, at Halifax, and Allen Jones proposed Richard Caswell for president, who was accordingly unanimously chosen. Theretofore all votes in the several congresses, as also in the council, had been by counties and towns; now it was determined, against the vote of the Albemarle section and the towns of Brunswick and New Bern alone, that all questions should be determined by the voice of the several members. A majority of the members were to govern, not a majority of the counties. At once the congress appointed a committee composed of the president, Thomas Person, Allen Jones, John Ashe, Abner Nash, Willie Jones, Thomas Jones, Simon Bright, Christopher Neale, Samuel Ashe, William Haywood, Griffith Rutherford, Henry Abbott, Luke Sumner, Thomas Respis, Archibald Maclaine, James Hogun, and Hezekiah Alexander to frame a constitution. In the formation of this committee the eastern members largely predominated, there being from the west only one member each from Granville, Rowan, and Mecklenburg, while Dobbs, Craven, Chowan, and New Hanover each had two members. Subsequently, however, as other members came in, there were added to that committee Waightstill Avery, Whitmel Hill, Thomas Eaton, John Birdsong, Robert Irwin, Joseph Hewes, Cornelius Harnett, William Sharpe, and John Spicer, four of whom were from the west. It would seem that where one conservative was appointed on the committee he was immediately followed by a democrat, the committee being about

C. R., X,
913

1776

Proceedings
in the
congress
C. R., X,
903

Additional
battalions

Criminal
courts

Bayard
vs.
Singleton,
1 North
Carolina
Reports

evenly divided, and doubtless well representing the sentiments of the congress. It at once began its work, but weeks were to elapse before it completed its plan of government.

An attack on South Carolina being feared, for a large fleet bearing a considerable number of troops had sailed from New York supposed to be destined for Charleston, the congress ordered General Moore to march with the continentals for the relief of that city, and a committee was raised to consider the most speedy method of embodying five thousand militia to aid in defence. Three additional regiments of continentals were also provided for, to be commanded respectively by James Hogun, James Armstrong, and John Williams. Hooper and Hewes were re-elected delegates to the Continental Congress, but Penn now gave place to Dr. Burke, of Orange County. It is to be observed, however, that although Penn was not chosen a member by his county, nor retained in the Continental Congress, he was appointed one of the committee "to revise and consider all such statutes and acts of assembly as are in force in North Carolina, and to prepare bills to be passed into laws consistent with the new form of government." He was not entirely ignored. And Sam Johnston was named second on this very important committee, the first being Thomas Jones. A seal of State being necessary, the congress directed Hooper, Hewes, and Burke to procure one; and in the meantime the private seal of the governor was to be affixed to all grants and other public acts of the State.

To enforce the criminal laws, temporary courts of oyer and terminer were established to be held in the several districts of the State, two persons learned in law in each district being appointed by the governor to hold them. It was enacted that all of the former statutes and such parts of the common law as were not inconsistent with the freedom and independence of the State should continue in force until the next Assembly.

The royal government being subverted and a new State erected on its ruins, the people felt as if "they had been marooned on some desert island," without a constitution, government or laws, and the congress addressed itself to organizing civil affairs. All glebes and lands formerly held

1776

S. R.,
XXIII,
996, 997

Citizenship
established

by any religious society were declared vested in their owners; and the congress ordained that all regular ministers of every denomination should have power to celebrate matrimony according to the rites and ceremonies of their respective churches, they, however, observing the rules and restrictions provided by law. It was particularly necessary to establish citizenship. The congress directed the governor to offer free pardon and protection to all persons who should within ninety days take the oath of allegiance to the State, and those who refused to take the oaths were declared incapable of bringing any suit, or purchasing any lands, or transferring their lands, which were declared forfeited to the State. All persons residing within the limits of the State were held to owe allegiance; and it was declared that any one who should thereafter levy war against the State or adhere to its enemies or give them aid and assistance or intelligence shall be adjudged guilty of high treason and suffer death, and forfeit his property; but on conviction the judge might make provision out of the forfeited estate for the wife or children of the criminal; and it was declared that any person owing allegiance to the State who should deny the supreme authority of the people, or assert that those who had taken up arms were rebels, or deny the lawfulness of defending the State, or do any act tending to propagate and spread sedition, should be adjudged guilty of a misdemeanor.

The principles of government

The matter of ordaining a new government had received thoughtful attention.* In every colony much consideration had been bestowed on fundamental principles. The people were embarking on unknown seas, and the principles of government were much discussed. Articles on the subject were widely circulated. It seems to have been generally considered that the legislative power ought to be vested in two

*Apparently after the failure to agree on a constitution at the previous session some one wrote to John Adams for an expression of his views, and his reply is preserved in Governor Caswell's letter-book. Governor Swain said it was addressed to Burke. We should think that it was addressed to Caswell. The constitution contains some of the principles he advocated. (N. C. Uni. Mag., 1856, 232.)

S. R., XI,
321

1776

bodies, not one, as in Pennsylvania; while there was difference of opinion as to whether the executive should have any legislative function. Other points of difference were as to the election of the chief executive and other great officers, whether by the people themselves or by the Assembly; and particularly as to the election and term of office of the judges; also as to the qualification of the electors. In some of the colonies all freemen could vote; in North Carolina only freeholders had enjoyed that right.

Sovereignty of the people

C. R., X, 870ƒ

The fundamental principle of the sovereignty of the people was universally accepted. It was held that political power is of two kinds—one the principal and supreme, the other the derived and inferior; the first possessed only by the people, the other by their servants; that what is ordained by the people cannot be altered but by them; that the legislature must observe the limitations and restrictions imposed by the supreme power; and that the executive, legislative, and judicial powers are distinct and independent. These principles were embraced in a set of maxims, which doubtless were extensively disseminated throughout all the colonies. They were embraced in the instructions given by the people of Mecklenburg and of Orange for the guidance of their delegates in the congress; and, indeed, the exact agreement of the seven principles first declared in these instructions indicates that they had a common source.

The Orange instructions

C. R., X, 239, 870a, 870g

Among the Orange instructions was one to the effect that all officers should give an assurance that they "do not acknowledge supremacy, ecclesiastical or civil, in any foreign power, or spiritual infallibility, or authority to grant the divine pardon." This was in the handwriting of Dr. Burke, himself a Roman Catholic. Similarly, Mecklenburg instructed that no atheist nor any one who denied any of the Persons of the Holy Trinity, or the divine authority of the Old and New Testament, or who should be of the Roman Catholic religion, should hold any office in the State. Orange County provided for two branches of the Assembly, one to be elected by the freeholders and householders and the other by freeholders only; while Mecklenburg, whose instructions were in the handwriting of Avery, required that both branches of the legislature should be elected by "the good people of the State"; and further, that "all judges should be appointed by the General Assembly, and that their term of office should be for one year only." Mecklenburg also directed that there should be a land tax, and that all should be taxed according to their estates; and that a college should be handsomely endowed in that county.

1776
The Mecklenburg instructions

Both Hewes and Penn returned to North Carolina at that time, and Hooper, feeling constrained to remain in attendance on the Continental Congress, wrote his views for the consideration of the congress. "Let us consider," said he, "the people at large as a source from which all power is to be derived. . . . Rulers must be conceived as the creatures of the people. . . . A single branch of legislation is a many-headed monster, . . . and its members become a tyranny, dreadful in proportion to the numbers which compose it. . . . I am now convinced that a third branch of legislation is at least unnecessary. But for the sake of execution we must have a magistrate solely executive." He urged that the constitution of Delaware, which had been promulgated in September, had great merit: "I admire," said he, "no part of the Delaware plan more than the appointing judges during good behavior. Limit their political existence, and make them dependent upon the suffrages of the people, that instant we corrupt the channels of public justice. Rhode Island furnishes an example too dreadful to imitate." Besides the Delaware plan, the congress had also the new constitutions of Virginia, South Carolina, and New Jersey for reference. The committee doubtless availed themselves of every aid in performing their important duty; but the prevailing ideas were, not unnaturally, similar to those that found expression in the bill of rights* and constitution of the adjoining State of Virginia.

C. R., X, 867, 868

*The Bill of Rights of Virginia was written entirely by Thomas Jefferson, while the body of the constitution was prepared by George Mason. (Wirt's Life of Patrick Henry, 215.)

1776
S. R.,
XVIII, 139
Although some members exercised more influence than others, it would seem that the work of the committee was the joint product of the intelligence of all of the members.

The framers of the constitution
In 1787 Judge Ashe said to the legislature: "If my opinion of our constitution is an error, I fear it is an incurable one, for I had the honor to assist in the forming it, and confess I so designed it, and I believe every other gentleman concerned did also"; from which it would be inferred that the constitution was the joint product of the members who "designed it."

Debates in convention in 1835, 43, 318
Although Thomas Jones was the chairman, the president of the convention, Caswell, was perhaps the most influential member. Of him the venerable Nathaniel Macon said: "He was certainly one of the most powerful men that ever lived in this or any other country"; and Judge Toomer said: "Such was his influence in the convention that tradition says he dictated the principles, if not the terms, of the instrument." On that committee were also Harnett, Thomas Jones, Willie and Allen Jones, Maclaine, Avery, John and Sam Ashe, Thomas Person and Abner Nash.

These and others as well, members of the committee, were men of decided convictions and were not overshadowed by any of their associates. Still Caswell, being president of the convention, probably exerted a strong influence not only in the committee, but in the congress, and as he had apparently sought the views of John Adams and preserved Adams's letter in his executive letter-book, it is an inference that he agreed with the sentiments of the New Englander, which were conservative.

S. R., XI, 504; XIII, 31
That Dr. Burke had a principal hand in devising the legislative plan may be gathered from Johnston's writing to him of it as "your plan"; while Caswell said if there is any blame to be fixed on those who formed the constitution, his good friend, Mr. Harnett, ought to take a very considerable part of it to himself for cramping so much the powers of the executive. To Harnett also, by tradition, is assigned the authorship of the thirty-fourth article, placing all denominations on the same footing, granting entire liberty of

orship, but not exempting preachers of sedition from legal unishment.*

Mr. Wilson, of Perquimans, remarked in the convention f 1835 that the "constitution is thought to have been as uch or more the work (the thirty-second section excepted) f Willie Jones than any other one individual." But if so, Villie Jones was not such a radical democrat as some have upposed.

Doubtless there were many concessions and compromises.

he draught reported

For three weeks the committee was framing the instru- ent; and then, on Friday, December 6th, Thomas Jones iformed the house that the committee had prepared the orm of a constitution, which he read in his place and sub- itted to the house. It was thereupon ordered that a copy iould be made for each county and for each district, and it iould be taken under consideration the following Monday.

Of the first draught we have no copy and but little infor- ation of its provisions, for the instrument as perfected was robably much amended by the congress itself. It may be onjectured that the committee followed the plan indicated y Thomas Jones in the preceding congress and provided or two branches of the legislature, one elected by the free- olders and the other by the freemen. The justices were to e elected by the people. Johnston on December 7th wrote: There is one thing in it which I cannot bear, and yet I m inclined to think it will stand. The inhabitants are em- owered to elect the justices in their respective counties, vho are to be the judges of the county courts. Numberless iconveniences must arise from so absurd an institution." his was changed by the congress. There was no religious est for office in the committee's report, but one was inserted y the congress. On Monday and Tuesday the house con- idered the constitution, when it was read paragraph by aragraph, amended and passed the first reading. On hursday it was again read and debated paragraph by para-

*It is said that Governor Swain once mentioned that a large part f the original draft of the constitution was in the handwriting of Vaightstill Avery.

1776

Debates in convention, 1835, 394

C. R., X, 954

C. R., X, 1040

1776

graph and passed its second reading. Thomas Jones then reported the bill of rights, which he read in his place; and this was taken up on Saturday, debated paragraph by paragraph, amended and passed its first reading.

McRee's Iredell, I, 339

On December 13th Johnston wrote: "One of the members from the back country introduced a test by which every person before he should be admitted to a share in the legislature should swear that he believed in the Holy Trinity and that the scripture of the Old Testament was written by divine inspiration. This was carried after a very warm debate, and has blown up such a flame that everything is in danger of being thrown into confusion. They talk of having all the officers, even the judges and clerks, elected annually, with a number of other absurdities." This was the talk in the house, not in the committee. It was a departure from the Virginia constitution and from the committee's plan, and it precipitated a contest.

The following Tuesday the bill of rights was read paragraph by paragraph, amended, passed and engrossed. It contains many of the principles of Magna Charta. For several days the constitution was yet further considered, the house reading it paragraph by paragraph and amending it. Finally it was perfected, passed, engrossed, and ordered to be immediately printed and distributed. The committee was appointed November 13th, reported on December 6th, and the constitution was under consideration by the entire body for twelve days, when it was adopted on December 18th. Each word in it was often weighed, debated, and passed on by the house itself.

C. R., X, 974

Whatever may have been the particular zeal of this man or that in the committee, or in the house, every principle contained in the instrument and every provision of it was responsive to the will of the majority of the members.

Similarity to Virginia constitution

As perfected, it nearly approached the Virginia constitution with its bill of rights. The second branch of the legislature, which in every other province but Virginia was known as the council, was denominated the senate, Virginia being the first to introduce that word in American history. Senators were to be elected only by freeholders, while assemblymen were to be voted for by all citizens who had paid their public taxes. The governor and other great officers were to be elected by the General Assembly, and the judges were to hold their offices during good behavior, as in Virginia. The justices of the peace were to be recommended to the governor by the representatives in the Assembly, and when commissioned by him were to hold their offices during good behavior, and were not to be removed from office by the General Assembly unless for misbehavior.

Thus was established a representative republic far removed from the pure and simple democracy which some have said that Willie Jones advocated. Indeed, the Constitution conformed in many respects to the views of Johnston, although he was not a member of the congress. There were to be annual elections of assemblymen, and a governor annually elected and ineligible after three years of service until a like period had elapsed; and the judiciary was entirely independent. Still Johnston remained opposed to the plan for constituting the legislature, and became discontented, perhaps the more because the people had burned him in effigy.

A representative republic

S. R., XI, 504

Mecklenburg's voice for the establishment and endowment of a school in that county seems to have been answered by a provision that a school or schools should be established by the legislature for the convenient instruction of youth, with such salaries to the masters, paid by the public, as may enable them to instruct at low prices; and all useful learning should be duly encouraged and promoted in one or more universities. The western member who offered in the house that legislators should swear that they believed in the Holy Trinity, as required by the Mecklenburg instructions, may have been Rev. Dr. David Caldwell, of Guilford, who was not a member of the committee. The introduction of that test raised a flame. Many of the public men of that era were deists; some were atheists. It is said that some of the leading members of the convention were of that mind, and it was for that reason, perhaps, that this proposed section caused such excitement. Besides, if the original proposition followed the Mecklenburg instructions throughout, it excluded from office all Roman Catholics, and Burke was of that faith, as well, perhaps, as others of the congress. The

Public schools

The religious test

1776
§32 of
Constitution

Mecklenburg proposition was, however, somewhat altered before adoption;* but still no one who denied the truth of the Protestant religion or the divine authority of the Old and New Testament, or should hold religious principles incompatible with the freedom and safety of the State, was to be admitted to office. This apparently was not thought to exclude Roman Catholics, who from the first held office unquestioned. It did exclude atheists and infidels, but none of the public men of North Carolina appear to have fallen within that category, although tradition attributes to some of them a little laxity in their religious beliefs. No public man, Roman Catholic or of atheistical inclinations, ceased to hold office.

The congress was apparently more conservative than the committee, for the committee's plan of electing the justices of the peace, who were to hold the county courts, by a vote of the inhabitants, was rejected by the congress.

The
instrument
conservative

From first to last the instrument as perfected by the congress was conservative, and the government it established must have been a great disappointment to those who favored a pure democracy. Nor did the congress submit it to the people for their approval, and it took effect immediately on its adoption. It, however, was well received by the people, and was the subject of eulogy for many years. It remained unchanged for two generations, although in the course of time complaints began to be made at the west against the plan of representation, and in 1835 the people preferred to choose their own governors, and twenty years later the requirement of a freehold to constitute a senatorial elector was abolished.

C. R., X,
991

The constitution being adopted, two days later the congress chose Richard Caswell to be governor of the State until the next session of the General Assembly; and Cornelius Harnett, Thomas Person, William Dry, William Haywood, Edward Starkey, Joseph Leach, and Thomas Eaton members of the Council of State; and in case of the death or other disability of the governor, the president of the

---

*A writer in the Wilmington *Herald* of 1844 ascribed that article as written to Cornelius Harnett. Harnett doubtless amended Dr. Caldwell's first proposition.

council was to succeed him. The congress having provided
for the establishment of courts of oyer and terminer in the
several districts of the State, proceeded to appoint justices
of the peace, sheriffs and constables for the several counties,
and establish county courts until the Assembly should meet.
As Caswell, on becoming governor, resigned his office as
treasurer of the southern district, John Ashe was elected to
that office; and Cornelius Harnett was elected vice-president
of the congress. The common law and the laws of the
province that were not inconsistent with the freedom and
independence of the State were declared in force. Having
performed its work, the congress, after sitting all day Sunday, on Monday, December 23d, adjourned *sine die*.

1776
December
S. R.,
XXIII, 992

C. R., X,
988

CHAPTER XXXIII

Caswell's Administration, 1776-80

Caswell's administration.—Military movements.—Political power.
—The first Assembly.—Tories banished.—Sheppard's regiment.—
Conditions within the State.—The task of the patriots.—Johnston
dissatisfied. — Loyalists depart. — Arrival of Lafayette. — Trade
through Ocracoke inlet.—The Continental Line joins the Grand Army.
—Brandywine.—Germantown.—Death of Nash.—New battalions.

1777
January

Caswell's administration

On the adjournment of congress Richard Caswell found
himself in power as the first governor of the sovereign State
of North Carolina. His title was "his Excellency." Shortly
after the Christmas holidays he seems to have taken possession of the governor's palace at New Bern, and there
on January 16th he held his first council, Cornelius Harnett

S. R.,
XXII,
880, 907
being chosen president of the board. On the same day
judges were appointed to hold the courts of oyer and
terminer. Among those appointed were John Penn, Samuel
Spencer and Sam Ashe; and the criminal courts again began
to be held. Penn, however, declined to serve, so no court
was held in the Orange district. His action in this matter,
disappointing Governor Caswell, was the probable cause of
an estrangement between them.

A few days later the fine furniture and effects of Governor Martin with which the palace was filled were sold at
auction under an order of the congress, and his Excellency
bought largely of them, doubtless to furnish the palace.

S. R., XI,
393
Notwithstanding the treaty of peace that had in the fall
of 1776 been informally agreed on with the Indians, in

Indians
hostile
February they again became hostile, and a detachment of
militia was ordered to range in the district of Washington
to prevent depredations, and General Rutherford was directed to raise eight independent companies, four for Washington and four for Tryon, Burke, and Surry, to be employed

1. MAURICE MOORE   2. ABNER NASH
3. ALEXANDER MARTIN   4. ROBERT HOWE

building stockades, in scouting and in protecting the
people.

William Sharpe and Waightstill Avery were appointed commissioners in conjunction with representatives of Virginia to
make a treaty with the Over-hill Cherokees and fix the boundary between their hunting grounds and the white settlement,
and during the summer they accomplished this purpose, extending the boundary line into the Great Iron Mountains.

Military movements

In anticipation of a southern campaign, General Moore
marched his entire command to South Carolina, being likewise accompanied by two battalions of militia under the
command of General Allen Jones, appointed by the congress
then in session at Halifax. On January 14th General
Moore's continentals were at Charleston, and the apprehension of a southern campaign having passed away, and
Washington's army being hard pressed, on February 6th the
Council of State directed that the ranks of three of his
regiments should be filled by transfers from the others and
he should lead them to the north. The considerable number
of inhabitants in western North Carolina led to the belief
that that was a favorable region for securing recruits. Indeed, General Rutherford made a return of over ten thousand men for his militia brigade in the Salisbury district
alone, and Nash, who on February 5th was promoted by the
Continental Congress to be brigadier-general, was directed
to repair to the western part of the State and superintend
the recruiting for the new regiments; but rapidly succeeding
this first order came a second directing that Moore and
Nash should proceed with all the continentals to the aid of
General Washington. Moore was then at Charleston in command of the department. On receiving these orders he
returned to North Carolina to arrange for the long march
of the troops, ordering Nash to follow him with the regiments. In April they reached Wilmington and went into
camp temporarily. There, unhappily, on April 15th, General Moore died from an attack of gout in the stomach. On
the same day his brother, Judge Maurice Moore, also died

Same house

1777
Nash
marches
north
in the same house. General Nash assumed command an
marched to the north. A camp was established at Halifa
where were concentrated the continental battalions the
forming, whose ranks were not yet filled; and another cam
and hospital were located at Georgetown, Md., where all th
North Carolina troops who had not had the smallpox wer
inoculated before joining the army. The brigade reache

May
the Potomac toward the close of May, and while man
were detained there to be vaccinated, two hundred wer
found to have already had the dread disease, and these wer
hurried forward to reinforce Washington. Under Colon
Sumner, they joined the army at Morristown on July 5th.

1777
Political
power
The new constitution apportioned the political power o
the State very differently from what had been the custor
in colonial times. In former assemblies the Albemarl
counties had each five representatives and the others bu
two. In the revolutionary bodies each county and boroug
had but a single vote without regard to the number of rep
resentatives they sent. Under the new constitution ever
county was entitled to one senator and two representative
and the borough towns to a representative. By this innova
tion the counties were all put on the same footing.

The first
Assembly
The division of the legislature into two houses, each con
sisting of a relatively small number of members, resulte
S. R., XII,
I
in lessening the influence of many of the old leaders. Whe
the Assembly, elected in March, met in April, the personne
of the representatives was greatly changed. Many of th
prominent public men were either in the military or civi
service, occupying positions that rendered them ineligibl
as members. Sam Johnston, being one of the treasurers
was not a member; nor was Harnett, who was a member o
the council. In the senate, Archibald Maclaine, Allen Jones
Griffith Rutherford, and Sam Ashe were men of the mos
influence. In the house, Abner Nash, Avery, Benbury, John
Butler, Alexander Lillington, Willie Jones and William
Hooper, and John Penn were among the leaders; but th
disappearance from the legislative halls of many who ha
exerted a controlling influence in former years was ver
observable.

egislative action

It does not appear that there were any party lines. Ten days after the session opened Abner Nash wrote: "We are ll harmony, and a perfectly good agreement, as far as I an see, is likely to prevail in our houses of legislature." Nash was elected speaker of the house of commons and am Ashe was chosen to preside over the senate.

A mass of important business, much of it of a delicate nature, confronted the Assembly; and despite the absence f so many men of experience who had been accustomed o manage public affairs, the laws passed at that and the djourned session attest the industry and high capacity of he assemblymen. Maclaine in the senate and Hooper in the house were probably the most influential in managing business. The former was in particular a strong, learned and painstaking lawyer and a patriot of the first water. The Assembly now levied an *ad valorem* tax on land, negroes, and ll other property, thus inaugurating a great change in the system of taxation. It established two new counties at the west, one named in honor of the governor and the other for Dr. Burke, "a compliment never before paid to a private citizen," so high was the popular regard for the talented Irishman, who was then representing the State in the Continental Congress with much ability. At the east, also, a county was created and called Camden, in grateful recognition of that nobleman's efforts in Parliament to befriend the colonies.

The election of officers by the congress in December had been merely for a temporary purpose, and now the Assembly re-elected Caswell and the members of the council. County courts were provided for, and courts of oyer and terminer were established, and Samuel Spencer was chosen to hold these courts in four districts, while Bonfield and James Davis were appointed for the Edenton and New Bern districts. Associated with these were others not lawyers. Because of the uncertainty of the times, it was considered best to postpone the establishment of civil courts until the next session, and the senate rejected the bill introduced to create them. Courts of admiralty were established and collectors of customs appointed for the various ports.

1777
April

S. R., XI, 720

S. R., XXIV, 6

Property tax

Caswell, Burke, and Camden Counties

S. R., XII, 109; XXIV, 39

An act was passed regulating the militia, dividing each company into four classes, which should in turn be called out when the necessity arose for making a draft. The brigadiers-general were all re-elected except Thomas Person who was succeeded by John Butler;* but General Vance dying soon, General Simpson was appointed by the council to take his place. A particular act was passed to encourage volunteers in the existing Indian war, and a premium of £10 was offered for each scalp taken from and "fleeced off the head of an Indian man" by a captor being in the service of the State, and £40 for each scalp taken by one not in the pay of the State, "who shall voluntarily undertake to make war upon the said Indians." Particular efforts were also made to promote recruiting for the continental service. To suppress the Tories, the county courts were authorized to require every inhabitant who should refuse to take the oath of allegiance to depart from the State in sixty days. For this purpose the counties were to be laid off into small districts, in which a justice of the peace was to warn the inhabitants to come and take the oath, and on the failure of any to do so, they were to be banished. Banished persons had the right to sell their property before leaving, but in case they did not, their property became forfeited to the State. The patriots of that day realized the necessity of reducing the number of the disaffected within the limits of the State as far as practicable, and although these were harsh and rigorous exactions, yet they seem to have been necessary and wise.

Sam Johnston and John Ashe were re-elected treasurers, and apparently there was no particular contest over any appointment, except alone for one of the delegates to the Continental Congress. Penn was a member of the house, and desired to replace Hewes. He made a determined and personal effort, alleging that Hewes, who as a member of the Marine Committee was transacting very important business for the congress, was holding two offices, a method of

---

*General Butler, like Rutherford, had been one of those county officers of whose excesses the Regulators complained. He was sheriff of Orange in December, 1770, although his brother William was one of the Regulators.

lectioneering that greatly disgusted Hewes and his friends.
A warm struggle ensued, and Penn succeeded by ten votes.
The delegates chosen were Burke, Hooper, and Penn.
Hooper declined, for the expense had been too heavy for
his purse, and his friend Harnett was chosen to fill the
vacancy. It was, however, said that had Hewes then been
willing to accept he would have been chosen unanimously
to replace Hooper, but his friends asserted that he would
not accept under the circumstances. If his great and patriotic service at Philadelphia was not appreciated by the
Assembly, he was content to attend to his private affairs.

At that time the militia battalions sent to South Carolina
were still in that State, one of them being commanded by
Colonel Abraham Sheppard. It being resolved to raise a
new continental battalion, Sheppard was appointed colonel
of it, and he was directed to select his own officers and
recruit his men. He had been Caswell's lieutenant-colonel
at Alamance, had commanded the Dobbs militia with Caswell at Moore's Creek, and was in service on the Cape Fear
under General Ashe. He was regarded as particularly efficient, and Caswell reposed the highest confidence in him.

Eventually, after a session of a month, in the course of
which the new State was launched with its officers and laws,
suited to the changed conditions, the Assembly adjourned.

Conditions within the State

The counties now became organized with their courts,
justices, clerks, sheriffs, registrars and other officers, and
there was a general feeling of stability, and that the new
government was permanently established. But yet the
inhabitants were by no means of one mind on the subject
of independence. Disaffection manifested itself more or
less in every community. In July there were Tories in
arms in Surry, and trouble in Guilford; and in that month
the Council of State, writing to General Rutherford, told
him that they could not send any troops from the Hillsboro
brigade, as he "well knew how many disaffected persons
reside in that district and neighborhood."

Indeed, this was a time of fearful commotion and anxious
solicitude in many parts of the State. A test oath being

1777
April
McRee's
Iredell, I,
359

Sheppard's
regiment
S. R., XI
457

July, 1777
S. R., XI,
526

S. R., XI,
521-523, 526

required of all citizens, and those refusing to take it being ordered to depart the State within sixty days, a dread alternative was presented that brought sorrow and lamentation

The Tories Deplorable in the extreme was the situation of a great number of inhabitants who determined to abandon their home and become wanderers on the face of the earth rather than engage in what they considered unjustifiable rebellion. A very large part of Cumberland, estimated at two-thirds of the county, prepared to leave the State, and in other communities considerable numbers had the same gloomy prospects. The Scotch refused to take the oath almost to a man. They preferred exile to renouncing their allegiance and being much exasperated, they became very troublesome

S. R., XI,
534, 560

The salt riots

The interruption of regular commerce resulted in general privation of the necessaries of life. Chief among the indispensable articles for domestic use was salt, and of this there was a scarcity. The first highways known to history were made by the denizens of the interior seeking the seashore for this commodity. The human system hungers for it, and when the supply among the inhabitants of the interior ran short they fell into great commotions—the people demanded salt and would have it; and now began a disturbance that might well be denominated the salt riot. The State had a quantity stored at Cross Creek for the use of the public and thither bodies of men began to congregate. It was reported that a thousand assembled in Orange alone, and crowds gathered in Duplin, Guilford, Chatham and other counties with such a threatening aspect that an alarming insurrection was feared. It was apprehended that the ultimate purpose was to seize the military stores at Wilmington Colonel Williams, in command of the continentals at Halifax, and Colonel Sheppard, whose Tenth Regiment was at Kinston, were directed to move on Cross Creek, and General Ashe was ordered to call out the militia of that district The rising, however, seems only to have been with a view of taking the salt, and it was that which drew together the crowds in the disaffected territory.

S. R., XI,
527, 533
et seq.

June

S. R., XI,
560

On July 30th a mob of one hundred and forty persons

from Duplin and Johnston entered Cross Creek, but Robert
Rowan met them with his company, and having required July
them to take the oath, sold them salt at $5 per bushel. Five
hundred more came in somewhat later, and probably were
appeased in the same way.

The task of the patriots

Just at the same time, July, 1777, a conspiracy was dis- S. R., XI, 521
covered among the eastern Tories to rise and fall upon their
neighbors. "I am sorry to inform you," wrote Colonel Irwin
to Governor Caswell, "that many evil persons in Edgecombe
and the neighboring counties have been joined in a most
wicked conspiracy. About thirty of them made an attempt
on Tarboro, but luckily I had about twenty-five men to oppose them, and I disarmed the whole and made many take
the oath."

Had there been more unanimity, the task of the patriot
leaders had been easier; but their daring, their constancy,
and fortitude would not have entitled them so thoroughly
to the gratitude and admiration of succeeding generations.
Notwithstanding the division in sentiment of the inhabitants,
it is to the honor of the public men of that period that no
man who had been honored with the confidence of the people
flinched when the test came or failed to move forward
through the gloom and obscurity of the doubtful and hazardous issue. They doubtless felt as Franklin in the Continental Congress expressed it, "we must all hang together, or
we will be sure to hang separately."

There were, however, two Englishmen who, after the S. R., XI, 539
formation of the State government, withdrew their support
from the cause. One, William Brimage, of Edenton, was Brimage
appointed by Governor Caswell to hold the court of oyer in
March. He declined, and not long afterward planned an
insurrection, proposing to join the British vessel at Ocracoke. For this he was arrested. The other prominent inhabitant who fell from the cause was John Slingsby, a mer- Slingsby
chant of Wilmington, who at first entered zealously into the
revolutionary measures, but subsequently adhered to the
Crown, and in 1781 was colonel of the Loyalist militia of
Bladen, and lost his life at the battle of Elizabethtown.

1777
July

S, R., XI,
488, 504

Johnston dissatisfied

Samuel Johnston, although always true to the cause, was much dissatisfied with the form of government, and doubtless suffered mortification at his treatment by the people of Chowan. Governor Caswell offered to appoint him to hold the court of oyer in the Edenton district, but Johnston questioned Caswell's right to make the appointment. The legislature in April re-elected him one of the state treasurers, but he declined, saying: "In the infancy of our glorious struggle, when the minds of many were unsettled and doubtful of the event, I joyfully accepted every appointment that was offered by my fellow-citizens, and readily stood forth to give testimony of my concurrence and approbation of every measure which tends to the security of the most inestimable rights of mankind; at this period, when the constitution of this State is happily, and, I flatter myself, permanently established, when all doubts and apprehensions are entirely removed, . . . I . . . request . . . the favor of being permitted to decline that very honorable and lucrative appointment." The cause of his declination was deep-seated. He was dissatisfied, mortified, and doubtless animated by resentment. The people had framed a government without his aid, and he had been treated by the inhabitants of his own county as if he were an odious character. Two months after he declined the treasureship he wrote to Dr. Burke: "I have had an opportunity of seeing an experiment of the new legislature, and am as little pleased with it in practice as I was formerly in theory, and am still of opinion that though your plan might, for aught I know, be well adapted to the government of a numerous, cultivated people, it will by no means be attended with those salutary ends which were in the contemplation of its framers." He characterized many of the representatives as "fools and knaves, who by their low arts have worked themselves into the good graces of the populace." "I saw with indignation such men as Griffith Rutherford, Thomas Person, and your colleague, J. Penn, . . . principal leaders in both houses, you will not expect that anything good or great . . . from the counsels of men of such narrow, contracted principle, supported by

:he most contemptible abilities. Hewes was supplanted . . . in congress by the most insidious arts and glaring falsehoods, and Hooper, though no competitor appeared to oppose him, lost a great number of votes." He concludes: "I am now out of office and totally abstracted from all political concerns." But in less than two years his resentment was mollified, and he again took his place in the Assembly as senator from Chowan, and in the dark days of the war he put forth his best efforts for success.

Loyalists depart

Throughout the province, however, there were large numbers of local standing who remained fixed in their opposition to the new government. These malcontents interfered with the recruiting and were a menace to the public peace, threatening the magazines in the different sections of the State, and it was desirable to free the inhabitants from their influence. Toward the last of July a large vessel sailed from New Bern having on board a great number of Tories with their wives and families, chiefly Scotchmen. Among the passengers were Martin Howard, the late chief justice of the province, and his wife and daughter. Since the beginning of hostilities he had been living quietly in seclusion on his plantation, Richmond, in Craven County. October 27th another transport sailed from New Bern for Jamaica, having on board John Hamilton and his brother Archibald, of Halifax, and many other Scotchmen. In January Governor Martin wrote from New York that many refugees from North Carolina had arrived there, "among them John Hamilton and Mr. MacLeod, the former a merchant of considerable note, long settled there, and the latter a Presbyterian clergyman of good character, who have formed a very spirited . . . and well-concerted plan by drawing out of that province for his Majesty's service the loyal Highlanders, of whom they have two hundred and seventy odd men actually under the most solemn engagements to join them on a summons." Later these men were embodied in a regiment under Hamilton's command, and were actively engaged during the war.

S. R., XI, 656, 765; XIII, 368

The Hamiltons

Arrival of Lafayette

In July, while the continental battalions were being filled at Halifax, there passed through that village a bevy of French officers who had just landed at Georgetown, S. C. and were making their way to the headquarters of General Washington, being the first practical indications of French sympathy with the colonies in their struggle for independence, the forerunners of that great assistance which later brought the war to its glorious close at Yorktown. On July 18th Major Ashe wrote to Caswell: "I haven't any news to write your Excellency, only th't one of the royal bloods of France (the Marquis de Lafayette), recommended by Mr. Franklin, passed this [place] a few days since, on his way to the Grand Army." Lafayette at that time was not twenty years of age, but at once he burst on the American horizon as a star of the first magnitude, and the glory of his name approaches that of the great Washington.

Ocracoke Inlet

British cruisers undertook to close the channel of commerce through Ocracoke Inlet, but many vessels still came in bringing salt, ammunition, and other needed supplies, and privateers were constantly sallying forth to prey on British commerce. Among those fitted out at New Bern were the *Sturdy Beggar* and the *Nancy,* while at Wilmington the *General Washington* was equipped as an armed vessel for the State.

In the middle of September two large English frigates suddenly appeared at Ocracoke, where many vessels lay ready to sail. They took several, particularly a large French brig, but the most of the fleet escaped by returning into Neuse River. The British tars then made capture of the fat mutton on the banks; but the *Sturdy Beggar,* fourteen guns, and *Pennsylvania Farmer,* sixteen guns, at once sailed to clear the harbor.

The Continental Line joins the Grand Army

On July 1st the long march of Nash's brigade came to an end, and it went into quarters at Trenton. This addition to Washington's army was important, adding largely to its strength and enabling him to present a bold front to Corn-

vallis, who threatened Philadelphia from the Elk. To form
a corps to hover about the enemy and give him all the annoyance possible, Washington now organized a light division,
composed in part of a hundred men taken from the North
Carolina brigade, under Colonel Martin, the command being
bestowed on Major-General Maxwell. The brigade itself
was assigned to General Sullivan's division, and participated
in the battle of Brandywine, September 11th; but the management was so wretched that none of the brigades in Sullivan's division won great renown. Colonel Martin's detachment had better fortune. Maxwell held his position at
Chad's Ford with remarkable tenacity, and particularly did
Captain Jacob Turner, of the Third Battalion, greatly distinguish himself, bringing honor to his corps.*

At the battle of Germantown, October 4th, the brigade
had a better opportunity of displaying its courage, and its
vigorous conduct was highly honorable to the State. Nash's
and Maxwell's brigades supported those of Sullivan and
Wayne that led the attack on the centre. They were successful from the beginning, drove the enemy pell-mell
in their front and pressed on resolutely through the long and
straggling village of Germantown. Eventually they routed
the British left, which had made a stand against their onslaught. Nash's brigade was on the extreme right, and
gained a more advanced position than any other of the
American troops. The victory was won when an untoward
incident changed the face of affairs. A great fog prevailed,
and at a point some three miles from where the engagement
began Wayne's division, on Nash's left, mistook some of
General Greene's troops, who formed Washington's left
wing and were approaching from that direction, for a large
British force on their flank. Alarmed at their supposed
peril, they broke and could not be rallied. Their flight from
the front turned victory into disaster. The British renewed
the contest with spirit. The brigades of Nash and Sullivan,
far in advance, unsupported and threatened on both flanks,
were compelled to withdraw. The army retired many miles,
pursued by the enemy.

Maxwell's
Light
Division

S. R., XIII,
262, 263

1777
Oct. 4th,
German-
town

S. R., XI,
789, 828

Irving's
Washing-
ton, III, 284

*Hugh McDonald, whose diary has been preserved, was apparently
a member of Colonel Martin's detachment with General Maxwell.

Death of
Nash

Biog. Hist
N. C., III,
301

The North Carolinians suffered heavily. How many of the rank and file were killed and wounded was not reported, but the loss was great. Among the higher officers, General Nash, Colonel Polk, Colonel Buncombe, Colonel Irwin, Captain Jacob Turner, and Captain Lucas, adjutant of the Third, fell on the field of battle. Colonel Polk, although badly wounded, fortunately recovered. Colonel Hogun, who particularly distinguished himself, escaped. Colonel Buncombe, badly wounded, was conveyed from the field, where he was found by an acquaintance in the British army, to Philadelphia, and died from his wounds shortly afterward. A cannon ball passed through the horse General Nash was riding, and tore through his leg, also killing Major James Witherspoon, an aide of General Maxwell. As he fell, Nash called to his men: "Never mind me, I've had a devil of a tumble; rush on, my boys; rush on the enemy; I will be after you presently." He was borne fainting from the field and died, after lingering in great agony for three days. He was interred in the Mennonite Churchyard at Culpsville, Pa. His death was truly lamented. It was a sad blow to his brigade, the men and officers alike having the greatest confidence in him and affection for him. At home, when the legislature met, it put on record a memorial of his worth and virtues, made an appropriation to erect a marble monument in his honor, and created a county, called by his name, to perpetuate his memory. On Nash's death, congress not being ready to appoint additional generals, the command of the brigade was assigned by Washington to General McIntosh, of Georgia.

The new battalions

S. R., XI,
605, 729, 738

After Nash moved north, the first efforts of the authorities were directed to filling the ranks of the older regiments, but these efforts were measurably checked by the activity of those officers who were seeking to enlist men for the Seventh, Eighth and Ninth battalions, upon whose prompt completion depended their commissions. While the officers of Sheppard's Tenth battalion offered the additional inducement that that battalion was for local service, and would not have to leave the State, numerous recruiting officers, representing every regiment and company, were scouring the State. The first impulse of patriotic ardor had somewhat subsided, and recruiting for the war proceeded but slowly. The camp at Halifax was left in charge of Colonel John Williams, and as rapidly as possible recruits were collected and sent forward in detachments, and eventually, on September 1st, Colonel Williams broke camp and moved the entire force northward to join the Grand Army. In July, likewise, Colonel Sheppard's regiment was taken into the pay of the Continental Congress and also ordered north.

Williams's Battalion

CHAPTER XXXIV

Caswell's Administration, 1776-80—*Continued.*

The second session of the Assembly.—Articles of confederation.—
Valley Forge.—Supplies from North Carolina.—The North Carolina
line destitute.—Feeling in England.—Treaty with France.—The second Assembly.—Dr. Burke in congress.—The battalions consolidated.
—Nine months' Continentals.—Defection prevalent.—The North
Carolina brigade.—The judges appeal to the people.—At the adjourned session.—For the southern campaign.—Importations continued.—The fall of Savannah.—Militia for the South.—Ashe surprised at Briar Creek.—Boyd's defeat.—Light horse at the North.
—Sumner and Hogun brigadiers.—The hardships of the officers.—
Prices and taxes.—Internal perils.—Movements of troops.—Battle
of Stony Point.—The second Assembly.—Efforts to increase the Continental force.—Tory movements.—Battle of Stono.—Davie wounded.
—Battle at Savannah.—Hogun's brigade ordered South.

The second session of the Assembly

Nov., 1777
S. R., XII,
114, 418 The Assembly reconvened in November and again sat a
month. It established superior courts, electing Samuel
Ashe, Samuel Spencer, and James Iredell the judges, and
Waightstill Avery the attorney-general. Courts for the
trial of civil causes that had been suspended since 1773 were
S. R.,
XXIV, 128 thus reopened in the spring of 1778. Many important
measures engaged the attention of the Assembly. It being
represented that a large force would probably be needed
at the north, the legislature empowered the governor to
draft five thousand militia, and to command them himself,
or to appoint a major-general in his place.

In the Continental Congress Dr. Burke had been particularly active and very efficient. He communicated to the
governor full details of the proceedings of the congress
and of his action on the various measures proposed, his
S. R., XI,
380-389, 417 letters being in the highest degree creditable to him. He
participated largely in the discussion upon the articles of
confederation and transmitted a brief of the argument.
These articles were laid before the General Assembly at its

November session, and that body declined to ratify the
entire instrument. As the Provincial Congress had rejected
Franklin's plan two years earlier, so now the Assembly was
careful about entering into any agreement with the other
states that might injuriously affect the rights of the people.
Indeed, the permanency of the connection with the other S. R., XII,
411
colonies was so far from being regarded as finally established that in the state constitution it was provided that the
delegates to the Continental Congress, "while necessary,"
should be annually chosen.

Although Johnston ascribed to General Person a controlling direction of the house, yet the few records of the
ayes and nays preserved in the journals of that body indicate
that that leader of the democrats was frequently in the
minority. He proposed without avail a tax reduction and a S. R., XII,
441; XXIV,
141-144
reduction in the compensation of the governor; and similarly other movements in the way of seeking popular favor
appear to have been defeated. Honors were paid to General Nash, for whom a new county was named; and a
county also was named in honor of Wilkes; and Washington district beyond the mountains, which had been accorded
representation in the Provincial Congress and in that
Assembly, was now converted into a county. For purposes
of intercourse with it a public road was directed to be
constructed across the mountains leading into Burke.

A fort was built at Ocracoke, and one of the row-galleys,
named the *Caswell,* was purchased from the State of Virginia for the better protection of the commerce through that
inlet. Commissioners were appointed also to repair Fort
Johnston and build a new fort commanding the bay at Point
Lookout. The academy at Charlotte was revived under the
name of Liberty Hall, and early in 1778 trustees were appointed to establish a similar academy in the neighborhood
of Hillsboro. Toward the end of the session some friction
appears to have arisen between the two houses, especially
over the election law, but eventually the house concurred
with the senate and passed the act fixing the time of the
annual meeting on April 1st and rendering ineligible delegates to the general congress and certain other officers. To S. R.,
XXIV, 79
take the place of the old-time vestries, the freemen in the

1777
December
counties were directed to elect overseers of the poor and county wardens, and this change marked the final separation of church and State.

Colonel Sheppard had been so dilatory in moving the Tenth Regiment to the north that a legislative committee investigated the causes of his inaction, and although some excuse was found in the dearth of supplies, on the whole the committee reported that his reasons were frivolous and insufficient; and toward the end of November he was again instructed to join the Grand Army.

S. R., XII,
134

Valley Forge

1777-1778
That winter, the British having occupied Philadelphia, General Washington went into winter quarters at Valley Forge, twenty-three miles west of that city. There the nine North Carolina battalions passed the winter subjected to the most trying vicissitudes. Terrible, indeed, were the sufferings of all the troops in that famous encampment. While for the most part the army remained in their cantonments, a special corps was organized for rapid march to harass the British outposts and keep in check their foraging parties. The returns show that about one-half the North Carolinians fit for duty were engaged in these commands outside of the regular quarters. As the season advanced with its unusual severity, the unhappy situation and destitute condition of the North Carolina line called for vigorous measures of relief. The only communication was to the southward, and except such provision and clothing as could be obtained from the unwilling Pennsylvanians, the army had to be furnished from Virginia and North Carolina, and Governor Caswell was unremitting in his endeavors to provide needed supplies. Now the value of Ocracoke became still more apparent. Governor Martin wrote in January from New York to Lord Germain: "The contemptible port of Ocracoke . . . has become a great channel of supply to the rebels. . . . They have received through it very . . . considerable importations." To close that inlet a British ship of war, two sloops, a brig, and privateersmen from New York and England hovered along the coast, charged with the duty of capturing American vessels. But,

S. R., XI,
688, 689, 703

Supplies
from North
Carolina

S. R., XIII,
367

1777
December

on the other hand, efforts were made to drive them off, and in addition to the fortifications and state vessels, the New Bern merchants fitted out the *Bellona,* carrying eighteen guns, and the *Chatham* to make reprisals. To pay for imported goods, tobacco was shipped to foreign countries, the State purchasing and sending out large quantities of that commodity. Salt brought in by the State was exchanged for pork, and Caswell employed men in every section packing pork for Washington's army. All sorts of skins and leathers and all cloths fit for blankets were likewise obtained for the soldiers, sometimes resort being had to impressment. In the Albemarle section, where there were so many industrious Quakers, large quantities of shoes were manufactured, and these were purchased not only for the army, but by northern merchants, who paid high prices for them. Importations were also made on account of the Continental Congress, and these supplies were stored at South Quay, on the Blackwater. From there they were moved by wagons to Valley Forge. Means of transportation were limited, and at length four brigades of wagons were sent from Pennsylvania to haul stores from Edenton and South Quay for the use of the army, and these supplies contributed to relieve the sufferings which the soldiers had so unmurmuringly endured. On February 15th Caswell wrote: "I find our nine regiments . . . very far . . . short of their complement of men, and those in camp almost destitute of clothing. . . . The officers of the Sixth Battalion are sent home as supernumeraries. . . . I am to buy leather, skins, shoes and other clothing, procure manufacturers, set them to work, purchase salt and provisions, and procure boats and wagons for sending those articles on. All this I am constantly, almost busily, employed about myself, receiving very little assistance."

Early in March General McIntosh reported that of the North Carolina line at Valley Forge since January 50 had died in camp; that 200 were then sick in camp, and an equal number were in hospitals in Pennsylvania and New Jersey. The number then at Valley forge was 900; in May there were 1100 privates, while of rank and file there were 1450. Colonel Sheppard's regiment, having lingered in North

Supplies for army at Valley Forge

S. R., XIII,
16, 17, 42, 74
et seq.
1778

1778
S. R., XIII,
377, 428

The North Carolina troops

Carolina until cold weather set in, spent the winter in the smallpox camp at Georgetown, Md., where more died with measles than from the effects of innoculation.

That winter was indeed terrible to the patriots; but it was also discomforting to the British. Burgoyne's entire army having surrendered in October, that general reached England in December, and such was the gloom and despondency in Great Britain that there was much sentiment in favor of a cessation of the war. In the House of Commons only 33 majority was cast against assenting to the independence of America. Lord North, in urging money for another campaign, declared as the alternative that they would have to furnish money to bring the troops home. This favorable news gave great hope throughout the colonies; and then in May came the treaty with France, followed quickly by the declaration of war by France against England and the promise of an immense fleet and four thousand veteran troops to end the struggle. When a copy of this treaty reached New Bern it was immediately published under a display of American and French colors and a triple discharge of thirteen pieces of cannon by the town company of militia, mustered for that purpose. And as the *Gazette* quaintly remarked: "Universal joy appeared in every countenance, great plenty of liquor was given to the populace, and the evening concluded with great good humor and social mirth."

The second Assembly

The new Assembly met on April 14th at New Bern, Whitmel Hill being chosen speaker of the senate and Judge John Williams speaker of the house. Among the new members was James Hunter, who now co-operated heartily with the Whigs. Governor Caswell gave a full account of public matters in a message to the legislature. He was again elected governor, and the other members of the council were re-elected, Richard Henderson taking the place vacated by Harnett. A new county was formed and named in honor of the victor over Burgoyne, General Gates; another in honor of Willie Jones; others for Montgomery and Randolph, while the names of Bute and Tryon were obliterated, and those counties were respectively divided into Franklin and Warren and Lincoln and Rutherford.

S. R., XI, 562, 750

On the death of General Moore, Dr. Burke, instead of recommending one of the North Carolina colonels to fill the vacancy, urged the appointment of Colonel Hand, of Pennsylvania, a gallant Irishman, his action in that matter calling forth a vigorous protest and remonstrance from the North Carolina officers. At the annual election in April he was not chosen a deputy, Abner Nash being elected in his place. Nash, however, declined, and John Williams, of Granville, the speaker, was then elected, Thomas Benbury becoming speaker.

But if Burke lost favor because of this incident, he soon re-established himself in the affections of North Carolinians. At the very time he was denied a re-election his action at Philadelphia was so patriotic that he gained renewed favor. A majority of the congress had drawn a communication to General Washington which Dr. Burke thought contained an unmerited reflection on that general, and he combated it with great warmth, and with indignation retired from the chamber, his withdrawal breaking the quorum. On being sent for, he expressed himself so vehemently to the messenger that congress considered his action a contempt of that body. He explained that he did not understand that the congress had sent for him, and offered some apology. His explanations, however, did not satisfy the irate members, and then Burke manfully reasserted his position, caused the matter to be fully spread on the records, and claimed that he was responsible only to the legislature of North Carolina. The record of the proceedings being submitted to the next session of the Assembly, that body approved his course, and again elected him a delegate in congress. For a time, however, he was retired, and when the articles of confederation were ratified on behalf of North Carolina, on July 21, 1778, they were signed by John Williams, John Penn, and Cornelius Harnett.

S. R., XIII, 87, 105, 209

Dr. Burke at Philadelphia

Articles of Confederation ratified

The Assembly took measures for filling up the continental battalions; but on May 29th congress resolved that the battalions in camp should be consolidated, and a call was made on the State to raise four additional ones, which, however,

1778
S. R., XI,
761

were to remain at home until ordered elsewhere. Pursuant to this resolution, the battalions in service were reduced to four. The Sixth, originally commanded by Lillington, and later by Colonel Lamb, was merged with the First, of which Thomas Clark was colonel. The Fourth, commanded by Colonel Polk, was merged with the Second, Colonel Patten remaining colonel. The Fifth was merged with the Third, Colonel Sumner continuing in command. Colonel Martin had resigned the previous fall; Colonel Polk now resigned, and Colonel Hogun and the supernumerary officers, of whom there were a large number, were directed to return to North Carolina for service in the new battalions when raised. Efforts to obtain recruits under the system of volunteering, even with the large bounties offered, proved unavailing, and the legislature directed that twenty-six hundred men should be detached from the militia to serve in the continental army for nine months. These were known as the "nine months' men." A certain quota was apportioned to each county, and this number was again apportioned by the colonel of the county among the militia companies, so that every militia company in the State had to furnish its proper share of these troops. It was the same system that had been devised for calling out militiamen. Volunteers from each company were first to be called for, and to these a bounty of $100 was offered; and then, to make up the deficiency in its quota, each company by ballot selected the other men, and these were to receive a bounty of $50. Every one so selected became a continental, and those who faithfully served for nine months were to be exempt from any military service for a period of three years. All through May and June the militia companies were assembling in the various counties and making their selections of nine months' men, and thus again the war was brought to the very homes of the people. In many communities there was great opposition, for defection was painfully prevalent. In Rowan Captain Johnston was appointed to adminster the oath of allegiance to the inhabitants of his district. They attended at the time and place advertised, but when the oath was read and proposed to them, one of the company hurrahed for "King George," whereupon about

The
battalions
consolidated

S. R.,
XXIV, 154

The nine
months'
continentals

S. R., XII,
862

hundred withdrew in a riotous, turbulent manner; and when the captain undertook to raise the quota of men required of his company he found that the majority were Tories, and that the disaffected element controlled the draft. In many other sections the condition was not far different. It was with difficulty that the law could be enforced, and the drafted men responded but slowly. Those from the eastern counties were to assemble at Halifax, while those from the west were to proceed to Paytonsburg, in Virginia, where Colonel Thackston was in command. Boards of continental officers convened at Halifax and Moore's Creek to arrange officers for the new battalions, and Colonel Hogun was elected to command the first that should be organized. In July his regiment was sufficiently organized at Halifax for him to march, and he moved northward with six hundred men.

S. R., XIII, 190

The three consolidated regiments and Colonel Sheppard's Tenth Regiment had been thrown into "the North Carolina Brigade," Colonel Clark being in command, and were with Washington when, at the end of June, he attacked Sir Henry Clinton at Monmouth. They did not form a part of Lee's advanced corps that made the disorderly retreat at the beginning of the engagement, but under Lord Sterling they held the left of the second line and repulsed the enemy, and later were thrown forward close to the British right to renew the engagement. Night, however, closed in, and under cover of darkness Clinton escaped.

S. R., XIII, 531

The brigade at Monmouth

During that fall and winter the brigade remained with Washington at Fredericksburg, near the Connecticut line, while Colonel Hogun with his new regiment of six hundred men was engaged in throwing up fortifications at West Point, which afterward became the fort so famous in history.

S. R., XIII, 496

Hogun at West Point

The other companies of nine months' men in the summer of 1778 went into camp, some at Duplin Court House, some at Salisbury, at Hillsboro, and at Paytonsburg; but, congress having failed to send the bounty money, most of them were placed on furlough to remain at home until the ensuing March.

As the clergy had urged the people forward, so now the bench sought to enforce constancy. Judge Iredell forcibly

1778

S. R., XIII,
442, 443

Reanimat-
ing the
people

urged patriotism; and at the June term of the Wilmington
district Judge Ashe, in calling the attention of the grand
jury to crimes against the State, adverted to the spirit of
disaffection, saying: "When I consider our present temper
and conduct and compare them with our past, I lament our
depravity. When the accursed plan to enslave us was first
formed and ready to be enforced against us, a noble spirit
animated us, our resentment kindled, every age and order
of men glowed with zeal; each became emulous who should
succeed in resisting the encroachment; to effect it all seemed
determined to venture everything; no danger was thought
too hazardous, no difficulty was too great. Then were companies formed and trained in every neighborhood; . . . the
example was forcible, our youths catch noble passion; nay,
our children of a few years old imbibe it. But, alas! how
are we changed of late; that noble spirit no longer inspires
us; the celestial fire is extinguished, the flame ceases, it
glows no more. We have suffered a fascinating spirit of
avarice and extortion to take place instead. . . . Lamentable
defection! Strange infatuation! Can we think the eager
pursuit of riches will preserve us? . . . Or is there no danger because the enemy are not instantly at our doors? . . .
Our fate is inseparably linked with our sister States. If
they fall we perish. America united must stand or fall
together. . . . For God's sake, then, let us rouse from our
supineness! Let that spirit which at first animated us revive. . . . Let the love of our country rise superior to the
. . . base passion for gain. In a word, let us adopt an equal
spirit, an equal love of liberty and firmness, with the brave
Corsicans, who, oppressed by Genoese tyranny, in their military oath thus solemnly swore: 'That we will sooner die than
enter into any negotiation with the Republic of Genoa or
return under its yoke.'" Every opportunity to impress the
people was seized by the patriots to strengthen the cause.

1778

The
delegation

In August there was a short session of the Assembly held
at Hillsboro. Because attendance on the congress brought
so many deprivations, it was resolved to increase the number of deputies to five, requiring that three should always
be present, while the other two could be on leave at their
homes. Whitmel Hill, the speaker of the senate, and Thomas

1778

Burke were elected as additional members, and Allen Jones succeeded Hill as speaker of the senate. James Iredell, one of the judges, having resigned, Richard Henderson was elected in his stead, but he did not accept, and Archibald Maclaine was then chosen. A new issue of £850,000 was ordered to discharge all debts, and with the hope of counteracting the efforts made by disaffected persons to depreciate the bills of credit, which were now rapidly falling in value.

In the early autumn it became evident that the southern campaign threatened the year before was to become a reality, and South Carolina called loudly for assistance, and urged that congress should ask Caswell himself to command the troops sent by North Carolina to her aid. In response congress called on the State for three thousand men for service at the south; and Caswell, with his accustomed zeal, at once entered on the work of organizing and preparing this force. He ordered out the nine months' continentals, who were then on furlough, and called on the generals of the militia brigade to send forward their quotas for this expedition.

The South threatened

Oct. 16, 1778

General Allen Jones, however, and many others as well, interposed objections, saying that Caswell had no authority to send the militia from the State; and the want of harmony led to great delay in drafting the men.

S. R., XIII, 246

Importations continued, and in January there were brought in on the ship *Holy Heart of Jesus* twenty-three pieces of heavy cannon, to pay for which a hundred and forty hogsheads of tobacco were necessary, and the agent of the State, Robert Salter, was directed to buy enough tobacco for that purpose.

Importations

S. R., XIII, 692

Indeed, privateering as a commercial venture was carried on with great energy. In the spring of 1779 Captain Biddle sent out the *Eclipse,* fourteen guns; Captain Snoaye, the *Rainbow* and the *Fanny,* each fourteen guns; while Captain Ellis had three ships at sea taking prizes; and about the middle of May it was reported that five vessels had come into New Bern with valuable cargoes. The more readily to import military supplies, the Assembly appointed commissioners to purchase and hire swift ships for the State, and Colonel Benjamin Hawkins was empowered as state agent to conduct that business. He was to buy and export tobacco and

1778

pork, and, going abroad, was to purchase the needed military supplies. Notwithstanding the doubtful issue of the struggle at that time, the State already had some credit abroad, and Colonel Hawkins was directed to borrow £20,000 sterling in the West Indies for state purposes.

S. R., XIII, 225

Howe in Georgia

General Howe, who had been promoted by congress to the rank of major-general, still remained in command of Georgia and South Carolina; but he was not agreeable to the South Carolina authorities, who found it irksome to be defended by a North Carolinian, and application was made for his removal. So in September he was ordered to join Washington, General Lincoln being directed to relieve him. In November, as he was about to depart from Charleston, he, however, received an express from Georgia urging the imminent danger of that State, and requesting his aid. Sending forward what troops could be spared, he hurried to Savannah to meet the invasion. He could muster but seven hundred and fifty men besides the Georgia militia. With these he took a position, deemed impregnable, about half a mile below the town, and was sanguine of repulsing the enemy. But the British commander, Colonel Campbell, directed a body of seven hundred infantry, under the guidance of a negro, to penetrate a swamp that had been thought impassable, and suddenly Howe found his position untenable. A brisk engagement ensued, and the Americans were compelled to retire. In this retreat the Georgia brigade ignored their general's orders and suffered severely. Driven from Savannah, Howe recrossed into South Carolina, intending to protect Charleston. General Lincoln reached North Carolina in November, and urged that the intended reinforcements for the southern army should be hurried forward, indicating that arms and equipments, of which there was a great scarcity, could be furnished at Charleston. He arrived at Howe's camp on January 2d, and Howe went north to the Grand Army.

Lincoln takes command

1779

S. R., XIII, 30, 55, 256, 289

Caswell offered the command of the detachment about to be raised to General Ashe, who expressed a disinclination to accept it. But the governor insisted, saying that one or the other must go, and that the situation in the State rendered his own presence imperative. To remove an objection, he promised to perform personally Ashe's duties as treasurer. Ashe finally accepted the commission of major-general, and proceeded to organize the detachments as they reached Elizabethtown, where the drafts were directed to assemble. To fill the vacancy made by Ashe's promotion, on January 1st Alexander Lillington was appointed brigadier-general of the Cape Fear district.

It becoming apparent that the British were to make a great effort at the south, congress called on North Carolina to increase her re-enforcements to five thousand, and Caswell ardently sought to respond. In addition to the eastern levies, General Rutherford was directed to call out his brigade and reinforce Lincoln. The Indians had become hostile at the west, so that no troops could be drawn from beyond the mountains, but Rutherford hastily assembled some seven hundred men, and toward the close of November began his march.

Colonel Lamb was collecting the nine months' continentals at the east and Major Lytle at the west, while Sumner, the senior officer then in the State, had general supervision. Early in December Major Lytle, with a contingent of continentals, joined Rutherford; but it was a month later before Colonel Lamb crossed the Neuse with two hundred more, and then he was detained at Kingston* several weeks waiting for other detachments to come in; while Ashe was still delayed at Elizabethtown, as only one-half of the militia drafts had assembled. Rutherford, being the first to reach Charleston, was fortunate in obtaining a fair supply of arms, but the other militia detachments were so ill supplied as to give great concern. Caswell was convinced "that little service could be expected from them with what they have." When the Assembly met, about the middle of January, he reported to that body that of the five thousand troops desired by congress, he was fearful that not more than half had marched, and those badly armed. The continentals were in better plight. They were formed into two battalions, Sumner being in command.

*This name was afterward changed to Kinston.

1779
John Ashe, major-general

Aid for the South

S. R., XIII, 317

Rutherford

Ashe

The nine months' continentals

S. R., XIII, 629
XIV, 48

1779

February

Ashe defeated at Briar Creek

The British, having taken Savannah, had established posts at Augusta and at various intermediate points on the river Toward the close of February, Lincoln, with a considerable force, was on the South Carolina side, near Savannah Above him was Moultrie's camp, while Rutherford's brigade was twenty miles below the point where Briar Creek empties into the river on the Georgia side. General Williamson, with twelve hundred South Carolina militia, was higher up toward Augusta. Notwithstanding Ashe's force was so badly equipped and only raw militia, Lincoln selected it to make the first movement. By his direction Ashe marched rapidly from the vicinity of Charleston, passed the other detachments, and, leaving his baggage, hastened toward Augusta. On his approach the British evacuated that post and fell down the west bank of the river. Lincoln having ordered him to take position at Briar Creek, because of information as to the insecurity of that position Ashe advised him that it was hazardous. But, crossing on the 25th, he vigorously pursued the retreating enemy, reaching Briar Creek on the 27th. His swift march and energetic action was well in keeping with his decision of character. In the swamp at the forks, as ordered, he made his camp. He directed his baggage to cross at a point some eight miles above, sending six hundred men under Colonel Smith to guard it, and he despatched four hundred men under Colonel Caswell beyond the creek to surprise an outlying British post. Summoned by Lincoln to attend a council of war at Rutherford's camp, he left his army, now reduced to about six hundred men, under the command of General Bryan, with whom was Colonel Elbert, an experienced continental officer of Georgia, and Major Lytle, equally experienced. At the council it was decided that Williamson should cross and join Ashe and they should press down the west bank of the river and clear the way for Rutherford and Lincoln to cross into Georgia.

On Ashe's return at noon of March 2d he found vague rumors that the British were in his vicinity, and that Bryan was apprehensive. There had been friction between General Bryan and himself from the beginning of the march from Elizabethtown, almost resulting in a rupture, and Ashe made

S. R., XIV, 33, 39, 51 *et seq.*

February

1779

light of Bryan's apprehensions. Two small parties of horse had been sent out to reconnoitre, and a strong line of pickets had been established three-quarters of a mile from the camp. Discrediting the rumors that could be traced to no definite source, and receiving no information from the reconnoitring parties, Ashe made no preparations to resist an attack, but busied himself in preparing for the forward movement. He was arranging to cross the creek some two miles south of his camp when, to his dismay, on the next afternoon Colonel Smith, who was guarding the baggage up above, despatched information that a large British force had passed around the swamp and was approaching from the north. Almost immediately the pickets became engaged; but the British column, consisting of nine hundred regulars, brushed them aside, advancing rapidly with fixed bayonets to surprise the camp before preparations could be made to receive them. In the absence of preparation there was almost no hope of a successful defence. Nor was there any road open for retreat. The position assigned the North Carolina force by Lincoln was a *cul de sac,* from which there was no escape. The drums beat an alarm, the outlying detachments on the creek were ordered in, and the troops were hastily formed into two lines and served with cartridges; but it was too late. "We marched out to meet the enemy, some carrying the cartridges under their arms, others in the bosoms of their shirts, and some tied up in the corners of their hunting shirts." The first line, with a few Georgia continentals under Colonel Elbert, and Colonel Perkins's regiment on the right, resolutely engaged the enemy. The Halifax regiment on the left of the second line almost at the beginning of the engagement broke and took to flight. The Wilmington and New Bern regiments after two or three rounds followed their example. The Edenton regiment remained on the field, but after two or three more discharges they, too, gave way just as Major Lytle with his command of light infantry and a brass piece came up. That the first line and a part of the second firmly stood their ground is attested by the heavy loss of one hundred and fifty killed and wounded on the battlefield.

The six hundred raw militia were not able to withstand

1779

S. R., XIV, 33

Ashe surprised March 3d

S. R., XIV, 52

The battle

1779

Ramsay,
Hist. U. S.,
II, 296
S. R., XIV,
45, 275
et seq.

The
Loyalists
defeated

nine hundred British regulars. The sight of the gleaming bayonets was too much for the untrained militia, hurriedly assembled and taken by surprise. The panic-stricken second line fled, and the others soon following, Elbert and his thirty-five continentals alone remained, fighting desperately; but these were quickly overcome.* The militia sought safety in the swamp, but one hundred and sixty-two privates and twenty-four officers were captured. The loss in killed was about one hundred and fifty. Those who succeeded in crossing the river, about two hundred, Ashe marched into Rutherford's camp; but as most of them had thrown away their arms they were now an incumbrance rather than of further use to Lincoln. The others who escaped through the swamp toward Augusta, about two hundred and fifty, were long collecting. Ashe asked for a court of inquiry, which found much to his mortification, that he had not taken all the precautions proper to secure his camp. But considering the position in which Lincoln had placed him, and the great superiority of the attacking force, in any event only discomfiture awaited him. As the North Carolina militia were to be discharged on April 10th, on that day they began their return home, although their general and many of the officers sought unavailingly to persuade the men to voluntarily remain. This detachment was, however, immediately replaced by another under General Butler.

When Hamilton was organizing his Loyalist regiment in Florida, as he had prior to his departure arranged with leading Tories in the State to join him, his adherents were watchful of his movements. His regiment formed a part of the force that captured Savannah, and on the fall of that town the Tory leaders became active. Colonel Boyd, a resident of the lower Yadkin, collected a force of Loyalists, and, marching through South Carolina, was joined by others, who as they proceeded plundered the defenceless settlements through which they passed. Colonel Pickens, determined on revenge, hastily embodied some three hundred men and

*Colonel Elbert, desperately wounded, had fallen, and a British soldier was in the act of bayonetting him when he made a masonic sign, and his life was saved. He recovered, became greatly distinguished, and later was governor of Georgia.

ame up with them near Kettle Creek as they were making their way to Augusta. In an action that lasted three-quarters of an hour the Tories were routed, about forty of them being killed, among whom was Colonel Boyd, and the others dispersed. Seventy of them were tried for treason by the South Carolina government and condemned to death, but this wholesale sentence was respited, and only five of the ringleaders were executed. General Prevost had counted much on the aid of the Tories of upper Georgia and of the two Carolinas, and the quick suppression of this first rising somewhat disconcerted his plans.

Dickerson's company of light horse had been taken into the service of congress soon after its organization, and served in New York and later in Pennsylvania, and always as a very efficient corps; but toward the close of the year 1778 its numbers were so reduced that by direction of congress it was returned to the State, and early in 1779 was discharged from further service. Major Phifer's light horse and Vance's artillery also were at the north with the Grand Army, and served at Brandywine and elsewhere.

In December, 1778, Colonel Hogun was directed to march his regiment from West Point to Philadelphia, as its time was soon to expire. The weather was very severe, but after a trying march he went into barracks at Philadelphia early in January. While he was there, on January 9, 1779, congress found time to make a tardy appointment of brigadiers for North Carolina. Sumner and Hogun were appointed, these being the senior colonels.* The former was directed to return to the south, organize the continental force then being raised in North Carolina, and join General Lincoln; while General Hogun was assigned to the command of the brigade, which continued during the winter and summer in the vicinity of West Point under the immediate command of Washington.

Although congress and the state authorities made pro-

*Colonel Clark had long been in command of the brigade, while Hogun had only his own battalion; and the Assembly urged Clark's appointment as brigadier, but Hogun's commission as colonel was two months older than Clark's, and he had so greatly distinguished himself at Germantown that Congress did not heed the wishes of the Assembly.

1779

The distress
of the
officers

vision for the continental soldiers, the officers had to depend
on their pay for supplies; and because of the depreciation
of the currency and the scarcity of cloth, their condition
became insupportable. They complained bitterly that the
legislature paid no attention to their distresses; and at length,
in the spring of 1779, they held a meeting at West Point
and resolved that they would resign to a man unless the
General Assembly supplied their needs. This action was not

Pref. Notes,
S. R., XIV;
viii, 302

without effect. The Assembly directed that they should have
provisions furnished them at the following prices: Rum,
8 shillings per gallon; sugar, 3 shillings per pound;
tea, 20 shillings; soap, 2 shillings; and tobacco, 1 shilling; and that they should have a complete suit of clothing
at what it would have cost at the time they first went into
service; and, moreover, that they should have half pay for
life, and that the lands granted to them, as well as to the
soldiers, should be exempt from taxation while owned by
them or their widows. This provision was accepted as satisfactory, and the storm that was brewing passed away.

S. R., XIII,
812

In the Assembly it is to be noted that General Person was
still proposing low salaries without avail; the house was
largely against him. The paper currency, which at the be-

Currency
depreciation

ginning of 1777 was at par, a year later was three for one,
and in 1779 opened six for one. To mitigate the hardships
of taxation, commodities were to be received for one-half of

Taxation

each assessment. The price of corn was fixed at 33 cents
per bushel; wheat, 43 cents; rice, 81 cents; pork, $3\frac{1}{4}$ cents;
beef, $2\frac{1}{2}$ cents; tallow, 9 cents; flour, $2\frac{1}{4}$ cents; salt, $2\frac{1}{4}$ cents
per pound; tobacco, $3 per hundred; salt pork, $9.37 per
barrel. The money of that period was so bulky that Treasurer Skinner made a remonstrance to the Assembly that it

S. R., XIV,
255

was unsafe to carry large cartloads of currency through the
country without a guard.

The better to supply the troops, each county was required
to supply a certain number of hats and shoes and stockings,
yards of woollen or cotton cloth and of linen, apportioned
according to their population. Rowan's contribution was
124 hats, 248 pairs of shoes and stockings, 248 yards of
woollen cloth, and 524 yards of linen; there was no cotton
cloth to speak of made at that time. There were thus to be

ollected about 3000 hats, twice that number of shoes and 1779
S. R., XII,
639 tockings and yards of woollen, and more than 12,000 yards f linen for the use of the troops. The value of these articles as to be ascertained by three freeholders in each county, he amount being deducted from the taxes assessed.

There had been much opposition to the movement of roops to the southward, but when the legislature assembled n the middle of January events of such importance had 1779 appened that there was no longer any opposition to Caswell's patriotic course. The governor was empowered to rder out at any time so many of the militia as he should eem necessary, and to march them wherever needed. In ddition to preparing against foreign invasion, the Assembly ow had to apprehend domestic insurrection. British emis- S. R., XIII,
296 aries were actively stirring the people up to sedition. As part of their plan for invasion, George Carey, a British aval officer, came in a vessel to the Cape Fear, under a flag f truce, to distribute manifestoes offering terms of settlement to the people, without regard to continental or state authorities. He was promptly seized and thrown into jail by Francis Clayton and John Walker. The vigilance of the Whigs detected movements in the central counties that excited grave apprehension. Realizing the danger, the Assembly directed Governor Caswell to embody with all possible expedition two hundred and fifty infantry and twenty-five horsemen to take possession of Cumberland County, and to disarm all persons in Cumberland, Anson, Guilford, Tryon, and other counties, who might give trouble to the cause.

Before any action could be taken, early in February Colonel 1779
S. R., XIV,
261 John Moore, a Tory of Tryon County, raised three hundred men, and he claimed that there were two thousand more ready for enrolment. Caswell, now fully authorized, acted with his customary decision. A force of seven hundred and fifty light horse was called out, Allen Jones being appointed to command it, and two thousand militia were drafted to meet at Salisbury on March 25th.

The command of this corps, whose ultimate destination S. R., XIV,
273, 287 was to replace the detachment at the south, then about to return home, was bestowed on General John Butler, of the

Hillsboro district. Calling his council together, the gov
ernor proceeded with them, along with the troops from th
east, first to Campbellton and then to Charlotte, where h
arrived early in April. The disaffected inhabitants wer
readily overawed, Moore fleeing the country and joining

Gen. Butler

Colonel Hamilton's regiment, and on April 11th Genera
Butler took his departure with seven hundred militia fo

Gen.
Sumner

Augusta. General Sumner likewise reached Moultrie's camp
about the end of March, and in May reported seven hun
dred and fifty of the nine months' men on his rolls, of whom
four hundred and twenty were present fit for duty, divided
into two regiments designated as the Fourth and Fifth Con
tinentals, commanded by Colonel Gideon Lamb and Major
Lytle.

In April the nine months expired for which the regimen
organized by General Hogun at Halifax* had enlisted, and
Colonel Mebane was directed to march it from Philadelphia
back to the State. He reached Halifax on May 10th, and
the regiment was soon disbanded. The time for which Gen
eral Butler's detachment was called out was to expire in
July, and when the Assembly met in May it directed that
two thousand new men should be sent to replace that force

On May 31st the British had captured Stony Point, about
thirty miles below West Point, and Washington resolved to
retake it. General Wayne was selected for this purpose. In
organizing a force for the secret expedition he chose, among
others, the Second North Carolina Continentals. It was to
be a night attack, and the approach was over a quagmire
crossed by a single causeway. A forlorn hope was necessary, and Major Hardy Murfree volunteered with two of
his companies for this post of honor. Just before midnight,
with unloaded muskets, the assault was made. A deadly
discharge of grape and musketry swept through the advancing column, but without avail. The enterprise was
successful, and the entire garrison were either killed or

---

*The four new battalions sent to the North were raised for twelve
months, and on the termination of their enlistment many joined
the other battalions. But these in time came to be so reduced that
the brigade consisted of only two battalions, Clark's and Patton's.
Hogun's battalion thus was at first spoken of as the seventh, but
later as the third.

1779

ptured. General Wayne himself was wounded, and Cap-
in John Daves, second in command under Murfree, was
ngerously wounded, but eventually recovered. This most
illiant feat of arms brought great credit and honor to all
gaged in it, and none deserved higher commendation than
e North Carolinians.

The new Assembly was to meet at New Bern, but the
nallpox was raging so violently in that vicinity that Gov-
nor Caswell suggested that it should assemble at Smith-
ld, where it convened May 3d. Allen Jones and Thomas
enbury were again chosen speakers, and in the senate
amuel Johnston reappeared as senator from Chowan.
aswell was continued as governor. Maclaine declined the
dgeship, deprecating his own abilities, and recommended
e appointment of John Williams, who, having served a
ear in the Continental Congress, was now willing to aban-
on a post of honor whose compensation was so insufficient;
d he was elected to the vacancy on the bench. As honor-
le as was the service in the Continental Congress, the great
xpense attending it rendered the position undesirable, and
ose chosen delegates were not eager to go to Philadelphia.
deed, for long periods, only one delegate from North
arolina was in attendance. The congress therefore
commended an increase in the delegation, and Burke,
harpe and Hewes were added to the other delegates, the
ssembly agreeing to pay their actual expenses and to leave
eir compensation to the next Assembly. General Bryan,
n his return from Briar Creek, having resigned, Colonel
Villiam Caswell was chosen to succeed him; and in the
bsence of General Butler at the south, Ambrose Ramsay
vas appointed to serve temporarily in his stead. The
egislature, considering that it would be well for the General
ssembly to meet at some fixed place near the centre of the
tate where the offices could be kept, appointed a commis-
ion to select the most convenient places in Johnston, Wake,
nd Chatham counties, and report a description of each place
o the next Assembly. Thomas McGuire was chosen attor-
ey-general in the place of Waightstill Avery, who had reigned that appointment, and John Pugh Williams was
lected brigadier-general in the place of General Skinner,

May, 1779
S. R., XIII,
784, 792

John
Williams
succeeds
Iredell

Changes in
officers

S. R., XIII,
753

1779
who resigned; and the State being divided into six treasu districts, William Skinner, William Cathey, William John ton, Green Hill, Richard Cogdell, and John Ashe we chosen treasurers of their respective districts.

S. R., XXIV, 254

It being evident that continental troops, trained and di ciplined in long continuous service, would be more effecti than short-time militia called from their fields to action ar anxious to return to cultivate their farms, unusual effor

Efforts to enlist continentals

were made to enlist continentals. To that end it was pr posed that any ten militiamen who should furnish one co tinental recruit to serve eighteen months should themselv be exempt from all military service for that period, exce only in case of actual invasion or insurrection. By th means, together with a liberal bounty, it was hoped that tw

S. R., XIV, 319, 320

thousand continentals could be recruited by July. But a these hopes were disappointed, and only about six hundre were raised, so that in July Governor Caswell was oblige to make another call on the militia districts for a force relieve General Butler, the command of the new levies bein

July, 1779 S. R., XIV, 181

conferred on General Lillington. As the detachments we being collected, however, a large force from Virginia passe through the State to the aid of General Lincoln, relievin his necessities; so for a time Lillington's drafts returne to their homes. And, indeed, there were other consider tions that pressed Governor Caswell to defer this exped

The Tories active

tion. In Edgecombe, Nash, and Johnston Tory leaders we harboring deserters who had signed articles of associatio to prevent the militia from being drafted, and who inaugu rated a reign of lawlessness, requiring a military force t

S. R., XIV, 321

restore civil authority. While at the west the Tories wer again active, and Rutherford reported that there was a organized band in Burke publicly robbing the friends c America and murdering them, and that a conspiracy wa

June, 1779 S. R., XIV, 129, 137 Lee's Memoirs, 130

forming for a rising immediately.

On June 20th General Lincoln attacked Colonel Maitlan at Stono, in the vicinity of Charleston. General Butler'

Stono

militia composed the right and General Sumner's con tinentals the left of the attacking force. In the front of th British line was Colonel Hamilton with his regiment o Loyalist North Carolinians. Both militia and continental

:haved admirably. General Butler, much gratified, reported Governor Caswell that he could with pleasure assure him :at the officers and men under his command behaved better :an could have been expected of raw troops. Lieutenant harlton, of the continental brigade, was killed and Major [al Dixon was wounded, as also was Major William R. Davie. t was the twenty-third birthday of this young officer, des-ned in after years to attain eminence both in military and ivil life. He was in command of a detachment of cavalry. n a cavalry charge he was wounded and fell from his horse. Iis company soon began to retire, when a private, although ne enemy were but a few yards distant, deliberately placed ne wounded officer on his horse and led him from the field.)avie never knew the name of his deliverer. The wound n his leg was so severe that the major was incapable of urther service during that year.

S. R., XIV, 312, 315
Death of Charlton

In July, the British having retreated from their demon-tration against Charleston, General Sumner marched his :ontinentals to Camden, and being in ill health, he returned o North Carolina and addressed himself to securing more :ontinental recruits. The enlistment of many of his men :xpired in August, but others were constantly being sent to nis camp, and about August 1st Colonel Lamb led a large letachment from the east to Camden, where he was joined oy others from Salisbury. The sand hills of the Peedee were found to be most healthful and admirably located for a camp, and the continentals remained there until the last of the month, when they marched to Charleston.

S. R., XIV, 157, 325, 338

The continentals on the sand hills

But hardly had they reached Charleston when a French fleet, bearing an army of thirty-five hundred men, arrived in the Savannah to co-operate with Lincoln in an attack on the British garrison of that post. The allies concentrated there early in September, but a month passed before the French were ready to attack, and North Carolina militia were hurried forward, but were detained at Charleston by General Moultrie. In the attacking column were the North Carolina continentals; with the defenders were Hamilton's Loyalist regiment. Though ultimately unsuccessful, the attack was made with great resolution, and for a time the standard of the North Carolinians floated over the parapet

S. R., XIV, 344

Savannah, October 9th

McRee's Iredell, I, 435

1779
Lee's
Memoirs,
142

Hogun's
brigade

Feb., 1780
S. R., XIV,
798

of the Spring Hill redoubt. The French lost 700 men and the continentals 240 out of a corps of 600.

As the British plans developed, the invasion of the South wore such a threatening aspect that toward the close of September congress directed the North Carolina brigade to reinforce General Lincoln, but Washington detained them for a time, and it was not until November 23d that the brigade broke camp on the Hudson and began its long march to South Carolina. About the middle of February General Hogun reached Wilmington with about seven hundred men, and on March 3d went into camp at Charleston. A little later Washington also sent all of the Virginia continentals south.

In 1779 the counties of Wayne, Montgomery and Richmond were established, the last named for the Duke of Richmond, while its county seat was called Rockingham, in honor of two friends of the colonists in Parliament.

CHAPTER XXXV

NASH'S ADMINISTRATION, 1780-81

The confiscation act.—Lillington's brigade.—The fall of Charles-
on.—The prisoners suffer.—Death of Hogun.—The delayed rein-
orcements.—Tarleton's quarters.—Invasion apprehended.—Caswell
major-general.—De Kalb's reinforcements arrive.—Gates to command.—Activity of Rutherford.—Ramseur's Mill.—Rutherford pur-
ues Bryan.—Plans of Cornwallis.—De Kalb encamps on Deep
River.—Davie's enterprise.—Gates advances.—Battle of Camden.—
Death of De Kalb.—Gallantry of Gregory and Dixon.—Gates's ride.
—The disaster.—At Charlotte.—Sumter's negligence.—Davie in ad-
ance.—The spirit of the people.—New supplies.—Preparations for
efence.—The Assembly acts.—The Board of War.—Smallwood
upersedes Caswell.

The confiscation act

The Assembly convened about the middle of October. 1779
The members felt that they had temporized long enough with S. R., XXIV, 263-268
he malcontents, and a bill was passed to carry into effect the
act of 1776, confiscating the property of Tories. It was a
strong and sweeping act of confiscation. Willie Jones and
a dozen other representatives entered a vigorous protest S. R., XIII, 992
against it. "It involves such a complication of blunders and
betrays such ignorance in legislation as would disgrace a
set of drovers," protested Jones, with emphasis. At that
time, as later, hundreds of hogs were driven in droves from
one part of the State to another where a market could be
found, and the men so employed were known as "drovers."
But notwithstanding Jones's disgust, the measure was
passed, although later its severity was tempered, and it
was not carried into full operation. Many of those who
would not take the oath of allegiance were allowed to remain in the enjoyment of their homes, but became known
even in the acts of the Assembly as "non-jurors."

General Jones having been appointed a delegate to congress, William Eaton became brigadier of the Halifax dis-

1779
November

Gen.
Lillington

S. R., XIV,
223

S. R., XV,
336

1780

Lee's
Memoirs,
148

trict, and, John Pugh Williams declining in the Edenton district, Colonel Isaac Gregory was also promoted.

To aid General Lincoln, a detachment of three thousand men was ordered to be embodied and sent to South Carolina and toward the end of December General Lillington led it southward. This brigade served at Charleston. The period of the enlistment expired just as Charleston was being closed up by the besieging British, and for the most part these troops remained and were surrendered.

From the first there had been a law that continental officers were not to command militia, and although there were in the State many fine officers trained in the continental army unemployed, this regulation debarred them from service with the militia detachments. But somehow Major Hal Dixon and Major Nelson served with Lillington, who during the campaign wrote to the governor: "I think myself very happy" in their appointment, "and could freely wish your Excellency would recommend these gentlemen to the Assembly if there should be more militia sent to the southward." That recommendation was followed, and Major Dixon subsequently had command of a militia regiment that did great credit to the State.

The fall of Charleston

The British being in possession of Savannah, it was apprehended that Charleston would be their next point of attack, and strenuous efforts were made to put that city in a state of defence. On February 10th Sir Henry Clinton, having arrived with an additional force from New York, disembarked on John's Island, and at the end of March he passed the Ashley River above Charleston, taking possession of the Neck, across which Lincoln had, as defensive measures, cut a canal, constructed abattis, and built strong redoubts and batteries. It was thought that the British fleet could be successfully opposed; but on April 9th it passed the bar, ran by Fort Moultrie, and took possession of the harbor. To prevent its ascent, the channel of Cooper River was hurriedly obstructed by sinking there the entire American fleet, and so the way was still open for General Lincoln to retire from the city if he had chosen to do so.

But the citizens entreated him to hold the city, and in
the vain hope of relief, he yielded to their earnest appeals.
It was expected that the Virginia continentals, as well as
militia from that State and the two Carolinas, would come
to his aid, and that he would be able to raise the siege when
these succors came. On April 6th Colonel Harrington, with
some of the North Carolina militia, arrived, having entered
the city by way of Addison's Ferry, and Governor Rutledge
was collecting the South Carolina militia on the Peedee, and
awaiting the arrival of the Virginia troops and Caswell's
brigade.

S. R., XV, 24-46

Day by day the enemy approached nearer and nearer, until
at length, on April 24th, Lincoln made a determined sortie
to drive off their working parties. The detachment for this
assault numbered three hundred men, composed of Hogun's
North Carolinians, Woodford's Virginians, and twenty-one
South Carolina continentals. The interruption to the operations of the enemy was ineffectual; and other than this one
effort, Lincoln simply endured the trying ordeal of his unfortunate predicament. The fire of the British along the
lines was continuous, and daily a few of the brave defenders fell at their posts. In all, the American loss
was 89 killed and 140 wounded; that of the besieging
force being about the same. At length, all hope of
relief having faded away, and all avenues of escape being
closed, and the citizens wearying of the siege, General
Lincoln convened a council of his officers, and by their advice agreed to surrender. The capitulation took place on
May 12th. His army at that time numbered two thousand
continentals, five hundred of whom were then in the hospitals. In addition, there were more than a thousand militia,
nearly all North Carolinians, for there were but few South
Carolina militia in the city.

S. R., XV, 398

May 12

Marshall's Washington, 333

By the surrender the entire North Carolina line, embracing
the new battalions as well as Hogun's brigade, was eliminated from the contest, all that were left being those on
sick leave and such officers as were at home unemployed.
Included in the surrender were General Hogun, Colonels
Clark, Patten, and Mebane and fifty-nine other officers and
eight hundred and fourteen rank and file. Under the terms

S. R., XIV, 816, 817, 821
Destruction of the Continental Line

1780

of capitulation the militia were paroled and allowed to re
turn to their homes, but the continentals were kept in the
harbor.

The
prisoners
suffer

The officers were located on Haddrell's Point, opposite
the city, while most of the men were confined on the prison
ships. The privates were subjected to horrible ill-usage, and
many died from confinement on shipboard in that hot climate
without suitable provision being made for them. The condition of the officers was somewhat better.* But while the
officers had some conveniences, and engaged in gardening,
and had some amusements among themselves, still they
underwent great privations. Notwithstanding some supplies
furnished by North Carolina under a flag of truce, food was
very scarce, and a petition to fish, in order to add to their
limited supply, was refused by the British commander. To
relieve the pressure of feeding these prisoners, Lord Ger-

Pref. Notes,
S. R., XV,
xiv, 297

main, writing to Cornwallis, said: "What appears to me the
most practicable measures for the purpose are the inducing
the prisoners to enter on board the ships of war or privateers
or to go as recruits to the regiments in the West Indies, or as
volunteers to serve upon the expedition against the Spanish
settlements from Jamaica; and your Lordship will therefore take the proper steps for dispersing as many of them
as possible in these several ways, or in such other ways as
may occur to you as more practicable and effectual." Conformably to these directions, a considerable number of the
prisoners were sent to the West Indies and were in a
measure forced by the British into their service.

Death of
General
Hogun
Biog. Hist.
N. C., IV,
196

General Hogun sought to counteract the influences exerted by the authorities to detach the prisoners from the
American cause, and although offered leave to return home
on parole, he refused to be separated from his men. He
knew that his absence would facilitate the efforts of the

*On March 27th, Colonel Washington while reconnoitering had
come up with a party of the British, and in the engagement that
ensued killed seven and took several prisoners, among whom was
Colonel Hamilton. Thus it happened that Colonel Hamilton was
a prisoner in Charleston at the surrender and was retaken by his
friends. Of a kindly and generous disposition, he rendered much
service to the North Carolinians, whose misfortunes appealed to his
sympathy.

S. R., XV,
386

British in seeking recruits among the half-starved prisoners, and he fell a victim to his sense of duty. He died at Haddrell's Point January 4, 1781, a striking illustration of devotion and self-sacrifice. Of the eighteen hundred regulars who went into captivity on May 12, 1780, only seven hundred survived when they were paroled. After an imprisonment of twelve months an exchange of officers was agreed on; those who had not died in captivity were landed on James River and those exchanged returned to the army.

1780
S. R., XV, 451

General Lincoln, in determining to hold Charleston, was in expectation that great efforts would be made to relieve him. The South Carolina militia were collecting; continentals were ordered to his aid from Virginia, and North Carolina sent forward a brigade of seven hundred men under Brigadier William Caswell. As Caswell marched from Cross Creek, the advance of the expected reinforcements, four hundred Virginia continentals under Colonel Buford reached the Santee, but the entrance to the city was then closed, and toward the end of April these detachments went into camp near Lanier's Ferry, on the Santee, where President Rutledge was then concentrating the South Carolina militia.

The delayed reinforcements

Pref. Notes, S. R., XIV, xi

Lee's Memoirs, 164

Quickly after the fall of Charleston the British occupied Augusta and Ninety-six, and Cornwallis led a heavy force toward Rutledge's camp, Caswell and Buford falling back before him toward Camden. There they separated, and Caswell retreated to Cross Creek, where he arrived June 2d, while Buford took the upper route to Charlotte.

S. R., XIV, 827

On reaching Camden Cornwallis despatched Colonel Tarleton with his cavalry and some mounted infantry in pursuit of Buford, who was overtaken at the Waxhaws, thirty-five miles from Charlotte. Tarleton demanded an immediate surrender on the same terms agreed on at Charleston. These Buford refused. While the flags were passing Tarleton made his disposition for an assault. The instant the truce was over his cavalry made a furious charge upon the unsuspecting continentals, who had no orders to engage. In dismay and confusion, they offered no effective resistance, but threw down their arms and asked for quarter. No quarter was given. More than 100 were butchered on the spot, and 150 were so badly hacked up that

Lee's Memoirs, 165

Buford's defeat

1780

they could not be removed and for that reason had to be paroled where they fell. Only 53 were preserved as prisoners. Buford, with a few cavalry and less than 100 of the infantry, being the advance guard, managed to escape. He fled to Charlotte, where Colonel Porterfield, of Virginia, had arrived with a detachment of cavalry and artillery as well as infantry. Alarmed at the situation, Porterfield withdrew his force at once to Salisbury, and Tarleton returned to Camden. This butchery at Waxhaw aroused great indignation, and was commonly spoken of as "Tarleton's Quarters." While it created some dread of falling into his hands, and made him and his corps particularly odious, it inflamed the passions of the Americans and added increased animosity to the conflict.*

invasion apprehended

South Carolina being, like Georgia, occupied by the British, the inhabitants generally were subjugated; and it was expected that Cornwallis would make no delay in invading North Carolina, which lay defenceless at his feet. A fleet was daily looked for to take possession of Wilmington, and it was apprehended that columns from Camden would penetrate to Cross Creek and Charlotte; but happily Cornwallis postponed further operations until he had established civil government in South Carolina.

April, 1780

Abner Nash, governor

While the siege of Charleston was in progress the new Assembly met at New Bern on April 17th. Governor Caswell being no longer eligible as governor, Abner Nash was chosen to succeed him. For three years Caswell had been the most important man in the commonwealth. He had discharged with great zeal and efficiency every patriotic duty. Probably no other man could have done so well. Unfortunately, under the constitution he could not be longer re-

---

*Banastre Tarleton was then less than twenty-six years of age. A student of the law, this was his first military service. He was below middle size, but muscular and active, and was a daring officer, capable of great endurance. Of a dark complexion and piercing black eye, he became noted for the violence of his temper and his sanguinary disposition. In his warfare he disregarded every prompting of humanity.

1780
May

tained in the discharge of executive functions. But he was not to remain unemployed.

S. R.,
XXIV,
331, 339, 341

So urgent now was the necessity for prompt and decisive action that the Assembly at once created him commander-in-chief of the militia, with the rank of major-general, and ordered a draft, in addition to that commanded by William Caswell, of four thousand men. As usual, the men were slow in turning out, some declaring that they would not leave their homes until their bounty was paid, and no money had been provided for that purpose. His son having returned to Cross Creek, Major-General Caswell ordered the eastern drafts to assemble there, and he also hastened to that point.

On the departure of Clinton from New York on his southern expedition, congress, realizing the importance of making determined resistance, ordered south, in addition to the unfortunate corps of Colonel Buford, detachments under Colonel William Washington and Colonel Armand and the First and Second Maryland regiments and a regiment of artillery, all to be under the command of Major-General De Kalb.

De Kalb's reinforcements arrive

These troops were too late to save General Lincoln, but their appearance in North Carolina was timely. The surrender of the southern army at Charleston and the destruction of Buford's corps caused great dismay among the patriots, while, on the other hand, the Tories were jubilant. The arrival of De Kalb with his regulars, well supplied with ammunition, tended in some measure to restore confidence; but yet all military movements were delayed and hampered by the want of provisions, that could not be immediately supplied.

On the surrender of Lincoln, as De Kalb was not thought equal to the command of the department, Gates, wearing high honors as the victor over Burgoyne, was despatched to direct affairs at the south; and Colonel Morgan, who had achieved a great reputation by his operations with his corps of light infantry, but who had been temporarily in retirement from illness, was urged to again enter upon active service and aid in defending the southern states.

Gates in command

Activity of Rutherford

Although the interior of North Carolina was now open to the victorious British, Cornwallis found it necessary to devote some attention to affairs in South Carolina. Nor did he desire to enter on a campaign until a plentiful supply of provisions could be assured from the maturing crop. So while relying much on the assistance of the Tory inhabitants, he directed them to remain quiet in their homes until he should call them to action. Thus for a time there was a period of quietude.

Graham's
Graham,
213 *et seq.*

But because of the proximity of the enemy, early in June General Rutherford, always zealous and resolute, called out his brigade, of whom eight hundred promptly assembled, and on the 14th of that month, at Mallard's Creek, somewhat to the east of Charlotte, he organized his command. A battalion of light infantry was committed to Colonel William L. Davidson, a continental officer, and two small troops of cavalry under Captains Simmons and Martin were assigned to Major Davie. On that evening Rutherford received information that the Tories were embodying in Tryon County, some forty miles to the northwest, and fearing to reduce his own force, he directed Colonel Locke and Captains Falls and Brandon, of Rowan, and Major Wilson, of Mecklenburg, to make every effort to disperse them. He himself advanced to the south of Charlotte.

Ramseur's Mill

Colonel John Moore, whose family resided near Ramseur's Mill, on the south fork of the Catawba, had joined the British army the preceding winter, and now had returned home, announcing himself as lieutenant-colonel of Hamilton's regiment. He was soon joined by Nicholas Welch, a major of the same regiment, and the Tory inhabitants, feeling certain that the time had come for a rising, on June 20th nearly thirteen hundred of them assembled at Ramseur's Mill.

Tories rise

In view of this movement, Rutherford made such dispositions that Colonel Locke felt strong enough to attack Moore and his followers. The Tories were encamped on a hill half a mile north of the present village of Lincolnton, with a gentle slope in front and a clear fire for two hundred yards. Locke having reached their neighborhood at daybreak, the attack was made by the mounted companies of Captains Falls, McDowell, and Brandon, the infantry under Colonel Locke being near at hand. The Whigs got the better of the battle. At times the two parties, having no distinctive uniforms, mingled without being aware of it. Eventually the Whigs obtained possession of the ridge at first occupied by the Tories, who, however, reformed across the neighboring creek, being much more numerous than their assailants. Rutherford, however, had advanced into that vicinity, and after some parley the Tories dispersed. Moore sought safety in flight, and with thirty men succeeded in reaching the British camp at Camden; the others returned to their homes. The loss on each side was about the same. Fifty-six lay dead on the ridge where the battle was hottest, with others scattered on the flanks. In addition, a hundred of each party were wounded. Fifty of the Tories were taken prisoners. "In this battle between neighbors," says General Graham, "near relations and personal friends fought on either side, and as the smoke would from time to time rise from the field they could recognize each other engaged in deadly contest. In the evening and on the next day the relations and friends of the dead and wounded came in, and a scene was witnessed of affliction and distress quite indescribable. Of the Whigs, Captains Falls, Dobson, Smith, Bowman, and Armstrong were killed, and Houston and McKissick wounded; while of the Tories, Captains Cumberland, Murry, and Warlick were killed and many well-known inhabitants wounded. So distressing was the result of this first encounter between the Whigs and Tories of that immediate section that from that time onward the Loyalists never actively engaged against their Whig neighbors."

On the second day after the dispersal of Moore's Tories at Ramseur's Rutherford received information that a considerable number were embodying in the forks of the Yadkin, at the north end of Rowan, near Surry, some seventy-five miles distant, under the command of Colonel Bryan. He immediately despatched Davie with his cavalry to Waxhaw Creek to watch the British, while he himself hastened to

Tories
dispersed

Graham's
Graham,
226

Rutherford
pursues
Bryan

1780
June

attack Bryan. That active commander, however, crossed to the east of the Yadkin and continued his route through those settlements which were much disaffected, being joined so generally by the inhabitants that by the time he passed Abbott's Creek his force had swollen to seven or eight hundred men. Rutherford hoped to intercept him, but Bryan, panic-stricken by the result of the affair at Ramseur's, marched night and day until he was able to form a junction with a British force under Major McArthur, whom Cornwallis had thrown forward, and who advanced to Anson Court House.

Cornwallis's plans

S R., XV,
252

These movements of the Tories were premature. Cornwallis wrote on June 30th that he had established satisfactory correspondence, and had seen several people of credit from North Carolina, and they all agreed in assuring him of the "good disposition of a considerable body of the inhabitants," but that it would be impossible to subsist troops there until after the harvest. He therefore had sent emissaries, recommending in the strongest terms that they should attend to their harvest and remain quiet until the king's troops should enter the province. He referred to Moore's rising as having been "excited by the sanguine emissaries of the very sanguine and imprudent Lieutenant-Colonel Hamilton," and hoped that no evil would result from that "unlucky business." Although advised of every detail of the American movement, Cornwallis had no apprehensions but that North Carolina would at his pleasure be "perfectly

S. R., XIV,
501, 502

reduced." Expecting an immediate invasion of North Carolina, following the complete pacification of South Carolina, the American troops had been concentrated well to the north, to give time for the arrival of reinforcements; but toward the end of June De Kalb determined to move forward, and established a camp on Deep River, awaiting a supply of provisions to carry him into the Peedee section.

De Kalb
encamps on
Deep River

There was a sandy barren, virtually destitute of provisions, as of inhabitants, lying between the Deep River and Cross Creek, and extending to the west and south toward the South Carolina line; but in the Peedee section supplies were generally very abundant. About the middle of July De Kalb took post at Coxe's Mills, on the Deep River, where General Caswell with the militia joined him, while General Rutherford and General Harrington moved cautiously down near the Cheraws, Sumter and Davie being still further in advance.

1780
S. R , XIV,
512
July

Davie's enterprise

In the meantime, Davie, with his small body of cavalry, was manifesting a spirit of enterprise that has rarely been equalled in partisan warfare. Being in the vicinity of Hanging Rock, one of the British outposts, on July 20th he intercepted a convoy of provisions and clothing intended for that garrison. The dragoons and Loyalists who guarded the convoy were captured and the horses and arms safely brought off, but the wagons of provisions had to be destroyed. A few days later he unexpectedly appeared at Hanging Rock, intercepting three companies of mounted infantry who were returning from an expedition, and in plain view of the garrison cut them to pieces, securing one hundred good muskets and sixty horses by that adventure. His own loss so far had not been a single man. He and Colonel Sumter, of South Carolina, and Colonel Irwin, of North Carolina, now arranged for a combined attack on Hanging Rock, to be undertaken on August 5th. Davie's force had increased to about five hundred men and Sumter's to three hundred. Among the garrison were Hamilton's regiment and Bryan's Tories, and North Carolinians again faced each other on the battlefield. Just after break of day the assault was made, and the Americans took the garrison by surprise. At first they routed the enemy and possessed themselves of the camp; but the pursuit and the plunder of the camp threw the Whigs into great confusion, and the enemy rallying, a retreat became necessary. An hour was spent in plundering the camp, taking the paroles of British officers and attending to the removal of the wounded, and then the men, loaded with plunder, marched off cheering for the American cause.

Lee's
Memoirs,
169, 176

Wheeler,
Hist. of N.
C., II, 189
et seq.

1780
August

Schenck,
North
Carolina,
1780-81,
76-79

Activity at
the West

S. R., XIV,
522, 528, 530

Musgrove's Mill

While Davie was active in that quarter, the mountain men were operating farther to the west. Colonel Charles McDowell, having been joined by Colonel Shelby and Lieutenant-Colonels Sevier and Clarke at his camp near Cherokee Ford, on Broad River, despatched them with some six hundred men to attack the Loyalist leader, Patrick Moore, who had a fortified post on Pacolet River. They were successful, Moore surrendering some ninety-three Loyalists and two hundred and fifty stands of arms. Immediately afterward Colonel Ferguson arrived in their vicinity, and a skirmish took place at Cedar Springs, the Americans retreating, but carrying off some fifty prisoners from the field. McDowell, learning that there were five hundred Tories encamped at Musgrove's Mill, on the Enoree, some forty miles distant, again detached Shelby, Clarke, and Williams, with seven hundred horsemen, to surprise them. Skilfully avoiding Ferguson, they reached the Tory camp at dawn on the morning of August 19th, and meeting a strong patrol party, a skirmish ensued. At that juncture Shelby learned that the Tories had been heavily reinforced by a regiment of British regulars. Shelby at once constructed some breastworks, and sent forward a small party to lure the advancing force into ambush. The stratagem succeeded. The British, hastily pursuing the retreating party, rushed in disorder to where the Whigs were concealed, and their commander, Colonel Innes, and all the other British officers except one subaltern having been killed or wounded, the pursuit was turned into a rout, and the Americans drove them beyond the Enoree. The British loss was 63 killed and 160 wounded and taken, while that of the Americans was only 4 killed and 9 wounded. General McDowell, having now received information of the disaster at Camden, withdrew his forces, and Colonel Shelby retired beyond the mountains, while Colonels Clarke and Williams conveyed the prisoners to Virginia.

Gates advances

On July 31st General Caswell united his forces, composed of the eastern brigade under General Isaac Gregory

THEATRE OF OPERATIONS
IN THE
SOUTHERN CAMPAIGN,
1781–1783.

REFERENCE.

Route of Greene's Marches
"   " Morgan's   "
"   " Lee's   "
"   " Cornwallis's "
"   " Rawdon's   "

SCALE OF MILES
0   10   20   30   40   60   100

1780
August

nd that of General John Butler, with Rutherford's at the Cheraws, and General Gates, who had joined De Kalb, was about to make a junction with him. Colonel Porterfield, of Virginia, with three hundred Virginia continentals, was also coming up, while General Stevens, with seven hundred Virginia militia, was at Coxe's Mills getting supplies to subsist his troops while en route to the advanced forces. By August 7th Gates reached Caswell, and a week later the combined forces encamped at Rugeley's Mills, in the vicinity of Camden, where the British had established their headquarters. Since the defeat of Buford all that region had been harried by strong bands of Loyalists. The Tories had joined their partisan leaders, and those inhabitants who sympathized with the American cause had either fled from their homes or had been captured and carried away by their enemies. The country was deserted and was a scene of desolation. It was with the greatest difficulty that food could be obtained for man or beast from day to day.

Being informed by General Sumter that a convoy of stores for the army at Camden was approaching from Ninety-six, and that he could intercept it at the ferry, one mile below Camden, if supplied with artillery, Gates now detached four hundred men under Colonel Woolford, of the Maryland line, with two light pieces to aid Sumter in that service. Lee's Memoirs, 179

Gates having brought together his remaining troops determined to take an advantageous position, which had been carefully selected, about five miles from Camden, and on the night of August 15th moved his army forward for the purpose of occupying it.

The battle of Camden

In the meantime Cornwallis, having been apprised of the advance of the American army, left Charleston with a large re-enforcement, and reached Lord Rawdon at Camden on the 14th. In that extremely hot season it was convenient to make military movements at night rather than in the day. At ten o'clock on the night of the 15th Cornwallis set his troops in motion with the purpose of attacking Gates at early dawn. Gates had ignored the value of cavalry, and knew nothing of Cornwallis's movements. Assuming that Rawdon's force Aug. 16,1780 Lee's Memoirs, 181 et seq.

1780
August

was largely inferior to his own, on the same night, the 15th he marched with confidence, taking no precautions. About half-past two o'clock that night, while leisurely on the march, his army came unexpectedly in collision with the British force that had moved out to surprise him. The meeting was unexpected to both. The British quickly routed Armand's troop of a hundred horse, in the advance, which recoiled at the unexpected discharge, became disordered and retired. Close behind were Porterfield's corps on the right and Major Martin Armstrong's light infantry, North Carolina militia, on the left. These resolutely withstood the enemy and brought them to a halt, but unhappily the gallant Colonel Porterfield fell in this first encounter. Prisoners being taken on both sides, the commanding generals soon became aware of the unexpected situation. The two armies remained through the night, excited, ardently looking for the approach of day, anxious for the conflict. Gates arrayed his army promptly, Maryland and Delaware continentals under Gist on his right, North Carolina militia under Caswell in the centre, Virginia militia under Stevens on the left. The First Maryland Brigade under Smallwood formed the reserve. De Kalb took post on the right, while Gates placed himself between the line of battle and the reserve. Cornwallis's right wing under Webster, composed of disciplined regulars, at dawn made a furious assault on the Virginia militia, and the brave Stevens had to endure the mortifying spectacle of his brigade seeking safety in flight, throwing away their arms without exchanging more

S. R , XV,
383

than one fire with the enemy. Caswell's militia in the centre, now threatened both in front and flank, soon followed this shameful example. Stevens, Caswell, and Gates struggled hard to rally the fugitives, but in the entire absence of cavalry the attempt was hopeless and the panic continued. General Rutherford acted with distinguished gallantry, but received a musket ball through his thigh, which disabled him, and he fell prostrate on the field. General Butler vainly endeavored to keep the centre of the North Carolina line

Ramsay's
Hist. U. S.,
II, 350
Gen.
Gregory

in position, but it quickly gave way. General Gregory on the right was more fortunate. His courageous example was followed by a large part of his brigade, and he stoutly maintained his position and adhered to the Maryland line; but he, too, was wounded in the thickest of the fight. Indeed, twice was he wounded by the bayonet, and many of his brigade had no other wounds than from the bayonet. But the odds were too heavy. On the American right the continentals and Major Hal Dixon's regiment of North Carolina militia stood their ground with devoted courage. They made stubborn resistance. Indeed, they not only repelled the attack, but ·drove the enemy back from their first advanced position. Although greatly outnumbered, resorting to the bayonet, they rushed the enemy before them, taking many prisoners. Smallwood, advancing, covered their left flank, but soon was borne down by Cornwallis's heavy columns. De Kalb made one last resolute attempt for victory, and fell with eleven wounds. Again the bayonets of bloody butchers were about to pierce him, when his aide-de-camp, Colonel Du Buysson, covered the prostrate general with his own body and received the bayonets thrust at his friend. The old hero poured out his life blood for American liberty and shortly expired, honored by his foes and lamented by his friends. The Delaware regiment was nearly annihilated. More than one-third of the continentals were killed and wounded and a hundred and seventy taken prisoners. A hundred of the North Carolina militia also fell on the field, and three hundred were captured. Rutherford, badly wounded, was taken, and for a time North Carolina lost his valuable services. As resolute and courageous as were this brave man and General Gregory, neither won higher commendation than Major Dixon. "None," says Lee in his "Memoirs," "can withhold applause from Colonel Dixon and his North Carolina regiment of militia. Having their flank exposed by the flight of the other militia, they turned with disdain from the ignoble example. . . . In every vicissitude of the battle this regiment maintained its ground, and when the reserve under Smallwood, covering our left, relieved its naked flank, forced the enemy to fall back." Dixon's troops emulated the noble ardor of their leader.

Dr. Hugh Williamson, who was surgeon-general on Caswell's staff, attended the prisoners, of whom, however,

1780
August

Hal Dixon

The fall of
De Kalb

Lee's
Memoirs,
186

S. R., XV,
166

1780
Booth Boote

no satisfactory returns could be obtained, as the British commissary of prisoners was, says the doctor, "one Booth Boote, whose character does not appear to be diversified by a single virtue, and who would never do anything that would prove acceptable to us."

Gates's ride, Wheeler, Hist. North Carolina, II, 194

General Gates hardly waited to learn the issue of the battle. Not succeeding in rallying the Virginia militia, although he and General Caswell made a third and last attempt, more than half a mile distant from the battle, he made no new dispositions, gave no further orders, but abandoning his army and his stores, he made such hot haste that at only a few miles from the field he was the first, except alone one frightened horseman, to meet Major Davie, then advancing to unite with the army. He was the first to give Davie information of the disaster. Davie proposed to proceed and bury the dead. "Let the dead bury the dead!" exclaimed the excited hero of Saratoga as he resumed his speedy way, attended by General Caswell and some members of his staff. About eleven o'clock on the night of the 16th Gates reached Charlotte, seventy-two miles distant from the battle ground, bringing the news of his sad reverse. He did not stop, but pressed on to Salisbury, and thence to Hillsboro.

Graham's Graham, 243

Caswell, however, remained a day at Charlotte, giving some directions for the movements of the eastern regiment, that fortunately had not reached his camp in time to join the army, and ordering out the militia of Mecklenburg and Rowan and Lincoln counties; and then, like Gates, he rode on to Hillsboro.

The disaster, Ramsay's Hist. U. S., II, 351

In the action every corps was broken and dispersed. The fugitives, pressing down the main road, were pursued some miles by Tarleton's legion, and the way was covered with arms, baggage and wagons. Many took to the woods and sought to escape into the swamps. It was a painful rout, the men without officers, without provisions or baggage, and great numbers without arms, the wounded and sick borne along without conveniences, and the weather extremely oppressive. The suffering was intense. Indeed, the horrors of that fearful rout cannot be adequately portrayed.

S. R., XIV, 569, 570

Soon Charlotte became crowded with troops in retreat

rom the disaster and with militiamen who were hastily col-
ecting. Neither the officers nor soldiers of Gates's army, August
lowever, remained at Charlotte, but kept moving toward
Salisbury. General Smallwood, whose brigade was the last Smallwood
on the field, being hotly pressed, turned from the road, and
t was supposed that he was either killed or taken, but on
he third day after the battle he arrived in Charlotte, to the
great joy of every one. His conduct gained for him the con-
idence not merely of the regulars, but of the militia, and he
was at once consulted as to what action should be taken.
He encouraged the militia to embody and to make strenuous
resistance if the enemy should advance. On the 20th, however, he and all the other officers and men who had come in
et out for Hillsboro.

On learning the woeful news, Davie, realizing Sumter's Sumter
langer, at once despatched a courier to inform that kindred routed
spirit, who had been so recently associated with him in dar-
ng enterprises, of the catastrophe. Sumter had been entirely successful in his last undertaking, and had captured
forty wagons of booty and nearly three hundred prisoners.
He immediately decamped, but Cornwallis hurried Tarleton Lee's
in pursuit. On the night of the 17th Sumter halted at Rocky Memoirs,
Mount, thirty miles from Camden, and the next morning 188
proceeded eight miles farther, when, because of the heat
and the fatigue of his troops, he again rested, ignorant of the
pursuit. His arms were stacked, his troops scattered, many
asleep, he himself asleep under a wagon, when Tarleton,
having gained his rear unperceived, fell upon the unsuspecting Americans, who were seized with consternation at
the assault. There was but slight resistance and then general flight. Out of eight hundred men, only three hundred
and fifty escaped; while Tarleton recovered the British
wagons, stores, and provisions, and took Sumter's artillery,
arms, and baggage, killed many and preserved some
prisoners.

When information was received of the catastrophe that Graham's
had befallen Sumter's corps, the people of Mecklenburg, Graham,
alarmed at their exposed position, held a meeting to deter- 246
mine on a course of action. It was resolved that Colonel
Irwin, the colonel of that county, should form a camp some

seven miles to the south of Charlotte, and Davie's cavalry should patrol toward Camden. In a few days Colonel Locke arrived with some militia from Rowan; and Governor Nash learning that Rutherford was a prisoner, commissioned Colonel Davidson as temporary brigadier-general and Major Davie as colonel of cavalry, and every exertion was made to offer resistance.

The spirit of the people

Severe indeed was the disaster, and for it Gates was vigorously condemned. "There are three capital . . . errors ascribed" to General Gates, wrote Davis to Willie Jones. "First, in not ordering a place of rendezvous in case of a defeat; secondly, in not having the baggage secured, it remaining all the while with the army; and thirdly, in quitting the field of action some time before the regulars gave way, and riding post to Hillsboro, two hundred and thirty miles in seventy-five hours. He is . . . execrated by the officers, unrevered by the soldiers and hated by the people."*

North Carolina Uni. Mag., IV, 81 (1855)

Not only was the large army that had been collected at great pains and expense destroyed, but all the artillery, two thousand stands of arms and nearly all the military stores sent to the south by congress fell into the hands of the enemy. Following so swiftly on the loss of the entire continental line at Charleston, this blow was an immeasurable calamity to the State. The dark hours that try men's souls had indeed come. The loss of brave and courageous soldiers at the north and the annihilation of the continental battalions robbed the State of thousands of her choicest spirits. But those who remained did not falter; the resolution of the North Carolina patriots never wavered, and their courage rose higher and higher under the calamities that had befallen them. As deplorable and distressing as the situation was, it was bravely met. Immediate preparation was made

---

*On the other hand, consider the opinion of Lee, a soldier, and compare it with Davis, the civilian: "This rapid retreat of General Gates has been generally supposed to diminish his reputation. Not so, in truth. It does him honor, as it evinced a mind capable, amidst confusion and distress, of discerning the point most promising to renew with expedition his strength; at the same time incapable of being withheld from doing his duty, by regarding the calumny with which he was sure to be assailed." (Lee's Memoirs, 100, ed. 1827.)

to resist the invasion that was now imminent; but for the moment North Carolina was defenceless and lay open to the conqueror.

Fortunately, other supplies were within reach. Trade between our ports and the West Indies was never entirely arrested, and many valuable cargoes continued to be imported; nor had the practice ceased of sending out privateers to prey on British commerce and make prizes of merchantmen. So it happened that several vessels came in just about the time Gates lost his stores, bringing cargoes tending to supply those losses. In particular, on September 4th there arrived in the Cape Fear two prizes made by the privateer *General Nash,* one cargo being invoiced at £10,000 and the other at £40,000 sterling, the latter being one of the most valuable captures made during the war, and having on board nearly everything desired for the soldiers. About the same time the Marquis of Bretigny also reached New Bern, bringing a quantity of powder, four hundred stands of arms, pistols, saddles, and accoutrements; while Dr. Guion's schooner likewise arrived with additional supplies. In fact, the enterprise displayed by the merchants was no less remunerative to them than beneficial to the State. It was also harassing to the enemy. Governor Nash in December mentioned in a letter to General Washington: "The enemy have not been entirely free of trouble off Charleston; and on the coast in that quarter during this summer they have suffered very considerably by our privateers, particularly by open rowboats. These boats, with forty or fifty men aboard, take almost everything that comes in their way. Two that went out in company returned here this week after a leave of about twenty days, in which time they took and sent in twelve valuable prizes, besides burning, I think, four."

All now was activity in the State. Smallwood established a camp at Salisbury, where the sick and wounded were assembled. Such ammunition and stores as remained at Mack's Ferry were speedily brought to the same point, and there began the nucleus of a new organization. General Harrington, with several companies of militia from Duplin, Onslow, Bladen, Cumberland and some of the Albemarle

Importations

S. R., XV, 70, 72

Enterprise on the water

counties, aggregating in all four hundred and fifty men, kept a vigilant watch and guarded the stores at Fayetteville. In his front, toward the coast, was Marion with a few horsemen, and over in Anson Colonel Kobb,* while down the Peedee the brave and energetic Kenan, of Duplin, patrolled with his squadron of horse. Farther to the west Davie and Davidson kept watch and ward.

Governor Nash had called the Assembly together to meet at Hillsboro on August 12th, but a quorum of members had not reached there on the 23d. Time being precious, the members who had convened united in recommending that the governor should call out one-half of the militia of the State and direct the commanding officers to appoint commissioners to obtain the necessary supplies, either by purchase or impressment. Accordingly, the militia was directed to assemble at Hillsboro, Salisbury, and Charlotte. General Caswell despatched messengers to intercept the militia regiments of Jarvis, Exum, and Pasteur, and to direct them to Ramsey's Mills, in Chatham, where a few days later he himself arrived, the strength of the brigade being some eight hundred men. To command it Governor Nash assigned General Sumner, as the most experienced officer of the State. On September 3d Caswell and Sumner proceeded with the brigade by way of Pittsboro to the encampment at Salisbury.

Sumner given a brigade (margin)

S. R., XIV, 573 (margin)

The Assembly acts

S. R., XXIV, 344 (margin)

When the Assembly met, and it was not until September 5th that a quorum was assembled, it addressed itself with vigor to preparations of defence. Responding to the recommendation of the governor, it levied a tax in kind to be at once collected out of the abundant harvest. For every £100 value of property each inhabitant was required to furnish one peck of Indian corn or three pounds of good pork,

*Colonel Kobb was afterward murdered by the Tories. "Among the many murders and house burnings perpetrated by this banditti," says Lee in his Memoirs, page 553, "that of Colonel Kobb was singularly atrocious. A party of them, led by a Captain Jones, surprised the colonel on a visit to his family. He defended his house until he was induced by a promise of personal safety to surrender as a prisoner of war, when he was immediately murdered in the presence of his wife and children and his house burned."

or other provisions enumerated in the act, except that the
inhabitants of Carteret might deliver instead a gallon of
salt; and the Quakers, Moravians and "non-jurors" were to
pay their entire tax in provisions. A loan of £1,000,000
was also directed to be made, while for the present the
confiscation act was suspended. Many persons being in
custody on the charge of opposing the State in its defence,
for the "speedy trial of traitors" the magistrates of the
different counties were given authority to try them, no
counsel being allowed either for or against any prisoner,
who, however, was at liberty to make his own defence, and
should have reasonable time to prepare for trial; and there
was to be no arrest of judgment in any case if the proceeding was of sufficient substance to convict.

The Board of War

Governor Nash had reported to the Assembly that the
members of his council did not attend its meetings and gave
him no aid; and he urged that other appointments should
be made; and he also recommended that a Board of War
should be created, who would share with him the responsibility of conducting military matters when the Assembly
was not in session. Accordingly the Assembly created a
Board of War, composed of Colonel Alexander Martin,
John Penn, and Oroondates Davis, investing it with great
powers, especially for concerting a general plan of operations for the defence of the State and carrying it into execution. General Harrington had somewhat earlier been appointed brigadier-general of the Salisbury district during the
absence of General Rutherford, and now that Rutherford
had fallen into the hands of the enemy the Assembly elected
Colonel Davidson to that position. Harrington promptly
tendered his resignation, but nevertheless, because of the
emergency, he continued to act under his commission as
brigadier, rendering efficient service on the southeastern
border. General Smallwood, of the Maryland line, was enjoying a high reputation because of his admirable conduct
at Camden, quite in contrast with the prevalent idea of the
conduct of Gates and Caswell; and the Assembly tendered
him the position of major-general and commander-in-chief

1780

of all the militia of the State, thus superseding Caswell, and giving Smallwood precedence over all the officers in the southern army except alone General Gates. This action virtually retiring him, Caswell indignantly resented; and he returned to his home at Kingston. A month later he wrote to Governor Nash, reminding him that "in the spring he had not only been appointed major-general to command the militia, but as well a member of the board to conduct trade in behalf of the State; and that as the Assembly had been pleased to dismiss him from the command of the militia, it is probable it would have dismissed him also from the Board of Trade had it occurred to them that he had been appointed a member of that board"; and so with some warmth he tendered his resignation of this latter position. For a time he remained entirely quiet.

S. R., XV, 131

1. JOSEPH WINSTON   2. JOSEPH GRAHAM
3. JOSEPH MCDOWELL (Quaker Meadows) 4. WILLIAM POLK

CHAPTER XXXVI

NASH'S ADMINISTRATION, 1780-81—*Continued*

Cornwallis moves to Charlotte.—Davie's gallant defence.—The
activity of the Mecklenburgers.—Governor Martin's proclamation.—
Movement on Augusta.—Ferguson marches westward.—The frontiersmen assemble.—Battle of King's Mountain.—Death of Chronicle.
—The victory gives great joy.—Its effects.—Cornwallis retires.—His
gloomy outlook.—Leslie in Virginia.—Moves to Camden.—Gates
moves forward.—Cornwallis's disappointment.—Arrival of Greene.—
His activity.—His forward movement.—The new year.—The Council
Extraordinary.—Caswell reinstated.—Four new continental battal-
ons.—No party divisions.—During Caswell's administration.—Nash's
administration.—Dr. Burke's zeal to correct abuses.—Sam Johnston
declines the presidency of congress.

Cornwallis moves to Charlotte

After the rout of Gates's army Cornwallis occupied himself at Camden arranging for the administration of civil
and military affairs in South Carolina, and then the time
being at hand for him to invade North Carolina, he moved
to Waxhaw on September 8th, resting there for the Tories
to embody and join him. Tarleton was thrown on his left
toward Ferguson, who was operating on the frontier. At
first while the British army lay at Waxhaw Colonel Davie
alone was at its front. With a command not exceeding
one hundred and fifty men, that enterprising officer on September 20th, by a circuitous march, fell on a detachment of
some three hundred of the enemy at Wahab's plantation,
routed them and brought off ninety-six horses, a hundred
and twenty stands of arms, returning to his camp that same
evening, having marched in less than twenty-four hours no
less than sixty miles. On the same day Sumner and Davidson reached his camp with a thousand militia. Four days
later Cornwallis renewed his movement, advancing on
Charlotte, and Sumner and Davidson fell back toward
Salisbury.

1780

Lee's
Memoirs,
193-196

Wahab's

Sumner at
the front

S. R., XIV,
647

1780
S. R., XIV,
389, 410, 681,
778 ; XV, 89

Davidson turned to the west, while Sumner took post a
McGowan's Creek, where early in October General Butler
brigade of seven hundred joined him. General Jones wit
the Halifax brigade had been ordered to join Harringto
New forces
concentrate
in front of Campbellton, but he, too, was now marching wit
all haste to Sumner's camp. Colonel William Washingto
had enlisted some hundred troopers also in the easter
counties, and he with other partisan leaders were concen
S. R., XIV,
412
trating at Salisbury. General Smallwood and Colonel Mo
gan already in high reputation on October 7th, left Hillsbor
for the front. Everywhere there was displayed the sam
energy and spirit. It was estimated that there were fiv
thousand men concentrating for defence. The Board o
War, however, was emphatic in directions that a genera
engagement was to be avoided, for a second defeat at tha
time would have had a most disastrous effect on the inhabi
tants and on the spirit of the militia, who had now in som
measure rallied from the depression caused by the disaste
at Camden.

Davie's gallant defence

Graham's
Graham,
251
Davie with his troop of horse, now augmented by a few
volunteers under Major Joseph Graham, remained to ob
Sept., 1780
serve the enemy. On the night of the 25th he took a num
ber of prisoners, and then himself retired to Charlotte
Early the next morning Tarleton's legion with some ligh
infantry was seen advancing, followed by the main body
Determined to make a defence, Davie disposed of his smal
force advantageously at the court-house, and when the
At Charlotte
enemy, sounding a charge, advanced at a full gallop, he
opened fire and drove them back with great precipitation
A second and third charge was similarly repelled; but a
length the infantry turned his flank, and in good order
Davie withdrew his companies, each in turn covering the
other, and made a successful retreat. The enemy followed
cautiously for some distance, when they ventured to charge
the rear guard. They were stubbornly resisted and driven
Locke killed
off, but unfortunately not without loss; Lieutenant Locke
and four privates were killed, and Major Graham and five

others were wounded.* The following day after this brilliant affair at Charlotte Davie joined the army at Salisbury, but on the union of some mounted infantry from Granville under Colonel Taylor with his corps he felt strong enough to return to the immediate front of Cornwallis, who established himself at Charlotte.

The activity of the Mecklenburgers

As trying as were the difficulties which beset the American commanders for the want of provisions, the troubles of Cornwallis on the same score were much greater. His foraging parties brought in but little, and they were so sorely harassed by Davie that the British army fell into sore distress for want of forage and supplies.

At Charlotte there were but a few houses, but it was a desirable location for an army because of the numerous mills in the immediate vicinity, at which corn and wheat could be ground for the use of the troops. At Polk's Mill, two miles distant from Charlotte, Cornwallis stationed a detachment of fifty men, and on September 28th Major Dickson with sixty cavalrymen made the entire circuit around Charlotte and attacked that post. He was repulsed, but the assault added to the disagreeable position of the British commander. Five days later he despatched a detachment of four hundred and fifty infantry, sixty cavalry and forty wagons under Major Doyle toward the fertile fields of Long Creek, some ten miles to the northwest of Charlotte, to bring in forage and supplies. At McIntyre's farm a party of a hundred men and ten wagons was left to gather forage, while the others continued on. Captain James Thompson and thirteen of his brave neighbors resolutely attacked this party, and so vigorously that eight of them were killed and twelve wounded. Doyle was so alarmed by this unexpected assault that he hastened back, picked up his dead and wounded and then fled precipitately, having obtained only forage enough to load four wagons.

Graham's Graham, 258, 260

Polk's Mill

McIntyre's

*In this encounter at the Cross Roads, St. George Locke, a son of General Matthew Locke, was literally cut to pieces in a most barbarous manner, while Captain Joseph Graham, in addition to being wounded three times with balls, received six sabre cuts and was left on the field for dead.

1780
~
October

Governor Martin's proclamation

Accompanying Cornwallis was the royal governor, Josiah Martin, who now entered the State for the first time since he departed from the Cape Fear in May, 1776. Hoping much from the Tories and disaffected inhabitants, who he conceived were attached to him personally, on October 3o he issued an earnest address seriously and solemnly calling on the faithful subjects of his Majesty with heart and hand to join and unite with the army, and exhorting all the young men to testify their loyalty and spirit by enlisting in a provincial corps to be under his immediate command; and offering a bounty of three guineas, full pay and free grants of land at the end of the rebellion. Couriers were at once sent off to disseminate this proclamation both to the west and to the east, but before it could have operation came the news of the destruction of Ferguson's corps, which effectually suppressed all Tory risings.

Graham's
Graham,
264, 265

Movement on Augusta

Although the southern Indians adhered to the British looking to the king of Great Britain for protection against the inroads of the colonists, intercourse with them was constantly maintained by Colonel Joseph Martin, specially employed in that service, and he managed with such skill, wisdom and prudence, that during that critical period of the war, they remained quiet, and the western borders were not menaced with the peril of a savage warfare.

Joseph
Martin

This fortunate circumstance left the frontiersmen free to take the field away from home when called upon. Somewhat earlier than Cornwallis's advance several detachments had embodied under local leaders with the purpose of attacking Augusta, where a large supply of arms, ammunition, blankets, salt and other commodities intended as the annual present to the Indians was then stored. Eventually all these united under Colonel Clarke, who marched toward Augusta. The British commander, Colonel Browne, having information of their approach, retired toward Ninety-six, but was overtaken at Garden Hill, where he fortified and gallantly defended himself, awaiting relief. After four days of siege relief came, and Colonel Clarke was forced to retire, carry-

Lee's
Memoirs,
198, 200
S. R., XV,
94

Garden Hill

S. R., XIV,
424

ng with him, however, a large amount of the Indian goods
hat had fallen into his hands. In the meantime other
movements had been made among the frontiersmen, even
as remote as Watauga and western Virginia.

Ferguson marches westward

To counteract these movements Cornwallis had detached
Major Ferguson, an accomplished officer, with three hundred regulars and a small body of Loyalists, to proceed
toward the frontier, arouse the Tories, collect provisions
and suppress the Whig inhabitants. He was not only S. R., XV, 163
supplied with ammunition, but carried with him a thousand
stand of arms for the Loyalists who were expected to join
his force. Marching through upper South Carolina and
then into North Carolina, Ferguson himself stopped at Gilbert Town, but a detachment penetrated as far as Morganton, and word was spread that he proposed to destroy all
the Whig settlements. This information, instead of acting Davidson's orders
as a deterrent, aroused the Whigs of the frontier, who were
already embodied ready for action. On September 14th S. R., XIV 615
Gen. William Lee Davidson ordered Armstrong, Cleveland
and Locke to unite their forces and arrest Ferguson's progress; and the other Whig leaders were also moving. They The corps unite
resolved on Ferguson's destruction. Campbell, from Virginia,
joined Shelby and Sevier at Watauga, their united forces
numbering nine hundred men, and on September 25th
crossed the mountains, where they were met by Colonel Mc-
Dowell with a hundred and sixty others, and on the 30th,
on the banks of the Catawba, they were reinforced by Cleveland with three hundred and fifty men of the counties of
Wilkes and Surry. Marching south on the evening of Octo- S. R., XV, 94
ber 6th, they were joined near Cowpens by Colonel Williams's force of four hundred. There information was received that Ferguson was near the Cherokee ford of Broad
River, about thirty miles distant. A council of the principal S. R., XV, 106
officers was held, and it was thought advisable to set out
that night with nine hundred of the best horsemen, leaving
the others to follow as fast as possible. Marching all night,
at three o'clock the next afternoon they reached the vicinity
of Ferguson's corps.

1780
King's
Mountain,
Oct. 7th
Ferguson, having information of the approach of a Whig column, had taken a strong position on the top of King's Mountain, twelve miles distant from the ford, and in full confidence that he could not be forced from a post possessing such natural advantages. The assailants were formed into three divisions, and coolly ascended the mountain from different directions. The day was wet, and their approach being fortunately undiscovered, the Whigs easily took the British pickets. As the column was arranged, the Washington and Sullivan regiments, gaining their positions first, began the attack on the front and left flank; to the North

S. R., XV,
116, 164
Carolinians under Winston, Sevier and Cleveland was assigned the attack on the rear and other flank. Campbell on the centre opened a destructive fire, but Ferguson re-

S. R., XV,
164
sorted to the bayonet and forced him back. At that instant, however, Shelby poured in a volley, alike effective. Ferguson turned furiously on this new foe, advancing with the bayonet; but Shelby, having reached the summit of the eminence, drove the British along the ridge to where Cleveland commanded, and his brave men stopped them in that quarter. Undismayed by this unexpected resistance, Ferguson now made a grand rally, his men fighting desperately; but all the Whig divisions acting in co-operation, the Tory

Death of
Ferguson
force could make but slight impression. Ferguson used the Shelby, Sevier, Hambright, and Winston, and Major Shelby, and for an hour the battle raged without abatement. At length the British commander sought to escape on horseback, but fell dead trying to force his way.

The victory
The fire of the beleaguered Tories now slackened, and soon there was unconditional surrender. Of Ferguson's force 300 were killed or wounded; 100 regulars and 700 Loyalists were taken, and 1500 stands of arms fell into the possession of the Whigs. The loss of the assailants was small, but among the killed was Colonel Williams,* of South Carolina, distinguished as one of the most active and reso-

*Colonel James Williams, a native of Granville County, N. C., then resident in South Carolina, on application had been allowed by North Carolina $25,000 to raise troops for the defence of North Carolina. He had under him troops raised in North Carolina, as well perhaps as in South Carolina. (S. R., XXI, 75; Graham's Graham, 263.)

te of the partisan leaders, and Major William Chronicle, 1780
hose loss was greatly lamented. It was night before the
risoners were all secured, and the victors slept on the bat-
efield; but early the next morning they set off northward
ith their prisoners under the command of Colonel Camp-
ell.

Later, General Gates directed that the eight hundred S. R., XV,
risoners should be conveyed to Fincastle, Va.; but on 115
aching Surry County they were turned over to Colonel
Martin Armstrong, and within two months all but a hun- The
red and thirty of them were either dismissed, paroled or prisoners
nlisted in the military service for three months. There
as great hope of using these prisoners for the purposes
f exchange to set free an equal number held by the British,
nd much disappointment was felt when this design was
ustrated by Colonel Armstrong's inexpedient conduct; nor S. R., XVII,
id he escape without severe and indignant criticism, and 668
ne Assembly deprived him of his commission.

he victory gives great joy

The movement of the Whigs at the west was not unknown
Davie, Sumner, and Gates, and they were in anxious
xpectancy.

Three days after the battle the news of the victory was S. R., XIV,
rought by a courier to Sumner at his camp on the Yadkin, 685;
ho forwarded it to Gates at Hillsboro. Whatever com- XV, 117
nent might be made on General Gates's course up to this
eriod, and he was thoroughly execrated by the people, it
ppears that in adversity he rose to the height of the occa-
ion. With resolution and promptness he was preparing Gates' spirit
o renew the conflict. With joy and hope he hurried an
xpress to Jefferson, then governor of Virginia, bearing
"the great and glorious news"; and, urging forward prom-
sed help, he said: "We are now more than even with the
nemy. The moment the supplies for the troops arrive . . . I
hall proceed with the whole to the Yadkin." Smallwood
nd Morgan were already on their way, Morgan with his
ight infantry then eighteen miles beyond Guilford Court
House and Smallwood with the cavalry was following fast. S. R.,
A new inspiration pervaded every heart, and when the XVII, 697

1780
Effects of
the victory
Assembly met, with grateful eulogium on their patriotism
and heroism, it resolved that Colonels Cleveland, Campbell
Shelby, Sevier, Hambright, and Winston, and Major Shelby
should each receive an elegantly mounted sword for their
voluntary, distinguished and eminent services.

Indeed, the victory at King's Mountain was no less extraordinary as a feat of arms than potent in its results.
That undisciplined and unorganized volunteers operating
under neither state nor continental authority should have
achieved such a victory over a force equal in numbers, amply
supplied with ammunition, ably commanded and so advantageously posted, attested the fighting qualities of the untrained inhabitants and gave new hope to those who had
been disappointed at the conduct of the militiamen on other
fields. It buoyed the hearts of the patriots in that dark
hour and nerved them to greater efforts for resistance;
while, on the other hand, not merely were the eight hundred
Tories who had joined Ferguson eliminated from the contest, but all of the disaffected inhabitants west of the
Catawba were suppressed during the remainder of the war.
Ramseur's Mill was a disaster to the western Loyalists, but
King's Mountain was their conquest.

S. R., XIV,
692-8
Nor was this the only catastrophe that befell them.
Colonel Wright, a zealous Loyalist, embodied three hundred
of the disaffected at Richmond, in Surry County, and began
his march to unite with Cornwallis at Charlotte; but Sumner
and Davidson hurried detachments against them, routed
and dispersed them.

Cornwallis retires

S. R., XV,
285
Cornwallis was so hemmed in at Charlotte that for some
days he received no information of the battle of King's
Mountain. Indeed, he was also in utter ignorance of what
was passing in South Carolina, as for nearly three weeks
he had no intelligence from Camden, every express for him
having been taken by the active partisan bands in his rear.
No wonder he declared Mecklenburg "the most rebellious
section of America," and that Tarleton spoke of it as "a
veritable hornet's nest."

When the information reached him of Ferguson's death

and the complete annihilation of that corps, he was no less shocked than grievously disappointed. Not only did it unsettle all his plans, but it rendered his own situation alarming. Realizing that he could not rely on the assistance from the inhabitants which he had confidently expected, and apprehending that Ninety-six would be at once attacked, he determined to immediately retire from North Carolina. So on the evening of October 12th he abandoned Charlotte and turned toward the south. So far the tide of good fortune had rushed on without interruption, bringing him victory and well-earned fame, but now began a series of mishaps that led step by step to irretrievable disaster and ultimately to the final abandonment of British hopes of subjugation and an acknowledgment of the independence of the colonies.

Forced by untoward circumstances to retire from his advanced position, Cornwallis found South Carolina ready to rise against British rule. In its dire extremity that State had offered to remain neutral during the contest and to abide by the general result of the struggle elsewhere. Clinton, not content with such a submission, required the subdued inhabitants to enroll themselves as Loyalist militia and take up arms for the king. Many now determined to throw off this yoke and fight, if they must, for the success of the American cause; and partisan leaders were drawing around themselves corps of determined patriots that were a menace to British occupancy.

Contemporaneously with the departure from Charlotte a rainy season set in, and the troops suffered severely from sickness, while Cornwallis himself became so ill that he had to relinquish the command of his army, committing it to the care of Lord Rawdon. It was not until October 29th that he reached the country lying between Camden and Ninety-six, making his camp at Winnsboro the more readily to support those two principal posts.

Leslie in Virginia

As there was expectation that North Carolina would be subjugated and held, as had been the fate of Georgia and South Carolina, it was designed that after that event Corn-

Margin notes:
1780
October

S. R., XV, 288, 289

Lee's Memoirs, 162, 163

Partisan corps

Sumter

Marion

S. R., XV, 287

1780

Albemarle
threatened

S. R., XV,
143, 149

wallis would continue his victorious march into Virginia. To keep the Americans from concentrating against the Earl, General Leslie with a considerable force had been despatched from New York to the Chesapeake. During the month of October Leslie had penetrated down the Blackwater to South Quay, and, nearer the coast, to the Great Bridge. General Benbury at once embodied his brigade and marched to oppose him. After the battle of Camden General Gregory returned home to the Albemarle section, and now he gallantly took the field with his militia and checked Leslie's advance, repulsing the British with some loss on November 8th at Great Swamp.

S. R., XV,
285, 286,
292-299, 307

Defeated in his purposes, Cornwallis now desired Leslie's aid at the south, but hesitated to order him to come to his relief. Clinton, however, left him free to co-operate with the southern army, especially as he had been sent to the Chesapeake to make a diversion in favor of Cornwallis's operations. Leslie, knowing that Cornwallis hoped much from the Loyalists on the upper Cape Fear, and that taking possession of Wilmington would encourage them to rise, determined to transfer his operations to that region. He therefore sailed from the Chesapeake on November 23d for Wilmington. Cornwallis being ill and the situation of his army dangerous, Rawdon, in temporary command, despatched vessels to intercept the fleet at Frying Pan Shoals and direct Leslie to come to his immediate assistance. So it happened that the corps lately operating near Norfolk made an unexpected appearance at Camden. Still further to ease Cornwallis, Clinton now hurried a new army under General Benedict Arnold to the Chesapeake; but for personal reasons, as he was obnoxious to the people, Arnold soon retired, leaving the command with General Phillips.

Leslie
sails for
Wilmington

Oct. 21, 1780

Gates moves forward

S. R., XV,
151, 160

Quickly following Cornwallis's withdrawal, Gates moved his continentals, numbering a thousand, to Charlotte, while Smallwood, who had superseded Sumner, much to the latter's disgust,* took post with the militia and Morgan some

---

*Sumner, like Caswell, resented the appointment of Smallwood as major-general of the militia and declined to serve under him, so when Smallwood reached his camp Sumner returned home.

ifteen miles farther to the front, calling his camp New Providence. General Stevens with five hundred Virginia troops, almost naked and unarmed, remained at Hillsboro.

In the meantime, as the consequence of Gates's misfortune at Camden, congress had directed Washington to commit the Southern Department to another general, and Washington appointed Nathanael Greene to that command. Accompanying Greene to the south were Baron Steuben and Light Horse Harry Lee with his corps of dragoons, three hundred in number. The baron was, however, left in Virginia to conduct operations in that State, which was within Greene's department.

The Board of War organized at Hillsboro on September 12th, but soon all the members left except John Penn, who for some time conducted military affairs without any aid. The board relieved Governor Nash largely of his responsibilities, and in a measure encroached on his powers. It was active in giving direction and stimulating the county officers to renewed exertions, and zealously co-operated with General Gates and afterward with General Greene in preparing for defence.

Cornwallis was thoroughly disappointed with the result of the campaign. He had been led to invade North Carolina at that time because of the difficulties of a defensive war, and the hope that the Tories in North Carolina, who were said to be very numerous, would be active in aiding him. The defeat at King's Mountain, however, suppressed all Tory risings at the west, while to the east Harrington and the state militia kept the disaffected much in check; so Cornwallis found that their friendship was only passive, and he derived little assistance from their co-operation. He reported that only about two hundred had been prevailed on to join his camp. His chief difficulty, however, was the absence of supplies. These could not be furnished from abroad, and his army necessarily had to subsist on the country; and in this matter such Loyalists as engaged with him were found very efficient and a great help to his distressed troops.

1780
S. R., XV,
173

Arrival of Greene

General Greene reached Charlotte on December 2d, and at once Gates departed northward. The new general immediately began to take measures for the organization and efficiency of his army.

Greene in
command

His presence inspired zeal and confidence. Colonel Lee, who accompanied him, in his "Memoirs" says: "This illustrious man had now reached his thirty-eighth year. In person he was rather corpulent, and above the common size. His complexion was fair and florid; his countenance serene and mild, indicating a goodness which seemed to shade and soften the fire and greatness of its expression." Every element combined to commend him to the good-will and affections of his soldiers.

S. R., XV,
173, 174, 185

The neighboring country was so bare that General Greene's first step was to request the Board of War not to call out any more militia until satisfactory arrangements were made to subsist the troops. Writing to Washington, he reported that: "Nothing can be more wretched and distressing than the condition of the troops, starving with cold and hunger, without tents and camp equipage. Those of the Virginia line are literally naked. A tattered remnant of some garment, clumsily stuck together with the thorns of the locust tree, forms the sole covering of hundreds, and we have three hundred men without arms, and more than a thousand are so naked that they can be put on duty only in case of desperate necessity." To facilitate his purpose of transporting supplies he caused the Dan, the Yadkin, and the Catawba to be explored, hoping to utilize water transportation. He established a hospital at Salisbury, and the osnaburgs and sheetings in store were distributed among the women to be made into shirts for the soldiers. Colonel Polk, who was the commissary-general, retired, and Greene asked the Board of War to appoint Colonel Davie to that most important position.

S. R., XV,
184

Desiring to cover Cross Creek, Greene directed Colonel Kosciusko, of the engineers, to select a camp on the Peedee where provisions could be obtained, and after some delay, caused by terrible rains and bitter cold, on December 20th he broke camp and moved his army to a location at the Cheraws.

1781

Morgan had already been advanced beyond the Broad with a detachment of three hundred Maryland regulars and the Virginia militia and Washington's dragoons, along with some four hundred militia embodied in the adjacent counties of North Carolina and some others from South Carolina and Georgia. General Smallwood, whose appointment to the command of the militia had resulted in the retirement of Caswell and Sumner, now himself returned to Maryland in order to hasten on re-enforcements and supplies from that State, and also to have settled a question of rank between himself and Baron Steuben.

January

S. R., XV, 184, 185

The opening of the new year was not without a bright lining to the clouds that had overcast the skies. There was at least a rainbow of hope in the heavens. Greene was now in command, Morgan in the advance, the State was again free from the presence of a hostile army, and renewed zeal was apparent among the inhabitants of every section.

The General Assembly was to have met at Halifax early in January, but the members arrived so slowly that it was the 26th before a quorum appeared. The Board of War, however, was in session and had control of military affairs. The army had suffered much from the inefficiency of the commissary department. In each district there was a commissary to obtain supplies, but no general head. General Greene had urged the appointment of Colonel Davie to be commissary-general for the State, but the Board hesitated to make such an innovation, not warranted by the act of Assembly; but finally, on January 16th, it conferred on that active and accomplished young officer the office of "superintendent commissary-general." Difficult as was the task imposed on Colonel Davie he performed it with a capability that rendered him one of the most useful men in the army, but it removed him from that branch of the service where he had won much fame by his daring exploits.

S. R., XIV, 490

Davie commissary-general

The Council Extraordinary

On the meeting of the legislature, Governor Nash complained bitterly that the Board of War had encroached on

Jan., 1781 S. R., XVII, 653, 720

1781
S. R.,
XXIV, 378

S. R., XVII,
786

S. R.,
XVII, 662

S. R., XV,
425, 426

his powers and duties as governor, and he offered to resign.
The Assembly thereupon dispensed with that board and substituted a Council Extraordinary, electing Governor Caswell,
Colonel Alexander Martin, and Allen Jones as members.
Caswell was now a member of the house, and Smallwood
having left the State, it was proposed to restore Caswell to
his former command as major-general of the militia. Indignant at his former treatment, he, however, was not inclined to be complacent; and to placate him the Assembly
passed a resolution declaring the reasons which had induced
the appointment of General Smallwood, "and the high sense
the Assembly then had and still have of the merits of General
Caswell, and of the singular services by him rendered this
State"; and he was appointed again to command the militia,
and as president of the Council Extraordinary to conduct
military affairs.

His health, however, was poor, and his operations lacked
his former energy. He established a camp near Halifax,
and ordered out the various militia brigades, but the zeal
and force that earlier distinguished his actions were not now
so apparent.

He was directed by the Assembly to raise a regiment of
light horse in the Wilmington and New Bern districts, and
General Butler one in the Hillsboro district. Colonel Malmedy was appointed to command the latter and Colonel Read
the former. Both of these officers later served in South
Carolina.

There were many continental officers in the State unemployed, and as Sumner was the ranking continental Greene
urged him to have these officers to repair to the camp and
assist Caswell in organizing the militia. Sumner tendered
his own services, and Colonel Ashe and Major Murfree also
reported to Caswell and placed themselves at his disposal.
But in addition to the indisposition to put the militia under
the continental officers, the militia officers themselves held
out for their own privilege of commanding their organizations; so that while a few experienced officers were employed, such as Major Dickson as inspector-general, Major
Armstrong with the forces at Salisbury, and Colonel Read
as commander of a regiment of horse, the services of many

of the most efficient regulars were not utilized by the State. Sumner hoped for the command of a brigade of militia, but met with disappointment. The General Assembly, however, made provision for four new regiments of continentals, and extraordinary measures were devised for filling up the ranks.

In order to raise these battalions, the Assembly offered a bounty of £2,000, and promised to every person who should enlist and serve one year "one prime slave . . . and six hundred and forty acres of land"; and provision was made for a draft from the body of the militia for the continental service. A tax in kind was levied, a large issue of bills was authorized, and the confiscation act was further suspended.

No party divisions

All seemed to vie in patriotic resolve. Indeed, during the period of the war, when every nerve was strained to accomplish success, all the public men were in accord, and there does not seem to have been any party divisions, except between Whigs and Tories. That there were differences in council based on policy and expediency is probable, extending to matters of finance and of taxation and to the treatment of the disaffected inhabitants; and certainly there were clashings arising from the natural ambitions of the leading men. But amid the turmoils and alarums of war it is not likely that there were discussions between candidates on the hustings, and no newspapers were published at that time in North Carolina. One of the differences among the people arose from the uncertain value of the currency, which depreciated because of excessive issues. Traders and speculators took advantage of the condition of affairs, still further depreciating it, and these became odious among the more patriotic inhabitants; but probably none of the public men were concerned in such proceedings.

The course of political action appears to have been influenced merely by natural considerations. If any divisions were evolved at the time of the formation of the State constitution, they do not seem to have been fostered and perpetuated. They passed away. Caswell and his council tendered appointments to Sam Johnston and other conservatives, as well as to their Democratic friends. Allen

1781

S. R., XXIV, 369

No newspapers, 1778-83

Jones was year by year honored by the Assembly, while his brother, Willie, received no particular mark of its confidence, although Jones County was named for him. Iredell was appointed to the bench, and when he retired Maclaine, certainly a conservative, was elected. He declined, recommending John Williams, who was in high favor with the Assembly. On Avery's resigning the office of attorney-general, Iredell was elected to that position. The officers first appointed were generally re-elected to the same positions. The senate continued year after year of the same mind, while Benbury was constantly re-elected speaker of the house. In 1780 Willie Jones and Sam Johnston, supposed to be in antagonism, were elected delegates to the Continental Congress. Caswell, while governor, was not on good terms with Penn, nor later with Governor Nash. The Assembly, after Camden, deprived him of his command, and creating a Board of War, made Penn a member of it; and Caswell indignantly withdrew from all public employment. Six months later the Assembly smoothed his ruffled feathers, displaced Penn from the board and restored Caswell to power as major-general commanding the state forces and as president of the Council Extraordinary charged with the direction of military affairs. Next to him, Colonel Alexander Martin was apparently the favorite among the representatives. On the promotion of Howe he had become colonel of the Second Battalion, but was charged with bad conduct in battle, of which, however, he was subsequently acquitted. He resigned, and was chosen speaker of the senate, next in succession to the governor, and made president of the Board of War.

Harnett, one of the prime favorites earlier, had been compelled to withdraw from public employment because of impaired health; and General Ashe, still more advanced in years, likewise was a great sufferer, but continued as treasurer until 1781. Many of the first men in talents and in energy, having entered the military service, had become separated from the civil administration, while death had made considerable inroads in the ranks of the patriot leaders.

During Caswell's administration three years passed without invasion; and except local manifestations of disaffection

nd the great efforts made to sustain the army and to send
ssistance to South Carolina, it was a period of repose, if
ot of peace. The inhabitants were measurably engaged in
heir customary vocations, the fields were tilled, the courts
vere held, the churches were open, schools kept, and the
eople lived much as usual. In general, the inhabitants Life in the State, 1776 to 1780
eared in the forests had always been dependent on their
wn exertions for the comforts of life. But few articles
ad been imported from abroad, and the isolation of war
rought no great change in the mode of living. Indeed, com-
nerce was still continued, and necessary goods to some ex-
ent were imported; the spinning-jenny and the hand-loom
vere constantly employed, and the people were dressed in
abrics of their own manufacture. Salt was made on the
oast, and iron, another essential, was forged at the Gulf,
n Chatham County, in Johnston, in Nash, in Surry, Lincoln
ind other counties. The dividing line between Virginia and
North Carolina had been run to the mountains by commissioners, those on the part of Virginia being General Joshua
Fry and Peter Jefferson, and on the part of North Caro-
lin, Daniel Weldon and William Churton; but population
had extended into the wilderness beyond that line, and in
1779 commissioners were appointed to continue the line, sep- S. R., XXIV, 223, 224, 300
arating Washington County from Virginia, and later Sul-
livan County was laid off. These two counties were to
extend west to the Tennessee or Ohio River—for even then
the course of those streams was not accurately known.

James Davis continued to publish his newspaper at New 1776–78
Bern, to print the laws and disseminate information; and
for the speedy transmission of intelligence posts were established between New Bern and the several counties, while S. R., XV, 223
on special occasions horsemen were employed to carry news
with despatch.

During Nash's administration the surrender of Charleston Nash's administra-tion
and the disaster at Camden and the invasion of Mecklenburg
caused distress, and the extraordinary efforts made to organize a new army and sustain the troops in the field bore
hard on the people and brought them to realize more fully
than ever the dire calamities of war and the doubtful nature
of the struggle in which they were engaged. As the years

1781

passed many began to despair and grow weary of the sacr fices they were constantly called on to make. The successiv drafts, the heavy taxes, the worthless currency, the impress ments and the privations of the war disheartened hundred who had once been zealous in the American cause.

Dr. Burke's zeal to correct abuses

S. R., XV, 769, 771

In July, on the return of Dr. Burke to his home in Orang County from the Continental Congress, he found the troop who had recently arrived from the north in great distres for the want of food and forage, and that the quarter masters were committing the most wanton destruction o property. "Every mouth was filled with complaints, ever countenance expressing apprehension, dejection, indigna tion, and despair had the place of the animated zeal" which he had before observed. Immediately he interposed to check the abuses, and he undertook that all who should vol untarily furnish supplies should be paid without depreciation and should be protected from all violence and injury. Much

July, 1780

of the situation he attributed to ill-advised acts of the Assembly passed to restrain speculation, which prevented retailers from purchasing from the merchants and put a stop to importations. Natural trade and commerce, made the more necessary by the prevalent conditions, were totally arrested, and this evil he sought to remedy.

S. R., XV, 772, 773

The State had ordered out eight thousand militia, one division of which was already in the field, and the other was on its march to the general rendezvous; but the men were without arms, and none were procurable. At that time Governor Nash was at the east, and Dr. Burke urged him to come to Hillsboro, attended by his council, where he would be in more close communication with the army and could better deal with the important matters of the day. Even after the return of General Gates from Camden Dr. Burke was pressing on that general to correct the irregularities of his quartermasters in their dealings with the people. His interposition to protect the inhabitants from unnecessary exactions was greatly appreciated, spread his fame and increased his popularity, and at the next election he reaped his reward by being chosen governor.

Sam Johnston declines the presidency of Congress

In the fall of 1780 Willie Jones attended the Continental Congress, but returned home on the opening of winter. On December 29th Samuel Johnston took his seat. The articles of confederation, having been agreed to by all the other States, were finally accepted by Maryland on March 1, 1781, and on the day following they were ratified in the Continental Congress by all the delegates from the several states, who then signed them on behalf of their respective states, and the confederation went into effect. For North Carolina they were signed by Burke, Sharpe, and Johnston. Samuel Huntington, of Connecticut, had been the president of the congress under the old system. On July 9th an election for president took place under the new system. Although Samuel Johnston had been but six months a member of the body, such was his recognized capacity, his learning and high patriotism that he was chosen by the Continental Congress its first president under the articles of confederation. Unfortunately, circumstances forbade his accepting the high honor, and on the following morning he declined "for such reasons as the congress regarded satisfactory." The day following Johnston found himself constrained to return to North Carolina. His family had fled from Edenton, and the inhabitants of his immediate section were in such distress that he felt compelled to hasten home and share their fortunes or aid in repairing them.

Journals of Congress, VII, 115

CHAPTER XXXVII

Nash's Administration, 1780-81—*Continued*

The battle of Cowpens.—Cornwallis pursues Morgan.—The death
of Davidson.—Invasion of the State.—Greene crosses the Dan.—
The endurance of the troops.—Cornwallis at Hillsboro.—On the
Cape Fear.—The movements of the armies.—Pyle's massacre.—
Greene at Troublesome Creek.—Battle of Guilford Court House
—Cornwallis moves east and Greene pursues.—Cornwallis reaches
Wilmington, Greene goes to South Carolina.—Craig occupies
Wilmington.—Death of Harnett.—Cornwallis's plans.—Cornwallis
marches to Virginia.—The inhabitants distressed.—At Edenton.—
The Whigs rally.—Greene in South Carolina.—Death of Major
Eaton.—Cartel of exchange agreed on.—Atrocities lead to threats
of retaliation.—Gregory defends the Albemarle region.

The battle of Cowpens

1781

Lee's
Memoirs,
222-225, 227
et seq.
S. R., XVII,
981, 292

Strengthened by the arrival of Leslie's regiments, and
pressed for provisions, Cornwallis with the opening of the
new year determined on renewing his campaign. Engaging
Greene's attention with Leslie's corps, he threw Tarleton
on Morgan, while he prepared to advance, hoping to separate the American columns and beat them in detail. On
January 17th Tarleton, confident of easy victory, came up
with Morgan at the Cowpens, near the North Carolina line,
some forty miles west of Charlotte; but after a stubborn
contest of fifty minutes his famous corps, that had been
regarded as invincible, was broken and dispersed and the
larger part of it taken prisoners. In arranging for the
battle Morgan established at his front two light parties of
militia, one hundred North Carolinians under Major
McDowell, of Burke County, and about fifty Georgians
under Major Cunningham. To these picked riflemen were
given orders to feel the enemy as he approached and to
maintain a well-aimed fire, and then, when they fell back,
to renew the conflict along with the first line of battle. This
main line was composed of about two hundred North Caro-

1. Banastre Tarleton
2. Horatio Gates
3. Daniel Morgan
4. Charles, Marquis Cornwallis

a militia and near a hundred South Carolinians, and was
nder the command of General Andrew Pickens. Further
the rear, on the crown of an eminence, were posted the
ree hundred Maryland regulars and two companies of
irginia militia and a company of Georgians, all commanded
y Colonel Howard, of Maryland. Washington's cavalry,
einforced by a company of mounted militia, was held in
serve. The field of battle was a sparse, open pine forest,
d the bright beams of the rising sun heralded the opening
f a glorious day.

Tarleton on reaching the ground impetuously rushed on
strike his prey. On being attacked, the advanced riflemen,
fter some skirmishing, fell back and joined the main line
nder Pickens. The enemy, shouting, rushed forward, but
ere received by a close and heavy volley; their advance
as not checked, however, and resorting to the bayonet, they
rove Pickens's line from its position. A part of that corps
ok post on Howard's right, and as Tarleton pushed for-
ard he was received with unshaken firmness. The contest
ecame obstinate, each party, animated by the example of
s leader, nobly contending for victory. Outflanked, how-
ver, Howard's right began to yield, and the line retiring,
Iorgan directed it to retreat to the cavalry. There a new
osition was assumed with promptness. Mistaking this
novement for flight, the British rushed on with impetuosity
nd disorder. As they drew near Howard faced about and **Howard**
oured in a close and murderous volley. Stunned by this
nexpected shock, the advance of the enemy recoiled in con-
usion, and Howard's continentals rushed upon them with
he bayonet. The British reserve, having been brought close
o the front, shared in the destruction of the American fire,
nd there was no rallying point offered for the fugitives.
\t the rear the battle also went well. Two companies of
Tarleton's cavalry having made a detour to cut off the
Americans, Washington struck them with his dragoons and
lrove them before him. Thus simultaneously the British
nfantry and cavalry engaged were routed. Morgan with
promptness and resolution urged his victorious troops to
enewed efforts, and the pursuit became vigorous and gen-
ral. Colonel Washington having dashed forward fully

1781

thirty yards ahead of his troops, Tarleton, in the rear of his own, attended by two officers, turned and advanced to meet him. Here a personal contest ensued between these two heroes of the battlefield. Both, however, escaped the imminent peril. An anecdote has been preserved that some months later, when Tarleton was at Halifax, he remarked to the wife of Willie Jones that he understood that redoubtable leader, Washington, could not write, whereupon Mrs Jones replied: "You at least, sir, can bear witness that he can make his mark," referring to a wound Tarleton received on his hand in that encounter. Turning then to Mrs Ashe, the colonel said that he had never had the pleasure of meeting Washington, and she answered quickly: "Had you looked behind you at Cowpens you would have seen him.

Wheeler,
Hist. N. C.,
II, 186

The loss of the Americans was comparatively small, the British, it was supposed, shooting too high—only 11 killed and 61 wounded. The British suffered much more severely 150 were killed, 200 wounded, and 400 prisoners, chiefly infantry. The artillery, 800 muskets, 2 standards, 35 baggage wagons and 100 dragoon horses, besides the prisoners fell into Morgan's possession.

A part of Tarleton's horse that had early fled from the field of battle carried information of the disaster to Cornwallis. That general fully realized the reverse following so quickly the destruction of Ferguson's corps. A peer of the British realm, trained from early youth to arms, now in his forty-second year, a man of great ability and self-poise always accustomed to independent action and relying on his own judgment, he was quick to decide the course to be pursued. He resolved by celerity of movement to regain his prisoners or to cut off Morgan's force before it could be joined by the other part of Greene's army. On being joined by Leslie he moved with despatch toward the fords of the Catawba.

Cornwallis pursues Morgan

Lee's
Memoirs,
233

Immediately after the engagement Morgan had hurried a messenger to Greene with news of his victory, and that general, comprehending the situation, on the 25th directed General Huger to conduct the army to Salisbury, while he himself with a few dragoons hastened to the scene of active operations.

Morgan, intent on evading pursuit, despatched his prisoners under guard of General Stevens and the militia northward beyond the South Mountains toward Morganton. Reaching the state road, Stevens turned eastward, crossing the Catawba at Island Ford;* and thence the prisoners were conveyed beyond the Dan into Virginia. The general himself with his continentals pursued a lower route, and forded the Catawba at Sherrill's. On the 28th Cornwallis reached the vicinity of Beattie's Ford, ten miles below, and there rested. He now determined to convert his army into light troops by destroying his baggage. He set the example himself by committing to the flames the baggage of headquarters. Everything save a small supply of clothing, hospital stores, salt, ammunition, and conveniences for the sick was destroyed.

S. R., XVII, 997

On the afternoon of the 31st General Greene arrived at Beattie's Ford, where by appointment General Morgan was waiting for him. By Greene's direction, General Davidson, who had collected about five hundred militia, divided his force and stationed some at different fords, of which there were several to be guarded. He himself with about two hundred infantry took post at a horse ford some two miles distant from Cowan's Ford, where a small picket force was stationed.

Graham's Graham, 286

The death of Davidson

At dawn of February 1st the British army began to cross. The first movement was by way of Cowan's Ford, and the pickets there gave speedy notice by their prompt firing. Davidson hurried to the scene with his infantry, he himself being on horseback. The enemy's vanguard had already reached the eastern bank before his arrival, and there was desultory firing while he was placing his men in position. The British advance now pressed on Davidson's unformed line, and that practised officer ordered his men to withdraw about fifty yards to the cover of some trees, where they could fight to better advantage. Hardly had he given his order

S. R., XVII, 998

Graham's Graham, 293

*In the vicinity of Statesville.

1781

when he fell, pierced by a rifle ball. He was a trained continental officer, courageous, efficient and enterprising, and he was much beloved by the inhabitants of his section and greatly esteemed throughout the State. His death was a great loss to the American cause and was widely lamented the Continental Congress itself ordering a monument to be erected as a memorial of his distinguished worth.

The invasion of the State

Having effected a crossing, Cornwallis hurried toward Salisbury, hoping to overtake Morgan, who had moved the evening before. While the opposition to his crossing had not delayed him, it had been so strenuous that the next day in general orders he made his warmest acknowledgments to the cool and determined bravery of the advance column in accomplishing it.

Cornwallis's Order Book in Caruthers's Old North State, II, 391 *et seq.*

On entering North Carolina his Lordship issued frequent orders forbidding excesses by any of his troops. No negro was to be allowed to have arms. The strictest discipline was to be enforced, and there was to be no wanton destruction of property or any unnecessary exactions from the inhabitants. He came, he said, to establish and maintain the rights of the people as British subjects, and his army should not be disgraced by any outrages. He required the punishment of any soldier or camp follower who should disobey his orders in this respect.

In the meantime Huger had been directed by Greene to move on to Guilford Court House or the fords of the Yadkin and there await further orders. At midnight of the 1st Greene left the Catawba for Salisbury. An anecdote is related in Johnson's "Reminiscences" that on his arrival at the tavern in that hamlet, in reply to inquiries of Dr. Read, the general could not refrain from answering: "Yes, fatigued, hungry, alone and penniless." The benevolent landlady, Mrs. Steele, overheard this remark, and hardly was the general seated at a comfortable breakfast when she presented herself, closed the door, and exhibiting a small bag of specie in each hand, said: "Take these, for you will want them, and I can do without them." Such was the

pirit that had ever animated the patriotic women of
alisbury.

There had been heavy rains on February 1st, and Mor-
an's continentals passed the Yadkin at Trading Ford,
even miles from Salisbury, just before the stream rose
apidly from the flood.

Some of the militia, being the rear detachment, were over- Graham's
aken after night at the river bank by General O'Hara, who Graham, 300
/as in hot pursuit, and a slight skirmish ensued. While
he Americans succeeded in escaping, the wagons and bag-
age of that detachment fell into the hands of the enemy.
he river being impassable, Greene, now safe, rested on the Huger unites with Greene
astern bank and then moved toward the upper fords, where
e knew Cornwallis must go in order to cross. The British
ommander, debarred from crossing lower, also turned
orthward and pursued the road on the western side of
he river. Time having been thus afforded for Huger's
rrival, Greene marched eastward and reached Guilford
court House on the 7th, where Huger joined him later on
hat day.

Greene crosses the Dan

The united force of Americans, including five hundred
militia, somewhat exceeded twenty-three hundred men,
f whom nearly three hundred were excellent cavalry.
Cornwallis's army was estimated at twenty-five hundred
rained veterans. At a council of war held by Greene Lee's Memoirs, 236 *et seq.*
t was determined not to give battle, but to cross the Dan
nd await the arrival of more militia. Colonel Carrington
vas directed to collect boats for the passage at Irwin's Ferry,
ome seventy miles distant and well to the eastward; and
n order to delay pursuit a light corps of seven hundred
nen was organized, the command of which was offered to
General Morgan. General Morgan had been in retirement
rom illness when, at the instance of congress, in October
e accepted employment at the south, and the exposure to
which he had been subjected now resulted in an attack of
heumatism, which incapacitated him for this active duty.
He therefore declined the command, and retired to his home
n Virginia. Colonel Otho Williams was then selected to

conduct the operations of that corps. He so manœuvred that the British commander mistook his detachment fo Greene's main body, and he delayed the pursuit unti Greene on February 13th succeeded in crossing the Dan

The pursuit More than once was Williams's rear guard, Lee's legion within musket shot of O'Hara's van, and it was with diffi culty that the men were restrained from bringing on an engagement; but that was no part of Williams's purpose Eventually he, too, about three o'clock on the evening o: the 13th, reached the vicinity of the ferry, and by sunse his infantry gained the river and were transported. Lee had been left to keep the enemy in check, and about dark he succeeded in withdrawing his cavalry, and between eight and nine o'clock that night his men embarked in the boats making the horses swim the stream. Thus ended this long arduous and eventful retreat. "No operation during the war," says Lee in his "Memoirs," "more attracted the public attention than this did; not only the toils and dangers en countered by a brave general and his brave army interested the sympathy of the nation, but the safety of the Soutl hanging on its issue, excited universal concern." "When we add the comfortless condition of our troops in point of clothing—the shoes generally worn out, the body clothes much tattered, and not more than one blanket for four men— the rigor of the season, the inclemency of the weather, our short stock of ammunition and shorter stock of provisions— the single meal allowed us was always scanty though good in quality and very nutritious, being bacon and corn meal— and contrasted with the comfortable raiment and ample equip ment of the enemy, . . . we have abundant cause to honor the soldier whose mental resources smoothed every difficulty, and ultimately made good a retreat of two hundred and thirty miles . . . without the loss of either troops or stores." This tribute to General Greene is but the expression of the universal praise which has been bestowed upon that great commander, not only by his countrymen but by the agreeing voices of all men; and yet something, too, is to be said of those suffering patriots who constituted the rank and file of his gallant army. Their endurance, their un flagging zeal, their spirit of self-sacrifice, entitle them to

nstinted praise and the grateful remembrance of pos-
erity.

Writing to Washington immediately on his arrival at
rwin's Ferry, Greene himself said: "The miserable situa-
ion of the troops, the want of clothing, has rendered the
narch the most painful imaginable, many hundreds of the
oldiers tracking the ground with their bloody feet. Your
feelings for the sufferings of the soldiers, had you been with
s, would have been severely tried."

Cornwallis, baffled in his purpose, yet apparently master
of the situation, took post at Hillsboro, where he erected
the king's standard with great formality, saluting it with
wenty-one guns, and Josiah Martin, who had accompanied
im, once more essayed to enter upon the administration of
his office as royal governor. But neither the commander nor
the governor was to receive much comfort.

Cornwallis at Hillsboro

The British on the Cape Fear

While these matters of moment were passing at the west,
the east as well had become greatly disturbed. Although
General Leslie had in November been diverted from occupying the lower Cape Fear, that purpose was not abandoned,
and contemporaneously with Arnold's invasion of the Chesapeake and Cornwallis's advance, such a movement was
undertaken. With a fleet of eighteen sail, carrying four
hundred regulars, artillery and dragoons, Major James H.
Craig was despatched to occupy Wilmington. His vessels
reached the harbor toward the last of January, and on
the 28th he approached the town. Taking possession, he at
once began to fortify by erecting batteries on the hills to
the north and south, and so strengthened himself that he
could not be attacked with any hope of success. At that
time it was also apprehended that there would be a movement in the interior from Camden, and such stores as the
Americans had to the southward were moved across the
Cape Fear River. Aroused by the presence of their British
friends, the Tories of Bladen and Anson became active, and
it required strenuous efforts on the part of the local leaders
to suppress them. General Lillington at once called out the
militia of that section, but so many of them had been taken

1781
S. R., XV,
423

1781

at Charleston and were on parole, and the country had been
so drained of adherents of the Whig cause, that but a small
force could be collected. To keep Craig in check, General
Caswell was ordered with the New Bern brigade and General
eral Butler with the Hillsboro brigade to the assistance of
Lillington. Such was the situation when Cornwallis was
pursuing Greene across the western part of the State and
invading the western counties.

Movements of the armies

Graham's
Graham,
311

After Davidson's death, although the militia of the western
ern district had no commander, some seven hundred of them,
all horsemen, collected in the rear of the British army, and
in the absence of a brigadier chose General Andrew Pickens,
of South Carolina, as their commander. In the troop was
a company under Captain Graham that subsequently became

S. R.,
XXII, 123

greatly distinguished. They followed the route taken by
Cornwallis through Salem and Guilford Court House, and
reached Hart's Mills, near Hillsboro, about the time that
Cornwallis established himself at that place.

Graham's
Graham,
317

There, on February 22d, Lee's corps was joined to Pickens's
brigade, all under the command of the brigadier-general
Other re-enforcements of North Carolina militia were also expected, and to facilitate their union and re-establish confidence
three days after Cornwallis entered Hillsboro Greene himself
crossed the Dan and passed to the west of his adversary. In

S. R.,
XXII, 141

response to Cornwallis's call, the Tories began to embody, and
some two hundred of them were collecting under Dr. Pyle
in Chatham and western Orange when Lee and Pickens were
advancing into that section. Tarleton, hearing that the
Whigs proposed to suppress the Tory rising, moved out
to protect Dr. Pyle and his recruits. Ignorant of the move-

Lee's
Memoirs,
253

ment of the Tories, Lee pursued his way to the southward,
and on the 24th, at a point south of the Haw, near the site
of the present town of Burlington, accidentally met the
Tories in the road, who, expecting Tarleton, and with no
information of the presence of any Whig force, arranged

S. R.,
XXII, 124

themselves along the road to allow their supposed friends

Graham's
Graham,
319

to pass. As soon as Lee's dragoons had reached the extremity of the Tory line, the character of the Loyalists being

discovered, a signal was made for an onslaught, and Pyle's unsuspecting men were quickly despatched. Ninety of them were killed outright and most of the survivors were wounded. Those not thrown to the ground dispersed in every direction, but were not pursued. Lee lost in this slaughter only one horse—not a single man. At the time Tarleton was hardly a mile distant, but he was not advised of the encounter or of the presence of a Whig force until some fugitives brought him information.

Greene established himself between Troublesome Creek and Reedy Fork, in the vicinity of Guilford Court House, having his light corps interposed between his main army and Cornwallis. His report of men fit for duty on the 17th indicated a thousand continentals, less than two hundred cavalry and a hundred mounted infantry—an effective force of some fourteen hundred men; but he was expecting a regiment of regulars from Virginia that had been hurried forward and several thousand militia to join him. General Butler's brigade, that had been despatched to the assistance of Lillington was ordered to return to the west, and the Halifax brigade was collecting for the march. General Allen Jones, having to return, invited Sumner to take command, but General Eaton claimed the right and refused to relinquish it. Colonels William Campbell and Preston, of Virginia, were also hurrying to Greene's camp, as well as smaller detachments under Majors Winston and Armstrong. General Stevens, too, who had conveyed the prisoners taken at Cowpens to a place of security, was now returning with his brigade of Virginia militia. To prevent the junction of these re-enforcements and to strike Greene before he was further strengthened, on February 26th Cornwallis himself marched to the westward, establishing his headquarters at Hawkins's, to the west of Alamance Creek. Doubtless he also hoped for accessions from the Tories. One band of Loyalists from Deep River, consisting of about a hundred, approached his camp on a night march. But Graham's company had been so bold and daring, even in the vicinity of the British headquarters, that a troop of Tarleton's dragoons, discovering the approach of an unknown body of men at night, thought them Graham's troop, and fell

1781
February

Massacre of Pyle's Tories

Greene at Troublesome Creek

S. R., XV, 427

Re-enforcements

Lee's Memoirs, 269

Graham's Graham, 339

on them and hacked up about thirty of the Loyalists before the mistake became known. As Pyle's Tories had suffered by mistaking Lee for Tarleton, so this party from Deep River suffered at Tarleton's hands by being mistaken for Graham's company. These mishaps tended to dissipate the zeal of the Tories, so that but few united with the British army. Indeed, Cornwallis was so disappointed at the luke warmness of the Regulators, from whom he had expected much aid, that he wrote to Clinton: "I could not get one hundred men in all the Regulators' country to stay with us even as militia."

S. R., XVII, 1011

Graham's Graham, 329

To avoid a battle until ready, Greene directed the several detachments of his army to be constantly in motion, changing their location every night, so that Cornwallis would not know where to strike. During the period of manœuvring there were several affairs between the cavalry and Tarleton's legion: one at Clapp's Mill on March 2d, followed by several minor collisions the next day; and at Whitsell's Mill on March 6th there was a hotly contested battle. In these encounters Pickens's brigade, embracing Graham's troopers, participated with much credit.

Lee's Memoirs, 265

But the time of that brigade expired on the 3d, and after remaining a few days longer, the men were dismissed and returned to their homes.

Battle of Guilford Court House

Finally, about March 7th, the British commander moved farther west, near the Quaker settlement at New Garden, and four days later Greene, having been joined by sufficient reinforcements, prepared to give him battle. Several important highways met at Guilford Court House, and on the 14th Greene took post on the New Garden, or Salisbury, road leading to the west from that hamlet. He had carefully selected his ground; indeed, it is thought that on his hasty march some weeks before he had chosen that battlefield For his first line he placed on the right of that road Eaton's militia, and on the left Butler's, both being protected by a rail fence that skirted an open field which lay in their front. On either flank there were stationed some three hundred regulars to give stability to the militia. In the rear of this

Lee's Memoirs, 272

1. GUILFORD COURT HOUSE BATTLEFIELD TO-DAY
2. NATHANAEL GREENE

1781
March 15th

ne there was a woodland, in which three hundred yards
istant he posted the Virginia militia under Lawson and
tevens; while the continentals were reserved for his main
ne some five hundred yards still farther to the rear.

The British moved with precision, being well-trained vet-
rans. Cornwallis's own regiment was renowned and had
ought many battles. The Welsh Fusiliers, distinguished by
aving the Prince of Wales nominally for its colonel, was
ommanded by Colonel Webster, one of the most accom-
lished officers in the army. The Seventy-first Scotch High-
anders, known in the annals as the Black Watch, had a
ecord of great glory; and the Queen's Guards, com-
nanded by Colonel Stuart, was a famous corps. The
ield pieces, as usual, began the engagement. As the
3ritish regulars advanced with fixed bayonets, they gained
he open field and approached within forty yards before
perceiving the North Carolina militia behind the fence. For Lee's
Memoirs,
277, 280
a moment the two lines stood in silence, then Webster, as
gallant in action as wise in counsel, ordered a charge, and
his troops rushed forward, receiving a hot fire from the Lamb's
Hist. Am.
Rev., 361
American line. Dreadful was the havoc on both sides at
his initial point of the conflict. The fire on the right was Schenck's
North
Carolina,
1780-81, 345
deadly, some of the Americans fighting like heroes. The
militia, however, speedily broke before the British bayonets, McRee's
Iredell, I,
493
Eaton first, then Butler's, and retreating, passed through the
Virginians posted in their rear, throwing them into con- S. R., XVII,
1003
fusion. Lawson's Virginians likewise gave way, but
Stevens's brigade made a firm stand. Eventually they, too,
were pressed back on the continentals. Here the Second
Maryland Battalion, a new organization, never before under
fire, followed the example of the militia; but the First Maryland, after a well-directed volley, charged with the bayonet,
routed the enemy and pursued them. Bloody and fierce now
was the battle, the continentals and Washington's cavalry
fighting with courage and resolution seldom surpassed. The
British loss bears witness to the valor of their foe. Greene's
army had, however, been severed into detached fragments,
and he feared to risk a prolongation of the contest. The
enemy rallying and threatening his rear, he prudently and
skilfully withdrew his forces from the field.

1781

A similarity is to be observed on the American side be
tween the arrangement of the troops in this and in the battle
of Cowpens, and also in the course of events during the
progress of the battles up to the breaking of the Second
Maryland Continentals. But on the British side there was
much difference. At Cowpens the action of Tarleton's corps
was not comparable to the steady conduct of the regulars
in this great battle, comprising some of the most famous or
ganizations in the history of the British army. Apparently
they might have been destroyed, but could not have been
driven from the field.

Great slaughter

The American loss was 14 officers and 312 of the continental troops killed, wounded and missing. Many of the
militia were missing, although no prisoners were taken. Of
the militia, 4 captains and 17 privates were reported killed,
a dozen officers and 60 privates wounded, as was also Brigadier-General Stevens. The slaughter of the British was
much greater. The official report states their loss at 532, of
whom 93 were left dead on the battlefield. Colonel Stuart
and Lieutenant O'Hara, brother to the general, and many
other officers, were killed outright; but few escaped without
wounds. Many, among them Colonel Webster, died of their
wounds. Seldom has an army suffered so severely. At the
outset there was terrible slaughter, the Highlanders being
piled upon each other. In the progress of the battle Cornwallis himself was unhorsed, his guards lay weltering in
their blood, the gallant Webster on the ground, O'Hara
disabled by his wounds, Tarleton with a rifle ball through
his hand, Howard borne off the field, and Stuart still in
death. The rank and file suffered alike. But the culmination of the carnage was in the final encounters of that fate-

Lee's Memoirs, 284

ful day. It was the immolation of an army of veterans
intent on victory. The battle being joined, Cornwallis resolved on destruction rather than defeat; and while he
gained the victory, he lost his army.

The terrible night

The night succeeding this day of blood was dark and
cold, much rain falling. The dead lay unburied, the wounded
unsheltered, and the groans of the dying and the shrieks
of the living cast a deeper shade over the gloom of nature.
Fatigued as the British troops were, without discrimination

1781

they took the best care of the fallen soldiers the situation admitted; but without tents and the houses being few, many of both armies were exposed to the deluge of rain, and it was said that not less than fifty died during the night. The next morning was spent in burying the dead and in providing comfort for the wounded, Cornwallis paying equal attention to friends and foes. He was a man of generous and lofty spirit, and rancor was foreign to his nature. In Parliament he had been a friend of America and had opposed the measures of the ministry. Now he treated the fallen without discrimination. The dead being buried, he returned to New Garden, leaving some seventy of his wounded, incapable of being moved, to the humanity of General Greene. There on the 18th he issued a proclamation calling on the Loyalists to return actively to their duties and contribute to the restoration of government.*

S.R., XVIII, 1007

On the 18th he began to move eastward by easy marches, having care for the comfort of his wounded, and being obliged to subsist on the country. Greene at once notified Colonel Lee: "I mean to fight the enemy again, and wish you to have your legion and riflemen ready for action on the shortest notice." But it was not until the 20th that he could move, for ammunition had to be supplied, cartridges made and provisions collected. In the meantime Lee's legion and Campbell's riflemen pressed the rear of the British commander, who dared not hazard another encounter.

Greene pursues Cornwallis

Willie Jones, who after the battle was appointed lieutenant-colonel of Read's militia regiment, while on the pursuit wrote: "We expect to come up with them in a day or two and to take a part, if not the whole British army." The men were now in fine spirits, and were so resolute that had Greene overtaken Cornwallis the British army would doubtless have been destroyed and Ramsey's Mills would have been an historic spot.

McRee's Iredell, I, 499

On the night of the 22d the British army lay at Dixon's Mills, on Cane Creek, in Chatham County. From there it

*Cornwallis wrote to Clinton: "Many of the inhabitants rode into camp, shook me by the hand, said they were glad to see us, and to hear that we had beat Greene, and then rode home again."

S. R., XVII 1061

1781

London,
Revo. Hist.
Chatham
County

Lee's
Memoirs,
290

marched to Pittsboro, and thence to Ramsey's Mills.* Here Cornwallis found it necessary to build a bridge and to collect supplies to carry him across the barrens to Campbellton. So quick had been his pursuers on the track that while he was yet at Ramsey's Greene reached Rigsden's Ford, on Deep River, twelve miles above, but hesitated to cross, uncertain of Cornwallis's intentions. The bridge completed, the British commander, finding himself in peril, decamped with such speed that he left some of his dead unburied, and was unable to burn the bridge behind him. The next day, the 28th, Greene's main force arrived; but it was considered impossible to subsist his army in the wake of Cornwallis's, and the pursuit was reluctantly discontinued.

S. R., XVII,
1011
1781

At Cross Creek Cornwallis suffered another disappointment in finding that his Loyalist friends were yet passive and had not brought in supplies for his army. He remained there several days, and then departed for Wilmington, where he arrived on April 7th. On the way it became his painful duty to bury the remains of the lamented Colonel Webster, who, borne on a litter between two horses, was found dead near Elizabethtown. The interment was on the plantation of Colonel Waddell.

Greene goes
south

Greene rested his army for a week, dismissed nearly all of his militia, and just as Cornwallis was entering Wilmington set out to recover South Carolina. At his camp on Deep River he left General Butler, who remained for some weeks on duty at that post. But notwithstanding Greene's

McRee's
Iredell, I,
497
S. R., XV,
434, 440, 443

departure from North Carolina, there was no relaxation in efforts to strengthen his army. The council ordered that those of Butler's and Eaton's brigades who had abandoned their posts at the battle of Guilford Court House should be drafted into the continentals for twelve months; and four days after Greene marched Butler sent forward two hundred and forty of these twelve months' continentals, and on the same day Major Pinketham Eaton received in Chatham a hundred and seventy of Eaton's brigade and conducted them to the south. This corps, reduced somewhat by desertions, under Major Eaton, later performed excellent service, especially at Augusta.

*Now Lockville.

Arriving in South Carolina, Greene, divining the probable
movement of Cornwallis, directed Sumner that if the British
general should come south to the relief of Rawdon he should
hurry with every available man to his assistance; but if
Cornwallis marched to Virginia, then Sumner with his continental drafts should go to the aid of Baron Steuben.
Greene, as commander of the department, had direction of
operations in Virginia as well as in the Carolinas, and he
ordered Steuben to be very cautious and conservative and
not to hazard a battle unless under very favorable circumstances.

Craig at Wilmington

The approach of the British fleet bearing Major Craig's
detachment caused the greatest consternation among the
Whigs of Wilmington, and many families hastened to leave
the town, seeking safety with friends in the country, while
others thought it more prudent to trust to the humanity
of the British officers. At that time Brunswick, which contained about sixty houses, was entirely deserted, and Wilmington, where there were about two hundred houses, contained but a thousand inhabitants. At the first information
of peril Bloodworth, the receiver of the tax in kind, stored
his commodities on a vessel, which he hurried up the Northeast Branch of the Cape Fear; but Craig made pursuit, overtook and burned the vessel some twenty miles from the
town. Of the inhabitants a considerable proportion were
disaffected, and soon a petition was circulated for all to sign,
praying to be received as British subjects, and those who
declined this abasement fell under the ban of displeasure.

Hardly had Craig settled himself on shore before squads
of troopers were scouring the country to arrest those who
were particularly obnoxious to the British, and the leading
patriots fled for safety. Harnett had withdrawn to Onslow
County. He had a considerable quantity of public funds
in his care, and he hastened to place it in safe hands, and
then proceeded to Colonel Spicer's. There he was seized
with a fit of his malady, the gout, and became unable to
travel farther. His place of refuge was betrayed by some
Loyalist, and he speedily was captured and, notwithstanding

S. R., XXI,
694

S. R.,
XXII, 543

Death of
Harnett

Biog. Hist.
of N. C., II,
162

1781

his illness, was conveyed with indignity to the British quarters. He suffered much ill-treatment, which his enfeeble
frame could not endure, and a few weeks later died, abou
April 30, 1781. Thus passed away "the Pride of the Cap
Fear," who from the beginning had been the ardent advocate of his country's freedom.

Similar efforts were made to capture every Whig of consequence, and many were taken by the Tories and Britisl
dragoons. But the patriot leaders, while beset by difficulties

Lillington at
Heron
Bridge
were not dismayed. General Lillington, having embodie
his militia, took post at Heron Bridge, ten miles up the
Northeast River, where he was joined by Kenan with the
Duplin militia and Moore with a detachment from Brunswick and some companies from Onslow; while Colone
Brown sought to hold in check the Tories of Bladen. The
brigades of Caswell and Butler were at first ordered to his
aid, but Cornwallis's operations at the west required that
all the militia possible should be withdrawn to reinforce
General Greene, and for a time Lillington was left to his own
resources.

About the end of February Craig advanced to dislodge
him, making a night attack. Lillington's advanced guard
Dickson's
Letters, 3
was surprised and dispersed, and a smart skirmish occurred
at the bridge, the British using their artillery on the Whig
S. R., XXI,
829
entrenchments on the farther side of the river. The militia,
however, maintained their position, and at the end of two
days Craig retired to Wilmington. He had occupied the
McKenzie place, known as Mount Blake, and when he withdrew a party of the Whigs crossed the river and burned that
residence. Lillington continued quietly in his camp, with
headquarters at the Mulberry plantation, near by, keeping
watch and ward. For a time Craig busied himself in con-
McRee's
Iredell, I,
531
structing fortifications around Wilmington; but numerous
were the forays of the British troopers, and often murderous
in their execution. Tradition still survives of the massacre
Bloodworth
at the "eight-mile house," where butchery as a pastime added
to the horrors of warfare. Some of the Whigs, too, displayed boldness and enterprise. Bloodworth had kept the
ferry from Point Peter across the mouth of the Northeast
River in the outskirts of Wilmington, and was familiar with

hat locality. Taking post within a large hollow tree on the Point he fired day after day, across the river, at the troopers as they brought their horses to water, several victims falling at the unerring hand of their unseen and mysterious foe. Finally a party being sent to dislodge him, Bloodworth successfully escaped.*

Cornwallis's plans

When the wounded of Cornwallis's army reached Wilmington the church building there was converted into a hospital, and later it is said was used by Craig's cavalry.

Although Cornwallis had succeeded in avoiding a second battle with Greene, he now found himself in a fearful dilemma. The generalissimo at the south could not remain inactive. He must move either in one direction or the other. Conflicting indeed must have been his emotions when reflecting on his painful situation. He found himself under the necessity of abandoning Lord Rawdon to his fate, and almost in despair he resolved to seek his own safety in Virginia. "By a direct move toward Camden," he wrote, "I cannot get time enough to relieve Lord Rawdon; and should he have fallen [back] my army would be exposed to the utmost danger." He dwelt on the exhausted state of the country, the numerous militia, the almost universal spirit of revolt and the strength of Greene's army, whose continentals alone were as numerous as his own force. Still he hoped to draw Greene back from the game of war in South Carolina by threatening the interior of North Carolina. He resolved to march by Duplin Court House, pointing toward Hillsboro, expecting that this might lead to Greene's return; and yet with his depleted ranks he feared to meet Greene again in battle. Ultimately he had in view to form a junction with General Phillips. But he realized that the attempt would be exceedingly hazardous and might prove wholly impracticable, and he warned that commander not to take any steps "that might expose your army to the danger of being ruined."

On April 23d he wrote to Clinton: "Neither my cavalry

S. R., XVII, 1019, 1020

---

*According to the tradition as the author heard it in 1847, Bloodworth, a gunsmith, used a long conical ball for his rifle on that occasion. The minie ball came into note some years later.

1781
S. R., XVII,
1018, 1019

or infantry are in readiness to move; the former are in want of everything, the latter of every necessary but shoes; . . . I must, however, begin my march to-morrow. . . . My present undertaking sits heavy on my mind; I have experienced the distresses and dangers of marching some hundreds of miles

The effects of Guilford Court House

in a country chiefly hostile, without one active or useful friend, without intelligence and without communication with any part of the country. The situation in which I leave South Carolina adds much to my anxiety, yet I am under the necessity of adopting this hazardous enterprise hastily and with the appearance of precipitation, as I find there is no prospect of speedy reinforcement from Europe and that the return of General Greene to North Carolina . . . would

S. R., XVII,
1921

put a junction with General Phillips out of my power." To Phillips he said: "My situation here is very distressing. Greene took advantage of my being obliged to come to this place, and has marched to South Carolina."

Indeed, Cornwallis's discomfiture at Guilford Court House altered the situation so greatly that Clinton wrote to Phillips that, it has "considerably changed the complexion of our affairs to the southward, and all operations to the northward must probably give place to those in favor of his Lordship, which at present appear to require our more immediate attention." Phillips had with him in Virginia thirty-five hundred men, and Clinton embarked seventeen hundred more to strengthen that corps for the benefit of Cornwallis.

Cornwallis marches to Virginia

After a fortnight's rest at Wilmington, the remnants of his shattered regiments again fell into ranks and began their march to the northward. Gloomy indeed must the outlook have been to the commander-in-chief of the British armies at the south when, baffled, disappointed, defeated, and distressed, in the closing days of April he bade farewell to Major Craig and Josiah Martin, the whilom governor of North Carolina, and with a heavy heart once more essayed the chances of doubtful war.

His progress was unopposed. When information of this movement was despatched to Governor Nash at New Bern he directed Lillington to fall back to Kinston, where Major-General Caswell, the commander-in-chief, had his headquarters, and the governor sent Baron Glaubeck to the front

1781
N. C. Uni.
Mag., IV,
83 (1855)

o watch the enemy. He ordered the militia of Halifax and
f the neighboring counties to assemble at Tarboro, and he
imself hastened to that point.

On reaching Kinston, presumably under the orders of
Major-General Caswell, Lillington disbanded his militia, ex-
ept one company retained to guard the artillery and stores,
nd the men returned to their respective homes to protect
heir families from marauders.

The inhabitants distressed

The march of the British column was slow and delib-
rate. The Whigs, unable to resist, scurried into the swamps
r fled to a distance. The disaffected rose in numbers and
gave every manifestation of loyalty. They now wreaked
vengeance on their neighbors for all they had suffered since
he beginning of the Revolution. The track of the army was
a scene of desolation, and the Whig settlements were
scourged as by the plagues of Pharaoh.

In Duplin the whole country was struck with terror,
almost every man leaving his habitation and his family to the
mercy of the merciless enemy. Horses, cattle and every kind
of stock were driven off from every plantation, corn and
forage taken, houses plundered, chests and trunks broken,
and the clothing of women and children, as well as that of
the men, was carried away. These outrages were committed for the most part by the camp followers, who, under
the protection of the army, plundered the distressed inhabitants. There were also many women who followed the
army in the character of wives of the officers and soldiers,
a certain number of women being allowed for each company.
These were generally mounted on fine horses and were Dickson's
Letters, 15
dressed in the best clothes that could be taken from the
inhabitants as the army marched through the country.

On May 6th Cornwallis reached Peacock's Bridge, on S. R., XV,
456
the Cotechney, and there was the first clash of arms. Colonel
Gorham with four hundred militia made a stand at the
bridge, but Tarleton by a bold dash drove him off, and there
was no further opposition. All the stores and the men
drafted for the continentals and the militia were moved to
the westward, and Governor Nash and General Sumner, in

1781

Warren, listened for news of the British progress. Glau
beck, trained from early youth a soldier, was seeking to
procure arms for the men assigned to his command, and in
the absence of swords, improvised weapons made of hickory
clubs. With these he hung on the outskirts of the British
lines and kept in check the barbarous camp followers. In
Nash a squad of Tories, who had risen on their neighbors
were roughly handled and hotly pursued.

S. R., XV,
461

"Not a man of any rank or distinction, or scarcely any
man of property," wrote Colonel Seawell, "has lain in his
house since the British passed through Nash County. We
are distressed with all the rogues and vagabonds that Corn
wallis can raise to pest us with. . . . A certain Robert Beard
with fifteen others on Friday last seized the person of John
Ferrell, Isham Alford and Robert Melton, together with
seven horses and I think three guns, . . . and carried them
all off. Our men after collecting, pursued them; but night
coming on, and drawing near the enemy's lines, they returned without any luck."

On May 10th Cornwallis entered Halifax, and after a
short rest marched on to Petersburg, where he arrived on the
20th, finding to his sorrow that a week earlier General Phillips had died from disease. His departure, however, was
not followed by a calm. From Heron's Bridge to Halifax
the Tories had their day of rejoicing, and the Whigs fled
to hiding places, their farms ravaged and the sanctity of
their homes often violated. For days and weeks the Tory
bands held high carnival, and no Whig dared sleep in his
house for fear of capture. Many were seized and carried
to Wilmington, where some were thrown into irons and subjected to cruel indignities.

McRee's
Iredell, I,
514

Terrible were the reports that were spread of the horrible
misdeeds of the soldiers and camp followers. Plantations
were despoiled, women outraged, even members of some of
the best-known families of the State. The most painful
apprehensions were excited because of their shameful conduct. The culmination of these outrages occurred in the
vicinity of Halifax, where, says Stedman, "some enormi-
ties were committed that were a disgrace to the name of

man"; and Tarleton states that there "a sergeant and a dragoon were executed" for their crimes against society.

1781

Lee's
Memoirs,
413

At Edenton

The Albemarle region was swept over by a storm of fears. The near approach of the British from the Chesapeake, the passage through neighboring counties of Cornwallis, rumors that a body of two thousand negroes had been sent to forage and collect supplies for the British army, the invasion of the sound by boats belonging to privateersmen too strong to be resisted, caused widespread alarm, and the inhabitants of Edenton dispersed. Edenton itself was raided, vessels taken, some burned and others carried off. But quickly the people recovered their resolution, and parties were formed to rid the sound of the raiders. The enemy was driven out, one of the British galleys taken and some of the vessels recaptured. "The inhabitants in general and the sailors turned out unanimously. I never saw, nor could even hope to see," wrote Charles Johnson in the midst of that turmoil and confusion, "so much public spirit, personal courage and intrepid resolution. I am convinced that was the measure adopted of fitting out one or two armed vessels we might laugh at all attempts of the enemy's plundering banditti."

McRee's
Iredell, I,
506-511

McRee's
Iredell, I,
515

The Whigs rally

In other sections also the same spirit was displayed, and the Whigs rallied and beat down the Tories and re-established the authority of the State.

James Armstrong, writing from Martinboro at the end of May, said: "We have been alarmed for ten days past by the Tories embodying about us, but they seem to drop off. Thirty horse from this county and a few from Craven . . . went up to Edgecombe, took Benjamin Vichous, one of their ringleaders, and twenty-one head of cattle, which they had collected for the British army; since, they wrote to me for peace, and was granted it provided they gave up their arms."

S. R., XV,
467

In Duplin, wrote Mr. Dickson, "the Tories rose and took several of our leading men and carried them to Wilmington. There were numbers of our good citizens, thus betrayed, who perished on board prison ships. This so alarmed the inhabitants that none of us dared to sleep in our houses for fear of being surprised. Matters being thus in confusion, there was no subordination among men, but all the proprietors raised and commanded their own little parties and defended themselves as they could. At length, however, Colonel Kenan embodied some four hundred of the militia, and quiet was restored." Many inhabitants because of these disturbances removed their families to the west, and even to Virginia, abandoning their plantations entirely. In New Hanover it was still worse. That county was measurably depopulated and a scene of universal desolation. It was at this time that General Ashe was wounded and captured and imprisoned at Wilmington, where he contracted the smallpox. This plague generally accompanied the British camp and became a fearful scourge. When convalescent, broken in health, Ashe was paroled in October only to die a few days later at Colonel Sampson's in Duplin County. The first to take up arms in North Carolina, he passed away ignorant of Cornwallis's surrender, and without a view of the promised land of independence.

Death of Ashe

Greene in South Carolina

After breaking camp on Deep River, Greene hurried across the barrens and soon reached the bountiful region of the Peedee. He lost no time in striking his blows. On April 20th he approached Camden, taking post at Hobkirk's Hill, where on the morning of the 25th Lord Rawdon attacked him, both suffering severely. The loss of each was somewhat more than two hundred and fifty, about one-fourth of their respective commands. In this battle, except those attached to Colonel Washington's cavalry, there were only about two hundred and fifty North Carolinians, being a militia battalion commanded by Colonel James Read; and these, having been placed in the reserve, although they gallantly and bravely marched forward to relieve the retreating continentals, were not in the thickest of the engagement. Their conduct, however, won them encomiums.

Lee's
Memoirs,
337

Hobkirk's
Hill

On May 10th, by Greene's strategy, Rawdon was compelled to abandon Camden, so that only Ninety-six and

Augusta were retained as British posts in the interior. Quickly Greene determined to drive the enemy entirely from the country and to hedge them in at Charleston. With this view, he detached Colonel Lee's and Major Eaton's continentals, who had just joined him, to attack Augusta, then held by Colonel Browne and Colonel Grierson, in whose honor one of the forts was named. Fort Grierson was the one first attacked. In the assault the American loss was trivial, a few wounded and fewer killed. But unhappily among the latter was Major Eaton, who had endeared himself to both officers and soldiers, and who fell gallantly at the head of his battalion in the moment of victory.* The siege of Augusta was then continued until June 5th, when Colonel Browne capitulated. During its continuance the North Carolina continentals behaved with the utmost gallantry. Greene's prisoners now numbered eight hundred, and he sent them to Salisbury, guarded by a detachment under the command of Major Armstrong and other continental officers.

Augusta taken

Lee's Memoirs, 357

Death of Eaton

In May Greene had himself undertaken the siege of Ninety-six, a strong fort admirably defended. Lord Rawdon, having received considerable re-enforcements at Charleston, now pressed forward to relieve that garrison, and on the near approach of this superior force Greene resolved if possible to carry the fort by assault.

Ninety-six besieged

On June 18th he led his army to the attack. A desperate conflict ensued, but without avail, and the next morning Greene withdrew beyond the Saluda, proposing if pressed to seek safety in North Carolina. Rawdon, however, determined to abandon Ninety-six and retire to Charleston, and Greene returned, taking post on the high hills of the Santee awaiting re-enforcements from North Carolina, for North Carolina was now his only dependence.

June 18

Cartel of exchange agreed on

On the Peedee on May 3, 1781, Colonel Carrington, on the part of General Greene, and Captain Cornwallis, on the

---

*Major Eaton commanded the new continentals, composed largely of men from Butler's and Eaton's brigades who had behaved badly at Guilford Court House.

1781

part of the Earl, had a meeting and agreed on an exchange of all prisoners. Pursuant to their action, the commissaries of prisoners at once gave notice that all militia taken on either side were absolutely exchanged, and were liberated from their paroles. This set free such of the North Carolina militia as had been captured at Charleston, at Camden and elsewhere, and tended somewhat to strengthen the militia force of the State. The continentals, officers and men, had to suffer longer delay, but it was agreed that the delivery would begin toward the end of June, and these prisoners were to be conveyed to the James River and then be at liberty to return to military service.

Painful indeed had been the period of their captivity and distressing the mortality among the men, which perhaps was quite equal to that horrid record of the hulks off Long Island, which shocked humanity. Many of the exchanged officers late in the summer were able to take their places in the continental battalions and served with Greene until the end of the war.

Atrocities lead to threats of retaliation

The excesses and atrocities of the Tories were intolerable, and the animosity which was felt against them assumed the character of ferocity. Many of them, when taken, were summarily executed as murderers and robbers. "I heard," wrote Mrs. Blair toward the end of May, "that some of the people about New Bern who had intended joining Lord Cornwallis had been taken and nine executed. The man who brought the account said he saw one of them hanged. Captain Pasteur, one of the party who made the capture, while riding with a prisoner behind him, was fired at in passing through a swamp and so badly wounded that he survived but three days." On June 20th Major Craig addressed Governor Nash on "the inhuman treatment" of the king's friends, the deliberate and wanton murders committed on them, which called for vengeance. "Had I listened only to the first emotions excited by the account of Mr. Caswell's conduct in murdering five men at Kinston, . . . Mr. Samuel Ashe and his comrades, who were put in irons for the purpose, would have become the immediate victims to his unwarrant-

McRee's Iredell, I, 517

S. R., XXII, 1024

ble cruelty." Major Craig threatened that if the acts he
described were continued he would give the people who
had taken arms in the king's favor ample revenge, and
"I shall not hesitate to deliver over to them those prisoners
who from character or situation are most likely to gratify
them in those sentiments." This communication was received by Governor Burke, who had just been elected successor to Governor Nash. It appears that Major Ashe, his
younger brother and others taken by scouting bands of
Tories, had been thrown into irons, confined on shipboard
and threatened to be delivered up to the Tories for their
vengeance. Burke answered with resolution: "Should you . . .
continue your treatment of those citizens or listen to any
emotions which may dictate any measure against them on
the ground of retaliation, . . . I shall find myself under the
unhappy necessity of taking similar measures against British
prisoners, though all such measures are utterly repugnant
to my disposition." "There are at present," he added,
"some prisoners in my power."

Burke's threatened retaliation resulted in checking Craig
in his measures of revenge. Many of these prisoners, not
taken on the field of battle, were, however, conveyed to
Charleston and paroled to James Island, where were congregated a large number of Tory refugees, men driven from
their homes, animated by a relentless hostility toward the
Whigs, some of desperate and despicable characters, who
were a menace to the lives of these unfortunate captives.

But Craig, foiled in his purpose as to Major Ashe, conceived the design of wreaking vengeance on the person of
Burke himself should the occasion arise. He devised the
capture of the governor, and planned to hold him for purposes of retaliation in case any of his Tory lieutenants
should fall into the hands of the Whigs and be severely
dealt with.

Gregory defends the Albemarle region

While attention was centred on the larger movements at
the south and west, the Albemarle region was constantly
threatened.

In the fall of 1780 there was sharp skirmishing, with some

1781
Biog. Hist.
N. C., IV,
144
loss of life, between Leslie's foraging parties and the militia
under General Gregory, who had taken post near the Great
Bridge. And early in 1781, when Arnold's corps arrived
Gregory again was quickly in service. It was about the end
of February that a circumstance occurred from which it appeared that a British officer sought to place the American
general in the light of a traitor, but the affair afterward was
shown to be a joke and without foundation. Still, to have
been suspected of being a traitor grated terribly on the feelings of that sterling patriot. Despite his mortification, he
continued to hold his camp at the Northwest Landing, and
although once compelled to withdraw, he soon occupied it
again. One of the few who won honor at Camden, his good
fame was never tarnished by an unworthy action.

3. R., XV,
507, 508, 618
"During the winter and spring," wrote Dr. Hugh Williamson, "I had not so much as an assistant . . . in General
Gregory's camp." "Nothing but frenzy could have tempted
the general to . . . remain a minute in his camp, after the
enemy had arrived at McPherson's"; but he added: "General Gregory has again taken possession of his camp with all
his cannon and stores." All the spring and summer the
general remained on guard, but toward the end of August,
the British having abandoned Portsmouth and proceeded to
Yorktown, General Gregory deemed it unnecessary for the
militia to continue in service longer than to reduce some of
the disaffected to terms, and then he dismissed his men,
who had so effectively protected the Albemarle region.

CHAPTER XXXVIII

Burke's Administration, 1781-82

Conditions in North Carolina.—Major Craig at Wilmington.—The
Assembly meets.—Burke governor.—Action of Assembly.—Governor
Burke's zeal.—Fanning embodies the Tories.—Pittsboro taken.—Conditions in Bladen.—Wade's victory.—Cornwallis's plans.—South Quay
captured.—New continental battalions.—Craig invades the eastern
counties.—Lillington forbidden to fight.—New Bern taken.—Tory
atrocities.—Battle of Elizabethtown.—Governor Burke's plans.—Fanning defeats Wade.—The governor captured.—The battle of Cane
Creek.—Butler surprised at Brown Marsh.—The battle of Eutaw
Springs.—-The gallantry of the North Carolinians.

Conditions in North Carolina

General Sumner had been directed by General Greene to
remain in North Carolina and organize the men drafted into
the continental service, and he was during the spring active
in the performance of this duty. Every thirtieth man had
been called out for this service, but they were to be selected
in their respective neighborhoods and clothing provided for
them, and progress was slow. In April these drafts were
assembled at Harrisburg,* doubtless with the view of co-
operating with Steuben in Virginia; but later General
Greene ordered such as were then ready to join him in South
Carolina, and May 26th Major Armstrong sent forward one
hundred and eighty from Salisbury. There was much delay
incident to the fearful times. About the middle of June
Captain Doherty, writing from Duplin Court House, said
that the "tumults in this part of the country have been the
cause of the delay in collecting the men, but at present some
little respite from the cursed Tories, but cannot say they are
entirely subdued. More than half the draft made in Duplin
have been among the Tories, or of men so disaffected that
they will not appear. The men have been so harassed by

*Near Oxford.

being kept in arms that hitherto they could not attend to providing the clothing, and without clothing they cannot march."

Colonel Joseph Hawkins, a zealous officer, with his regiment of light horse was at the same time on the head of Black River among the Tories; the people there, except one family, he reported "as being all disaffected." "The Tories," he said, "continued to carry great quantities of beef from that part to the enemy at Wilmington." He himself sent a detachment in and brought off fifty-two beeves and six prisoners.

S. R., XV, 487

Major Craig at Wilmington

Major Craig was a very efficient officer. He sought by strenuous endeavors to restore royal authority. Proclaiming that the inhabitants, being British subjects, were Loyalist militiamen, early in July he directed that they should be enrolled as such, and he issued commissions to zealous Tories as officers of their counties. He fixed August 1st as the last day of grace for those who would not obey, and all not then returning to their allegiance were to be harried as rebels. While the Whigs had measurably neither arms nor ammunition, he bountifully supplied the Tory bands with both, and inspired them to zealous activity by giving them special marks of favor.

S. R., XV, 511

The Scotch especially responded to his calls and up the Northwest strong detachments of Loyalists held the country. To the northward he threw out the British dragoons, and he established a post at Rutherford's Mills, some seven miles east of Burgaw, and there he constructed a bastion fort, whose outline still remains in perfect preservation, a memorial of those historic times. Lillington, who had after the passage of Cornwallis returned to the vicinity of Heron Bridge, now stationed himself at Richlands, in Onslow County; and on June 28th, when a British column advanced in that direction, called on the Duplin horse and foot to assemble at the rendezvous with despatch. However, before opposition could be made, Craig's troopers penetrated into Onslow, and secured in that fertile section needed supplies; but when the people collected, finding that warm work

Rutherford's Mills

S. R., XV, 496

Craig in Onslow

was to be expected, they hastily returned to their strong-hold.

The movements of Cornwallis, the perils threatened by Craig, the defection of the Loyalists, and the drafting of men in every part of the State caused a deep gloom to enshroud the people, and public affairs were thrown into great confusion.

In the midst of all this turmoil and distress the General Assembly met on June 23d at Wake Court House. The session was held in the old Lane residence, still standing in the suburbs of Raleigh. So threatening were the bands of Tories that a regiment of militia was stationed in the vicinity to protect the body during its sitting. Alexander Martin was chosen speaker of the senate, and Benbury again presided over the house. Governor Nash declined a re-election because of ill health, but perhaps there were other reasons as well. The creation of the Board of War and later of the Council Extraordinary had divided power and responsibility and had resulted unfortunately, so that the government had lost much of its efficiency. The council had ordered that one-fifth of the provisions upon every farm should be taken for the public use, and heavy taxes in kind had been imposed. Impressments having been resorted to, Major Murfree toward the end of May impressed, at Pitch Landing, two thousand gallons of rum, nine hundred weight of sugar, a thousand of coffee, six or seven hundred yards of canvas, a small quantity of ammunition and other commodities, which the merchants had imported. Much dissatisfaction resulted from these measures, tending to render the administration unpopular, while the currency, both continental and state, had become almost worthless, and the feebleness of the military arm in checking the Tories and the scarcity of ammunition, guns and clothing for the soldiers were causes of adverse comment and grave apprehensions. To succeed Governor Nash, the Assembly chose Dr. Burke, who qualified on June 26th.

On accepting the office of governor, Burke communicated to the Assembly with emphasis that he did not wish a continuance of the Council Extraordinary, but that he himself would discharge the functions of commander-in-chief. The

S. R., XVII, 877
The Assembly meets at Wake Court House

McRee's Iredell, I, 497
S. R., XV, 475

S. R., XXII, 1038, 1041
Burke governor

1781
June

Measures of
defence

council therefore ceased, but General Richard Caswell remained nominally as major-general in command of the state forces. The Assembly acted with promptness and vigor. The Marquis of Bretigny, having offered his services to the State, was appointed a special agent to procure a fast sailing vessel, and go to the French islands in the West Indies and obtain five thousand stands of arms, ten thousand pounds of powder and other military supplies, twenty thousand pounds of tobacco being placed at his disposal for the purpose. A regiment of state troops was directed to be raised, and Benjamin Williams was chosen the commander, Joel Lewis first major, and Baron de Glaubeck, who had been so active and efficient, was appointed major of horse. In view of the condition of affairs in Chatham, Cumberland, and Randolph, it was resolved that a company of light horse should be raised for two months in each of those counties. An exception was made in the operation of the confiscation act of all persons, theretofore disaffected, who should serve with General Sumner in the continental battalions for the term of ten months.

S. R., XV,
533; XVII,
930-975

The militia that had acted badly at Guilford Court House having been drafted into the continentals, the Assembly now requested the governor to recommend to General Greene to discharge them "whenever the situation of affairs would admit of such an act of benevolence." Samuel Johnston, Charles Johnson, William Sharpe, and Ephraim Brevard were on July 12th elected delegates to the Continental Congress. The value of the currency had now fallen so low that the Assembly rated a day's work at $250, allowed Joel Lane £15,000 for the use of his house and pasturage for one month, and paid $12,000 for a single horse. On July 14th, the body adjourned to meet again in November at Salem, more removed from the seat of war.

The
depreciated
currency

Governor Burke's zeal

Undismayed by the adverse circumstances of that unhappy period, when Burke assumed the reins he was all activity. Three days after his election he directed General Butler to post five hundred men between the Cape Fear and the Neuse, covering the lowest fords on each, and to patrol with

avalry toward the enemy's lines, requiring daily reports of 1781
he situation. He lost no time in urging the Assembly to S. R., XVII, 910 June
ction. "I perceive," said he, "the country everywhere un-
repared for defence; without arms, without discipline, with-
ut arrangements, even the habits of civil order and obedi-
nce to laws changed into a licentious contempt of authority
nd a disorderly indulgence of violent propensities. Indus-
ry is intermitted, agriculture much decayed, and com-
nerce struggling feebly with almost insuperable difficulties.
The public money is unaccounted for, the taxes uncollected
r unproductive," the individual creditors of the public unpaid for years, "and the treasury totally unable to make
payment." Dark indeed was his portrayal of the situation. The depressing conditions
And to that were to be added the perils and dangers of that
gloomy period when the British were threatening the State
from the north, the sounds and coast infested with privateersmen bent on spoils, and from Guilford to Brunswick
civil war raged, its horrors heightened by passion, butcheries
on either side being of daily occurrence.

Even before the adjournment of the Assembly Governor Burke's activity
Burke began to move from point to point in the State, in-
spiring confidence by his presence and assuming direction.
He had full power to act, and his known energy and resolute will brought new hope to the Whigs in the terrorized
sections. While urging the Assembly on he busied himself
supervising operations; and he began to plan a movement
not merely to suppress the Tories, but to drive Craig out of
his stronghold on the Cape Fear. Indeed, he was aroused
to the utmost exertions by the earnest appeals that constantly came for immediate assistance.

General Lillington, writing from the Trent on July 6th, S. R., XXII, 540
complained most bitterly that no aid had been furnished his
district by the other counties. He represented that the The Cape Fear region
Whigs of that region, distressed as they were, felt that they
were to fall a sacrifice to the enemy; expelled from their
homes, their plantations ravaged, their negroes carried off,
and those caught compelled to accept allegiance or to go
into captivity. His own immediate section was desolate and
deserted, and doubtless the iron had entered into the soul

1781
S. R.,
XXII, 543

of the old veteran, whose heart bled for the misfortunes of his friends and kindred.

From Bladen, Cumberland, and the upper Cape Fear also, came cries for help that appealed most strongly to the governor for prompt and effective action.

Fanning embodies the Tories

Although Cornwallis suffered continuous disappointment while at the south from the passiveness of the North Carolina Loyalists, yet after his departure from the State they became very active. While many of their partisan leaders

Fanning's
Narrative in
S. R.,
XXII, 180
et seq.

attained great prominence, chief among them was David Fanning, a native of Johnston County, but from boyhood a resident of South Carolina. In the fall of 1780 he came to Deep River and made himself acquainted with many persons who had received commissions from Colonel Hamilton the preceding July. He watched and waited. He was concerned with Dr. Pyle in the raising of that band of Tories that Lee cut to pieces in February, 1781, but was not himself present at the massacre. Immediately afterward he began to collect another body, and he gave information to Cornwallis, and was with him on his march to Ramsey's Mills, accompanying him to Cross Creek. At that time Cornwallis's plans were not matured, and he expected that he might return to Hillsboro. Fanning established himself with some seventy Loyalists at Coxe's Mill* and interfered with Greene's communications in North Carolina. Shortly afterward he attacked a detachment under Colonel Dudley, of Virginia, coming from Greene's camp with baggage, drove off the guard, capturing the baggage and nine horses. Colonels Collier and Balfour, of Randolph, embodied one hundred and sixty men, and on June 8th reached his vicinity, but he made a night attack on them, and then sought safety in concealment. A few days later Fanning contrived a general meeting of the Loyalists, who selected him as their commander. Accordingly he repaired to Wilmington and obtained on July 5th from Major Craig a commission as

1781

---

*Coxe's Mill is on the western side of Deep River, at the mouth of Mill Creek, in Randolph County, about five miles from the Chatham line.

colonel of the Loyalist militia of Randolph and Chatham counties. A week later he had a general muster at Coxe's Mill and organized a force of a hundred and fifty men. There had been appointed by Colonel Hamilton captains and other officers for seven companies in Randolph County, for six in Chatham, two in Orange, four in Cumberland, and three in Anson. These all were more or less in touch with Colonel Fanning, affording means of embodying men and directing their movements that rendered his operations very effective. On the same day that he held his muster on Deep River there was a court martial and Whig muster at Pittsboro, some twenty-five miles distant. Fanning determined to strike them a blow. By seven o'clock the next morning he reached the hamlet and surrounded it. The members of the court had dispersed for the night to country homes. As they approached the village in the early morning Fanning successively took them prisoners, among them being all the militia officers of the county except two, a captain of the continentals and three members of the General Assembly, his captives numbering fifty-three. He paroled most of them, but conducted fourteen of the most prominent and influential Whigs to Major Craig, at Wilmington. Among those taken were Herndon Ramsey and James Williams. Excesses committed by Major O'Neal, Colonel Robeson, of Bladen; Wade, of Anson; Phil Alston, and other vigorous patriot leaders, which the Tories complained of as being "barbarous murders," led Fanning and his associates to practise retaliation, and these Chatham prisoners, when they reached Raft Swamp, were threatened with execution. They apprehended they were to fall victims to partisan rancor. Accordingly, their "situation being very unhappy," from that point they addressed a letter to Governor Burke detailing the complaints made by the Tories and asking that Tory prisoners "may be well treated in future." In view of this intercession, their lives were spared, and after a month's detention at Wilmington some of them were paroled, while others were conveyed to Charleston.

On his return to Deep River Fanning received information that Colonel Alston with a party of twenty-five was watching for him. He surprised Alston at his house, and

1781
July

Pittsboro taken
July 18, 1781
N. C. Uni.
Mag., II,
80
(1853)

S. R.,
XXII, 550

N. C. Uni.
Mag., II,
83
(1853)
S. R.,
XXII,
203, 557

in an action lasting several hours killed four and wounded all the rest except three, when they surrendered. His own loss was but two men killed and four wounded. Again did Colonel Balfour make an effort to capture him, but without success.

While Fanning was operating in the Deep River country two active Tories in Bladen, McNeil and Ray, collected the Loyalists lower down, and proved much too strong for the local Whig leaders.

S. R.,
XXII,
543, 546, 548
In Bladen On July 10th Colonel Robeson wrote to Governor Burke of the situation in Bladen: Distressed by a large body of Tories and robbers, who range through the county from Wilmington up to Drowning Creek and the waters of the Little Peedee as far as Richmond—a hundred miles in length and fifty across—a country much encumbered with very large swamps and thick places, difficult for a small party of troops to be of much service; and the friends to their country that live in this part so distressed by their property being taken from them daily, and they in constant danger of their lives by a set of Tories and robbers protected by the British, that if we can't have assistance, we must unavoidably fall a prey to those villains—must in a very short time be obliged to leave our homes; and at this time obliged to leave our habitations every night to take our rest. The inhabitants of the county consisted of fifteen companies, and now there can't be raised more than seventy or eighty men that dare move in behalf of their country. Five days later he again wrote to the governor that there were but fifty men to oppose some four hundred under McNeil and Ray, and McLaurin Colvill* appointed colonels of Bladen County; that Colvill had said he would have three hundred more men from the lower part of the county and one hundred from Brunswick; that August 1st was the time limited for the people to come in by the proclamation of General Clinton and Arburthnot, which had been industriously spread among the people, and if they did not go in they were to be destroyed. McNeil was encamped at McFalls Mill, between Drowning Creek and Raft Swamp, and Colvill was ordering a general muster at Elizabethtown.

*Called by Dickson Maturin and generally so written.

Colonel Brown was the commanding officer of Bladen County, but it was impossible to get men to join him without assistance. Colvill, however, did not live long to enjoy his new honors. Colonel Emmett wrote to the governor on the 19th: "A small party of our people in Bladen, . . . without orders, went to the house of Mr. Colvill, who had accepted from the English a colonel's commission, killed him, and plundered the house of what property was to be found in it."

On July 30th Colonel Brown and Colonel Robeson joined in a pathetic letter to Governor Burke, which was borne by Colonel Owen himself, urging help. For six months they said they had been seeking to defend themselves and property, but the Tories were largely increasing, and robbers were "daily plundering and destroying our stock of cattle and our houses of everything, . . . and now at this time old Hector McNeil is encamped with a large body of men within eight or ten miles of our court-house, and is increasing in number very fast, and Colonel Duncan Ray is encamped in another part of our county with a large body of men and is giving out notice to the inhabitants that all that do not come in by August 1st will have all their properties destroyed and laid waste; and we, being but few in number that stand in behalf of our country, are not sufficient or able to stand in our own defence without immediate assistance. . . . Our number is not one hundred . . . to oppose between four and five hundred. . . . We shall be all broke up and obliged to give way and leave the place, which will be greatly to the advantage of our enemy and will still increase their number."

Wade's victory

As Colonel Owen passed through Campbellton, Colonel Emmett, commanding in Cumberland, sent by him a similar letter advising the governor that there were four or five hundred Tories embodied at McFall's Mill, on Drowning Creek, thirty-five miles from Campbellton, and that unless Campbellton itself were occupied by the State, the Tories would take it. In the meantime, however, Colonel Wade, of Anson, was not inactive. Ascertaining that these Loyal-

margin notes:
1781
July

S. R., XXII, 1043

S. R., XV, 590

1781
August 4th

ists were engaged in disarming the settlers within twent
miles of the Peedee and carrying off men fit for duty an
driving off all stock over Drowning Creek into what the
called "protected land," where McNeil and Ray had thei
"flying army," Colonel Wade called out half his regiment
and was joined by parties from Montgomery and Richmond

Wade's
Report,
Graham's
Graham,
376

and proceeded into that territory. On Saturday, August 4th
he came up with them at Beattie's Bridge, on Drowning
Creek, and after a sharp engagement, lasting until twelve
o'clock at night, the Tories drew off. A dozen of them
were killed and some fifteen wounded, while Wade suffered
no other loss than four men wounded.

Cornwallis's plans

In the middle of July news came from Virginia that was
at once disquieting and hopeful. Lafayette wrote that a par

S. R., XV,
508

of the British troops were designed to embark for New
York; the rest "will garrison Portsmouth; but from thei
number of cavalry I imagine they will push to the south
land." Other developments led to the belief that Tarleton
with a large force of cavalry would pass through the in
terior of the State to the aid of Rawdon. And preparation
were made to harass if not destroy him should the movemen
be undertaken.

Governor Burke at once directed the commanding officer

S. R., XV,
549, 550, 551,
556, 557

of Granville, Orange and Caswell to collect all their rifle
men and march to Boyd's Ferry, on the Dan, and Kemp's
Ferry, on Roanoke, to drive back Tarleton's cavalry. But
Cornwallis changed his plan, were it ever contemplated to
send that corps to the southward.

South Quay
captured

A party of the enemy pushed from Suffolk to South Quay
on July 16th and destroyed all the stores and warehouses

S. R., XV,
560

at that place. The next day they came within twelve miles
of Murfree's Landing, burning dwellings and storehouses;
and also at Weyanoke they destroyed large quantities of
rum, sugar, coffee, and other articles stored by the merchants. They threatened Pitch Landing, but Major Murfree
having raised some seventy men and taken post at Skinner's
Bridge, on Meherrin River, they retired to Suffolk.

S. R., XV,
535

At the south, Craig, too, was displaying energy. He

1781
August

ebuilt the Heron Bridge, and announced his intention of
giving no more paroles, but would seize and sell the property of every man who did not join him. Many of the
Whigs were overawed. From Cumberland came the report:
"We had a muster on Monday last, where the third and
fourth numbers were ordered to meet in order to march
after the Tories; but there were neither officers nor men
met—only eight or ten; the colonel never came at all."
And Lillington reported to the governor that he had not
three rounds of ammunition, and knew not where to apply.

S. R., XV,
569

New continental battalions

In South Carolina General Greene, always prudent, was
chafing at his enforced inactivity because his force was inadequate to renew hostilities. He was anxiously awaiting
the arrival of more men before risking another battle.
Urged by his repeated calls, Major Armstrong hurried forward two hundred of the continental drafts; while on
July 14th General Sumner wrote to Greene from Salisbury:
"I arrived here Wednesday last with about five hundred
rank and file badly equipped; however, I have . . . received near three hundred good arms, . . . which I have
put in the hands of some good men, who will march to join
you under the command of Lieutenant-Colonel Ashe early
to-morrow morning." To Colonel Ashe he gave orders that
on his arrival at General Greene's camp he was to take
charge of all the continental troops of this State and incorporate them as the First Regiment.

S. R., XV,
530, 533

Ten days later Sumner himself marched, leaving Armstrong, Hogg, and Blount to organize and bring forward the
drafts from the districts of New Bern, Halifax, Edenton,
and Wilmington, all of whom were still delayed. When assembled, these were formed into the Second Battalion.

At that time General Greene had in contemplation the relief of North Carolina by carrying the garrison of Wilmington, and then to hasten on to Virginia, and to once more try
conclusions with Cornwallis. With this view, on August 2d
he gave orders for Lee's Legion, Kirkwood's Delawares,
and Handy's Maryland continentals, to prepare for an expedition against Wilmington. Secrecy and despatch were

Greene
proposes to
take
Wilmington

Lee's
Memoirs,
447

1781
August

necessary elements of success. Captain Rudolph, with a small party of the legion, was hurried to the Cape Fear to acquire information and to collect boats to cross that river. His mission was entirely successful; but at the moment when Greene was about to strike the blow he received information from General Washington that required a change of plans. Ordering Lafayette to continue his cautious conduct, he again addressed himself to driving the British into Charleston. Washington planned to capture Cornwallis himself.

Craig invades the eastern counties

All inhabitants had been required by Major Craig to come into the British camp and give in their adhesion by August 1st, and those failing to do so were to be regarded as enemies subject to the death penalty and to having their homes plundered. The alternative was fearful to those within his power. The dog-days of August indeed ushered in a period of horror and relentless warfare. The British commander issued his proclamation that the Loyalists should be ready to march with him, and on August 1st he began a tour through the eastern counties. Colonel Kenan with a hundred and fifty of the Duplin militia had taken post at Rock Creek (some two miles east of Wallace), and now was joined by a detachment of a hundred and eighty from the brigade of General Caswell, and two hundred under Colonel Brown of Bladen. On the approach of Major Craig with two hundred and fifty regulars and about eighty Tories, Kenan proposed to contest his passage. His ammunition, however, was soon exhausted; and on being charged the militia broke and fled, closely pursued by the British light horse, who succeeded in taking some twenty or thirty prisoners.

For ten days the British column lingered in Duplin, living on the country, embodying the Tories, exacting allegiance of the people and carrying out the programme announced in Craig's proclamation. The moderate and conservative policy of Cornwallis at his entrance into the State was no longer enforced; on the contrary, fire and sword now took the place of conciliation and regard for the inhabitants as subjects of Great Britain. Those who did not attach them-

S. R., XV, 569, 593

Battle of Rock Creek

Dickson's Letters, 17

Aug. 2, 1781

S. R., XXII, 568

1781
August

selves to the British camp were held outside of the pale of protection and given over to the vengeance of the Tories.

Having thoroughly harried Duplin, the column, now increased by the accession of three hundred Loyalists, turned its head toward New Bern, and General Lillington, who was encamped at Limestone Bridge, in Duplin, moved his force on the road to the Trent to intercept its progress.

Lillington forbidden to hazard a battle

General William Caswell with a party of one hundred and sixty horse operated on the enemy's lines, and before Craig had reached Kinston had a skirmish with about fifty of the dragoons. He found, however, that his mounted militia could not stand a charge; the gleaming swords of the enemy terrified them. Craig hastened on to surprise Lillington, who would have given him battle if permitted. But under orders, he avoided a meeting. Yet again were the British horse attacked, and with some loss. Caswell reported to the governor on the 17th: "General Lillington is between New Bern and the enemy, and I am fearful will risk an action. . . . I have done everything in my power to prevent it, and have let him have a sight of your Excellency's letter, wherein you mention that no general action must take place." General Lillington's force was about six hundred, drawn from Onslow, Jones, Craven, Dobbs, and Pitt, while Caswell commanded one hundred and fifty horse. The crying need was for ammunition, and arms were very scarce. It is probable that the want of ammunition determined Governor Burke to order that no general engagement should be risked. Lillington had taken position at Webber's Bridge, on the Trent, had removed the planks and had placed a strong guard to hold it. At that point there was a slight collision with a reconnoitring party, three of the enemy being killed and five wounded. On the evening of the 19th Craig reached New Bern. In his progress he had ravaged every Whig plantation and brought ruin and distress on the inhabitants of the country. On leaving Wilmington he had with him only about eighty Tories, but as their route lay through a country much disaffected, many inhabitants

S. R.,
XXII,
564, 565

New Bern
occupied
Aug., 1781
S. R.,
XXII,
564, 566, 568,
569

1781
~~
August
joined them. Those above fifty years of age were required
to take an oath of allegiance, while the younger men were
prevailed on to enroll in their ranks, and their numbers were
augmented by hundreds. General Caswell was apprehensive
that almost all of the inhabitants in the vicinity of New Bern
and most of those in Beaufort and Hyde counties would
enlist with Craig. "What force we can raise and arm,"
he said, "will not be superior to the Tories," and arms could
not be had for the men they could raise. He proposed to
establish a post at Webber's Bridge and at Bryan's Mills, on
the Neuse. General Lillington, now quite old and much
fatigued, was to leave the camp the next day.

Lillington was resolute, and doubtless eager for a battle,
but it appears that he was restrained by the prudent orders
of the governor from making a stand against the British
force. His plantation and those of his friends at Rocky
Point had been desolated, their negroes carried off, and
themselves reduced to poverty. Some of his friends had
been captured and subjected to inhuman ill-usage, and he
doubtless chafed that he was not permitted to strike a blow
at the enemy, even though he might not hope for absolute
victory.

Death of
Gaston
On entering New Bern, the British met with a cordial reception from some, but the patriotic citizens sought to escape. As Dr. Alexander Gaston with his wife and two small
children were about to depart in a boat one of the Tories
ruthlessly shot Dr. Gaston down, and the son, afterward
the eminent jurist, was literally baptized into patriotism in
Biog. Hist.
of N. C., II,
99; VII, 111
S. R., XV,
623
the blood of his murdered father. After despoiling the
town, robbing the citizens, burning vessels and committing
other excesses, Craig with his Tory followers departed
toward Kinston.

Tory atrocities

S. R., \V,
626
He rapidly advanced to Bryan Mills, on the Neuse, where
Colonel Gorham commanded a detachment. There a skirmish ensued, but Gorham was easily driven off.

The British remained at that point one night, burning the

1781

S. R., XV,
627; XXII,
593

iouses of General Bryan, William Heritage, William Coxe, and Longfield Coxe, and much distressed and abused their families. Their intention was to proceed further into the interior, but General Wayne with a body of continental troops, who was operating against the British near Suffolk, now drew near to North Carolina, and a report spread that he was at Halifax. Craig, receiving this information, turned to the southward, crossed the Trent and moved to Richlands, thence returning to his fortifications at Wilmington. His loss on this raid was about fifteen killed and captured and about the same number wounded. The great scarcity of ammunition prevented much skirmishing on the part of the Americans. The destruction of the residences at Bryan Mills led to severe retaliation; the inhabitants who had suffered raised a party and burned up all the houses of the Tories in that vicinity. General Caswell ordered such troops as could be raised in Duplin, Wayne and Onslow to fall in the rear of the retreating enemy, and to annoy them on their return to Wilmington. But without serious opposition Craig regained his fortifications. In this foray he carried into effect the terms of his proclamation. The Tories especially were jubilant. They burned houses, seized many negroes and destroyed many farms. In retaliation, the Whigs devastated the plantations of their Tory neighbors, and a reign of terror and relentless warfare was inaugurated. William Dickson, of Duplin, writing three years later, says: "The enemy stayed several days in Duplin—the first week in August, 1781. The Royalists gathered together very fast, and we were now reduced again to the utmost extremity. . . . Some men collected and formed a little flying camp, and moved near the enemy's lines, and made frequent sallies on their rear flanks. . . . The Tories in Duplin and other counties . . . become more insolent than ever; but Craig having returned to Wilmington, the Whigs again resumed their courage, and determined to be revenged on the Loyalists, our neighbors, or hazard all. Accordingly, we collected about eighty light horse and . . . marching straight into the neighborhood where the Tories were embodied, surprised them; they fled, our men pursued them, cut many of them to pieces, took several and put them to instant death."

August

Craig
returns to
Wilmington

Retaliation

Dickson's
Letters,
17-19

Tories
massacred

Battle of Elizabethtown

While Major Craig was harrying the Whigs of the easter
counties, Fanning and the other Tory leaders were devasta
ing the settlements on the Northwest Branch of the Cap
Fear. On August 11th Fanning, Slingsby, McNeil, an
Ray all met, with their respective forces, at Cross Creek
and together they scourged the country on either side o
the river, taking prisoners, ravaging plantations and desolat
ing the Whig settlements. Colonel Slingsby on the assassi
nation of Colvill had been appointed to command the Blade
Loyalists, and when Fanning, toward the last of August, re
turned from Wilmington, he found Slingsby with his com
mand at Elizabethtown in possession of many Whig pris
oners.

Colonels Brown, Owen, Robeson, Morehead, Irwine and
others who had been forced to abandon their homes by these
Tory bands, had been anxiously seeking aid and re-enforce
ments to return and drive them from Bladen. But the
people of Duplin and the neighboring counties were themselves harassed by troopers from Wilmington and the
Tories of their own section, so that assistance could not be
obtained. At length, however, they collected some one hundred and fifty Bladen men, who like themselves had been
expelled from their homes, and on the night of August 29th
they forded the river in the vicinity of Elizabethtown, and
just before daybreak made an attack on Slingsby's post
Although the garrison, consisting of four hundred, largely
outnumbered the small party of assailants, this night attack
resulted most fortunately. In the camp were many Whig
prisoners, and this circumstance probably contributed to induce the early flight of the garrison. The Whigs, by a sudden and violent onslaught, just before daybreak, threw the
surprised Tories into disorder; and as their principal officers
sought to marshal them, they soon fell before the unerring fire of the resolute assailants. Deprived of their leaders,
the Tories, in consternation, precipitately fled, many of them
leaping pell-mell into a deep ravine, which has since been
known as "Tories' Hole." "In this action," wrote Archibald Maclaine from Sampson Hall some three weeks later,
"we had only one man wounded; killed, wounded and taken

f the enemy, nineteen. Slingsby since dead of his wounds."
Colonel Godden fell dead in his tracks, as did most of the
ther officers of the garrison. Knowing that their small
umbers could not successfully resist the Tories in an open,
itched battle, the Whigs collected the arms and stores in
he camp and retired to the other side of the river, carrying
heir booty with them.

This battle of Elizabethtown,* as it was one of the most
aring in conception, was one of the most brilliant in the par-
isan warfare of that region, so remarkable for its many bold
ncounters. In its results it was equally important as it
vas successful. Not only were the Loyalists of Bladen dis-
eartened and suppressed, but the supply of arms and ammu-
ition obtained by the Whigs equipped them for larger
operations, and the Tories of that part of Bladen made
ead no more.

Governor Burke's plans

During all that heated season the efforts of the governor
vere untiring. In August he was mollifying the outraged
merchants of Edenton, whose commerce had been arrested
oy the impressment of their cargoes, and then at Halifax he
vas preparing to delay the progress of Cornwallis should
ae again turn southward, escaping from Virginia to reunite
vith Rawdon in South Carolina. Certain information had
come that in consequence of the arrival of the French fleet,
Cornwallis was moving from York to Jamestown, intending
to cross the James River, and hoping to pass unopposed
through North Carolina. Perhaps it was to facilitate that
possible movement that Craig had made his inroad into the
eastern counties somewhat earlier. Now Burke was busy
securing the boats on the lower Roanoke and embodying the
militia to obstruct the expected march of the enemy until

S. R.,
XXII,
578, 573-88

S. R., XV,
630

---

*There has been some confusion as to the date of this battle. It
was evidently after Major Craig had passed through Duplin; and
Fanning says in his Narrative that it was two days before the defeat
of Colonel Wade, which was on September 1st. Dickson says
Colonel Brown was in command of the attacking party (Dickson's
Letters, pp. 17 and 19. Maclaine's Letter, *Univ. Mag.*, 1855. Fanning's Narrative). Fanning, ignorant of the assault by the Whigs
under Brown and Robeson, ascribed the affair to the uprising of the
Whig prisoners Slingsby had in his camp.

1781
September

McRee's
Iredell, I,
542

S. R , XV,
595

The
situation

Lafayette and Steuben and Wayne might bring him to battl
On August 24th he ordered out the militia of all the cou
ties; those in the east to oppose Cornwallis; those of th
centre and west to suppress the Tories on the Cape Fea
The detachments from Granville and Wake were to assemb
at Wake Court House; from Caswell, Randolph, Chathan
and Orange, at Ramsey's Mills. It is said he was projectin
a great movement and intended to lead the militia himself.

The danger of Lord Cornwallis's situation being eviden
it was not doubted that he would endeavor to make good hi
retreat through the State. Governor Burke resolved to pu
the whole force of North Carolina in motion to act as th
occasion might require, either to oppose Cornwallis or t
attack Craig or to re-enforce General Greene so as to giv
him a decisive superiority. Realizing that everything de
pended upon prompt execution, he gave his personal exer
tions, influence and authority to accomplish his design, an
early in September moved toward Salisbury, where h
proposed to complete the dispositions he had directed at th
West.

He spent the early days of September in Granville an
then set out on his journey to Salisbury. On the way h
stopped a day or two at Hillsboro. He was constantly re
ceiving and answering appeals for military aid made b
the distressed inhabitants of the Cape Fear section. Bu
insurmountable obstacles and difficulties met him on ever
side. There was pressing need for the continental drafts t
be hurried to Greene's aid in South Carolina, and calls wer
made by General Steuben for both continentals and militi
to assist him in Virginia. General Rutherford and Colone
Isaacs, who had been conveyed as prisoners to Florida, ha
just returned from their confinement; Davidson was dead
Colonel Locke had marched a detachment to the southward
William Caswell in the east and General Butler at the wes
were the main reliance for active work. Butler early ir
September was gathering a force on the Haw and the Deep
to hold in check the formidable bands of Tories that wer
scourging that region. Next to Rutherford he was the
most efficient of the brigadiers.

1781

anning defeats Wade

On his return from Wilmington, with a fresh supply of
ammunition, Colonel Fanning after passing Slingsby at
Elizabethtown continued to McFall's Mills, about sixty
miles distant. There he received information of the disaster
to his friends at Elizabethtown, and he despatched ninety of
his men back to render assistance; but it was too late, the
Whigs had gathered their booty and had retired. He likewise received information that Colonel Wade was marching
to attack Colonel McNeil in the vicinity of Raft Swamp, and
he set out to re-enforce that Loyalist partisan, whom he joined
in the morning of September 1st. S. R.,
XXII,
205, 584

He found that Wade had crossed the bridge to the eastern
side of Drowning Creek, and had taken post on the highland
near a mile distant from the bridge, the intervening road
being a narrow causeway. Fanning directed McNeil to
turn down the swamp to cut off Wade's retreat in that direction, and, confident of victory before midday, began the
battle. At Wade's first fire eighteen horses of Fanning's men
were killed, but the Tories at once dismounted and made
a deadly assault, continuing to fire as they advanced; and
when they approached to within twenty-five yards of Wade's
line the Whigs broke and fled in the utmost confusion. Had
McNeil obeyed directions closely Wade's force would have
been entirely destroyed; but he did not take the position
assigned him, and the causeway and bridge were open for a
safe retreat. Fanning pursued some seven miles, and took
fifty-four prisoners, four of whom died that night, while
nineteen of the Whigs lay dead on the ground. He states
his own loss at only one killed and a few wounded. Having
taken two hundred and fifty horses, he distributed them
among those of his troops who were not mounted in the
action. The prisoners were paroled, except thirty, who were
sent to Wilmington; and then Fanning returned to McFall's
Mills, where he was joined by the detachment he had sent
to Slingsby's assistance. The misfortune that befell Wade's
force in this encounter had a dampening effect on the ardor
of the Whigs; but General Butler, Colonel Balfour, Colonel
Mebane, Colonel Collier and their associates redoubled their

1781

efforts to restore confidence and bring the militia togethe
to make head against the aggressive Loyalists.

The governor is captured

September

While Fanning was at Wilmington toward the end o
August, that bold partisan agreed with Craig that Gov
ernor Burke should be captured; and after defeating Wade
Fanning resolved to carry the design into execution
On September 9th he was joined by Colonel McDougal, o
Cumberland, with two hundred men, and Hector McNei
with a detachment from Bladen, and more than four hundred others had responded to his call for the Loyalists t
embody. He thus found himself at the head of several hundred active partisans. Marching directly toward Coxe's Mill
as if to attack General Butler, who was in that vicinity, he
suddenly changed his route, pushed on during September 11th and all the following night, and reached Hillsboro
in the early morning. His presence in that vicinity was not
at all suspected.

S. R.,
XXII, 207

Governor Burke on September 10th received information
of the movement of Fanning toward Butler's camp, and
sent a warning to the general to be on his guard. Little did
he suspect that the object of the enterprising partisan was
nothing less than his own capture. On the night of the 11th
no particular precautions were taken by the detachments at
Hillsboro. The little hamlet was rejoicing in the presence
of his Excellency and those who attended him, and its sense
of security was not at all disturbed by the movements of
the enemy. Hillsboro was in a measure the seat of government, and there were stored some cannon, supplies and provisions, and it was the headquarters of the continentals at
that time, a number of whom were congregated there preparing to march to the southward. Suddenly the next morning, a foggy, disagreeable morning, it was rudely awakened
from its peaceful repose. A clap of thunder from a clear
sky would have been no greater surprise. At seven o'clock
on the morning of the 12th Fanning's Tories entered the
town in three divisions. Several shots were fired from different houses upon the invaders, but without inflicting any

S. R., XVI,
12 *et seq.*

At Hillsboro

Sept. 12, 1781

1781
S. R.,
XXII, 207

erious loss. "We killed fifteen of the rebels," said Fanning, "and wounded twenty, and took upward of two hundred prisoners. Among them was the governor, his council, a party of continental colonels, captains and subalterns, and seventy-one continental soldiers taken out of a church. We proceeded to the jail and released thirty Loyalists and British soldiers, one of whom was to have been hanged on that day." He took the guns from the guard and put them in the hands of the prisoners, and turned the guard into the prison quarters. It was there that most of the Whigs were killed.

Battle of Cane Creek

Colonel Mebane made good his escape during the melée, and hastened to advise General Butler. Seeking to intercept Fanning on his return, Butler took post at John Alston's mill, near Lindsay's, on Cane Creek.

The Tory commander, having secured the object of his expedition, hastened away with his prisoners, thinking by celerity of movement to escape without molestation. By twelve o'clock he began his march. That night he reached the vicinity of Cane Creek, and the next morning the march was resumed. His force was composed chiefly of two bodies, one, several hundred Scotchmen, under McNeil and McDougal; the other, loyal inhabitants, not Scotch, under Fanning and militia officers. The Scotchmen were in the advance, while Fanning's Tories were in the rear with the prisoners. Butler had posted his men along the high banks on the south side of the stream, where the road coming from Caruthers, Old North State, I, 207-219 the ford skirted through a narrow piece of low ground. As McNeil advanced along this open roadway the Whigs from the brow of the hill delivered a deliberate fire with murderous effect. S. R., XXII, 207 The Scotchmen, utterly surprised, at once recoiled. Fanning hastened to send his prisoners off under a detachment so as to secure them at all events, and then crossed the stream higher up, and a desperate and bloody McRee's Iredell, I, 545 conflict ensued. By Fanning's attack from an unexpected quarter the Whigs were thrown into momentary confusion, but soon rallied, and nearly every Whig killed in the action fell at this time. The engagement lasted four hours, resulting in

1781
September

Fanning
disabled

Caruthers,
I, 214

S. R., XV,
651

Butler
surprised at
Brown
Marsh

Graham's
Graham,
365

Biog. Hist.
of N. C., V,
36

Martin
acting
governor

the retreat of the Whigs. The loss of the Tories was twenty-seven killed, sixty so badly wounded that they could not be moved, and thirty others wounded, who, however, continued with the main body. The loss of the Whigs, while great, was not so heavy. Several of the highest officers on both sides were killed. Among the slain were Colonel Lutterell and Major John Nalls; while on the Tory side John Rains, Edward Edwards, Colonel Dushee Shaw, and Colonel Hector McNeil, the elder, fell dead on the field. At the very end of the battle Colonel Fanning received a wound in his arm that shattered the bone and disabled him. It is related that Colonel Robert Mebane signalized himself by a bold and deliberate act of courage in the hottest of the battle. The ammunition of the Whigs was about expended, and he advanced along the line slowly distributing powder and ball to the men as needed, a target for every man in the Tory ranks. Fanning, being unable to travel, was conveyed to a secret place on Brush Creek, and for some weeks was disabled by his wounds. At his request, Colonel McDougal assumed command and hurried toward Wilmington, successfully delivering, on September 23d, the person of Governor Burke to Major Craig, who had advanced to Livingston Creek to receive his distinguished and valuable prisoner. Fearing to be overtaken, the Tories made such haste that although General Butler hotly pursued them even to the vicinity of Wilmington, it was without avail. However, he had a slight engagement at Hammond Creek, and he then took post at Brown Marsh, in Bladen County. There about October 1st the British marching from Wilmington in the night surprised him, attacking his camp with some success; and he retired toward Campbellton. And now for a time the State was left without a head, but Colonel Alexander Martin, as speaker of the senate, quickly assumed the reins of government and began an energetic administration.

Governor Burke was regarded as a political prisoner and not a prisoner of war. He was denied the right of exchange, and was held at Major Craig's suggestion as a hostage for the safety of Fanning, should that venturesome Tory fall into the hands of the Whigs.

The battle of Eutaw Springs

Greene had now received considerable re-enforcement from North Carolina. The continentals led by Colonel Ashe were formed into the First Battalion; those brought by Major Armstrong and General Sumner about the close of July became the Second Battalion; and toward the middle of August Major Blount arrived with such other continental drafts as had then been embodied and provided with arms. These became the Third Battalion. They were all thrown into a brigade commanded by General Sumner in person. There had also reached camp two battalions of North Carolina militia commanded by Colonel Malmedy, a French nobleman, trained to arms, who was appointed by the Assembly early in July for that purpose. Taking into account those North Carolinians who had enlisted with Colonel William Polk, of Mecklenburg, Colonel Wade Hampton, and Colonel Hill, and in other corps then with Greene, North Carolinians formed one-half of Greene's entire army.

Strengthened by these accessions, Greene resolved to take the initiative and put an end to his enforced inactivity. At last, at the very time when Fanning was compassing his great stroke against his enemies—the capture of the governor, Greene brought on the battle of Eutaw Springs on September 8th. As before, the militia was placed at the front; those from North Carolina, under Colonel Malmedy. The second line was composed of continentals, the North Carolinians now under Sumner on the right. The British army was drawn up in a single line. The militia advanced with alacrity, and the battle became warm. The fire ran from flank to flank, the American line still advancing; but after a fierce contest the militia, having fired seventeen rounds, eventually gave way, and Greene instantly ordered Sumner to fill the chasm. He came handsomely into action, and the battle grew hotter and hotter, the British being driven back to their first position. The American line persevered and advanced, and the fire became mutually destructive, when General Greene, determining to strike a conclusive blow, brought up his reserves, and all pressing forward with a shout, the battle raged with redoubled fury. The conquering Americans pressed the advantage they had gained, pur-

Lee's
Memoirs,
467

Lee's
Memoirs,
468

McRee's
Iredell, I,
553

1781

suing the foe, and possessed themselves of the British camp, which was yielded without a struggle. The British line gave way, and in the pursuit the Americans took three hundred prisoners and two pieces of artillery. The British general, however, later restored his broken line and advanced; and the action was renewed, the battle terminating in the British re-possessing their camp, taking two field pieces, the Americans in turn retreating. For three hours it was a fierce contest, every corps in each army bravely supporting each other. It was one of the bloodiest of the great conflicts in the course of the war. More than one-fifth of the British and one-fourth of the American army were killed and wounded. The British took sixty prisoners, while the Americans captured about five hundred. Of the six commandants of continental regiments, only Williams and Lee escaped unhurt.

The bloody battle

The gallantry of the North Carolinians

When Sumner moved forward, the battalions of Ashe, Armstrong and Blount so promptly filled the gap with such admirable and soldierly precision that Greene in a burst of enthusiasm exclaimed: "I was at a loss which most to admire, the gallantry of the officers or the good conduct of their men." These men had just been raised as new drafts, and were in part the very militia who under adverse circumstances had retired disorderly at Guilford Court House, and had been enrolled by the Council Extraordinary into the continental service for one year on that account. Now they were drilled and disciplined, themselves had bayonets and had been taught how to use them. They had officers trained and experienced, and they gave to the world an example of courage and endurance that reflected the highest credit on American soldiery. The loss of North Carolina was particularly heavy in that sanguinary battle. Of her continentals, three captains and one lieutenant were killed, and one captain and five lieutenants were wounded. Major James Rutherford, son of General Griffith Rutherford, was killed, and Captains Goodwin, Goodman, Porterfield, and Lieutenants Dillon and Polk, and Ensign Lamb were killed. The militia as well as the continentals suffered severely both in killed and wounded.

McRee's
Iredell, I,
554, 555
S. R., XV,
638

CHAPTER XXXIX

Martin's Administration, 1781-83

Rutherford marches to Wilmington

Although the abduction of the head of the commonwealth disorganized the administration and threw matters of state into disorder, it did not entirely disarrange the plans Governor Burke had set on foot to subdue the Tories and expel the British from Wilmington. In August General Rutherford, having returned from his captivity in Florida, resumed command in his district. His zeal had not been quenched by his misfortunes, but rather the remembrance of the sufferings he had endured inspired him with a firmer resolution. Conformably to the governor's programme, he quickly called out a part of his brigade, and asked volunteers to meet him at Little River, in Montgomery County, by September 15th, urging as many as possible to bring their horses and act as cavalry. Governor Burke was on his way to Salisbury in connection with this movement when he was captured, and doubtless this startling, shocking event caused some delay in the assembling of Rutherford's troops. A fortnight was passed in organizing the companies and in training the cavalry, the command of the horsemen being assigned to Colonel Robert Smith, assisted by Major Joseph Graham and Captain Simmons and others who had served under

1781
October

Biog. Hist.
N. C., III,
35

S. R.,
XXII, 209

Graham's
Graham,
363

Major Davie in previous operations. Rutherford, intent on victory, took every precaution to bring his raw levies up to a state of efficiency. On October 1st he broke camp and moved by slow marches toward Campbellton, being joined constantly by new accessions. At that time General Butler, who had shortly before suffered discomfiture at Brown Marsh, had withdrawn from below and was in the vicinity of Cross Creek; and later he united his force with the new levies. On reaching Rockfish on October 15th, Rutherford's cavalry had a slight engagement with a detachment of Tories, and from prisoners information was obtained that a body of six hundred Loyalists under Colonels Elrod, Ray, McNeil, and McDougal then lay in Raft Swamp. Fanning was still in hiding on Brush Creek, in the Deep River section, his wounds not yet healed; but he had so far regained his strength that somewhat earlier he despatched messengers to Wilmington for a supply of ammunition, which Major Craig sent him on October 13th, and he was preparing to take the field again. The corps of Tories then at Raft Swamp was, however, a part of those who had been with him in the expedition for the capture of the governor and their leaders were wily and astute. In order to expel them from their stronghold, Rutherford arranged his men in a single line, five steps apart, and beat through the swamp, but without avail. The game had flown. The vigilant Tories made good their escape.

Rutherford encamped at Brown Marsh, some fifteen miles south of Elizabethtown and thirty miles from Wilmington, as General Butler had done several weeks before. While there, Colonel Alexander Martin, who had succeeded to the office of governor, visited the camp, remaining several days with the soldiers, and enthusing them by his presence. General Rutherford now determined to divide his force, leaving on the south side of the river Colonel Robert Smith with the mounted infantry and dragoons, some three hundred in number; while with the infantry he himself should invest Wilmington on the north side. Carrying this plan into effect, on October 23d he crossed the Cape Fear at Waddell's plantation and proceeded into New Hanover. Colonel Smith at once drew near to Wilmington, had several brushes with parties of the enemy, and found that some fifty of the regulars occupied a brick house about two miles from the town, while a hundred Tories were encamped at Moore's plantation close by. He proceeded to attack the latter, and was so favored by fortune that twelve of them were killed outright and some thirty wounded; while on the part of the Whigs neither man nor horse was hurt. Finding the brick house* well garrisoned, protected by abattis, and the doors and windows barricaded, Colonel Smith despaired of reducing it without heavy loss, and after a fruitless attack retired beyond Livingston Creek.

When Rutherford reached the bridge over the Northeast River, ten miles north of Wilmington, he had a slight engagement with a British garrison established there, easily driving them off. He established his camp on the adjacent sand-hills, near the river swamp, and cut off all approach to the town from the northward. While investing Wilmington on the north and west Rutherford received information that Craig was obtaining provisions by boats from Lockwood's Folly.† He therefore directed Major Graham to make an excursion to cut off that source of supplies. Major Graham having proceeded in that direction, encamped after a cold, rainy day at Seven Creeks, not far from the South Carolina line. During the night his detachment was aroused by a full volley discharged into their camp by a band of Tories under Major Gainey, a noted partisan of that section. The enemy, however, fired too high, and only one of the men was wounded. Quickly the Whigs turned out and a night encounter ensued, but the attacking party successfully escaped into the neighboring swamp. The loss to the Whigs was Lieutenant Clark killed and three others wounded. Of the Tories, only one was killed.

On November 17th, while Rutherford was still hemming

---

*The brick house was still in existence in 1857, its walls indented by balls, within sight of the town, on the rise of the hill just beyond Brunswick River, on the right of the Fayetteville road leading over Eagles Island from Wilmington (McRee's Iredell, I, 562).

†Lockwood's Folly, some ten miles west of Southport, was the scene of a settlement made by a man named Lockwood many years before the permanent settlement of the Cape Fear. But he incurred the enmity of the Indians, and the settlement had to be abandoned.

1781

Oct. 19, 1781
Surrender of
Cornwallis

Wilmington
evacuated,
Nov. 18, 1781

The
rejoicing

McRee's
Iredell, I,
563

in the British garrison, Light Horse Harry Lee* arrived in camp on his way to General Greene, bringing the great news that on October 19th Cornwallis and his entire army had surrendered at Yorktown; and that General Wayne and a considerable number of troops were marching to the south to aid in bringing the war to a close. With joy and gladness the news was proclaimed, and Rutherford drew up his army and peal after peal of musketry resounded through the neighboring country as he heralded the glad tidings in a *"feu de joie."* On the same day came the information that Major Craig was evacuating Wilmington, and Rutherford moved down to Shaw's, four miles from the town. The following morning, November 18th, all the British troops boarded the vessels which were then falling down the river. While they were yet in sight General Rutherford and a part of his troops arrived and took possession. Thus swiftly following Cornwallis's surrender, the last British soldier was expelled from the soil of North Carolina and the dominion of the enemy was over.

It is impossible to describe the enthusiasm and happiness these events diffused among the Whig inhabitants of the State. It is narrated that when the news that Cornwallis was taken was announced to the congress, an officer of that body fell dead with joy. Throughout the State there was a season of great rejoicing. Even grave and reverend seignors gave a loose rein to hilarity. "One reason why I did not come to Edenton last term, as I promised," wrote Judge Williams to Iredell, "was that upon the confirmation of the news of the capture of Cornwallis we were all so elated that the time elapsed in frolicking." In the Cape Fear region, where there had been such a protracted reign of terror, the exaltation of the Whigs must have been unbounded.

*Early in October General Greene, hoping that after Cornwallis should have been taken Washington would despatch a force to his aid, sent Colonel Lee to Virginia to represent the situation of affairs in South Carolina. Washington assented to the suggestion and proposed that the French admiral should convey a detachment under Lafayette to the Cape Fear; but eventually the admiral found it inconvenient to delay his departure from the coast longer, and the plan was abandoned. General Wayne, however, marched some troops from Virginia to the south and operated in Georgia (Lee's Memoirs, p. 518).

But the distresses of the people of Wilmington were not quite over. They had grave complaints to make of the spoliation of their property at the hands of Rutherford's militia, who appear to have regarded that the town had been captured and was subject to plunder. The depredations were inexcusable. When requested, however, guards were placed by the general to protect the homes of the inhabitants. Such salt as the British had left was seized, and that being insufficient to load all the wagons, an additional supply was taken from the storehouses of the merchants, for that was a commodity of prime necessity, and was greatly needed at the west. When the army returned home, as it arrived at the place where a company was mustered out, the salt was distributed, one bushel to each man as his compensation, and it was of more real value than the auditor's certificates which they subsequently received for their services. ·General Rutherford, quiet being restored, marched his army to the interior, having first given orders to Major Graham to take all the dragoons and mounted infantry and effectually disperse such Tories as were still embodied along the South Carolina line.

1781
November

Graham's
Graham,
374

While the investment of Wilmington was in progress, Fanning, having received a supply of ammunition, toward the close of October gathered around him a hundred Tories and renewed his operations on Deep River. The Whigs, however, soon embodied and marched against him. On their approach he gave them battle, at first driving them off, but on their returning to the attack he himself retreated, and made good his escape. Fearing utter discomfiture if he maintained a large camp, he then separated his men into small parties, and these bands passed here and there through the Whig settlements, committing many depredations.

Fanning re-
news opera-
tions

The Assembly at Salem

The Assembly had adjourned to meet at Salem in November, and on the 8th of that month Colonel Martin, the acting governor, arrived, bringing with him two companies of soldiers. General Caswell and sixty-three members of the legislature also appeared, but twenty-eight members of the house and ten members of the senate were absent. Two

1781
November

Clewell's
Wachovia,
158
weeks passed in listless inaction. Then on the night of November 24th the alarming news was received that a large body of Tories was approaching with the purpose of seizing the person of Governor Martin. It was a cold November night, rain falling; and all night long the two companies were in anxious expectancy.

However, no attack was made; but the peril and the hopelessness of profiting by longer delay led to an adjournment, and on November 27th, without having transacted any business, the legislature adjourned to meet again on January 25th.

S. R.,
XXII, 211

Tories not
suppressed
Deep River was still the scene of great disturbance, for although Fanning had certain intelligence of Craig's departure, he and his lieutenants continued their depredations and murders, until at length on December 10th Colonel Elijah Isaacs, who had been taken at Camden and was Rutherford's companion at St. Augustine, "came down from the mountains" with a party of three hundred men and established his camp at Coxe's Mill, in the settlement where the Tory bands had their headquarters. For some weeks he remained there, but although his presence had some effect, he was unable to entirely suppress the roving bands, whose appetite for blood and plunder seemed insatiable. Nor, notwithstanding the departure of Craig's regulars and the operations of General Rutherford, were the Tories of the lower Cape Fear entirely subdued. In Bladen they still gave trouble. General Marion had made a truce with Colonel Gainey, a South Carolina Tory, in June, 1781, establishing a large truce-ground adjoining Anson and Bladen, in which the Tories could live in a state of neutrality, not to be interfered with, they undertaking to commit no depredations. Toward the end of January many coming from Gainey's truce-land did much mischief in Bladen, and Colonel Robeson wrote to Governor Martin that the worst of the Bladen Tories continued to stand out and would not surrender, "and I am of the opinion won't until they can be beaten or killed." Further, about a hundred of these irrepressible sympathizers of the British had gone over to the truce-land, and were a menace to that part of North Carolina. Colonel Robeson urged that the S. R.,
XXII, 608 State regiment should be stationed on Raft Swamp and

Ashpole, as a means of repressing them, but that regiment was not then fully organized, and was not sent.

Governor Martin's action

In order to hasten a restoration of normal conditions, Governor Martin, considering that an end ought to be put to all hostile operations now that there was no longer any British force to contend with, determined to enforce the civil law while offering the olive branch of peace.

He ordered that special terms of court should be held for the trial of the prisoners in jail, and such other criminals as might be captured; and on Christmas day he issued a proclamation pardoning all who had taken up arms against the State who should surrender before March 10th, on condition that they would enlist in the continental battalions for a term of twelve months; but such as had been guilty of murder, robbery or housebreaking were excepted from this offer.

Those inhabitants who had taken sides against their country were regarded by the administration as mere law-breakers and amenable to punishment.in the courts. On January 17th a session of the court was begun at Hillsboro. Four culprits were arraigned for high treason, and convicted; one of them, Thomas Dark, had figured as a captain in Fanning's band, and was as enterprising and nearly as dangerous as Fanning himself. From his cruelty to prisoners, in cutting, hacking and wounding them, he had acquired among his followers the name of "young Tarleton." At that term of the court Colonel Alfred Moore conducted the prosecutions on behalf of the State, and gained great reputation for legal acquirements. At Wilmington court others were tried and convicted; and at the March term of Salisbury court Samuel Bryan, John Hampton, and Nicholas White were likewise found guilty of high treason and condemned to death. These men were the leaders in the Tory movement in June, 1780, escaping Rutherford and joining Major McArthur with the British dragoons at Anson Court House, then occupied as a British post. The judges in a statement made to the governor said that Bryan and Hampton were generally considered as very

1782

S. R.,
XXII, 910

Tories tried
and
convicted

S. R., XVI,
268, 270

1782

honest men; and it did not appear to the court that they had on their march through the State committed any unusual violence, there being no proof that they had been guilty of any murder, or house-burning, or even plundering except for the use of the army. Governor Burke at once reprieved the prisoners until May 10th, when the Assembly might determine on the proper course to pursue with regard to them, or they might be exchanged; and as some of the people about Salisbury were threatening violence against these prisoners, he directed Major Lewis, who was in command there, to be very attentive and prevent any interference with them.

The return of Governor Burke

Toward the close of October, Governor Burke, who had been held a close prisoner at Wilmington, was conveyed to Charleston, and was at first confined in a fort on Sullivan's Island; but on November 6th he was paroled to James Island, then infested by desperate refugees, full of hatred toward those who had expelled them from their homes. They had been accustomed to murder Whigs without compunction, and Governor Burke was often threatened and considered himself every moment in danger of assassination. At length a party of revengeful Loyalists fired on a small group who were at the governor's quarters, killing one man on one side and wounding another standing on the other side of him. The next morning the governor wrote to General Leslie portraying the perils of his position and requesting a parole within the American lines, or that he might be removed to a place of safety. General Leslie took no notice of this reasonable request. Finding that he was to be sacrificed to the rage of the exasperated Tories, whenever his assassination could be effected, and that he was not held as a prisoner of war, Governor Burke determined that he was perfectly released from all obligations to remain on James Island. His situation involved mutual obligations to which General Leslie seemed indifferent. Having resolved to escape, he succeeded in doing so on January 16th. He reached General Greene's headquarters safely, and at once wrote to General Leslie asking to be exchanged, and saying that he would return on parole provided General Leslie would

S. R., XVI, 15 *et seq.*; 178, 181

Burke escapes, Jan. 16, 1782

1782

pledge himself to treat him not differently from the continental officers. General Leslie acceded to neither of these propositions. At the end of January the governor therefore returned to North Carolina.

On the day fixed for the meeting of the Assembly, Governor Martin and a number of members arrived at Salem; but a quorum did not attend. Five days later, January 30th, while the members were still lingering in hope of additional arrivals, Governor Burke unexpectedly appeared on the scene. At the election in March, Colonel Martin would cease to be the speaker of the senate and therefore it was argued he could not act as governor after that date. This consideration induced Governor Burke to assert his right to resume the administration; and the next day, January 31st, Colonel Martin delivered to him all the papers in his possession as governor, and gave him all the information possible about public matters. As no quorum appeared, the Assembly then adjourned.

Clewell's Wachovia, 159

He resumes the administration

Entering promptly on the administration, Governor Burke immediately undertook to remedy the great derangement of public affairs, and applied himself to the work of establishing peace in the State and making the people secure in their homes. His attention was first given to the condition of supplies and provisions for the army, and to the accounts of those in charge of public property. But he was not unmindful of the Tory bands. On February 5th he directed General Butler to send parties into the disaffected settlements, for Fanning was gaining strength and it was feared that he would seize Butler himself and other principal officers. To form the nucleus of an army Burke directed the state drafts to rendezvous immediately at Hillsboro. Indeed he was now all energy and acted with spirit. Having ordered Glaubeck to meet him at Halifax, and Glaubeck not attending, he at once put him under arrest; and similar action was taken as to others who were not prompt in observing his directions. Calling his council together, it was determined that the general plan the governor had in mind at the time of his capture should be now carried into effect, and a

January 31st

S R., XVI, 500

S. R., XVI, 181, 196, 540

strong and efficient force should be marched into the disaffected region and the Tories quieted or expelled from the State. And inasmuch as it was thought that the regulations restricting exportations had worked to the injury of the State, he by proclamation gave permission for the free and unlimited exportation of all commodities, and otherwise sought to re-establish commerce in its natural channels. Some of those who had been convicted of treason by the courts he allowed to be executed, but he pardoned others on condition that they should serve twelve months in the continental service, they being thereafter regarded as citizens of the State.

Major Bennet Crofton was the senior officer of the state battalion authorized by the last Assembly, among the other officers of that battalion being Captain George Farragut, a native of Minorca.* Governor Burke did not think Major Crofton equal to the command of the expedition which he had in mind, and so selected Major Hogg of the continentals for that duty. Major Crofton, however, refused to abdicate, and although the governor placed him under arrest, his disobedience of orders interfered so seriously with the collection of the drafts that the proposed expedition came to naught.

S. R., XVI,
560-562.

Fanning's brutality

To the proclamation of Governor Martin offering pardon, Fanning made some objections, and proposed other terms, saying that if his terms were not agreed on his sword would be continually unsheathed, as he was determined he would not leave one old offender alive that had injured any of his Majesty's friends. The general conduct of this relentless partisan at this time is well illustrated by some extracts from his diary: "We wounded two of them mortally and several slightly. . . . The day following we pursued them to Cumberland County, and on my way I burned Captain Coxe's house and his father's. On my return to Little River, . . . fell in with one of Captain Golson's men who had been very assiduous in assisting the rebels. I killed him . . . And I went with a design of burning Captain Golson's

*Afterward the father of Admiral David Glasgow Farragut.

1782
S. R.,
XXII, 213
Negotia-
tions with
Fanning,
Feb., 1782

house, which I did, and also two others. In my way I fell
in with a man, . . . and on observing me that day he attempted to escape, but I shot him." Pending negotiations,
however, Fanning remained more quiet; and eventually in
February he and his officers made a proposition for a truce
to last at least six months, and not to exceed twelve, similar
in terms to the truce granted to Colonel Gainey in South
Carolina by Marion the preceding June: the truce-land to
be from Cumberland County twenty miles north and south,
and thirty east and west, to be kept totally clear of light
horse. Every man who had been in arms in behalf of the
British Government was to have a right to withdraw himself into that district, and to have free trade with any port,
but not to carry arms.

After making his proposition for a truce, for a time Fanning remained passive; but having heard of the execution of
some of his men under the sentence of the court, he could
control himself no longer, and wrote to the governor: "I
understand that you have hung three of my men, and have a
captain and six men under sentence. If the effusion of blood
is not stopped and the lives of these men saved, I will retal-
iate, blood for blood, and tenfold for one; and there shall
never an officer or private of the rebel party escape that falls
into my hands hereafter, but they shall suffer the pain and
punishment of instant death. If my request is not granted
by March 8th, I shall fall upon the severest and most inhuman terms imaginable." March 8th came and his proposition for a truce-ground had not been agreed to; and, moreover, he had heard that Colonel Balfour, of Randolph
County, had said that there should be no "resting place for
a Tory's foot on the face of the earth." This excited his ire,
and, accepting the challenge, he wreaked a fearful vengeance.
Having equipped a party, he set out for Balfour's plantation.
Margaret Balfour, the colonel's sister, has preserved an account of that affair: "On March 10th," she wrote, "about
twenty-five armed ruffians came to the house with the intention to kill my brother. Tibbie and I endeavored to prevent
them, but it was all in vain. The wretches cut and bruised
us both a great deal, and dragged us from the dear man.
Then before our eyes the worthless, base, horrible Fan-

Balfour
killed,
Mar. 10, 1782

Biog. Hist.
N. C., II, 18

ning shot a bullet into his head, which soon put a period to the life of the best of men and most affectionate and dutiful husband, father, son and brother. The sight was so shocking that it is impossible for tongue to express anything like our feelings; but the barbarians, not in the least touched by our anguish, drove us out of the house, and took everything they could carry off, except the negroes, who

happened to be all from home at the time." Fanning, detailing the adventures of that raid, writes in his diary: "We also wounded another of his men. We then proceeded to their colonel's (Collier), belonging to the said county of Randolph. On our way we burned several rebels' houses, and catched several prisoners. . . . It was late before we got to Collier's. He made his escape, having received three balls through his shirt. But I took care to destroy the whole of his plantation. I then . . . came to one Captain John Bryan's. . . . I told him that if he would come out of the house, I would give him parole, which he refused. . . . With that I immediately ordered the house to be set on fire. . . . As soon as he saw the flames increasing, he called out to me, and desired me to spare his house for his wife's and children's sake, and he would walk out with his arms in his hands. I immediately answered him that if he walked out his house should be saved for his wife and children. When he came out he said, 'Here, damn you, here I am.' With that he received two balls through his body. He came out with his gun cocked and his sword at the same time. . . . I proceeded on to one Major Dugin's house, and destroyed all his property, and all the rebel officers' property for a distance of forty miles."

Such were some of the scenes of the barbarous warfare, waged even after the surrender of Cornwallis, in the Deep River region.

Progress of events

A new election occurred in March, and the Assembly convened at Hillsboro on April 13th. Conditions had greatly changed. The surrender of Cornwallis, the successes of Greene, and the departure of Craig, put a new aspect on the face of affairs. The end of the long struggle was now in sight. Indeed, although then unknown in America, Parliament had declared for peace. On February 27, 1782, it was moved and carried in the British House of Commons that the war ought to cease. The king, however, was not of that mind. He was still eager to press hostilities notwithstanding the apparent hopelessness of victory, and his answer to the address of the House was so unsatisfactory that on March 4th that body solemnly resolved that "it would consider as enemies to the king and to the country all who should advise a further prosecution of the war." This language could not be misunderstood. Sullenly and reluctantly George III yielded when he could contest no further. Lord North resigned, the ministry was changed, and Rockingham came into power on the principles of a restoration of peace. Unhappily he soon died, but his policy had prevailed, and now it was only a matter of negotiation. His attitude toward the colonies struggling for independence had been so humane and based on such high principles, that three years after his death North Carolina erected a memorial in his honor by creating a new county and bestowing upon it his name.

But while it seemed that the victory had been won, North Carolina did not abate her efforts to maintain an army in the field so long as any British troops remained on the borders of the State.

Indeed both General Washington and the Continental Congress apprehended from information received from Europe that King George was seeking to form foreign alliances, and would again prosecute an active campaign; and great pressure was made on the State to fill up her continental battalions. Moreover, General Greene gave alarming intelligence that a force consisting of four vessels was preparing in Charleston to plunder and destroy the town of Beaufort, where there was a large quantity of public and private stores, and then perhaps intending to enter the sound and take New Bern and Edenton. Apprehensions of this invasion led to renewed activity; and Governor Burke ordered General Caswell and General Jones each to raise five hundred men and protect the coast.

1782
March

S. R., XVI,
553

Besides, in March the Tories to the southward gave signs of renewed hostility. They embodied to the number of five hundred, and were very bold. They threatened to march on Wilmington, and it was supposed that their purpose was to plunder the inhabitants of that town. The Whigs quickly embodied, and Colonel Kenan hastened with the Duplin militia to the aid of Colonel Robeson, and together they confronted the hostile malcontents. It developed, however, that the object of the Tories was merely to possess themselves of some vessels in the river and make their escape from the country. Defeated in their purpose, they retired to the truce-ground in South Carolina, and this was the last of their formidable demonstrations in that quarter.

S. R., XVI,
558

Further in the interior Fanning continued his operations, and was irrepressible. Indeed his audacity was such a menace that Governor Burke deemed it necessary to have a party of both horse and foot at Hillsboro to secure the safety of the Assembly when it should meet. When the Assembly convened, it was therefore protected by a military force under the command of Major McCauley. Quietude reigned until April 30th, when a report gained credence that the fearful Fanning was approaching, and the members and the governor thought themselves in danger of being carried off into captivity. In the emergency the members took arms and bravely paraded; but happily the alarm was without foundation, and the session of the Assembly was not interrupted by any untoward event. Fanning's proposition for a truce land was rejected by the Assembly, and in May he determined to abandon the contest and leave the State. He married a girl on Deep River, whose father had been useful to him when in distress, and found a refuge in the truce land in South Carolina.*

Fanning
departs,
May, 1782

S. R., XVI,
534

As the election for governor was coming on, Colonel Martin began to court popularity with great avidity. Burke had gained popular favor the preceding year by the stand he had taken against the excesses of forage masters and those im-

*In June this redoubtable partisan leader, whose boldness, enterprise and resolution, had he been on the patriot side, would have ranked him high in American annals, made his way to Charleston, and later he passed some time in Florida, but eventually settled in Nova Scotia, where he lived to a green old age.

1782
April

pressing and seizing provisions for the army; now Martin sought popularity by a severe attitude toward disaffected persons. Governor Burke apparently desired a re-election. Major McCauley was a friend of the governor's, and on Sunday morning, April 14th, he visited the different rooms occupied by the members of the Assembly, and gathered from their conversation their views about the approaching election. He reported to the governor that Samuel Johnston, William Sharpe, and Colonel Martin, as well as himself, were much talked of; but that he was supposed to be still under parole, and that the way he had left Charleston was much debated. However, he said: "Your friends are very steadfast, and with a little of your assistance when a house is made I doubt not but to have success."

Burke desires a re-election

S. R., XVI, 593

But Burke saw that sentiment was against him. He ceased his efforts to secure the election, and when the Assembly was organized, in an elaborate address he referred to his financial embarrassment and the necessity he was under of devoting his attention exclusively to his private affairs. However, doubtless with the hope of softening the adverse opinion that prevailed because of his breach of his parole of honor, he laid before the Assembly all the correspondence relative to his flight from Charleston. Although some steadfast friends still adhered to him, he was not a candidate for the office. Samuel Johnston, William Sharpe, and John Williams were among those voted for, but Colonel Alexander Martin, who had so recently been the acting governor, won the prize.

Alexander Martin chosen

On being elected governor, Colonel Martin on April 22d made a spirited address to the Assembly, declaring that "British pride, long supported by riches and power, late drunk with the idea of conquest of these states, with reluctance at last must bend to superior force." But he called on the Assembly to maintain the army, and be prepared for any emergency. He recommended mercy to those citizens who having been in revolt had surrendered themselves to the justice of the State; and in particular he said: "The education of your youth demands your serious attention; savage manners are ever attendant on ignorance, which, without correction in time, will sap the foundation of civil govern-

S. R., XVI, 295-297

ment. Those states who want knowledge and wisdom in their councils have generally fallen a prey to their wiser neighbors, or require their guardianship. This will never be our fate while those seminaries of learning now established be further supported by your authority, and others created when they are wanting." Although not the father of the university, he broke ground in favor of education before the echoes of the war had even subsided.

New legislation

The Assembly now proposed to carry into effect its purpose of establishing a permanent seat of government near the centre of the State, and resolved that thereafter the legislature should always hold its sessions at Hillsboro; but a year later this action was annulled. The palace at New Bern was directed to be repaired, rented out, or sold.

When the superior courts were established in 1777, equity jurisdiction was denied to the judges on the ground that all issues of fact should be tried by a jury. Session after session the lawyers combated this view and urged that the judges should have the powers of a chancellor, and now at the end of the war this change was made, and the title of the courts became "Superior Courts of Law and Equity." A new judicial district was created, embracing Washington and Sullivan counties across the mountains, and Lincoln, Burke, and Wilkes on the eastern side; and while terms of court were to be held at Morganton, two sessions a year were directed to be held west of the mountains.

Courts of Equity

S. R., XXIV, 441

Because of the impoverished condition of the people in the Wilmington district, who had suffered so much from the depredations of the Loyalists, those inhabitants of that section who should be excused by the county commissioners were exempt from the payment of taxes; and the residents of Bladen were required under penalty of fine to carry with them their arms and six rounds of ammunition whenever they attended courts or elections or any public meeting, for the Tories were not yet entirely subdued in that region.

S. R., XXIV, 474

The Moravians had been fearful that their lands would be regarded as subject to the confiscation acts. In 1778 they applied for some alteration in the form of the oath of

The Moravians

allegiance, and that they might on the payment of the regular tax be exempt from military service.   At first their request was not favorably considered, and without some relief,
under the orders of the court of Surry County, they would
have been compelled to abandon their homes in sixty days
should they further delay taking the prescribed oath.
Mr. Hooper befriended them when all seemed dark in the
Assembly, and satisfactory legislation was obtained.   Still
doubts were entertained lest their lands were subject to the
confiscation act, and at this session all uncertainties were
finally removed.

The depreciation of the currency

The public accounts being in great confusion, the office of
Comptroller of Accounts was created, and Richard Caswell
undertook its duties.   The depreciation of currency was such
that while in December, 1778, the decline in value was only
5 per cent., a year later it was 30 per cent.   During the following year it went by leaps and bounds, until in December,
1780, it fell 200 per cent., and the next December its value
had declined 725 per cent.   No greater depreciation than
800 per cent. was, however, recognized by the Assembly.
The value of a Spanish milled dollar was fixed at 8 shillings,
making a shilling in North Carolina 12½ cts.   A tax was
laid by the Assembly of one penny on the pound of value
of all property embracing land and negroes; but two-thirds
of this tax could be paid in commodities.   Quakers and other
non-combatants were, however, subjected, as they had been
during the war, to a threefold taxation.   Inasmuch as there
were many worthy citizens of the State still confined on
prison ships and suffering the most cruel hardships, the
legislature directed the governor to send Samuel Bryan and
others under sentence of death to be exchanged for militia
officers of similar rank, and that he should cause a sufficient
number of Tories to be sent on to General Greene's camp
to be exchanged for the citizens held by the British, sending also the wives and families of the Tories; and the governor was directed to continue to do this from time to time.
And if General Leslie would not carry out in good faith

this proposition, the treason laws of the State were to be rigidly enforced.

The Assembly addressed itself to giving effect to its confiscation acts, and appointed commissioners to sell the property of those who had adhered to the enemies of the State. Provision, however, was made for unfortunate families, and where a wife or widow or children of a Tory remained in the State, the county courts were directed to set aside so much property, both real and personal, as would provide them adequate support.

The Continental Line

On March 30th a board of officers of the North Carolina line had held a meeting to arrange the continental officers of the State to command the four continental battalions which had been provided for. Thomas Clark was assigned to command the First Battalion; Colonel John Patten the Second; Lieutenant-Colonel Selby Harney the Third, and Lieutenant-Colonel Archibald Lytle the Fourth. There were ninety-six officers embraced in this arrangement. Some, Colonel James Armstrong, Colonel James Thackston, and Captain Francis Childs, were allowed to retire on half pay. The Assembly approved of this arrangement, and the officers took the commands assigned them.

While under the exchange many officers as well as men were returned to duty, yet as late as November Colonel Clark, Major Nelson, six captains and eight lieutenants of the North Carolina line were still unexchanged, although paroled.

The Assembly was not indifferent to the hardships endured by the soldiers, and took measures for their relief; while in order to manifest its appreciation of their patriotic service, it granted to every soldier who should continue in the ranks until the end of the war 640 acres of land, and to every officer a larger quantity according to his rank, a colonel receiving 7200 acres; a brigadier, 12,000 acres, while to General Greene was given 25,000 acres. This land was set aside for the soldiers in the wilds beyond the mountains, now in the State of Tennessee.

The Indians had long been quiet, and **General Greene**

1782

on taking command of the Southern army had made a particular treaty with them to preserve their neutrality, but now, although the British cause no longer wore a hopeful outlook, they were suddenly inflamed to renew hostilities. They were active in Georgia and in South Carolina, and against the inhabitants of Washington County, where, under the direction of the legislature, lands intended for the soldiers were to be located. In July Martin Armstrong wrote: "The Indians are very troublesome in this side of our new county." Colonel Crawford with four hundred and eighty men was totally defeated by them, aided by the British Tories.

S. R., XVI, 627

A year later, in August, 1783, Governor Martin, understanding that there were still some Cherokee prisoners held in Rutherford and Lincoln counties, directed General McDowell to have them given up to Colonel Joseph Martin, in command across the mountains, that he might send them to the Indian nation in exchange for the white prisoners the Indians held.

Nor were the Tories pacified; even in October they made a demonstration in Bladen. When the judges issued warrants against some rioters in that county they threatened to disturb the court, and Governor Martin felt that the menace was so great as to require General Lillington to protect the court with his militia.

After the battle of Eutaw, on September 8th, the British commander, Colonel Stuart, took post at Monk's Corner, and Greene on the high hills of the Santee. Lord Rawdon, having previously sailed for Europe, General Leslie, then serving in Virginia, was appointed by Cornwallis to command in the Carolinas, and he soon made his headquarters at Charleston. Although there were some slight conflicts, a period of inactivity set in between the contending armies. Greene took post at Camp Round O, on the Edisto, about forty miles from Charleston, hemming the British in to the coast. In the spring of 1782 General Leslie proposed a cessation of hostilities, which, however, was not agreed to. Not supplied with provisions from abroad, Leslie was forced, in order to relieve the distress of his troops, to forage on the country as far as he could make incursions, but his field of operations was so restricted that only an insufficient supply could be ob-

General Leslie remains at Charleston 1782

1782

tained. His troops suffered severely, and so did those in the Whig camp.

The deplorable condition of the army

Indeed, the condition of the army in South Carolina was deplorable. No clothing or provisions could be obtained from Virginia or Maryland, while South Carolina was ut-

S. R., XVI, 518, 634, 645, 687

terly unable to supply their necessities. North Carolina was their only resource. Colonel Dixon reported to General Sumner in February that "some of our officers are so bare of clothes that they cannot mount guard or keep company with decency." On May 15th Colonel Murfree wrote that the men were almost naked, and a great many were returned not fit for duty for want of clothes. Officers felt compelled to resign because they could get no pay and could not live. The legislature having taken steps to keep the ranks of the battalions filled, all during the year drafts were being collected and sent forward. General Greene had urgently requested that at least three thousand head of cattle should be sent to camp, together with some rum and salt, for the army was in great distress for the want of these neces- saries. And in August Governor Martin wrote to General Bryan, the superintendent-commissary for the New Bern district, that General Greene is still in great distress for beef. "Must General Greene," said he, "retreat before a conquered and despairing enemy, abandon all his conquest, give up

S. R., XVI, 703

South Carolina for the want of food, and return to this State? . . . Rather than he should be compelled to this alter- native, which would disgrace the State to eternity, I would through all opposition drive to him everything in the shape of a cow or steer" to be found in North Carolina. Truly, the situation of the army at that period was most distressing ; not merely were the troops ragged and without decent cloth- ing, but subsistence was scarce, and their deprivations exces- sive and heartrending.

All during the summer the opposing forces in South Carolina watched each other, waiting for some development. At length, in August, General Leslie announced in general orders his intention of evacuating Charleston. To stop the further effusion of blood, he addressed General Greene, ask- ing permission to purchase from the country such supplies as might be furnished him until he should be ready to sail. As desirable as this practical suspension of hostilities was for the advantage of the naked and destitute American soldiers, General Greene felt constrained to refuse the accommodation. How deplorable was the situation of the army was portrayed by General Greene in a report: "For upward of two months more than one-third of our army was naked, with nothing but a breech-cloth about them, and never came out of their tents. . . . Our condition was little better in the articles of provision." In September the preparations for evacuation were apparent; but autumn passed without action, and it was not until December 14th that the British, having embarked, took their departure. General Greene with his continentals at once occupied the city, which the next day was restored to the civil authorities.

1782

Lee's
Memoirs,
572

Charleston
evacuated

Dec. 14,
1782

The number of troops furnished by North Carolina

It is impossible to ascertain with entire accuracy the number of North Carolinians who were in the field during the war for independence. There were originally six battalions of continentals of 500 men each, and later the battalions of Colonel Hogun, of Williams, and Sheppard marched to the north, so that 4500 continentals might be computed for these. There was Vance's artillery company and Dickinson and Ashe's cavalry, and Phifer's cavalry, numbering about 400. In the spring of 1779 there was a battalion of continentals with Lincoln and in the fall General Sumner had a brigade of new continentals in South Carolina, altogether 1500. All these disappeared on the surrender of Lincoln. Major Eaton's battalion in the early summer of 1781 numbered about 400; Sumner's brigade at Eutaw Springs, 1000. The returns of this brigade in April, 1782, showed 1000 on the roll. The Assembly of April, 1782, directed that every thirtieth man in the State should be drafted for eighteen months to fill up this brigade, and these drafts were being sent forward in May and later. They were calculated to raise 2000 men, and even in September selections from the militia were being made to complete these drafts, so that probably 1000 new men became continentals after the summer of 1782. These figures aggregate 8800 continentals. On the reorganization, in 1781, the new battalions were numbered the First, Second, Third, and Fourth, the former ones having been obliterated.

There were originally 3000 six-months' minute men; 500 militia marched in the "Snow campaign"; 1500 with Rutherford against the Cherokees. Colonel Williams had 300 with the Virginia troops at the same time. There were probably 3000 militia besides minute men and continentals on the Cape Fear in the Moore's Creek campaign, and in May, when the British fleet was in the harbor; for it is stated that the number of troops in arms at that time was 9400. In the fall of 1776 General Allen Jones's brigade was in South Carolina, numbering, say, 600. General Rutherford carried 700 and Ashe 2000 to the aid of General Lincoln; to take their place, Butler carried 700 to Lincoln in June. Early in 1780 Lillington carried, say, 800 to Charleston, where Colonel Lytle already had a detachment of two regiments, numbering perhaps 400. A thousand North Carolina militia were surrendered by Lincoln. General William Caswell marched to the relief of Charleston with 800. At Camden, under Richard Caswell, there were 1600. In June General Rutherford had his brigade of, say, 800 and Davie, say, 200. The First Brigade commanded by Sumner, three regiments, 800; Butler's brigade, assigned to Sumner, 800; Harrington, 450; the North Carolina detachments at King's Mountain, 1000; General Gregory, in defence of the Albemarle section, 600; with Morgan at Cowpens, 300; Davidson's brigade, after his death commanded by Pickens, 700; Lillington, near Wilmington, 600; Eaton's brigade and Butler's, at Guilford Court House, 1600; Colonel Kenan, 400; General Caswell, 150; General Lillington, in August, 600; Colonel Hawkins's cavalry, 150; Wade, Brown, Robeson, 800; Malmedy, at Eutaw Springs, 600; Rutherford, Butler, Smith, and Graham, in October, 1200; Colonel Isaacs, 300; State troops, 500; sailors and companies stationed at the forts on the coast, 600. These aggregate 27,800. Certainly there were many duplications; how many is a mere matter of conjecture. It is to be remembered that the inhabitants of the State were divided into militia companies, and these companies into five classes, and when a draft of militia was made for three months, the regular term, one of these classes only was embraced in the draft, until all the five drafts, being all the militia, had been called out into service, so that the error of duplication is largely minimized. Indeed, first and last it would seem that every man, not a Tory, in the State capable of bearing arms was at one time or another called into active service, although for only one tour of duty. It has been computed that there were 22,000 different names on the muster rolls of the North Carolina troops. Probably that is a correct statement. Were there no duplications the number would be 36,600.

Except in the territory where the Highlanders and the Regulators resided, and in Tryon County, there was but little disaffection. In Bladen fifteen companies of the militia out of eighteen were inclined to the British; in Cumberland and Anson, at least one-half of the people were disaffected, and similarly in the Deep River country. Elsewhere the proportion was not near so great.

On January 29, 1783, Captain Eve brought the ship *Dawes,* bound from Jamaica to New York, which was still held by the British, into Wilmington. Lord Charles Montague, lieutenant-colonel of a British regiment, Captain Montague, and four or five other British officers had taken passage for New York. When well at sea, Captain Eve informed these officers that they must consider themselves his prisoners, and he brought them into the Cape Fear and delivered them to General Lillington. It was at once reported to Governor Martin that the regiment raised for Lord Charles Montague was chiefly composed of captive continentals taken at Charleston, who were compelled to enlist into the British service, under Montague's own direction, on the pain of severe penalties. For this conduct Governor Martin thought that Montague should suffer some punishment. The other officers were paroled as prisoners, but allowed to go abroad, while his Lordship was paroled only to North Carolina. There was some delay in communicating these circumstances to General Greene, and before he was informed of Governor Martin's purpose to deal with his Lordship differently from other prisoners, General Greene paroled him with permission to go to New York. On inquiry General Greene found that Lord Charles did enlist

The capture of Lord Montague S. R., XVI, 741

American soldiers into the British service, but it was said that it was by the voluntary act of the prisoners themselves. The punishment in contemplation by the North Carolina authorities was thus defeated, as the parole by General Greene could not be annulled.

The condition in 1783

The eight years that had elapsed since the first provincial convention assembled in August, 1774, had brought many changes. Harvey had died while the colonists were just entering on the struggle to maintain their rights as British subjects, and year by year the leaders who had set in motion the ball of revolution mourned the loss of some of their number. James Moore, Francis Nash, James Hogun, Harnett, Hewes, Buncombe, Davidson, John Ashe, Gideon Lamb and many of their associates had perished without beholding the glorious consummation of their patriotic desires and unselfish sacrifices. It is to be observed that among the North Carolinians who had enrolled themselves under the banner of the American cause there was not a single desertion during the whole course of the conflict. The contest had been doubtful. It brought many vicissitudes and much suffering. The state as well as the continental currency had ceased to have value. Many families had been utterly impoverished. Misery and desolation were diffused through innumerable households. Civil war and carnage had raged from Surry to Brunswick. Murder and pillage had stalked through a large section of the State, and families expelled from their homes had sought asylums in distant parts, and were too impoverished to return. Many mothers and children were bereft of their last support, their sacrifices in the cause of independence being irreparable. In the desolated region of the Cape Fear even the wealthiest of the patriots were ruined by the ravages of the war. They had cheerfully laid their all on the altar of their country. Hard had been the conflict, but in the darkest hours the brave hearts of the North Carolina patriots became still more courageous, and in their adversity they bore their sufferings with resolution and fortitude. At length the storm-clouds passed away, the sky was no longer obscured, and hope gave place to assurance. The ardent longing became a joyful realization.

On September 21, 1782, Lord Shelburne being then at the head of the administration, the King of Great Britain acknowledged the independence of the American States, and authorized Oswald, the British commissioner at Paris, to make a treaty of peace, which, however, was not to be operative until agreed to by France also. On November 30, 1782, preliminary articles were drawn up requiring a cessation of hostilities, and on January 20th France gave her assent. The war was over. Independence had been won. The long and arduous struggle had closed, and everywhere, in the household of every patriot, there was great rejoicing. But in the bosoms of many there burned a strong resentment against the detested Tories.

S. R., XVI, 752

At the next session of the Assembly Governor Martin in his opening address said: "With impatience I hasten to communicate the most important intelligence that has yet arrived in the American Continent," the acknowledgment by Great Britain of the independence of the American States and the appointment of commissioners to conclude a treaty of peace, which was signed on January 20th. He continued: "Nothing now remains but to enjoy the fruits of uninterrupted constitutional freedom, the more sweet and precious as the tree was planted by Virtue, raised by Toil and nurtured by the Blood of Heroes. To you, gentlemen, the representatives of this free, sovereign, and independent State, belongs the task, that in sheathing the sword, you soften the horrors and repair those ravages which war has made, with a skilful hand, and thereby heal the wounds of your bleeding country." He recommended an act of pardon and oblivion, with some exceptions, and said: "Let the laws henceforth be our sovereign; when stamped with prudence and wisdom, let them be riveted and held sacred next to those of Deity. . . . Happy will be the people, and happy the administration when all concerned . . . contribute to this great end."

Governor Martin's address, April 18, 1783

Preliminary Treaty, Jan. 20, 1783

S. R , XIX, 240

Governor Martin's re-election was strenuously contested by Governor Richard Caswell, but without avail, Martin's majority being 17. There were those who never forgave

1783
April
Caswell for withdrawing from the service of the State in the dark hours after the battle of Camden, although he continued to wield a great influence, and later again enjoyed the gratification of directing the affairs of the commonwealth.

The
sovereign
State
Although the last British soldier had departed from the southern states, General Greene continued to hold the remnant of his army together at Charleston. The regiments,
S. R., XVI,
725
however, constantly grew smaller by the expirations of enlistments. By January 5, 1783, all the North Carolina battalions except one had been sent home on furlough and finally on April 23d Greene was instructed to furlough his troops, and the last of the North Carolina continentals relieved from further service, returned to their homes.

Definitive
Treaty,
Sept., 1783
After much delay, in September, 1783, the Definitive Treaty of Peace was signed. By it Great Britain formally acknowledged the United States, naming North Carolina and each of her sister States separately and particularly, to be "free, sovereign, and independent States," and relinquished all claims to any right in them. And thus North Carolina entered on her career as a separate, distinct, and sovereign State.

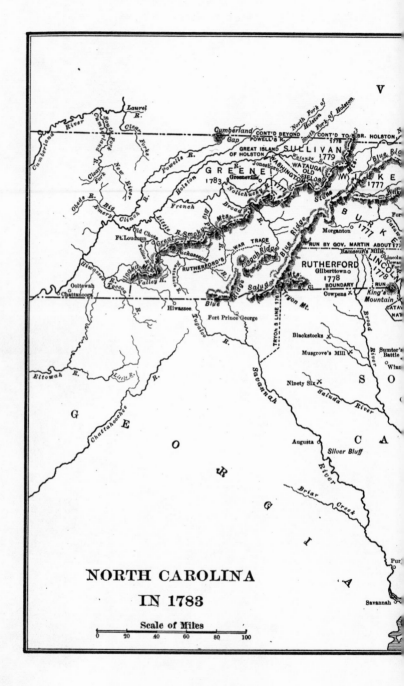

NORTH CAROLINA
IN 1783

Scale of Miles

0   20   40   60   80   100

INDEX

Abercromby, James, pp. 294, 295.
Accounts, Public, p. 354.
Admiral's Island, p. 30.
Admiralty, Courts of, p. 573.
African Company, p. 84.
Almance River, Battle at, p. 364ff, 370ff.
Albemarle, Duke of, p. 52.
Death, p. 94.
Albemarle, p. 69.
Settlement, p. 88; Proprietary government, p. 88ff, pp. 94, 95; Beginnings of government, p. 90; Agreement with Maryland and Virginia, pp. 92, 93; Influence of Virginia, pp. 96, 97; Becomes Palatine, pp. 104, 105; County government and activities, p. 112ff; Culpepper's Rebellion —Free government, p. 126ff; Extent in 1677, p. 130ff; Becomes North Carolina, p. 141; Boundary dispute with Virginia, p. 148; Complaints against changes.—Life in colony, pp. 149, 150ff.
Albemarle County, Quarrel for seat of Assembly, p. 268ff.
Conditions, p. 154ff.
Albemarle Governors under proprietary Government, List, p. 52.
Albemarle River, p. 66.
Name given, p. 69.
Alexander, Abraham, p. 455.
Alexander, Hezekiah, p. 530.
Alexander, John McKnitt, Mecklenburg resolves, p. 437.
Provincial Congress, p. 475.
Algonquin Indians, p. 85.
Allen, Eleazar, p. 54.
Receiver of rents, p. 251; Commissioner on boundary settlement, p. 255; Deserts Johnston, p. 258; Treasurer—Death, p. 276.
Amadas, Philip, Account of voyage to America, p. 1ff.
Voyage to America, pp. 25, 26.
Anne, Queen, Attitude towards slavery, p. 84.

Anson County, p. 267.
Actions of regulators, p. 342; Attitude toward King—Clashing of interests, p. 465.
Archdale, John, pp. 53, 138ff.
Governor, p. 146ff.
Armada, p. 44.
Armstrong, p. 475.
Armstrong, Col. Martin, pp. 633, 635.
Armstrong, Maj., To unite with Greene, p. 657; Battle of Eutaw Springs, pp. 697, 698.
Army, p. 523; p. 590.
Conditions, 1781, pp. 654, 655; Condition, 1782, p. 718; North Carolinas quota, p. 719ff.
Army, Continental, p. 462; p. 481.
Articles of Confederation, p. 647.
Ashe, John Baptista, pp. 53, 54.
Conflict with Burrington, p. 234; Imprisonment, p. 236; Speaker of Assembly, p. 302; Speaker of Assembly, p. 307; Rebellion against Stamp Act, p. 321; Treasurer, p. 331; General—Treasurer, pp. 365, 366; To be exchanged, pp. 370, 371; Description, p. 378; Colonel of militia, p. 430; Provincial Congress, p. 475; Recruiting, p. 485; At Cross Creek, p. 500; At Rockfish Creek, p. 502; General, p. 524; Work on Constitution, p. 564; Treasurer, p. 569; Major-general, pp. 594-595; Battle at Briar Creek, p. 596ff; Treasurer, p. 604; Death, p. 670.
Ashe, Samuel, p. 378.
Actions against governor at Fort Johnston, pp. 468, 469; Provincial Congress, p. 475; Committee to frame constitution, p. 527; Chosen judge, p. 570; Treasurer, p. 574; Judge, p. 584; On spirit of people, p. 592; Battle of Eutaw Springs, pp. 697, 698.
Ashley, Lord Anthony, p. 51.
Fundamental constitutions, p. 98.
Asiento, p. 84; p. 260.
Assembly, p. 107.

I

INDEX

Brunswick, Taken by Spaniards, p. 271.

Brunswick County, Adopts new Hanover Association, p. 466.

Bryan, William, p. 475.
General, p. 524; Briar Creek Battle, p. 596.

Bryan Mills, Skirmish at. p. 688.

Buford, Col., pp. 611, 612.

Buncombe, Edward, p. 523.

Burke, Dr., pp. 475, 477.
Committee to frame Constitution, p. 527; Elected to Continental Congress, p. 560; One of Framers of Constitution, p. 564; Delegate to Continental Congress, p. 575; Loses re-election for Continental Congress—Action at Philadelphia—Elected again, p. 589; Delegate to Continental Congress, p. 603; Efforts to relieve distress, p. 646; Threats of retaliation of atrocities, p. 673; Governor, p. 677ff; Capture, pp. 694, 695; Escape from James Island, p. 706; Resumes administration as governor, p. 707ff; Desires re-election, p. 713.

Burke County, p. 573.

Burrington, George, p. 53.
Governor—Administration, p. 208ff; Denunciation of Everard, p. 218; Quarrels with Assembly, p. 226ff; Enemies in power, pp. 248, 249.

Bush Assembly, p. 259.

Bute County, Name obliterated, p. 588; Butler, Gen. John, Against Tories, pp. 601, 602.
Battle of Stono, pp. 604, 605; Union of forces—Battle of Camden, p. 619; At McGowan's Creek, p. 630; Unite with Lillington, p. 656; To unite with Greene, p. 657; Battle of Guilford's Court House, p. 658ff; On Deep River, p. 662; Patroling toward enemy lines, pp. 678, 679; Battle of Cane Creek, pp. 695, 696; Joins Rutherford, p. 700.

Butler, William, Regulator, pp. 336, 338ff.
Indicted, p. 344; Outlaw, p. 374;

Butler, William, Regulator.
Pardon, p. 397; Letter from James Hunter, pp. 404, 405.

Byrd, Valentine, pp. 115, 118, 122.

Caldwell, David, Sermon for Revolution, pp. 478, 479.

Camden, p. 605.
Abandoned by British, pp. 670, 671.

Camden, Battle of, p. 619ff.

Camden County, p. 573.

Campbell, John, p. 54; Speaker of Assembly, p. 287.

Campbell, Col. William, Battle of King's Mountains, pp. 633, 634, 636.
To unite with Greene, p. 657.

Campbellton, p. 407.

Cane Creek, Battle of, p. 695ff.

Cape Fear, Conditions in 1664-1665, pp. 76, 77.
Abandoned by British, p. 554; Civil War, p. 681ff.

Cape Fear Region, Rebellion, p. 319ff.

Cape Fear River Explorat'ons, pp. 63, 64.
Settlement, p. 72ff; Colony abandoned, p. 80ff; Explored by Burrington, p. 209; Settlement of the region, p. 213; Preparations for defence, p. 533.

Carolina, The, pp. 124, 126.

Carolina Province, p. 50.

Carolina Sound, Settlement, p. 58ff.

Cartagena, p. 261.

Carteret, Sir George (see also Granville), pp. 51, 52.

Carteret, John, Lord, p. 52.

Carteret, Peter, p. 52.
Governor of Albemarle, p. 105.
Administration, resignation, pp. 110, 111.

Carteret Precinct, p. 207.

Cary, Thomas, p. 53.
Governor, p. 160; Suspended, p. 163; President of Council, p. 165; Dispute with Glover—Head of Government, pp. 166, 167; Rebellion, p. 169ff; Impeachment — Freedom — Contest with Hyde, pp. 173, 174ff.

Cary Rebellion, p. 169ff.

Cary's Usurpation, p. 168.

3

INDEX

Caswell, Richard, p. 54.
Speaker of Assembly. p. 357; Delegate to Continental Congress, p. 422; Delegate to 2nd Congress, p. 435; Provincial Congress, pp. 475 476, 477; Opposes Loyalists, p. 499; At Moore's Creek Bridge, pp. 503, 504; Report to Harnett, p. 510; Influence in Continental Congress, p. 542; President of Congress, p. 559; Influence in framing Constitution, p. 564; Governor, pp. 568, 569; Administration as Governor, p. 570ff; Administration, p. 584ff; Re-elected Governor, p. 588; End of exelutive. —Commander-in-chief of Militia, p. 613; Battle of Camden.—Flight from, p. 620; Member Council extraordinary—Command of militia, p. 642; Offices, pp. 644, 645; Comptroller of Accounts, p. 715.

Caswell, William, General, pp. 603, 611.
Unites with Lillington, p. 656; Skirmish with Craig, p. 687.

Caswell County, p. 573.

Catawba Indians, p. 86.

Catawba Massacre, p. 548.

Catchmaid, George, pp. 53, 60, 65, 66.

Cathay, William, p. 604.

Cedar Springs, Battle of, p. 618.

Charles II, Charters in America, p. 51. 51.

Charleston, Founding of present city, p. 83.
Lee stationed—Fort Moultrie attacked, p. 573; Falls to British, p. 608ff; Held by Gen. Leslie p. 717; Evacuated, p. 719.

Charlestown, Name given, p. 75.
Conditions in 1664-1665, pp. 76, 77; Desertion by colonists, p. 81.

Charlotte, Schools, pp. 391, 407.
Mecklenburg resolves, p. 437; Liberty Hall, p. 585; Cornwallis occupies, p. 629ff; Held by Tarleton, p. 630; Abandoned by Cornwallis, p. 637.

Chatham County, p. 359.

Cherokee Indians, p. 86.
Influence towards joining Revolu-

Cherokee Indians.
tion, p. 487ff; Begin warfare, p. 548; Boundary settlement, p. 571.

Cherokee Line, p. 332.

Chief Justices, List of, p. 54.

Christian, Col., pp. 550, 552ff.

Church, State, p. 381ff.

Church of England, Established in colony, pp. 196ff, 303, 382.

Citizenship, p. 561.

Civil War of Whigs and Tories, pp. 682, 683, 686ff.

Clapp's Mill, Skirmish at, p. 658.

Clarendon, Earl of, Lord Proprietor, p. 68; Banishment, p. 94.

Clarendon County, p. 75.
Assembly in 1665, p. 78ff; Desertion by colonists, p. 81.

Clark, Colonel Thomas, pp. 590, 591, 716.

Clarke, Col., Attack at Garden Hill, p. 632.

Cleveland, Col., pp. 633, 634, 636.

Clinton, General, Arrives in the Chesapeake, p. 531.
Actions in Virginia, p. 532; Proclamation—Actions in North Carolina, pp. 533, 534, 535; Attack on Fort Moultrie, p. 538ff; Capture of Charleston, p. 608ff; Rule in South Carolina, p. 637.

Cogdell, Richard, p. 604.

Colleton, Sir John, Death, pp. 9, 51.
Grant in Carolina, pp. 67, 68.

Colleton, Sir Peter, pp. 52, 74.

Colleton Island, p. 66.

Collett, Capt., p. 468.

Colony, Lost, pp. 9. 10, 14, 15.
Attempts to find, p. 18; Probable fate (Lawson), pp. 19, 20, 21, 43, 45, 47, 48, 49.

Colvill, McLaurin (or Maturin), Tory leader, p. 682.

Concessions, p. 91.

Confederation, Articles of. p. 647.

Confiscation Act. p. 607ff.

Congaree Indians, p. 86.

Congress, Continental, pp. 421, 422, 424, 425.
Declares Independence, p. 540ff.

Congress, Provincial, 1775, pp. 473ff, 479ff, 513.

Conscience, Freedom of, pp. 92, 103.

4

INDEX

INDEX

Jenkins, John, p. 53.
Land in Albemarle, p. 60; Buys land, pp. 65, 66; Deputy governor of Albemarle, p. 111; Governor of Albemarle, p. 115; Conflict with Miller, p. 118ff; Deposed, p. 119; Governor of Albemarle, p. 135.

Johnson, Charles, Delegate to Continental Congress, p. 678.

Johnson, Nathaniel, Governor, p. 157.

Johnston, Gabriel, p. 53.
Governor—Administration, p. 247ff.

Johnston, John, p. 527.

Johnston, Samuel, Riot Act, p. 360.
Calls convention, p. 468; President of Provincial Congress, p. 474; Leader in Congress, p. 475; President Provincial Congress, p. 516; Committee to frame Constitution, p. 527; Idea on democracy, p. 528; Work on Constitution, pp. 529, 530, 531; Defeated in election—Reason, p. 558; Committee work, p. 560; Treasurer, p. 574; Dissatisfied with form of government, pp. 578, 579; Delegate to Continental Congress, p. 644; Declines presidency of Continental Congress, p. 647; Delegate to Continental Congress, p. 678.

Johnston, William, p. 604.

Johnston County, p. 265.
p. 342.

Jones, Allen, Leader in Congress, p. 475.
Elected general, p. 524; Committee to frame Constitution, p. 527; Speaker of Senate, p. 593; Command against Tories, p. 601; Speaker, p. 603; Member council extraordinary, p. 642.

Jones, Frederick, p. 54.

Jones, Thomas, Committee to frame Constitution, p. 527.
Committee to frame Constitution, pp. 564, 565, 566.

Jones, Willie, Leader in Congress, p. 475.
Work with Indians, p. 487; Committee to frame Constitution, p. 531; President of council, p. 555; One of framers of Constitution, pp. 564, 565; Protest at Confiscation Act, p. 607; Delegate to Continental Con-

Jones, Willie.
gress, p. 644; Lieutenant-colonel, p. 661.

Jones County, p. 588.

Judiciary, pp. 305, 328, 565.

Justices, Chief; List, p. 54.

Kenan, Leader in Congress, p. 475.
At Rockfish Creek, p. 502; Battle of Rock Creek, p. 686.

Kennon, Member of Congress, pp. 475, 476.

Kentucky, p. 430.

Kettle Creek, Battle of, p. 599.

King's Mountain, Battle of, p. 634.

Knight, Tobias, p. 54.
Complicity, pp. 200, 201ff.

Lafayette, Arrival, p. 580.

Lamb, pp. 475, 595.

Land, Grants—Rents, p. 90.
Grants and deeds recorded, p. 91; Grant—Rents, p. 92; Rent—Great deed, p. 96; Divisions of, for Lords Proprietors, p. 100; Laws, p. 103; Patents, p. 206; Quit rents, pp. 229, 230; Quit rents, p. 232; Quit rents, p. 237; Quit rents, p. 255; Quit rents, pp. 261, 262; Quit rents, p. 285; Quit rents, p. 393; Quit rents, p. 401.

Land Tax, p. 392.

Lane, Ralph, Starts colony in America, p. 5ff.
Governor in Virginia, abandons colony, pp. 7, 8; Governor of new Virginia colony, p. 29; Expedition up the Moratoc, pp. 32, 33ff.

Lane, John, At Roanoke Island, p. 31.

Law, Debtor, pp. 96, 97.

Law, In fundamental constitutions, p. 102.

Law, Marriage, pp. 96, 97.

Law, Naturalization, p. 99.

Lawson, Captured by Indians—Death, p. 181.

Lawson, Battle of Guilford Court House, p. 659ff.

Lawyers, p. 394.

Lee, Gen. Charles, Command of Southern department, p. 531.
Follows Clinton in Virginia, p. 532; Arrives in Halifax, p. 532; Stationed at Charleston, p. 537; Expedition to Florida, p. 539; With

10

INDEX

Walpole, Horace, pp. 493, 494.
Wanchese, pp. 4, 27; 30; 32.
War, Board of, pp. 627ff; 630; 639; 641, 642.
Warren County, p. 588.
Washington, George, Visit to Ohio country, p. 283.
Attitude on tax, p. 350; Commander-in-chief of Continental Army, p. 462; Valley Forge, p. 586ff.
Washington, Col., Battle of Cowpens, p. 649ff.
Washington County, pp. 585; 717.
Washington District, p. 549.
Watauga, p. 333.
Waxhaw, Battle at the, pp. 611, 612.
Wayne County, p. 606.
Webber's Bridge, Skirmish at, p. 687.
Webster, Col., Commander of Welsh Fusiliers, p. 659.
Death, pp. 660, 662.
Welsh Tract, p. 254.
Whigs, pp. 493, 494, 495; 498; 499ff; Policy toward Tories, p. 520.
White, James, pp. 367, 368.
White, John, Narrative concerning Lost Colony in Virginia, p. 9ff.
Voyage to America, p. 12ff; Member of Virginia colony, p. 29; Colony in Virginia, p. 39ff; Governor of new colony in Virginia, p. 40; Colony in Virginia, p. 41ff; Black Bay, pp. 367, 368.
White, William, pp. 367, 368.
Whitsell's Mill, Battle at, p. 658.
Wilkes County, p. 585.
Wilkinson, Henry, p. 53.
Governor of Albemarle, p. 136ff.
Williams, Benjamin, Commander of state troops, p. 677.

Williams, James, pp. 633, 634.
Williams, John, Member of Congress, pp. 475; 583.
Speaker of House, p. 588; Delegate to Continental Congress, p. 589; Judge, pp. 603; 644.
Williams, Joseph, pp. 550, 552.
Williams, Col. Otho, pp. 653, 654.
Williams, Roger, In Carolina, p. 60.
Land patent, p. 66.
Williamson, Major, p. 550ff.
Willoughby, John, p. 119.
Wilmington, Incorporation, p. 252.
Seat of government, p. 307; protest at Stamp Act, p. 316; Fire, p. 398; Committee of safety, p. 427; Fortified, p. 500; Meeting of council of safety, p. 535; Taken by British, p. 655; Craig holds, p. 663; Evacuated by British—Entered by Rutherford, p. 701.
Wilson, Sarah, pp. 400, 401.
Wingandacoa, pp. 3; 27.
Wingina (see also Pemisapan), pp. 3, 27, 32.
Winslow, Moses, p. 475.
Winston, Member of Congress, p. 475.
Thanked for actions, p. 636; To unite with Greene, p. 657.
Woodward, Thomas, p. 60.
Yamassee Indians, p. 194.
Yardley, Francis, pp. 57, 58.
Yeamans, John, Exploration of Carolina coast desired—Results, p. 75ff.
Yeamans, William, Exploration of coast desired, p. 76.
Governor of colony, p. 82.
Yellow Jacket, p. 273.